The Killing Wind

The Killing Wind

A Chinese County's Descent into Madness during the Cultural Revolution

BY TAN HECHENG

TRANSLATED BY STACY MOSHER
and
GUO JIAN

OXFORD
UNIVERSITY PRESS

OXFORD
UNIVERSITY PRESS

Oxford University Press is a department of the University of Oxford. It furthers
the University's objective of excellence in research, scholarship, and education
by publishing worldwide. Oxford is a registered trade mark of Oxford University
Press in the UK and certain other countries.

Published in the United States of America by Oxford University Press
198 Madison Avenue, New York, NY 10016, United States of America.

© Tan Hecheng 2017

Library of Congress Cataloging-in-Publication Data
Names: Tan, Hecheng, 1949 – author. | Mosher, Stacy, translator. | Guo, Jian, translator.
Title: The killing wind: a Chinese county's descent into madness during the cultural revolution /
by Tan Hecheng; translated by Stacy Mosher and Guo Jian.
Other titles: Xue de shen hua. English | Chinese county's descent into madness
during the cultural revolution
Description: New York, NY: Oxford University Press, [2017]
Identifiers: LCCN 2016016713 (print) | LCCN 2016031266 (ebook) |
ISBN 9780190622527 (hardcover: alk. paper) | ISBN 9780190622534 (E-book) |
ISBN 9780190622541 (E-book)
Subjects: LCSH: China—History—Cultural Revolution, 1966–1976. | Political violence—China—Dao
Xian—History. | Dao Xian (China)—History—20th century.
Classification: LCC DS778.7.T35513 2017 (print) | LCC DS778.7 (ebook) | DDC 951.2/15—dc23
LC record available at https://lccn.loc.gov/2016016713

1 3 5 7 9 8 6 4 2

Printed by Sheridan Books, Inc., United States of America

CONTENTS

MAP

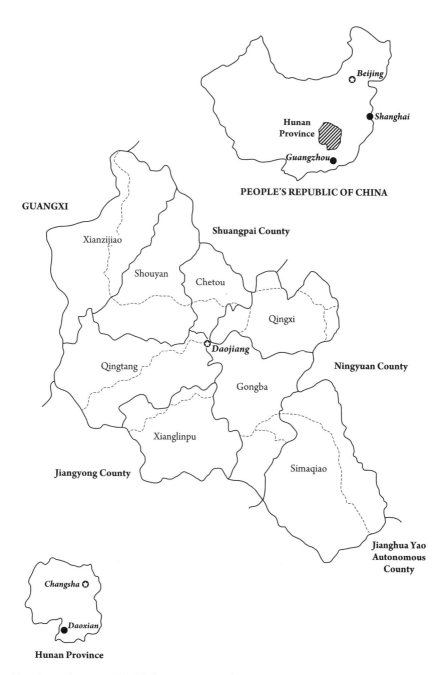

PEOPLE'S REPUBLIC OF CHINA

Beijing

Shanghai

Hunan Province

Guangzhou

GUANGXI

Xianzijiao

Shouyan

Shuangpai County

Chetou

Qingxi

Daojiang

Qingtang

Gongba

Ningyuan County

Xianglinpu

Jiangyong County

Simaqiao

**Jianghua Yao
Autonomous
County**

Changsha

Daoxian

Hunan Province

Daoxian at the time of the Task Force investigation

FOREWORD
BLOOD AWAKENING

I've never written a foreword or the like for anyone else's book, primarily because I lack the requisite fame and heft; I'm merely an ordinary reader and journalist. Nevertheless, when Tan Hecheng's work of historical journalism was set before me, I decided to break with precedent and write this foreword in recognition of a fellow speaker and seeker of truth. I know very well what it is to undertake this kind of journalistic inquiry in mainland China, and the risk and political pressure it entails. It is the tragedy of our age that those expressing common sense and truth are regarded as outliers or hailed as "especially courageous," and that any intention to seek and tell the truth requires preparing for all sorts of contingencies.

The first draft of this book was written in 1986, when a work assignment gave Tan Hecheng access to a large quantity of classified documents relating to the mass killings in Hunan's Dao County (Daoxian) and surrounding counties and cities in 1967, about 15 months into the Cultural Revolution. In compiling these records, Tan took a heavy cross upon himself, and his life entered a new trajectory. The author subsequently made repeated visits to Daoxian to interview sources in order to verify, correct, and supplement his first draft. The current draft, completed in 2007 on the eve of the 40th anniversary of the massacre, represents in some respects a qualitative leap from the original version. Over the past 20-odd years, the author has made every effort to publish the facts of this horrific event in hopes of stirring reflection among China's people. Let me say in passing that most of the information currently circulating in China and abroad regarding this massacre is the result of Tan's reporting and is only the tip of the iceberg; a much more detailed and in-depth exploration is presented in this book.

This work of historical journalism uses authentic documents and evidence to let the facts speak for themselves. Although Tan Hecheng has no formal training in social sciences, his research methods fully conform to the basic requirements of modern socio-scientific research. He collected nearly 400 documents totaling millions of words and interviewed nearly every key individual who agreed to speak with him. This cushion of information has allowed him to assemble a clear-cut and almost seamless narrative. He used this large quantity of valuable primary sources and his own experiences during the Cultural Revolution to assemble this secret history, taking the reader back to the 1960s to consider how a nation with such a long civilization and history descended into madness and barbarity.

In the Daoxian massacre, more than 9,000 innocent people lost their lives in horrific violence that the author categorizes into ten main killing methods, blood chilling even in the abstract. Even more dreadful, however, is the slaughter of conscience and humanity. My profession has brought me in frequent contact with humanity's weaknesses and society's black holes, but even I was shocked by what I read here. Some details are almost unbearable to read, all the more so as they issue unfiltered from the direct participants. The author has ripped away the carefully placed bandage from this running sore in our people's history and has dissected its cancerous core to probe the essence of the "Great Revolution." How and why the Daoxian massacre occurred is a theme explored throughout this book. The roots are deep, but their tendrils are evident everywhere. The bulk of historical material shows that the Daoxian massacre was not an extreme or chance occurrence triggered by a spontaneous incident or by any individual or group. Many killings of varying degrees of similarity occurred throughout China during the Cultural Revolution. In the capital city of Beijing alone, during the "Red August" of 1966, Red Guard militants killed 1,772 people, a full year earlier than the Daoxian killings, and under similarly horrific circumstances. Our generation should not leave it to posterity to expose these incidents, or dupe future generations by obliterating all memory of them.

Mr. Zhu Houze[1] once told me: "A nation that loses its memory is a nation of fools; a party that forgets history can only be a fatuous party; a regime that intentionally obliterates historical memory is an extremely dubious regime; a country that deliberately and thoroughly imposes amnesia is one that instills dread in the human heart." By triggering memory, this book serves as a touchstone, and its fate in China will explicitly reveal the condition of our country and our people.

This book is all the richer in its implications for the complex ecosystem that emerges from its many survivor testimonies. The book richly details the actions and circumstances not only of the victims but also of the killers, as well as others who were implicated in the incident. This multifaceted portrayal provides readers with a comprehensive understanding of the tragedy, and future researchers with invaluable material.

The fundamental cause of this horrific incident was China's system. "Feudalism" has long been the accepted term for China's political system over the millennia. In fact, since the reign of China's first emperor, Qin Shihuang, China has not been feudal but rather autocratic, or, under Mao Zedong, totalitarian. Totalitarianism is characterized by powerful centralized rule that imposes coercion and repression to control and direct all aspects of people's lives. Totalitarianism imprisons an entire society within a state apparatus that monopolizes the economy, politics, truth, and information with a dominance that penetrates every aspect of life.

Under this totalitarian system, a portion of the people (perhaps 5 percent or more of China's population) were labeled as members of a political underclass (landlords, rich peasants, counterrevolutionaries, bad elements, Rightists, capitalists, and their family members). Year in and year out, day after day, the media tools of the state apparatus demonized this political underclass until they were considered worthy of death. Lacking any means of resistance, members of the political underclass became targets of class struggle, and any political campaign turned them into fish on the chopping block, as expendable as grass or insects. Those who were not members of the political underclass were victims, in their own way, of the state monopoly over economics, politics, truth, and information. They knew only what the regime allowed them to know, and they believed what the regime allowed them to believe. Politically ignorant, they existed in poverty and fear and lashed out in whatever direction the regime pointed. The Daoxian tragedy was a slaughter perpetrated by the politically ignorant on the politically downtrodden and was driven by political power.

Up to now, histories of the Cultural Revolution published in mainland China have focused largely on victims who were officials and on the evils of the rebel faction. Some accounts also mention intellectuals who were victims, but without pointing out that the instigators of this persecution were officials. This book exposes another side of the Cultural Revolution that may be even more important, which is the victimization of ordinary people. This aspect allows us to excavate deeper layers of the Cultural Revolution.

Before the Cultural Revolution, bureaucratic cliques dominated China, and bureaucrats enjoyed special privileges based on rank. Workers and peasants enjoyed nominally higher political status but had no genuine participation in policy-making, and they were stripped of anything beyond a guarantee of basic livelihood. Deeply dissatisfied with this bureaucratic system, the public responded quickly to appeals to "smash" the "state apparatus." Mao himself was dissatisfied with this system and wanted to change it. The reasons for his dissatisfaction were many: populism, utopianism, a loathing of any bureaucratism besides his own, and perhaps a fear of losing power. Hoping to "smash" this system, and "through great chaos to attain a great order," Mao called on the people to revolt against the bureaucrats. Given the deification of Mao in years of personality cult campaigns, and the popular loathing of bureaucrats, Mao's appeal immediately raised a tsunami of antibureaucratism. Bureaucrats were attacked (deservedly or not), the bureaucratic system disintegrated, and society devolved into chaos. Mao provided nothing to replace the bureaucratic system, and China could not be allowed to continue in a state of total disorder over the long term, so Mao was forced to compromise by gradually restoring the bureaucracy. Bureaucrats who regained power avenged themselves on those who had responded to the call for rebellion, by mounting campaigns aimed at ordinary people. During the Cultural Revolution, political power was in a state of flux, with one group of bureaucrats in power today and a different group in power the next day, and ordinary people on the wrong side at any given time became the victims.

The 10 years of the Cultural Revolution were followed by 30 years of reform and opening, but the bureaucratic system remains unchanged. China is still ruled by bureaucrats, with those below submissive and loyal to those above. The difference is that present-day bureaucrats control even more assets, the privileges they enjoy are much greater, and they wield their power to enlarge their interests even further. Before the Cultural Revolution, bureaucrats concealed their personal interests behind idealistic banners, but today's bureaucrats see no need to camouflage their brazen amassing of wealth. Thirty years of reform have enlarged China's economic "cake," but bureaucrats have seized the largest and tastiest portions for themselves, while tossing a few scraps to the ordinary people who have borne the costs of reform and who still have no role in policy-making. The power-market economy[2] resulting from 30 years of reform is a departure from pre-reform totalitarianism but is still a long way from a democratic system. Under this system, lust for power joins with lust for riches in an unholy alliance that precludes social justice and harmony.

Bloodshed can shock and awaken. Those who were awakened pushed forward reform and opening, which allowed the political underclass to achieve equality, and the politically ignorant have also gained awareness. The efforts of these newly liberated and politically aware people will someday transform the bureaucrat-led power-market economy into a constitutional democracy of the people, by the people, and for the people.

This is the real value of reclaiming historical memory.

Yang Jisheng

PREFACE

DECONSTRUCTING THE MYTHOS OF MAO ZEDONG'S PEASANT REVOLUTION

As someone engaged in research on massacres that occurred during China's Cultural Revolution, I am happy to write a preface for Tan Hecheng's book, not only because it is an outstanding record that reinforces the Chinese people's collective memory of the Cultural Revolution, but even more so because it provides a powerful deconstruction of Mao Zedong's mythos of peasant revolution.

Mao's peasant movement is undoubtedly a quintessential element of the mythos of the Chinese Communist Revolution. In his early years, Mao advocated the Hunan peasant revolution of the Northern Expedition era and directed training for the Guangzhou peasant movement, and he later took special delight in claiming that it was his understanding of peasant issues that ultimately led to his victory over Chiang Kai-shek. The first political campaign after the founding of the People's Republic was the Land Reform movement, which set the first cornerstone for the new China. Although victory does not always go to the just, history has almost always been written by the victors. That is why the injustice and inhumanity of Mao's peasant movement mythos has seldom received the challenge it deserves from the academic or even the dissident community.

At first glance, it would appear that Tan's firsthand investigative record of what occurred in Hunan's Dao County (Daoxian) and its environs from August to October 1967 has nothing to do with Mao's peasant movement. It is hardly a coincidence, however, that this tragic incident occurred in Hunan, and that many of its organizers and perpetrators declared that they were imitating the peasant revolution that Mao led in that province a half century earlier, and referred to their actions as a "second Land Reform." Tan Hecheng's massive record of blood and tears thus presents the reader with a very simple and convincing inverse logic: if the spillover from Mao's peasant movement could cause such catastrophic lawlessness and terror in peacetime a half century later, during the Cultural Revolution, how could it claim even the most basic humanity and justice in its original manifestation during wartime and then as "violent land reform" at the dawn of the People's Republic?

One of the pillars of the revolutionary mythos that Tan Hecheng deconstructs is that of the legitimacy of struggle against the "class enemy" (landlords, rich peasants, and their offspring) and the justice of their physical extermination. The Daoxian massacre resulted in 9,093 deaths by unnatural causes, and around 90 percent of the victims were landlords and rich peasants or their offspring. According to a "conservative estimate" that the American scholar Yang Su arrived at on the basis of figures published in 3,000 county gazetteers, some 750,000 to 1.5 million people died of unnatural causes through the phenomenon of "collective killings" that became pervasive in the Chinese countryside during the Cultural Revolution, and the majority of these victims were "black elements" and their offspring. Although the killers of Daoxian used all sorts of pretexts, claiming that "landlords and rich peasants were joining the rebel faction to prepare for an insurrection" with the intention of "killing poor and lower-middle peasants," the facts have proven that this was a complete fabrication and falsehood.

Tan Hecheng's investigation shows us that "black elements" and their offspring were an underclass suffering horrendous social bias who had become so disempowered under the long-term dictatorship of the proletariat that even as they faced their deaths, they didn't dare ask the simple question, "Why do you want to kill me?" Furthermore, "the ages of victims ranged from 78 years to ten days old." There is no justification, whether in international law, in China's own laws, or even in the superficial policies of the Chinese Communist Party (CCP), for killing unarmed and peaceful citizens, not to mention women, the elderly, and children. For a long time, there was a popular saying in China's official and even academic circles that "everyone made mistakes" during the Cultural Revolution. After reading Tan Hecheng's record, however, the reader will quickly realize that there was a social grouping of at least hundreds of thousands of people—the black elements—who never did anything wrong during the Cultural Revolution; they were victims, pure and simple. In my view, the fault that can be found with them is that in facing this cataclysmic slaughter, they never rose up in resistance to protect the lives and rights of themselves and their families.

The second pillar of the revolutionary mythos that Tan Hecheng deconstructs is the sacredness of class struggle. His investigation shows that many of the "poor and lower-middle peasant" killers had previous histories of hooliganism, graft, pillage, rape, and acts of sadism, and that they acted not out of some glorious revolutionary ideal but out of naked lust, rapacity, and evil. Furthermore, around

11 percent of the victims were themselves "poor and lower-middle peasants" who had previously offended their killers in political campaigns or through some kind of financial dispute.

It is worth mentioning that according to the internal documents revealed by Tan, this terrifying incident involved about half of all of Daoxian's cadres and CCP members. For a party and regime that have always extolled their "communist ethics," this intense irony lays bare the bloodthirsty nature of the revolutionary mythos.

Incidents such as the Daoxian massacre have often been depicted as "spontaneous movements" by the masses that spun out of control. Yet, Tan's in-depth investigation provides ironclad evidence that there were hardly any instances of spontaneous killing among the "poor and lower-middle peasants." Rather, in every case there is evidence of instigation by cadres and People's Armed Forces officers. Furthermore, most of those who directly participated in the killings were militiamen whose brutality was rewarded with extra allowances and work points from their production teams. Clearly, the Daoxian massacre and the many other notorious slaughters of the Cultural Revolution were results and extension of the actions of the Chinese Communist state machinery.

Given that the organizers and perpetrators saw themselves as engaging in a "second Land Reform," the author felt compelled to carry out even more in-depth investigation and comparison, which helps the reader perceive the violence in Daoxian as a continuation and development of the earlier Land Reform movement. As during this movement, killing orders were issued at rallies by "people's courts" and were carried out through savage means by ordinary people. Some killers openly referenced the "Land Reform experience" by demanding that their victims hand over "movable assets" allegedly hidden away during the first Land Reform movement, and dividing the spoils pillaged from victims' homes.

Tan Hecheng's investigation goes even further back to investigate how victims came to be designated "landlords" or "rich peasants" during the first Land Reform movement. He finds that these people were not the kind of tyrannical landlords depicted in revolutionary operas, but that they were hard-working, law-abiding people whose assets technically qualified them as members of the rural middle class. I believe that after reading Tan's book, every reader with a sense of conscience will understand the injustice and inhumanity of the Chinese Communist revolution and will recognize the innately bloodthirsty quality of Mao's revolutionary mythos.

Regrettably, mainland China still has many people loyal to Mao and his revolution, and Tan's investigation tells us that some of these Maoists were the killers in the Daoxian massacre. In May 1984—eight years after Mao's death—China's new leadership decided to send a task force to Daoxian to investigate this shocking incident. "As soon as the Task Force arrived, it was surrounded by opposing voices. . . . Some said, 'Chairman Mao is dead, and the landlord's restitution corps has arrived!' Some said, 'What are you doing and why are you speaking for the landlords and rich peasants?' Some went hungry and sleepless as they wailed, 'Chairman Mao, Chairman Mao! Come back and save us!' Some even poisoned or hanged themselves in protest." This abnormal phenomenon presents the reader with a simple and compelling logic: if mainland China does not thoroughly denounce Mao Zedong's revolutionary theory and deconstruct the mythos of his peasant movement, China could someday experience another Cultural Revolution and further tragedy on the scale of the Daoxian massacre.

We must be deeply grateful for the courage of Tan Hecheng. Although living in mainland China in an environment bereft of freedom of expression, he has provided the world with this outstanding record of historical truth and a monumental subversion of the revolutionary mythos.

Song Yongyi
(librarian and professor at John F. Kennedy
Memorial Library of California State University)

TRANSLATOR'S NOTE

This English translation is roughly two-thirds the length of Tan Hecheng's monumental Chinese original. In carrying out the editing work (with Mr. Tan's permission and with invaluable input from cotranslator Guo Jian), I focused on preserving the richness of the original content while paring away extraneous material to improve flow and clarity for non-Chinese readers. This entailed removing duplicative narratives, cutting out names of less significant individuals, excerpting documents rather than reproducing them in full, and summarizing some blocks of text in tables. I also carried out some reordering of the text with the needs of an English readership in mind. I take full responsibility for any infelicities resulting from this process.

The chief objective of the editing was to highlight Tan Hecheng's exploration of how atrocities such as the Daoxian massacre occur, and his search for the switch that turns ordinary people into bloodthirsty murderers. Tan Hecheng is not the first or last writer to investigate this theme, but his nuanced description of the processes and individuals involved should contribute significantly to our understanding of mass killings, not only in China but also elsewhere in the world.

I would like to thank the Open Society Foundations for essential support of this translation.

Stacy Mosher

CHRONOLOGY OF THE CULTURAL REVOLUTION KILLINGS IN DAOXIAN

Date	Deaths in Daoxian	Event
1966		
May 16		The Cultural Revolution is formally launched in Beijing.
August 16		The "Sixteen Articles" stipulate that the purpose of the Cultural Revolution is to purge "capitalist roaders" from the CCP.
September		100,000 "Rightists" and other political targets are detained in Hunan Province.
Late October		Massive rebel faction mass organization Xiang River Storm is established in Changsha, Hunan Province.
1967		
January		Shanghai's existing CCP establishment is overthrown in the "January Storm," which spreads throughout China.
First half of 1967		Splits develop among Hunan's rebel factions, with different groups gaining the favor of the central authorities at different times.
Late summer		In Daoxian, the Red Alliance and Revolutionary Alliance become antagonistic factions.
July 18		A mass rally is organized in Beijing to criticize President Liu Shaoqi.

Date	Deaths in Daoxian	Event
August 2–5		Daoxian Leading Group to Seize Revolution and Push Production calls an urgent meeting of district seize-and-push groups to present the "new situation in class struggle."
August 5		Liu Shaoqi, Deng Xiaoping, and Tao Zhu are denounced at a mass rally at Tiananmen Square; People's Daily publishes Mao's essay "Bombard the Headquarters."
August 8		Gun-snatching incident at the county PAFD armory by the Revolutionary Alliance.
August 9		Red Alliance stalwarts decide to withdraw from the county CCP committee compound to Yingjiang Commune.
August 11		District PAFD heads and Red Alliance heads hold a battle-readiness meeting in Qingtang Commune and decide to organize militia to attack the Revolutionary Alliance headquarters.
		County seize-and-push group holds a telephone conference urging districts and communes to strengthen dictatorship over class enemies and organize militias.
Aug 13	1	First victim: Zhu Mian, in the Xiaba brigade of Shouyan District's Jiujia Commune.
		Armed conflict between the Red Alliance and Revolutionary Alliance in Daojiang results in two deaths in the county seat.
Aug 15	7	The killing campaign begins in Yangjia Commune and Shouyan Commune.
		Meeting of PAFD cadres at the Red Alliance headquarters in Yingjiang to discuss how to prevent the Revolutionary Alliance from establishing contacts in the countryside.
		Late at night, county CCP deputy secretary Huang Yida and others head for Changsha to alert the provincial authorities to rising tensions in the county and to request intervention.

Date	Deaths in Daoxian	Event
Aug 16	3	Killings begin in Lingling County.
Aug 17	15	Qingtang District holds a killing-mobilization meeting, and killings begin in that district and Qiaotou District.
		Killings begin in Jiangyong County.
Aug 18	17	The Red Alliance formally establishes its frontline command post in Yingjiang.
		Killings begin in Ningyuan County.
Aug 19	20	Lingling Military Subdistrict joint investigation group arrives to investigate killings.
		Killings begin in Gongba District.
Aug 20	23	Killings begin in Chetou (Meihua) District.
Aug 21	30	Leaders of the Lingling Military Subdistrict and Daoxian PAFD make an inspection visit to Yingjiang.
		Killings begin in Hongyan (Xianzijiao) District.
		Beginning of first major upsurge in killings throughout Daoxian.
Aug 22	87	Killing rally in Shangguan Commune launches killings in Shangguan District.
Aug 23	205	Ganziyuan Commune's "Supreme People's Court of the Poor and Lower-Middle Peasants" is formally established, launching the killings in Qingxi District.
		Qiaotou Commune holds a mass killing rally.
		Killings begin at the Xiaoshui Forestry Management Bureau in Shuangpai County.
Aug 24	135	Shangguan Commune holds a killing rally. Killings begin in Xianglinpu District.
Aug 25	350	Gongba Commune's Yanhetang brigade kills off all of its black elements.

Date	Deaths in Daoxian	Event
Aug 26		Lingling Military Subdistrict joint investigation group leaves Daoxian.
		The 47th Army transmits the Lingling Military Subdistrict's "Cable on the Social Situation" to the districts and communes.
		After many delays, Huang Yida and others gain access to the provincial leaders and tell them of the killings in Daoxian.
Aug 26–28	638	The Red Alliance calls a "political and legal work conference" in Yingjiang to transmit the 47th Army's Cable on the Social Situation.
		New upsurge in killings begins.
		The provincial leadership sends cables to the Central Cultural Revolution Small Group, Lingling Military Subdistrict, and Daoxian PAFD to take measures to halt the killings.
Aug 27	590	PAFD leaders in Xianglinpu District launch a three-day "clean up" during which 569 people are killed.
Aug 28	501	The 47th Army and Hunan Province Cultural Revolution Committee Preparatory Group send a cable to the Lingling Military Subdistrict and Daoxian PAFD headquarters ordering an end to the killings.
Aug 29	452	Troops from the 47th Army's 6950 Unit are stationed in Daoxian to end factional battles and to stop the killings.
		Youxiang Commune's Yuejin brigade releases its "killing satellite."
Aug 30	273	Major battle between the Red Alliance and Revolutionary Alliance.
Aug 31	176	Killings begin in Jianghua County.
Sept 1	155	
Sept 2	142	
Sept 3	88	
Sept 4	91	Killings begin in Qiyang County.

Date	Deaths in Daoxian	Event
Sept 5	156	The Lingling Military Subregion transmits the cable from the 47th Army and provincial revolutionary committee preparatory group prohibiting further killings.
Sept 6	75	
Sept 7	36	
Sept 8	47	Killings begin in Xintian County.
Sept 9	72	The Red Alliance and Revolutionary Alliance sign the September 9th Agreement.
Sept 10	25	Killings begin in Lanshan County.
Sept 11	13	
Sept 12	12	
Sept 13	5	Huang Yida and others arrive in Changsha from Daoxian.
Sept 14	5	
Sept 15	22	
Sept 16	9	
Sept 17	2	
Sept 18	2	
Sept 19	1	
Sept 20	3	
Sept 21	11	
Sept 22	1	
Sept 23	1	Huang Yida and others arrive in Daoxian.
		Major battle between the Red Alliance and Revolutionary Alliance.
Sept 26	2	
Sept 27	0	The 47th Army and provincial revolutionary committee preparatory group issue an urgent notice prohibiting further killings.
Sept 30	7	
Oct 1	0	Aircraft drop leaflets throughout Hunan Province printed with the urgent notice prohibiting further killings.

Date	Deaths in Daoxian	Event
Oct 2	0	Further airdrops of leaflets.
Oct 10	1	
Oct 15	1	
Oct 17	1	The last victim: He Yuxiang of Qiaotou Commune's Shangba brigade.
Total	4,509	

Introduction

In the summer and autumn of 1967, a massacre in Hunan Province's Dao County (Daoxian) and nearby counties and cities left more than 9,000 dead. Officially referred to as the Daoxian Cultural Revolution Killing Incident, it is popularly known as the "Killing Wind." A "living fossil" of this incident wrote in a complaint sent to the Chinese Communist Party (CCP) Central Committee and Hunan provincial committee: "If a single word I've written is false, may I be beheaded in the public square." It is on testimonies avowed in such terms that I have based this record of historical events. These heart-rending events and chilling narratives have a mirage-like quality, almost impossible to believe, yet everything in this book actually happened, and every person, every incident, every detail, every sentence spoken, and even every song comes from original and authentic accounts; there are no fictional characters, no fabricated events, and no aliases. In some cases, only a surname is given, but only for very good reasons. Any errors that remain are due to lapses of memory or heavy accents among the persons concerned. In summation, I've done all in my power to create a faithful record of the plain and unvarnished truth.

In May 1984, Lingling Prefecture assigned more than 1,300 cadres to a "Task Force to Deal with the Aftermath of the Cultural Revolution Killings." The task force spent more than two years, from June 1984 to the end of 1986, investigating and dealing with the aftermath of the killings that occurred in and around Daoxian in late summer and early autumn 1967. Without their hard effort, I could never have completed this record. The incident was simply too chaotic and involved too many individuals and facts. For various historical reasons, much was obscured, and truth was mixed with falsehood; getting to the bottom of it was more than any individual could accomplish. My reporting partner and I had the good fortune to interview some members of the Task Force, and this rare opportunity was a turning point in our inquiries. We're grateful for the large amount of firsthand material they provided—records, data, and investigative reports—which gave us an overarching view of the killing. The passage of time had created layers of fog that prevented seeing things with crystal clarity, but these unforgettable scenes were captured. As agreed in advance, I can never under any circumstances reveal the names of my sources, for which reason I once again express my deepest gratitude to them here.

I carried out numerous interviews and investigations regarding the Daoxian killings. The first and most important was when I visited Daoxian for more than a month in late summer and early autumn 1986, 19 years after the incident occurred. I made this visit in the company of Mr. Zhang Minghong, who at that time headed up the Lingling Prefecture office of Hunan Radio and Television. After gathering information on what Zhang Minghong called "an incident as shocking to one's worldview as the Tangshan earthquake," we agreed that I would write up the report and that we would jointly bear any consequences. In September 1986, we quickly compiled a 100,000-word report titled "Blood Myth," which had been commissioned by a major and highly influential mainland Chinese magazine. For reasons that are no doubt obvious, it was never published. A number of other periodicals subsequently expressed an interest, but to date this essay has not been made available to the Chinese public at large.[1] I am especially grateful to Mr. Yue Jianyi, formerly deputy chief editor of the Workers' Press magazine *Kaituo*, who devoted great effort to publication of this historical reportage and paid a great price. Like us, he "took a heavy cross upon himself."

I shouldn't have been the one to write this book. It should have been the reminiscences and confessions of survivors, and the research of historians and sociologists, compiled, written, examined, and authorized by an authoritative editorial committee. Yet, 10 years passed, then 20, 30, and even 40 years, and none of these reminiscences, confessions, or research papers have appeared, not to mention any collective repentance or genuine spiritual revival. Many people who should bear more responsibility for the future of our country and our people persist in closing their eyes to iron truth and bloody revelation.

Those who know about and experienced this incident are becoming fewer as time passes, while others hope that time will obliterate all vestiges of the incident. What should we do?

As an observer of the tragedy of what people did to each other, individually and collectively, so horrific and irrational that it is almost beyond comprehension, I'm compelled to examine my own conscience and ask: If I had been there at the time, would I have been a killer or a victim? I shudder to contemplate this question. Since fate has given me a glimpse of all this, I have no right to keep silent and no choice but to reveal the truth to the world. I cannot allow future generations to impugn ours for covering up our errors, or for amnesia, apathy, impotence, reticence, stupidity, and a lack of soul and dignity.

This book is dedicated to all those who are concerned with the fate of China, in hopes that it will not wrong the dead or disappoint the living or future generations.

PART ONE

THE ORIGIN OF THE MASSACRE

1

The River of Death

In China's south-central region lies the province of Hunan, and in the south of Hunan is a county ancient, fertile, and rich in culture—Daoxian.

Daoxian is nestled among several mountain regions in the middle reaches of the Xiaoshui tributary in Lingling Prefecture, abutting the Guangxi Autonomous Region to its west. An aerial view of the county shows a verdant basin encircled by green hills and networked with rivers. Jiucailing, the highest peak of the Dupang mountain range on the county's western border, rises more than 2,000 meters above sea level and is the second-highest peak in Hunan Province. Sixty-three rivers of varying sizes crisscross the basin like veins in a leaf, but the main waterways are the Xiaoshui, Fushui (also known as Yishui), Yanshui (also called the Yongming River), Paoshui (Gongba River), Lingshui (Ningyuan River), and Lianxi. The Xiaoshui, Daoxian's main waterway, nearly bisects the county from south to north, flowing into the Shuangpai Reservoir north of Daoxian. The Lianxi, Yongming, and Ningyuan Rivers and the Paoshui and Fushui tributaries intersect with the Xiaoshui from the east and the west. This geography explains why, during the Daoxian massacre, so many corpses followed the Xiaoshui through Daojiang Town, the county seat of Daoxian, and into the Shuangpai Reservoir. According to observers at the time, at the peak of the massacre, nearly 100 bodies flowed past in a single hour, an average of 1.6 per minute. Many fish died from gorging on the bodies, and so many stinking corpses clogged the reservoir's dam that the hydroelectric plant was shut down for half a year.

The hundreds of bodies flowing into this medium-sized reservoir stained its water and filmed it with a rancid, reddish, oily scum. The seventh and eighth months of the lunar calendar are the hottest time of year in Hunan, and the blazing sun combined with foehn winds produced an overwhelming stench that afflicted everyone within miles. Clearing the corpses from the reservoir became a major headache. The decision at the time was to assign the odious task to the offspring of "black elements."[1] This had the advantage of "puncturing the arrogance of the class enemy" and "facilitating the ideological remolding" of black-element offspring, while cleansing the reservoir area and restoring the Shuangpai's waters to their original limpid beauty.

A friend of mine, Yang XX, a well-known writer in Lingling Prefecture, told me of his personal experience of the Daoxian massacre. Yang was from a "rich peasant" family in Shuangpai County, and having recently graduated from middle school at the age of 17, he had returned home to farm. After Daoxian's killing wind spread to Shuangpai, many people were also killed there. Yang's family was fortunate enough to have been spared, but his production brigade sent Yang to the reservoir for voluntary service. The task seemed simple enough, consisting of rowing boats out to the corpses and towing them ashore for burial. Although the stench was appalling, it was infinitely better to bury another's corpse than to be buried oneself. One day, while looking out on the water, Yang saw a dozen or so corpses floating together in a circle, looking from afar like a flower in bloom. He promptly rowed his little boat out to deal with them, and as he drew nearer he saw that the corpses had been strung together with wire through their collarbones. As Yang snagged them with the hook on his bamboo punt pole, a female corpse turned over, and he saw an infant clutched in her arms.

The Xiaoshui River had nurtured millions of lives without the devastation of flash floods, its placid waters shaded with trees and dotted with sandbars like strings of jade beads. Like the people who lived along its banks, the river was docile and not easily stirred. Its waters were dotted with fishing boats and timber rafts, the latter driven along at a leisurely pace by men, some burly and some rail thin, wearing only sackcloth trousers, if even that, their skin bronzed and glistening under the sun as they gripped their bamboo punt poles tipped with sharp iron hooks. When they saw housewives and girls washing clothes and vegetables along the shore, they puffed up their chests and bellowed uncouth highland ditties, the women responding with playful scolding. During the massacre, however, the raftsmen and washerwomen were replaced by corpses bloated to the size of water buffalo, male and female, young and old, floating singly or strung together like fish. The Xiaoshui wordlessly declined responsibility for this unaccustomed cargo by beaching the corpses among its phosphorous jags, sodden willow groves, and sandbars.

Most of the bodies were naked, or at most covered with only shreds of clothing, usually skeletal or dismembered, and often headless. They'd been rendered unrecognizable by the gnawing of hungry fish, which left deep pits for eyes and a horrible, yawning cavity in place of the lips that had recited Chairman Mao's quotes and begged for the revolutionary masses to punish them for their crimes, their joyous laughter and cries of grief having been eternally silenced.

When the corpses first began floating through Daojiang Town, crowds lined the riverbanks in wide-eyed astonishment, discussing among themselves. After the sight became common, however, people took no more notice than of trees felled by a storm. Although rumors were rampant and explanations varied, who these corpses were and what had happened to them soon became an open secret. People quickly turned away at the sight of the corpses, because the weather was hot and the stench sickening, and because they had a faint inkling that the day might come when they themselves must kill or be killed. Some itched for the opportunity, while others lived in dread of that day.

Here in Daojiang Town, people encountered the same problem as at the Shuangpai Reservoir, as some of the bodies became stranded among the town's piers, wharfs, and culverts, an offense to the senses and public health. The Jiefang Neighborhood Committee, located along the river, bore the brunt of a practical issue that had to be addressed. But it was more difficult in the county town to recruit black-element offspring as had been done at the reservoir, so the neighborhood committee was obliged to hire a mentally ill man to handle the cleaning work. His task was even simpler than that at the reservoir; he need only push stranded corpses back into the water with a bamboo pole and allow the current to carry them out of town. Many of Daojiang's elderly still remember this man, though his name is long forgotten; he was called the Black Lunatic. His age, impossible to ascertain, appeared to be somewhere between 30 and 50. Dark and thin, with a stubbly beard, he wore only a pair of ragged pants of a murky blue-black color and a shabby coir hat hanging down his back. All day he carried his bamboo pole along the river bank, pushing corpses into the current. It was said that the Black Lunatic was a "peach blossom manic" who favored female corpses. Some young scamps enjoyed teasing him by spotting a male corpse but telling him it was female. The Black Lunatic would run off to deal with it, and upon learning the truth, he'd raise his pole and scold the naughty boys, who by then would be doubled-up with laughter.

With classes suspended and adults all caught up in the Cultural Revolution, packs of untended children ran wild in the streets day and night. They liked to run up to the watchtower on the city wall and gaze out on the Xiaoshui and Lianxi Rivers to see who could spy the most floating corpses.

"One, two, three, four . . . I see seven," said one child.

"No, there's eight," another argued.

Two of the Xiaoshui's most notable sandbars could be seen from Daojiang's Kou Gong Watchtower. One of Daoxian's great historic sites, the watchtower had been built during the Northern Song dynasty (960–1127) by Kou Zhun, a respected prime minster, after he was demoted to the position of a deputy commissioner of Daozhou, a larger administrative region of that time. Back then, the watchtower had been adorned with a placard personally inscribed by Kou Zhun with the words "Peaceful Prospect," but the placard had been destroyed by Red Guards when the Cultural Revolution began in 1966. As the corpses floated past a sandbar, it was possible to determine that the boy who'd guessed eight was correct, because one female corpse carried a child's body on her back.

Those boys are now grown, and remembering those times is like living in a dream.

These little vignettes hardly seem worth mentioning against the backdrop of Daoxian's Cultural Revolution massacre. I've given them space in this narrative as examples of the recollections passed along to me by local people who greatly assisted me when I first began looking into the Daoxian massacre in 1986. In particular, it would have been all but impossible for me to make contact with surviving family members of the massacre's victims without others acting as intermediaries. They felt that the Daoxian massacre was a disgrace not only to the people of their county, but also to the Chinese people as a whole, and that it must be written about so that all could reflect on its lessons.

It was, in fact, such local outrage that eventually brought the Daoxian atrocities to the attention of officials in the central government. This information was relayed in petitions that the families of victims submitted to the central government in hopes of redress. China's petitioning system has existed for centuries as an alternative means for ordinary citizens to obtain the justice deprived them in more-institutional settings. It is a last-ditch and often-unsuccessful appeal to officials who may be far enough removed from the matter to give it an objective hearing. In the case of the Daoxian massacre, petitions of this sort spurred China's top officials into appointing the Task Force that eventually investigated the incident.

I read some of these petitions before I went to Daoxian to report on the Task Force's investigations, and they gave me a sense of the terror that shrouded Daoxian's towns and villages at the time. Here are some scenarios depicted in those petitions:

Rumors abounded of "class enemies" organizing "black killing squads" that would "organize in August, rebel in September, and carry out a massacre in September," "killing first Party members, then cadres, then half of the poor and lower-middle peasants, so the landlords, rich peasants, counterrevolutionaries, and bad elements can eat their fill." These lies were not mere back-alley rumormongering but were transmitted through official or semiofficial channels or through Chinese Communist Party (CCP) meetings, cadre meetings, militia rallies, and mass rallies.

The streets were flooded with "highest-level directives" exhorting people to "sharpen our knives as the enemies are sharpening theirs," and ubiquitous posters called for "exterminating the seven black categories and keeping China eternally red" while reporting killings by the Supreme People's Court of the Poor and Lower-Middle Peasants.

Militia checkpoints and sentry posts were set up along blockaded highways, in shady mountain villages, along wave-lapped ferry piers, in fields crisscrossed with footpaths, and at bus stations, wherever people came and went. Militiamen wearing red armbands and carrying rifles, hunting guns, or homemade weapons interrogated passersby day and night. At the slightest movement, they would grip their sabers or cock their rifles and call out, "What's going on?" or "What element?," then check travel permits, carry out body searches, and interrogate. At the slightest suspicion or hesitation, they would tie up and grill the suspect, and failure to give a good accounting could be fatal.

In one instance, a secondary-school student named Yang Yuekun, whose home village was part of Dapingling Commune, was coming home for the summer school break when he was interrogated by militiamen as he passed by Xingqiao Commune. As elsewhere during the Cultural Revolution, Daoxian hosted two opposing "rebel factions" known as the Revolutionary Alliance and the Red Alliance. When a phone call to his commune raised suspicions that Yang Yuekun was a "spy" for the opposing Revolutionary Alliance, he was escorted to his production brigade to be executed with other black elements. Before his execution, Yang cried out, "Long live Chairman Mao! Long live the Communist Party!," at which his eyes were gouged out and his tongue sliced off, and the executioner stabbed Yang Yuekun 16 times with horrendous brutality. The Task Force subsequently categorized Yang Yuekun's case as revenge for an incident back in 1963, when Yang's father had criticized the local CCP secretary and led to his dismissal. This turned out to be a common pattern during the Daoxian killings.

In another case I read about, Jiang Xiaochu, a 22-year-old student of mechanics at Hunan University, made the fatal error of deciding to avoid the Cultural Revolution turmoil in Changsha by returning to his home in the Huangtuba production brigade of Daoxian's Shenzhangtang Commune.

Jiang Xiaochu's father, Jiang Xun, had graduated from Hunan University in 1942 with a degree in history and had been teaching ever since then. Many years later, a leader of the county's education bureau described Jiang Xun as "an upright and diligent man who made an indelible contribution to Daoxian's education efforts." But back in 1964, during the Socialist Education movement (also known as the Four Cleanups campaign),[2] Jiang Xun's family background caused him to be labeled an "alien-class element who had infiltrated the party." He was stripped of his CCP membership and dismissed from his job, and he and his wife were sent back to his home village, Huangtuba.

Aware of his "class enemy" status, Jiang Xun was prepared to remold himself by working diligently and without complaint, and he instructed his wife and children to do likewise, hoping that good behavior would win them a promising future. And indeed, the family made a positive impression on the other villagers in the two years following their return.

When Jiang Xiaochu returned to Huangtuba in August 1967, the "killing wind" was already blowing through Daoxian, and Jiang Xun's joy at his son's return was offset by a sense of impending disaster. That night, Jiang Xun killed the household's two ducks so his family could at least have one good meal together, but Jiang Xiaochu was the only one with an appetite that night. Jiang Xun gave a long sigh and said, "You really shouldn't have come back . . . ," at which point tears began flowing from his eyes and his chopsticks clattered to the floor. Jiang Xiaochu tried to comfort his father, saying, "Papa, don't be impatient. As long as we listen to Chairman Mao and follow the party, the villagers won't hold our background against us. Executions are carried out only on criminals and with permission from the judicial organs." Jiang Xun gave a bitter smile and said no more.

The next day, the village held a meeting, and Jiang Xun and his second son, Jiang Xiaozhung, along with a dozen or so other "landlords and rich peasants" and their offspring, were rounded up and locked in the brigade headquarters until they could be executed. When Jiang Xiaochu learned what had happened, he dashed off to the headquarters, hoping to persuade the irrational grassroots cadres with Mao Zedong Thought, only to be locked up as well.

At midnight that night, Jiang Xiaochu and his younger brother were bound hand and foot and taken to the Jiujing River, where they were shot and stabbed and then kicked into the river, sending scarlet ripples downstream. The next day, Jiang Xun and the other black elements were divided into batches for execution; in a little mountain village of just over 100 households, 15 people were killed. Jiang Xiaochu's mother and younger sister were gang-raped by the executioners. The devastated women later fled to Xinjiang, where they somehow managed to survive.

Yet another petition describing the murder of Xiong Yunyou, a medic at the county's Shouyan District Public Health Clinic, showed how arbitrary killing became in Daoxian.

Xiong Yunyou, born in 1930, was from an upper-middle peasant family. A native of Lianghekou Village in Daoxian's Cenjiangdu Township, he was a secondary-school graduate who joined the People's Liberation Army (PLA) in 1950, serving as an educator and political instructor. Xiong wanted to marry a young woman from his home village named Wu Xiuqin, but at that time, the prospective spouses of military personnel had to be vetted, and since Wu Xiuqin had an "overseas connection" (her father was in Hong Kong), permission to marry was withheld. Xiong Yunyou was insistent, however, and finally CCP officials told him, "If you must have her, you'll have to be demobilized." That's how Xiong ended up back in his native village in Daoxian.

After returning to Daoxian and marrying Wu Xiuqin in 1962, Xiong Yunyou began working at the Veterans' Convalescent Hospital and then became a medic in the Shouyan District Public Health Clinic in 1964. The couple had just had their third son in July 1967, and Xiong Yunyou was killed on the way back from visiting his wife and baby on August 31, 1967. Although killings had become rampant in Daoxian by then, Xiong wasn't a member of any "black category," nor had he taken part in any rebel faction organizations, so he never expected to be killed. But when he was stopped at a militia blockade and was found not to be carrying identification, the militiamen suspected him of being a black element and took him to their headquarters in Yingjiang for further interrogation.

As luck would have it, just that morning the commander of Shouyan Commune People's Armed Forces Department (PAFD), Zhou Yuanbing, and several cadres had come to Yingjiang out of concern over the direction the Cultural Revolution was taking in Daoxian. Shaoyan District public-security deputy Chen Zhixi[3] was also there, and Chen told Zhou and the others, "Xiong Yunyou has been captured, and comrades from the clinic tell me this fellow has been AWOL for three days. He must have run off to the high school. He's no good and should be shot." Daoxian's No. 2 High School had become the headquarters of the local Revolutionary Alliance, and Chen Zhixi suspected Xiong of being on a secret mission. The leaders of the Red Alliance at Yingjiang decided that the militia should execute Xiong Yunyou while escorting him back to Shouyan.

That afternoon, Chen Zhixi called in the Shouyan militia platoon leader, Tang Zu, and told him to have militia escort Xiong Yunyou to Donglingjiao. "We'll go ahead and wait for them there. Once they arrive, we'll decide how to deal with him." But when the militia escort headed by deputy platoon leader He Wanxi arrived with Xiong Yunyou at Donglingjiao, Chen was nowhere to be found, so they proceeded to Shouyan.

As they passed by the Tangfu production brigade, they spied commune PAFD head Zhou Yuanbing resting and eating watermelon with production brigade leader He Shenghong and other cadres under a large tree by the well. He Shenghong asked why the men hadn't killed Xiong Yunyou at Donglingjiao: "I order you to find a place up ahead to kill him." He Wangxi found a quiet place about 250 meters off, and since he wasn't carrying a gun, he motioned for one of the militiamen, Yi Zhichang, to shoot Xiong Yunyou in the back.

Although Yi Zhichang claimed to be a demobilized veteran, he had never killed anyone, and trembling with fear, he managed to miss, even at such close range. Alerted by the gunfire, Xiong Yunyou ran for his life, quick as a rabbit even with his hands tied, and the militiamen gave chase, gasping with their effort. He Wangxi impatiently grabbed the gun from Yi Zhichang and fired at Xiong Yunyou. His aim was true; Xiong fell to the ground, twisted a few times and was still.

After reading about these killings, some readers may ask: weren't the main targets of the Daoxian killings supposed to be black elements and their offspring? It appears that these examples don't qualify. Why is that?

While the victims in the examples above were not classified as black elements in the strictest sense, all of them were educated and had seen something of the world. That's why their survivors were more daring and "incautious" and ceaselessly petitioned the county, prefectural, provincial, and even central authorities, demanding that their loved ones be rehabilitated and that action be taken against their killers. In the case of actual "black elements," however, very few surviving family members dared to protest the injustice done to their loved ones, the vast majority maintaining their silence to this day. Only as our interviews prodded deeper did the details of these deaths gradually float to the surface. To these people, the process of painstaking investigation and gradual advance toward truth was in its own way an extension of the massacre.

Trying to understand this bloody historical episode nearly 20 years later required courage and conscience, but also timing and opportunity. History had been waiting for our government and historians to provide clear answers to our people, our society, and future generations; even now, decades later, our society maintains a profound silence, as if nothing ever happened, or as if it were all part of some remote and mythic past.

In Daoxian, however, people still remember. People told us how in the town of Daojiang, while not so badly affected as the rural areas, rumors spread like wildfire that the Red Alliance wanted to wash the streets with blood. People going out to the street stalls to buy their daily necessities were confronted with big-character posters, and a gust of wind stirring up a clump of litter or the clank of an upset pail was enough to send people yelling and scurrying in all directions like scared rats. People referred to the phenomenon as "mental dust storms," and these occurred almost daily in Daojiang, where people's nerves were stretched to the breaking point. Those with bad family backgrounds, and especially those who belonged to one of the 21 categories,[4] never knew which day would see their heads tumbling to the ground. Every day at dusk, Daojiang became a ghost town. Some neurotics found it impossible to sleep at night, any sound outside their homes leaving them wide-eyed until dawn.

The owner of a small restaurant told us: "At that time, even though I'd never broken a single law and had never taken part in activities organized by any faction, I was scared out of my wits, never knowing if I'd live to see another day. Back then, there was no way to defend yourself against what was going on."

The people of Daoxian, accustomed to drinking cool, clear river water, no longer dared use the water polluted by corpses. The county town's five wells suddenly became tremendously precious. Every day at dawn, long lines formed at the Anjia well next to the county militia headquarters and the Qijia well on Wuxing Street, and quarrels were frequent.

The people of Daoxian loved eating fresh fish. The old county town had a place called Plank Bridge (Banziqiao) where the river intersected with the street, and beneath the bridge's boards hung numerous bamboo baskets of fish being kept alive in the river water while awaiting purchase. In normal times, the locale was packed with buyers first thing in the morning, but now customers were few. The price of fish dropped from 2 yuan per kilo to 20 cents without attracting buyers. The reason was that some people had found human eyes, hair, and fingernails in the fish's bellies. Nearly two years passed before eating fish became popular again.

This was the case in neighboring Shuangpai County as well. My friend Yang who worked at the Shuangpai Reservoir told me: "That year, the reservoir's fish were especially fat and numerous. Every morning we'd find fish weighing more than 5 kilos floating belly-up in the water, having died from gorging on human flesh. No one scooped them out or dared to eat them, but you couldn't avoid seeing them."

Daoxian was famous for its tofu, and most of the county town's tofu shops were located along the river for easy access to water. But who would eat tofu made with water that had carried corpses? And there wasn't enough well water for basic consumption, much less for making tofu. The tofu makers switched to a recipe for rice tofu that used less water, but even so, when the tofu makers took their trade to the streets with cries of "Well-water rice tofu!," there were few takers.

Big-character posters went up exhorting "Drink river water for the revolution!," and some brave revolutionaries publicly demonstrated their own willingness to drink the river water.

Meanwhile, the Xiaoshui River, which had nurtured generations of Hunan's sons and daughters, sorrowfully licked her wounds and flowed silently through the Daozhou basin like an enormous question mark.

These are the images described by eyewitnesses. At that time, they couldn't understand the enormous historical implications contained in these scattered images, much less realize the full truth. Even now, aware of the implications, they still have no way of knowing the whole truth.

The tragedy of China is that experience has accustomed our people to disaster and bloodshed, and even to apathy and forgetfulness.

Similar massacres and other types of large-scale death have occurred throughout Chinese history, and as recently as the Three Years of Hardship in 1959–1961,[5] more than 34,000 people died of starvation or illness in Daoxian—7.5 times the number that were killed during the Cultural Revolution. It is unprecedented, however, to carry out such large-scale, brutal slaughter of innocent people in a time of peace, as in the case of the Daoxian killings. It's not death that's the issue, but how it occurred and for what reason.

For the victims, life as a biological function ended without further argument. The survivors, however, are left to ponder it, because they want to keep on living, and even more because someday they will also die. Death makes us understand sorrow, learn pity, and acquire the capacity for mercy. Indeed, in all we do today, the responsibility we bear for the living must surpass what we do for the dead.

One comrade assigned to the Task Force told us of an incident in spring 1985, when he was questioning a killer about his motives. The killer replied in a righteous tone of voice, "They were class enemies. If we didn't kill them, we would have suffered from the revival of capitalism." Another Task Force investigator was dumbstruck when a malefactor replied even more simply, "The higher-ups told me to kill, and I killed; if someone told me to kill you now, I would do it, too!"

I wonder what China's leaders today would think at hearing these words.

Any incident can be said to have its reasons and historical background at the time it occurs, and I'm in no position to analyze and explore each and every factor. I only hope to pull back the thick veil of history and let the world see the basic truth. We know that the government never welcomes the exposure of national wounds long enveloped in the fog of history, and that some "patriotic" citizens consider it "harmful" to the national image of an ancient country with a long history. For example, a leader in the Daoxian CCP committee who had no involvement whatsoever in the killings still felt that "the best way to deal with this matter is to let it gradually fade with time." But in truth, the greatest sorrow for any people is not disaster and hardship, but rather spiritual castration and psychic fracture. Just as wounds left covered will fester and breed further misfortune, attempts to whitewash the historical calamities of millions of people will foment even-greater historical calamity. As George Santayana said, those who forget the past are doomed to repeat it.

2

My Destiny with Daoxian

Although not religious, I believe some invisible and mysterious hand predestined my connection with the Daoxian Cultural Revolution killings. The first sign of this mysterious hand came at the end of 1967, just months after the slaughter and nearly 20 years before I undertook my reporting assignment in Daoxian. At that time, I was a high-school student in Changsha, and in what proved to be a vain attempt to avoid being sent to the countryside, I accompanied my elder cousin (a former "educated youth" who had been sent down in 1964 to Jiangyong County, next to Daoxian) and a few others who were returning to their second home to "seize revolution and push production." As we passed through Daoxian, my cousin and I got off the bus to meet up with those other friends.

In my recollection, the county town of Daojiang was only about one-tenth of its current size. It had a desolate atmosphere, its granite city wall rimmed with irregular growths of trees and vines and an arc of clear, blue water marked where the Xiaoshui and Lianxi Rivers met at the town's southwest border and flowed southeast toward the city's east gate. Standing on the city wall, one could see, beyond Daoxian's No. 2 High School, the 135-meter Shuinan pontoon bridge that connected Daoxian with Ningyuan and Lanshan. The town of Daojiang itself had probably fewer than 20 streets lined with green-tiled, two-story wooden structures. Most of the buildings had balconies, making the already narrow streets even more claustrophobic, and many had their windows, and even some doors, partially bricked up, giving them a lopsided appearance. Most of the roads, 3 to 4 meters wide, were cobbled with river pebbles, which gave them the local nickname of "corn roads."

The town had few pedestrians and even fewer shops. In front of the single long-distance bus stop was a pond, next to which a shack constructed from tree branches served as a restaurant—I think it was called the Red Star Cafe—and that's where we ate lunch. Inside the crude structure were several eight-person tables with benches for seating, and the smoke-blackened walls carried gaudy images of the "Great Leader" Chairman Mao, along with the latest "highest directives" and slogans along the lines of "Swear to pursue the Proletarian Cultural Revolution to the end." One I remember with particular clarity: "If the enemy refuses to surrender, he must be destroyed!"

We ordered a few dishes, warmed a bottle of rice wine, and sat down to eat. The stewed fresh fish, incredibly cheap and in an amazingly large serving, had a delicacy and freshness that kept our chopsticks in constant motion. Locals at the next table stared incredulously as we wolfed down the fish and its broth. (Fortunately we didn't understand the implications of this gaze, or we might have vomited up our insides along with the food.) We examined ourselves and each other without finding anything amiss, and I thought disdainfully, You hicks, all we're doing is eating!

After we'd eaten and drunk our fill, I suggested a stroll through Daojiang Town. This was the first time I'd gone to the countryside or to a distant town, and everything was novel to me. My cousin and the others weren't interested, so I went off on my own while they waited at the bus station. The main sound and fury of the Cultural Revolution had passed by then, and its "smashing of the four olds"[1] and big-character posters were no longer in fashion, although their traces were detectable in the ruined walls, memorial archways, stele inscriptions, and wall towers of the old city. The inscribed placard in the Kou Gong Tower had been destroyed by then, and a rusty lock secured the tower's moldering door, but from the wall I could see the shimmering river and its distant tree-covered sandbars. Climbing down, I detoured around a smashed memorial arch and reached the riverbank through an archway in the city wall. At the north end of the Shuinan pontoon bridge, clear water beat against jagged rock, and although the granite pagodas at the end of the bridge had been knocked down, the scene was still heart-achingly beautiful. Walking back from the bridge, I was shocked to find posted next to the city wall archway a notice by the "Supreme People's Court of the Poor and Lower-Middle Peasants." The succinct notice, written in a fine hand, went something like this:

> An investigation of reactionary landlords XXX, XXX, XXX . . . has found them guilty of heinous crimes including persistent reactionary standpoints, score settling, and resistance to remolding and poor work effort; public wrath demands their execution. Following a decision by the Supreme People's Court of the Poor and Lower-Middle Peasants, they are sentenced to death, effective immediately.
>
> The Supreme People's Court of the Poor and Lower-Middle Peasants of the XX Production Brigade
>
> Head Judge: XXX
>
> Deputy Head Judge: XXX
>
> [Date]

I remember with particular clarity that each of the names of those sentenced to death had been crossed out with a brush dipped in red ink.[2]

My heart began thundering in spite of myself, my scrotum shriveling into a tight little ball as my scalp tingled. I read the notice once more to make sure I hadn't misread or misconstrued it. Although I'd long become inured to the many fantastical oddities emerging from the Cultural Revolution, this notice and this "court" took me completely by surprise. I wondered if it might simply be some malicious prank, or at most a threat.

Upon returning to the bus stop, I immediately told my cousin and the others of my discovery and was surprised by their nonchalance. My cousin said, "What's so strange about that? It wasn't only here that people were killed. They were killed where we were, too [i.e., in Jiangyong], but it wasn't quite as bad as it was here." His friends who had been sent to Daoxian's villages had even more knowing expressions on their faces: "That's nothing. Lots worse things went on. In our village, they tied people together and blew them up with dynamite. Flesh and bone flew all over the place. The villagers called it 'the Celestial Maiden scattering flowers.' "[3] But when I asked why these people were killed, they couldn't come up with a reason. By the time of the killings, they had returned to their homes in Changsha to carry out revolution, and all they knew was what others had told them, which was that black elements had been killed and entire families had been massacred, even suckling infants. Heads had rolled and blood had flowed in rivers.

After leaving Daoxian and arriving in Jiangyong, I looked up an educated youth nicknamed Karl Liu, who was notable for rooting himself in the villages to "grasp revolution and promote production." As someone well versed in Marxist-Leninist ideology, he could be expected to have a good knowledge and understanding of the Daoxian killings. Karl Liu said, "This was the inevitable result of the intensification of class struggle," and as he went on I became only more bewildered.

According to Karl Liu, "The 'killing wind' in Daoxian arose because a small minority of black elements took advantage of the Great Cultural Revolution to establish reactionary organizations such as 'black killing squads' to kill poor and lower-middle peasants, but they were discovered, and the poor peasants turned around and killed them. But then things got out of control, and that's what led to the indiscriminate killing."

Liu's explanation didn't stand up under even the simplest follow-up questioning. I asked, "How do you know all this?" He replied, "I heard it from the poor and lower-middle peasants in our production team."[4]

I later learned that this was the favorite explanation Daoxian officials gave for the killings. A slightly later version, still widely believed today, had it that the Daoxian killings were spurred by an ultra-Leftist ideological trend and by killings in Guangxi.[5] This was also a complete fabrication; the truth was exactly the opposite, as I will later discuss in detail. What I found most chilling was that someone such as Karl Liu, who could not be regarded as ignorant or gullible, would express not the slightest suspicion toward such obvious fabrications. Even so, it took nearly 20 years for me to come any closer to the truth.

A few months after my first visit to Daoxian, in early 1968, I left Jiangyong and returned to Changsha to "resume my studies and make revolution." Soon after that, I was sent to Leiyang, Hunan Province, as part of the mass campaign to send educated youth "up the mountains and down to the villages." The events in Daoxian receded from my mind as I spent eight years being "reeducated" by the peasants. Finally, as the great tide of rusticated youth returned to the cities, I used the pretext of "health problems" to return to Changsha. I passed the college entrance exam to attend university, and after graduation I was assigned work in a school-run factory. Preferring my creative pastime, I eventually resigned and became a writer, and by 1986 I had gained a following. My life course seemed to have chosen me, and part of it was the opportunity to go to Daoxian to report on the Cultural Revolution killings.

This life-changing opportunity was the result of efforts by a few senior officials to get to the bottom of the Daoxian atrocities. According to a source in the Lingling prefectural Chinese Communist Party (CCP) committee, on December 22, 1980, just before Hu Yaobang became general party secretary, he went on an inspection tour of the five south-central provinces and made a point of stopping in Hunan's Lingling Prefecture to hear a report from the prefectural CCP committee on the killings in Daoxian. While listening, Hu Yaobang fidgeted and grimaced, popped up and down in his seat, and finally demanded, "What hasn't yet been dealt with must be taken care of, especially the arrangements for the victims." But discretion was required. As Hu Yaobang put it, "We can't let this matter become public. Once it's been taken care of, leave it alone and let it gradually fade away."

In spring 1982, Jiang Hua, then president of the Supreme People's Court, went back to his home village in Jianghua County, Lingling Prefecture, for a family visit. When the prefectural CCP secretary reported to him on the random killing of innocent people in Daoxian during the Cultural Revolution, Jiang Hua abruptly asked, "How many monks do you have in Daoxian?" The prefectural CCP secretary expected only a serious question from a senior cadre, so he answered truthfully, "I haven't heard of any monks in Daoxian." "No monks?" Jiang Hua demanded, his voice rising an octave, "Yet killing so many so lawlessly!" He was making a pun on the word "lawless," *wufa*, which sounded the same as the term for "no hair," a defining characteristic of monks. Jiang Hua's own cousins had been among the innocents killed in this massacre.

Eventually the indignation of such officials, and a brief period of openness and reform in the government, let to the establishment in May 1984 of the special Task Force to investigate the Daoxian massacre. The Task Force carried out all its work behind closed doors, and its findings were never made public.

That was not the original intention, however. In 1986, just as I was making my name as a writer, there was still an official desire to understand and learn from the tragic events in Daoxian.

At that time, a certain Hunan literary magazine was influential throughout China, and its editors had the ambition of raising it to a higher level and making it more relevant to the life of China's people. With historical reportage popular at that time, the editors decided to publish a series of groundbreaking reports on actual events, one of which was the Cultural Revolution killings in Daoxian. The honor of that assignment was entrusted to me. Through internal information and the grapevine, we'd learned that Lingling Prefecture had organized a huge task force under the central and provincial leadership to investigate and deal with the Daoxian killings, and that the task force had investigated the cause and effect of the killings, settled matters with the survivors of the victims, and dealt appropriately with those whose crimes and errors were responsible for the killings. In official parlance, the Task Force had "sorted out issues of right and wrong, absorbed important historical lessons, and enhanced the concepts of law and discipline"; 85 percent of the victims' families had reportedly expressed satisfaction with the results, and most of the investigated individuals had admitted their wrongdoing. The diffusion of rancor between cadres and the public had united hearts and minds and set the groundwork for the Four Modernizations,[6] and the Central Committee had expressed its satisfaction in a four-phrase assessment: "Attention to leadership, clear-cut policies, steady pace, and competent measures."

One of the magazine's editors said: "We hope this article will comprehensively and realistically reflect the killing incident, while also emphasizing the great effort and enormous achievements of the Lingling prefectural party committee and its Task Force in thoroughly negating the Cultural Revolution, liberating thought, and bringing order out of chaos under the spiritual guidance of the Third Plenum of the Eleventh Central Committee. We hope you can come up with something as powerful as the article on the Tangshan earthquake."[7]

Taking the hint, I replied, "I understand. I'll be forward looking and will thoroughly cover the healing process."

That editor was normally a very stern individual, but at this point he allowed a little humor to creep in with a well-known quote by former president Liu Shaoqi: "Yes, problems must be discussed thoroughly, and accomplishments must be discussed adequately."[8]

That's how I arrived in Lingling Prefecture (also known as Yongzhou) to embark on the most important assignment of my journalistic career, the Cultural Revolution killings in Daoxian. It never occurred to me that this trip would completely change the course of my life.

Through friends, I first arranged interviews with some members of Lingling Prefecture's "Task Force to Deal with the Aftermath of the Cultural Revolution Killings" (referred to hereafter as the Task Force). The Task Force, established in May 1984, carried out all its work behind closed doors and never made its findings public. Our interviews were subsequently referred to as "secret," but in fact we received help and support from leaders in Hunan Province and Lingling Prefecture; our inquiries were not secret, but it could be said that they were not open. Without the help and support of those officials, we could never have gained access to so much confidential data or carried out so many sensitive interviews. We read those records, data, and investigative reports trembling and with tear-drenched faces. It was as if we stood disoriented in the middle of a desert with the wailing of thousands of people assaulting our ears while gales of wind sent human body parts dancing through the air around us. The horrifying details will come later, but here I will extract some figures from the reports to summarize this killing campaign.

The Daoxian killings occurred over the course of 66 days, from August 13 to October 17, 1967, affecting all of the county's 10 districts and 37 communes, 468 (93.4 percent) of its rural production brigades, 1,590 of its production teams, and 2,778 of its households (2.7 percent of the total), with 117 households completely wiped out. A total of 4,519 people died, composing 1.17 percent of the county's population at the time. Of these, 4,193 were killed and 326 were driven to suicide. In terms of class breakdown, 1,830 (41.4 percent) of the victims were classified as black elements, 2,207 (49.9 percent) were classified as the offspring of black elements, 352 (8 percent) were poor or lower-middle peasants, and 31 (0.7 percent) belonged to other categories. In terms of occupation, 4,208 (95.2 percent) of the victims were peasants, 17 (0.38 percent) were state cadres, 141 (3.19 percent) were educators, 20 (0.45 percent) were health workers, and 34 (0.77 percent) were workers. Those killed included eight CCP members and 13 Communist Youth League members. Following the killings, family members of the victims were also targeted through the confiscation of assets of 2,423 households, the occupation or destruction of 3,781 homes, and the seizing of 53,000 household implements, while 629 people were forced to flee the county and 635 elderly or children were left without family support.

Under the influence of Daoxian, the other 10 counties and cities of Lingling Prefecture also experienced killings to a greater or lesser degree. The entire prefecture (including Daoxian) recorded 9,093 unnatural deaths during the Cultural Revolution, of which 7,696 were killings and 1,397 were suicides, and another

2,146 people were gravely wounded or crippled. In terms of class breakdown, 3,576 of the dead were black elements (including Rightists), 4,057 were the off-spring of black elements, 1,049 were poor or lower-middle peasants (some of whom had varying degrees of "historical problems," and some of whom were killed in revenge for their killing of others), and 411 belonged to other catego-ries. The victims included 826 minors, and ranged in age from 78 years to 10 days old.

Some 15,050 people were directly implicated as organizers, supervisors, or those who actually did the killing. In Daoxian, for example, it was initially ascer-tained that 426 state cadres were directly involved, composing 22.6 percent of all the county's cadres (and the majority of the county-level leadership), along with 4,665 (66.5 percent) of the county's rural grassroots cadres, and 3,880 (36.9 percent) of its CCP members.

There were ten basic killing methods:

(1) shooting (with rifles, shotguns, fowling pieces, blunderbusses, etc.);
(2) stabbing (with sabers, broadswords, hatchets, spears, etc.);
(3) drowning (in ponds or in rivers, known as "releasing a raft");
(4) explosion (known as "flying the homemade airplane" or the more evoca-tive "Celestial Maiden scattering flowers");
(5) pushing over a cliff (or into an abandoned mining pit);
(6) live burial (usually in abandoned kilns previously used for roasting sweet potatoes);
(7) beating (with cudgels, hoes, rakes, and shoulder poles);
(8) hanging or strangling;
(9) burning (including smoke inhalation);
(10) other methods.

I should note that when I was unable to publish the initial draft of this book, I compiled the above data for inclusion in someone else's book,[9] which brought the Daoxian killings to the public eye for the first time. At that time, I gave the 10th killing method as "dropping," believing that other killing methods would fall under one of the listed categories. During later supplementary interviews, a source told me of a production team that tied up a "rich peasant," dropped him into an abandoned limekiln, and covered him with quicklime, then poured on water, which ignited the quicklime and incinerated him. This method was known as "lime-roasted egg." I had difficulty believing this method actually existed, since lime is hard to come by, yet it is essential for neutralizing Daoxian's acidic red earth and for construction, and using it for killing would be wasteful. But my source contacted me after I returned to Changsha and said he'd found witnesses who could confirm the report: "Next time you come to Daoxian, I'll take you to

see them." That's how I learned that Wanjiazhuang Commune's Ganzhepu production brigade (Shangdong Village) used this method to dispatch 14 victims.
The victims were lowered into two abandoned pits in a stone quarry near the
village, after which 500 kilos or so of quicklime was poured in. Witnesses say the
people in the pits screamed pleas for a quick death as their skin blackened and
rotted from their bones. I was simply flabbergasted.

That's why I changed the 10th method to "other," to ensure that even the most
inconceivable killing method would not be left out.

All the evil of which humans are capable was displayed to shocking effect in
this mass frenzy. What was it that stripped these killers of all conscience and
made them so determined to eliminate their victims? With few exceptions, no
prior ill will existed between killers and victims, and some were even distant
relations. To this day, the killers have been unable to claim any threat presented
to them by the victims, or any improvement to their own lives resulting from
these deaths. The vast majority of the dead had been honest, law-abiding citizens
who minded their own business and worked hard to maintain the most basic
standard of living.

The investigation by the Task Force found:

(1) Among the more than 9,000 people killed, scarcely anyone had engaged
    in any form of counterrevolutionary activity, and very few even resisted or
    dared protest their innocence.
(2) The seven major "counterrevolutionary organizations" that Daoxian
    claimed to have uncovered during that time all were found to be bogus.
(3) Being a black element was reason enough to be killed; if you weren't a
    black element, you could be labeled as one or as a collaborator and then
    be killed.

After gaining this basic understanding of what had occurred, I devised a
work plan with my reporting partner, Zhang Minghong, who at that time was
the Lingling station chief for Hunan Provincial Radio and Television. A native
of Ningyuan County, Zhang was a journalist with a genuine grassroots background. At his home we discussed and formulated a rough plan for our reporting and set three rules of conduct for ourselves: (1) to maintain complete
objectivity and fairness during our reporting, not to make any false repre-
sentations or act against our convictions, and not to be swayed by personal
feelings; (2) to listen carefully and not ask leading questions or express our
own viewpoints, and not to involve ourselves in any specific case; (3) if during
our reporting any conflict or disagreement arose between us, we should not
argue or become divided but should resolve the matter after our reporting was
completed.

Looking back, I can see that our ability to carry out our reporting without a hitch was dependent on these three rules, and it was my careless violation of them that caused the serious obstruction we later encountered.

We set off for Daoxian by bus early the next morning, without any specific local interview targets or any work unit or individual to receive us. Minghong said jokingly, "We're going fishing in choppy waters."

The weather was gray and drizzly, and my attempts to recall the details of my visit 19 years earlier were just as clouded. I must have traveled the same road twice before, but it seemed to become only increasingly unfamiliar and mysterious. The precipitous, twisting slopes of Shuangpei Mountain made my head spin, while a misty rain made me feel that the bus was carrying us deep into a treacherous lair of no return. Yet, as the bus descended through the folds of Zijin Mountain and passed the Huyan Dam, the vista opened onto a gradually leveling and expansive landscape. A road sign appeared in bold, black script: Daoxian. At that moment, the clouds parted to reveal a brilliant sun. Minghong told me this was the southern Hunan microclimate: rain amid sunlight and sun amid the rain. The bus barreled on toward the county town, through alternating bands of golden ripening paddy and newly planted green sprouts enclosed by screen-like mountain ranges.

Upon disembarking from the long-distance bus, I found Daojiang completely transformed from the place that had been lingering in my dreams, as if the past 19 years had wiped clean the stains and scars of that time. The pond and snack shop had been replaced by a market where multicolored garments rippled in the wind. Across the road stood the Daoxian No. 2 High School, which during the Cultural Revolution had served as headquarters for the Revolutionary Alliance and had been the locus of Daoxian's three main incidents of mass armed conflict.

A concrete bridge replaced the steel cable bridge that had once spanned the Xiaoshui. Wide, straight concrete streets were lined with shops and crowded with pedestrians. The bus station restaurant's walls were full of information on the latest merchandise, and the fruit store wall offered an advertisement for a "secret family recipe curing impotence and flaccidness." A red banner proclaiming a 20 percent discount emblazoned a nearby store, while on a roadside billboard, a beautiful woman called for striking hard against the evil people and deeds that sabotaged family planning. The county radio station broadcasted tips on preventing sunstroke in the fields, and the cosmetic uses of loofah gourds.

The cobblestone streets, city wall, and pontoon bridge that had so deeply impressed themselves in my memory had subtly receded into the background, and without making an effort to seek them out, I would easily have missed them.

The coastal road ran along the Xiaoshui for about a kilometer before crossing a concrete bridge that took us to the county CCP committee hostel. Behind the hostel's enclosing wall, a pre-revolutionary screen wall commemorated the Chinese Workers and Peasants Red Sixth Army stopping in Daoxian in August and September 1934 while heading westward for the Long March: "China for the underprivileged: Long live the Chinese worker and peasant revolution!"

Along the way, I looked for anything that might make the town or its people stand out, only to find Daoxian indistinguishable from any other county in the People's Republic of China. The Cultural Revolution killings had led other people (including myself) to wrongly view Daoxian as a closed-off, backward, unruly place full of barbarians who attacked each other at the drop of a hat. Before my departure, my wife had been sleepless with worry and had repeatedly urged me to mind my safety and remember that our children were still young, while an old comrade who supported my reporting project wrote a letter for me to take to a former subordinate working in Lingling Prefecture, asking him to guarantee my safety. Even people in Lingling Prefecture who had never been to Daoxian shared this excessive apprehension. One comrade from the Task Force later told us that he'd been so anxious about his transfer to Daoxian that he'd brought a handgun with him. It was only after his arrival that he realized the gun was an unnecessary bother, and that what he should have brought was an extra stomach; the people of Daoxian put such an emphasis on civility, friendship, and respect that they would cut off their own heads for you to sit on if necessary. We repeatedly experienced this same feeling in the course of our reporting.

That evening, under our lamps, we browsed through the *Daozhou Gazetteer* and other related materials to prepare for our reporting work, hoping to gain a better understanding of Daoxian's history. The *Gazetteer* recorded that tribal settlements had existed here as far back as the Neolithic period. The locality had undergone many transformations and jurisdictional changes from prehistoric times through the reign of China's first emperor, Qin Shihuang, and on through the dynasties, merging with and then splitting from other counties and known successively as Yongyang County, Yingdao County, Hongdao County, and Daozhou, finally taking its current name in the second year of the Republican Era, 1913.

In its 2,000-year recorded history, Daoxian had been the birthplace of the Song-dynasty scholar Zhou Dunyi (1017–1073) and the Qing-dynasty calligraphy master He Shaoji (1799–1873), among other notables. Indeed, scholars have established that the great modern writer Lu Xun and the People's Republic of China's first premier, Zhou Enlai, had their family roots here. In short, the county could be said to have produced more than its share of talent.

Daoxian contributed to the development of the Chu culture in the first millennium BCE and then gave rise to the Baiyue culture of southern China. The legendary Emperor Shun passed through here when he toured the south. Here Kou Zhun had erected his tower, dreaming of peace, and here the Taiping Rebellion leader Hong Xiuquan had paused to issue his proclamations against the Qing in 1852.

Outside the window of our room, the county town was a vision of tranquility as the Lianxi River shimmered under a starry sky and refreshing winds surged across the basin from Mount Jiuyi. Standing in the placid moonlight, I sensed an insistent murmur beside my ear, but when I listened for it, all returned to silence.

Daoxian on the Eve of the Massacre

As noted earlier, our reporting trip to Daoxian was ideally timed. By the time we arrived, the 1,300 cadres of the prefectural Task Force (nearly half of whom were in Daoxian) had completed two years of inquiries and had just begun preparing a summary report. Had we arrived earlier, they would have still been dealing with their investigation, and had we arrived later, the material would already have been sealed up in top-secret files. It was our arrival at just this moment that gave us access to such a large quantity of comprehensive firsthand material.

Arriving under the official banner and actual intention of "reporting the achievements of the Task Force," we got off to a smooth start. Indeed, having anticipated all kinds of difficulties and obstructions, I instead found my arms loaded with files; for so much valuable material to be presented to us without fanfare or subterfuge was beyond my wildest imagining. Two years of effort by hundreds of people had gradually peeled away the layers that obscured the Daoxian massacre, and apart from some details requiring our further inquiries, a rough picture of the incident was now clear.

The occurrence and development of any incident are related not only to its deep historical context, but also to a unique sequence of self-generating factors. In tracing the origins of the killings of Daoxian, the narrative that follows draws on the following sources:

(1) materials gathered by the prefectural Task Force from 1984 to 1986;
(2) materials from the 1968 "exposure study sessions" on the Daoxian massacre;
(3) our reporting;
(4) firsthand material from survivors of the massacre.

The first step in comprehending what happened in Daoxian in the summer of 1967 is understanding the political backdrop to the events.

In 1967, China was mired in chaos. July not only brought the steadily increasing heat of summer but also saw the Chinese people's revolutionary fervor reach its boiling point. On July 18, at the Chinese Communist Party (CCP) head-quarters in Zhongnanhai, a mass rally was organized to criticize President Liu Shaoqi, whose home was ransacked. Former defense minister Peng Dehuai was subjected to brutal criticism and struggle from July onward, and following factional clashes in Wuhan in late July, Jiang Qing called for "verbal attack and armed defense," resulting in an intensification of violence throughout China. On August 5, as Liu Shaoqi, Deng Xiaoping, and Tao Zhu were denounced at a mil-lion-strong mass rally at Tiananmen Square, *People's Daily* published Mao's essay "Bombard the Headquarters: My First Big-Character Poster," accompanied by an editorial titled "Bombard the Headquarters of the Bourgeoisie." On August 7, Public Security Minister Xie Fuzhi called for "smashing the public-security, procuratorial, and judicial organs," and a new state apparatus was established under military control.

These directives reached every corner of the People's Republic of China (PRC), including this little Hunan border county. The streets and lanes of Daojiang were full of "cables from Beijing" and "extraordinary glad tidings." Everyone held aloft Mao's "little red book" as they recited its quotations; a throb of gongs and drums echoed through the streets, hailing the latest directive from Chairman Mao.

Since its founding, the People's Republic had already experienced at least 10 major "mass movements," all on orders from the CCP Central Committee, and in each case the masses of China had eagerly thrown themselves into the campaigns, attacking whatever the CCP told them to attack. The Cultural Revolution was no exception. The difference was that once the masses became involved in this campaign, they quickly split into multiple factions with intensely antagonistic viewpoints. Even the Central Committee was split between a "pro-letarian headquarters" led by Mao Zedong and a "bourgeois headquarters" led by Liu Shaoqi. But all factions claimed to be defending "Chairman Mao's rev-olutionary line" and endorsing the "proletarian headquarters represented by Chairman Mao."

Initially confused about the intentions of the Beijing leadership, the Hunan provincial CCP committee treated the Cultural Revolution as a combination of the ongoing Socialist Education movement and the 1957 Anti-Rightist cam-paign. As a result, the early stage of the Cultural Revolution in Hunan adopted past methods of dispatching "work teams" to schools and work units and "cleansing the class ranks" of various "black elements"—targeting not only the usual classes such as landlords and rich peasants, but also new groups such as "reactionary academic authorities" and other alleged "anti-party cliques." In the popular parlance of that time, the campaign aimed to "sweep away all ox demons and snake spirits."

The "cleansing of the class ranks" that I refer to here was not the well-known Cultural Revolution campaign to "Rectify the Class Ranks" that began in late 1967, but rather one that began during the Socialist Education movement, a campaign of class struggle and political education that Mao launched in September 1962 in response to efforts by some leaders to scale back disastrous economic policies such as the Great Leap Forward. The Socialist Education movement first targeted corruption in Hebei and Hunan and then proceeded nationwide as a campaign to "clean up accounts, warehouses, assets, and work points" in communes and counties, through which it came to be known as the "Four Cleanups campaign," while in the urban areas it targeted corruption, profiteering, waste, decentralism, and bureaucracy (the "Five Antis").

The special feature of this movement in Hunan (to which Mao gave a particularly high appraisal) was the reorganization of the class ranks, in particular the formation of "poor- and lower-middle-peasant associations" (hereafter "poor-peasant association" or PPA). The first secretary of the provincial CCP committee, Zhang Pinghua, also held the position of chairman of the provincial PPA, while the second-in-command of the Daoxian CCP committee, Xiong Bing'en,[1] was also chairman of the county PPA. This was true in other counties as well. The PPAs, which play a crucial role in the tragic narrative that follows, were a major outcome of the Socialist Education movement. In Hunan, this movement lagged behind Beijing, lasting for more than three years from 1962 until the middle of 1966, and involved two major stages. The second stage, which began in 1965, included "clarifying politics, investigating class background, and launching a struggle against class enemies" (the stage that I refer to in this book as "cleansing of the class ranks"), which lasted through the first half of 1966 and overlapped with the launch of the Cultural Revolution on May 16, 1966. In Daoxian, specifically, the Cultural Revolution did not really begin until student Red Guards began attacking teachers and "black element" students in mid-August 1966. At that point Hunan's Socialist Education movement hastily transitioned into the Cultural Revolution, and decisions made to purge people during the earlier campaign's "cleansing of the class ranks" were actually carried out during the early stage of the Cultural Revolution. During the Cultural Revolution killings in Daoxian, a substantial number of the people who were killed had been sent back to the countryside as a result of the Four Cleanups campaign, while many others were targeted because they had criticized cadres during the campaign. Throughout this book, any reference I make to "cleansing of the class ranks" refers to that particular stage of the Socialist Education movement (Four Cleanups).

As a result of its misunderstanding of the Central Committee's (in fact, Mao's) intentions, the Hunan provincial CCP committee in September 1966 made a decision to "seize Rightists," and in a matter of days, some 100,000 "Rightists," "political pickpockets," and "black demons" had been detained, with "black material" compiled against many others targeted for a new and expanded round. In this way, tens of thousands of ordinary people were sucked into the whirlpool of political struggle. These moves by the Hunan provincial CCP committee were not in line with Mao's strategic planning, however, and they were criticized by Mao and the Central Cultural Revolution Small Group as "implementing and executing Liu Shaoqi's bourgeois reactionary line." The unanticipated result was that people initially labeled as "counterrevolutionary students" and "Rightists" were transmogrified into "militant Red Guards" and "valiant revolutionaries." These former "black demons" eventually made their way to Beijing and submitted complaints to the Central Cultural Revolution Small Group, and with the support of Beijing's Third Command Post and other rebel faction student groups, they established their own organizations.

These developments in Beijing exacerbated the uncertainty and chaos as the Cultural Revolution progressed elsewhere in the country. There had been no freedom of association since the founding of the PRC in 1949, and no organizational base for ordinary people outside of the CCP, but people were suddenly able to form their own groups, such as the Red Guards and various "rebel factions," from mid-1966 to mid-1968. Xiang River Storm was one of the large-scale mass organizations formed in Hunan Province during this stage of the Cultural Revolution, and it serves as a prime example of how a product of chaos became an impetus for the worst kind of violence.

On October 24, 1966, a young teacher at Changsha's No. 1 Secondary School, Ye Dongchu (who subsequently changed his name to Ye Weidong), and an art designer at the Silver Star Cinema, Zhang Jiazheng, joined with others in Beijing to establish the Maoist Red Guard Xiang River Storm Troopers, more commonly referred to as Xiang River Storm. In late October, Xiang River Storm returned to Changsha and burgeoned into an enormous rebel faction mass organization with some one million members, including many of the workers, cadres, and ordinary people who had earlier been attacked as "black demons."

Then in Shanghai in January 1967, former propaganda official Zhang Chunqiao (eventually a member of the infamous Gang of Four) headed an overthrow of the city's existing CCP establishment. This power seizure, referred to as the "January Storm," was replicated elsewhere in China as campaigns criticizing the "bourgeois reactionary line" shifted their emphasis to seizing power from an alleged "capitalist-roader faction in power" within the CCP. In compliance with Mao Zedong's directives, the People's Liberation Army (PLA) made a full-scale intervention to "support the Left, industry, and agriculture, and establish military control and training," a de facto military junta. The "Support the Left" campaign in Hunan Province was the responsibility of the provincial military district.

At this point, the question of how to carry the Cultural Revolution forward caused a split in Hunan between organizations such as Xiang River Storm and the Hunan Province College Red Guard Revolutionary Rebel Faction Command Post (known as the College Command Post), giving rise to two camps, the "moderate faction" (also known as the "revisionists") and the "radical faction." The Hunan provincial military district unequivocally supported the moderate College Command Post and sent a report to the Central Cultural Revolution Small Group depicting Xiang River Storm as a "conservative organization engaged in violent activities." On February 4, 1967, a brief directive by the Central Cultural Revolution Small Group designated Xiang River Storm and another group called the Red Flag Army as "reactionary organizations" against which immediate dictatorial measures should be taken to "divide and demoralize the hoodwinked masses." The provincial military district launched its operation that night, and all key members of Xiang River Storm were rounded up before dawn. According to conservative estimates, during this three-day campaign more than 10,000 individuals were arrested throughout the province, and many were subjected to public denunciation.

One of the key characteristics of the Cultural Revolution was constant reversals. Even as Xiang River Storm and the Red Flag Army were being suppressed, divided, and demoralized, an energetic movement to reverse the verdict against these groups had already been launched and was intensifying, with a rebel faction made up largely of workers as its nucleus. Even more critically, the central leadership did not completely approve of the Hunan provincial military district's "Support the Left" operations and had not endorsed the power-seizing movement led by the College Command Post.

On June 3, the provincial military district declared that Xiang River Storm was not a counterrevolutionary organization but did not allow it to resume its activities. The next day, however, Xiang River Storm held a rally to reestablish itself and its headquarters and began engaging in public and organized activities. Conflict intensified between the College Command Post faction and the Hunan Province Working Class Revolutionary Rebel Faction Alliance Headquarters (the Worker Alliance, which included Xiang River Storm), presaging armed conflict between the two factions. The violence reached a climax in August and September with heavy gunfire exchanged in localities between Changsha and Xiangtan.

This phenomenon was not unique to Hunan; most other regions of China experienced similar chaos and violence, in particular where actions by "revolutionary rebel factions to seize power from capitalist roaders" did not initially gain the support of the central leadership. The conflict between antagonistic mass organizations deepened and gave rise to larger umbrella factions, with successive rounds of mass factional violence becoming increasingly intense.

In the early morning of July 27, at a reception for representatives of Hunan's various factions who had come to Beijing for negotiations, the central leaders who were present explicitly instructed that Xiang River Storm be rehabilitated. On August 10, the Central Committee formally issued "Certain Decisions regarding the Hunan Issue" (known as the "August 10 Decision"), which reversed the Central Cultural Revolution Small Group's February 4 directive.

This mass confusion and repeated reversals from the Beijing leadership form the general backdrop to the events in Daoxian in late summer 1967. In Daoxian, as in other parts of China, two irreconcilable mass organizations emerged: one was called the Mao Zedong Thought Red Warrior Alliance Headquarters, or "Red Alliance," and the other was called the Proletarian Revolutionary Struggle-Criticism-Transformation Alliance Headquarters, or "Revolutionary Alliance." The Red Alliance referred to the Revolutionary Alliance as the "Revolutionary Bandits," and the Revolutionary Alliance referred to the Red Alliance as the "Red Fogies." The two groups indulged in mutual recrimination and frequent small-scale clashes. Each was determined to defeat the other.

The Revolutionary Alliance was a hodgepodge of students and teachers, townspeople, craftsmen, lower-level intellectuals, and a few cadres. Its members were relatively well educated, and many had suffered injustice that engendered resistance toward the bureaucratic class and the status quo. This faction was stronger in the county town of Daojiang, its stronghold in the No. 2 High School blaring constant strident broadcasts of "Forge On against the Tottering Foe," the editorial published on the first anniversary of the Central Committee's formal decision concerning the Cultural Revolution.

The Red Alliance had inseparable ties both to the new and old powers in the locality, most of whom were CCP stalwarts on whom the regime depended either nominally or in terms of vested interests. This group tended to defend the entrenched political order and felt a deep antipathy toward those who boldly claimed the right to revolt. The Red Alliance enjoyed the support of the entire local government and CCP organization as well as the de facto leadership, which was composed mainly of the county's People's Armed Forces Department (PAFD).

County-level PAFDs were the grassroots appendage of the PLA's local regiments and came under the departmental jurisdiction of the provincial military district as well as the geographic jurisdiction of the county CCP committee. In a sense, members of the PAFD were both military personnel and local cadres. For example, at that time, Daoxian PAFD commander Cui Baoshu and political commissar Liu Shibin also served on the standing committee of the Daoxian CCP committee. China had been gradually moving toward virtual military control since January 1967, when the CCP Central Committee, State Council, Central Military Commission, and Central Cultural Revolution Small Group issued the

"Resolution regarding the People's Liberation Army Resolutely Supporting the Revolutionary Masses on the Left." Daoxian had established governing bodies at the county, district, and commune levels under the name of "leading groups to seize revolution and push production" (known as seize-and-push groups). In the national context, these tripartite entities consisting of cadres, military personnel, and ordinary people were usually called revolutionary committees. In Daoxian, this new power establishment of seize-and-push groups included PAFD cadres, representatives of revolutionary mass organizations, and "cadres who had taken sides with the revolution," with PAFD personnel at its core, and it effectively governed the county.

Daoxian's climate has been described as a "year-round summer refreshed by rain," suffering neither cold winters nor sweltering summers. However, some elderly people recalled that the summer of 1967 was unusual, with an overcast August unrelieved by rain and oppressively hot and humid; they remarked, "Heaven knew what was coming!"

The people of Daoxian have a tradition of composing doggerel, and one was dedicated to the "killing wind" of the Cultural Revolution:

> The August 5 meeting sent up the flare;
> The August 8 gun snatching planted the fuse;
> The Xiaba production brigade started the killing;
> Xique Zhengjia set the fire.

Accordingly, we will examine each of these key events in detail.

The August 5 county seize-and-push meeting

From August 2 to 5, the Daoxian Leading Group to Seize Revolution and Push Production called an urgent meeting of the leaders of all district seize-and-push groups. Some people say it went beyond its ostensible purpose and actually mobilized the killings. The minutes of that meeting include the following quote from Xiong Bing'en, county CCP secretary and deputy head of the county seize-and-push group:

> At present a new situation has emerged in class struggle: the class enemy's activities have become highly aggressive. A few days ago, a reactionary poster appeared in District 6. The class enemy was creating rumors of war, saying the Chiang Kai-shek gang is about to launch an offensive on mainland China, that the American imperialists

are about to launch a world war, and that once the war starts, CCP members will be killed first and then probationary CCP members. District 1 has an old collaborator who goes every day to the production brigade CCP secretary and the chairman of the poor and lower-middle peasants' association and argues about getting rehabilitated. In District 11's Tangjia Commune, the landlords and rich peasants of the Xialongdong production brigade openly launched an attack to settle old scores, claiming they were going to take back the property distributed to poor and lower-middle peasants. . . . In some places we've had land divided among households, disputes and fighting, an outflow of the labor force, speculation, and profiteering. Comrades, we must raise our revolutionary guard against these new trends in class struggle and not lower our defenses for an instant. District 6 has done well in this regard, taking the initiative to attack class enemies and showing signs of improvement in revolution and production. This shows that seizing class struggle is the answer, and that failure to seize class struggle makes it impossible to push production and development. . . . We must boldly seize the net and pull the string of class struggle and strike hard against sabotage by class enemies. We must organize the masses to criticize and struggle against the incorrigible Four Black Elements and mobilize the masses to impose dictatorship. We must mercilessly attack the most heinous offenders by assembling dossiers and reporting them to the higher levels for punishment in accordance with law.

This is an opportune moment to introduce the three main leaders of the Daoxian CCP committee and county government at that time:

(1) County CCP First Secretary Shi Xiuhua, 39, was from a poor peasant family in Hebei's Yutian County and had been sent south as a cadre. Shi had an explosive temper and an overbearing attitude that earned him the nickname Nan Batian.[2] In addition, he had "fallen into the class enemy's honey trap" by marrying the daughter of a landlord, which made him a target for overthrow. After being exposed by the Red Alliance, he was sent to a rural village to labor under the supervision of poor and lower-middle peasants.

(2) County CCP secretary Xiong Bing'en, 39, was a local cadre from a farm-hand family in Dongmen Township. Xiong had come under attack early in the campaign for "executing a bourgeois reactionary line" but was now stepping forward to take charge of operations as a "cadre taking sides with the revolution."

3) County deputy CCP secretary and county head Huang Yida, 33, was a local cadre from an upper-middle peasant family in Shenzhangtang Township. In the early stage of the Cultural Revolution, he had been attacked for "executing the bourgeois reactionary line," and by this time he was locked up in the Revolutionary Alliance headquarters (the No. 2 High School) to "confess his problems and accept the criticism and struggle of the revolutionary masses."

The crux of the matter was Xiong Bing'en's position in Daoxian's political life at that time, combined with the content of his speech on August 5.

Available evidence indicates that among those seated on the rostrum, no one could be said to have directly issued orders to kill, but the implication of killing was there, in particular the implication of killing black elements.[3]

The heads of most of the district seize-and-push groups were also the heads of district or commune PAFDs or public-security or political-affairs cadres. Once the meeting ended, they dashed back to their respective districts and communes to relay the gist of the meeting and arrange follow-up.

The August 8 gun-snatching incident

The August 5 county seize-and-push meeting was closely followed by a sudden occurrence that accelerated the advent of the slaughter. This was the August 8 gun-snatching incident constantly alluded to with such notoriety in the course of Daoxian's Cultural Revolution. The process was in fact quite simple. On August 8, the Daoxian Revolutionary Alliance (which at that time enjoyed the advantage over the Red Alliance) with the help of Lingling Prefecture rebel faction organizations obtained a letter of introduction from Deputy Commander Zhao of the Lingling Prefecture Military Subdistrict, then burst into the office of the county PAFD, broke down the door to the armory, and forcibly "commandeered" firearms and ammunition. The next day the Revolutionary Alliance returned and seized firearm parts (specifically firing pins) stored in the ceiling. Most of the seized firearms were taken by Xiang River Storm and another local rebel faction organization, with the Revolutionary Alliance retaining 150 guns and firing pins for its "verbal attack and armed defense."

Differing versions of this key event demonstrate the difficulty of establishing the facts behind the Daoxian massacre.

An "exposure and confession" written one year later by Red Alliance leader and county production command post cadre Zhang Mingchi provides collateral verification of the August 8 incident. Zhang said that when he went to political commissar Liu Shibin to get weapons for the Red Alliance, Liu showed him the shattered armory door and claimed that the Revolutionary Alliance had carried out a counterrevolutionary coup d'état:

> He told us, "The Revolutionary Alliance has taken armed occupation of our headquarters. I've lost my personal liberty, and they're watching everything I say and do. They're treating us like the enemy. I never guessed the Cultural Revolution would turn out this way. Those above won't let us rebel; otherwise, I'd go to Beijing and rebel!" When he avoided the topic of weapons, we insisted that he take us back to his room at the production office. After inviting us to sit down, he told us, "Class struggle has become intense in Daoxian. It's very complicated. The actions of the Revolutionary Alliance fully expose their reactionary character. I understand how you're feeling now, but we haven't any weapons; if we did, we would support you. The Revolutionary Alliance has snatched the guns and left you unarmed, but don't worry, the district and commune PAFDs have guns, and there are more guns in the villages than the Revolutionary Alliance has. . . ." Liu also divulged to us, "The Revolutionary Alliance is planning to bring all the district and commune PAFD heads to the county seat so they can round them up and leave the district and commune militia without leadership. I'm not in a position to make telephone calls, but you should get word to all the districts and tell them not to fall for it."

A report by a Revolutionary Alliance leader and former chairman of the Daoxian Grain Bureau Labor Union, Liu Xiangxi, verifies the gun-snatching incident from another angle:

> Around 7:00 p.m. on August 8, 1967, the county PAFD's deputy commander, Zhao Decai, and two staff officers rushed over to the Revolutionary Alliance headquarters at the No. 2 High School and reported . . . that the head of the Lengshuitan Paper Mill's production department, Mao Jiansheng, and the head of the Lingling Resistance (a Lingling Prefecture rebel faction organization) had brought a letter of introduction from the Lingling Military Subarea Headquarters (this letter is now filed in the county archives) authorizing them to take control of the weapons and ammunition in the county PAFD's armory, and to remove everything that night. Deputy Commander Zhao said, "In consideration of the urgency of anti-airdrop defense at Qianjiadong and the Xiangyuan tin mine, the PAFD hopes Revolutionary Alliance

leaders will rush over in person to the PAFD headquarters to take part in negotiations between the PAFD and Lingling Xiang River Storm and Lingling Resistance, urging them to place national interests first and leave some weapons and ammunition behind for defense against air-drops of enemy agents."

... The next day that I learned that ... the outcome of the negotia-tion was that all of the good weapons (Soviet-style carbines) were taken over by Xiang River Storm's Lengshuitan "Fire Spark Detachment"; Lingling Resistance required only one heavy machine gun and some small firearms. The remaining 150 guns, which had parts missing and were malfunctioning, were handed over to the Revolutionary Alliance for anti-airdrop defense. These guns were subsequently repaired by a demobilized serviceman, Wu XX.

Liu Xiangxi's statement was written after 1986 and was filtered by memory. I have in hand a six-part report from September 16, 1967, titled "Report Material by the Hunan Province Daoxian Revolutionary Alliance Headquarters to the 47th Army." The fifth part describes the August 8 gun seizure as follows:

The possession of the guns on August 8 transpired as follows. Around eight o'clock in the evening, the Xiang River Storm Lingling Regional Headquarters and the Lingling Resistance Headquarters dispatched two vehicles full of people to the armory and sent someone to tell us to send someone to the armory as well. Comrades Mao [Jiansheng] and Huang [Chengli] of the Leftist organizations Xiang River Storm and Lingling Resistance Headquarters had a letter of introduction from the military subdistrict, and from midnight until 3:00 a.m., they met in the PAFD conference room with PAFD commissar Liu [Shibin] and leader Zhao [Decai] to discuss the question of handing over arms to the rebel faction. Hu Xianzong also took part in the negotiations, and following study by the four sides it was unanimously agreed to turn over guns and ammunition to the Daoxian Revolutionary Alliance Headquarters. After 3:00 a.m., the handover was carried out in accordance with formal procedure. Our people lined up to accept the weapons.

Conflicts in the versions of events are natural, given the different interests involved as well as the timing of the statements. At the time, gun snatching was a glorious revolutionary action of proletarian revolutionaries, but after the Cultural Revolution, during investigations of people and incidents tied to the Gang of Four, taking part in gun-snatching incidents qualified one as a "beating, smashing, and looting element."[4] What is indisputable is that from late July to early August 1967, such gun-snatching incidents occurred throughout China; in some places, even cannons and tanks were seized. This may have been a strategic plan on the part of the proletarian headquarters, since documents show that in late July, Mao Zedong explicitly instructed Jiang Qing to distribute arms to the revolutionary Leftist factions. That is the only way to explain how unarmed civilian organizations were able to seize such a large quantity of arms and ammunition from the PLA.

After the August 8 gun-snatching incident, the Revolutionary Alliance considered themselves the Leftist victors, and the opposing Red Alliance, which had seized power in January, now felt under enormous pressure. On August 10, 1967, the CCP Central Committee issued "Certain Resolutions regarding the Hunan Issue," but the gist of its content had by then already spread throughout Hunan in the form of "cables from Beijing" and "extraordinary glad tidings." The main content of these resolutions was:

(1) The standing committee of the Hunan Province Military District CCP committee had committed political errors by attacking Xiang River Storm and suppressing the Worker Alliance and other revolutionary rebel factions during the previous phase of its "Support the Left" work but had carried out sincere self-criticism and displayed a good attitude. The Central Cultural Revolution Small Group's memo on the Hunan Provincial Military District's February 3 report regarding Xiang River Storm was also in error. On this issue, the Central Committee took responsibility.

(2) The Central Committee decided to reorganize the provincial military district and set about establishing a Hunan Province Revolutionary Committee Preparatory Committee, led by Li Yuan, Hua Guofeng, Zhang Bosen, and others, and including representatives of revolutionary mass organizations, military representatives, and revolutionary leading cadres, which would lead the province's Great Proletarian Cultural Revolution and industrial and agricultural production.

(3) All mass organization should, under the leadership of the Hunan Province Revolutionary Committee Preparatory Committee, firmly seize revolution and vigorously push production. They should be on guard against the enemy's creation of division and plots to instigate violence and should carry out internal rectification of work styles to bring about the great revolutionary alliance.

(4) The "Agreement on Immediately and Resolutely Curbing Violence" signed by the Hunan Province delegation reporting to Beijing was very good, and all mass organizations should resolutely put an end to violence. From this time forward, no faction was authorized under any pretext to seize weapons from the PLA or to loot military armories.

The day before the formal publication of the resolutions, on August 9, the head of the Red Alliance's logistics department, Zhang Mingchi, called an urgent meeting of Red Alliance stalwarts to explore emergency measures. After this noisy and argumentative meeting, it was finally decided that the Red Alliance would withdraw from the county CCP committee compound to Yingjiang Commune and would adopt Mao's anti-Kuomintang tactic of "rallying the villages to surround the town and eventually capture it." Yingjiang Commune was less than 4 kilometers west of Daojiang and was a commune under the direct jurisdiction of the county, with equivalent status to a district or township.

At this point, Daojiang Town was basically under the control of the Revolutionary Alliance, while anything outside of town was Red Alliance turf.

Following the August 8 gun-snatching incident, the Daoxian PAFD (at the county level organized by the PLA, and at the district and commune levels organized by local bureaucracy) became even more at odds with the Revolutionary Alliance, and its ties with its old comrades-at-arms in the Red Alliance became even closer. County PAFD commander Cui Baoshu, commissar Liu Shibin, and others regularly went to the Yingjiang Red Alliance headquarters to direct operations, and the PAFD's operations chief and logistics head were stationed at Yingjiang. Evidence shows that in the slaughter that followed, the Daoxian PAFD played a key role in creating rumors, exacerbating conflict, and hatching plots, and that it bore an undeniable responsibility for the killings.

On August 11, the heads of all the district PAFDs (most of whom were also the heads of their district seize-and-push groups) and some of the Red Alliance heads held a battle-readiness meeting at the clubhouse of Qingtang Commune's Yingleyuan production brigade. They decided to assemble the core members of people's militia in each district (those possessing weapons) to attack the Revolutionary Alliance headquarters and root out that "fortified village." District 6 (Qingtang District) PAFD commander Zheng Youzhi and others formed a frontline command post, with Zheng as commander in chief and Red Alliance leaders providing logistical support and intelligence work. The meeting also looked into establishing a solid "rear base area" and other such measures, emphasizing the need to strictly manage black elements (and offspring) and firmly suppress any "careless words or actions."

On that same day, at the county production headquarters, county PAFD political commissar Liu Shibin and county CCP secretary Xiong Bing'en held a telephone conference with the heads of all district and commune seize-and-push groups. After arranging for districts and communes to focus on rushing the harvest of midseason rice and sweet potatoes, Xiong Bing'en once again emphasized the need for ruthless class struggle and also stressed the looting of the PAFD and public-security arms as an indication that class enemies were planning a rebellion. Indignantly tapping on the microphone, he said, "Every locality must mobilize the masses to take decisive action, strengthen dictator-ship over the class enemies, and organize people's militias ... to defend the safety of the people's lives and property, and to safeguard the 'double rush' plant-ing and harvesting."

Everything followed as a matter of course. No one appeared to arrange for any killings, yet the killing wind intensified and only awaited a spark to ignite it.

4

The Random Killings Begin

First blood at the Xiaba production brigade

A distance of 12 kilometers northwest of Daojiang lies Shouyan Town, named for Shoufo Temple in the center of town and Yanfeng Mountain behind it.[1] In 1967, Shouyan Town was considerably smaller than it is now, consisting of two streets intersecting to form a T. The top stroke was formed by the Dao(xian)-Quan(zhou) Highway, constructed in 1964, which turned Shouyan Town into a transport hub and Daoxian's largest rural market town. It hosted a supply and marketing collective, a grain shop, a blacksmith and carpentry collective, and a school and a health clinic and served as the official location of district and township government organs.

In the district office one night in early August, Chen Zhixi lay on a bed, tossing and turning as he struggled to sleep.[2] He was tormented by a chronic illness, but also by the meeting he'd just attended as head of the Shouyan District seize-and-push group and deputy of the district public-security bureau. Ever since taking part in the Land Reform movement, he'd been engaged in public-security work and had all of the district's black elements recorded in his mental notebook. Comparing the county leader's remarks with the actual situation in his district, Chen flicked through each black element as if on a movie screen in his mind. The most infuriating image to keep flickering in his mind was that of Zhu Mian, a member of Shouyan Commune's Xiaba production brigade, whose service in the army and as township head under the old Kuomintang (KMT) regime had resulted in a 12-year prison sentence as a "pre-Liberation counterrevolutionary."

A bachelor from a lower-middle peasant family, Zhu Mian was still grumbling about his recently completed prison term, and while Chen Zhixi had been heard threatening to smash that dog's head, Zhu Mian had taken the wind out of his sails by declaring, "Director Chen has a sharp knife, but it's not that easy to kill a law-abiding citizen." Now Chen Zhixi was convinced that if the black elements attempted to seize control, Zhu Mian would lead the charge.

The next day at noon, Chen Zhixi called a meeting of the district's cadres to communicate the gist of the county seize-and-push conference and to expound on the district's "enemy situation." He said, "Comrades, class struggle in our district is intense! Over at Niulukou Village the enemy has set up a radio transmitter, and the production brigade's landlord class is being united with rumors that Chiang Kai-shek is planning an assault on the mainland. That insufferably arrogant pre-Liberation counterrevolutionary in the Xiaba production brigade, Zhu Mian, is forming a counterrevolutionary organization."

As Chen Zhixi piled up vivid but groundless criminal accusations against Zhu Mian, the Shouyan Commune cadres were shocked, completely unaware that Zhu Mian was engaging in so many counterrevolutionary activities right under their noses. (During this meeting, Chen Zhixi also mentioned Tang Song, a Rightist in the commune's Xialiantang brigade who was also subsequently killed.)

After the meeting, Chen Zhixi made a suggestion to district head Li Laiwen: "Zhu Mian is no good, and the masses should tie him up and struggle him to puncture his arrogance." Li Laiwen whole-heartedly agreed. But was it really enough to "tie up and struggle" such a thick-skinned fellow? Such dangerous elements as he would cause no end of trouble if not eliminated.

August 11 was market day in Shouyan, and its location on an important thoroughfare attracted a bustling crowd. Standing along the side of the road, Chen Zhixi spotted the head of Shouyan Commune's women's committee, Zhu Qinghua, and called her into his office. He told her, "Go back and talk with Fatty" (referring to Zhu Jiaxun, Chinese Communist Party [CCP] secretary of the Xiaba brigade) "about whether we should do away with Zhu Mian." In the Chinese language, the word for "do" has rich implications and can be applied to anything from class struggle to sex, but its meaning is always clear in context. Zhu Qinghua lived in the Xiaba brigade, and after returning to the village, she immediately went to Zhu Jiaxun and relayed Chen's message.

Zhu Jiaxun wasn't sure how to handle Zhu Mian, and that night he called a meeting of brigade's cadres and production team political instructors to consider the matter. A dozen or so cadres squeezed into the generator room of the brigade's rice mill, glancing furtively at each other in an indescribably tense atmosphere. Someone said, "We should just do away with him. That fellow Zhu Mian should have been done away with long ago." Another cadre disagreed: "Even killing a pig requires paperwork, so how can you do away with a person on the basis of a verbal instruction?" Another chimed in: "We can do away with him, but Director Chen needs to put it in writing." The discussion went on until midnight with no agreement reached, and the notion of doing away with Zhu Mian was temporarily shelved.

In the meantime, on that same day, the chairman of Shouyan Commune's Cultural Revolution Committee (CRC) and commander of the commune's Red Alliance, Xu Shanming, had talked with district head Li Laiwen about a specific plan for Shouyan Commune to take on class struggle: first, the production brigade public-security heads should convene "admonishment meetings" for black elements; second, misbehaving black elements would be handed over to the masses for criticism; third, preparations would be made for Zhu Mian and Tang Song to be tied up and beaten to puncture their arrogance.

Li approved of taking the initiative. "There's nothing wrong with mobilizing poor peasants to struggle black elements and knock someone around. Even if someone is beaten to death, no one will know who did it. Go back to the commune and forge ahead!"

Xu Shanming went back to Shouyan Commune and met secretly with commune People's Armed Forces Department (PAFD) officer He Jianxi, who said, "The situation's getting complicated. If we keep shouting slogans without taking action, people are going to stop listening."

The more experienced Xu Shanming said, "The crux of the matter is who gets attacked. District head Chen says that Zhu Mian from the Xiaba production brigade has been holding secret meetings on market day and has threatened to kill brigade cadres. Shouldn't you and Fatty take the opportunity to do away with him once and for all?"

He Jianxi immediately agreed: "Let's get it over with!"

On the morning of August 13, Shouyan Commune convened a "five chiefs" conference (involving brigade-level CCP branch secretaries, poor-peasant association [PPA] and CRC chairs, militia commanders, and public-security heads) to look into organizing personnel for a march into the city. As soon as Zhu Jiaxun arrived, He Jianxi hurried over to him and asked, "Fatty, has that fellow Zhu Mian in your production brigade been done away with?"

"No."

"Do away with him as soon as you get back—the sooner the better."

At the conference, the head of the commune PAFD gave a speech in which he repeatedly mentioned Zhu Mian's name, saying he had ties to the Revolutionary Alliance, was forming a counterrevolutionary organization, wanted to kill all the poor peasants, and so on. District leader Chen Zhixi's speech was even more vivid: "The Revolutionary Alliance wants to kill members of the Communist Party and Communist Youth League and revolutionary cadres. If you don't take action, how will you be able to sleep at night?"

After the meeting, Zhu Jiaxun and the others from his brigade hurried home with the commune leaders' directives in mind. It was about 2 kilometers from the district office to Xiaba along a shaded gravel tractor path.

"The higher-ups have given the word. What do you think we should do?" Zhu Jiaxun asked the others brigade leaders as they walked.

Public-security head Cheng Fu said, "What's to discuss? We just have to do it."

The men paused under a tree and decided to convene two meetings that evening. The first, held in Cheng Yuezu's home, would call in production brigade and production team cadres, CCP members, and PPA representatives to communicate the gist of the commune "five chiefs" conference; the second would be an "admonishment meeting" for black elements convened at the brigade's primary school, during which they would drag Zhu Mian out to the hills and do away with him. This would allow them to impress ideology on the masses while also ensuring that black elements such as Zhu Mian would cause no further problems.

This was the first killing in the Daoxian massacre, and we can see the effort that went into it, with repeated mobilization and discussion, for the very simple reason that someone stated: even slaughtering a pig required paperwork, so no one dared to kill a human being without verified instructions from upper-level officials. The villagers of Daoxian can't be accused of a poor sense of legality. Even the *Daozhou Provincial Gazetteer* of olden times recorded: The people of Daozhou "are simple and unadorned; they love to fight, and if one word displeases them, they will raise their fists. They esteem knowledge and respect the law, and ask officials to resolve matters."

There was no moon that night, and the weather was oppressively muggy. The village's older residents recalled a rainstorm after midnight.

During the "admonishment meeting" in the brigade's primary school, a dozen or so black elements (and offspring) were lined up against the wall with their heads lowered, the chiaroscuro effect of a storm lantern giving their wan, thin faces a grotesque appearance. Zhu Mian, having no family, stood there nonchalantly and showed none of the terror or servility of the others. According to an elderly resident of Xiaba Village, Zhu Mian had read quite a few ancient books and talked in a faux-cultured fashion, and he might well have risen in the world if not for the political label that weighed him down. The admonishment meeting was managed by brigade militia leader Zhou Jilan and public-security chief Cheng Fu. As was customary at such meetings, Cheng recited a quote from Chairman Mao: "If you don't strike down reactionary things, they will not fall. It's like sweeping the floor—if you don't sweep up the dirt, it won't run away on its own." After this and other "directives from the highest level," the admonishment began.

Cheng first commended several landlords and rich peasants for their good behavior, then he went on to criticize Zhu Mian by name. Zhu looked askance at him, considering his comments completely out of line. Cheng Fu then sternly demanded, "Zhu Mian, why did you go to the market without requesting a leave of absence?" Zhu said carelessly, "Going to market isn't leaving the area, so why should I apply for leave?" At that point, someone shouted, "Zhu Mian is dishonest. What should we do with him?" The crowd cried out in one voice, "Tie him up!" Two militiamen brought out a rope prepared in advance and bound Zhu Mian hand and foot, just as Zhu Jiaxun rushed in with the cadres and others he had been meeting with at Cheng Yuezu's home. As arranged in advance, someone said, "Take Zhu Mian to the agricultural secondary school for labor reform," and someone else said, "Take him to the commune." Then seven or eight militiamen took Zhu Mian away.

Nineteen years later, militia commander Zhou Jilan recalled the killing of Zhu Mian this way: "When we took Zhu Mian out, he still didn't know we were going to do away with him. He walked out calmly, saying 'If you want me to go, I'll go; I'm under labor reform no matter where I am.' When we reached a three-road junction about halfway there, one road led to the commune's agricultural school, where a lot of people were already being held for labor reform, and another went up the mountain, and we began pushing him toward the mountain. At that point, Zhu Mian realized disaster was looming, and he sat down on the ground and wouldn't go further. Someone gave him a kick, and Zhu Mian cried out 'Aiyo!,' and then everyone began punching and kicking him. Zhu Ming died without so much as a groan, and then he was thrown into the pond. I'd never killed anyone before, and I was so scared that my heart was in my throat. After I got home, I couldn't get to sleep for a long time, my heart was pounding so, and even when I finally fell asleep I could hear the rain pouring down outside."

Dawn broke to an autumn coolness brought by the rain shower. The heavy cumulus clouds had dispersed, and only a few wispy clouds floated across the azure sky as sunlight shimmered on the shallow pools of water formed in the hoof prints of cattle. The villagers of Xiaba Village went out to their fields as usual to gather the midseason rice or to plant sweet potatoes, and it was as if nothing at all had happened the night before. This kind of morning brought to mind a story based on the Bible: "God said, I give life to the world. The Devil said, I use death to punish it. God angrily said, I make the sun rise in the east, and who can prevent it from setting in the west? The Devil could say nothing in reply."[3] Is this a poem, a picture, or an eternal philosophical question?

Uneasy after killing Zhu Mian, Zhou Jilan hurried to the market first thing the next morning to report what had happened to the commune's public-security deputy, He Longxi, and district public-security deputy Chen Zhixi. Chen Zhixi said, "Well done! Don't worry about killing him—there are plenty of other bad guys who still need to be killed."

The commune women's committee head, Zhu Qinghua, who had passed along the message that Zhu Mian was to be killed, also reported the matter to the head of the district women's committee and district head Li Laiwen. Seeing Zhu

Qinghua's stricken face, Li Laiwen said, "So he was beaten to death—it's nothing to be afraid of! Tell Fatty [Zhu Jiaxun] that the masses beat him to death out of righteous indignation; who will ever know who actually did it?"

On the same day that Zhu Mian was beaten to death, violence broke out between the Red Alliance and the Revolutionary Alliance. The day before, on August 12, the Revolutionary Alliance had held a mass rally demanding publication of the CCP Central Committee's August 10 "Certain Decisions regarding the Hunan Issue" and then had sought to secure the Daoxian No. 2 High School as a "revolutionary stronghold" by forcibly expelling more than 20 teachers and students who supported the Red Alliance. On August 13, the expelled students and teachers, backed up by the Red Alliance, arrived at the door of the No. 2 High School and staged a protest demanding that they be allowed to return to the school to make revolution, but they were refused. Around one o'clock in the afternoon, a large group of farmers carrying shoulder poles and rakes charged at the school and clashed with armed members of the Revolutionary Alliance who were guarding the door. The Revolutionary Alliance members opened fire, killing a farmer from Yingjiang Commune's Baiditou production brigade, Wen Taiji, and injuring several others. A pregnant female worker from the Daoxian sugar refinery, Mo Dangui, was out shopping just then, and as she paused by the high school to watch, she was killed by a stray bullet.

There are many different versions of this incident, but essentially it was an extreme reaction by the Revolutionary Alliance and Red Alliance to the Central Committee's "August 10 Decision." The Revolutionary Alliance considered itself the victor and believed that it had won the Central Committee's support and endorsement as Leftist revolutionaries, but the Red Alliance considered itself the genuine proletarian revolutionary faction and insisted that the "August 10 Decision" had resulted from deception by reactionary organizations such as the Worker Alliance and Xiang River Storm. If the "February 4 Memo" could be overturned, so could the "August 10 Decision."

The life-and-death factional warfare between mass organizations during the Cultural Revolution was really a kind of revolutionary competition. There were no genuine ideological differences between the groups, who were merely vying for who could demonstrate the greatest loyalty toward the same political authority.

The Red Alliance lifted up the dead bodies and marched through the streets, chanting, "Vow to fight the Revolutionary Bandits to the bitter end!" and "Blood must be repaid with blood!"

This was the "August 13 battle" that shook Daoxian. At that time, similar conflicts were occurring throughout China. In terms of scale, the conflict in Daoxian was not as large as those at the provincial or prefectural level, but it was one of the larger ones at the county level.

Some say this fight set off the Daoxian massacre, but that's hard to prove. What can be said, however, is that this battle at the No. 2 High School did draw out a certain person who was being held there for criticism by the revolutionary masses—the county head and deputy CCP secretary Huang Yida. Huang played a crucial role in curbing the spread and development of the Daoxian massacre and in revealing the truth of what happened. Since his story is tortuous and complicated, I won't interrupt the narrative of the killings at this point but will devote a chapter to Huang Yida near the end of the book.

Xique Zhengjia sparks off the massacre

Following the violent confrontation at the No. 2 High School on August 13, the Red Alliance found itself at a disadvantage in the county seat, Daojiang, but with the support of the county PAFD, it retained political control over the entire countryside. Now the Red Alliance's members needed a release for their fury and to prove their orthodoxy and revolutionary spirit, and black elements were dragged onto the sacrificial altar as a matter of course. History had borne out time and time again that the peasantry was the easiest to command and manipulate, and that there was nothing easier or more risk-free than punishing black elements.

A senior official on the Task Force later told us, "The killing of Zhu Mian in Xiaba didn't have much effect on the county overall. Very few people even knew about it until we carried out our large-scale investigation. The incident that had a truly negative influence was the killing of Zhong Peiying's family in the Zhengjia production brigade of Yangjia Commune in Simaqiao District (see Map 1). This can be called the curtain raiser to the random slaughter in Daoxian."

The Zhengjia brigade was situated in the northeastern corner of Daoxian, bordering Ningyuan County and about 40 kilometers as the crow flies from Xiaba. The Zhengjia brigade killings were prompted by the telephone conference convened by the county seize-and-push leading group on August 11. Yangjia Commune's secretary, Jiang Wenjing, had taken the call and recorded notes, and after the conference, Yangjia Commune convened a cadre meeting to "study the spirit of the upper-level directive" and consider a "battle-readiness plan." When discussing the monitoring of black elements, commune CCP secretary Chen Shuneng said, "If black elements start causing trouble, do away with several of them." Jiang Wenjing said, "It's better to speak of 'dictatorship' than to put things so baldly. Why not use this formulation: if black elements rise up in rebellion, we'll adopt drastic dictatorial measures."

After the meeting, the commune's main cadres split up to transmit this message to the production brigades. Just as the Xiaba production brigade was

Map 1 Communes of Simaqiao District

imposing the iron fist of the dictatorship of the masses on Zhu Mian on August 13, more than 20 cadres and rebel faction leaders were being briefed at a meeting at Hongdong Temple in Zhengjia Commune on August 13.

Inside the temple, a lantern flickering in the shrine of a long-deposed deity accentuated the shiny cheekbones of Jiang Wenjing as he communicated the "battle-readiness plan" passed down from the upper levels. A youth in his late 20s, Jiang was also the Red Alliance's deputy regional commander and commune commander. After leading a recitation of Chairman Mao's quotations on class struggle, Jiang transmitted the message from the upper levels: "First, each production brigade must organize militia to stand guard; second, we must adopt effective measures to prevent the Revolutionary Alliance from establishing ties in the countryside; third, we must mobilize the poor peasants to keep an eye on black elements; fourth, if black elements begin talking or acting irresponsibly and try to cause an insurrection, the brigades must unite and take drastic measures."

After Commander Jiang spoke, the representatives of the various brigades began discussing the plan. A liaison officer for the Zhengjia brigade's CCP branch, Zheng Fengge, was the first to speak: "The class enemies in our production brigade are becoming very aggressive. They've already organized and held several secret meetings. Zhong Peiying, the wife of a pre-Liberation counterrevolutionary, Zheng Yuanjun, has been contacting class enemy off-spring to go to Jingyuan to join up with Xiang River Storm. She's already drawn two months' pay to bring back some guns to use against poor peasants. There's also a landlord bastard, Zheng Shengyao, who's been sleeping in party secretary Zheng Fengjiao's doorway for several nights now, and Secretary Zheng has gone into hiding out of fear of being killed."[4] In a deeply anxious tone of voice he concluded, "With the class enemy so aggressive, who knows when we poor peasants will die at their hands!" Brigade CCP secretaries chimed in with their own fears and their need for Mao's guidance.

Jiang Wenjing directed everyone to open their Little Red Books and study one of Chairman Mao's directives: "Chiang Kai-shek holds a knife in each hand, and we must accordingly take up our knives. . . . Now Chiang Kai-shek is sharpening his knives, and so must we." In a grave tone of voice, Jiang said, "Comrades, Chairman Mao has spoken, but we didn't understand him! The only question now is how to organize the masses!"

The commander of the Zhengjia brigade militia, Zheng Huijiu, asked, "How should we deal with someone like Zhong Peiying?"

Jiang Wenjing unambiguously replied, "The moment she starts an uprising, we have to do away with her!"

After that, a concrete plan was devised for killing Zhong Peiying. At first, someone suggested secretly nabbing her on the way to the fields and taking her into the hills, but ultimately they decided on a plan similar to that used against Zhu Mian.

The next evening (August 14), Jiang Wenjin and the others went to Fuzuwan to meet with CCP and Youth League members of the Fuzuwan and Laowu brigades. Apart from "strategic planning," this meeting also covered a new item of business: the criminal counterrevolutionary rebellion that the black-element Zhong Peiying was organizing right under their noses.

On the evening of August 15, at the Zhengjia brigade, Zheng Huijiu and Zheng Fengge convened a black-element admonishment meeting as planned. At the meeting, Zheng Huijiu shouted at Zhong Peiying, "Why didn't you request leave to go to Ningyuan?"

Zhong Peiying replied, "I'm not a black element, so why should I request leave?"

Before she could finish speaking, Zhang Huijiu shouted, "Zhong Peiying is dishonest. How should we deal with her?"

"Tie her up and take her to the commune!" everyone yelled.

What followed was basically the same as what happened to Zhu Mian, with the exception of three details. First, when Zhong Peiying was bound up, her two sons (ages 18 and 20) shouted "Use words and not violence!," at which point they were ferociously "taught a lesson" by the poor peasants and beaten until they spit blood; second, when Zhong Peiying was dragged into the hills, she was beaten to death with hoes and shoulder poles; third, after doing away with Zhong Peiying, her killers thought of something they hadn't considered before: her two whelps were still alive and would certainly avenge their mother's death, so how should they be dealt with? Someone suggested "Let's just get rid of them." Immediately someone chimed in, "If we take care of both of them at once we can rest easy."

The killers proceeded to Zhong Peiying's home, where her two sons had already gone to bed, never dreaming that their mother had been taken out to be killed, but believing that she had actually been taken to detention at the commune. That was nothing new; people were always being taken to the commune and subjected to various torments and punishments. Exhausted from the rush planting and harvesting and required to go back to it first thing the next morning, they had hurried home, washed up, and gone to bed. Now they were dragged from their beds and up into the hill behind their homes, where they were finished off with hoes and shoulder poles.

After half a night's violent exertions, the killers gathered at Zhong Peiying's home and turned it over from top to bottom, seeking evidence of her crime. After a long search with no results, they slaughtered the family's chickens and ducks and spent the rest of the night feasting on them with strong rice liquor. When the cooking pot had been drained of its last drops of broth, a rooster's crow reminded the mob that it was time for them to go out to the fields, so they hurried off.

According to the "exposure and confession" material that militia commander Zheng Huijiu subsequently submitted to the Task Force, after doing away with Zhong Peiying and her sons, Zheng skipped breakfast the next morning, worrying that there might be repercussions and perhaps even an investigation by the upper levels. Burning with anxiety, he rushed to the commune and reported the matter to Jiang Wenjing. Jiang responded by laughing out loud and saying, "Excellent! You acted with speed and boldness!" This put Zheng Huijiu's mind at rest for further killings.

After the deaths of Zhong Peiying and her sons, random killings quickly spread throughout the county. Yangjia Commune naturally bore the brunt of this development. On the morning of August 17, Jiang Wenjing convened another "five chiefs" meeting and highly commended the "revolutionary action" of the poor peasants of the Zhengjia brigade. After the meeting ended, the other brigades leaped to action, and in short order 31 people were killed in the Hezuo, Tangping, Zaohetian, Chenjia, and Sanjiaohe brigades.

The subsequent investigation found that during the Daoxian massacre, the Simaqiao District in which Yangjia Commune was situated had 533 deaths, with 55 households completely extinguished.[5] Among that district's four communes (Yangjia, Simaqiao, Dapingling, and Hongtangying), Yangjia Commune experienced the largest number of killings, totaling more than 190, among whom 95 were ordered killed by Jiang Wenjing himself. This man whose hands were stained by the blood of so many innocent people was later promoted to CCP secretary of Xiajiang Commune.

Regarding the killings in Yangjia Commune that followed the murders of Zhong Peiying and her sons in the Zhengjia brigade, we refer to the Task Force's investigative report on commune CCP secretary Zheng Fengjiao:

> In early August 1967, Zheng Fengjiao left the village and went into hiding when he suspected that the landlord offspring Zheng Shengyao was plotting revenge. He returned in mid-August after learning that his production brigade had started killing landlords and rich peasants. On the morning of August 27, Zheng Fengjiao called a cadre meeting during which he said, "The previous three rounds of killing have gone very well. Now that I'm back, let's do another round." He asked each team to come up with a list of names, after which it was decided to kill seven landlords, rich peasants and offspring. . . .
>
> On September 14 of that same year, Zheng Fengjiao presided over a meeting of the production brigade CCP branches, during which he said, "We need to discuss whether to kill another batch." Yangjia Commune public-security officer Fan Shushou pointed out, "The September 5 Order[6] has already been sent down. The killings have had major repercussions, and no more killing is allowed." Zheng Fengjiao would not be dissuaded, saying, "We have so many black elements in our production brigade, and they're so evil, we have to kill them even if it's not allowed." Because some production brigade cadres supported Zheng Fengjiao, commune head Peng Xinming felt obliged to say, "Gentlemen, if you must, do it over by the Ningyuan border so it doesn't affect our commune."
>
> That afternoon, Zheng Fengjiao organized and convened a cadre meeting to assign tasks. The next day, Zheng Fengjiao ordered the militia to take 19 landlords and rich peasants and offspring to Ningyuan's Ouchonglei Hill and kill them.

Most of the people in this last batch of victims were elderly women or minors, including a blind woman more than 60 years old and two children under 10.

They were buried alive in four pits on a deserted hillside, which was subsequently renamed Sigekeng, or "Four Pits."

During our reporting, we visited the mountain village of Zhengjia, which is also known as Xique (Magpie) Zhengjia. During the Cultural Revolution, 37 people were killed in this production brigade, and it was the actual eruption point of the Daoxian massacre. About a hundred shabby brick houses were scattered around a lowland field surrounded by hills denuded during the communal canteen and iron-smelting projects of the Great Leap Forward and now covered only with scrub and low masson pines. Poor transport links had mired generations of the villagers in lives of hardship. Upon our arrival, the current CCP secretary, Zheng Fengqiao, wanted to kill a chicken for us, but we firmly declined. When we mentioned Zhong Peiying, Zheng Fengqiao said, "She was a very dignified woman in her 40s, educated and able to do both skilled and unskilled work and also to make clothes. They say she came from an influential family over in Lanshan, and that she ran off to Guizhou during the early years of Liberation and married Zheng Yuanjun, a man from our production brigade who was working there at the time. Zheng Yuanjun was sent back here during the cleansing of class ranks in 1965."

We asked about Zheng Yuanjun's class background and whether he'd been involved in any misdeeds. Zheng Fengqiao replied, "During Land Reform, Zheng Yuanjun wasn't assigned a class. He'd been working elsewhere all along, and no one in the village knew of any wrongdoing on his part. But he had a cousin, Zheng Yuanzan,[7] who back in 1950 headed up a bandit gang that staged an insurrection in Ningyuan, and the head of our county party committee's organization department and two cadres were killed. All those participating in the insurrection were suppressed except for Zheng Yuanzan, who escaped to Taiwan. We've heard about this matter, but we don't know all the details."

"Did Zheng Yuanjun also take part in the Ningyuan insurrection?"

"I've never heard anything to suggest that. He was ferreted out in 1964 during the Socialist Education movement and sent back with the label of a pre-Liberation counterrevolutionary. He'd been working as a clerk in a warehouse in Guizhou, and he was killed in a traffic accident in Hengzhou (now Hengyang City) in 1965."

"So, if Zhong Peiying wasn't classified as a black element, why was she killed when there were so many black elements in the production brigade?"

Zheng Fengqiao said, "Ai! At that time, Zhong Peiying had the kind of social relationships that made it hard for her to just stay home and not get into trouble. She was involved with Xiang River Storm and had counterrevolutionary ties. I was on the party committee at the time, and on the day of the meeting, when they brought up Zhong Peiying, I was shocked to hear that she was involved in so much without my knowing anything about it. In any case, she died in a

horrible way, and she was left over by the mountain pool for days without anyone burying her."

"So she was killed for participating in Xiang River Storm? There was no other
reason?" Somehow I felt the killing of Zhong Peiying was not that simple.

"I'm not clear about any other reason. You can ask the people at the Task
Force; they probably know more about it than I do."

In fact, we had asked the Task Force, and they also said they didn't know. It
had happened so long ago that it was impossible to ascertain the details. Another
version had it that Zhong had been killed for rejecting a persistent suitor, but
there was nothing to substantiate that claim, either. One comrade came right
to the point: "Why does everything have to be so clear? We need just the basic
information, how she was killed and who ordered it, and who did it and where,
and that's good enough."

This was certainly reasonable, but given that this killing was the prelude
to a massacre, wouldn't it be better to investigate it in more detail and understand it more clearly? Especially since after Zhong Peiying was killed, rumors
circulated that she had been the mistress of Zheng Yuanzan, the leader of the
1950 Ningyuan counterrevolutionary insurrection (how had she suddenly
been transformed into Zheng Yuanzan's mistress?), and that she was under
orders to organize black elements into a counterrevolutionary organization.
It was also said that Zheng Yuanzan had secretly arrived in Lengshuitan from
Taiwan and was preparing to take over from Zhong Peiying in carrying out the
bloodbath in Daoxian. Jiang Wenjing and others had repeated these rumors
at meetings—didn't they have a responsibility to state the source of their
information?

We learned that back then the brigade's leaders had selected several people
from among the black elements as "earphones" to "make secret inquiries into the
enemy situation" and report back regularly. The Task Force's files revealed that
for the fourth round of killings at that brigade, CCP secretary Zheng Fengjiao
had announced that black-element offspring who killed a black element would
be given a guarantee that their families would be spared. I wondered if "earphones" were included, and the current CCP secretary, Zheng Fengqiao, confirmed that they were.

"Did any of the 'earphones' kill people?" I asked.

"Some did, but some didn't."[8]

At this point I asked Zheng Fengqiao if it would be possible to talk to one of
the "earphones."

"He might be threshing in the responsibility fields.[9] It's pretty far off. Let me
go get him."

Secretary Zheng went off, and we took that opportunity to walk around the
village, hoping to find family members of victims who might be able to tell us

more about the killings. We had heard rumors that during the third round of killings in the Zhengjia brigade on August 26, one of those killed was a heavily pregnant woman who had been horrendously tortured. First her eyelids had been cut off, then her nose, then her lips, then her breasts, and finally her belly had been cut open and her fetus removed. What evil had that woman done to deserve such treatment? Surely it hadn't been merely the joy of killing that led to this? Secretary Zheng said he hadn't been present when the woman was killed, and he didn't know the details, so we could only try to get more information from a survivor.

Someone gave us directions to a newly refurbished, tile-roofed house with a little rice mill in front of it. An old woman was chopping vegetables inside the house, while a middle-aged woman was spreading rice out to dry in the sun. One look at the house indicated that it belonged to a survivor family. At that time, the policy for compensating families of victims of the Cultural Revolution in Daoxian went more or less like this: those whose homes had been dismantled or divided up were paid compensation of 300 yuan. If family members had been killed, compensation of 150 yuan would be paid for each (known as a "head fee"). The loss of farming tools and home furnishing and other necessary items would be compensated at one-fourth of their 1967 value. At that time, 300 yuan was equivalent to three months' salary for me, and while it wasn't enough to build a home, it could be combined with savings to build a very basic two-room house. Many such houses had appeared in Daoxian, and this was clearly one of them.

"We'd like to ask you about the killings here during the Cultural Revolution," I said to the middle-aged woman.

She raised her head and glanced at me. "I don't remember anything about that."

"Please don't misunderstand. I just want to ask whether anyone in your family was killed," I stammered.

"Ask all you want, but I don't remember," she said impatiently, her eyes reddening. I will never forget her blank expression and those dejected eyes. She lowered her head and went back to spreading the rice without paying me further attention.

At that point, Zheng Fengqiao returned from the field and said that the "earphone" had gone to work at his watch repair stall in Simaqiao Market. I realized that this man wasn't willing to talk to me, and that may have been Secretary Zheng's preference as well.

Standing beside me, Minghong gave me a quizzical smile: "Wasn't it rather spiteful of you to want to meet the 'earphone'?"

I was speechless for a moment, but on further thought, there was something less than generous in my keen anticipation. How hard it must have been for that man just to survive! In the long years since, dragging out a shameful existence might have been a sustained mental torment even more painful than death. Who was I to pour salt in his wounds? But Minghong disagreed with my thinking: "Don't worry that he's been tormented by spiritual interrogation; if he were that kind of person, he wouldn't have survived." Somehow Minghong was always better than me at seeing the essence of the matter.

The Lingling Task Force's inquiries found that news of the killing of Zhong Peiying and her sons spread quickly throughout the county, along with rumors that black elements were planning a revolt. Around the same time, the districts of Qingtang, Shouyan, Meihua, and Qiaotou falsely reported the existence of seven counterrevolutionary organizations (all bogus) and began extorting confessions, creating tension throughout the region. "With the region in a state of anarchy, and with law and order seriously undermined, starting on August 17, commune and production brigade cadres in Qingtang, Qingxi, Meihua, and other districts began holding meetings to mobilize and orchestrate killings."

The killing wind progressed as shown in the following table:

District	Date killings began	Production brigade and targets
Shouyan	August 13	Xiaba brigade "puppet" (KMT) township head Zhu Mian
Simaqiao	August 15	Zhengjia brigade pre-Liberation counterrevolutionary family member Zhong Peiying and her sons
Qingtang	August 17	Da Village No. 1 brigade Rightist Tang Yu
Qiaotou	August 17	Shengli brigade black elements He Guangzhao and Xie Susu
Gongba	August 20	Guangjialing brigade pre-Liberation counterrevolutionary Yang Jingcheng, landlord He Qingsong, small-plot lessor Xiang Qijia
Chetou (Meihua)	August 20	Lijiaping brigade "puppet" police officer Tang Linxian
Hongyan	August 21	Jixin brigade black element Hu Xiang
Shangguan	August 22	Jixin brigade "puppet" village chief He Guangqin

District	Date killings began	Production brigade and targets
Qingxi	August 23	Qingkou brigade landlord Wei Yongcheng, class enemy offspring He Jingdong
Xianglinpu	August 24	Songliu brigade three fugitive class enemy offspring

In practical terms, although factional fighting was intense at that time and had resulted in violence, the county's three-level administration was still largely operational. In particular, the county PAFD effectively controlled the county with the "imperial sword" of the People's Liberation Army's Support-the-Left campaign on its side. If someone at the county level had stepped forward and said the word, the indiscriminate killing would never have occurred, and even if it had started, it could have been brought under control before it reached a significant scale. Regrettably, all the evidence indicates that at that time, some of the county's leading cadres tacitly supported and even instigated the killings. There were even some who used Mao Zedong's 1927 *Investigative Report on the Hunan Peasant Movement* to commend this random killing of innocent people as an "excellent" revolutionary action. From then on, the killing wind rapidly spread throughout the county.

PART TWO

ASSEMBLING THE MACHINERY OF SLAUGHTER

The Killing Wind Spreads
through Administrative Lines

The narrative thread of the Daoxian massacre is complex. In terms of strict chronology, it should progress from the initial killing of Zhu Mian to the prelude and then to the wider massacre, then to the August 17 "killing mobilization meeting in Qingtang District," the "August 20 reporting meeting in Yingjiang," and so on. This narrative organization works well initially, but further on it develops into a chaotic tangle of people and incidents. Relations of time and space make it impossible to shape a concise narrative thread for the entire incident.

The collected material shows that the origin and development of the killings proceeded in distinct and unambiguous veins within each district, with a progression from the district level to the communes, then to the production brigades of each commune, and to the individual production teams under each production brigade. It was rare for a commune to have any relation to the killings occurring in a production brigade of a different commune, for example. The killings were generally mobilized, engineered, and carried out within the various levels of the individual administrative districts. At the county level, however, the problem looks much more complex. After long consideration, I've decided to describe the killings as they spread through each district, in the way Uyghur maidens comb their hair into many small braids. This provides an obvious advantage, but also a drawback in that it leads to a fragmentation of the origin and development of the Daoxian killings. For this reason, I would remind the reader to pay attention to how the killings began in each district, after which the overall cause and effect of the killings become clear.

Accordingly, I will now return to Shouyan District (see Map 2), where the first victim, Zhu Mian, met his death, and describe how the killings developed there.

Shouyan District, also called District 1, included Shouyan, Tangjia, and Niulukou communes as well as Shouyan Town. It was where the Daoxian killings began, but it did not experience the greatest number of killings.

Shuangpai County

Xianzijiao District

Lefutang*

Chetou District

Niulukou

Fushui (Yishui) River   ●Tangjia

Shouyan

Qingtang District   ○ Daojiang

*At the time of the massacre, Lefutang was part of Qiaotou District.

Map 2 Communes of Shouyan District

According to the Task Force's investigations, a total of 535 residents of Shouyan District were killed (including 97 suicides), and 12 households were entirely wiped out.[1]

Tangjia Commune experienced the greatest number of killings. The main people responsible for inciting, planning, and arranging for the killings were the commune's deputy Chinese Communist Party (CCP) secretary, deputy commune head, public-security deputy, and the commune accountant and Red Alliance head. The first official in the entire county to explicitly order a killing was Tangjia Commune's deputy CCP secretary, Zou Yunlong. According to a cadre from the commune's Zhuzifu production brigade, on August 11, 1967, Zou issued the following instructions to the production brigade's CCP secretary: "Zhuzifu's black elements have gotten completely out of hand. Go back and arrange for cadres and commune members to attack them. Just make sure not to kill anyone on the spot—let them die slowly."

This happened to be the same day that the district seize-and-push chief, Chen Zhixi, directed the CCP secretary of the Xiaba production brigade to "do away with Zhu Mian." Could this have been pure coincidence? As it turned out, however, Zou Yunlong's more sweeping directive was more difficult to implement than Chen Zhixi's; Zou didn't specify which individuals should be targeted, and it was difficult to calibrate beatings in such a way that targets would not be killed at the scene but would still eventually die. That's why the first blood of the Daoxian massacre was ultimately drawn at Xiaba rather than Zhuzifu.

Although Tangjia Commune ultimately racked up the largest number of killings, during the first wave of the massacre (August 17–26, 1967), only 19 people were killed there in a cool and deliberate fashion as other localities engaged in riotous slaughter. Starting on August 28, however, more than 100 people were killed in just five days. The Task Force investigation found this was entirely related to the commune's leaders and to a "political and legal work conference" that the Red Alliance convened in Yingjiang from August 26 to 28. I will later describe in detail the cause and effect of this meeting in relation to the second wave of killings.

During the first stage of the killings in Tangjia Commune, although Zou Yunlong and the others repeatedly tried to stir up violence and even ordered specific killings, they weren't very forceful, and their attitude was somewhat ambivalent and even coy. However, once Zou and the other leaders came back from the county political and legal work conference in Yingjiang on August 28, it was as if they'd been given an adrenaline injection; they immediately called a "five-chiefs meeting" of all the commune's production brigades to mobilize manpower and arrange for more killings.[2] Zou Yunlong explicitly ordered: "After you return to your production brigades, carry out a careful examination and then kill a couple of troublemakers." Red Alliance leader He Xueneng praised the Tangjia and Wenjia brigades for the speed and number of their killings, and he criticized brigades that were lagging behind: "You brigade party secretaries need to get involved and step up for revolution! If you don't come forward under these complicated circumstances, you betray the revolution." Public-security deputy Xie Lintong was even more specific: "I want you to kill a couple of those bad guys, the real scoundrels. A lot of landlords and rich peasants have run off to mountain lairs to become bandits. Organize militia to search the hills and suppress them where you find them—don't haul them back, and don't kill people at Victory Bridge—too many people pass by there, and pools of blood would be unsightly. When you kill, do it in the hills, and post guards lower down so the cat doesn't get out of the bag."

Killings in the commune reached a climax after that meeting.

The largest number of killings in the district occurred at the Tangjia brigade, where 50 people died (including two suicides). In the county overall, four production brigades recorded 50 or more killings, and Tangjia didn't break into the top three,[3] but it had one killer named Lei Kanggu who broke the county record with a claim to having single-handedly beheaded 36 people with a saber. The Task Force eventually ascertained that Lei actually killed only half that many, the discrepancy apparently related to the taking of "commission." Killings were rewarded in Daoxian at the time, and the typical commission for one killing was

2 to 5 yuan, supplemented with work points and material rewards such as 10 or 15 kilos of unhusked rice. The Tangjia brigade was relatively prosperous, so the commission was at the higher end, 5 yuan per person. Lei Kanggu reportedly earned 180 yuan in commission on that one day (likely partly in the form of grain), which is more than he would normally have earned in an entire year.[4]

Among the victims in the Tangjia brigade was Hu Xiangxian, a 23-year-old man from a class enemy family[5] described as quiet, honest, and hard-working. During the killings, the production brigade cadres said, "We don't need to kill this one." That should have been enough to spare Hu Xiangxian, but he had the disadvantage of a pretty wife who was also a hard worker, the kind referred to as good in the field and in bed, and this made Hu a target of envy. An unmarried poor peasant named Xiong Tiangou who had his eye on Hu's wife insisted that Hu be "suppressed." It was common during the Daoxian massacre for men to be killed for the sake of a woman; I found at least 40 instances in the material I collected, and the actual number was certainly much higher, given that the authorities investigated only if the woman concerned filed a complaint. What distinguished the case in the Tangjia brigade was that while Xiong Tiangou joyfully anticipated becoming a bridegroom, he unexpectedly encountered two rivals, both likewise poor peasant bachelors who wanted Hu's wife for themselves. Xiong Tiangou subsequently said, "Those two were worse than Chiang Kai-shek. When it was time to kill landlords, they hid out in the mountains rather than risk their lives in revolution, but once it came to sharing the spoils, they ran down to steal the peaches."[6] None of the parties would back down, and when it looked like a fight would break out, Xiong stabbed the woman to death rather than provoke a conflict that would "damage class sentiment."

Someone in the Task Force summarized 15 notable cases during the Daoxian massacre, including the mass killer Lei Kanggu in the Tangjia production brigade. We reported on most of these cases, and they will be integrated into subsequent narratives relating the districts or communes where they occurred. The truth is that all individual cases in the Daoxian massacre are at once classic and distinctive, and understanding any case in depth always brings distinctive and inherent qualities to the surface. The difficulty of such in-depth reporting was immense, however; grassroots cadres were unwilling to cooperate, killers would say only as much as they wanted to, and the families of victims were wary of us and displayed clear signs of post-traumatic stress. Some of these family members were referred to as "squealers," and if we weren't careful in our handling of sensitive matters, we'd be accused of "creating new chaos with the intent of intensifying conflict." This was a source of constant vexation to me, and I felt frustrated in my attempts to get to the truth. Minghong took a wider view and said, "Don't worry; just being allowed to do this reporting is already a major accomplishment. Don't beat your head against a wall. Just publishing the names of the 4,000 victims would require writing down more than 10,000 characters, so why obsess over details? As long as we get the basic facts, that's enough." What he said made a lot of sense, and even though I had misgivings, I could only do my best to carry out my mandate.

Let's now turn again to Simaqiao District, where the killing of Zhong Peiying's family sparked off the massacre in the rest of the county.

After Jiang Wenjing and the others killed Zhong Peiying and her sons at Yangjia Commune, another meeting of the district's Red Alliance leaders was held at Simaqiao on August 17. At this meeting, Zhong Peiying was transformed into the mistress of a counterrevolutionary rebellion leader, an underground secret agent of the Kuomintang, and the commander in chief of a black-element insurrection. The commune's poor and lower-middle peasants were now on high alert against a black-element insurrection, and Jiang Wenqing's vivid rendering of its timely discovery and suppression mesmerized the meeting's participants, some of whom expressed regret that their own communes didn't have villains of similar stature to battle against.

After that meeting, Dapingling and Hongtangying Communes invited Jiang Wenjing and the other Yangjia Commune leaders to come over and pass along their valuable experience on August 18 and 19.

Hongtangying Commune (now known as the Hongtangying Yao Ethnic Township) was situated in the Jiuyi mountain range in southeastern Daoxian. Its majority Yao population was highly assimilated into the dominant Han culture and was indistinguishable from their Han neighbors. Among Daoxian's 37 communes, Hongtangying Commune covered the largest area and had the smallest population, its rugged physical environment a source of hardship to its residents. A folk song passed down to the present day explains why this locality had more bachelors than average: "Don't marry off your daughter to the distant hills / to freeze and starve all year, / living in a wood plank thatched hut / and eating yams and corn ears." Women were a factor, and possibly the main reason, for many of the killings that occurred in this commune.

After absorbing the "real-life revolutionary experience" of Jiang Wenjing and the others, the leader of Hongtangying Commune's People's Armed Forces Department (PAFD) and seize-and-push group, Lai Xinghao, called a "four chiefs" meeting for the production brigades on August 20, 1967, during which he played up the rumors passed along by Jiang Wenjing and related what had happened at Yangjia Commune's Zhengjia brigade. He declared the formation of a Supreme People's Court of the Poor and Lower-Middle Peasants, and said that poor and lower-middle peasants were allowed to kill any class enemies who were "acting up," specifically directing the Honghua production brigade to "lead the commune in the struggle against the enemy." After the meeting, a total of 43 people were killed within five days.

On August 26, Hongtangying Commune's deputy CCP secretary, Pan Jiarui, demonstrated his revolutionary mettle by establishing ad hoc people's militias and calling another "four chiefs" meeting, during which he criticized some brigades for "conservative thinking and tardy action" while commending the Honghua, Zhengjia, and Huangjiatang brigades for their quick action and numerous killings. Pan Jiarui then said, "Following discussion by the poor and lower-middle peasants, a couple more of the worst black elements can be killed." The production brigades took immediate action, resulting in 47 killings that day. Some of the brigades criticized at the meetings made a special effort to catch up with the others. Another 86 people were killed in Hongtangying Commune on August 27, with Lai Xinghao and Pan Jiarui directing operations by telephone from the commune office. On August 28, Pan Jiarui and two commune cadres went to the Dongjiangyuan brigade, which was too remote to take part in the "four chiefs" meeting, and pushed the brigade to kill some of its black elements. Pan observed, "If you don't kill a batch, won't you waste a lot of manpower keeping them shut up in their houses?" After discussion, the brigade decided to have nine black elements killed by lepers from the nearby leprosarium.

On August 29, the situation changed somewhat; following the Red Alliance's "politics and law cadre conference," a telephone call came from the upper level saying there could be no more random killings, and the commune summoned all the principal production brigade cadres to an urgent meeting the next day, August 30. When the militia commander of the Dongjiangyuan production brigade telephoned the commune to confirm the time of the meeting, Pan Jiarui told him to focus on the killing instead of attending the meeting. Accordingly, the Dongjiangyuan brigade had the lepers come and kill 22 people—13 more than originally designated.

That brought the total in Hongtangying Commune to 189 deaths (including five suicides), with 133, or 70 percent, killed in just two days, August 26 and 27. The Honghua brigade led the field with 42 deaths.

One commune member, Li Boqing, became addicted to killing and repeatedly took the initiative, ultimately killing 26 people. He was probably responsible for the largest number of deaths in the entire county, given that Tangjia Commune's Lei Kanggu exaggerated the number of people he killed. At that time, Li Boqing was 45 years old, which made him nearly elderly at a time when death at 60 was not considered at all premature. In examining the data, I found that Daoxian's famous killers were typically around 20 years old, and it was very uncommon for a killer to be over 40 years old unless revenge, material gain, or a woman was involved. What could have led Li Boqing to become such an eager killer? After the Task Force began its work, Li Boqing was quickly arrested, and when asked to explain his motivation, he replied, "To earn more work points." At first, this may seem absurd and hard to credit, but on further thought it makes sense. If killing became a revolutionary act that brought no blame but rather reward in the form of monetary payments, grain rations, and work points, many would be willing to do it.

Stories of Li Boqing's killings spread far and wide, with inevitable exaggeration and embellishment. The Task Force's official report, the content of which Li Boqing himself fully admitted to, found that Li had voluntarily pushed 24 of the brigade's class enemies and offspring into a mine pit on the night of August 26. Then, on August 27, when escorts of three class enemy offspring from the Huangjiatang brigade asked Li for directions to the mine pit, Li led them there and pushed two of the victims into the pit himself. Li Boqing was undoubtedly rewarded for the killings in his own brigade, but was he able to collect work points for killing the two class enemies from another brigade? This casts doubt on Li Boqing's claim that he killed people just for the work points, and leaves us with much to ponder.

During my reporting, I posed this question to local cadres: most of the production brigades at Hongtangying Commune had few killings, ranging from a minimum of one or two to twenty-odd. Why was the Honghua brigade so exceptional? One comrade involved in the aftermath work gave the following answer:

The Honghua production brigade was less than a kilometer from the commune, close enough to hear a dog bark, and its proximity meant that the production brigade's cadres were in close contact with the commune leadership. During the "killing wind," commune leaders Pan Jiarui, Lai Xinghao, and others established this brigade as a focal point of class struggle and repeatedly went to the brigade to supervise and encourage the killings—that's one reason. The second reason is that the Honghua brigade had always been the commune's most advanced, so it had to kill more people than any other brigade and take the lead in "suppressing a class enemy insurrection," "safeguarding Chairman Mao's proletarian line," and "safeguarding the Red regime." So the cadres of the Honghua brigade enthusiastically took the lead. The brigade's CCP secretary, Chen Mingfeng, personally took the lead in killing people, and the 25-year-old poor-peasant association (PPA) chairman, Yang Longkuan, was absolutely rabid; whenever there were killings, he grabbed a fowling gun and rushed to set an example by killing people himself. The head of the brigade militia, Zou Jinggui, was also head of the commune militia, and he led militia all over to assist with the killing. He was a really vile character, not only killing people but also taking the opportunity to rape the womenfolk. With top cadres such as these leading the way, how could other cadres stand back? And once production brigade and production team cadres took the lead, how could ordinary people do nothing?

The third reason is that the Honghua production brigade killed a wider range of people. Although the killing wind is referred to as random killings, there actually were limits, but once the limits were breached, the number of people killed multiplied, from black elements to offspring to women and children. Some people killed for the sake of a woman, and in order to prevent future trouble, the woman's family would be wiped out. The Honghua brigade killed not only class enemies, but also "capitalist roaders among poor and lower-middle peasants"; for example, someone who engaged in a sideline occupation without handing money over to the production team, or a slacker, or someone who argued with cadres. Nowadays we would consider these minor issues, but at that time, it became a matter of principle and two-line struggle, and being accused of undermining the foundations of socialism or resisting the CCP's leadership was enough to put your head on the block! The truth is that the Honghua brigade stuck pretty close to official policy; otherwise they'd have killed double the number they did.

Even so, the number of killings increased with each batch, and apparently they had a fifth round in the works when the communes were ordered to halt the killings on August 29. That night, Lai Xinghao held a meeting of administrative cadres[7] to pass on the order and separately notified all the production brigades. The Honghua brigade, being located closest to the commune, stopped all killing immediately, but the Dongjiangyuan production brigade, where Pan Jiarui was, somehow got left out, as a result of which nine more people were killed there on the morning of August 30, and a few more the next day.

Yet, what is most shocking, or perhaps most distinctive, about the Cultural Revolution killings at Hongtangying Commune is not the Honghua brigade, which recorded the most killings, or the Dongjiangyuan brigade, which pushed through a last round at the end, but rather the Huangjiatang brigade, which doesn't stand out in any way at first glance. The killings at this production brigade were not orchestrated by commune cadres, but by a telephone operator named Deng Jiayu. It was the only instance of its kind that we heard of. A commune telephone operator was at best a contract worker for the county postal and telecommunications apparatus. What would qualify him to issue a directive to kill people, and why would anyone in the production brigade obey him?

We asked a Task Force comrade, "Did a commune leader tell Deng Jiayu to pass along this directive?"

That comrade answered, "No, he did it on his own. We initially made the same assumption you did, but after repeated inquiries, we established that not a single commune cadre had instigated his behavior; Deng was simply sitting by the telephone with nothing better to do, and when he saw that all the other brigades were killing people but nothing was happening at Huangjiatang, he telephoned the brigade and told them to get going." Huangjiatang wasn't on our original itinerary, but when we learned of this case, we decided to go there to find out more.

The production brigade (village) of Huangjiatang was situated in the northernmost portion of Hongtangying Commune, bordering Gongba Commune and squeezed into a saddle-shaped dip between Mao'er Mountain on its east and Fengmu Mountain on its west. Its geographical position suggested that it was the closest to Daojiang of all the commune's production brigades, but this was belied by its inferior transport links. At that time, all of southeastern Daoxian had only one basic highway, a gravel road running from Daojiang to Tanshuiping via the Xiangyuan tin mine, and Hongtangying was linked to it by an even-cruder roadway, followed by a 7-kilometer walk along a winding mountain path. The alternative was to reach the village by ferry from Simaqiao Market. We took the highway to the village to do our reporting, and then returned by ferry.

In spite of a less-than-warm reception by the production brigade cadre, we were able to learn essentially what happened. After the Huangjiatang brigade's CCP secretary, Zhu Yuliang, and others attended the commune mobilization meeting on August 20, they discussed the matter back at the brigade. Unable to identify any class enemies who absolutely had to be killed, they decided to simply put these individuals under "supervision and control" for the time being, and Huangjiatang continued focusing on "pushing production" instead of "seizing revolution" even after most of the other production brigades had already taken action. This came to the attention of the commune telephone operator, Deng Jiayu. Although he was not a commune leader, Deng sat all day at the switchboard listening in on the telephone calls between the commune and the various production brigades (at that time, only the most politically reliable individuals could be telephone or switchboard operators), so he knew everything about the killings throughout the commune.

Deng Jiayu later said, "I noticed that Huangjiatang hadn't taken any action up to then, and I knew the commune would be holding a 'compare and assess' meeting and thought they would come under criticism, so out of the goodness of my heart, I telephoned to warn them. I never guessed they would accuse me of ordering the killings. I'm just a commune telephone operator, not even at the rank of an administrative cadre, so how could I order any killings?"

It's hard to argue with Deng Jiayu's logic. However, the Huangjiatang brigade's cadres and masses gave a slightly different version of events. Zhu Zhongcheng, who was the brigade's accountant at the time and who took the call, said:

> At noon on August 25 [1967], I was working at the brigade headquarters when a phone call came from Deng Jiayu, the chairman of the commune's "killing office." He asked why our brigade hadn't done anything,

criticized us for holding the entire commune back, and told us to get moving. I quickly reported the call to party secretary Zhu Yuliang and brigade leader Zhu Yusheng. The production brigade held a special meeting and decided to kill five class enemies before Secretary Zhu had to attend the commune meeting. We also telephoned Chairman Deng to report it to him. The next morning, Chairman Deng telephoned again, and this time party secretary Zhu Yuliang took the call. Chairman Deng said that two class enemies (in fact, offspring) had escaped from our brigade and had been apprehended at District 1 (Gongba District), and we should send someone to fetch them. Secretary Zhu asked, once we've brought them back, what should we do with them? Chairman Deng said we should do away with them along the way. So those two people were also killed. After the commune meeting on August 27, the brigade still had several class enemies in custody, and we telephoned the commune and asked Chairman Deng for instructions on whether or not to kill them. Chairman Deng said "Kill them all," so those three were also killed.

I should add here that Deng Jiayu categorically denied the official title of "chairman of the killing office." He said, "Of all the terrible titles, 'killing office chairman' is the worst! I would never be that stupid!"

In any case, this is a minor quibble; whatever the title, the crux of the matter is the perception of the poor and lower-middle peasants of the Huangjiatang production brigade.[8] It would thus appear that the main difference between the killings in Huangjiatang and the other production brigades was that the commune's directives to other brigades were the "real thing," while the directive to Huangjiatang was "counterfeit."

But there's something Zhu Zhongcheng didn't mention about his August 27 telephone call to Deng Jiayu: he also asked, "Some people aren't class enemies, but they don't pull their weight in production and just roam around engaging in sideline occupations. Should we kill this sort of people?" Deng Jiayu replied, "Capitalist roaders can also be killed!" Having received this directive, Zhu Zhongcheng went with others the next day to arrest and kill Zhu Zhongdao, who was engaged in a sideline occupation outside the village. Zhu Zhongcheng then conveniently forced the dead man's wife to marry his younger brother. During the aftermath work, this case was classified as one of killing a man to seize his wife.

Qingtang District and the Rise of the Peasant Supreme Courts

In the hometown of the philosopher

In 1967, Daoxian's administrative area was divided into ten districts, one commune (Yingjiang), and one town (Daojiang), but in 1984 it was reorganized into eight districts and the town of Daojiang. The following chart summarizes these changes:

Daoxian's districts during the Cultural Revolution and after reorganization

District Number	*Name*	*Post-1984 Name*
District 1	Shangguan	eliminated; reorganized under Meihua, Qingxi, and Qingtang
District 2	Chetou	Meihua
District 4	Qiaotou	eliminated; reorganized under Xianzijiao and Shouyan
District 5	Xianzijiao	Xianzijiao
District 6	Yueyan	Qingtang
District 7	Xianglinpu	Xianglinpu
District 8	Simaqiao	Simaqiao
District 9	Qingxi	Qingxi
District 10	Gongba	Gongba
District 11	Shouyan	Shouyan
	Yingjiang Commune	put under Qingtang District
	Daojiang Town	Daojiang Town

Only Gongba remained essentially unchanged. The complications that these administrative changes caused to the subsequent aftermath work will be described elsewhere in this book.[1]

The Task Force ascertained that killings were planned and arranged at the district level in eight (72 percent) of Daoxian's districts: Shangguan, Qiaotou, Qingtang (Yueyan), Xianglinpu, Gongba, Qingxi, Meihua (Chetou), and Shouyan (the exceptions were Xianzijiao and Simaqiao), while killings were arranged at the commune level in 18 (48.6 percent) of the county's communes. Killings occurred in 485 (93.4 percent) of the county's production brigades. Among these, 27 brigades had 30 or more killings, 7 brigades had 40 or more killings, and 4 brigades had 50 or more killings (Appendix I provides a more detailed breakdown).

The main portion of Qingtang District (see Map 3) was known as Yueyan District in 1967. It was the district where the commander of the Red Alliance's Yingjiang Frontline Command Post, Zheng Youzhi, served as People's Armed Forces Department (PAFD) commander, and it was the first place where a district-level meeting was called to mobilize manpower for the killings. By the time of the Task Force investigation, the district's original three communes, Qingtang, Jiujia, and Wutian, had been increased to include Yingjiang and Wanjiazhuang Communes. Those five communes accounted for 269 killings.

Qingtang District is located in the western region of Daoxian, less than 10 kilometers from the county seat, Daojiang. The Lianxi River originates within its borders, and Hunan's second-highest peak, Jiucailing, rises from the Dupangling

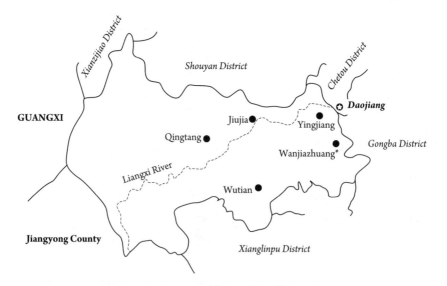

* At the time of the massacre, Wanjiazhuang was part of Shangguan District.

Map 3 Communes of Qingtang (Yueyan) District

mountain range in the district's western portion. Below Dupangling lies the limestone cavern that gave the district its original name, Yueyan, meaning Moon Rock, named for light patterns resembling the different phases of the moon that are cast into the cavern by an opening in its roof.

A distance of 4 kilometers west of Moon Rock lies Loutian Village, the native place of Zhou Dunyi, one of China's greatest philosophers and originator of the idealist school of Confucianism, who lived in the 11th century during the Northern Song dynasty. When we visited Qingtang District, we made a point of starting with Loutian Village.

At the time of our visit, Loutian had still not fully recovered from the catastrophe of the Cultural Revolution, and scars from the political campaign to "smash the four olds" were apparent everywhere. The ancient village was still breathtakingly beautiful, with its misty mountains and a crystalline rivulet where Zhou Dunyi was said to have experienced enlightenment while fishing. But the philosopher's stone image had been smashed to pieces, and there was hardly anyone left in the village who understood the "dispositional reasoning" of the cosmic philosophy he had founded.

While in Loutian, we interviewed a 25th-generation descendant of Zhou Dunyi named Zhou Minji. He was 68 years old at the time and was the village's former Chinese Communist Party (CCP) secretary. As a young man during the Japanese occupation in 1944, he had survived the shocking Loutian Massacre, during which Japanese troops killed more than 400 villagers hiding in a cave. Twenty-three years later, he became one of the killers in the Daoxian massacre:

> After Liberation, I took up my work with an intense feeling of class and national vengeance. Eventually I joined the party and became party secretary of my production brigade. While I was secretary, I did a lot of good things for the masses, but also quite a lot of foolish and wicked things. . . . But I never acted against my conscience until that incident during the Cultural Revolution, which filled me with remorse. At that time, I was too fanatical to tell true from false, and I believed the lies others told, thinking that landlords and rich peasants really were organizing "black killing squads" to kill us party members and cadres. At the commune meeting, a commune cadre said, "Someone's holding a knife to your neck, and you can still sleep at night?" They wanted us to go back and kill any troublemakers, saying taking the initiative would give us the upper hand. After I came back, I discussed things with the militia commander and others, and we decided to take advantage of the killings that were going on elsewhere by doing away with the class enemies in our village. We ended up killing nine people. In fact, once we started, it was easier than killing chickens. We just tied them up

and led them to the river next to the village, and after we killed them we dumped them in the river. We first thought of killing them in the hills behind the village, but someone said that might damage the village's *feng shui*, so we changed to the other location. No one resisted; they were all very well behaved. There was just one rich peasant, Zhou Minzheng, who said, "In the old society we ate the rice of exploitation, and we deserve to die. But our kids were born in the New China and grew up under the Red Flag. Can't they be spared?" But you know how it is, we'd had our meeting and discussed the matter, so how could we spare anyone? We needed to kill them all. All these years my heart has been uneasy, and whenever I think of this incident, I feel an ache in my gut. My conscience won't let it pass. The fact is that those nine people were all members of our Zhou clan; they were 25th- and 26th-generation descendants of Zhou Dunyi. Now I'm being punished for it, and I have no one to blame but myself. I'm grateful for the leniency of the party and the government.

Looking at this old farmer with his callused hands and etched face standing where a great Confucian philosopher had come into being, we didn't know what to say. Sometimes words become meaningless, and it's better to say nothing at all.

The rise of the peasant supreme courts

At noon on August 17, 1967, the club room of Qingtang Commune was packed with cadres at the level of production team leader and above who had been summoned from all over the district for an impromptu meeting.

At noon the day before, Zhou Renbiao, who was a district tribunal cadre and vice chairman of the district seize-and-push group, had made a special trip to Yingjiang to pass on hearsay about the "enemy situation," reworked through his personal embellishments, to the district PAFD commander and Red Alliance head, Zheng Youzhi: "Commander Zheng, in the few days since you arrived in Yingjiang, we've unearthed two counterrevolutionary organizations. One is the 'Peasant Party' led by the old counterrevolutionary Wang Feng at Dashen Mountain, which had grown to 400 or 500 people, and the other is the 'New People's Party' led by the landlord whelp Jiang Weizhu in Jiangjia, which had grown to 700 or 800 people and had its own radio transmitter. These two counterrevolutionary organizations were coordinating with agents of the United States and Chiang Kai-shek to mount an insurrection to attack the mainland." Zhou Renbiao ended his report by suggesting that Zheng Youzhi come to Qingtang and hold a meeting of CCP members and cadres to stabilize the masses, who were "in a state of confusion."

That was how Zheng Youzhi, dressed in full military uniform and with a Mauser pistol slung over his rump, jumped on his tractor early in the morning of August 17 and chugged over to Qingtang to preside over the meeting,[2] which the competent Zhou Renbiao had managed to put together in just half a day.

Some muddy-footed grassroots cadres had rushed over from nearly 10 kilometers away. Zheng Youzhi had served in the army, so there were two sentries posted at the entrance to the clubhouse, which was festooned with banners proclaiming "Never forget class struggle!," "Once class struggle is grasped, all problems will be solved!," and "The enemy is sharpening his knife, and so must we!" The space was too small for the hundreds of people crammed inside it. The farming folk of Daoxian had a habit of carrying long-stemmed pipes with them, and some managed to pull them out for a drag on the pungent local tobacco. Some district and commune cadres had more recently upgraded to self-rolled trumpet-shaped cigarettes or cheap packaged cigarettes. The air of the clubroom was hazy with choking tobacco smoke and the stench of sweat, exacerbated by the heat of the day. Meetings of rural cadres were generally disorderly, with the higher-level cadres holding the main meeting while those below held their own smaller meetings, and the clubhouse rang with the clamor of voices.

The meeting finally began in earnest at 10 o'clock as Zhou Renbiao directed the participants to take out their Little Red Books and stand at attention before a portrait of Chairman Mao. That was an essential procedure in any meeting, large or small, and it brought the clubhouse to a sudden and miraculous silence.

Zhou Renbiao began: "First, let us present our respectful wishes to the reddest, reddest, red sun in our hearts, our most esteemed and beloved great teacher, great leader, great commander in chief, and great helmsman, Chairman Mao!" At this, all the assembled cadres brandished their Little Red Books in rhythm as they chanted in unison, "Long life! Long life! Long, long life!" Zhou Renbiao then led them by saying, "Let us present our respectful wishes to the esteemed and beloved comrade-in-arms of our great leader Chairman Mao, deputy commander in chief Lin!"[3] At this, all assembled again brandished their Little Red Books in unison and cried out, "Good health! Good health! Eternal good health!" Zhou Renbiao then invited PAFD commander Zheng Youzhi to deliver the mobilization speech. Over the last few days, Zheng Youzhi's emotions had been somewhat subdued; taking on the job of frontline commander in chief was a perilous task since the Revolutionary Alliance had snatched PAFD weapons and was growing in strength and aggressiveness by the day, and the PAFD's failed attack on the No. 2 High School on August 13 still infuriated him. Today, at last, he had a satisfying channel for venting his feelings, and he delivered his speech with great animation, alternately rising to his feet and sitting down again, and punctuated it with thunderous pounding on the table.

A transcript of Zheng Youzhi's August 17 speech was miraculously preserved. After outlining the general threat posed by the August 8 gun snatching and the armed conflict on August 13, Zheng Youzhi employed considerable artistic license in describing the "complexity of the current struggle between the two classes, the two roads, and the two lines":

> Our District 6 is a focal point for air defense and riot prevention. After the weapon snatching on August 8, a handful of class enemies have taken advantage of a chaotic stage in the Cultural Revolution to carry out sabotage and create disturbances and are prepared to make trouble! We've already uncovered two counterrevolutionary organizations. Likewise, in the Zhengjia production brigade of District 8's Yangjia Commune, the mistress of puppet county head Zheng Yuanzan organized an "Anti-Communist National Salvation Army." One evening, the production brigade called an admonition meeting for black elements, and after listening for a while, Zheng Yuanzan's mistress gave a flick of her cattail-leaf fan, and all the black elements rose in unison and began attacking our cadres with their stools. The party secretary quickly called in the militia, who dragged out six or seven black elements and killed them, quelling the riot. During an admonishment meeting in the Xiaba production brigade of District 11's Shouyan Commune, puppet township head Zhu Mian openly provoked the cadres by saying "You're messing with us now, but if you'd waited three more days, we would have been organized enough to kill every one of you." Everyone was furious when they heard that, and they beat him to death on the spot. . . .
>
> We must comply with Chairman Mao's instructions: "The people rely on us to organize them; China's counterrevolutionaries rely on us to organize the people and overthrow them." The enemy is sharpening his knife, so we must sharpen ours. The enemy is swabbing his rifle, so we must swab ours.

Zheng Youzhi called for each production brigade to keep black elements in line through admonishment meetings and close surveillance, and to kill those who seemed predisposed to staging a revolt. As the meeting was about to end, Zheng Youzhi turned to Zhou Renbiao, who was sitting with him on the podium, and asked, "Comrade Renbiao, is there anything you'd like to add?"

Zhou Renbiao made a name for himself in that instant by saying, "I'd like to add a few words. The public-security, procuratorial, and judicial organs are paralyzed, so once the poor and lower-middle peasants decide to do away with heinously criminal black elements, they don't need to request instructions in advance or report afterwards; the supreme people's court is the poor and lower-middle peasants. We have to do away with any traitors among us, even if they're administrative cadres or those who wear wristwatches and leather shoes." He then spoke again of the bogus "People's Party," saying that one of its members, Tang Yu of Jiujia Commune, wanted to become the district head. He laughed coldly and said, "Today I'll send him packing to become district head in hell!"

The meeting erupted into chaos, with everyone talking at once. Many were hearing these things for the first time and were thoroughly shocked. Some became agitated, others became apprehensive, and all stared at the men on the podium, whose orders they were accustomed to obeying.

After the meeting adjourned, Zhou Renbiao told Jiujia Commune public-security officer Jiang Bozhu to lead 30 or 40 commune members to Tang Yu's home in Dayicun.[4] Tang Yu was already bedridden with a broken leg from a denunciation meeting on August 14. Now Jiang Bozhu dragged Tang Yu from his bed and out to the rice yard, where the crowd pounced on him and beat him to death and then dumped him in the pond next to his home.

What exactly had Tang Yu done to deserve such treatment? Tang came from a middle peasant family and had once been a primary-school teacher; he was outspoken and something of a busybody. After being labeled a Rightist in 1957, he had been sent back to the countryside to engage in agriculture. When Jiang Bozhu was sent to Tang's production brigade for work experience as a public-security deputy, he had raised hackles by "jumping a woman." While others choked with silent fury, Tang Yu had imprudently put his writing skills to work by writing a complaint on behalf of the victim. This resulted in a reprimand for Jiang Bozhu, affecting his career prospects and making him Tang Yu's sworn enemy. As for Tang Yu's desire to become district head or such like, we learned that on one occasion, while "giving vent to his hatred of the party," Tang had said, "If I were allowed to be district head, I could certainly do no worse than they have." Even if he'd really said such a thing, it was hardly worth a death sentence.

The thing we heard most often during our inquiries was that "Tang Yu was a good man!" But if so, why were so many people willing to beat him to death? "When he was beaten, I didn't hit him hard," one participant told us. In fact, Tang Yu would probably have been better off with harder blows. In the killings we looked at, many of the victims were reported to have said, "Please get it over with quickly."

After the August 17 meeting, five production brigades in Jiujia and Qingtang Communes rapidly exercised the authority of the Supreme People's Court of the Poor and Lower-Middle Peasants and killed 13 people in four days. In the course of the Daoxian massacre, Jiujia Commune killed 36 people (including four suicides) and Qingtang Commune killed 75 (including nine suicides).

At Qingtang Commune, a poor peasant named Zeng Baobao in the Yueyan brigade had criticized poor-peasant association (PPA) chairman Chen Zhicai and others during the Socialist Education movement, so Chen and the others took their revenge during the "killing wind." Zeng was more than six months pregnant at the time and was dragged to the killing field with her stomach bulging. She pleaded, "I was wrong, I'll change. Please don't kill me! If you must kill me, please wait until my baby is born." Chen Zhicai said, "We're not falling for your delay tactics!" He then sliced open Zeng's belly with a saber, and the fetus spilled out squirming in the blood and gore.

I believe that the "supreme people's courts of the poor and lower-middle peasants" that became so ubiquitous in Daoxian during the massacre first emerged in Qingtang District, and that Zhou Renbiao and the others were its originators. Before August 17, only 11 people had been killed throughout the county. Most of these killings were concentrated in the area of Simaqiao District's Yangjia Commune, and investigations found no evidence of a peasant supreme court. After the meeting in Qingtang on August 17, however, peasant supreme courts sprang up like mushrooms at the commune, production brigade, and even production team levels. Our inquiries found that with few exceptions, Daoxian's peasant supreme courts had no organizational structure and were simply set up to demonstrate the legitimacy, propriety, and revolutionary nature of the killings by declaring "death sentences" in the name of the PPAs. Most of the "chief judges" and "execution supervisors" of the peasant supreme courts were PPA or Cultural Revolution Committee (CRC) chairmen.

The only place where such a court was formally established and hung out a shingle to handle official business was in Qingxi District's Ganziyuan Commune,[5] which decided to establish a peasant court on August 23 after hearing that Yingjiang Commune had done so. The commune's PPA chairman, Liang Yu, who was a locally funded teacher at the local primary school, was chosen as chief judge, and Liang immediately put his fine penmanship to good use by creating a sign for the court. Worried that the title Supreme People's Court might be construed as usurping the power of the central authorities, Liang proposed the name "Ganziyuan Commune Higher People's Court of the Poor and Lower-Middle Peasants," and a sign to that effect was hung over the commune office door amid the thundering of blunderbusses and firecrackers.

The Ganziyuan court's first trial considered the case of six members of the Hongwei brigade who had allegedly fled to the hills to mount an insurrection, even though they were actually arrested while laboring in the fields for the double-rush planting and harvesting. Given the manifest absurdity of the charge, balanced by the pressure to do away with "troublemaking black elements," Liang Yu and other commune leaders decided to show "leniency" by sparing two of the men.

The Ganziyuan peasant court tried a total of 13 people, among whom eight were condemned to death and five were granted "leniency." That was a relatively civilized outcome at the time, since some kind of "process" was involved and the "criminals" were allowed to defend themselves (whether it actually served any purpose was another question). Notably, among the condemned men were Zhu Yongjin and his two sons, whom Liang himself proposed because Zhu was constantly threatening him over a personal grievance. Eventually, in order to "simplify procedures," "authority" was delegated to the peasant supreme courts of the production brigades, and the commune's court became no more than a shell, existing in name only.

Given the checkered history of the peasant supreme courts as an institution, Zhou Renbiao and the others declined the patent on this invention. Some of them defended themselves by saying, "The killings in Daoxian and the supreme people's courts of the poor and lower-middle peasants were influenced by Guangxi and were a carryover from Guangxi's Quanzhou County." Is there any truth to this? We consulted large quantities of documents regarding the Cultural Revolution,[6] which show that there was in fact a massacre in Quanzhou County, which adjoins Daoxian, and that Quanzhou did in fact have peasant supreme courts as well as special committees of poor and lower-middle peasants to suppress and eliminate counterrevolutionaries (which Daoxian did not have). However, these organizations emerged after October 1967, so the chronology would suggest that it was Guangxi that came under the influence of Daoxian rather than vice versa. Task Force files related to this issue reveal that organizations such as the peasant supreme courts were the collective creation of a small number of Daoxian's grassroots cadres. The first to propose such a court was Zhou Renbiao, and the first to carry out a killing in the name of such a court was Tang Zuwang, the CCP secretary of Shouyan Commune's Pingdiwei brigade.

The Task Force's investigation established that during the Cultural Revolution killings, Zhou Renbiao on multiple occasions directed, supervised, and encouraged killings in the communes and production brigades under his jurisdiction, that he authorized the killing of 17 specific individuals in several Qingtang Commune production brigades, and that he personally initiated killings at the Jiangjia brigade as an example to the militia. Peasants of Qingtang Township still recall with relish how Zhou brought two bold and brave female "militia officers" along with him to supervise and encourage the killings. He was one of the very few administrative cadres who personally dirtied their hands in the Daoxian Cultural Revolution massacre.[7]

A commune Communist Party secretary's story

Qingtang District's Wutian Commune deserves its own section because of its former CCP secretary, Xiong Liheng, who later became deputy CCP secretary of Daoxian.

During the 1967 massacre, Xiong Liheng was still CCP secretary of Wutian Commune. As a member of the ruling faction, he underwent some trivial attacks at the outset of the Cultural Revolution, but this didn't stop him from playing a role in Wutian's political arena as a "revolutionary leading cadre." When we went to Wutian to interview people about the massacre, one grassroots cadre offered the following assessment of "our Secretary Xiong": "He's quite remarkable— able, competent, and audacious." So how did Xiong Liheng use his abilities, competence, and audacity during the Cultural Revolution killings? During our reporting, we found that Xiong utilized his subsequent power and prestige to obscure his role in the killings.

During the killing wind, 42 people were killed at Wutian Commune (including three suicides). Four meetings were held during this time, the first three to mobilize and engineer the killings and the fourth to end the killings. Xiong figures in both types of activities. Most of the killings occurred in two rounds: the first around August 23, when 12 people were killed under the influence of Qingtang District's three-level cadre conference, and the second around August 26, when 28 people were killed through the arrangements of the commune's August 24 "seize-and-push" meeting. The worst of the killers was the commune's PAFD commander, He Mengxiang, and the greatest number of killings occurred in the Wutian brigade, where 11 died under He Mengxiang's personal instigation. The second-highest number of killings occurred in the Jiangjiadong brigade, with eight dead, and we detected Xiong Liheng's hand in these killings.

After cadres from the Jiangjiadong brigade took part in the August 24 commune seize-and-push meeting, they immediately held a meeting to inform other cadres of the commune leadership's instructions and to draw up a list of people to kill. A meeting later in the evening for cadres and PPA representatives added two more names to the list, for a total of 12.

At nightfall on August 26, the production brigade militia brought in all the killing targets and locked them up in the brigade's storehouse, except for one class enemy offspring who resisted and was killed on the spot. Brigade militia commander Zhu Baosheng then telephoned the commune to request instructions from Secretary Xiong, telling him that the brigade had already drawn up a name list and reporting on their class status, performance, and other details. Xiong recited two of Chairman Mao's quotes: "The core power that guides our undertaking is the Chinese Communist Party, and the theoretical foundation that guides our thought is Marxism-Leninism," and "Policy and strategy are the life of the party; leading comrades at all levels must pay close attention to this and must never be negligent." He then instructed Zhu: "I'll leave it up to you whom to kill. I have no opinion on the rest, but you have to take note of policy and strategy, and you need to distinguish between black elements and offspring."

After Zhu Baosheng hung up the phone, he and production brigade head Zhu Yongsheng quickly held a meeting with 11 militia cadres and passed on the instructions from Secretary Xiong. After discussion it was decided to show leniency to five people (all offspring) and to kill only six, five of whom were black elements and the other of whom was a troublemaking landlord offspring whose killing could serve as a warning to others. The five handled leniently were released after being "educated" that night. (On this point, Xiong Liheng told the Task Force that he not only didn't order any killings but actually saved five people.)

The next day (August 27), a mass rally was held for the entire production brigade to "promote democracy" by having everyone raise their hands in a vote. The six condemned people were led bound onto the stage. Presiding over the meeting, Zhu Baosheng announced the crimes of the six, then read out a name and asked, "Whoever agrees to kill this person, raise your hand." The masses cried out their agreement in unison, and all raised their hands.

After completing this process, the militia took the six out to the hills behind the village and shot them with fowling pieces. Counting the man killed during the roundup, this brought the death toll to seven. One other landlord offspring was later killed after fleeing and being captured elsewhere. By the time he was brought back, the commune had already transmitted the 47th Army's prohibition of further killings, and everyone said to just let him be. But Zhu Baoshen and others disagreed, saying, "If he hadn't fled, we wouldn't need to kill him. But once he's fled and been brought back, how can we not kill him? During Land Reform it was the same: landlords and rich peasants who ran off all had to be killed after they were caught and brought back." They then led several militiamen to secretly kill this eighth man in the middle of the night.

Wutian Commune's Xincha brigade didn't kill anyone during the first or second wave of killings. It wasn't as if this production brigade had no black elements, or that the brigade's black elements were particularly well behaved; in the words of one of the brigade's cadres: "Behavior is what you say it is, good or bad." So why were there no killings in this brigade? It turns out that members of the brigade who might have been targeted had rather complicated backgrounds: someone in the family was a cadre somewhere, or the clan was especially powerful. In any case, their deaths would be noticed, unlike the class enemies in other brigades who could be killed without anyone raising a fuss. The cadres and masses of the Xincha brigade didn't want to get tangled up in this kind of controversy. Even when they came under pressure from cadres sent from the regional and commune headquarters to monitor the situation, the leading cadres of the Xincha brigade just gritted their teeth, and the word "kill" never passed their lips.

On September 8, Wutian Commune convened a cadre meeting to discuss the issue of "seizing revolution and pushing production." At the meeting, Xiong Liheng specifically criticized the Xincha brigade for its conservative thinking, fuzzy understanding, and softheartedness on the cardinal issue of struggle with the enemy: "That fellow Zhu Mei in the Xincha brigade is incorrigible, always causing trouble and committing sabotage. He was a trainee pilot under the Kuomintang and comes from a powerful family. Letting him live won't help build our country and is dangerous to the leadership of your brigade. If you don't kill him now, it will only be harder for you later. If your brigade is afraid to do it, we can send people from the Tangxia and Xiawen brigades to assist you." Cadres from the other brigades began jeering, humiliating the cadres of the Xincha brigade. Smirking, Xiong Liheng asked the Xincha cadres, "Do you agree to the killing?" The cadres replied in unison, "We agree!" "Do you want the Tangxia and Xiawen brigades to help you make revolution?" "No, we'll make revolution ourselves!"

That day after lunch, Xincha militia commander Tang Guilong summoned Zhu Mei, repeated what Xiong Liheng had said word for word, and then represented the brigade's peasant supreme court in pronouncing the death penalty. Several militiamen came forward and killed Zhu Mei with their fowling pieces, thus carrying out Secretary Xiong's directive less than four hours after the commune meeting adjourned. Zhu Mei was the Xincha brigade's only victim during the Daoxian massacre.

In practical terms, Xiong Liheng's behavior was nowhere near the worst in the Daoxian massacre; the commune he led killed only 42 people, fewer than many production brigades, not to mention other communes. Few offspring of black elements were killed, and there were few instances of household annihilation, gang rape, or killing for financial reasons. In a sense, Xiong was actually a moderate, and killings at Wutian Commune commenced only after a district meeting from August 20 to 22, during which Jiujia Commune was praised for its swift action while Wutian was criticized as conservative. I have no intention of defending Xiong Liheng, but given that so many other cadres were so much worse, he can be considered among the more circumspect, and since I've related his story, it's my responsibility to make this clear. At the same time, seeing how an able, competent, and policy-minded commune leader such as Xiong Liheng became caught up in the killing wind also deepens our understanding of the nature of this massacre.

The Red Alliance Role in the Killing Wind

Establishment of the Yingjiang Frontline Command Post

In summer 1967, the two most important places in Daoxian were the No. 2 High School, where the Revolutionary Alliance had its headquarters, and Yingjiang, where the Red Alliance established its headquarters after retreating to the countryside. Almost all the key incidents in the massacre are somehow related to one of these two places.

The Red Alliance called a meeting of People's Armed Forces Department (PAFD) cadres at Yingjiang on August 15, 1967. As the cadres ate watermelon beside a pond in the cool of the moonlight, District 6 PAFD commander Zheng Youzhi described the August 8 gun-snatching incident and other "counter-revolutionary crimes" by the Revolutionary Alliance, drawing intense indignation from those in attendance. A plan was formulated to prevent the Revolutionary Alliance from establishing contacts in the countryside and organizing an insurrection by class enemies: (1) each commune should transfer 20 militiamen to Yingjiang for verbal attack and armed defense, (2) they must establish and consolidate rural base areas and follow the path of "the villages surrounding the cities and ultimately scoring a victory," and (3) every district had to organize militia and set up sentry posts, with Qingxi District responsible for the waterways, Simaqiao District responsible for roads to the Xiangyuan tin mine, Chetou District responsible for the Lingdao Highway, and Shouyan District responsible for the roads toward Guangxi. The cadres also discussed a preliminary plan for removing the Revolutionary Alliance headquarters from the No. 2 High School, and while discussing stronger supervision of black elements, Zheng Youzhi said, "Several troublemakers among the black elements can be done away with."

After presiding over the killing-mobilization meeting at Qingtang on August 17, Zheng Youzhi rushed back to Yingjiang to set up the Yingjiang Frontline Command Post. Following the evening meal on August 18, 1967, Zheng Youzhi, District 2 PAFD commander Zhong Changyou, District 4 PAFD commander Liao Mingzhong, Red Alliance political commissar He Xia, and Red Alliance commander Zhang Mingchi strolled over to a fallow field in the Baiditou production brigade to discuss the arrangements.

By then the sun was sinking behind the mountains with a scarlet glow, but it was the busy season of rush planting and harvesting, so farmers could still be seen laboring in the fields. Zheng Youzhi said, "Call everyone in for a short meeting to organize militias, strengthen leadership, unify command, and prepare for the establishment of a battle command organ. . . . We're at the frontline, so we can call it the Frontline Command Post. Do you all agree?"

With the others expressing their support, Zheng Youzhi moved on to who should man the command post. Zhong Changyou proposed Zheng Youzhi as commander and He Xia as political commissar.

Zheng Youzhi said, "Comrade He Xia has other important tasks at this time—he's preparing to go to Beijing to file a complaint, so it would be better for Zhong to serve as political commissar. Liao, are you prepared to take on the responsibility of deputy commander?"

Liao Mingzhong said, "I have to hurry back to district headquarters tomorrow. I've been neglecting my duties there, and I can't take any more time away."

Zhong Changyou said, "Fuck that! We have to focus on the big picture now. Who cares about petty matters in the districts when the situation of class struggle is so grim?"

Zheng Youzhi agreed: "What's the use of going back? If the Revolutionary Alliance overthrows the government, everything's finished."

Zhang Mingchi joined in: "Commander Liao, take up this responsibility. We'll all support you."

At this, Liao Mingzhong grudgingly agreed, with He Xia put forward as deputy political commissar. Zhang Mingchi, a cadre in the county goods-and-materials office, was recommended as logistics head, and he immediately declared, "I pledge to supply you with whatever you need!"

Once the most important leadership positions were decided, other matters were quickly dealt with, and Zheng Youzhi said, "Call in the Red Alliance leaders and PAFD cadres tonight to unify everyone's thinking, and tomorrow we'll hold our inaugural meeting."

Around eight o'clock that night, Yingjiang's Red Alliance leaders and PAFD cadres gathered at the Yingjiang seed multiplication farm. Zheng Youzhi announced the establishment of the "frontline command post" as the supreme power organ as well as the decision to organize two armed militia companies and one independent platoon: "After this meeting, all actions will be under the direction of the command post."

Early the next morning (August 19), Zheng Youzhi had just gotten out of bed when he received a telephone call from Zhou Renbiao in Qingtang District: "Commander Zheng, I have good news to report. The poor and lower-middle peasants of the Liaojia brigade have started taking action, and they killed six bad guys last night."

Upon hearing this, Zheng Youzhi cried out, "That's wonderful! Comrade Renbiao, I have good news for you, too. We established the Yingjiang Frontline Command Post today, so the poor and lower-middle peasants of the Liaojia brigade have honored the command post's establishment with a valuable gift!"

After breakfast, Zhong Changyou presided over a militia rally during which the Frontline Command Post was declared formally established. Zheng Youzhi gave the "keynote speech," and he and others greatly exaggerated the so-called enemy situation of class struggle, describing the killings at Yangjia Commune and the Liaojia brigade as "revolutionary actions by the poor and lower-middle peasants" and as "the gold standard for who is revolutionary and counterrevolutionary."

A special Red Frontline Politics and Law Headquarters was also established to set up blockades and arrest "suspicious persons" as well as to investigate and interrogate "ringleaders of counterrevolutionary organizations" sent up from the districts and communes. The Politics and Law Headquarters was staffed full-time by county cadres Yao Yuesong, Li Xianzhong, and He Rongsheng, whom local people referred to as the first, second, and third "presiding judges." Several storerooms in Yingjiang's seed multiplication farm were converted into prison cells, and 62 people were taken into custody and interrogated by the Politics and Law Headquarters. (Twenty were still detained there when the Frontline Command Post later evacuated Yingjiang, and some were killed after the Red Alliance notified their brigades to bring them back.)

After this inaugural meeting, Zheng Youzhi and the others quickly created and hung a 3-meter-long banner for the "Red Alliance Frontline Command Post."[1]

On the day that the Frontline Command Post was established, county seize-and-push group head and PAFD commander Cui Baoshu made a special trip from the county headquarters to inspect Yingjiang. As Zheng Youzhi and He Xia reported to Cui on their work, the discussion turned to the killings in the countryside. Quoting Mao, Commander Cui instructed them: "Political power comes from the barrel of a gun. Daoxian's problems arose mainly from gun barrels, so killing a few black elements is a small matter. Once the Military District leaders and 47th Army representatives arrive and seize all the guns, everything will be easier."

On that same day, the vice chairman of the county federation of trade unions made a special trip to report to county Chinese Communist Party (CCP) secretary Xiong Bing'en on killings in the countryside: "Secretary Xiong, down in the villages they've put up blockades everywhere, and in some places they've started killing people. Everyone's terrified. Why doesn't the county party committee step forward and put a stop to it?"

Xiong Bing'en said, "Cadres have all run off, the PAFD's guns have been snatched, and the public-security, procuratorial, and judicial organs have all been disbanded. Who's going to listen to me?"

Xiong had taken a different tack, however, when Red Alliance heads He Xia and Zhang Mingchi had asked for his comments, saying, "This time the masses have truly been mobilized, and the poor and lower-middle peasants have the clearest understanding of who is good and who is bad."

The August 21 Yingjiang reporting meeting

Leaders of the Red Alliance's Yingjiang Frontline Command Post

Name	Command Post position	Official position
Zheng Youzhi	Commander	PAFD commander, Qingtang District (6)
Zhong Changyou	Political commissar	PAFD commander, Chetou District (2)
Liu Houshan	Deputy commander	PAFD commander, Shangguan District (1)
Liao Mingzhong	Deputy commander	PAFD commander, Qiaotou District (4)
He Xia	Deputy political commissar	County CCP committee agricultural department
Wang Xianzhi	Deputy political commissar	PAFD commander, Xianzijiao District (5)
Huang Tao	Chief of staff	County public-security bureau cadre
Zhang Mingchi	Logistics department head	County goods-and-materials office cadre

The Yingjiang Commune seed multiplication farm where the Red Alliance's Yingjiang Frontline Command Post was situated was rather impressive. The compound had a two-story building at its main entrance flanked by a row of red-brick, one-story houses on each side, with an open area about the size of a soccer field in the middle. In this compound and two hamlets that surrounded and protected it, nearly 1,000 militiamen had amassed from various districts and communes to form two militia companies and one platoon. They wore an assortment of garb with leather belts or sashes tied around their waists, and they carried various types of weapons: core militiamen carried rifles, while rank-and-file militia carried fowling pieces, sabers, or spears. The most impressive were those wearing yellow military uniforms, most of whom were army veterans and served as the backbone of the militia. All were united by the common goal of earning revolutionary work points from their work teams in addition to subsidized food supplies.

Zheng Youzhi and the others also arranged for specialized personnel to manufacture homemade cannons and hand grenades at Dapingpu Farm. They succeeded in producing a cannon that could fire about 1,000 meters, but it wasn't very accurate or deadly. Production of hand grenades was halted after an explosion killed someone.

The command post was headquartered in a crude and simple upstairs committee room, where Commander Zheng Youzhi and the other leaders handled factional battles with the Revolutionary Alliance as well as directing class struggle in the county's villages and establishing a strong base area. It was hard work, and Zheng Youzhi was so absorbed in it that his eyes were bloodshot from days and nights of endless toil.

Especially given their location only 2 kilometers from the No. 2 High School, the Frontline Command Post needed to be on guard against surprise attacks from the Revolutionary Alliance's "flying tiger brigades." After experiencing the rapacious cunning of those "desperados" on August 13, Zheng Youzhi and the others were sleeping with their guns under their pillows. Open and covert sentry posts were set up along the small bridge and highway in front of the headquarters. Once night fell, the silence was broken by shouted calls for passwords, raising barking from nearby dogs and making Red Alliance members so tense that their temples throbbed. Not until the barking receded and silence gradually returned did their hearts drop back down from their throats.

On August 21, the deputy commander of the Lingling Military Subdistrict, Zhao Erchang, accompanied by county PAFD commander Cui Baoshu and political commissar Liu Shibin, arrived travel-worn and weary at the Yingjiang Red Alliance Frontline Command Post. Due to conditions at the time, Zhao had taken the long route via Ningyuan rather than the direct route through Daojiang in an effort to avoid the Revolutionary Alliance. Readers may find it baffling that a powerful military subdistrict commander was afraid of a mass organization in a small county town. But please keep in mind that this occurred during the Cultural Revolution. Throughout the country, CCP and government organs were in a state of paralysis or even stripped of their power, but the People's Liberation Army (PLA) apparatus was still solid as a rock and had taken on the heavy responsibility of simultaneously "supporting the Left" and stabilizing public order. The crux of the problem was the term "support the Left."

Although the PLA enjoyed the highest possible prestige, the local armed forces of the Hunan Provincial Military District (including subsidiary organs such as the Lingling Military Subdistrict and the Daoxian PAFD) were by now in an awkward position. The central government's reversals over which factions it supported (described in chapter 3) had resulted in the Central Military Commission sending a cable on July 27, 1967, to the field army in Hunan, the 47th Army, directing it to take over "Support the Left" work from the provincial military district, and provincial military district commander Long Shujin had carried out a "profound self-criticism" before the Central Committee on July 31. The Central Cultural Revolution Small Group's "August 10 Decision" criticizing the Hunan Provincial Military District for line errors on the "Support the Left" issue had also implicated the Lingling Military Subdistrict and the Daoxian PAFD—that is to say, they'd supported the wrong "Left" and now had to turn tail. But how easy was that in reality? There were myriad connections, and things couldn't be clarified in two or three words.

That was why Deputy Commander Zhao and his party skirted the political hot seat of Daojiang and arrived in Yingjiang bronzed from traversing dozens of kilometers of mountain roads under the broiling sun. A local peasant who saw them at the time remembers clucking his tongue and thinking, "Deputy Commander Zhao is really something! Such a senior official, and here he is on such a hot day, walking on his own two feet, covered in sweat, but in full uniform and with his insignia all in order."

As soon as he sat down, Deputy Commander Zhao didn't even bother to mop the sweat from his brow before calling in the district PAFD commanders and leaders of the Red Alliance's Yingjiang Frontline Command Post to report on the situation. Some 30 people were crammed into the little conference room. There were no air conditioners back then, and even electric fans were considered bourgeois luxuries, so the conference room was stifling. Deputy Commander Zhao was wearing a polyester uniform and a military hat, his hook-and-eye clasps all fastened tight, and he sat bolt upright looking straight ahead. Zheng Youzhi and the other PAFD commanders were dressed in more-casual rural garb, and when they saw Zhao, they busied themselves with tidying their appearance.

Zheng Youzhi reported first, indignantly condemning the "heinous crimes" he'd learned about while making the rounds of the districts: "Class struggle in Daoxian's villages is very complicated right now. . . . In Yangjia Commune's Zhengjia production brigade, the counterrevolutionary Anti-Communist

National Salvation Army led by the mistress of puppet county head Zheng Yuanzan has grown to more than 3,000 members. She's commanding black elements in an assault against the production brigade's public-security head. In Gongba Commune, some black elements have been holding secret meetings to form a counterrevolutionary New People's National Salvation Corps. In District 6 [Yueyan District], the landlord Jiang Weizhu[2] has a radio transceiver, and she herself is the dispatcher, drawing funding from a secret agent with the code name '609' in Lengshuitan. They're preparing to attack the arsenal in Dazishan, Hubei Province, and mount a military insurrection. Some 200 to 400 bandits are holed up in the mountains on the border of Yangjia Commune and Ningyuan County and are planning to kill our party members, cadres, and poor and lower-middle peasants. These bandits killed six children from Xinche Commune who were grazing cattle in the hills." (According to the Task Force's subsequent investigations, not a single one of these stories was true.)

Before Zheng Youzhi could finish his report, Zhong Changyou cut in: "In our Chetou District, black elements in Jiaping Commune have staged a revolt and seized the militia's weapons, and at least 100 black-element bandits are hiding in the hills behind Xiganqiao. . . ."

Unfamiliar with local conditions, Deputy Commander Zhao and the other military men were shocked by the reports, their faces expressing bitter hatred of the common enemy.

Zheng Youzhi continued: "Now the poor peasants have mobilized and have organized militia to enhance surveillance over black elements. In some places, class enemies have also been killed."

Deputy Commander Zhao asked, "How many have been killed?"

Zheng Youzhi replied, "Maybe a hundred or so."

Deputy Commander Zhao said, "You need to give us an accurate count."

Zhou Renbiao took his turn to report, and apart from relating how he had "uncovered" the reactionary operations of two counterrevolutionary organizations, he added some new content: "These two counterrevolutionary organizations are in contact with the No. 2 High School. They want to overthrow the government, carry out a counterrevolutionary coup d'état, and kill the poor and lower-middle peasants. Poor peasants in the villages have risen up and killed a bunch of class enemies."

At this point, someone interrupted: "Not everyone agrees with the killings in the villages."

Zheng Youzhi stood up and retorted: "The poor peasants were right to kill those class enemies! It's an expression of the class consciousness of poor and lower-middle peasants, and this is a good thing, not bad! We should support the revolutionary actions of the poor peasants. Better a thousand wrongful killings than even one poor or lower-middle peasant being killed."

Deputy Commander Zhao said, "With class enemies in the villages rising up in insurrection to kill poor peasants, if poor peasants rise up and kill class enemies, this is what comrade Jiang Qing calls 'verbal attack and armed defense.' The PAFD's guns have been seized, the political and legal departments are in disarray, and black elements are trying to overthrow the government. I understand the hatred of the poor peasants toward black elements; I myself am from a poor family, and I resolutely side with the poor and lower-middle peasants."

When the reporting ended, Deputy Commander Zhao said, "Your reports and suggestions are excellent and have helped us understand the actual situation in Daoxian. We'll take this back and report it to the 47th Army so the problems in Daoxian can be resolved as quickly as possible. On the basis of the current situation, you'll need to enhance surveillance over black elements and must quickly assemble the manpower to unearth counterrevolutionary organizations, collect solid data, and resolutely attack them."

Zheng Youzhi took this opportunity to request weapons. Zhao replied, "We can supply arms only under orders from the upper level."

After the Yingjiang reporting meeting adjourned around three o'clock that afternoon, Zheng Youzhi convened a joint conference of PAFD commanders at the Baiditou production brigade. This small-scale inner circle meeting was attended by just eight people: Red Alliance commander Zheng Youzhi; district PAFD commanders Zhong Changyou (Chetou), Liao Mingzhong (Qiaotou), Liu Houshan (Shangguan), Liu Fuxi (Simaqiao), Jiang Youyuan (Qingxi), and Yang Yansheng (Gongba); and the commander of the Yingjiang Commune PAFD, Peng Zhongqiu. The meeting passed an important resolution to prepare to exterminate the Revolutionary Alliance if the 47th Army didn't take measures to eliminate it. Each district selected 60 of its best army veterans to assemble at District 1's Zhengjia brigade on the evening of August 23 to await orders. Liu Houshan held overall responsibility, his assignment being to hold the highway to Ningyuan and the Xiangyuan tin mine, cutting off the Revolutionary Alliance's land and water access in a unified action that would close in on the No. 2 High School from both sides and obliterate the "Revolutionary Bandits." In addition, with the entire county's militia and masses mobilized not to deliver their grain taxes or go to town to sell vegetables, they would see how long the "Revolutionary Alliance bandits" could maintain their stubborn resistance. After the people's militias were organized, they could be fed with the grain meant for agricultural tax wherever they were stationed.

The joint conference adjourned around six o'clock, and on the road back, Zheng Youzhi inquired about the killing of black elements in each district. Liu Houshan, Jiang Youyuan, and Yang Yansheng all said they were unaware of any killings in their districts. Liu Fuxi reported "seven or eight" killed in Yangjia, while Zhong Changyou said one had been killed in Meihua, and Liao Mingzhong reported one "struggled to death" in Qiaotou. Zheng Youzhi said,

"In our district's Liaojia brigade, six were done away with in one night. In Wuhan and Changsha many have been killed in armed conflict, and what's done is done. Commander Cui [Baoshu] said that what matters now is to solve the problem of the Revolutionary Alliance; once this problem is taken care of, all the other problems will be easy to handle."

Meanwhile, after returning to Lingling, Deputy Commander Zhao carried out no further inquiries to confirm the reports he'd been given in Yingjiang but summarized them in a "Cable on the Social Situation" that he sent to the 47th Army. After adding some editorial comments, the 47th Army transmitted this cable down its ranks and then to every district and commune in Daoxian. I was fortunate enough to obtain a copy of this cable:

> According to various partially verified reports, Daoxian's black elements have recently engaged in aggressive activity, distributing reactionary leaflets, killing poor and lower-middle peasants, retaliating to settle old scores, organizing counterrevolutionary organizations, and plotting insurrection. With the county PAFD and public-security organs paralyzed, the poor and lower-middle peasants are in fear of a government overthrow by black elements, and some have proactively taken action. According to incomplete figures, since the end of July, and especially since August 22, they have killed a total of 207 black elements (including a minority of black-element offspring) with fowling pieces, hoes, and carrying poles, and the situation is similar in other localities. We maintain that apart from dealing with killers and the most evil, aggressive, and rebellious of the black elements in accordance with law, black elements should not be indiscriminately killed. Black-element offspring should not be regarded as black elements, and in accordance with policy should be unified[3] and educated. The boundary between those who are and are not the targets of dictatorship cannot be blurred; this is the only way to win over the offspring of black elements. . . .

In its comment on the "Cable on the Social Situation," the 47th Army stated:

> The Central Cultural Revolution Small Group transmits the Lingling Military Subdistrict's report on black-element activities in Daoxian. Pay strict attention to the activities of black elements, but peasants must be advised to proceed in accordance with policy (August 26, 1967).

It is claimed that this "Cable on the Social Situation" entailed genuine investigation, since the Lingling Military Subdistrict had already sent a joint investigation group to Daoxian and other counties on August 19 to investigate the killings. The

18-member group that went to Daoxian, led by company commander Liang of the 6952 Unit, carried out eight days of on-the-spot inquiries in Shouyan, Yangjia, Gongba, Shangguan, Qingtang, and other localities. What remains a mystery is why the results of the inquiry diverged so greatly from reality. Furthermore, why were only 43 people (0.96 percent of the total) killed before the investigation group arrived, while 1,488 people (one-third of the total) were killed while the investigation group was in Daoxian from August 19 to 26?

In fact, the "partially verified reports" in this cable were subsequently found to be completely unsubstantiated. Yet, through this cable, gossip and even intentionally manufactured rumors became part of an official document transmitted to Daoxian's base-level political organs, turning fiction into "ironclad evidence of an overthrow by class enemies" and even a basis for inciting or implementing killings. When we were carrying out interviews in Daoxian, many of those responsible for the killings spoke of this "Cable on the Social Situation" as the source of the "killing wind." They said, "The 'Cable on the Social Situation' fueled the flames of the killing wind at that time. When the poor and lower-middle peasants read this cable, they believed that black elements had actually mounted an insurrection and had become bandits in the mountains. They were in a panic and killed black elements without distinguishing black from white."

After reporting in Yingjiang, Zhou Renbiao told a three-level cadre conference in Qingtang District the next day that "Yesterday I reported to Deputy Commander Zhao on our class struggle in District 6 and the rising up of the masses to kill black elements, and Deputy Commander Zhao praised me. This has bolstered my confidence."

I compiled my record of this incident on the basis of the Task Force's records and from interviews with many people who were discreet yet very sincere. Even so, I must say that I still feel some apprehension regarding to what extent it reflects the original situation. Regarding what those who reported or accepted the reports actually did or directed at that time may be a matter of selective memory on the part of some of those involved at the time. Some people, facing irrefutable evidence that comes to light, still gritted their teeth and refused to admit their errors, greatly impeding the Task Force's efforts, and I had even less recourse. Some informed sources said these people had "engaged in a lot of activity behind the scenes" and wanted to use human blood to "call out the Left," but lacking proof, I have no right to publish such allegations as fact.

Deputy Commander Zhao's main purpose in visiting Yingjiang was to gain an understanding of the situation and to end the violence. Yet statistics reveal this reality: August 21, 1967, was in fact a great leap forward for the Daoxian massacre. The report that the Task Force ultimately submitted to the Lingling prefectural CCP committee and Hunan provincial CCP committee divided the massacre into four phases:

The first phase was August 13–20, 1967, and was mainly manifested in the form of scattered and spontaneous killings. This initial eight-day phase resulted in 81 deaths, or 1.8 percent of the total, and involved only Shouyan, Simaqiao, and Qingtang Districts.

The second phase was August 21–25, and during this phase a countywide upsurge of killings emerged. Killing-mobilization meetings were held in various forms in most districts and communes. During those five days, 807 people were killed, composing 17.9 percent of the total, and only a minority of the county's communes had no killings.

The third phase was August 26–30, and mass killings occurred in many localities for the purpose of "catching up" or "evening out," creating a new upsurge of violence. During this phase, killings were carried out according to the guideline of "no random killings" and "killing one or two of the most heinous criminals." In those five days, 2,454 people were killed, composing 54.5 percent of the total, and killings occurred in every one of the county's 37 communes.

The fourth phase was from August 31 to October 17. This was the period when the killing wind was curbed and began to subside. In these 48 days, 1,177 people were killed (many of them driven to suicide), composing 25.8 percent of the total.

Each of these phases has a symbolic incident:

(1) the August 8 gun-snatching incident;
(2) the August 21 Yingjiang reporting meeting;
(3) the August 26 Yingjiang political and legal work conference;
(4) the August 29 stationing of the 47th Army's 6950 Unit in Daoxian.

The facts make it clear that August 21 was a key date in the massacre, and that from this day forward, Daoxian's killing wind swept rapidly through the county in the form of organized and large-scale killings. Not only did the number of killings increase radically, but the previous situation, in which some kind of accusation had to be fabricated against those who were killed, changed into one in which people could be killed arbitrarily and for no reason whatsoever. What exactly happened that day? It's a matter deserving further thought.

The Yingjiang Political and Legal Work Conference

A report the Task Force wrote for the county CCP committee and prefectural CCP committee clearly outlines the key role that the Red Alliance and its

Yingjiang Frontline Command Post played in igniting, agitating, and orchestrating Daoxian's killing wind:

> A minority of Red Alliance leaders (including some cadres who supported them) fought factional wars and engaged in violent clashes with the Revolutionary Alliance on the one hand, while on the other hand spurring on the "random killing wind" in the villages through a range of activities.

The first activity was creating public opinion in favor of killings.

The second activity was actually mobilizing and engineering the killings. All the killing-mobilization meetings held in the districts and communes were carried out by Red Alliance leaders and the cadres who sided with them, and the Red Alliance headquarters and frontline command post leaders all took part in these activities. . . .

From August 26 to 28, the Red Alliance called a meeting of the county's uniformed political and legal cadres, ostensibly to stop the killings, but it actually served as a further step in mobilizing killings. . . .

The third activity was organizing the people's militia to control the villages throughout the county. . . . All districts and communes in the county assembled militia and established "command posts," "militia barracks," and "self-defense corps," withdrawing people from production to man sentry posts and checkpoints to block, intercept, search, and investigate people and vehicles as they came and went. . . .

The fourth activity was that the Red Alliance arranged a unified solution for funding and feeding the militia and providing the districts and communes with explosives, covering their costs with public funds and grain collected for state tax. When some districts and communes questioned this practice, the Red Alliance leaders said, "This is not the time to think about a little money or grain; the Revolutionary Alliance wants to stage a counterrevolutionary coup d'état. We'll eat first and resolve this later."

The fifth activity was to establish and strengthen peasant associations throughout the county. On August 11–17 and 30, the Red Alliance convened two meetings of the county congress of poor and lower-middle peasants and its standing committee to organize the poor and lower-middle peasants to take part in the "random killing wind." Many districts, communes, and production brigades established poor and lower-middle peasant associations (PPAs), and in many places, the trials for killing people were run by the heads of PPAs. . . .

The sixth activity was organizing specialists to interrogate members of so-called counterrevolutionary organizations. In the latter half of August, the frontline command post arranged for members of so-called counterrevolutionary organizations in all districts and communes to be sent to Yingjiang. . . . Most of the people who underwent interrogation were killed after their release. . . .

The seventh activity was carrying out upward and downward liaison work. In mid-August, after the Red Alliance withdrew to the country-side, it left three people in the county seat to carry out liaison work: Tang Mingzhi acted in the name of the Daoxian Red Guard Headquarters, while Liu Changlin and Wang Enchang acted in the name of peasant associations, regularly telephoning districts and communes to gain an understanding of developments and to collect statistics on the number of people killed, to share information on major situations throughout the county, and to communicate the views of the Daoxian Red Alliance Headquarters. . . .

Given the key role of the Yingjiang Frontline Command Post, this is a good time to describe the event that marked the third stage of the massacre, the Yingjiang Political and Legal Work Conference. Because the massacres continued over a period of weeks in most districts, understanding this event is essential to comprehending the progress of the killings in each locality.

The escalating violence in Daoxian had intense repercussions not only on the county, but also on Hunan Province and even throughout China, and not only through the spread of violence to surrounding counties and cities, but also in the intense resistance it began to engender. The circumstances of the killings (truth mixed with fiction) were passed along through private, military, and government channels to the provincial capital of Changsha, and from there to Beijing, arousing considerable concern and cautious attempts to arrest the progress of the killings. Around this time, both the Hunan Provincial Revolutionary Committee Preparatory Group and the 47th Army's Support-the-Left Group made numerous telephone calls to the Lingling Military Subdistrict and the Daoxian PAFD Headquarters inquiring about the killings.

Yet, Daoxian's killing wind continued to rip through the county's charming scenery like a plague that killed wherever it landed. The targets of the killings expanded from black elements and their offspring to anyone with "historical issues" or even people who were merely the subject of personal grudges or differences of opinion. People lived in dread of the next meeting that would send a new batch of corpses drifting down the Xiaoshui River. As the threat spread like a prairie fire, banners emblazoned with the slogan "Exterminate the Seven Black Categories" began appearing at Hunan University and other institutions of higher learning.

On the afternoon of August 26, 1967, the county PAFD's political commissar, Liu Shibin, rushed to Yingjiang with a copy of the 47th Army's "Cable on the Social Situation" and told Zheng Youzhi to quickly pass it on. Zheng Youzhi immediately notified all districts and communes of a three-day conference for political and legal cadres to be held in Yingjiang starting on August 27 for the purpose of transmitting the "Cable on the Social Situation" and discussing how to end the indiscriminate killing. On that evening, a telephone conference for district and commune seize-and-push group heads was also held to communicate the content of the cable.

Yet this meeting, ostensibly called to end the indiscriminate killing, turned into a killing-mobilization meeting that led to a new upsurge of violence. A comrade from the Task Force described to us how this paradoxical phenomenon came about:

> The guiding ideology of the meeting that the Yingjiang Frontline Command Post called at Yingjiang Commune for the PSB [public-security bureau] duty officers and PAFD commanders of each district [the Yingjiang Political and Legal Work Conference] was that "indiscriminate killing is forbidden" and "in the case of heinous crimes, one or two can be killed," but the emphasis was still on the word "kill." During the meeting, there was a lot of talk about the gravity of class struggle and the sabotage being carried out by class enemies, and confessions forced from people through the use of torture racks, chili water, and branding irons were used to greatly exaggerate the existence of so-called counter-revolutionary organizations. Frontline Command Post commander Zheng Youzhi, Red Alliance commander Zhang Mingchi, and political commissar He Xia all gave speeches on the so-called current situation, the problem of the Revolutionary Alliance, and their views on the killings in the countryside. Some comrades effusively praised the random killing of innocent people as the revolutionary actions of the poor and lower-middle peasants. Some raised the killings to a theoretical level, saying they were "supplemental lessons in democratic revolution" and calling for everyone to seriously study Chairman Mao's *Investigative Report on the Hunan Peasant Movement* to enhance their ideological awareness.[4]
>
> At the meeting, Zheng Youzhi said, "This has made Daoxian famous; even the Central Committee knows who we are. The Central Cultural Revolution [Small Group] has issued a memo.[5] Although the center didn't praise us, they also didn't criticize us, which shows that they support the revolutionary actions of the poor and lower-middle peasants. . . . The enemy wants to launch an insurrection, and the poor and lower-middle peasants have taken up their hoes, shoulder poles, and lances to kill the rebelling black elements, just as Chairman Mao described in the *Investigative Report on the Hunan Peasant Movement*. Is this excellent

or deplorable? I say it's excellent; everyone has to accurately recognize the problem of poor and lower-middle peasants killing landlords and rich peasants."

Of course they also talked about killings requiring files being compiled and submitted for approval, and about distinguishing between black elements and their offspring and so on, but this was mere formality. Summing up the conference on August 28, Zheng Youzhi said, "In the earlier phase, there was some random killing; some who shouldn't have been killed were killed, and some who should have been killed weren't killed. You have to persuade the masses not to kill just anyone; too much killing leads to chaos and factionalism and the wrongful killing of good people. But in the case of people who commit heinous crimes, one or two can be killed if the masses demand it."

Zheng Youzhi also convened a telephone conference at noon on August 29, and although he spoke of the prohibition against killing, he still talked about the seriousness of class struggle throughout the county and said black elements wanted to launch an insurrection and kill CCP members, cadres, and poor and lower-middle peasants. The speeches by Zheng Youzhi and others can be considered to have added fuel to the fire of the killing wind. Of course it wasn't just him saying these things; he was just a typical example. Another reason, and in a certain sense an even more essential reason, was that left-deviating thought had confused people's thinking. Let me tell you a joke. At that time, if there was flash flooding from the mountains, what should you do? Denounce class enemies. If the reservoir began leaking, what should you do? Denounce class enemies. If there was a meningitis outbreak, what should you do?[6] Denounce class enemies. If grain output declined, what should you do? Denounce class enemies. . . . Every problem could be solved through class struggle. It sounds ridiculous now, but at that time, it was such a sacred formulation that you could lose your head over it. People talked about class struggle every month, every day, and every hour, and it led people to draw a simple conclusion: since class struggle was a fight to the death, killing black elements was perfectly justified, and if we don't kill them, they'll kill us.

Another factor was factionalist mischief-making. At that time the Red Alliance and Revolutionary Alliance were in a life-and-death struggle, and the Red Alliance vented its hatred of the Revolutionary Alliance on the black elements. What connection might actually exist between black elements and the Revolutionary Alliance was immaterial.

Before the Yingjiang Political and Legal Work Conference ended, there was a second upsurge of killings in every district.

As will be seen in the narratives that follow relating to the various districts and communes, commune delegates who attended this conference quickly telephoned their production brigades or held meetings immediately upon their return to arrange "catch-up" killings before bureaucracy came into play. In Shouyan District, for example, only 40-odd people were killed before the conference, but more than 400 were killed in the days immediately following. All in all, in the five days from August 26 to 30, a total of 2,454 people were killed throughout the county, comprising just over half of the killing wind's total death toll. All of the county's 37 communes experienced killings, including communes that had delayed killing up until then.[7]

PART THREE

CHETOU AND SHANGGUAN DISTRICTS—MURDER AS SPECTACLE

8

Chetou District's Model Killings

The real story of Chetou District's "landlord and rich-peasant insurrection"

When during the August 21 Yingjiang reporting meeting, Chetou District People's Armed Forces Department (PAFD) commander Zhong Changyou reported to Military Subdistrict deputy commander Zhao Erchang and the others on the situation of class enemies staging a revolt, seizing the PAFD's weapons and hiding in the hills, what was he referring to? He'd made no mention of this matter two days earlier, when the Yingjiang Frontline Command Post was established, so how had he come across such a major piece of intelligence overnight?

After the inaugural meeting to establish the Yingjiang Frontline Command Post, Zhong Changyou found time to hurry back to Chetou District on August 19. For all his insistence on focusing on the "big picture," Zhong was head of his district's seize-and-push group and felt compelled to monitor what was happening in the district.

(I previously noted that the administrative reorganization of Daoxian after the Cultural Revolution led to Chetou District being renamed Meihua District[1] and losing Lijiaping Commune to Shuangpai County while retaining Meihua, Chetou, and Futang Communes under its jurisdiction (See Map 4). As in other cases, this somewhat muddied the waters when the Task Force subsequently tried to establish cause and effect in the Daoxian massacre.)

Yingjiang was only around 7 kilometers from Chetou, and traveling this route was a routine matter for a veteran grassroots cadre such as Zhong Changyou. Crossing the Lianxi and Fushui Rivers slowed things down, however, so Zhong didn't reach Chetou until midafternoon. By then, public-security deputy He Tian and others had been waiting for him in the district office for quite some time. He Tian quickly called Zhong Changyou into his office and grilled him on how the Cultural Revolution was progressing in the county, and about the establishment of the Frontline Command Post in Yingjiang. After answering He Tian's questions as concisely as possible, Zhong Changyou said gravely, "The current situation is very tense. It's by no means certain whether the Red Alliance or the Revolutionary

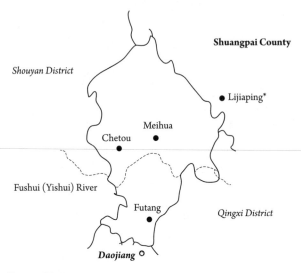

* Lijiaping Commune was part of Shuangpai County at the time of the Task Force investigation.

Map 4 Communes of Chetou (Meihua) District

Alliance will prevail in the end, and black elements are preparing to make trouble all over the county. According to Zheng Youzhi, the Liao clan's landlords and rich peasants staged a rebellion in their district, but fortunately the poor and lower-middle peasants quickly discovered it and suppressed six of them."

He Tian responded sympathetically, "We hear a dozen or so black elements are active in the hills of Xiganqiao."

When Zhong Changyou heard this, he became very anxious and said, "He Tian, you need to send people right away to look into this. If it turns out to be true, we have to arrest them immediately. For now we'll organize a militia to keep an eye on the black elements. If any cause trouble or try to settle old scores, the masses need to arrest them and kill the ones they think should be killed. We can't allow any lingering threat."

He Tian said, "Don't worry, Commander Zhong, we're on the case."

After speaking with He Tian, Zhong Changyou arranged for the next stage of operations in the district and then hurried back to Yingjiang. Zheng Youzhi had telephoned to chase Zhong back to Yingjiang as soon as he had arrived in Chetou; with the Frontline Command Post just established, there was much to do, and Zhong couldn't be spared.

As soon as Zhong Changyou set off, an "enemy situation" occurred in Meihua Commune. While the Shewan production brigade militia was carrying out routine checks on August 20, it came across a man around 50 years old, whose arms bore bruises and scars from being tied and beaten. When detained and interrogated, the man revealed that this name was Tang Linxian, and that he was a pre-Liberation counterrevolutionary from Lijiaping Commune's Lijiaping brigade. Although from a middle peasant family, he had served as a policeman under the Kuomintang regime, which meant he was no good. It turned out that on August 9, Tang Linxian had gotten into a dispute with his nephew's wife over some trivial matter. Tang felt that as a member of the older generation, he should get his way, but the nephew's wife saw things differently, saying that since he was a class enemy and she was a poor peasant, he should submit to her supervision and control. The production brigade had decided in favor of the woman and tied up Tang Linxian in preparation for puncturing the arrogance of the class enemy. Tang Linxian had managed to loosen the ropes and escape, but lacking a certificate from his production brigade, he could only roam around and support himself through odd jobs until he was finally captured on August 20.

The Lijiaping brigade was notified to fetch Tang Linxian, and Chinese Communist Party (CCP) secretary Wang Huanliang rushed off to Shewan with public-security deputy Wang Tianqing and core militia member Tang Liqiang, who happened to be Tang Linxian's nephew. Because Tang Linxian had "received counterrevolutionary training" as a puppet police officer, Wang Huangliang and the others were on their guard, and upon reaching Shewan, they hogtied Tang Linxian before taking him back to Lijiaping. Wang Huanliang later said, "We didn't intend to kill Tang Linxian, but only to take him back to the production brigade and request instructions from the commune on how to deal with him." However, on the way back, Tang Linxian misbehaved, pulling various stunts and dragging his feet instead of following along obediently, sometimes acting pitiful and claiming to have done nothing wrong and begging for mercy and other times complaining that the rope was too tight and demanding that it be loosened. His nephew Tang Liqiang finally lost his temper, snatched the gun Wang Tianqing was carrying, and aimed it at Tang Linxian. It went off, and Tang Linxian dropped to the ground. Wang Huanliang examined him and found he was dead.

At that moment, the three men panicked. Although by then some black elements and offspring had been killed during struggle sessions or had killed themselves, this was the first time someone had been shot in broad daylight, and Daoxian's "killing wind" hadn't yet reached the point where someone could be killed without worrying about the consequences. Wang Tianqing, the smartest of the group, told Tang Liqiang, "We'll say your uncle was shot while trying to grab the gun." Everyone thought this was a great idea, and that's what they reported to He Tian after hurrying back to the district. He Tian said, "It's intolerable for a class enemy to seize arms from the militia! He deserved to be killed."

This is the closest version to the truth regarding what later circulated throughout the county as "class enemies snatching militia weapons in District 2 to mount an insurrection." During the August 21 Yingjiang reporting meeting, Zhong Changyou and others passed on this rumor to Lingling Military Subdistrict deputy commander Zhou Erchang and the 47th Army as an example of how black elements were mounting insurrections.

At one point we asked a Task Force comrade, "It seems that this kind of counterrevolutionary gun-snatching case should have been a major incident at that time. The scene of the crime was less than an hour from the district office, even by sedan chair, so why didn't He Tian go there and investigate the matter himself? Wouldn't an experienced politics and law cadre like him think there was something fishy about the claim that a hogtied old fellow in his 50s could snatch a gun from three armed militiamen?"

The Task Force comrade said, "You can't view the matter from our current perspective. As soon as we went there to carry out our inquiries, people talked about Tang Linxian being shot in a gun-snatching attempt, and we immediately knew it was a lie. But at that time, if there were no cases of class enemies mounting an insurrection, they had to be invented. He Tian had come to take a nap, and when someone provided him with a pillow, he naturally put his head down and snored away."

An old Daoxian cadre said, "Class struggle was easy because it *could* be fabricated, but also hard because it *must* be fabricated."

Back in Yingjiang, Zhong Changyou continued to obsess over what was happening in his district, and on the afternoon of August 20, he telephoned Chetou to ask how things were going. He Tian wasn't there, but the head of the district women's association, Zhang Gui'e, answered the phone, and she told Zhong of the Tang Linxian incident. That night, He Tian himself telephoned Yingjiang to report the matter to Zhong Changyou. Zhong said, "The black element brought this upon himself. It's a good thing, not a bad thing. Quickly pull together the information, and I'll report it to Deputy Commander Zhao and the 47th Army comrade tomorrow." He added, "Have every production brigade carry out inspections to see if there are more of these miscreants around. Every brigade should kill two of the worst ones."

A Task Force comrade who investigated this case observed that Zhong Changyou had always been on good terms with He Tian, but once the Task Force began its work, the two of them had a falling out. He Tian said, "Zhong Changyou is always accusing me of killing people and still refuses to admit his errors." Zhong Changyou said, "He was the one who pushed for killing people, and now he's trying to put the responsibility on me. He's such a liar." Between the two of them, they turned a family quarrel into a counterrevolutionary incident.

Blood-soaked Meihua

Tan Linxian was the first victim of the Cultural Revolution's "killing wind" in Chetou (Meihua) District. Influenced by this incident, Chetou Commune's

Shewan brigade obtained commune-level permission to kill a 50-year-old landlord element named Wu Zhicheng on August 21.

On August 22, Chetou District called a Cultural Revolution Committee (CRC) meeting presided over by district CCP secretary Yang Jifu to discuss and implement the spirit of a telephone conference by the county seize-and-push leading group. During this meeting the "enemy situation" was greatly exaggerated.

The next day (August 23) at noon, a mobilization meeting was called for the district's administrative cadres, with district public-security deputy He Tian presiding and a speech by Wu Ronggao, the district head and deputy CCP secretary. In his speech, Wu played up various bogus reports of enemy activity and encouraged killings: "In Lijiaping, a counterrevolutionary seized a weapon to mount an insurrection but was suppressed by the poor and lower-middle peasants. This shows that in our district the masses have truly risen up and realize they're the masters of their own affairs. If we don't kill the most-heinous black elements, they'll turn around and kill us. From now on, the poor and lower-middle peasants are the ones who decide whether to kill the most-heinous criminals."

Just before the meeting adjourned, Wu Ronggao stood once more with a cryptic smile on his face and said, "Comrades, I have a suggestion: after lunch, let's all go have a look at the Meihua production brigade."

The formerly hushed meeting buzzed with excitement. Those familiar with Wu Ronggao's temperament and work style knew there would be something worth seeing at the Meihua brigade. Someone impatiently asked a Meihua Commune cadre sitting next to him, "What new moves is your commune going to show us?" The Meihua Commune cadre smirked and said, "Just come and see, then you'll understand everything."

It turned out that the day before the district mobilization meeting, Meihua Commune had held a "four chiefs" meeting to arrange some killings. Commune CCP secretary Jiang Yixin had presided over the meeting, with commune secretary Liao Longguo delivering the main speech. After the meeting adjourned, Liao Longguo had the Meihua brigade cadres stay behind and instructed them to hold a grand mass rally on the 23rd, during which a 50-year-old landlord element named He Wencheng would be killed to mobilize the masses and intimidate the enemy. Secretary Liao repeatedly told them: "There will be observers at the meeting, so don't do anything that will make the commune lose face."

After the rally, He Wencheng was taken to an abandoned limekiln, where public-security head He Xianfu asked him, "Do you want to live? If so, hand over your movable property, and your life will be spared." As someone who had experienced Land Reform, He Wencheng was familiar with this policy and repeatedly expressed willingness to pay for his life. He didn't realize that after paying the 180 yuan[2] he would still be killed. When the Task Force later carried out its inquiries, He Xianfu would admit to taking only 80 yuan, and what happened to the other 100 yuan was never determined. He Xianfu told the Task Force that after taking the payment, "We originally wanted to spare his life, but people had come to observe and we had to kill someone, so we couldn't come up with any other idea but to kill him."

After observing the killing at the Meihua brigade, Lijiaping's cadres rushed back and the next day held their own commune cadre meeting to transmit the spirit of the August 23 district meeting, report on what had happened at the Meihua brigade, and arrange for their own killing campaign. In the five days following the meeting, more than 170 people were killed in Chetou District (not including those killed in Lijiaping Commune[3]).

On August 25, He Tian left Chetou to attend the Yingjiang Political and Legal Work Conference and then communicated the gist of the conference at another meeting for administrative cadres in Chetou District on August 29, and Liao Longguo read out the Lingling Military Subdistrict's "Cable on the Social Situation" transmitted by the 47th Army. Giving the meeting's keynote speech, He Tian spoke of the previous killings by saying, "The poor and lower-middle peasants rose up and killed some troublemaking black elements who had committed heinous crimes. This was an excellent revolutionary act! We should vigorously support it. However, some errors arose and killings became random, and some who shouldn't have been killed were killed while others who should have been killed were not. We mustn't randomly kill people, especially the heads of reactionary organizations. We should spare them, not because they don't deserve to die, but because through them we can continue to dig deeper and round up the entire reactionary organization behind them. We can kill a few of the most heinous criminals if the masses insist, but there should be no indiscriminate killing."

He Tian was in fact repeating comments that Zheng Youzhi and others made at the Yingjiang Political and Legal Work Conference. After the August 29 meeting, Chetou District experienced a second upsurge in killings just like the rest of the county.

I'll sketch out the killings in Meihua and Chetou Communes, but not in Lijiaping Commune, which came under the jurisdiction of investigations in Shuangpai County.

I mentioned earlier that Meihua Commune had already held a killing-mobilization meeting before the district mobilization meeting was held, and that after its meeting, Meihua had assigned the Meihua brigade to serve as an "advanced model." Even so, the Meihua brigade recorded only seven deaths, with two more killings on August 26 and three killings and a suicide on August 29.

I consider the Meihua brigade emblematic, in that (1) it kept in close step with the upper-level leaders—when the upper level held a meeting, it carried out a round of killings in close coordination, and (2) the killings were few but carried out with great fanfare. In each case, a mass rally was called to denounce the victims, during which the poor-peasant association (PPA) represented the brigade's peasant supreme court in proclaiming the "nature of the offense," and then the victim was escorted ceremoniously to the execution ground. Black elements and offspring who weren't killed were brought to the execution ground for "reeducation."

The executions of the last three people on August 29 can serve as an example. After the district held its meeting to implement the spirit of the Yingjiang Political and Legal Work Conference, the Meihua brigade decided on another round of killings, saying, "We might not have another good chance in the future." They settled on a rich peasant, Mo Desheng, and a poor peasant, Wen Shangyi, along with his son, Wen Shoufu.

Killing Mo Desheng was understandable, since he was a class enemy, but why kill the poor peasants Wen Shangyi and his son? Inquiries determined that the cadre Wu Dexue took the opportunity to avenge himself against Wen Shangyi, who had criticized him back during the Socialist Education movement. He Guoqing, He Antao, and others went along with Wu, and they agreed to kill Wen's son, Wen Shoufu, at the same time to prevent future trouble. Aware that complications could develop over killing poor peasants, He Antao used his status as CRC chairman to request instructions from commune secretary Liao Longguo. Liao said, "Not all poor peasants are guaranteed Reds. If they need to be killed, then kill them."

When Wen Shangyi and his son were killed, Wu Dexue, He Guoqing, and the others bound them up with the rich peasant Mo Desheng and then blew them up with dynamite, a process known as "flying the homemade airplane." Because the amount of explosive used was inadequate, or for some other reason, Wen Shangyi and Mo Desheng were blown to smithereens, but Wen Shoufu only had his buttocks blasted off, and he writhed on the ground in agony. Wu Dexue ran over, used his fingers to gouge out Wen Shoufu's eyes, and stuffed them in his mouth. According to local lore, if Wen Shoufu went to hell blind, he would be unable to find his way back to the living world to wreak revenge. When Wen Shoufu continued to breathe, Wu Dexue cut his throat with a saber. After killing the father and son, Wu Dexue went to the Wens' home and pointed his dripping saber at Wen Shangyi's sobbing wife, saying, "Your son died on this knife. If you lick the blood off, I'll let the matter rest. Otherwise, I'll kill you, too." After forcing Wen Shoufu's mother to lick his blood off the saber, Wu Dexue took the matter no further.

When an elderly woman from the landlord class, Wu Nanzhu, witnessed the horrific deaths of Mo Desheng and the Wens, she was so terrified that she hanged herself that very night.

There are plenty of stories about the killing of landlords and rich peasants, so at this point I will just mention the killing of a poor peasant in the Xiepidu production brigade. Among the 4,500 people killed during the Daoxian massacre, more than 350 were poor or lower-middle peasants, and I need to explain how such killings came about.

After the killing-mobilization meeting at Meihua Commune on August 22, the commune's top cadres went down to the villages to encourage and supervise killings. Commune CCP secretary Jiang Yixin went to the Chiyuan brigade, while deputy CCP secretary Wang Guoxiang and commune director He Changbao went to the Tangjiashan brigade. The commune's Youth League secretary, Li Rentao, went to the Xiepidu brigade to guide operations because he had been assigned to this brigade during the earlier Socialist Education movement.

On August 24, Li Rentao presided over an enlarged cadre meeting at the Xiepidu brigade to implement the spirit of the August 22 commune-level meeting. Li Rentao talked about the brigade's production problems and the situation of class struggle throughout the county, and then he asked, "Does our brigade have one or two troublemakers we can kill?" Core militia members Li Junsheng and Li Cisheng (a blacksmith) stood up and replied, "Of course we do! He Zhonggong is one." But none of the representatives of the masses spoke up to endorse this killing as in other localities. There were three reasons for this: one was that He Zhonggong was a poor peasant; second, the Li brothers had a grudge against He Zhonggong; and third, the Li brothers were themselves highly problematic, involved in pilfering and messy sexual relationships. In particular, Li Cisheng had spent half a year in "reform through labor" for stealing, and although a steadfast revolutionary, he was a person of poor character and reputation.

After the meeting adjourned, Li Rentao had the brigade's main cadres stay behind for further discussion. Brigade CCP secretary He Rushun said, "He Zhonggong really is an incorrigible troublemaker, and it would be acceptable to kill him." But Li Rentao withheld his approval: "We have to be discreet about killing a poor or lower-middle peasant. Detain him first and investigate the matter further before we decide."

Treating this as a full-fledged delegation of authority, Li Junsheng and Li Cisheng immediately tied He Zhonggong up and locked him in the brigade storehouse. That night, He managed to escape and took his son, He Ruchang, with him. Perhaps he worried that if he fled on his own, the brigade would call his son to account, but he didn't consider how dangerous it was to take his son along. The entire county had militia manning a vast network of checkpoints, and the father and son were nabbed at Dongmen Commune within two days. After the Xiepidu brigade sent someone to bring them back, father and son were tied to a column in the brigade's ancestral hall. Someone asked, "How should we deal with them?" CCP secretary He Rushun sighed and said, "Now we have no choice but to kill them."

It had to be done discreetly, however, so Li Junsheng was sent to the commune to request instructions from Li Rentao. Li Rentao replied, "Strike while the iron is hot and get rid of them."

Li Junsheng trotted back to the production brigade and said, "Secretary Li has given us permission to quickly kill this fellow and his whelp."

He Rushun said, "Go to it, then."

When the time came for the father and son to be killed on August 30, Li Rentao came to personally oversee it. Because rifle bullets were precious, the two were shot with fowling pieces, and the first round of shots wasn't fatal. Stamping his foot anxiously, Li Rentao told He Rushun to get it over with. He Rushun was dressed in a white robe; afraid of soiling it, he fired from farther away, and when this shot was likewise ineffectual, Li Rentao berated him as useless. A core militiaman finally hurried over and finished the men off with his blunderbuss.

After He Zhonggong and his son were killed, an elderly woman of the landlord class, Wu Chengyuan, hanged herself on September 2.

The greatest number of killings at Meihua Commune occurred in the Dongfeng brigade. This was one of the notable cases highlighted by the Task Force, which observed that the killings were carried out with a bugle call. This production brigade, which included the natural villages of Xitian, Zhenggu, and Huangtudong, recorded 28 deaths during the "killing wind," including three suicides.

After presiding over the commune's killing mobilization meeting on August 22, commune CCP secretary Jiang Yixin went straight to the Dongfeng brigade on August 23 to oversee operations. The brigade immediately held a cadre meeting and came up with a list of names. The first batch of five people was killed on August 24. After a meeting of administrative cadres was called on August 29 to implement the spirit of the Yingjiang Political and Legal Work Conference, the brigade quickly killed another batch of 16 people on September 1, with piecemeal killings after that. This production brigade had a militia platoon leader named He Tiexian who killed 11 people single-handedly and raped the wives and daughters of many of his victims.

So what was the incident in which people were killed by bugle call?

A grassroots cadre from the Dongfeng brigade said, "When we weren't allowed to discuss killings, He Guosheng proposed using a bugle as a signal for all three villages to move at once. That idiot always wanted everyone to remember that he'd served as a bugler in the army, but all it did was make our brigade notorious once the Task Force brought it to light, even though Zhangwufang killed a lot more people."[4] He added, "The fact is that the people would have been killed whether or not the bugle was blown, so what does it matter?"

Words leapt to my throat, but I held them back, knowing that the only way to continue our reporting was to listen more and say less.

After the Dongfeng brigade killed 16 black elements and offspring on September 1, the upper-level prohibition against random killing reached the brigade and was transmitted during a cadre meeting on the morning of September 2. That evening, when a brigade member named He Ruobei returned from sideline work in the county seat,[5] a middle peasant named He Dingxin and his son He Ruoying came to chat with him. It was normal for villagers to want to hear what was going on in town, especially when there had just been an earthshaking battle between the Red Alliance and Revolutionary Alliance in Daojiang on August 30. There were rumors that class enemies had gained the upper hand and seized arms and that they had set up a base camp in the No. 2 High School, where they had hung a portrait of Chiang Kai-shek and distributed reactionary leaflets. He Dingxin and his son were experienced and knowledgeable men, and finding all this incredible, they came to ask He Ruobei what was really going on.

He Ruobei's neighbor noticed this and suspected that He Ruobei had come back from the Revolutionary Alliance's bandit lair to establish ties in the village. The report quickly reached brigade militia commander He Ziliang, who immediately summoned a dozen or so militiamen to arrest He Dingxin and He Ruoying. Why didn't they arrest He Ruobei? Supposedly, since He Ruobei had come back to the production team to hand over the proceeds of his sideline occupation, He Dingxin and He Ruoying had an additional motive for going to ask him about the "bandit's lair," showing how ruthlessly ambitious and venomous they were.

Since the cadre meeting prohibiting further killings had just been held, any demands for the killing of "heinous" criminals required compiling and submitting a file to the commune for permission. This posed no real difficulty to He Ziliang and the others, however; acting in the name of the brigade CCP branch, they quickly put together a file accusing He Dingxin of colluding with bandits, supplemented with a file on a "rich-peasant element who had slipped through the net" as a middle peasant, He Xisheng, and submitted them to the commune.[6] The commune agreed to the killings.

On the morning of September 5, He Ziliang and others called a mass rally of commune members to read out the crimes of He Dingxin and He Xisheng. After the rally, he personally led more than 20 militiamen who hogtied He Dingxin and He Xisheng and took them to Shizi Mountain to be executed. He Dingxin's son He Ruoying was also bound and taken along to witness the execution. He Xisheng was killed first, but when it was time to kill He Dingxin, He Ziliang halted the proceedings and asked He Dingxin, "Tell me, would you still dare to cut down my family's camphor tree?"

It turned out that in 1950, when He Dingxin was serving as a district representative, he had cut down a camphor tree near Zhongren Pond. His family and

He Ziliang's had fought repeatedly over who owned the tree, and He Dingxin had used his status to take possession of it by force. The two families pursued the dispute to the township and district levels, and eventually He Dingxin won the lawsuit. The two families had nursed a mutual grudge ever since. He Ziliang said, "You had the big mouth back then, and we couldn't out-talk you. But that tree belonged to my family—my granddad planted it with his own hands."

"What camphor tree are you talking about?" It had happened so long ago that He Dingxin couldn't recall it right away.

"What camphor tree? You may not remember, but I do, and when you see the King of Hell, you'll have lots of time to think about it."

After killing He Dingxin, He Ziliang worried that He Dingxin's son might try to avenge his father's death, so he claimed to have received a message from the commune saying that He Ruoying had joined a reactionary organization and had three militiamen bring He Ruoying in to be interrogated. But He Ruoying denied involvement in any counterrevolutionary organization: "You can go and investigate, and if you find out I was a member of a counterrevolutionary organization, you can throw me in jail or execute me as you like."

He Ziliang pounded on the table and yelled, "Since you won't cooperate, I'm tying you up."

Two militiamen went over and hogtied He Ruoying. Seeing how things were going, He Ruoying pleaded with He Ziliang for mercy: "Brother Ziliang, just give me some idea of what I've done wrong, and I'll think it through and confess everything."

He Ziliang said, "So you've never done anything wrong? Your old man cut down my family's camphor tree."

He Ruoying said, "That was my father's business. I was just an ignorant boy at the time, so how can you blame me? My father's dead, he's paid for his crime. . . ."

Fed up, He Ziliang interrupted He Ruoying and said, "Enough. You're wasting your breath."

When they reached the edge of the Panjia limekiln, He Ziliang ordered the militiamen to shoot He Ruoying. The three militiamen were reluctant, having been told only to take He Ruoying to the commune. He Ziliang berated them: "Fuck your mothers, if you let him live he'll overthrow us all!" He then grabbed a fowling piece and shot He Ruoying himself.

As he died, He Ruoying cried out, "He Ziliang, you dare to settle your private grudge in the name of public interest!"

He Ziliang laughed coldly: "So what if I did? You can bite my balls!" He ordered a militiaman to cut off He Ruoying's head and took it back for public display.

An advanced commune encounters a new challenge

Back during the Cultural Revolution, Chetou Commune had a formidable reputation. It was the model commune promoted by Hua Guofeng,[7] then secretary of the Hunan provincial CCP committee secretariat, and was Daoxian's famous "red flag"—during the 1958 Great Leap Forward, Hua Guofeng cited the high rice yield at the commune's Shixiadu production brigade in his essay "Victory Lies with the People Who Leap Forward Holding Aloft the Red Flag," which he submitted to the Hunan provincial CCP committee and CCP Central Committee. The most important highway linking Daoxian to the outside world—the Lingdao Highway running from Lengshuitan to Daoxian—traversed Chetou from north to south. When we went to Daoxian for our interviews and reporting, the first thing we saw through the drizzling rain was this stretch of lovely, fertile land.

Chetou Commune held its killing mobilization meeting on August 24. Commune deputy CCP secretary He Yongde, who at that time was in charge of the commune's operations, communicated the spirit of the district's August 23 meeting and arranged the commune's killing campaign.

That afternoon, He Yongde personally went to the Sikongyan brigade to "direct operations." The commune CCP committee's organization and supervisory committee member Yang Zhengdong, commune director Zhu Qiaosheng, commune secretary Pan Jitong, and others also went to various other production brigades to encourage and oversee killings.

Compared with Meihua, this advanced commune seemed somewhat backward. In fact, Chetou began its killings earlier than Meihua, but with less fanfare. Apart from the killing of the old landlord Wu Zhicheng at the Shewan brigade on August 21, the Xiantian brigade killed another old landlord, Huang Yongdu, on August 22, a day earlier than Meihua's killing of He Wencheng. On August 23, the Chetou brigade killed an old landlord named Zhou Jiapian at the instigation of commune deputy CCP secretary He Yongde.

Besides being the first brigade in Chetou Commune to start its killing, the Shewan brigade also killed the most people, a total of 15 (including three suicides). After the killing of Wu Zhicheng on August 21, a 59-year-old landlord element named Li Binqing was so terrified that he killed himself on August 23.

On August 24, the commune held its killing-mobilization meeting, and the Shewan brigade responded by killing four more people: two class enemy offspring (Wu Guangzheng, 20, and Li Qinshou, 23) and poor peasant Li Changrui, 44, and his son Li Zuwen, 17, a student at the Daoxian No. 1 High School.

The Task Force focused its investigations on four types of murder cases: those involving rape (including carrying out murder to seize someone's wife), money, or revenge, and the killing of poor and lower-middle peasants. The Task Force's inquiries established that the killing of Li Changrui and his son qualified for two of these categories: revenge and the killing of poor and lower-middle peasants. During the rural Socialist Education or "Four Cleans" campaign in 1962, Li Changrui had followed the instructions of the Four Cleans work team by criticizing public-security head Li Rongbao and the brigade's then CCP secretary Li Yikuan, among others. This led to Li Rongbao and the others being investigated and forced to pay restitution. Li Rongbao carried a grudge against Li Changrui because of this, and the Cultural Revolution gave him and others a chance to revenge themselves with brigade CCP secretary Li Yikuan's support. As a young student, Li Zuwen shouldn't have been killed, but he went around the village flaunting the red armband of a Young Red Guard Militant, so he seemed the kind who would avenge his father's death and consequently had to be killed as well.

There was a prevalence of this kind of revenge motive among the killings that occurred in Daoxian during the Cultural Revolution. While it can't be said that every production brigade had such a case, every commune had more than a couple; I have material on more than 60 such cases.

After the Shewan brigade killed Li Changrui and the others on August 24, they killed a woman in her 60s from the landlord class, Pan Duanying, the next day. That evening, Li Xinqing, the son of rich peasant Li Ronghui, fled out of fear of being killed. Feeling that he had no way out, Li Ronghui hanged himself after his son fled. On the 26th, a 56-year-old woman from the rich-peasant class, Liu Luanying, committed suicide "to escape punishment." After that, the production brigade killed a 19-year-old class enemy offspring on September 4, and four more offspring on September 10. The young man who had fled, Li Xinqing, was captured and killed on September 11.

I earlier mentioned the fame of the Shixiadu production brigade, and this is an appropriate time to speak of the killings there. This advanced production brigade, which created the myth of 5,000-kilo-per-*mu* rice yields, was far less "progressive" during the killing spree, recording only five deaths. The brigade had killed a 56-year-old woman from the landlord class, Pan Jinjiao, on August 26 to implement the spirit of the commune's August 24 meeting, but when the August 29 district meeting required permission from the upper level for any future killings, Shixiadu's cadres felt they had "missed out" and "appeared backward"; they said, "We killed too few in the previous round compared with other brigades. No matter what, we have to quickly kill a few more." They then held a meeting and decided on four more people to kill.

Although they were obliged to submit files to the upper level, this was a simple matter for a reputed "advanced brigade," and once they'd pulled the material together, brigade CCP secretary Wu Yaosheng personally delivered it to the commune to request instructions. Commune CCP secretary He Yongde was away at the time, so Wu took the file to commune secretary Pan Jitong. Pan said, "It's not as easy to kill people as it was before. The higher authorities require prior authorization from the frontline command post. I suggest you drop it."

When the Shixiadu cadres heard this, they felt they were in a spot. The killings weren't absolutely necessary, but they'd already arrested the four targets, and the peasant supreme court had already handed down death sentences. If all this had to be taken back, the brigade's cadres would lose credibility, and the black elements would become impossible to manage. When they pressed the matter, Pan Jitong reluctantly acquiesced: "Whatever you've decided, just do it. But when you kill them, do it along the river across from the Shangmo brigade, not over by Haitoumiao; blood all over the riverbank looks nasty, and the two households living at Haitoumiao will object."

That evening, Wu Deying (46 years old), Wu Yourui (57), Wu Youqiu (52), and Wu Yongzheng (38) were led to the riverbank across from Futang Commune's Shangmo brigade and were killed with explosives.

Shangguan District—in the Eye of the Storm

Shangguan Commune's on-the-spot killing rallies

During Daoxian's killing wind, killings were arranged by 18 of the county's 37 communes. Among these, Shangguan Commune's on-the-spot killing rally was the most distinctive.

Shangguan Commune was positioned on the southeastern border of the county seat of Daojiang, close to the Tuo River (as the Xiaoshui River was called where its upper reaches near Daojiang). Shangguan is now part of Gongba District, but at the time of the killings, it belonged to Shangguan District (Map 5), which no longer exists. The water and soil of Shangguan made it one of Daoxian's most prosperous communes. The garlic chives of Daoxian were famous far and near, and the best were from Shangguan, where they grew tall and lush, their color crisp and their fragrance delicate; they were absolutely scrumptious.

On August 22, Shangguan Commune's first on-the-spot killing rally was held at Baotajiao on the banks of the Tuo River.

Baotajiao lay less than 4 kilometers from Daojiang, and the pagoda (*baota*) for which the place was named could be seen from almost any point in the city, towering 25 meters above the red-clay hillocks under a mantle of blue sky, its brick and bluestone looking golden from afar. Constructed in 1764 during the Qianlong era to ward off the water demons of the Xiao River that brought calamitous floods upon the land, it became a local landmark. It was only natural that the stretch of fertile soil below the pagoda should be named Baotajiao ("foot of the pagoda"). During the Cultural Revolution's "smashing of the four olds," however, it was renamed the Qixin ("one mind") production brigade.

Now the spacious threshing ground of the Qixin brigade's Huziping production team was packed with heads and spears. Outside the meeting space,

Map 5 Communes of the former Shangguan District

militiamen wearing uniforms and red armbands stood guard. Apart from members of the production brigade, cadres, Chinese Communist Party (CCP) and Youth League members, and poor-peasant association (PPA) representatives from the Jianshe and Xiangyang brigades brought the attendance to more than one thousand. At one end of the threshing ground, a large table and several wooden chairs had been set up to serve as a rostrum. In order to enhance the impact, the theme of the meeting had not been divulged in advance. People whispered in each other's ears asking what it was all about.

Daoxian's climate is at its hottest in August, and invisible heat waves rippled from the fields under the broiling sun. The meeting began just as the heat became oppressive. After the usual ceremonial preludes of studying the "highest directive" and respectfully wishing long life to Chairman Mao, the deputy head of the Shangguan Commune seize-and-push group, Zhou Yuanji, delivered a report. Lacking a microphone, he had to shout each sentence at the top of his voice: "Poor and lower-middle peasant comrades, the black elements of Simaqiao have headed for the hills! Weapons have been seized at the No. 2 High School for a coup d'état! Poor and lower-middle peasants in Districts 8, 10, and 11 have taken action and killed black elements! What should we do?"

The assembly fell silent. Having been given no advanced warning, everyone looked at each other in blank dismay, wary of making a careless remark. Seeing the lack of response, Zhou Yuanji continued, "Shouldn't we kill some of those scheming, lowlife black elements?"

The meeting erupted into chaos as everyone began talking.

Zhou Yuanji went on: "Right now, no permission is needed for killing. The poor and lower-middle peasants are the Supreme People's Court, and killings can be carried out with their agreement." He paused for a moment while looking about portentously and waiting for his words to sink in, then shouted, "Today we'll take the knife to puppet security chief He Guangqin to serve as an example."

As soon as Zhou finished his report, the Qixin brigade's Youth League secretary, Luo Teliang, mounted the podium and pronounced judgment on behalf of the peasant supreme court, and a group of militiamen came from behind dragging a hogtied He Guangqin. After Luo Teliang finished reading out a "judgment" that commune Youth League secretary Wu Rongdeng had drafted, he imitated the drawn-out diction of movie judges to proclaim, "I now represent the Supreme People's Court of the Poor and Lower-Middle Peasants in sentencing He Guangqin to death, to be carried out immediately!"

He Guangqin thought he was only going to be subjected to the usual public denunciation, and when he heard his death sentence pronounced, he was so terrified that he fell senseless to the ground and soiled his pants. Holding their noses against the stench, two militiamen dragged He Guangqin like a dead dog to a harvested paddy field in front of the threshing ground. After forcing him to kneel, they brought a saber down upon his neck. Blood spurted all over the fragrant soil. Eyewitnesses said that the execution was so poorly handled that He Guangqin's body continued to twitch after he was beheaded.

Zhou Yuanji had been just an ordinary 33-year-old plant breeder at Shangguan Commune's agrotechnical station, but once the Cultural Revolution began and he became deputy head of the commune seize-and-push group, his temperament changed radically. Sloughing off his slack habits, he became fervent, speedy, and resolute, earning repeated commendations from his leaders.

This killing rally had been prompted by the Yingjiang reporting conference on August 21. Shangguan District People's Armed Forces Department (PAFD) head Liu Houshan and others had hurried home and convened a cadre meeting that resulted in the organizing of a militia and establishment of a militia base area in the Qixin brigade, setting up roadblocks and sentry posts and closely monitoring all black elements. Liu Houshan made an unmistakable knife-like gesture with his hand and said, "We have to make the first move against class enemies who are habitually disobedient, troublesome, and hard to manage." The cadres had decided to kill He Guangqin, who had served as a public-security head under the Kuomintang (KMT), as a means of mobilizing the masses. Liu Houshan had clapped Zhou Yuanji on the shoulder and said, "We'll hand over operations here in Qixin to you." Zhou Yuanji was very excited to have a leader place so much trust in him, and the on-the-spot killing rally was his first salvo, with representatives from the neighboring Jianshe and Xiangyang brigades invited to attend and learn from the rally.

After the killing rally at Baotajiao, Zhou Yuanji went straight to the Jianshe brigade in Longjiangqiao to arrange an even more spectacular killing rally.

On the morning of August 24, the beating of gongs could be heard, sometimes slow, sometimes urgent, as large and small groups of people converged on the roads leading to the Longjiangqiao transformer substation. Four troupes similar to dragon dance teams wound their way from the Dongfeng, Dongfang, Dongjin, and Dongyuan brigades. Those walking in front wore dunce caps and placards and struck cymbals and battered washbasins that they held in their hands. Bound together and escorted by armed militia, they included men, women, old people, and children. Behind this troupe ran a bunch of women dragging their kids to see what was happening, even though they would lose work points for attending.

"Granny Jiang, going to the rally at your age?"

"Sure, I'm going! We haven't seen anything so grand in years! How could I miss it!"

"You must have seen a lot of rallies at your age. Leader Zhou says this is unprecedented."

"Yes, I saw lots back when you were young, and they were splendid, but nothing like this."

"Better hurry! If you're late, you'll have to stand in back and you won't be able to see a thing."

"You're right. I lost out last time, standing in the back. Hey, Sister He, let me be blunt: last time your son really messed up, hacking at He Guangqin so many times to cut his head off."

"It wasn't his fault—they gave him such a dull blade!"

"This time they'll have sharpened it."

"They're not using a saber this time. Leader Zhou says they're using a 'foreign method.'"

"Really? You'd better get going!"

By the time the old ladies and housewives reached the plaza at Longjiangqiao's Shitouling transformer substation, it was already packed with more than 3,000 people. In order to prevent class enemies and the Revolutionary Alliance from sabotaging the event, Zhou Yuanji had gotten permission from district PAFD head Liu Houshan to borrow dozens of core militiamen from the nearby Baimadu militia command post to maintain order at the rally. The attending cadres and commune members stood in areas chalked in for each production brigade. Dozens of black elements and offspring knelt in a line with their heads bowed on the stage, which was festooned with red flags and a large red banner proclaiming, "Carry the Great Proletarian Cultural Revolution to the End!" Zhou Yuanji, who had instructed each brigade to submit black elements for killing,[1] stood on the stage, eyes directed solemnly ahead of him as people from surrounding localities continued to crowd onto the plaza.

Finally the rally began, and as soon as Zhou Yuanji opened his mouth, there was no more talking or coughing, and no children whimpered as everyone pricked their ears to catch whatever sound issued from Leader Zhou's lips. Only the wind continued to rustle through the bamboo and tree leaves.

"Today we are here to hold a large on-the-spot rally. Today's rally is the second signal flare our Shangguan Commune is sending up to suppress the class enemy following the first signal flare at the Qixin brigade yesterday. Each brigade needs to take immediate action to thoroughly puncture the arrogant bluster of the class enemy."

After that, the six black elements chosen by the various production brigades were executed by firing squad. When the onlookers realized that the "foreign method" was actually just shooting, they couldn't help but feel disappointed. This method had already been used back during Land Reform: people were bound up, had placards hung around their necks, and knelt down, and then the muzzle of a gun was placed at the back of their heads. Boom! The tops of their heads blew off, and their bodies toppled forward as red blood and white brains sprayed out, none of it getting on the executioners, unlike that fellow He using a saber and getting drenched. This method was good enough, but it was nothing new.

After the rally ended, the commune's administrative cadres stayed behind for a brief meeting during which each was assigned to several brigades for supervising and encouraging killings. We read the notebook Zhou Yuanji kept that year, which showed the specific brigades assigned that day to He Ruidi (commune head), Xiong Liji (commune deputy CCP secretary), Zuo Changci (commune organization cadre), Yang Guolong (Shangguan District deputy CCP secretary), Wu Rongdeng (commune Youth League secretary), and Yang Daoming (commune CCP secretary).

What exactly did these comrades do in the production brigades? An illustration is commune deputy CCP secretary Xiong Liji's actions at the Shuinan brigade. Located on the outskirts of Daojiang, Shuinan was well known as one of Daoxian's most prosperous villages, producing citrus fruits and melons that were the best in the county. The members of this brigade were also relatively prosperous, and it had quite a few black elements, but several of these households had members working outside the county, some as fairly senior cadres. When Xiong Liji called a meeting to discuss killings, the brigade's cadres showed a marked reluctance, and Xiong finally became so agitated that he drew out a dagger and drove it into the meeting table: "This is the watershed between revolutionary and counterrevolutionary. Who here is unwilling to distinguish himself from the class enemy?"

The knife handle quivered under the lantern light, and the faces of the cadres blanched white. Soon after that, the brigade drowned several class enemies and offspring.

Under the supervision and encouragement of district and commune cadres, the other production brigades likewise took action one by one, and in the eight days up until August 30, Shangguan Commune's 12 brigades killed a total of 112 people.

The Task Force's investigation verified that under the arrangements and direction of district PAFD commander Liu Houshan, commune CCP secretary Yang Daoming, and others, Shangguan Commune killed a total of 173 people during the Cultural Revolution massacre, mainly through the use of guns, knives, and drowning. One of the victims was Du Zhuzhong, an Army veteran and poor peasant from the Dongfang brigade who had rendered distinguished service during the Korean War. The Task Force's inquiries established that Liu Houshan personally talked grassroots cadres into "doing away with" Du Zhuzhong because Du had dared to argue with him in the past.

Killing turncoats as well as landlords

As mentioned earlier, during the Cultural Revolution "killing wind," Shangguan Commune was under the jurisdiction of the subsequently eradicated Shangguan District. Readers may wonder why this point is important enough to keep repeating. The reason is that the massacre occurred along administrative boundaries, from the districts to the communes to the production brigades, each level inciting the next one down to carry out killings. I can confidently say that there were almost no genuine instances of poor and lower-middle peasants spontaneously rising up against landlords and rich peasants unless it was out of personal revenge or to take possession of women or valuables, and that apart from these personal factors, the killings showed a clear chain of command from top to bottom. The adjustment of administrative boundaries in 1984 obscured this process when the Task Force investigated the killings, resulting in many errors and misunderstandings.

Viewing the sequence of events in Shangguan District from the perspective of the original boundaries, we see that the jurisdiction of Shangguan District (also referred to as District 1) included not only Shangguan Commune but also Futang (now under Meihua District), Dongmen (now under Qingxi District), and Wanjiazhuang (now under Qingtang District), forming the northern, eastern, and southern coordinates of a crescent shape enveloping the county seat of Daojiang. Adding Yingjiang Commune in the west completed the circle and ensured that Shangguan District, like Yingjiang Commune, became a key battleground between the Red Alliance and Revolutionary Alliance.

Due to constant infiltration by the Revolutionary Alliance, the four communes in Shangguan District experienced varying degrees of division within the "class ranks," with a small number of grassroots cadres and poor peasants switching over to the Revolutionary Alliance. For example, the core militia commander of Shangguang Commune's Shangguan production brigade, Li Chenggou, and some others brought guns to the No. 2 High School, and Li became head of the "Poor and Lower-Middle Peasant Revolutionary Rebel Headquarters" under the Revolutionary Alliance, while simultaneously serving as commander of the "Verbal Attack and Armed Defense Command Post." Such people were considered much more destructive than the average black element, because they masked the "reactionary character" of the Revolutionary Alliance. As a result, the killings in Shangguan District targeted not only class enemies but also a significant number of these "turncoats," a term applied specifically to poor peasants and grassroots cadres who sympathized with Revolutionary Alliance viewpoints or joined Revolutionary Alliance organizations.

In Dongmen Commune's Youyi brigade, a 26-year-old poor peasant named He Shanliang was considered one of the county's most outstanding students of Chairman Mao's works and had been an active participant in the Socialist Education movement. During the Cultural Revolution massacres, one would have expected him to be one of the most enthusiastic killers and least likely to be targeted. Instead, he perversely joined the Revolutionary Alliance and was consequently sentenced to death by the peasant supreme court, which declared him guilty of secret communications with the "Revolutionary Bandits" and undermining the foundations of socialism by stealing two cabbages from his production team during the hard times of the Great Famine in 1960. This second charge might strike the reader as ludicrously petty, but in 1960, when even chaff was hard to come by, one cabbage could save a life. An estimated 38,000 people starved to death in Daoxian during the famine, partly because of people such as He Shanliang, which makes it less surprising that during the Youyi brigade's meeting to discuss the killing, the poor peasants unanimously demanded He's death. Heeding the call of the masses, brigade CCP secretary Jiang Shiming[2] agreed: "Do away with him along with the class enemies." There were other such cases in other communes of Shangguan District.

In Wangjiazhuang Commune's Hongqi brigade (Xialongdong Village), He Ziyuan was a CCP member and principal of the Shenzhangtang Elementary School, and it may never have occurred to him that he would be designated a black element during the "killing wind." He was said to have been brought to justice by his village's poor peasants because he joined the Revolutionary Alliance. (A former Revolutionary Alliance leader had no recollection of He Ziyuan joining any of the alliance's organizations; it appears that he at most supported Revolutionary Alliance standpoints.) When the production brigade met to discuss who should be killed, the PPA and Cultural Revolution Committee (CRC) chairmen said He Ziyuan absolutely had to be killed. The first time He Ziyuan was taken out to be killed with several class enemies, he recited a quote from Chairman Mao: "The Great Leader Chairman Mao instructs us: the core power that guides our undertaking is the Chinese Communist Party, and the theoretical foundation that directs our thinking is Marxism-Leninism." He added, "I'm a party member, and whatever I've done wrong should be handled by party discipline and national law. Your Supreme People's Court of the Poor and Lower-Middle Peasants is not qualified to kill a party member." Some of the Hongqi brigade cadres thought this made sense, and they had the class enemies killed, but locked He Ziyuan up again to await a decision from above.

At that time, He Ziyuan's production team pointed out that although he was a CCP member, he had turned his back on the revolution and therefore should be handled as a "turncoat," so he was taken out a second time to be killed. But He Ziyuan played the same old trick, reciting a quote from Chairman Mao: "The Great Leader Chairman Mao instructs us: policy and strategy are the lifeblood of the party; leading comrades at every level must pay close attention to this and never disregard it under any circumstances." He added, "Poor and lower-middle peasant comrades, comrades of the revolution, in carrying out our revolutionary work we must do everything in accordance with party policy. If you want to kill me, you must first expel me from the party. I'm still a party member, and if you kill me, you're killing not only me but also a party member and the party!"

Amazingly, this drivel was actually effective in prompting dissention within the brigade. Some said, "Who cares, just kill him!" But others said, "It's fine to kill class enemies, but killing a party member requires instructions from the upper level." So again, He Ziyuan's life was spared.

The production brigade's militia leader, He Gouxiang, telephoned the commune to request instructions, and the call was taken by Jiang Zhi, the commune's Red Alliance head and a member of the commune CCP committee's organization, propaganda, and supervision committee. Jiang didn't dare make a decision without authorization, so he telephoned Peng Yuming, the district's Red Alliance head and a member of the district CCP committee's organization committee. Peng immediately directed him: "If the masses demand that he be killed, it doesn't matter if he's a party member. Kill him and then we'll discuss it."

After obtaining these instructions, He Gouxiang laughed and said, "A weasel has three farts to save his life. Let's see what He Ziyuan comes up with now!" This time He Ziyuan's glib tongue was unequal to the task, and he was finally put to death.

Why was such trouble taken to kill He Ziyuan? A comrade from the Task Force explained that the He family had a fairly high-class status, and before killing He Ziyuan, the brigade had already killed his wife and son. The brigade's cadres were afraid that if they spared He's life, he would eventually take revenge for his family, so they needed to find an excuse to kill him.

During the Cultural Revolution massacre, Shangguan District killed a total of 415 people (including 46 suicides). The district's main leaders who incited and planned the killings were deputy CCP secretary and propaganda committee member Yang Guolong; CCP committee organization, propaganda, and supervision committee member Peng Yuming; PAFD commander Liu Houshan; and district women's committee chair Wei Shuying.

In the district's four communes, the main people responsible can be categorized as in the following table:

Official position	*Commune*			
	Dongmen	*Futang*	*Wangjiazhuang*	*Shangguan*
CCP secretary				X
Deputy CCP secretary	X		X	X
Public-security deputy	X	X	X	
Militia commander	X			
Red Alliance leader	X		X	
Commune director		X	X	X
CRC chairman		X		
Organization and propaganda committee member	X		X	X
Youth League secretary				X

Note: in a few cases, an individual held more than one position.

The Shangguan Commune plant breeder Zhou Yuanji, whose role in the killings is described so colorfully above, was only a pawn and henchman in the chain of responsibility.

I would like to make three observations regarding the cadres involved:

(1) It's not the individuals who are important, but rather the official titles. I have often imagined these people as mere actors selected by some unfathomable and mysterious hand to play their role in this cosmic tragedy and to provide a lesson for our great nation. I have the names of more than 200 county, district, and commune cadres who are directly implicated in the killings, but there is little purpose in assigning personal blame; only raising national consciousness can prevent such a tragedy happening again. I originally intended to give no names at all in this book, but only the positions

of those responsible. However, I later decided that the information was necessary to allow others to verify the accuracy of this text. I myself have sometimes found its content difficult to believe, and if it were made more obscure, later generations might suspect it was pure fiction. Things published in black and white must be recorded word for word like sworn testimony in a court of law.[3]

(2) This listing reveals that the main people responsible for the killings were seldom CCP secretaries but were most often deputy CCP secretaries, committee members, PAFD commanders, and public-security deputies. Is this because most of the top officials (secretaries) had reservations about the killings? Or were their policy or strategic standards of a higher caliber? This is a point that those who experienced the Cultural Revolution will implicitly understand. The Cultural Revolution was a mass movement launched by Mao as the leader of the CCP, and it involved the top-down mobilization of nearly every individual who lived and breathed in China. None of the abominations of the Cultural Revolution were unique to that period, but its adherence to the slogan "Rebellion is justified" ensured that it proceeded largely, though not entirely, in accordance with Mao's personal will. The guiding principles of the Cultural Revolution, the "Sixteen Articles,"[4] stipulated: "The emphasis of this movement is to purge from the party those in authority who take the capitalist road." As a result, in the early stage of the movement, the persons in authority or "first in command" at every level, from the Central Committee down to every local work unit, came under attack to some degree. It was under this general environment that the Daoxian massacre took place. Consequently, apart from cadres who had already "stepped forward" to "strike a revolutionary pose," those who had "stepped aside" as "capitalist roaders" had little role to play, whether they agreed with the killings or not. By the time they achieved "Liberation" and resumed their administrative duties, the Daoxian massacre was a page that had been turned in the book of history.

(3) As mentioned before, but which bears repeating here, during the Cultural Revolution killings in Daoxian, the real power was held by the various levels of seize-and-push groups, with the county PAFD at their core. Evidence indicates that in the vast majority of cases, killings were incited and arranged through this channel.

10

Other Communes
in Shangguan District

Dongmen Commune: Graffiti on a cottage wall

"Moo. . . ." When we poked our heads into the "Dongzhou thatched cottage" that the famous Qing calligrapher He Shaoji had written about 200 years ago, we found it was now a cattle barn holding Dongmen Village's dozen or so fat plow oxen. Buffeted by the overpowering odor of hot, fermenting cattle dung, we quickly retreated to the vast yard outside, with its luxuriant grove of bamboo resembling a mass of ink pens.

The histories record that the "Dongzhou thatched hut" had at one point been destroyed by the army of the Taiping Heavenly Kingdom, but the extent of its decrepitude was still unexpected. He Shaoji's poem described the cottage as once having a study, rostrum, corridor, pavilion, bridge, cassia tree, and tangerine grove. By the time of our visit in 1986, all that remained was the tangerine grove. The narrow slab and cobblestone lanes between the farmhouses were covered with a treacherous slurry of mud and manure, while bubbles of gas oozing from the inky fluid in the roadside drains imparted a funk of humid rot. Only the crumbling village archway and courtyard beams and gables testified to the village's former glory.

During the Cultural Revolution, no one practiced calligraphy in He Shaoji's home village, but there were still quite a few people with a fine hand, as evidenced in the reports on killings and the violent posters and banners displayed around the village. The Dongmen brigade had someone whose bold cursive rendering of the word "kill" was particularly reminiscent of He Shaoji's style. He Shaoji once wrote a couplet that went, "Sitting up until the second watch, I fall asleep; with nothing in my heart, no fear of a knock at the door." During the Cultural Revolution, someone changed the wording: "Sitting up at the second watch, unable to sleep; nothing in my heart but fear of a knock at the door."

At noon on August 17, 1967, Dongmen Commune's Red Alliance political commissar, Xiao Jiawang, called a meeting of "reliable cadres, party members, and some administrative cadres" from all brigades at the Gaoche production brigade. At the meeting, Xiao Jiawang made the usual "battle-readiness arrangements" to organize militia and enhance control over black elements.

For a week after the meeting, not a single killing occurred, but on August 23, factionalist struggle resulted in one killing. Then on the night of August 24, the moon's reflection on the peaceful waters of the Xiaoshui River was spliced by the prows of two boats silently making their way toward Dongzhou. Two groups of people huddled in the boats: one group holding spears and sabers and the other group hogtied. When the boats reached the middle of the river, a murmured order broke the silence, and the people holding the weapons tied baskets of rocks around the necks of the bound individuals and then pushed them one by one into the river. With each splash, an eddy roiled as the river received its offerings. The victims were not gagged, yet no one wailed or cried for help and no one struggled; it was all inexplicably peaceful. Then, under the soul-stirring radiance of the starry sky, He Jiren, a landlord element from the Dongmen brigade, stood up and yelled out a slogan, his cries reaching far along the shore in the stillness of the night. His cries were still echoing when He Jiren was pushed into the river along with his 20-year-old son.

This "incident of the landlord element who yelled the reactionary slogan" became vivid teaching material for class struggle, and an additional punishment was exacted a few days later, when He's wife and 12-year-old son were drowned in almost the same spot, making his the only family to be completely extinguished in Dongmen Commune.

What was it He Jiren yelled that brought such disastrous consequences? An informed source replied evasively, "It was a reactionary slogan, and a particularly vile one."

"What was the reactionary slogan?"

"Something like 'Long live Chiang Kai-shek.' "

During our reporting, someone told us that He Jiren had once said, "Chiang Kai-shek did well for himself. After losing this country, he ran off to Taiwan to eat and drink and bathe in milk, leaving us to take the blame."

Of all the 9,000 people killed during the Daoxian massacre (including in the 10 surrounding counties), He Jiren was the only one reported to have yelled a "reactionary slogan" before he died. Yet, we heard another version as well, which was that before he was killed, He Jiren yelled, "Why are you killing us, you bandits!" This version seems more credible, but still made him culpable of "brazenly vilifying the revolutionary action of the poor and lower-middle peasants."

Someone discreetly told us that He Jiren was a descendent of the calligrapher He Shaoji.[1] Whether he was or not doesn't really matter; if He Shaoji himself had been alive then, he would have been killed without compunction. And it is likely that, as in Zhou Dunyi's home village of Loutian, He Jiren's killers also included descendants of He Shaoji.

We mentioned He Jiren's shouted slogan in passing while talking with a teacher surnamed Huang who had been a political commissar for the Revolutionary Alliance during the Cultural Revolution. Huang's response was unexpectedly vehement: "That's a complete fairy tale and an absolute lie made up by those people in the Red Alliance. A normal person simply can't imagine the kinds of stories they came up with. Back then they said that our No. 2 High School [the Revolutionary Alliance headquarters] was a den of black elements. They said we had Chiang Kai-shek's portrait hanging in the school and that the Kuomintang had air-dropped secret agents to secretly direct operations. They said we marched through the streets yelling, 'Long live Chiang Kai-shek,' and that killing black elements in the villages was killing the class brothers of the Revolutionary Alliance. The father of one of my students was the party secretary of a production brigade, and he made a special trip to the No. 2 High School to check out the rumors. I took him through every room in the school so he could see for himself. Nothing was displayed but portraits of Chairman Mao and Chairman Mao's quotes! They made up these rumors in order to label us counterrevolutionaries and provide an excuse for attacking the No. 2 High School and killing every one of us."

Huang's remarks were naturally flavored by partisanship, but a Task Force report dated December 25, 1984, cited the same rumors about the Revolutionary Alliance and the No. 2 High School.

At the Dongmen Township office, the township's current CCP secretary and the discipline inspection committee head told us of a tragic incident that occurred in the commune's Wujiashan production brigade.

On September 2, 1967, a militiaman walking home to the Wujia brigade saw a young woman sitting alone on the tea hill. She didn't look like a local, and when she saw him approach, she looked nervous. The militiaman stopped and questioned her, but the young woman refused to answer. Noticing rope marks on her wrists, the militiaman decided she must have done something wrong, and he took her back to the brigade for interrogation. In a stern voice he asked her, "Who are you? What is your class status? Where did you come from? Where are you going?" But the young woman stared at him in terror and didn't speak. Finally he held a saber to her neck and said, "If you don't speak, I'll butcher you!" At that point she finally stammered out what sounded like "Guangdong," and her accent sounded like she could have been from those parts. Since both parties spoke with heavy local accents, they couldn't understand each other.

Unable to get any further with her, four militiamen escorted the young woman to the commune militia headquarters. The headquarters was too preoccupied with other matters, however, and told the militiamen to take the young woman back to the production brigade. By then dusk had fallen, and as they walked along the road, the militiamen looked at the darkening sky and began to think wicked thoughts. One of them, named Guo Chengshi,[2] suggested, "Even the commune doesn't want this girl, so there's no point taking her back to the brigade. Let's have some fun." The other three agreed, and they stopped alongside a pond, stripped the young woman, and raped her. Afterwards, one of them said, "Now that we're done, let's let her go." But Guo Chengshi said, "What if she comes back and makes trouble? Let's just say she's a black element and kill her." So saying, they killed the young woman with rocks and a hoe and then dumped her body in the pond. Later, worrying that the corpse would be discovered, they went back and buried the body on the hillside. But the grave was too shallow, and eventually wild dogs dug it up and dragged parts of the body all over the hill, creating a horrific spectacle. The young woman was tall and thin and in her mid- to late 20s, but her name and hometown were never determined. How she turned up in Daoxian in August 1967 is likewise a mystery. In the records of unnatural deaths in Daoxian during the Cultural Revolution, only this record remains: "An unnamed woman from another place, aged around 30."

Dongmen cadres told us that 78 people were killed in Dongmen Commune during the killing wind. The main people responsible in terms of inciting, supervising, or directing the killings were district People's Armed Forces Department (PAFD) head Liu Houshan and district women's committee chair Wei Suying, along with the commune's Red Alliance leader, deputy CCP secretary, PAFD commander, accountant, and public-security deputy.

The only production brigade in Dongmen Commune that had no killings was the Beimen brigade. The reason was that the CCP secretary of that brigade, Ding Jinlong, never arrived at "mature consideration" of the killings. The absence of killings doesn't mean that no one died, however. The Beimen brigade had a former Kuomintang insurrectionist named Feng Fei who committed suicide, anticipating the worst after having been publicly denounced on several occasions in the past due to his historical problems and overseas relations.

The killings at Wanjiazhuang Commune

On August 21, 1967, Wanjiazhuang Commune called a meeting of reliable leading cadres from its production brigades. Commune CCP organization committee member Jiang Zhi presided over the meeting, with public-security deputy Liao Chengyuan delivering a "battle-readiness report" on the "grim situation" of class struggle in the commune, and calling for a crackdown on "troublemaking black elements" as in other districts: "With the class enemies so aggressive in our commune, we can't be softhearted; this is a battle to the death, and if we don't kill them, they'll kill us."

After the meeting, the Wuzhou and August 1st brigades took immediate action to implement the spirit of the meeting by killing "one or two trouble-makers." The other brigades just watched from the sidelines, however, and after discussing this, Jiang Zhi, Liao Chengyuan, and other commune leaders felt the need for a larger meeting to mobilize the masses and develop struggle against the enemy.

On August 24, the commune called a meeting of CCP members and cadres during which commune secretary Zhong Qiqi communicated the spirit of the upper-level directive and Jiang Zhi reported on the killings in the Wuzhou and August 1st brigades: "This was an excellent revolutionary action by the poor and lower-middle peasants! Now that action is being taken everywhere, what are you waiting for?" A cadre who attended this meeting told us that when Jiang Zhi said this, the masses became agitated and everyone began talking at once.

After the meeting adjourned, May 1st brigade CCP secretary Jiang Fangru requested instructions from Jiang Zhi: "At our brigade's primary school, Liu Fucai [a teacher] is mounting a campaign to establish ties among class enemies, and we want the commune to send him away."

Jiang Zhi quickly took Jiang Fangru to see Liu Fucai's direct superior, pri-mary-school principal Huang Xisheng, and said, "Principal Huang, we want you to transfer that person Liu Fucai. There are too many black elements in our bri-gade for us to manage, and Liu Fucai is having a negative effect here."

Huang Xisheng said, "Secretary Jiang, the brigade wanted him transferred and we should have done it, but now it's the Great Cultural Revolution, and we can't transfer him. Since he's teaching at your brigade's school, it's up to your brigade to manage him. If the masses say he should be publicly denounced, then do that, and if he should be killed, then kill him. Once he's been killed, we'll bring in a better one."

During our reporting we learned that Liu Fucai was not a troublemaker and was a diligent teacher. His only fault was a fondness for good students, and his failure to discriminate between "socialist grass" and "capitalist seedlings." The production brigade's school included two particularly good students from class enemy households, and during his visit with parents, Liu Fucai tended to linger a little longer in the homes of these good students, never imagining that this would have such disastrous consequences.[3]

Jiang Fangru explained Liu Fucai's killing this way: "Our brigade didn't intend to kill him but just to have him transferred. We didn't even want to kill the other class enemies. But then there was an incident of a class enemy running off and joining the bandits in the hills to mount an insurrection. At that point we real-ized that we had no choice but to kill people, so we finally requested instructions from the commune and did away with all of them."

What had happened was that on the morning of August 25, a class enemy offspring named Jian Liuming from the May 1st brigade attempted to escape, fearing that he would be killed and unaware of the dense network of sentries and watchmen all around him. Captured before he even left the brigade, he ended up dead and pulled Liu Fucai and others down with him.

After breakfast, the Wuzhou brigade sent invitations to the cadres and militia of all the production brigades to attend an on-the-spot killing rally like that in the Qixin brigade. Having been commended for killing a black element on August 23, the Wuzhou brigade was ready to kill another batch, and Liao Chengyuan and others wanted it done with great fanfare in order to puncture the arrogant bluster of the class enemy and kindle the flame of revolution throughout the commune.

After the rally, Jiang Fangru asked for militia from the Wuzhou brigade to help the May 1st brigade carry out its own killings, since some people at the May 1st brigade had a conservative mindset and needed a "hard shove from behind." On learning of the Wuzhou on-the-spot killing rally and the militia's assistance with killings at the May 1st brigade, Jiang Zhi said over and over again, "Excellent!" and told them, "You have to notice that all the brigades are monitoring each other; don't let information leak out, and if it does, handle it appropriately."

After this, the Wuzhou and May 1st brigades each killed another batch. All of Wanjiazhuang Commune's 15 production brigades carried out killings during the "killing wind," but the Wuzhou production brigade killed the most, at 31, and the May 1st brigade killed 13.

We'll now turn to two of the commune's other brigades.

The first is the Yanhe production brigade, which didn't initially implement the spirit of the August 21 commune killing conference. Commune accountant Zhang Guirong went to the brigade on August 23, and finding everything peaceful and quiet he scolded a brigade cadre: "People are taking action all over the county, so what's your brigade waiting for?"

The Yanhe brigade was then criticized with some other production brigades at the August 24 commune meeting where the Wuzhou and August 1st production brigades were praised for their enhanced awareness and quick action. The commune leader said, "This is a major event involving millions of heads hitting the ground. . . . Some of our comrades are softhearted now, but when the time comes, it will be too late for crying."

After the meeting was adjourned and the Yanhe cadres returned to their production brigade, CCP secretary He Shengzhi and deputy CCP secretary Jiang Liuluan felt a need to proceed with caution, so they called a cadre meeting on August 26 to discuss the killing issue. Everyone felt that since the upper level had spoken, they had to kill a few, especially since other brigades were already killing people and they were in danger of falling behind. At a meeting of cadres and core militia members the next day (the 27th) with Jiang Liuluan presiding, a list was drafted of people to kill, but problems arose over the specifics. They'd planned to kill one or two troublemakers, but Cultural Revolution Committee (CRC) chairman He Defu pointed out, "If we're going to kill, better kill them all and not leave any black elements behind. The other production brigades have been so ferocious, what are we afraid of?"

Poor-peasant association (PPA) chairman He Tiancheng said, "If we kill the adults, what about the young ones?"

He Defu said, "Don't think about too much at once; kill the adults first and then we'll deal with the kids."

One CCP committee member had great misgivings: "If we just kill whoever you say, isn't there a danger of error? A few years ago we had the Five Winds,[4] and all that rashness resulted in a lot of errors, didn't it?"

He Shengzhi said, "What the fuck is wrong with killing a couple of class enemies? The worst that will come of it is self-criticism, and I'll do that, so you don't have to worry."

After a commune cadre said the brigade's poor peasants could decide what to do, agreement was reached to kill all the class enemies. When the class enemies were led out to be killed, an old poor peasant bachelor took a fancy to a female landlord element and asked the brigade if she could be spared. Considering the hard life the bachelor had spent without a wife, the brigade leaders agreed and declared, "Condemned female landlords who agree to marry poor or lower-middle peasants will be spared, but the marriage must take place immediately." The other 13 people were killed.

The second production brigade I'll mention is the July 1st brigade. There's no need to go into the commune mobilization meeting, brigade meeting, and further discussions, which proceeded the same as with the Yanhe brigade. Instead I'll relate a story: on August 26, the brigade's peasant supreme court pronounced a death sentence on a black-element offspring named Liao Chengmao. When he was led out to be killed, Liao's mother, Jiang Zhiying, followed behind him weeping and scolding. Fearing that Madam Jiang was too foolish to see the danger of her actions, someone pulled her aside and said, "Just stay here and do your crying. If you keep following him, you'll be killed, too."

But Jiang Zhiying refused to listen to reason: "They might as well kill me. Once they kill my boy, who will take care of me? Either way, I'll die."

The Task Force comrade who told us the story said, "What else would an illiterate village woman go on about? It was, 'What has my boy done wrong? Why are you killing him? Whatever numbskull hurts us is going to die for it!' Back then, no black element even dared breathe too loud, and here she was ranting and raving. The result was predictable. The brigade's public-security head said, 'Jiang Zhiying is too unruly. If we don't kill her, we'll never be able to manage the other black elements.' Several militiamen went over and beat and kicked her until she couldn't cry anymore and then dragged her like a dead dog to the hill behind the village, dumped her and her son into an abandoned cellar, and buried them alive."

This aroused an intense reaction in the production brigade, and when a meeting was held to discuss killing a second batch, the head of the women's association, He Xinhua, pointed out, "We all have sons and daughters, fathers and mothers, and we should understand how others feel. Seeing loved ones killed is bound to cause antagonism. This talk about drawing a clear distinction is all a lie, and sparing offspring won't work. If black elements are killed, won't their sons and daughters take revenge? In my opinion, we either kill none or all of them." The majority of those in attendance agreed with her view. The original plan had been just to kill a few class enemies, but ultimately their families weren't spared, either, and a total of 17 people were killed.

The unbearable lightness of Futang Commune

After attending the district "strategy meeting" on August 19, the first thing Futang Commune director Ding Tianzhi did was send the commune militia to the Dongyang production brigade to apprehend Xiong Guanyi, a landlord and pre-Liberation counterrevolutionary.

This 29-year-old commune head later told me he was feeling the pressure of being "entrusted with a mission at a critical moment." With the Futang Commune CCP committee paralyzed and mass confusion reigning among cadres and ordinary commune members, the bulk of responsibility had fallen on Ding Tianzhi's shoulders. Ding had always taken his revolutionary responsibilities seriously and had acted with vigor and speed, but the Cultural Revolution had kept him guessing.

Although young, he had plenty of experience with campaigns big and small, including actively participating in the Anti-Rightist movement, the campaign against Rightist deviation, the rectification of incorrect work styles, and rectification of the cooperatives, as well as the Socialist Education movement. It could be said that he had grown up in these campaigns, and as soon as the Cultural Revolution began, it was second nature for him to stand at the frontline of struggle. But soon after the "Sixteen Articles" were issued, the Cultural Revolution work groups that the county had sent to every work unit were withdrawn and replaced with liaison officers to direct operations at various work units, and students from outside the county wearing Red Guard armbands rushed in to "establish ties" and inflame the masses. Everything devolved into chaos overnight as big-character posters went up attacking "Liu Shaoqi's reactionary capitalist road" and calling for the Daoxian CCP committee to be reorganized or even "bombarded."

Ding Tianzhi observed all this with an inward smile. After taking part in the Anti-Rightist campaign, he knew all about "luring the snake from its den" and how to make class enemies expose themselves. And as he predicted, after this latest batch of "reactionary slogans and big-character posters" came out, the county CCP committee held rallies, meetings, and conferences to arrange a campaign to "seize Rightists and push production" and to criticize "political pickpockets." Those who had launched frenzied attacks against the CCP immediately became objects of opprobrium.

But Ding Tianzhi never dreamed that soon afterward, the "political pickpockets" would spring back to life as "young militant Red Guards" and "valiant revolutionaries." It was thoroughly confusing. When the two radically opposing mass rebel organizations emerged in the county, Ding Tianzhi took the side of the Red Alliance, never anticipating that the Revolutionary Alliance would gain the upper hand in the county seat and force the Red Alliance to withdraw to Yingjiang.

The constant reversals regarding which faction was in favor at any given time were enough to bewilder even China's canniest political minds. Experienced as he was in class struggle, Ding Tianzhi was still just a young rural cadre, and in August 1967 he was convinced that the Revolutionary Alliance would have a lifespan no longer than a rabbit's tail: wasn't the CCP bound to rely on "strong revolutionary roots and shoots" such as him rather than those cack-assed sorts? Experience had deeply impressed on him that personal advancement required being groomed and trusted by the CCP, and this was earned through performance in campaigns. The crux of excellent performance was first of all a firm class standpoint; second, keeping in lockstep with his leaders; and third, an enhanced spirit of class struggle. Ding saw Futang Commune plagued with infiltration by Revolutionary Alliance forces, especially in the Dongyang production brigade adjoining Daojiang Town, and the district meeting had called on commune leaders to take drastic measures to put the class ranks in order and cut off the black hand that the Revolutionary Alliance was extending into the countryside. All this was in Ding Tianzhi's mind when he ordered the arrest of Xiong Guanyi, a move that would puncture the arrogant bluster of the class enemy while serving as a sharp warning to those in the Dongyang brigade who were making overtures to conspire with the "Revolutionary Alliance bandits."

When the militia went to arrest Xiong Guanyi, Xiong was working busily in the fields for the "double rush" planting and harvesting. He had been a routine target in every political campaign, and he was surprised and uneasy when the Cultural Revolution went on for more than a year without any moves being put on him. When the commune finally came for him, he felt almost relieved to see things proceeding as normal, never anticipating that this time he'd actually be killed, and in a particularly brutal fashion.

On August 21, the commune convened a "four chiefs" meeting, after which the Dongyang brigade's peasant supreme court sentenced Xiong Guanyi to death on August 23. In order to maximize shock value, they carried out the execution with explosives. According to our inquiries, Xiong Guanyi may have been Daoxian's first victim subjected to "flying the homemade airplane," given that this term came into common usage only following his death.

Ding Tianzhi later said, "We put Xiong Guanyi under control to implement the spirit of the district conference and to strengthen control over black elements; it was entirely justified at the time. The district's on-the-spot [killing] meeting required every commune to seize one or two classic cases. Our commune was no exception, and we were obliged to make Xiong Guanyi our first target of attack. This was a historical error, and there's no reason to make anyone take personal responsibility for it. If we hadn't killed Xiong Guanyi, we'd have killed someone else, and if I hadn't authorized it, someone else would have. In any case, compared with other places, Futang Commune was one of the most lightly affected by the 'killing wind.' We killed fewer people in our entire commune than a single production brigade in other communes."

Although we can't categorically accept Ding Tianzhi's claims, we have to admit he was right to some extent. Among Daoxian's 37 communes, the majority had 100 to 200 killings, with a small minority killing as many as 400 to 500. Futang, with only 24 killings, came in second from last.

Another victim in the Dongyang production brigade was a 19-year-old black-element offspring, Liang Xianlian, who was killed on August 26. It is said that this young woman was a local beauty who was also blessed with brains and talent and that the county theatrical company had considered recruiting her, but she hadn't passed the political vetting. Local villagers said, "It's a pity she was handicapped by her landlord background; otherwise she would have gone far." Back then, most girls in Daoxian's villages married at 17 or 18 and always before 20, but Liang Xianlian had ambitions beyond her status and wouldn't consider a match that was beneath her, while men with better backgrounds wanted nothing to do with her. A few years earlier, even with her political disadvantages, she would have been snatched up by some commune leader or leather-shod townie, but now even the most covetous didn't dare take her. Secretary Shi Xiuhua had taken a hit to his career by marrying a landlord's daughter while serving as a cadre down south, and no one else wanted to follow his example.

Liang Xianlian should have had enough self-awareness to realize that she would have to settle for what she could get. Others with slightly better political backgrounds and somewhat inferior personal qualities could hope to escape disaster by focusing on humble motherhood, but an unattached person such as

Liang Xianlian could easily go astray, and it was rumored that she had sneaked off to the No. 2 High School to join the Revolutionary Alliance and to accept their counterrevolutionary assignment to "establish ties" in the countryside. It was as if she were tired of living, a mouse toying with a cat's tail—she was doomed!

The leaders of Shangguan District paid close attention to the Liang Xianlian problem, and a special meeting attended by Shangguan District PAFD commander Liu Houshan and several commune leaders on August 18 reached the unanimous conclusion that Liang Xianlian was a classic case of a "black element plotting overthrow" in Shangguan District and required decisive measures. After the meeting, militia apprehended Liang Xianlian and locked her up in the Fengjia Elementary School (by then the stronghold of the Shangguan District PAFD) for interrogation.

What the interrogation entailed, whether it involved torture, and if so by whom, could not be determined by the inquiries 19 years later, since the dead cannot bear witness, but it has been ascertained that Liang Xianlian was forced to confess that she had engaged in "counterrevolutionary activities" to expose the reactionary activities of the Revolutionary Alliance. She is unlikely to have satisfied her interrogators, however, because she'd never actually been involved in the Revolutionary Alliance. A former Revolutionary Alliance leader told me that "I have no impression of Liang Xianlian participating in any Revolutionary Alliance matters, and I think it unlikely. Although we maintained the party's policy that 'class status was not a choice, and one could choose one's own road,' and we would not reject the participation of a person with a bad family background in the Cultural Revolution, we were under harsh attack from the Red Alliance, and in order to avoid providing them with a pretext for gossip, we normally wouldn't let any black-element offspring from the villages join us. We mainly developed our membership among the poor peasants and the grassroots cadres."

On August 25, 1967, the district notified the Dongyang brigade to fetch the reactionary organization member Liang Xianlian, after which the brigade's peasant supreme court ruled that "the people's wrath could not be assuaged except by her death." It is said that some of the militiamen holding Liang in custody felt it would be a great waste to let such a prime specimen be killed without enjoying the pleasure of her company, and they ensured that they would be freshly imprinted on her memory when she went to meet the King of Hell. After being gang-raped, Liang Xianlian flew to Paradise on the "homemade airplane" on August 26.[5]

Following the killing of landlord element He Lin on August 29, Liang Xianlian's 26-year-old brother, Liang Xianlang, was killed on September 4, followed by his wife, Zhou Pingzhou (age 20), on September 10. Like her sister-in-law, Zhou was gang-raped and was reportedly killed mainly to shut her up afterwards.

Of the five people killed in the Dongyang brigade during the "killing wind," the Liang family made up 60 percent, and all that was left was the siblings' 46-year-old mother and her grandson, Liang Yueming, less than three years old. After the killings, the elder Madam Liang took her grandson with her to Daojiang, where she married a shipping-company worker surnamed Jiang. Liang Yueming took his step-grandfather's surname and was raised by the older couple. His subsequent story makes one bemoan the random cruelty of fate and the complexity and darkness of human nature. Later in this book I will take the opportunity to tell readers more about him.

For now, we turn to Futang Commune's Wuxing production brigade.

Prior to the communization movement, the Wuxing brigade was known as Wuhou Village, and it has reclaimed that name in recent times. It's named after the ancient Wuhou (Five Immortals) Temple on Wulao (Five Elders) Mountain next to the village, which was built by a Tang-dynasty official named Yang Cheng in honor of five immortals who asked him to do well by the people of Daozhou. Yang Cheng (735–805) had been sent to Daozhou after being demoted by Emperor Dezong, and *The History of the Tang* records that he governed benevolently and was greatly loved by the people of Daozhou. Yang gained particular fame for abolishing the practice of sending dwarfs to serve the emperor's court as an amusement, an incident immortalized in a highly regarded poem, "The People of Daozhou," by the great Tang poet Bai Juyi. The people of China are so sincere and easily satisfied; whenever anyone does the least thing for them, they continue to express their gratitude through succeeding generations. But perhaps the Five Immortals genuinely blessed and protected the people here, because during the "killing wind," only four people were killed in the Wuxing brigade.

After attending the commune's "four chiefs" conference on August 21, 1967, brigade CCP secretary Jiang Longxiang decided that none of the brigade's black elements had misbehaved enough to be killed; if anyone was acting up, it was some of the brigade's poor peasants, but killing them wasn't an option. Of course, Jiang Longxiang couldn't openly say anything of the kind because this would be a standpoint problem that would be interpreted as taking the side of the class enemy, which would put his head on the block. This prudence caused Jiang to proceed slowly, and he did nothing at all for several days.

Eventually Jiang noticed that other brigades were enthusiastically killing people, and the commune had already telephoned twice asking the Wuxing brigade for its killing figures. This compelled Jiang to call a meeting of the brigade's cadres, and a decision was reached to kill a class enemy named Hu Rong and one other. When it came time to make the arrests, only Hu Rong was apprehended, the other fellow having apparently gotten wind of the matter and run off. Jiang Longxiang was infuriated: "We already reported two killings [to the commune]. Now we have to find one more to meet our quota." They decided to kill two class enemy offspring, Zhou Deji (age 16) and Hu Rongquan (25), and then a 53-year-old middle peasant named He Qingming. The Task Force investigated the killing of He Qingming and determined it to be a revenge killing by the brigade's deputy CCP secretary, Wen Shicai, who had been criticized by He during the Socialist Education movement.

In contrast to the Wuxing brigade, the Lijiayuan production brigade killed more people than any other in Futang Commune, with seven deaths including one suicide. After brigade CCP secretary Wu Yongmao attended the commune's August 21 "four chiefs" meeting, a landlord couple, Wei Zhengfu and Tang Yuan'e, were sent to their deaths on a "homemade airplane" on August 25. An informed source said, "Our production brigade had no experience and didn't know how to do it. They tied Wei and his wife together back to back and then stuck a bundle of dynamite between them with a detonator cap and fuse, like they did when working on the reservoir. Then they lit the fuse, but too much dynamite was used, and flesh and blood flew all over the place. It was absolutely horrific."

Perhaps because this scene was so hair-raising, greater mercy was shown to two other landlords, Nie Lianjie and Chen Yangrui, who were killed with knives instead. The next day (August 27), two more people were killed: a middle-aged rich peasant, Wen Shaofu, and his wife, Yang Yueying.

A rich peasant named Chen Fashou, fixated on the horrific deaths of Wei Zhengfu and his wife, hanged himself on September 1 when the militia knocked on his door to summon him for a production brigade admonishment meeting.

On August 29, Futang Commune held an enlarged meeting of more than 300 cadres to call a halt to the random killings. The meeting was held against the background of two events: the first was the Red Alliance's Political and Legal Work Conference. Although this meeting led to a second wave of killings in Daoxian, some districts and communes actually did hold meetings to curb the killings, and Futang Commune was one of them. Second, the 47th Army's 6950 Unit had entered Daoxian at noon on August 29 to disseminate Mao Zedong Thought and stop the violence. At the commune's August 29 meeting, one of the commune's leaders, Tang Xianshu, said, "We can't just go around killing anymore. Anyone who kills will be held accountable. Even if it's someone guilty of heinous crimes, a file has to be submitted to the upper level for permission before they can be killed."

As the meeting was about to adjourn, however, the commune's CRC chairman, Liu Anxian, stood up and said, "After listening to so much at this meeting, each production brigade should think it over. It's still a good idea to kill a few troublemakers. Once your hair's wet you need to shave; those who deserve killing should be killed, and if the poor peasants agree to it, you don't need to report it to the commune, just decide for yourselves."

After that, the Libu brigade pushed through three more killings, and three other people were killed at other brigades.

The Libu brigade had been slow to take action during the killing wind, mainly because its leadership ranks were rather slack. After brigade leader Cao Fakai attended the "four chiefs" meeting at the commune on August 21, he delayed holding a meeting until August 27, and some of the more conservative cadres prevented agreement being reached on whom to kill. It was finally decided to lock up black element He Gaochang and his son, He Rensheng, as well as middle peasant He Runsheng, and to deal with them after requesting instructions from the commune. However, when it came time to arrest them, all three men had fled. Clearly, an insider had leaked the information, in spite of commune leaders saying that anyone who tipped someone else off would be punished as a traitor. An investigation was planned, but it immediately became clear that there were too many suspects; the investigation would only disrupt local harmony, and if the miscreant was identified, he would have to be killed, so finally the matter was dropped. (To this day, the informant has never been identified.)

When Futang Commune held its meeting on August 29 to stop the killings, commune leaders said that the three fugitives from Libu had been caught, and the brigade was told to go fetch them, causing a great loss of face. After the three men were brought back, the brigade's cadres met to discuss how to deal with them. Since the commune leaders had already said there could be no more random killings, everyone just looked sheepishly at each other without speaking. Finally, PPA chairman He Nengchang stood up angrily and said, "Here's my opinion: kill them! If they hadn't run off, we could be lenient with them, but now that they've run off and we've brought them back, how can we let them go? If you're all afraid to take responsibility, I will, and if someone has to make self-criticism later, I'll do it." There seemed nothing more to say, so that night the three men were killed and their corpses were dumped into the river.

PART FOUR

GONGBA DISTRICT, THE COUNTY'S TOP KILLER

11

A Dubious Honor

Gongba District (District 10) is situated in the eastern portion of Daoxian (Map 6), with the district's government offices on the Gongba embankment located 21 kilometers from the county seat, Daojiang. This district recorded more killings than any other in Daoxian. During the Cultural Revolution, the district had three communes under its jurisdiction: Gongba, Xingqiao, and Xiaojia. When we did our reporting in 1986, the district also included Shangguan Township (formerly Shangguan Commune under Shangguan District). The killings in Gongba District were notable for being concentrated within a short timespan, and for their brutality. From August 23 to 30, 1967, the only production brigade with no killings was Gongba Commune's Lucaoping brigade, which due to its remote mountain location didn't receive notification to attend the killing-mobilization meeting. In the rest of the district's 59 production brigades, a total of 1,054 people were killed in those eight days, composing 1.98 percent of the district's population at that time, or one out of every 50 people, and one-fourth of the total number of people killed throughout the county. Another 20 people were subsequently killed, bringing the district's killings to 1,074, with an additional 122 suicides making a grand total of 1,196 dead. Forty-six households were completely obliterated.[1]

A major reason for the number of killings and the seriousness of their consequences was the top-down delegation of killing from the district to the commune and then to the production brigade level. The district convened a mobilization meeting between the district Chinese Communist Party (CCP) committee deputy secretary, district People's Armed Forces Department (PAFD) head, Red Alliance commander, and the commune heads; the communes then held "revolution meetings" for commune secretaries and PAFD heads and the key cadres of every production brigade and production team. The production brigades followed up with "discussion meetings" to implement the spirit of the district and commune meetings. Although referred to by different names, these meetings all served the identical purpose of spreading rumors and creating an "enemy

*Shangguan Commune was part of Gongba District at the time Task Force investigation.

Map 6 Communes of Gongba District

situation" out of thin air, inciting the masses to kill with an easy conscience and even arranging killing assignments and handing down directives.

Let's look at what happened at those meetings.

On the evening of August 20, 1967, Gongba District PAFD commander Yang Yansheng returned from a trip outside the district, and the minute he entered the district office, district Red Alliance political commissar and Youth League secretary Ye Chenghu ran down the hall toward him saying, "Aiya, Commander Yang, you're back! I've been waiting for you! Commander Zheng [Youzhi] called this morning and said you have to rush to Yingjiang tomorrow for a meeting. The Military Subdistrict and 6952 Unit commanders will be there."

Commander Yang knew that this meeting took priority over all else, but while young, he was steady and wanted to set an example for the younger cadre, so he responded casually: "Fine."

This only made Ye Chenghu even more anxious: "Commander Zheng is very unhappy with our district for its tardiness in assembling militia to take action. What do you think we should do?"

Yang Yansheng said, "What are you worried about? The duck is in the stew pot and you're afraid it'll fly away. Call in Secretary Zheng and Commander He for a discussion."

Ye Chenghu hurried off and contacted the district's deputy CCP secretary, Zheng Jitian, a cadre prone to revolutionary posturing, and the district's accountant and Red Alliance commander, He Changxue. The four sat under the big camphor tree next to the district office and held their discussion in the cool of the evening. After Yang Yansheng analyzed the various new trends in the current class struggle, he said, "I have to go to a meeting in Yingjiang tomorrow, so you should start taking action here at home and assemble a militia as quickly as possible. Otherwise, we'll lose out. We can't fall behind the enemy; the faster we move, the greater our advantage."

Zheng Jitian put in, "We'll need some of the grain tax to organize the militia. I'll deal with that problem."

Ye Chenghu spoke up vigorously: "If we don't organize the militia, the enemy will snatch our weapons, and the poor and lower-middle peasants will consider us a bunch of fatheads."

Zheng Jitian said, "The situation is very complicated right now, and everyone's confused. We need to call a meeting of commune heads and PAFD cadres to unite everyone's thinking and action. Commander Yang, what do you think?"

In terms of CCP ranking, Zheng was above Yang, but now that the People's Liberation Army (PLA) was carrying out its "Support the Left" campaign, Yang Yansheng's position as PAFD commander put him in control of the district. Seeing Yang Yansheng nod his head in agreement, Zheng Jitian went on: "Shall we hold the meeting tomorrow?" Yang said, "I'll leave that to you, Secretary Zheng."

Applying his accountant's mindset, He Changxue suggested, "Since we need to use the grain tax to assemble the militia, commune accountants should also attend the meeting." Everyone agreed.

The next day (August 21), while Yang Yansheng was at the Yingjiang reporting meeting described in chapter 7, Zheng Jitian presided over a meeting of the district's commune heads, PAFD cadres, and mass organization heads at Gongba Commune, where he greatly exaggerated the killings at the Zhengjia brigade and tasked each commune with organizing militia. The deputy commander of the district Red Alliance (and accountant of Xingqiao Commune), Wang Chengguang, elaborated, "The current situation between us and the Revolutionary Alliance now is no longer one of opposing organizations but of revolutionary versus counterrevolutionary. Striking the first blow gains the advantage, and falling behind will bring disaster!"

Finally, political commissar Ye led everyone in studying several quotations by Chairman Mao and then exhorted them: "Here in Gongba District we've never fallen behind anyone in carrying out our tasks. We all need to be good revolutionary promoters of progress, not promoters of retrogression, and you need to implement the spirit of this meeting when you return to your communes."

On August 22, Xiaojia Commune took the lead by holding a "revolution meeting" with more than 100 in attendance, including the key cadres of each production brigade and production team. Commune PAFD commander Liao Longjiu worried about lagging behind and called for "killing people as quickly as possible." That night, the Donglekou production brigade telephoned the commune requesting permission to kill five people, and commune secretary Yang Qingkui immediately authorized the killings. The next day (August 25), the Donglekou brigade escorted the five black elements to the entrance of the village and killed them with fowling pieces and hoes, then dumped them into an abandoned sweet-potato cellar.

Meanwhile, on August 22, district PAFD commander Yang Yansheng returned from the Yingjiang reporting meeting, and while passing through Xinqiao Commune he ran into deputy CCP secretary Zheng Jitian and Red Alliance leader Wang Chengguang. Wang Chengguang asked, "Commander Yang, we hear that black elements in District 2 [Chetou District] mounted an insurrection and were killed by the poor peasants. The poor peasants of District 6 [Yueyan] and District 8 [Simaqiao] have also taken action and have started killing class enemies."

Yang Yansheng said, "I haven't heard anything about District 2, but it's true that District 6 and District 8 have started taking action. Six miscreants were killed in one evening in Qingtang's Liaojia brigade. The revolutionary situation is very encouraging!"

Wang Chengguang reported to Yang Yansheng: "Not long ago, a counterrevolutionary element from Jinxing brigade, Yang Guiqing, went to the No. 2 High School, and now he's come back threatening to lead several more back to the school.[2] The poor peasants want to do away with him. What do you think we should do?"

Commander Yang replied, "If the masses want to do away with him, do it, but don't hold a rally—that would cause problems." After Yang Guiqing underwent a public denunciation that night, the militia pretended to escort him to the county public-security bureau for labor reform, but when they reached the riverbank at Shangguan, the militia stabbed Yang in the back with a saber and then dumped him into the Xiaoshui River.

On August 24, 1967, Xingqiao Commune PAFD commander Yang Youdao and Wang Chengguang called a meeting of Xingqiao Commune's production brigade cadres and then sent commune cadres to various production brigades to oversee killings. No one went to the Jinxing brigade, however, as a result of which that brigade was criticized at an August 27 commune meeting for "taking a hesitant and wait-and-see attitude, and being sluggish in its action." Stung by the criticism, the brigade's leaders called a cadre meeting and said, "Other brigades are killing more than us, and this situation can't continue." The brigade then proceeded to kill 23 people in one go, including a few "capitalist roader" poor and lower-middle peasants. A total of 29 people were eventually killed in the brigade.

The most characteristic trait of the killings in this production brigade was reflected in its final killing of a welfare recipient. By September 3, the brigade had killed 28 people and the commune had passed down the upper-level directive prohibiting further random killings. At that point, the poor peasants of the No. 4 production team discovered a practical problem: how could they have forgotten to kill the widow He Xuancui? She had been living off public welfare for many years and had become a major burden on her production team. He Xuancui was from the rich-peasant class and should have been killed with other class enemies right at the outset. Someone suggested just killing her anyway, but now that the prohibition had been handed down, whoever killed her would be held responsible. The head of the No. 4 production team didn't want to make the decision on his own, so he called a meeting of the team's poor and lower-middle peasants to discuss it. The view of the masses was that He Xuancui should be killed like all the others. The team leader said, "Since the masses have decided on this, we don't need to make a big deal about it, but just take her quietly back to the mountains and do away with her."

That night, several militiamen went to He Xuancui's home and dragged her from her bed. He Xuancui asked "Where are you taking me so late at night?" One of the militiamen joked, "We think life is just too hard for an old lady like you, so the production team has decided to take you to a better place where you'll never have to worry about food or clothing again." After dragging He Xuancui to Shishan Pond, they hacked her to death with sabers and buried her in a pit. No one seemed to notice this incident until the Task Force's investigation uncovered it.

After Yang Guiqing was killed at the Jinxing brigade on August 22, Red Alliance deputy commander Wang Chengguang telephoned commander He Changxue at the district headquarters and reported on the killing while at the same time asking him to exercise his authority by telephoning Xiaojia and Gongba Communes and directing every production brigade to select one or two especially troublesome black elements to kill. This was the first time during the Daoxian killings that a killing quota was handed down.

In Daoxian, the lower levels did whatever the upper levels told them to do; that was typical of China's peasants generally and even more so when killing became a job that brought work points and even "movable property." For a while, killing became a socialist work competition among communes, production brigades, and production teams. By August 29, 12 out of Xiaojia Commune's 13 brigades had carried out killings, and only the Xiaojia brigade, right under the commune's nose, had failed to take action. When that brigade held its meeting to discuss implementation of the commune's "revolution meeting," people raised two problems: First of all, even killing a pig required paperwork, much less killing a human, so it would be better to have everything in writing before they made a move. Secondly, if all the black elements were killed off, it would be hard to assign work afterward, especially for jobs no one else wanted to do, such as repairing roads and bridges. Furthermore, the brigade's black elements were largely resigned to their fates and performed well, and they didn't deserve such treatment. The cadres and masses of Xiaojia brigade therefore felt they shouldn't take action; one group reportedly even sided with the Revolutionary Alliance.

Commune head Yang Shengfang and PAFD commander Liao Longjiu repeatedly chased after the brigade's leaders and tried to "educate" them, but to no avail. Some brigade cadres even said, "If the commune wants someone killed, let them come down and do it. We won't." This infuriated the commune's leaders: "We can't allow a 'fortified village' to rise up under our very noses!"

Finally Yang and Liao called a summary commendation rally on August 29, during which the Donglekou brigade and others were praised for their "swift action and impressive results" and the Xiaojia brigade came under heavy criticism. Liao Longjiu said, "All the other brigades have had killings, so why haven't you made a move? The entire commune objects to what you're doing." Commune secretary Yang Qingkui said, "How can this be tolerated while there's a ticking time bomb on the commune's border? Are you going to kill anyone or not? If you're afraid to do it yourselves, just tie the people up and we'll send militia to help you out."

The next day, the commune actually sent core militiamen personally led by Liao Longjiu and armed with guns, sabers, and explosives to assist Xiaojia in "making revolution." The killing was a grand spectacle: 11 class enemies and offspring were tied together with a big bundle of quarrying explosives stuck between them, after which the fuse was lit and they were sent off on the "homemade airplane."

Nineteen years later, an elderly man from that brigade still shivered when he recalled the terrible sight: "There was this great 'boom!' and blood and flesh poured down like rain. There were hands, feet, and pieces of rumps, and some didn't die but wept for mercy as they rolled around in agony. . . . Commander Liao ordered the militiamen to go over and kill them with hoes and sabers. . . . After the crowd dispersed, a flock of crows flew over, cawing and fighting over pieces of human flesh in the trees and undergrowth. . . ."

Apart from the 11 people killed in the Xiaojia brigade, another person committed suicide. There were 326 suicides in Daoxian during the killing wind, 7 percent of the total fatalities, but the Task Force didn't investigate these deaths as a matter of principle, and the compensation paid for them was only

100 yuan, one-third less than the 150 yuan paid for those who were killed outright. The Task Force's files on these suicides were also very simple, usually consisting only of the name, sex, age, address, time of death, and amount of compensation paid. This was the Task Force's policy, and in our reporting we likewise focused more on classic killings and neglected the suicides; this has to be considered a major flaw in our reporting. The information on the case of suicide in the Xiaojia brigade resulted from supplementary reporting that I carried out later.

The suicide was Zhou Renjie, a native of Xiaojia Village under the Xiaojia brigade of Xiaojia Commune.[3] He was a middle peasant 60 years old. Prior to Liberation, Zhou Renjie had served for ten months as a village chief under the Kuomintang (KMT) regime, and he served three years in prison following the 1951 campaign against bandits and local despots. During Daoxian's Cultural Revolution massacre, "puppet village chiefs" were prime targets even where killings were few, and all the more so in a place such as Gongba District that had more killings than anywhere else. It was only because Zhou Renjie lived in the Xiaojia brigade that he had the "good fortune" of a peaceful suicide and burial.

On August 29, after being criticized at the commune's summary commendation rally, the Xiaojia brigade held an urgent meeting of its main cadres to unite everyone's thinking, given that further resistance to the commune's orders was impossible. Even so, it was hard to come up with a name list, having no standard to follow. In other places, this indecision usually had one of two results: either none was killed or none was spared—usually the latter. The Xiaojia brigade was a rare exception, and after a great deal of discussion, it was decided that one person would be killed in each class enemy household, with each production team deciding on the specific victim. A comrade from the Task Force told me that the main reason for this decision was that factional influence was very strong in Xiaojia. The Xiaojia brigade had quite a few natural villages, each made up largely of people from the same clan and with the same surname who gathered in their ancestral halls at the Qingming Festival to worship their ancestors, drink Qingming wine, and sweep graves. In the course of history, Daoxian produced 12 successful candidates in the highest imperial examination, and one of them was from Xiaojia Village, commemorated by a memorial gateway that was eventually destroyed by Red Guards.

When Zhou Renjie heard the news, he called his sons together to discuss how to deal with the situation. Zhou Renjie had seven sons and one daughter. His daughter had married and moved far away, but all his sons but the second and third worked in the production team. His second son had drowned as he tried to escape when caught illegally reselling homespun cloth. Zhou's third son, the best student in the family, had managed to become a state official but had been sent off to reeducation through labor during the 1957 Anti-Rightist campaign.

Among the brothers who remained in the production team, the eldest was relatively better off. He had married prior to Liberation, had children, and lived a life of no great incident or distinction in the village. None of the other brothers had found a wife. The fourth son had suffered brain damage from a high fever as a boy and was a simpleton. The fifth son had fled the village in search of food during the Great Famine and had been involved in a traffic accident that left him disabled. The seventh son was not yet 17 years old, while the sixth son, in his 20s, had passed the traditional marriageable age; although he had no shortcomings in terms of character, looks, or working ability, eligible girls would have nothing to do with him, and even a young widow introduced by a matchmaker refused to meet him after learning that his father had been a puppet village head.

Zhou Renjie called his five sons together and explained the situation to them. The youngest son, too young to understand, burst in: "We haven't broken any laws or done anything wrong, so why do we have to be killed? We shouldn't agree, and if they insist, we'll fight them."

The eldest son blanched with fear and quickly said, "Stop your careless talk—if it gets out, we're done for."

Zhou Renjie added, "Yes, we have to be careful what we say. Illness comes in by the mouth and disaster comes out of it. Your third brother opened his mouth and suffered for it, and you should remember that." He added, "I don't have any other thoughts except that unlike the other class enemies, I never exploited anyone, and I wonder if I can convince the production team to treat us differently."

The eldest son said, "How would you be treated differently? The production brigade says your problem is even worse. Even smaller families than ours have to kill someone, and given how many of us there are, how can we get away without one being killed?"

The sixth brother said, "Father, there's no point thinking any further. We have to run away and hide. We'll go to our sister in the mountains where they can't find us."

Zhou Renjie immediately rejected that idea: "That won't work. There's no escape. During Land Reform, some people escaped, but eventually they were caught and every one of them was killed—and they pulled their families down with them."

On hearing this, the seventh son said, "So if we can't escape, we're just supposed to sit at home and wait to be killed?" Once he said this, no one spoke.

Seeing the situation, Zhou Renjie said, "It's getting late, and we have to go to work. I'll think of a way to deal with this situation."

The five brothers went out with heads bowed. Zhou Renjie and his wife sat for a while without speaking, then Zhou got up and found a rope and told Wang Xiaomei, "Wife, I have to leave you."

Wang Xiaomei said nothing but just looked at her husband.

Zhou Renjie took the rope to the staircase next to the sitting room. Wang Xiaomei sat in the sitting room and listened to her husband move a stool, tie the rope, and then kick the stool away. After there was no more sound of movement, she rushed out and told her sons to come back and arrange for the funeral, and she sent the sixth son to the production brigade to report her husband's death.

The brigade leader sent militia commander Zhou Bingyuan to carry out a postmortem. After the examination, Zhou Bingyuan said, "We told you to hand someone over, not to have one of you hang yourselves. If everyone follows his example, what are we supposed to do when the commune tells us to hand people over?"

Wang Xiaomei wept in panic: "The man is dead, what more do you want?"

Zhou Bingyuan said, "I have to tell you right now, if the commune doesn't care, we don't either, but if the commune doesn't accept this, you'll have to hand over someone else." These words frightened the seventh brother so badly that he fled that very night.

During the Cultural Revolution massacre, Xiaojia Commune killed a total of 237 people, including 33 driven to suicide.

A special characteristic of the killings at this commune was the phenomenon of "admittance to the party on the battlefront," which required probationary CCP members and activists joining the CCP to demonstrate their indomitable spirit on the firing line. An example of this practice occurred at Xiaojia Commune's Jinghua brigade, which had killed 12 people (with an additional suicide) by the time the commune called a meeting to halt further killings on August 30. At lunch after the meeting, a member of the commune CCP committee's propaganda committee, Zhang Guangliang, said to Jinghua brigade cadres sitting next to him, "What was your production brigade thinking? He Qingyou was a Three People's Principles Youth Corps leader; it would be better to kill him than 10 others. He's a ticking time bomb, and if you don't take care of him, he'll explode." Hearing this criticism from a leader, the Jinghua brigade cadres had a discussion and decided to "detonate" He Qingyou and his wife, Zhang Zhiyu, on September 2. Brigade CCP secretary Jiang Shangchen ordered 10 probationary CCP members to carry out the executions as a test.

That afternoon, Jiang Shangchen led the probationary CCP members (including two women) in escorting He Qingyou and Zhang Zhiyu to a place called Yangmei Cave. The probationary CCP members encircled the two with spears in their hands, and at the count of three, they all stabbed He Qingyou and Zhang Zhiyu at once. One young female probationary CCP member was so frightened that the best she could do was dip her spear into the blood of the dead bodies and take it over to be examined. Her ruse was discovered, however, and as a result, her probation was extended for another year.

One day in Yanhetang

While Gongba District placed first in terms of the number of killings, Gongba Commune was tops in that district, its 524 deaths composing half of all the district's fatalities. Gongba Commune hosted the district government offices and was in lockstep with the district leadership. It maintained close surveillance and control over its black elements and their offspring, and the few who slipped through the net were recaptured and killed.

The classic Gongba Commune slaughter occurred in the Yanhetang brigade, which killed nearly all its black elements in a single day.

On the morning of August 26, 1967, Yanhetang Village was shrouded in a grayish mist. Usually by this time, the village's diligent peasants would have been out laboring in the fields, but today not a single figure could be seen where only the dark stubble of rice stalks remained from the early rice harvest. Instead, each production team poured out in separate ranks of vigorous young men carrying sabers, spears, fowling pieces, and hoes and escorting other strong young men bound hand and foot. They proceeded in one long line until they reached a crossroads in the mountains, where they gathered for what looked like a pilgrimage.

There the brigade's Cultural Revolution Committee (CRC) chairman, He Xinchang, made a headcount of the bound individuals as if they were draft animals, counting 21 in all and then recounting to make sure there was no mistake. Having satisfied himself, he delivered the command: "All together now, go!" The armed men cried out and slapped their sabers against the bound men as if driving cattle, guiding them onto a winding mountain path toward their doom.

Three days previously (August 23), the brigade's leaders had attended a killing-mobilization meeting convened by commune deputy CCP secretary Liu Fubao, PAFD commander Zeng Qingsong, and CRC chairman Mo Jiakun, and after returning to the brigade, they had discussed the possibility of carrying out killings, but without reaching agreement. After waiting for two days and seeing killing take place at the brigades around them, they felt they had to make a move. CCP secretary Zhou Jia'ai called a CCP branch meeting that night where it was decided to "eliminate the enemy's effective strength" and to start by killing "big tigers who might mount an insurrection," and these 21 men had been chosen and rounded up first thing the next morning.

The robust young men were calm and humble as they were bound, long accustomed to a life of subhuman status after being born into the wrong kind of family. They didn't know where they were being taken, but they knew it wouldn't be anywhere good, and they looked back with distress as the village gradually receded from view. It was their home, where they had aged parents and young wives and children, and, however hard, their lives had meaning. They could only wonder what would happen to their families now that they were being taken away. They must have had many questions, but as they proceeded to their deaths, not one of them asked why they had to die.

A place called Huluyan (Calabash Rock) had been selected as the slaughter site. A large cave there emitted cool air even in the summer, and in the winter a white mist was often seen floating from its inky depths. No one knew how deep it was; a dropped stone fell for a long time before making a sound. These men had often passed this place when collecting firewood or grazing cattle, and when hot and tired they would cool themselves at the mouth of the cave, never guessing that someday it would be their final resting place. It had been He Xinchang who had suggested pushing the men into the cave as a preferable alternative to shooting or drowning them.

By the time the black elements were brought to Calabash Rock, the mist had dispersed and the sun's scarlet rays had begun to push between the mountain peaks. He Xinchang ordered the militia to take the "criminals" to the edge of the cave, where he represented the peasant supreme court in condemning them to death. The condemned men were almost imbecilic in their silent immobility; having lost all their nerve as long-term targets of violent oppression, they submitted like sheep. As each name was called, a man was led to the mouth of the cave, at which point a militiaman used his saber, spear, or club to kill or daze him and push him into the cave; only at this point were cries of distress heard.

Suddenly, a class enemy named He Yuanyou rushed forward and knelt before He Xinchang, saying, "Chairman He, don't kill me. I haven't enjoyed a life of wealth; I've worked hard just like you all my life. I've saved up some money to get married, but I'll give it all to you. If you spare my life, I'll be your slave as long as I live."

He Xinchang said, "Yuanyou, I can't save you. It's not me that's killing you. Those above have told us to do it, and if I don't kill you, my own head is on the line."

The Calabash Rock grotto, as its name suggests, was a karst-type limestone cave with a small neck opening into a large hole. It is said that in the old days, the village dealt with unfilial sons or other corrupters of public morals by pushing them into this cave. Now, steaming fresh blood saturated the grayish rock and green moss at the cave's mouth. Some who were thrown into the cave didn't die immediately and continued to cry out. He Xinchang scurried around, ordering the militia to throw in rocks and burning bundles of straw. Finally he sent someone back to the village to fetch a pile of dynamite, which was lit and dumped into the cave. After a deafening explosion, silence returned to Calabash Rock.

Around noon, He Xinchang led the militia back to the village. The scorching white heat of the midday sun was both stimulating and vexing, and as they walked, the men discussed among themselves. "Now that we've killed the young and vigorous workers, who will look after their elderly and young ones?"

These were farmers, after all, and they were practical men, so this question became a major topic of discussion. "Do we have to support them? That'll be a huge burden on the production teams!" Someone thought even further ahead: "What will we do when their kids grow up and want to take revenge?" Someone said, "Might as well destroy them root and branch and do away with old and young as well so we don't have any rats left nibbling at the warehouse door."

He Xinchang had to admit that made sense. He hurried back to the brigade office and telephoned the district to report on the killings of the 21 "big tigers": "Now we have more than 30 little tigers left, and the poor peasants want to do away with all of them. Can we?"

The person taking the call was the secretary of the district CCP committee, and he hesitantly replied, "The big tigers were justly killed for their crimes, but it seems that killing the little tigers might not conform to policy."

Seeing that the district appeared to veto further killings, He Xinchang took it no further, but some in the production teams continued to push the matter after lunch. The head of the No. 2 production team, Zhou Jiaxiu, had already rounded up five children, and he announced, "If the brigade won't kill them, we'll do it ourselves." He Xinchang felt he had no choice but to telephone the commune for instructions. Deputy CCP secretary Liu Fubao took the call and ordered, "Do away with all of them." He Xinchang was still uneasy, however, not knowing whether to obey the district or the commune, so he telephoned the district again, and this time it was one of the district CCP committee's leaders, Ye Chenghu, who took the call. Ye's instructions were unequivocal: "Kill all of them." He Xinchang immediately notified the other brigade cadres and production team leaders and told them to make the necessary arrangements.

The sun had begun to set behind the hills, and its last rays tinged the Xiaoshui River a blood-red color. The Yanhetang brigade had sentries posted everywhere.

News of the morning's killings had already spread to every household, and the air was rigid with tension. The families of the dead men, young and old, huddled in their homes weeping into their arms, afraid to make a sound that might invite disaster on them as well. Some of the old people, having seen too much of the world, especially during Land Reform, knew their hour was at hand, and contrarily, their minds were at peace as they tremblingly pulled their good clothes from their trunks so they would look their best when it was time to go.

A female landlord element named Zhang Xiujiao had always been obedient, discreet, and diligent, enthusiastically doing what needed to be done without being told, joining her quiet and hard-working husband in repairing bridges and roads, and for that reason, Zhang and her husband had not been apprehended that morning. Now they sat across from each other discussing how they would die. The husband said he'd never eaten chicken, and he'd really like to taste some before he died. Zhang Xiujiao quickly killed their five laying hens, cleaned them, and cooked them. The caldron bubbled in the firepit as flames licked its bottom, filling the house with an alluring aroma. When the chicken was stewed, Zhang Xiujiao spooned out a bowl of broth and presented it to her husband, who took it with equal ceremony and raised it to his lips, then passed it to his wife. At this moment, there was a pounding at the door. They knew their time had come, and, placing the bowl on the table, they rose silently to their feet. A militiaman discovered the caldron of stew and said, "They always said you were honest, but here you are resisting death!" Saying nothing, they walked out the door, and this dutiful couple maintained their silence right until they died.[4]

The production brigade's threshing ground was packed with people. Children and old people wept. Apart from those about to be killed were those with a killing rage in their eyes and many who had gathered to watch. A haggard old man who'd been dragged from his sickbed asked the militiamen escorting him, "Where are you taking me so late at night?" A militiaman impatiently replied, "Your son was condemned to death. The production team can't afford to support you, so we're sending you to a better world." A little boy of three was unwilling to go and cried for his parents. A militiaman comforted him: "Your mom and dad are in the hills picking fruit. I'll take you there to find them." In this way, the old were tied with ropes and children were hurried along with cudgels, while bawling infants were carried in baskets.

The sun set like a gigantic wheel being pushed behind the hill, its last rays lingering high in the sky as night gradually descended with the chill of early autumn. There was no moon, but the stars were large and bright, and dogs could be heard barking in the distance. Some children began sobbing at being led into the darkness so late at night, but the militiamen sternly shushed them as the line of people tottered to the Baishi Crossing of the Xiaoshui River.

These people would not be pushed into the bottomless pit but rather "set adrift" (i.e., drowned), because practice had borne out that the cave was not a trouble-free method after all, not to mention the difficulty of dragging so many people up the hill by torchlight.

Unlike in the morning, there was no peasant supreme court, and no words were wasted declaring their "crimes" or "death sentences"; killers and victims alike knew exactly what was going on. Nevertheless, He Xinchang suddenly felt there were several things he needed to say. These old people and children all had ties of kinship and friendship with him, however distant, and there was no grievance between them; this was just the requirement of revolution and class struggle. He cleared his throat and said, "You mustn't blame me. Those above told us to kill you, so just blame your own fates. Go in peace, and next year we'll mark the anniversary of your deaths."

Having said that, he commanded the militia to drive the people onto wooden boats that had been prepared in advance, and a rock was tied around each neck; then, the boats were quickly rowed into the center of the river, and each person was dropped into the water like wonton. As the moon rose, the hills along the river took on the dismal aspect of people who had seen too much and had turned to stone.

The Task Force's inquiries established that 52 people were killed during the "killing wind" at the Yanhetang brigade, ranging in age from 74 years to 56 days. The victims composed 8.4 percent of the brigade's total population, and 72 percent of its black elements and their offspring. A few young women were spared and offered a "change of status."

The 56-day-old baby went to its death unnamed, being too small and born to illiterate parents. Brought into the world at the wrong time and to a family of the wrong status, this baby passed its short life in terror. Curled in the bosom of his trembling mother, Zhang Xiuhua, it stared at the men bearing spears and sabers who burst into its home and pulled out its 72-year-old grandmother, 37-year-old father, and brothers aged 12 and 3, sending up a heart-rending howl as its household of six was instantly reduced to two.

There was, of course, a reason why the baby's mother, Zhang Xiuhua, was spared. When the meeting had been held at noon to discuss further killings, a villager known as Loony Jiang had said, "Can Xiuhua be spared?"

Some young rascals joked, "You want a bite of that landlord woman's muffin?"

CCP secretary Zhou had been more understanding, and he'd scolded those scamps: "What are you laughing at? You hardly have pubic hair, so what would you know? It's tough being without a woman. Let's say that anyone who's willing to marry a poor or lower-middle peasant bachelor can be spared. We'll change their status." This local policy that Zhou came up with spared the lives of a number of young "landlord women" from the village.

That night, Zhang Xiuhua sat numbly beside her bed, weeping in silence as she clutched her baby, the only loved one left to her. There was a knock at the door, and Zhang Xiuhua nervously hurried to open it. Loony Jiang stood there smiling at her. A bachelor at 37 even though a third-generation poor peasant, he was too gluttonous and lazy to be considered a good match. But he'd exerted himself to have Zhang Xiuhua's life spared, and now he wanted to claim his spoils. As he pulled Zhang Xiuhua toward the bed, he discovered the infant clutched in her arms. All he could think was how this whelp would be a source of endless trouble in his future union. Snatching the baby from Zhang Xiuhua's arms, he sprinted to the river and tossed the baby in to "keep the rest of its family company." He then ran back to where Zhang Xiuhua's stood mute and paralyzed with shock. Thrilled at the prospect of finally having a woman, he clutched her to him and murmured, "Xiuhua, don't be afraid. Once you're with me you won't be a landlord woman any more, and no one will pick on you. Don't worry, Xiuhua, I'll treat you right."

The next day, Loony Jiang kept his word; in order to ensure that Zhang Xiuhua should be considered a poor peasant and spared further harassment, he resolved to marry her properly. He had the production brigade's seamstress, a very dignified person, go with a box of sweets and request Xiuhua's hand on his behalf. With his own hands, he tidied up his thatched hut and hung a festive wedding couplet on the door: "In your new life, don't forget the Communist Party; in your happiness, don't forget Chairman Mao."

On the night of the killings, the Yanhetang brigade established an "asset settlement committee" to divide up the "movable property." Having gone through Land Reform, they had experience in this area, and the process went smoothly. They dragged out several pigs from the homes of the victims, killed them, and held a feast. Also served was the stewed chicken that Zhang Xiujiao and her husband had never had a chance to eat. Brigade CCP secretary Zhou Jia'ai jubilantly raised a glass of liquor in a toast: "Today, we poor peasants are the victors! We scored a great victory, and now is the time for everyone to raise a glass in celebration." After downing his glass, his face flushed, he led them all in shouting, "Long live Chairman Mao's revolutionary line! Long live the Proletarian Great Cultural Revolution! Long live the poor and lower-middle peasants!"

The Killings at Daoxian's Deadliest Commune

The systematic push for killings by commune cadres made Gongba Daoxian's deadliest commune, even though it got a relatively late start. The first of Gongba's production brigades to begin killing people was Guangjialing on August 20, 1967; by then, more than 80 people had been killed elsewhere in Daoxian.

August 18 was market day for Gongba Commune, and when the Guangjialing brigade's militia commander, Yang Buzhao, went to the market, he ran into commune People's Armed Forces Department (PAFD) commander Zeng Qingsong and Cultural Revolution Committee (CRC) chairman Mo Jiakun. Zeng and Mo invited Yang to the commune office, where they told him all about the "enemy situation" and instructed him to find out if his brigade had any "troublemaking black elements," and if so, to "gain the advantage by making the first move" and "killing one or two." After returning to his brigade, Yang Buzhao quickly reported Zeng and Mo's instruction to brigade Chinese Communist Party (CCP) secretary Jiang Youyuan.[1] That night, the brigade called a cadre and militia meeting and decided to strengthen surveillance over black elements and hold denunciation rallies for some "troublemakers."

Apparently there was no talk of killings at that point; the "killing wind" had just begun blowing, and killings were still being done discreetly. However, the next day a landlord named Yang Meiji ran off,[2] and Yang Buzhao and public-security head Yang Caiji decided someone must have tipped him off. It was intolerable that the class enemy could have infiltrated the ranks of the poor peasants, and this called for decisive measures. Black elements He Qingsong, Xiang Jiaqi, and Yang Jingcheng were detained, and the decision was made to do away with them, but CCP secretary Jiang Youyuan said, "We have to request instructions from the commune first."

On August 20, Yang Buzhao telephoned the commune and requested instructions from CRC chairman Mo Jiakun. A vigorous young man of 25, Mo repeatedly praised the "elevated awareness and quick action" of Guangjialing's poor peasants and said, "This is the excellent revolutionary action of the poor and lower-middle peasants, and we fully support it; the commune will hold a meeting to commend you." The Guangjialing production brigade killed the three black elements that night.

Gongba Commune CCP secretary Deng Changchu and deputy CCP secretary Liu Fubao had attended the meeting that Gongba District leaders held on August 21 to brief commune heads, PAFD cadres, and mass organization heads on killings elsewhere. The commune then followed up by holding a "revolution meeting" for production brigade cadres on August 23 to implement the spirit of the district meeting. Zeng Qingsong presided and along with Mo Jiakun delivered a speech inciting killings. The Guangjialing brigade was singled out for praise, and other brigades were told to follow its example. In most cases, brigade cadres held meetings back at their brigades soon after the meeting and began arranging killings. Meanwhile, Zeng and Mo took command at Gongba Commune and directed operations over the telephone, while Liu Fubao, commune accountant and Red Alliance head Chen Daiqin, and others were sent to various brigades to supervise and encourage the killings. The influence of the commune's August 23 "revolution meeting" and the subsequent prodding of commune cadres can be seen in the timeline of killings at the commune's production brigades:[3]

Brigade	Date	Killings
Fulutian	Aug 23, 27	31 (2 suicides)
Jingtang	Aug 26	14 (2 suicides)
Majiangkou	Aug 23, 30; Sept 6–7	18
Taohuajing	Aug 25, 27; Sept 9	48
Jialuzhou	Aug 25	29 (1 suicide)
Shazihi	Aug 27	19 (6 suicides)
Jinjidong	Aug 23, 26, 30	45
Yanhetang		52
Lianhuatang	Aug 25	29 (1 suicide)
Mujingdong	Aug 23, 27	8
Huangjia	Aug 23	9 (2 suicides)
Xinyouzha	Aug 25	25 (1 suicide)
Shangyunba	Aug 25	13 (2 suicides)
Majialing	Aug 25, 30	33 (3 suicides)

Brigade	Date	Killings
Gongba	Late August	35 (6 suicides)
Houjiangqiao	Aug 25 and soon after	19 (4 suicides)
Fengcundong	Aug 26, 30	18 (3 suicides)
Xiahudong	Aug 24	3 (1 suicide)
Zhonghudong	Aug 23	18 (4 suicides)
Shalejiang		3 suicides
Changjiangwei	Aug 27, 31	27 (3 suicides)
Caoyutang	Aug 24	7 (1 suicide)
Guangjialing	Aug 20	22 (1 suicide)

In some production brigades, the influence of commune cadres was explicit and direct, either through telephone calls demanding that the brigades take action, or through the presence of commune cadres overseeing the killings on the spot.

For example, commune cadre Li Jiande was responsible for "igniting the revolutionary flame" at the Fulutian and Jingtang brigades, with killings taking place as soon as he arrived. Further killings occurred at Jingtang after Liu Fubao and Chen Daiqin arrived to "inspect, supervise, and encourage." At the Majiangkou brigade, seven people were killed under the direct instructions of Zeng Qingsong, and the Jialuzhou brigade carried out 21 of its 28 killings following direct authorization from Liu Fubao. At the Shangyunba brigade, Mo Jiakun telephoned the brigade to urge it to take "revolutionary action" against two specific black elements, and Mo and Zeng Qingsong arrived the next day to supervise and encourage the killings. Zeng Qingsong telephoned the Fengcundong production brigade on August 26 and harshly criticized their lack of action, instructing the brigade accountant to prepare a list of the brigade's black elements for discussion: "The masses know very well who's good, bad, and worst. Let them bring it into broad daylight so none of the scoundrels get off." That night, the brigade called an urgent meeting of CCP members and cadres and decided on nine people to kill. A second batch of six were killed on August 30. Mo Jiakun's repeated telephone calls also resulted in the killing of six people at the Caoyutang brigade.

At the Changjiangwei brigade, when the brigade cadres didn't immediately pass on the directive from the August 23 commune meeting, commune CCP secretary Deng Changchun, along with Zeng Qingsong and Mo Jiakun, came to the brigade to inspect operations on August 25 and called a meeting of the brigade's cadres, where Mo Jiakun reported on killings in other brigades and urged the Changjiangwei brigade to quickly take action. Commune secretary

Deng Changchun tactfully criticized the brigade's cadres: "Are your brigade's black elements all so well behaved that you don't have even one troublemaker?" That night, Mo Jiakun telephoned the brigade and pushed them to report some killings. The brigade's cadres met on the night of August 26, and CCP secretary Huang Shizhi said, "Those above have spoken, and we have to resolutely carry it out and not be softhearted as in the story of the farmer and the serpent.[4] This time, all the production teams have killed several troublemakers." The brigade subsequently killed 24 people, including three entire families.

At the Shazihe production brigade, the cadres who attended to commune meeting on August 23 communicated the message to other cadres but didn't call a meeting to take further action. However, Liu Fubao arrived at the brigade to inspect operations on August 25, and he told public-security head Zhou Liangcai, "Other production brigades are all going at it; what's holding you up? Are you waiting for an insurrection by the class enemy? When you suffer for it later on, don't say we didn't warn you." At a brigade CCP branch meeting on August 26, CCP secretary Fan Jingyue suggested, "I think we should handle these people through education and reform. Whether the odd troublemaker should be killed or not will depend on their behavior." Public-security head Zhou Liangcai disagreed: "We don't have to kill offspring for the time being, but the black elements should all be killed." Ultimately, 12 black elements were killed following a public rally, and 14 offspring were shown "leniency" and locked up in a primary school serving as a temporary prison. Six more people committed suicide out of fear of being killed.

Some brigade leaders were more successful in avoiding pressure from commune leaders. After the Xiahudong brigade's CRC chairman, Liao Yousheng, and poor-peasant association (PPA) chairman Chu Yugui returned from the August 23 meeting and reported to CCP secretary Sun Yuquan, Sun said, "We'll stick to the instructions and kill two troublemakers." The three of them reached a decision and the next day called a meeting of CCP members and cadres to carry it out. The brigade acted quickly and didn't deviate from its original plan, as a result of which no more people died there during the "killing wind" except for a landlord element who killed himself out of fear.

The Shalejiang brigade was the only production brigade in Gongba Commune where no one was killed. After brigade CCP secretary Zhu Zhibao and militia commander Zhu Xianming attended the August 23 commune meeting, they called a cadre meeting during which someone suggested, "Let's not be in a hurry. We can wait for the other brigades to kill people before we do anything." Most of the cadres supported this proposal, so they decided to impose control over four black elements but never killed them. However, landlord element Zhu Xiang and rich-peasant element Huang Guixiu and her daughter killed themselves after hearing of killings at other brigades.

While they were the prime instigators of the killings, commune-level leaders were occasionally capable of demonstrating a moral bottom line. After leading cadres and mass organization heads from the Jinjidong production brigade attended the August 23 commune meeting, they arranged for 22 black elements to be killed. But as in the case of the Yanhetang brigade, the problem then arose of what to do with the "little tigers" left behind after their parents were killed. On August 29, the production brigade decided to kill 15 underage class enemy offspring, but when they requested instructions from the commune, Zeng Qingsong, Mo Jiakun, Liu Fubao, and the others felt this was too inhumane, and they refused to approve it. However, no one came up with an alternative solution, and this put Jinjidong's poor peasants on the spot. If someone were willing to bear the expense to raise the "tiger cubs," it wouldn't be necessary to kill them, but no one resolved this practical issue. On August 30, the poor peasants of Jinjidong killed 14 minors, 4 of them young children.

Many atrocities were carried out with particular relish by brigade leaders, quite apart from prodding from the upper level.

The Jingtang brigade's CRC chairman, Yang Tingxiu, was implicated in many cases of gang rape during the killing wind. Yang and others raped Tang Maonü after killing her husband, primary-school teacher Tian Zibi,[5] and throwing their 18-month-old toddler into the river. A 17-year-old girl named Zou Yuhua was forced to marry a poor peasant bachelor in his 30s after the peasant supreme court, represented by Yang Tingxiu and others, killed her parents and two younger brothers and confiscated the family's belongings. When Zou Yuhua objected to the marriage, she was tied up and savagely kicked in her private parts while her oppressors shouted, "You cunt! Are you saving yourself for Chiang Kai-shek?" The badly injured Zou Yuhua was later gang-raped by Yang Tingxiu and others.

At the Majiangkou brigade, public-security head Xie Zhencheng suggested the killing of Huang Shijin, a class enemy offspring who had done some teaching at the primary school, along with his elder son, Huang Youqing. Huang's 15-year-old daughter, Huang Lihua, was spared because she was pretty and there were many in the brigade who wanted to marry her. Xie Zhencheng first tried to force her to marry his crippled nephew, but Huang Lihua refused. Then the head of the No. 5 production team tried to force her to marry his son, but she also refused. The brigade's leaders warned her, "You can only marry someone in our brigade. Don't say we didn't give you a way out." The spirited girl said, "After you killed my father and brother, you want me to marry one of you? I can't do it, and if that means you'll chop me into pieces, I'm resigned to my fate." Two months later, with the help of relatives, Huang Lihua managed to escape to faraway Heilongjiang Province and found a job as a casual laborer. She returned to Daoxian eight years later but stayed clear of Majiangkou, eventually marrying someone from Simaqiao Commune's Zhoujiashan brigade.

The Majiangkou brigade had a man named Huang Yiyi who had been trans-ferred to the countryside from a geological team in 1962. The state had paid him more than 1,000 yuan to cover his transfer, and, with eyes on that money, someone took the opportunity to have him killed during 1967 massacre. His home was ransacked, and each production team received more than 100 yuan in "movable assets."

At the Shangyunba brigade, although only 13 people were killed, CCP com-mittee member Zhang Xiaobing dispatched eight of them with his own hand, a fact that continued to generate comment and tongue clucking when we did our reporting nearly 20 years later.

The killings of 48 people at the Taohuajing brigade were considered partic-ularly horrific and were mainly instigated by CRC chairman Wang Changzhen and brigade head Wang Mingzhen. The circumstances behind the killings in this brigade were very complex, a particularly notorious case being the revenge kill-ing of a demobilized soldier named Zhang Mingyu.

Zhang Mingyu was born and raised in the brigade's Taohua Village, and his family was classified as middle peasant. After graduating from middle school, Zhang farmed with his family and then enlisted in the army, returning to the village after his demobilization in 1964. His time away had made him critical of local people and conditions, and, even worse, he was regarded as ruthlessly am-bitious and as trying to take control of the production team and brigade with a group of young followers. Production team head Zhang Ming'ai was grinding his teeth in rage and frustration, and even the production brigade couldn't figure out what to do with him. The enmity between Zhang Ming'ai and Zhang Mingyu fell just short of coming to blows, but Zhang Mingyu's status as a demobilized soldier protected him.

When the "killing wind" arrived and the Taohuajing brigade met to draw up its killing list, Zhang Ming'ai said, "If we don't kill anyone else, we have to start with Zhang Mingyu. He's more destructive than any class enemy." Other brigade leaders agreed with this view, and it was unanimously decided to punish Zhang Mingyu as a black element.

On the day Zhang Mingyu was to be killed, Zhang Ming'ai and the others nailed his hands and feet to a wall, and Zhang Ming'ai, knife in hand, vented his hatred by subjecting Zhang Mingyu to the feudalistic "death by a thousand cuts." With each cut he asked, "Who's tougher, you or me?" By then Zhang Mingyu had surrendered completely, and he begged for mercy: "Brother Ming'ai, I was wrong, I'll never do it again! Please have mercy on me!" Zhang Ming'ai said, "Should I have mercy on you and wait for you to come and kill me? This is a fight to the death—it's you or me!" He dismembered Zhang Mingyu bit by bit.

The circumstances at the Guangjialing brigade, which began this chapter, were different from the commune's other 22 production brigades in that other brigades began killing people after the August 23 commune meeting in what the Task Force referred to as "killing under orders," while the Guangjialing brigade began its killings on August 20. As a result, some termed the killings there as "spontaneous," but the cadres and masses of Guangjialing strongly disagreed with this assessment. The main person responsible for the killings, militia commander Yang Buzhao, said, "I had no personal grudge against them [the victims], so why should I kill them? It was the upper levels shouting at us to do it." Yang insisted that even after Zeng Qingsong and Mo Jiakun called him into their office on market day and urged the brigade to start killing people, the brigade initially didn't plan to kill anyone. "But then Yang Meiji ran off, and it was said he'd gone to join the bandits in the hills, so we felt we had no choice but to start killing. Before we killed anyone, I requested instructions from Chairman Mo at the commune, and he approved it. We shouldn't be blamed for this, because we were 'killing under orders,' too. The later killings were our responsibility. By then the production brigades and production teams were competing with each other, and we felt we had to kill people."

These subsequent victims included an 18-year-old girl, Xiang Xinzhen, and her parents and younger brother, who were among a second batch of people killed in the Guangjialing brigade on August 26. When the brigade was discussing the second batch of killings, someone suggested, "Chairman Mao taught us that 'Winning state power requires both the gun and the pen, and defending it likewise requires both.' If we're going to kill landlords and rich peasants, we can't just kill the troublemakers, but also those who wield pens, because they're the most-dangerous enemies." It was therefore decided that the primary-school teacher Xiang Longru, a member of the landlord class, should be killed.

Xiang Longru taught at the Gongba Primary School while his wife took care of the children and farmed on the production team, but when the schools were shut down to make revolution, Xiang had returned home. Like most people with bad political backgrounds and a measure of education, Xiang Longru knew something of the brutality of political struggle, but he was not mentally prepared for indiscriminate killing, and when the brigade's peasant supreme court pronounced a death sentence on him out of the blue, he was completely flabbergasted.

The original plan was to spare Xiang Xinzhen because one of the leaders of the peasant supreme court, a poor and shabby bachelor in his 30s surnamed He, wanted to marry her. After her parents and brother were led away, Xiang Xinzhen was panic-stricken and inconsolable, huddling in her home and weeping. A neighbor heard her and quickly reported to CCP secretary Jiang Youyuan. Jiang sighed, "We intended to spare her, but if she insists on being the dutiful offspring of the landlord class, we can't save her." After killing the parents and brother, the killers returned to the Xiang home, grabbed Xiang Xinzhen by the hair, and said, "Your father and mother are dead, and if you want to live, you have to marry one of us poor peasants."

When Xiang Xinzhen heard that her parents were dead, she began weeping and shouting hysterically. "I want my mother and father! I don't want to get married!" Seeing her ingratitude, the militiamen bound her up and took her weeping to an abandoned mine at Tuzhailing. As the killers pushed her to the edge of the pit, bachelor He, still hopeful, said, "If you're willing to reform your thinking and make a fresh start, all you need to do is agree to marry me, and you'll be released immediately."

Xiang Xinzhen stopped crying and opened her eyes wide. Perhaps in that instant she became aware of the fearfulness of death and the preciousness of life. She wouldn't have been the first in Daoxian to marry to save herself. . . . But by then, for Xiang Xinzhen, time was a luxury that could no longer be measured in days, hours, or even minutes. It was being measured in seconds. Uninterested in what answer she might give, someone in the group, long out of patience with this black-element whelp who didn't appreciate the favor shown to her and seeing no point in sparing her, raised his hoe and heaved it savagely onto the head of that 18-year-old girl. Afterwards, He berated the killer for depriving him of his lucky break.

The first victim from Gongba Commune to be cast into that abandoned mine, Yang Jingcheng, was also the one we heard the most about, partly because of Yang's distinctive personal history, and partly because his son subsequently filed countess petitions demanding justice for his father, making at least 200 trips to the county seat, Daojiang; the prefectural capital, Yongzhou; the provincial capital, Changsha; and the national capital, Beijing.

Yang Jingcheng, born Yang Houji in 1920, was from a rich peasant family, and his well-read father taught at a private school. When the War of Resistance against Japan broke out, Yang Jingcheng enlisted in the army, joining the Kuomintang's Student Volunteer Corps and rushing to the battle front, adopting the name Jingcheng ("there is a way") in honor of his personal motto, "Where there's a will, there's a way." He subsequently fled to Taiwan but then switched sides in 1948 and returned to Daoxian with a reward of two silver dollars in his pocket. When Daoxian was "peacefully liberated" in 1950, Yang Jingcheng followed in his father's footsteps and became a "people's teacher" at a primary school.

By the time the Land Reform movement arrived at Guangjialing Village, the Yang family owned 2.6 *mu* of paddy fields and six *mu* of nonirrigated farmland, which under the county's land reform standards barely qualified them as middle peasants. For some reason, however, Yang decided to set an example by classifying his family as rich peasants. Although they came to profoundly regret this decision, there didn't seem much to lose at the time, given their small fields and limited movable assets, and they didn't have any of their land redistributed, since each of Guangjialing's poor peasants was allotted two *mu* of land, and the Yang family owned less than two *mu* per person.

During the 1957 Anti-Rightist campaign, Yang Jingcheng didn't engage in any "erroneous speech" but was exposed as a "suspected latent secret agent returned from Taiwan." In June 1958, Yang was dismissed from his teaching position and was sentenced for three years of discipline for "counterrevolutionary crimes," and then he was sent back to his home village to labor under the supervision of the poor and lower-middle peasants. In 1962, Yang's wife divorced him and ran off, abandoning their four children. Yang Jingcheng was a truly capable person, a middle-aged man raising four children on his own, forced to take on farming work in the middle of his life yet managing to keep his home ship-shape and cozy. He had no aptitude for farming but somehow learned to raise geese and ducks, and the value of Daozhou gray geese as a key export item helped Yang Jingsheng and his family survive even the Great Famine. By August 1967, Yang's eldest son, Yang Qingxiong, was an able-bodied youth nearly 20 years old, and Yang began to feel that his worries were over.

One day, when Yang Qingxiong went out to work, a cousin who was a core militiaman for the production brigade told him, "Qingxiong, the upper level has had a meeting to discuss killing rich peasants. Your dad is in danger—tell him to find a way to escape quickly." Returning home after work, Yang Qingxiong passed this information to his father. By then, Yang Jingcheng had heard of rich peasants being killed in Daoxian, but he'd seen the world and had worked in a land reform team, and after thinking it over carefully, he said, "I can't run. If I do, how will you manage? If I run off, you'll have to pay the price."

Yang Qingxiong said, "Then let's both run off."

"Then what about your siblings? They're too young to get away."

"So what should we do?"

"Let's do this. I'll pretend to be going on a trip and run off into the hills. If things start to look bad at home, find a way to meet me at your grandfather's tomb. I know how the Communist Party works. First they mobilize the masses and create a terrifying spectacle, but after a little while, things will get back to normal and the situation will improve. Then they'll implement policy and treat people differentially. Everyone in the production team has seen how I've obediently accepted reform all these years, so if I can just avoid this first hurdle, there shouldn't be any major problems."

"Then I'll go with you."

Father and son packed up some quilts and ran off that day. After two days hiding near the grandfather's tomb, they didn't notice any untoward activity, and, worried about the other three children, they crept home under cover of night. That night, a core militiaman going home from a meeting discovered Yang Jingcheng and his son hoeing the chilies in their family garden plot. He quietly followed them home and then latched the door from outside and ran off to report them to the CCP secretary, and the brigade quickly sent militia to stand guard over Yang's home.

Young and vigorous, Yang Qingxiong grabbed a cleaver, preparing to rush out and attack the sentries. Yang Jingcheng held onto him for dear life and took away the cleaver: "Do you want to die and take the whole family with you?"

"So what should we do, sit here and wait to die?"

Yang Jingcheng was also anxious and afraid, but he was still thinking clearly: "Of course we're not going to wait to die, but we can't act rashly. We have to calm down and see what happens before we decide what to do."

This was around the time of the Ghost Festival on the 15th day of the 7th lunar month, and the production team had slaughtered a pig, distributing a piece to each family, including the Yangs. Whenever the production team killed a pig, any meat left over could be purchased by families who were better off. Yang Jingcheng sent Yang Qingxiong to fetch their portion and told him to buy an extra half kilo as well, but the butcher responsible for meat distribution, Yang Fengji, refused point-blank: "No matter how much I have, I wouldn't sell it to you."

Security head Yang Caiji, standing off to the side, said, "Fengji, just sell another half kilo to him." Yang Caiji was actually a kindhearted person, and he felt there was nothing wrong with Yang Jingcheng eating a little extra; even the emperor allowed a last meal to a condemned man. Yang Jingcheng drew the opposite conclusion, however; seeing his son come home with the extra meat, he was overjoyed and said, "It doesn't look like they plan to kill us." They cooked the meat that night, and the family celebrated with an excellent meal.

The next day was the Ghost Festival, and the production team called in core militiamen from the villages of Changxingdong and Hongjialei to help them arrest Yang Jingcheng. Because Yang had been a soldier and had a tough and unyielding character, they feared he would fight for his life, so they decided to claim they were taking him for reform through labor and then kill him at the abandoned mine at Tuzhailing on the way.

When Yang and his son saw the militia coming, Yang Jingcheng climbed on the roof to hide while Yang Qingxiong squeezed between the rails of the pigsty next door and hid in a haystack. The pigsty contained a massive hog weighing more than 50 kilos, and, startled by the human intrusion, it began ramming against the rails. When the militiamen saw this, they jabbed the haystack with their spears, shouting, "Surrender! We see you!" One of the spears struck Ying Qingxiong in the forehead, and with blood pouring out of his head, Yang Qingxiong stood up with his arms raised in surrender. The militia wanted to take him away with his father, but an older relative who was a leader of the brigade's PPA said, "Don't be hasty. Lock him up first and then kill him if he makes trouble."

By then, the pig butcher Yang Fengji had moved a ladder to the side of the house and climbed onto the roof, and seeing Yang Jingcheng hiding in the rain gutter, he said, "Yang Jingcheng, you can't get away, just come down. The district has ordered you to be sent for reform through labor." Yang Jingcheng believed him and obediently followed Yang Fengji down from the roof. As soon as his feet hit the ground, he was tied up like a rice dumpling for the Dragon Boat Festival and was led away.

At a crossroads about a quarter of a kilometer outside the village, the militiamen pulled Yang Jingcheng over toward the old mine at Tuzhailing. When Yang saw they weren't heading toward the district headquarters, he tried to resist, but there wasn't much he could do. The militiamen dragged him to the side of an abandoned prospecting pit, where Yang Buzhao represented the brigade's peasant supreme court in pronouncing the death sentence on Yang Jingcheng for being a "reactionary rich peasant and secret agent."

Standing at the mouth of the pit, Yang Jingcheng tried to reason with them: "I'm not a secret agent, and I've made a clean breast of all my past wrongs to the party. The party has never treated me as a secret agent."

Yang Buzhao said, "Enough talk. If you're not a secret agent, who is? Kneel down!"

Yang Jingcheng was unwilling to kneel: "I've broken no laws, why should I kneel?"

Yang Buzhao swung a cotton presser axle at Yang Jingcheng's head. Blood gushed out and drenched Yang Buzhao as Yang Jingcheng collapsed to the ground. Yang Buzhao ordered two militiamen to drag Yang Jingcheng into a kneeling position, after which he was killed with a saber and dumped into the pit. After that, they went back and seized all of the Yang family's livestock and other "movable assets."

After killing Yang Jingcheng, the Guangjialing brigade killed the other two "class enemies" and dumped them into the pit. A number of nearby production brigades chose this place as their execution ground, and the bones of 77 bodies remain inside it to this day.

Yang Qingxiong was among a third batch of 81 victims that was going to be slaughtered on August 30. But heavy rains on August 29 and 30 prevented the killings from going forward, and on the 31st the directive arrived from the commune prohibiting further random killings. The Guangjialing brigade's killings ended at 22, and Yang Qingxiong had his "dog's life" spared.

"We spared him and he went around filing complaints," a cadre from the production brigade fumed. "As a matter of fact, only his old man was killed. Other families with more people killed didn't say anything about it. It was only him who filed complaints for compensation and became a professional petitioner."

Yang Qingxiong's petitions give the impression of a desperate person leaving no stone unturned. I have a copy of one of Yang's "written complaints," which a friend at the provincial archives gave me while I was doing my reporting. My friend said, "This fellow has sent his petitions everywhere—not just to government offices, but even to universities and colleges, libraries, and archives." In his complaint, Yang Qingxiong detailed the killing of his father and the others and named the main perpetrators, adding that one of them, Yang Qingyu, head of the brigade's rebel faction, had also raped his wife:

> . . . I began petitioning for justice on my father's behalf on April 15, 1979. In the seven years since, I have submitted 244 petitions, the bus fares alone costing me more than 600 yuan. I am left destitute and in debt and cannot sustain even the most basic livelihood in the village. The issue has not been resolved, and some people have even enriched themselves through the relief money the state has sent down for the families of victims. Some of the chief instigators and killers of Daoxian's Cultural Revolution indiscriminate killing wind have been promoted as officials or cadres, and some have joined the party. They occupy every leadership position in Daoxian from the county to the production brigade level, wielding power and hoodwinking the public while the families of victims are forced to swallow their anger in the face of an insurmountable barrier to justice.
>
> Following the Third Plenum of the Eleventh Central Committee, order has been brought out of chaos, wrongful cases have been overturned, and the party's radiance has illuminated our land. On October 30, 1984, the Daoxian People's Court found on reexamination that . . . the judgment against my father for counterrevolutionary crimes in 1958 was in error. On this basis, the court rescinded Criminal Judgment 58-211 and granted redress (court judgment attached).
>
> Our entire family is deeply grateful for this, but up to now, the various policies that should have been implemented toward us have not been carried out. . . . The killers have not only gotten off scot-free but flaunt their strength. . . . Having no alternative, I can only once again bypass the immediate upper levels and prostrate myself in begging for an investigation, and I urgently request the following:
> (1) Restore my father's position and reputation and arrange for his proper burial and appropriate restitution.
> (2) Return or compensate all the private property confiscated from my family.
> (3) Restore the urban household registrations of myself and my siblings.
> (4) Severely punish the chief instigators and killers in accordance with law.
>
> Respectfully yours,

Yang Qingxiong, Guangjialing Village, Gongba Township, Dao County, Hunan Province

February 17, 1985

After the Beijing Olympics ended in 2008, I received a telephone call from a friend in Daoxian: "Mr. Tan, do you remember that victim family member named Yang Qingxiong?"

"Of course I remember him."

"He's dead."

"Dead? How did he die?" I was shocked. Yang was around the same age as I, and I had seen him just two years before. He'd been very healthy and seemed to have only some minor problems with his state of mind.

"This year he went off to Beijing to petition, and no one could talk him out of it, and as a result he was arrested for sabotaging the Olympics. After he was sent back to Daoxian, the township government detained him, and when he returned home, he hanged himself."

After hanging up the phone, I was plunged into grief. This insignificant little person's death reflected the anguish of our entire people. As I mourned, I wrote a poem titled "Back to Dust":

> Thinking there was brightness
> Thinking there was warmth
> I therefore
> Disregarded all else to fling myself there
> Whereupon
> I turned into gray dust
> Everything I've done
> Is what all living things do
> Only
> I am even stupider
> And more instinctive
> Than others
> I need even more warmth
> Long for even more brightness
> That is why
> I've turned into gray dust.

Interview with the Butcher of Gongba Commune

The situation described earlier in this chapter makes it quite clear that Gongba Commune militia commander Zeng Qingsong played a key role in making

Gongba Commune Daoxian's bloodiest commune. We had an unexpected opportunity to interview Zeng in the interrogation room of the Daoxian Detention Center.

Several of the commune's cadres had been imprisoned for what was one of the most serious mass killings in the county, but getting an interview with one of them was no easy matter. No one in Daoxian offered to help us, and, fearing that making such a request would create trouble for ourselves and others, we left it to chance.

It seems we were fated to meet Zeng Qingsong, having gone to the detention center to interview a completely different person. While we were carrying out our reporting work in Gongba, a young woman had run up to us and said, "Comrade journalists, I need to tell you about an injustice connected with the killings here." Our hearts leapt at what appeared to be the first instance of a surviving family member approaching us. Taking her measure, we saw a tidy person with pale skin and a steady gaze, not in the least resembling the typical jittery countenance of surviving family members. We promptly invited her to sit down and tell us her story, and that is when we realized she was actually the family member of a killer—the first and only person in Daoxian who spoke to us in that capacity. Specifically, she wanted to talk to us about the sentencing of her younger brother: "Comrade journalists, the barbaric killing of class enemies here during the Cultural Revolution was instigated by production brigade cadres. My brother was a member of the core militia under their orders, and if he was told to kill Zhang Three, he did it, or Li Four, he did it. . . . Now they're shifting all the blame on my brother. The Task Force has been boarding at the homes of these cadres, eating and sleeping with them, so they're protecting them. One of the brigades went after my brother, and he was unjustly sentenced to three years in prison. But in fact the cadres were much worse than he was, and they haven't been punished at all. Please, comrade journalists, tell our side of the story to those above."

During our reporting, we'd come across other such claims, but one of our guiding principles was not to get involved in any case even on behalf of victims, much less killers. We could only explain this to her and recommend that she appeal to the authorities. But the woman replied, "I've told them about it many times, but it's useless, and that's why I'm asking you to help me. No one pays attention to what we stupid peasants say, but the words of journalists soar upwards. There are many things we're unable to report to the district, county, or prefecture, but as soon as you journalists turn up, the report is accepted. I beg you to help us."

We could only respond more bluntly: "From what we've been able to understand, the Task Force hasn't been harsh with the killers, so it's highly unlikely that your brother has been treated unjustly. Even if others who behaved worse than him haven't been punished, that doesn't mean that your brother has been unjustly convicted. I would guess he must have at least five or six lives on his account."

At this, the woman became even more anxious, her eyes widening as she said, "That's absolutely impossible. You can ask anyone in the brigade. My brother was known for his integrity. At home he could hardly bear to kill a chicken, so how could he kill a person? It's because they saw he was easily browbeaten that they pushed the blame on him!"

She spoke with such certainty that we considered this might be a genuine case of injustice that would make a good story, so we agreed to look into the matter. That's how we came to make the trip to see that woman's brother at the county detention center, also hoping to flush out some more good cases.

As it happened, a friend of Minghong's held a minor position at the detention center, and that made things easier. After an exchange of conventional greetings, we got to the point of our visit. Hearing our tale, the man gave a great laugh and said, "You must be joking! Any of the killers locked in here have been treated too leniently if anything! We don't have anyone who's been unjustly convicted. Come here, I'll look it up for you. . . . See? This person took 11 lives by his own hand, not including other killings where he was a participant. This is an ironclad case. He not only confessed to everything, but there was thorough collateral evidence."

Sighing with disappointment, we continued chatting with him about the killings, especially those at Gongba Commune, and when he said that Zeng Qingsong was also jailed there, we asked if it might be possible to interview him. The official answered without hesitation, "Why not? I'll just go call him out."

Soon after that, we were sitting in the interrogation room with Zeng Qingsong.

He was a swarthy man of about 50 and big for someone of his generation, but while heavy-set, he didn't look obese under the dark singlet stretched taut over his frame. He had very large eyes, and his prison crewcut gave him a flatteringly guileless and vigorous appearance. He had been serving his sentence in the Daoxian Detention Center ever since being prosecuted for his crimes, and apart from being kept within its walls, he was given a free run of the detention center, helping in the kitchen and assisting the guards in managing the other prisoners. Even so, he resented his imprisonment.

When Zeng was brought to the interview room, Minghong immediately felt he'd seen the man before, but he couldn't remember when. We showed him our credentials and reassured him that all we wanted was to understand what had happened back then, and that he could refuse to answer any of our questions. He said he'd be more than happy to answer our questions, and he looked at us with the steady gaze of one with a clear conscience.

"Zeng Qingsong, do you know why you were arrested?"
"Yes, because of the random killings during the Cultural Revolution."

"What position did you hold at Gongba Commune at the time?"

"I was head of the commune PAFD."

"What were you doing prior to your arrest?"

He gave a bitter smile and said, "I was head of Xianglinpu District."

Zhang Minghong then recalled that the previous spring, flash floods had struck Xianglinpu from the upper reaches of the Yongming River, breaking a bridge and destroying homes. Minghong had accompanied a comrade from the prefectural CCP committee to the frontline of the disaster area and had seen Zeng Qingsong directing rescue efforts, performing impressively with his body soaked and covered with mud.

We asked some specific questions, but Zeng had little fresh information to offer because his memory had become a bit "hazy" regarding the killings. However, he repeatedly maintained that his superiors had approved everything he'd done.

"When did you request instructions, and from whom?"

"On August 8, 1967, I requested instructions from political commissar Liu [Shibin] at the county PAFD. That afternoon, I went to town with the commune cook, Zhang Jisheng, to see commissar Liu in his home. I reported three problems to him: the first was that weapons were very hard to protect, the second was what should we do if someone tried to snatch them, and the third was that killings had started in the villages, and what should we do about it? Liu Shibin said 'The county PAFD's weapons have already been stolen, so Daoxian is depending on the militia's firearms to protect the poor peasants. You have to hold your positions and take care of your weapons. Whether what's happening in the villages is killing or revolutionary action is not your concern. You need to focus on maintaining public order and protecting your weapons.' Early the next morning, under the grape arbor at militia headquarters, I encountered [military subregion deputy commander] Zhao, and I reported to him the matters I'd reported to commissar Liu. Deputy Commander Zhou said 'You need to purge your ranks; the people's militia can't risk having turncoats. . . . Don't concern yourself with the killing of black elements; you have to support the revolutionary movement of the poor and lower-middle peasants.' "

When I asked Zeng's feelings about how he'd been treated, he said, "I have two opinions. First, I didn't specifically direct or arrange for my subordinates to kill anyone; second, some people were yelling more ferociously than me, so why haven't they been called to account?" He then said in a wounded tone of voice, "It's always us district cadres who bear the brunt. We're the ones who have to do the work, and when problems arise, we're held responsible. They got us during the Five Winds and they got us this time, too."

"You say you didn't arrange for any killings, so why were so many people killed in Gongba Commune, where you were in charge? Why were the killings so focused and the methods so brutal?"

After a long silence, he stammered, "I've thought about this question for a long time, and I still don't have the answer."

It was no easy matter for the Task Force to send a cadre to prison. Without a dozen solid killings in hand, they couldn't put anyone away even if they wanted to. When I carried out interviews in Qingxi District's Qingkou Commune, I heard of a comment that a perpetrator made to a family member of a victim: "Others have only one head, but I have three—my party member head, my cadre head, and the head my parents gave me to eat with. Killing a couple of black elements means losing one head, but I'll still have two left to save myself and raise my kids, so you can bite my balls!" It was said that there was an unwritten rule for dealing with the perpetrators of the Daoxian killings: it took three killings to be dismissed from the CCP or from an official position. That suggests what it took to send Zeng Qingsong to prison. As for his "hazy" memory and his lack of an answer, that's irrelevant. In the course of my reporting, I encountered quite a few perpetrators, and almost none of them remembered "clearly" or seemed to understand what they had done.

13

Some Who Got Away

During the Cultural Revolution killings in Daoxian, 688 people were compelled to flee their villages and were accused of becoming bandits. Outside observers have always wondered how these people managed to escape. When we first did our reporting in Daoxian, we particularly hoped such people could give us firsthand accounts of the massacre, imagining that nothing could be easier than interviewing these 688 indomitable survivors. We were surprised to find that most were so traumatized by their experience that they were afraid of saying the wrong thing or had difficulty expressing what they'd been through. Instead, they told us of their gratitude to the Chinese Communist Party (CCP) and the government for rehabilitating them and helping them rebuild their homes.

Perhaps we took the wrong approach by "receiving" former fugitives in production brigade offices, in the presence of the local CCP secretary or a Task Force member. We didn't know how to go about interviewing them, and conversations inevitably languished after a brief exchange. Some others who would have been willing to speak freely were never introduced to us because others didn't want them to destroy the "excellent situation of stability and unity." We were obliged to use personal connections to contact such people in secret. We made our first breakthrough at Gongba Commune, where we interviewed three men who survived the massacre. Their accounts of their experiences follow.

Becoming a beast to survive: Xu Zhenzhong, a Rightist and retired schoolteacher, age 63 (in 1986)

Back then, brigade cadres or poor peasants just had to open their mouths, and whoever they want killed didn't have a chance.

I originally taught at the Dongyang Primary School in Daojiang Town. In 1957, during the campaign to help the party rectify itself,[1] my superiors mobilized me to offer some views, and I spoke a few truthful sentences, nothing important—I thought that since they wanted my opinion, I couldn't just sing their praises, but in fact I actually did praise them a great deal and included only a few suggestions besides. For that I was designated a Rightist, dismissed from my job, and sent back to my home village. During the turmoil in 1967, I was in the lineup to be "done away with," but I was fortunate, and by running fast I lived to see this day. If I'd stayed put like some other class enemies, my bones would be drumsticks by now.

In the Gongba brigade's No. 4 production team, where I lived, the killing began on August 24, 1967. It all happened so fast, we had no inkling of it beforehand.

I'd spent all that day harvesting rice in the fields, and my back was aching. I had a weak constitution from being a teacher, and it was hard for me to keep up with the others, but if I didn't I'd be denounced for slacking off or resisting remolding. I had to put all my strength into it, and after a day's work I'd just drop onto my bed and sleep. I had an 80-year-old mother who was largely deaf—she couldn't even hear thunder most of the time. That night, when the militia came knocking on our door, I was sleeping like a dead pig, and my deaf mother didn't hear them, either, so no one opened the door. I later learned that when they'd pounded on the door and heard no movement inside, they'd thought we weren't home and just left.

Early the next morning, I got up and went to the field as usual. Ever since being sent back to my village, I'd made a point of going out earlier than the others and leaving the field later. I'd just cut a row of rice when a poor peasant named Li Fashun came over to me, and while cutting rice he nudged my shoulder and said, "Hey, brother, I don't know if you've noticed, but some people didn't come out to the fields today." After he said this, I noticed that several "black elements" who always came out the earliest weren't there. Li Fashun whispered to me, "They were at it all night last night—you need to think of something as soon as you can!" After saying this, he walked off to the side and kept working without paying me any more attention.

At that moment, my heart was pounding like a drum. I didn't know what to do.

When I went home at noon, my mother had already heard rumors of the killings, and she told me, "Guixing (my childhood nickname), a person should know why he's dying. It's a waste to have someone grab you in the night like a chicken in a coop and throw you into a pit for no good reason! You need to leave fast. Don't make your old mother attend your funeral." When I heard her words, I sucked my tears right back into my belly. I felt I'd wronged my elderly mother. Our family had been a proper lower-middle peasant household. We had no money, and sending me to school had been a major sacrifice, and then I had to go running my mouth and getting myself labeled a Rightist, not only ruining my own prospects but also imposing the label of "black-element family member" on my mother. My mother had heard that the night before, the brigade had seized 20-odd black elements—in fact, most of them were only offspring—and had taken them to the Zuangzi Hills out behind the village, pushed them into an abandoned kiln, thrown in burning rice straw to suffocate them, and then covered them up with dirt. She was very worried and urged me to flee for my life. It had been nearly 10 years since I'd been labeled a Rightist. I'd been through the Anti-Rightist campaign and the "Five Unhealthy Tendencies,"[2] so I knew how bad things could get. It seemed that this time they really intended to annihilate all the black elements.

Although I'd obediently remolded my thinking since returning to the village and had performed very well, I knew this wouldn't matter—hadn't all those who'd been killed also worked hard and well? They were all as docile as the Buddha. They were mostly just offspring, but I was a straight-out black element, and I wouldn't get lucky a second time. I realized the brigade would be killing in batches just like they labeled people as Rightists in batches 10 years earlier. It seemed my only choice was to run off; even if I was eventually caught and the government sentenced me to death, it was better than waiting at home for them to bury me alive. I comforted my mother, saying, "Don't worry, fate governs our lives. Since I escaped last night, there may be a way out for me."

In the afternoon, I went out with the rest of the commune members as usual, and without showing my feelings, I set about cutting and bundling the rice while at the same time watching for an opportunity to escape. That opportunity never came. When it was about time to finish work, I took a moment when others weren't paying attention, nonchalantly walked over to a nephew of mine, and said, "Mongol (his nickname), I'm tired out today. Why don't you go on ahead and meet me up the road in a little while." He agreed to this, and when it came time for work to end, I brought up the rear carrying some moist, unhusked rice, lagging behind as the sky gradually darkened. After my nephew delivered a load of rice, he doubled back to meet me. He took up my shoulder pole, and I asked him, "Has there been any activity in the production team?" He said, "Nothing special." I pretended to feel a bit ill and told him to go on ahead while I washed my hands and feet in a gulley. Looking around and seeing no one, I turned and squeezed in among some tea shrubs and ran with all my strength into the hills.

I hid in the hills all night, and the next day I ran on blindly with no plan, only knowing that I had to run as far as I could. Finally I reached the stretch of flatland at the Xiaojia Dam. After running nonstop for two days, I was tired and hungry, having only dug up a few sweet potatoes to eat raw along the way, and I felt I had to risk leaving the hills to find some food. Just as I began heading for the lowlands, I ran into a member of my clan, Xu Zhensi, who was also on the run.[3] He asked, "Where are you going?" I said, "I'm going down to find some food." He said, "Don't go down! There are sentries everywhere, and they're questioning everyone who looks suspicious. Don't fall into their trap." He'd brought along some cakes baked for the Ghost Festival, and he shared some with me. It seems strange, but eating something and having someone with me was very consoling. After discussing things for a while, we decided to go together to his sister's home in Jianghua and set off with this objective in mind, not like headless flies buzzing around. We hid by day and moved by night, and after crossing the Da River [a tributary of the Xiaoshui], we bypassed Dapingling Commune and arrived in Mianzhujiang. Jianghua was within sight, but as luck would have it, we encountered militia searching the hills. They saw us, and one of them shot at us. We turned and ran and became separated as a result.

After we split up, I continued running aimlessly until I reached the barren and remote highlands of Sunchongyuan, where I spent the night. I slept under a tree on a bed of pine needles; you can't imagine what that was like unless you've experienced it. It was only the onset of autumn, but nights in the mountains were bitter cold; I was frozen, hungry, thirsty, damp, lonely, and bug-bitten . . . and I had to keep a lookout for poisonous snakes and wild animals as well as the militia. I was so exhausted that I fell half asleep, but then I awoke in the middle of a nightmare, scared half to death, and when I didn't see anything I started running again. Because I'd split off from Xu Zhensi and didn't know if he was dead or alive, I couldn't go to his sister's house. I wandered like a sleepwalker through the brambles and underbrush, every muscle in my body aching, my limbs exhausted, thistles ripping my skin, and the cuts leaving trails of blood. Fortunately my clothing was made of thick homespun cloth, so it didn't get torn to ribbons. I don't think I was even in control of my body; I was like a wild dog that's been whipped, spurred on by instinct, using all my strength to make my way through the impenetrable mountain vegetation.

Sometimes I came across the tracks of wild boars and panthers, but instead of being frightened, I was comforted by these signs of other living creatures. The feeling that constantly burned in my heart like an iron was of someone chasing me. I couldn't see them but never doubted they were there and close enough that they might appear before me at any moment, clutching their sabers and firing at me with their fowling pieces. I never even stopped to wonder what crime I'd committed; I felt like an escaped criminal, and that it was perfectly justified for them to chase me. A shrill, penetrating noise constantly buzzed in my ear and made me tremble from head to toe. I felt I was reaching the end of my rope. A person fleeing for his life has to become a wild beast in order to defend himself. He has to completely abandon everything that civilization has endowed him with; he has to rely entirely on instinct if he's to have any hope of evading danger and surviving in the remote highlands.

After scurrying around in the mountains for a couple of days, I reached Zhuyingzhai in Jianghua County. At that time, no one had been killed there, and there were no militia patrolling the roads and questioning people. Groping in my pocket, I found I had still had a little money and some grain coupons that I'd taken when I decided to flee, and I used them to get a haircut and something to eat. But at that time, leaving the village required a certificate from the production brigade and commune, and it was hard to do anything without these papers. In this remote village where I knew no one, had nothing to eat, and could sleep only out in the open, I began to lose heart and felt I couldn't keep going much longer. I would die either at the hands of others or from starvation, and I would be better off dying close to home so my spirit wouldn't have so far to roam. There's an old proverb that says, "A domestic chicken runs around in circles, a wild chicken flies all over." I turned back with a heavy heart, picking up a long stick and carrying a load of grass so I'd look like I was in the hills gathering kindling. On the way, I ran into some landlord offspring, Zhu Xianhou and his brothers, who were also fleeing for their lives.[4] I could see they weren't carrying guns or knives, and from their flustered manner and desperate appearance I could tell they weren't militia, so I joined up with them. When the brothers saw that I was a bit older and had some education, they asked for my advice. Good heavens! What bright ideas could I have! I didn't even know where to flee myself, but it was a comfort being with others.

At around two o'clock in the afternoon (we guessed the time from the sky), a dozen or so militiamen from the Dahe brigade came searching the hills with dogs, fowling pieces, bugles, and sabers, and when they discovered us they gave chase. I hid in the underbrush and escaped. Cornered, Zhu Xianhou and his brothers knelt on the ground and pleaded with them: "We're law-abiding, dutiful people. Our lives have been as hard as yours, and we haven't had a day of enjoyment or exploited anyone. We've done nothing wrong in the distant or recent past, so why bother capturing us? Please let us go, and we'll be in your debt for the rest of our lives." The search party said, "You've surrendered, and we're just obeying orders. We won't kill you, we'll just take you back." Further entreaties from Zhu Xianhou and his brothers were to no avail, so, steeling themselves, they stood up and said, "Since we have to die and you insist on capturing us, we might as well fight." All the brothers cried out together, "Let's fight!" This startled the militiamen so much that they let them go and ran down the hill blowing their trumpet.

Zhu Xianhou and his brothers ran for their lives deep into the hills. Having seen their resistance, I was afraid even more militia would be summoned to search the hills, so I didn't dare follow them but instead set off in another direction as fast as I could. Again I was separated from my companions. I don't know if Zhu Xianhou and his brothers ultimately lived or died. As for me, I hid in the cogon grass in the hills during the day and in a limekiln at night. When I was hungry I ate sweet potatoes, and when I was thirsty I drank from mountain springs, and in that way I endured half a month in the hills. By September 13, I couldn't sustain myself anymore, so I gritted my teeth and crept down the hill, and I found my cousin's home in Xiahezhou Village of Gongba Commune's Jinjidong production brigade. I quietly knocked on the door, and when my cousin saw me he was shocked, never imagining I was still alive. At first my cousin was afraid and didn't want to let me in, but his wife was kind and said, "It's been hard enough for him to escape with his life. We can't push him out of our home to his death." With his wife's persuasion, my cousin reluctantly allowed me to stay. During the day I hid in my cousin's wife's room, and I spent the night in the storage shed. After hiding for several days, I saw my cousin was becoming drawn with anxiety, and, afraid of involving them further, I decided to leave. My cousin said, "It's not that we don't want you to stay, but if something happens, I'm afraid we'll all be killed." After leaving my cousin's home, I ran to the home of my uncle Xu Xiude in Xingqiao Commune's Xujia brigade. By that time the killing wind had subsided somewhat, and besides that, my relatives were all poor and lower-middle peasants, so I was able to avoid detection.

It was just that my uncle would sometimes lose patience and scold me: "You were eating from the government's iron rice bowl and didn't know what was best for you, giving your opinions and courting death! If I'd had a chance to eat from your iron rice bowl, I'd kowtow every day in gratitude. But you didn't know your own good fortune and brought this all on yourself." As long as my uncle didn't chase me out, there was nothing I could do but follow his example and curse myself.

I never guessed that on September 23, when my uncle's son got married, someone from my production brigade would come to the feast, see me, and go back and report it. The Gongba brigade sent people to arrest me, saying I'd run to the hills to become a bandit. Luckily someone in my uncle's production team tipped us off, and I escaped by hiding in a pile of firewood in the attic. I couldn't stay with my uncle any longer and had to go on the run again. In early October, when the killing wind subsided, I got a message to my wife, who worked in the county seat, to come and get me, and after enduring so much hardship, I returned with her to Daojiang. By then, the 47th Army's 6950 Unit had arrived in Daoxian, and there was no possibility of any random arrests or killings in Daojiang Town. So it was that my life was spared.

I later learned that after I fled, the production brigade said I'd become a bandit, and they had sent people to track me down. Many others like me who wandered in the wilderness hiding from pursuers were accused of becoming bandits and mounting a resistance, and this was written up in reports to the upper levels and disseminated everywhere. Where is justice? Where is conscience? Such unprecedented and bizarre injustice leaves you with no tears left to weep!

"I never dreamed they'd kill my children": Xu Zhensi, primary-school teacher, age 55 (in 1986)

When the killings are mentioned, I feel I'm still in the middle of a dream.

I'd been a primary-school teacher ever since I began working in March 1950. Because of my class background, during the 1959 Socialist Education movement I was accused of imaginary crimes, dismissed from my job, and sent back to my home village. The truth was that I'd worked especially hard on the education frontline because of my bad family background. But even though I'd been so careful that no one could find any fault with me, I was still dismissed. After returning home, I went straight into agricultural production, working conscientiously. At that time all I thought about was making the best life I could and raising my kids to adulthood. No matter how harsh or unfair the circumstances, the thought of my family kept me calm. My wife, Jiang Langui, was kind and gentle and never complained of the hardship she endured with me. We had four sons and a daughter, the eldest 14 years old and the youngest 2, and all of them were clever and adorable. Everyone said we were high-quality goods from a shoddy landlord kiln. In fact, we weren't landlords at all, but only born to the landlord class, and I'd simply received a little education. I never dreamed that disaster would descend on us as we sat at home. When the killing wind began blowing in 1967, my entire family was killed, allowing only me to escape with my life.

I remember around three or four o'clock in the afternoon on August 26, 1967, not long after eating lunch, I was taking a nap after harvesting rice in the fields. News had spread of killings in the neighboring production brigade, so I was somewhat uneasy. Although I felt I'd performed well enough, my landlord status and having been sent down after being purged were crimes in themselves. Having received some education, my thinking was more complex, and I realized that once the killing started, it could easily become indiscriminate, so I was vigilant. Just then I heard a bell toll nonstop: "Dong! dong! dong! dong!" My heart began to tremble. This was not the normal time for ringing a bell! I quickly got out of bed and looked outside, and over by the pressing room I saw militiamen rushing over with fowling pieces, spears, and sabers. Two days earlier, people with bad class backgrounds had been put under watch, but perhaps I wasn't meant to die, because just at that time the poor peasant assigned to keep watch over me was home with diarrhea. Sensing that things were not right, I felt I had to try to escape. I quickly placed a pair of straw sandals next to the bed and pulled the mosquito net down around it as if I were still there napping, and then, wearing only a pair of shorts, I grabbed a sweat cloth and a bamboo hat and told my wife I had to leave. My wife told me, "Just save yourself, don't worry about anything else." She told our eldest son, Jiawen, to see me off: "Get some cakes for your dad and a pair of pants. We don't know if we'll ever see him again." Choking with sobs, I told her, "Please take care of yourselves. Don't think about where I might die." My wife said, "Just hurry, or you won't get away."

Jiawen carried a basket and followed me, and we slipped out the back door and ran over to the Fengcun Hills behind the village. Jiawen followed me all the way to the hills, but I was afraid it would be dangerous for him to accompany me, so I told him, "Son, go home. Take care of your brothers and sister." I was stupid, so stupid. I thought they'd kill only adults. I never thought they'd kill children. I thought only of my own danger and not of theirs. I never thought they would kill off entire families! How I regret it! I regret it to the depths of my soul. Even now, I cry just thinking about it. If Jiawen had gone with me, perhaps his life would have been spared, but I sent him home to die. It's all my fault. . . .

At this point, Xu Zhensi broke down in sobs. The sound of his hoarse cries as he beat his breast and stamped his feet shook us to the cores of our being. But apart from quietly weeping with him, we said nothing. He hadn't wanted to recall the past, but we'd made him do it; he hadn't wanted to speak, but we'd pushed him to. It was not only people in the government who wanted to forget what happened in Daoxian; many victims also wanted to forget. If they didn't forget, how could they go on living? After a long time, Xu Zhensi's sobbing gradually subsided, but it was still heartbreaking to listen to the hoarse breath heaving from deep within his breast.

I took the cakes that Jiawen had brought along—they were cakes for the Ghost Festival—and followed a narrow path into the mountains. Jiawen went down the mountain, and when he reached home they grabbed him. I later learned that when the militia came to my home, my 12-year-old son, Jiawu, hid in the pig barn, covering himself with rice straw, but he was so afraid that he trembled all over, so he was discovered and captured. My wife, Jiang Langui, and our five children were bound up by Li Yaode and the other murderers, and they were led to a muddy pond behind the village, where there was a pit about 15 meters deep and 2 meters in diameter left behind by a prospecting team, and they were speared one by one and thrown in. My production team threw 16 people into the pit that time. After pushing people in, they set rice straw alight and threw it in, and those who weren't dead screamed as they burned. They say that one of my sons wasn't burned to death at the time, and that people still heard him crying in the pit for days afterward. . . .

In the mountains, I encountered a Rightist from our production brigade, Xu Zhenzhong. . . .[5] After becoming separated from Zhenzhong in the hills, I just kept going, crossing hill after hill, river after river, all day and all night, until I reached my younger sister's home in Jianghua County. At that time they'd heard nothing of the killings. My sister asked why I'd come, and I didn't dare tell her, but just said I was stopping in while passing through. Because my brother-in-law also had a bad class background, I was afraid of implicating them, and I didn't dare tell them anything or weep in front of them. When I saw how things were in their home, I knew I couldn't stay long, and after asking for the latest news the next day, I took my leave. Seeing from my expression that something was wrong, my sister ran after me and asked, "What happened? Tell me!" I couldn't hold it back any longer and began to cry: "You can't imagine—they've started killing people in our village. They want to kill everyone with a bad family background. I don't even know whether your sister-in-law and niece and nephews are still alive, and I don't know when I'll die. I came to see you because I'm afraid we may never meet again." When my sister heard this, she began to weep. I said, "Don't cry—just take care of yourself. I'm putting you at risk by being here, and the sooner I leave the better." Telling me to wait, she ran back and got a little money from her husband to give to me, and then she walked with me a good long while, weeping the whole way.

After leaving my sister's home, where could I go? No matter how hard I thought, I didn't know which way to go. I hadn't been away from home at all since losing my job in 1959, and I didn't know what conditions were like elsewhere. After thinking about it, I decided I could only go back to Daoxian. I didn't know where the killing wind had blown up from, but I knew it had to have come from the upper levels; if people would have dared engage in random killing on their own, we'd have been killed long ago. One thing I knew for certain was that in implementing any policy, the lower levels always took things further than the upper levels. It would be best to go straight to the county government and give myself up to the county public-security bureau (PSB). I reckoned the worst they'd do to me was send me to labor reform rather than kill me, and if they insisted on killing me, I might as well die there.

Once I'd made up my mind, I followed the Wujiang Reservoir back to Daoxian. There were many sentries along the way, and they questioned everyone passing and arrested those without traveling permits. Through careful observation, I found that most of the sentry posts were set up on the main roads and at ferry piers, and there were few in the remote highlands. I tramped across the hills along small pathways, seldom seeing people, and when I saw a sentry I'd take a detour. My journey was endlessly perilous and confirmed my thinking that if I wanted to live, I had to turn myself in to the county PSB.

After several days, I reached a place just a few kilometers from the county seat. Sentries were thick on the ground, and they questioned people closely. People were being arrested everywhere. They were especially on the lookout for people with nothing in their hands. I could see it would be hard to get past them, and I was terrified, but the danger behind me was even greater. Just as I wrestled with this dilemma, I saw an old man carrying a load of chili peppers to sell in the county town. I ran over to him and said, "Uncle, that's such a big load of chilies. How about if I help you carry them?" The old man said, "How could I ask you to?" I said, "It's nothing at all—I'm just learning from Lei Feng!"[6] Without awaiting his reply, I took up his load while he carried his scale. Because the old man was a local, the sentries recognized him, and in that way I passed through this last barrier and entered Daojiang Town.

After reaching Daojiang, I ran to the PSB and turned myself in, but they wouldn't take me. I didn't have enough money to stay in a hostel, so all I could do was wander the streets. At that time, the atmosphere was tense in Daojiang as well, but there had been no killings. The Revolutionary Alliance headquarters was in the No. 2 High School, but the door to the school was barred, and no one was allowed in. In the open area in front of the school, where the bus station is now, a makeshift building had been put up with rice straw spread on the floor. It was filled with a couple dozen class enemies and offspring who had escaped, so I stayed there as well. The Revolutionary Alliance inside the school was afraid we'd cause problems for them, and they also ignored us. By this time, the 47th Army's 6950 Unit had entered Daoxian. We lined up at the People's Armed Forces Department (PAFD) headquarters for two meals every day. Eventually the number of people grew so large that the PAFD couldn't feed us all, and they told us to go home, saying a notice had been sent down forbidding any more killing. But we were all scared to death, and no one dared go back. We just waited at the PAFD headquarters every day for something to eat.

I stayed there for five days, and on the sixth day the roads were reopened, and the county arranged for 19 buses to take travelers back to Lingling. In order to protect the safety of the travelers, each bus had two People's Liberation Army (PLA) soldiers escorting it, one in front and one in back. Those of us from other places also scrambled onto the vehicles. By then we were all filthy and stinking, and one look was enough for anyone to know what kind of people we were. At that time, there was enormous prejudice against black elements and offspring. Some of the travelers were local people, and those who weren't local had been in Daoxian long enough to have heard of the killings in the countryside. They had pity on us and didn't make us leave the buses.

The bus set out from Daojiang Town, but when we reached Shili Bridge it was blocked by Red Alliance PAFD troops, who ordered us all to get out of the bus for questioning. When I heard this, I nearly passed out. I thought to myself, it's finished—after so many narrow escapes I've fallen into this trap! I looked at the others, and they were all blanching with terror. Fortunately, the PLA escorts refused to comply, and standing at the front and back of the vehicle, they said, "We already examined everyone on this bus while in Daoxian. We'll take responsibility for any problems, so please let us pass." When the PAFD saw the unyielding stance of their PLA comrades, they negotiated for a little while but finally raised the checkpoint barrier and let us pass. Once we'd crossed Shili Bridge, my heart dropped from my throat back into my stomach.

I took the bus all the way to Lingling. Although the atmosphere in Lingling was also tense, it was infinitely better than in Daoxian. In Lingling we went to the regional PSB to turn ourselves in, but they chased us away. When I saw that no one would take us in, I realized I'd have to find a way to survive. As an educated person, I was ashamed to beg, but looking for work, I couldn't even get my foot in the door. Just when I was feeling there was no way out, I encountered a craftsman who was willing to take me on. I went with him to Hubei, and there I learned carpentry, brickmaking, and other odd jobs—anything to feed myself. In any case, I didn't need much, just something to eat, and I wasn't lazy, so I was able to survive.

In 1969, I heard that things had returned to normal in Daoxian, so I went home. That's when I learned that my entire family had been killed. Someone else was living in our house, and all our belongings had been taken, but at that time I was so afraid that all I could do was grit my teeth and bear it.

After the Third Plenum, I came under the implementation of the new rehabilitation policies and had my job restored, and now I'm in charge of general affairs in the school. It can be considered a good ending. But when I think of my family, so unjustly murdered, I just can't stop crying all night long.

"A nightmare without end": Zhu Xianhou, peasant, class enemy offspring, 41 years old (in 1986)

I escaped from my production brigade [the Majialing brigade of Gongba Commune] around August 23, 1967. That morning, I was in the field harvesting rice while my elderly mother carried a load of chaff to Gongba Market to sell. But she rushed home from the market without selling her chaff and told me in a panic, "It's terrible—they're killing class enemies at Gongba Market!" My heart trembled at this news—I was only in my twenties at the time, so I was only an offspring rather than a landlord proper, but at that time if your family was designated as landlord class, everyone was considered a landlord, even a three-year-old kid, not to mention someone in his 20s like me. I asked my mother, "What should I do?" My mother said, "You won't be safe at home. Run away quickly!" I said, "We haven't done anything wrong, we've lived honest lives; why should I run?" My mother chided me, "Don't be stupid! Once they start killing people, none of that will matter—once the cry goes up, they'll kill everyone. If you go now, you may save yourself, but if you wait any longer, it'll be too late."

I was actually very anxious and wanted to run, but I was worried about my mother. She was 70 years old, and my elder brothers had married and set up their own households. I asked, "If I run, how will you manage?" My mother said, "Don't worry about me, I can still get around, I won't starve. Just save your own life."

By then I was resolved to run, but I had no money, so how could I manage? I looked around the house, but there was nothing of value. My mother pointed to two half-grown pigs in the sty and told me to take them to the market to sell. We'd bought them only a short time ago, planning to sell them after they were grown. I said, "It would be a waste to sell them when they're still so young." My mother became angry and said, "You're too stupid to live! Sell them fast or they'll become someone else's anyway." I quickly caught the pigs and carried them to Gongba Market to sell. We lived close to the market, just a walk across the bridge. I didn't know the killing wind was already blowing by then, but even someone blind and deaf could sense the terrorized atmosphere. After I reached the market, I was in such a hurry to sell off the pigs that I accepted a low price, 34 *kuai* for two pigs weighing more than 10 kilos each. I hurried home and tried to give some of the money to my mother, but she refused it and stuffed all of it into my hands. My mother said, "I have nothing to spend it on here. If you have more money with you, you'll be able to put it to use. Remember, once you leave, don't come back until you know things have settled down again!" My poor mother, a clever person all her life, understood only my danger and not her own—or maybe she did understand, but at her age, death was approaching in any case, and she didn't want to burden her children.

Around ten o'clock that morning, the brigade called a meeting. I felt things were taking a bad turn, so I slipped off into the hills behind the village.

After I escaped, the brigade began killing people. It was done in two batches, with more than 30 killed in all. I don't know all the details of how they killed people of other families, but I do know how they killed nine in my family and four in the family of my second cousin Zhu Liangrui. My mother, Chen Mei'e, was dragged to the bridge we crossed to Gongba Market and drowned in the river. My three elder brothers all were thrown in a kiln and buried alive, while the others, including my six- and three-year-old nephews, were drowned. My fourth sister-in-law died most horribly: when she was thrown into the Gongba River she didn't drown, but she hid among the willows along the bank. After hiding all day and night in the water, she still hadn't been found the next morning. But a lot of people walk that road along the riverbank, and my sister-in-law, alone and easily frightened, trembled every time someone passed by, causing the willow branches to shake. Finally someone discovered her and reported her to the brigade. The brigade sent militia over and ordered her onto the bank, but she hid in the water, quivering and afraid to come out. The production team's political instructor, Jiang Rutian, thrust a spear at her, and witnesses say the water was immediately stained red. My sister-in-law didn't even have a chance to cry out before she died—her body sank and disappeared. Jiang Rutian had always been a gluttonous and lazy man, and during the killings he was an enthusiastic participant, killing a dozen or so people all on his own.[7]

My sixth brother, Zhu Xianzhong, age 37 at the time, had not been labeled a landlord during the Land Reform movement but acquired the label during the Socialist Education movement in 1964. He had worked as a bamboo crafts-man elsewhere and was quick-witted, so when the production brigade began killing people, he also ran off. He wasn't as stupid as those of us who only knew how to run to the hills; he planned to escape to Guangxi, where he had worked before. At the Huluyan ferry pier in Shenzhang Commune, he ran into our second cousin Zhu Liangrui, which is fortunate, because otherwise we would never have found out how my brother died. Zhu Liangrui was also of the landlord class and was a member of our brigade's No. 5 production team. He had been arrested on August 24 and locked up in the production team's storehouse, but he'd squeezed out through the opening between the eaves and the walls and escaped that night. Zhu Liangrui was also a bamboo craftsman, and the two decided to go to Guangxi and make a living by their craft. After crossing the river, they fled to the home of Zhu Liangrui's aunt and stayed the night.

At that time, the killings hadn't started where Zhu Liangrui's aunt lived. But life was hard in that village, and our kinsmen lived hand to mouth, so early the next morning the two of them set off for Guangxi, only to be intercepted by militia interrogating people on the roads in Hongyan Commune. The militia asked what they were doing, and they said they were bamboo craftsmen on their way to Guangxi to ply their trade. But they weren't carrying travel certificates— which people had to get from the production brigade or commune or else be considered the remnants of capitalism—nor were they carrying tools, so this raised suspicion. My brother was a good talker and he said they'd left their tools and certificates in Guangxi and had just been back to hand over the proceeds of their sideline occupation to the production team. The militiamen were still skeptical of this explanation and took them to the commune's processing plant, where they gave each of them a bamboo knife and told them to split a stalk of bamboo. This was no problem for them, since it was how they made their living, and once it was clear that they were indeed craftsmen, they were released and told to go back to their production brigade to get travel certificates.

Having escaped with their lives, my brother and Zhu Liangrui didn't dare continue on to Guangxi, but they were even more afraid to return to the production brigade, so all they could do was turn around and follow the main road from Shouyan toward the county seat.

After they left, the Hongyan Commune militia was still uneasy and telephoned Gongba, and after learning that my brother and cousin were "escaped criminals," the militia chased after them. At that time, it took several attempts to put a telephone call through, so my brother and cousin had already gone a long way, and the militia didn't catch them. But my brother was unlucky; as they headed toward the county seat, the Red Alliance and Revolutionary Alliance were fighting each other, and the Red Alliance suffered a heavy defeat, so there were checkpoints on all the roads leading to the county seat to capture escaping black elements and Revolutionary Alliance spies. My brother and Zhu Liangrui had no way of knowing this and just bumbled their way through the devil's gate. When they reached the western gate of the county seat, they were tired and hungry. Alongside the bridge where the Lianxi and Tuo Rivers meet was an eatery selling noodles, so my brother and Zhu Liangrui went in for something to eat and drink. My brother sat with his back to the door, but Zhu Liangrui sat facing the door and was able to see armed militiamen approaching and questioning people. He quickly tried to signal my brother, but my brother had his head down drinking his noodle soup and didn't see it. Zhu Liangrui stood and walked into the kitchen, where a back door led to the riverbank, and he slipped out and ran along the river. My brother was caught by the militia, who called the production brigade to come and fetch him. On September 2, CCP secretary Jiang Huazong arrived with several militiamen to fetch my brother, and on the way back, as they crossed the Shuinan Pontoon Bridge, Jiang Huazong said, "Since we're just taking him back to be killed, we might as well send him to Paradise here." There in the middle of the bridge, they pushed my brother into the river.

Zhu Liangrui survived and is still living. After escaping out the back door of the eatery, he hid in the forestry bureau's pine oil cellar for seven days. After the county prohibited any more random killings, he went with some outlanders to Lingling and worked there as a bamboo craftsman, finally returning to his village a year or two later. By then, his grandfather, father, and uncle all had been drowned. His 18-year-old brother, Zhu Liangshan, escaped and headed toward an aunt's home in Xingqiao Commune but lost his way in the depths of night and was caught by the village militia at daybreak. The production brigade escort sent to bring him back chopped his head off on the way. They say the brigade had decided that whoever ran off would be executed where they were caught, and none would be spared.

Now I'll speak of my own narrow escape from death. After running off, that evening in the hills I ran into a young relative, Zhu Liangmou, who was accompanied by a class enemy offspring named He Dengyun who had escaped from Lianhua Village over by Baotajiao. The next night we encountered two more cousins from our brigade, Zhu Xianci and Zhu Xiankui, who were also class enemy offspring. When we spoke of the killings going on in the village, our legs turned to jelly. With nowhere to go, we joined up and fled together. Later we ran into Teacher Xu [Zhenzhong] from the Gongba brigade, a Rightist who had been sent to the countryside for labor reform.[8] We all were stupid peasants who had never left our village or seen the world, but Teacher Xu was older than us and had been a cadre outside, so we wanted to follow him, having a plan in mind. . . . But eventually militia searching the hills forced us to scatter.

On the fifth day, I remember running into Jiang Sanming, a rich-peasant offspring from our brigade. Several of us hid in the Liujia Hills at Jinjidong. We had no idea how hard it would be to stay in those hills. The mosquitoes were the least of it—the nights were freezing cold, and we had no blankets or anything to eat; if we hadn't been in fear for our lives, we would never have been able to tolerate it. At first we still had some solid food with us, but eventually we had to rely on wild fruit and sweet potatoes dug from the side of the hill in order to survive, while sleeping in a limekiln at night. We managed to stay in the hills for more than half a month. Finally it started raining, but we were lucky enough to find an empty shack that colliers had left behind after producing charcoal in the hills. During the day we split up to look for food, and then we would come back and spend the night there.

Jiang Sanming was more finicky than the rest of us; he couldn't take this hard living and felt it would be better to die at home, so one day he crept off and went back to the village. Most of the people in our brigade were surnamed Jiang or Zhu, and the Jiang surname was the most numerous and powerful, as a result of which more surnamed Zhu were killed. After Jiang Sanming secretly went home, his family advised him to "surrender and expiate his crime through meritorious service." Jiang Sanming was a real bastard—we'd all been through so much hardship together, and if you wanted to surrender, you didn't have to destroy us at the same time!

That night, I guess it was September 28, there was a rainstorm. When Jiang Sanming went down and didn't come back, we all worried that something had happened to him, never guessing that he'd inform on us. My cousin Zhu Xianci said, "We've been staying here too long—it's unsafe. We should find a new place." But it wasn't easy to find shelter in those hills, and we thought with it raining so hard, and so dark, who would come up into the hills? So we decided to look for a new place at dawn, right after the rain stopped. We never dreamed that as we slept, our brigade CCP secretary was leading dozens of militiamen through the rain with fowling guns, sabers, and spears. Afraid of giving themselves away, they hadn't brought dogs, just flashlights. But apparently we weren't destined to die, because my cousin Zhu Xiankui, getting up to relieve himself, discovered them and shouted, "The militia is here! Run!" As soon as we heard him shout, we woke up and ran out of the shed. Someone yelled, "Hand over your weapons and we won't shoot!" And then we heard the booming of fowling guns. I didn't think too much but just ran to a nearby path. I heard a booming sound behind me, and something hit me in the head and made me fall to the ground. I squeezed in among the bramble bushes along the path, and the militiamen following me jabbed their spears where they heard rustling, hitting me in the hand but nowhere more critical. I didn't even realize I was wounded at the time, not feeling any pain but only a burning in my arm and something flowing out of it. I just kept climbing deep into the brambles, and finally I got away.

Afterwards we learned that Zhu Xianci and He Dengyun were wounded and immobilized. Alarmed by the escape of the rest of us, the militia assembled and went back down the hill. The next day at dawn, they came back and trussed up Zhu Xianci and He Dengyun like a couple of wild boars, slung them onto two fowling guns, and carried them down the hill. By then, killing was no longer allowed, so both of them were taken back to their production brigades. Zhu Xianci starved to death in 1981. I don't know if He Dengyun is still alive.

I was seriously injured—I'd been shot in the left side of my head with a fowling piece, and the buckshot is still in there to this day. And I was jabbed with the spear here in my hand.

Zhu Xianhou took off his hat and had us rub his head, where we could feel little bumps from seven or eight pieces of buckshot under the skin. The scar on his left hand was still clearly perceptible after 19 years.

At sunrise, I came across Zhu Liangmou in the limekiln where we'd hidden before, and later I ran into Zhu Xiankui; both of them were fortunate enough to be uninjured. At this time we felt that staying together would be too dangerous, so we decided to split up. My fourth brother's wife's family lived in Congshanling Village over by the Shazi River, and they were poor peasants, so I thought I'd check out the situation there. Zhu Xiankui had no place to go, so I let him come with me. We arrived at Congshanling under cover of night. When my sister-in-law's elder brother and his wife saw the shape we were in, they were terrified. The brother didn't want us to stay, but his wife was kindhearted and said, "Where do you expect them to go at this time of night? Let them stay here tonight and leave tomorrow." She found a place for us to sleep in her firewood shed, wrapped my head in a kerchief, and cooked us some rice and a big bowl of taro. We hadn't eaten in a long time, and we wolfed the food down until we were too stuffed to breathe. After overeating like this, my stomach ached like mad, and I gripped it and groaned and panted all night long.

At dawn, the good woman came over and told us that the district and commune had handed down a prohibition against any more random killings; the 47th Army had arrived in the county to halt the killings, so we'd be better off going to the county seat and taking refuge there. That's how we ended up in Daojiang Town, and we told the 47th Army what was happening. They didn't seem very interested, but they did have a medic look at my wounds and apply ointment to them. By then there were a lot of people like us in Daojiang. A shed had been erected at the bus station, but we were too late to find a place there. I stayed for a while in a melon shack along the river next to the No. 2 Machine Factory, begging for food in town and sometimes lining up at the county PAFD headquarters for a meal. Fortunately I still had some money on me, and I was able to have my wounds treated in the town's clinic; otherwise, they might have become infected and gangrenous. I spent one month and three days this way, and then the county officials advised us to go back, guaranteeing that there would be no more random killings. Some who were craftsmen or had another trade were unwilling to go back and went off to other places to find work. I had no trade or skill to ply, and I was still thinking of my 70-year-old mother, so I agreed to return to my production team. When I got home I learned that everyone in my family had been killed and all our belongings had been taken away. But I didn't dare cry—I was afraid that someone might see me even if I shed a few tears quietly at home. The only good thing to come of it was that I had survived, so my family hadn't completely died out. All I could think was that if my mother hadn't urged me to escape, I would be dead like the rest of my family without even a proper burial.

Sometimes I get this stupid idea, wondering who was better off, those who died or people like me who survived. Those who died suffered much less hardship; by remaining alive, I've been tormented much more. Putting aside daily hardships, which I've been used to all my life, my health has suffered. Since being shot in the head, I often feel explosive pain. Sometimes it's so bad that I can't sleep all night, and when I do sleep I dream of my mother standing before me, covered in blood. . . . I wake with a start, my body covered in a cold sweat and my clothes soaked through. I've hardly had a decent night's sleep in all this time—those terrifying nightmares keep coming back.

Ai! Sometimes it's hard to keep on living.

14

Death before Marriage

Gongba Market is situated on the banks of the Paoshui (Gongba) River in the northeastern portion of Daoxian, about 20 kilometers from Daojiang and connected to it by a gravel road. The market itself is unimpressive and indistinguishable from other rural markets in the Hunan region, consisting of a main thoroughfare about half a kilometer long, lined with hundreds of houses and several open areas used for trading in pigs, plow oxen, and bulky agricultural byproducts. It's normally quite deserted, but on market day farmers arrive from all around, packing the market so densely that a person can hardly move through it. My deepest impression is of the old wooden bridge crossing the Paoshui River to Gongba Market, about 50 meters long and a meter wide and constructed entirely of wood. When I stood on that bridge and looked at the Paoshui River flowing beneath it and heard the pounding of footsteps on the bridge, it reminded me of blood surging through veins. Zhu Xianhou pointed to the bridge while telling us how his 70-year-old mother was thrown into the river below it.

In the Gongba production brigade, where this bridge was located, lived three girl cousins, all around 17 years old, named Tu Yuehua, Tu Meizhu, and Tu Qiulei. To these girls and their families, the Cultural Revolution was like a bus careening into them from behind as they walked along the road. Day after day, they went to the commune's fields for the "double rush" season, working themselves to exhaustion and drenched in sweat, with no time to do anything or think about anything but working, eating, and sleeping. They had no idea what was going on in Beijing, in the provincial capital of Changsha, or even elsewhere in Daoxian. All they knew was that if they didn't work, they wouldn't eat, and if they didn't work hard, they'd be criticized.

On the evening of August 24, 1967, the production brigade suddenly called a mass rally during which a dozen or so people were tied up, beaten, and denounced, and three "troublemakers and arch-criminals" were buried alive: a landlord in his 50s, a 17-year-old landlord offspring, and Huang Renfeng, the 43-year-old mother of Tu Meizhu, described as a "landlord's wife." Huang

Renfeng was seven or eight months pregnant at the time, and given that she herself was classified as a poor peasant, she dared to protest her treatment, as a result of which she was flogged. It is said that Huang Renfeng had not been on the production brigade's original killing list, but when her husband, Tu Hongchang, "fled to escape punishment," Huang Renfeng was forced to take his place.

We were unable to clarify the sequence of events that followed. Several other people had also been buried in the pit on August 24 but were then pulled out with ropes and "treated leniently." It could have been that the intention was to "kill one to warn a hundred" while obeying the upper-level directive to "kill one or two troublemakers." But then why, the next day, did the brigade suddenly hold a mass rally and kill 22 people at once, including those who had been shown "leniency" the day before? It remains a mystery. We asked a comrade from the Task Force about this, and he replied, "Many of those involved [in the killings] are dead now, and the others have put all the blame on them, saying that they said killing three was not enough and the revolution was not thorough enough, so more had to be killed. The dead can't speak, so we haven't been able to determine the truth."

The next day, August 25, was market day, and the brigade's leaders rushed to take advantage of this time when so many people were in one place to hold a rally to pronounce the judgment of the peasant supreme court. The brigade's black elements and offspring, young and old, including Tu Hongchang's eldest brother, Tu Hongguang, were bound up and brought forward, and after the death sentences were pronounced, the condemned were dragged to two empty sweet-potato cellars next to the market for execution. Because so many were "dumped in the cellar" that day, the brigade didn't use the live burial method of the day before but instead stabbed the victims before tossing them in and covering them with earth, with the production brigade leaders offering a reward to the person who killed the most.

After doing away with these 22 people, the brigade penned up more than 40 surviving women and children like livestock in the storeroom of the commune's supply and marketing cooperative to await an order from the peasant supreme court to take them to the killing ground. That order for the class enemy to be "obliterated root and branch" was finally delivered at noon on August 27. The condemned were escorted to the execution ground, with no one weeping or crying out. One little boy was bound so tightly that he had to hop along until his pants fell off, and even then he said nothing.

At that point, a district leader who was passing by and saw so many women and children in the group asked what was going on. The escorting militiamen said these were "landlord whelps" being taken for "root and branch extermination." The leader said, "The big tigers deserve to be killed for their crimes, but there's no need to kill children. If you insist on killing them, you need to wait for a central directive." The Task Force's subsequent inquiries determined that this leader was Ou Rifu, the head of Gongba District. Ou Rifu was one of the main people responsible for the killings in Gongba District, and he personally directed mass killings in Caoyutang, Xiaojia, and other production brigades. Ironically, his brief words were sufficient to save dozens of women and children in the Gongba brigade, including the three Tu cousins. It seemed that the Buddha preserved them.

The brigade's cadres discussed the matter and felt that the upper-level leader was truly taking the higher road and the longer view; since maggots could hardly overturn a millstone, the tiger cubs could be spared and reformed. In any case, the cadres held all the power, and dictatorship could still be imposed if the class enemy attempted an overthrow later. Besides that, it seemed a waste to kill so many women when many class brothers lacked wives; even some production team cadres were still unmarried. The group was therefore escorted back to the production brigade. Their parents were dead and their homes and belongings had been seized, but one house was set aside for the Tu cousins and several younger girls. By then the brigade Chinese Communist Party (CCP) branch had already begun considering how to "change their classes," and the brigade's poor-peasant association (PPA) chairman handed down an order assigning each of the three cousins to one of the brigade's bachelors. One of the men was mentally handicapped, and the other two were irredeemably shabby. The PPA saw this as the best outcome for the girls, whose daily needs would be met and who would gain a new lease on life through their change in class status. Yet much to everyone's surprise, all three refused to marry. The representative of the brigade's peasant supreme court was enraged: "If you don't marry them, we'll kill you!" The girls replied in a chorus: "We'd rather die!"

Perhaps those who have circled the gate of hell gain a clearer perspective on life and death, and their fear of death is no longer so intense. The girls probably thought: if our parents have died, why shouldn't we die as well?

Seeing how the landlord whelps remained entrenched in their reactionary standpoints and refused to reform their thinking, the PPA was enraged; if they'd known the girls would be so stubborn, they would never have let them off. Now the upper level had handed down a prohibition against random killings, and besides that, if the girls were killed, the three class brothers would still be left without wives. So the girls were bound up, beaten, and subjected to public denunciation. Incredibly, all three still refused to give in.

Since the stick hadn't worked, the carrot was plied, and someone was sent to carry out ideological work on the girls: "A girl is born to belong to another. Whoever heard of a woman not marrying? If you marry, you'll never have to worry about having enough to eat, and with your class status changed to poor peasant, how much better your life will be!" But the three girls stuck to their own rationale: if marrying these men was such a great idea, why didn't anyone else want them? They didn't dare say this out loud, of course.

Finally Tu Yuehua and Tu Qiulei managed to escape, but Tu Meizhu was left behind with the three younger girls to accept her fate.

Tu Meizhu may have been surprised to learn that while she looked down on her prospective husband for gambling, gluttony, laziness, and stupidity, she was deplored as politically undesirable and as a taint on three generations of poor-peasant purity; the soldier brother of the man to whom Tu Meizhu had been promised wrote a letter objecting that Meizhu's class status would harm his career prospects, and his firm rejection put an end to the match.

Nevertheless, one can only imagine how hard it must have been for a 17- or 18-year-old girl to support herself and three children. She finally married a youth from a poor peasant family in Dongmen Commune's Shuinan production brigade, whose poverty had prevented him from finding a wife, and who was willing to raise the three girls as well.

I can't help feeling a deep admiration for these three cousins. Although having no real education, given the choice between death and dignity, they chose the latter (how costly a luxury is dignity!) and became a thread of light in the depths of darkness. Because of them, when we look back at these days of insanity and bloodshed, we aren't rendered speechless with shame but have the courage to continue on as decent human beings.

Years later, while carrying out supplementary interviews regarding the Daoxian massacre, I met Tu Meizhu once more. By then she was in her 50s, and the hardships of the intervening years had etched her face like a knife. The only consolation was that as her living environment gradually improved, she had emerged from the deep shadows of her family's destruction and had gradually regained her human dignity. She still worked from dawn to dusk to improve her life, little by little. I spent a morning conversing with her.

This wasn't a formal interview, because that wasn't part of my plan for this particular visit. I had originally come because some of Daoxian's oldest survivors had begun expressing a willingness to talk. The passage of time makes individual suffering recede into the background, but surprisingly, as society began reconsidering the Daoxian killings, some people who had previously refused to speak of the tragedy now felt they couldn't take what they knew to their cremation urns but should share their experience for the sake of their grandchildren's generation. When I returned to the guest house to put my notes in order after interviewing some of these people, I became lost in thought again. Our interviews regarding the massacre, especially those conversations carried out in 1986, had been limited by time, opportunity, and our own mental conceptions to focusing on incidents and processes while neglecting the conditions and environment both of victims and killers. In a sense, we'd missed the essential part. I became convinced that the story of how Tu Meizhu's family was "revolutionized" provides an important reference both for officials and researchers, and with Tu Meizhu's cooperation, I present it here.

The Tu family was not originally from the Gongba brigade, but rather from the Shangyunba brigade (village). Tu Meizhu said, "The destruction of our family has to be traced back to my grandfather. If he had been a gluttonous idler, we would have been classified as poor peasants during Land Reform. Then during the Cultural Revolution, even if we hadn't killed others, at least we wouldn't have been killed ourselves."

So what kind of person was Tu Meizhu's grandfather? Simply put, he was a skilled stonemason. Stonemason Tu was born to an average peasant family in Shangyunba Village, and his parents left only two things to him: an intelligent mind and a robust physique. Of course they also had him learn a skill, but that was secondary: Tu would have excelled at whatever occupation he put his hand to. One year, when Daojiang was repairing its dockyard, Stonemason Tu was lucky enough to do the stonemasonry work and make some money. As it happened, there was a drought the next year, and with land selling cheaply, Tu took advantage of the hardship of others to buy some land, establishing himself as a small landlord.

Throughout his life, Stonemason Tu had a number of disagreeable qualities: first, whenever he saw a rich or powerful person, he would bow and scrape. Second, when he saw a poor person, especially a gambler or loafer, he would roll his eyes in disgust. Third, he was a miserly man who never spent a penny more than necessary on anything, and if he had 90 cents, he'd find a way to borrow another 10 cents and buy land. Fourth, he was a hard-hearted man, feeding his children nothing but congee three meals a day. If a son went out to work for someone else, he'd chase after him shouting: "Don't get fat! If you come back with a big belly, you won't be fed at home!" Tu Meizhu's father had acquired the nickname "Scar" from an overturned caldron of congee that scalded his leg as a child.

Stonemason Tu's wife was of a similar character, and apart from laboring from morning to night, she was always conniving to increase the family's fortune. If anything, her faults were more egregious than her husband's. Anyone who dared to steal a melon from their garden or pluck a leaf from their tea plants would be treated to a harangue of such deafening volume that half the village would know of it.

Envious of other families with a smattering of learning, Stonemason Tu after long consideration finally decided to send his second son, Tu Hongsheng, off to school. (Looking back, this may have been the one correct decision Stonemason Tu ever made in his life. Although this modest schooling brought Tu Hongsheng unending tribulations, it allowed him to avoid the slaughter that struck his village during the Cultural Revolution.)

The Land Reform movement began in Daoxian in 1951. On the eve of the campaign, Stonemason Tu's family resources were roughly as follows: 50 *mu* of land, a large tile-roofed house, hillside land for gathering firewood, five sons (the fourth of whom had left the village to seek his living prior to Liberation, and no one knew what had become of him), four daughters-in-law, and a number of grandchildren, bringing the number of family members to more than 20. His children all worked, and Tu also had long-term hired hands. The upshot was that during Land Reform, Stonemason Tu was "suppressed" (i.e., killed) as a despotic landlord.

Tu Meizhu observed: "My grandfather wasn't very good with people. He was mean to his family but treated outsiders pretty well. When my parents were still alive, I remember them saying that they never ate anything but congee, but my grandfather's long-termed hired hands were given proper rice to eat. If you don't feed people decently, they won't work well for you, but you can begrudge your own family members a cup of cold water. My grandfather's household had 50 *mu* of land at that time, which qualified him as a landlord. But at that time there were more than 20 of us, so that meant only around 2 *mu* of land per person, which was the standard for a middle peasant. After Land Reform, the poor peasants in our township were allotted 2 *mu* of land per person, which was about the same as what our family had before Land Reform. . . . It would be unreasonable to say that my grandfather acquired his property through exploitation, but even if you have to confiscate it, you don't have to kill for it, and if you insist on killing, even in the Old Society, only the exploiter himself was killed without pulling the rest of his family down with him. All my life I've relied on the labor of my two hands to support myself, and, if anything, I've been undercompensated, not overcompensated, for my work. Why should I be designated a member of the exploiting class? Back then, even a three-year-old child would curse you as an evildoer, but my parents and I, and my uncles and aunts who were killed, never did anything bad. . . . In the Old Society, people were allowed to have a little extra."

After land reform, the Tu brothers split up into individual households and began to lead separate lives. Luckily, they were used to hard living, and now they could even eat a little rice instead of congee three meals a day. In 1954, the Tu brothers sold off the house in Shangyunba and moved to Gongba Market to make a living from small businesses. At that time, Gongba Market consisted of nothing but a gravel road and a hundred-odd wooden, brick, and thatched houses. Because the Tu brothers were shrewd and capable, they quickly established themselves at Gongba Market. Perhaps they believed that by leaving their old village and no longer engaging in farming, they could permanently cast off their landlord status. They didn't realize that this cap was virtually imbedded in their heads, and that it would accompany them to even the remotest corner of the country. When the People's Commune movement began in 1958, small tradesmen and craftsmen such as carpenters and blacksmiths all were made part of large collectives, and the Tu brothers became members of the Gongba production brigade of the Weixing (Satellite) People's Commune, which was later renamed Gongba Commune. Eldest son Tu Hongguang and third son Tu Hongchang, who had shops in Gongba Market, were kept on to work in the commune's supply-and-marketing cooperative. They made decent enough livings, what locally would be considered middle-class standard or above.

Old Mother Tu had it the hardest, now dependent on her children and subjected to the temper of her daughter-in-law, who would be scolded at work and then come home and vent at her mother-in-law for not knowing how to eat and dress decently but instead buying land that only harmed her progeny. Aware of how she had gone wrong, the old woman just shrank silently into herself. When the Three Years of Hardship came, her children didn't have enough to eat themselves, much less to properly look after her needs. Old Mother Tu contracted edema, and after subsisting on chaff and pomegranate leaves she finally died of a bowel obstruction.

The educated second brother, Tu Hongsheng, had once served as a low-level officer in the Kuomintang army, so he was designated a pre-Liberation counter-revolutionary in 1953 and sentenced to 10 years of labor reform in Hengyang. After being released and returning home in 1962, he was much worse off than his brothers. Although clever and able, he had a weak constitution, having studied in his youth and then undergone labor reform, so he had difficulty with farming work. Fortunately, Stonemason Tu had arranged for him to marry a sturdy woman, who while lacking physical allure was a better worker than most men. Back then, quite a few people were eager to marry into the Tu family, and Stonemason Tu had only one standard for selecting a daughter-in-law: looks didn't matter, but anyone who wanted to marry one of his sons had to know how to sift rice, brew liquor, and pickle vegetables, and in particular had to be strong enough to lift the household's heavy caldron. Tu Hongsheng's wife, Qin Ji'e, met all these conditions, and while originally less than happy with his parents' choice, Tu Hongsheng now appreciated his wife's virtues; without her, the family would have been finished, and he would have starved to death.

Having taken up farming in midlife, Tu Hongsheng was not as competent as his brothers, and while plowing one day in 1963, he accidently struck a poor-peasant commune member on the forehead with his whip. Tu immediately begged for forgiveness, and since it had been an accident and no serious injury was caused, the peasant didn't blame him, and the matter should have ended there. But that evening, when work points were recorded, the public-security head made Tu go up on the podium, where he was surrounded by seven or eight others and beaten with carrying poles until he coughed blood and passed out. Watching from below, his brothers were struck dumb with fear and just bowed their heads without saying a word. After the meeting was adjourned, they carried the half-dead Tu Hongsheng home on a door plank and then furtively took him to Gongba Market for medical treatment the next day. After examining Tu Hongsheng's injuries, the doctor said, "You're too badly injured to treat here. You need to be taken to the city. I'll write you a prescription first. Go home and take the medicine and then get to the city hospital as quickly as possible; otherwise, even if you live you'll be crippled for life." After returning home and recuperating for a time, Tu Hongshen said to Qin Ji'e: "I'm neither dead nor alive and can't go on this way. I want to go to the city for treatment. . . . If I get better, I'll come back, and if I don't, I'll die there and you should just forget me." When Qin Ji'e heard this, she began weeping, but, unable to think of any alternative, she could only agree and told their son to go with Tu and look after him on the way. Tu packed a small toolbox (he was skilled in fixing clocks and watches, radios, and fountain pens) and set off secretly with his nine-year-old son.

A few years later the Cultural Revolution broke out, and the killing wind began blowing through Daoxian. Here I'll hand the story over to Tu Meizhu:

> When the killing began, it was during the double-rush season, and we went out with the production team every day for work, having no inkling what was going on. One day, the production brigade called my mom and dad in for a meeting. My father wasn't at home, and my mother, who was seven or eight months pregnant, went to the meeting with her big belly. I stayed home with my two younger sisters waiting for them to come back. I waited until late at night and still they didn't return. I was worried and went to my second uncle's home to ask what was going on. As soon as I opened the door, I saw my aunt [Qin Ji'e] sprawled out on her bed, covered with sweat, her arms swollen this big [while saying this, Tu Meizhu used her hands to show the size of a large bowl] and covered with blood. I was shocked and asked what had happened. They quickly waved at me to be quiet, or everyone in the house would be killed. That was when I learned that my mother had been buried alive in the pit. Apart from my mother, they'd also buried a class enemy offspring the same age as I, 17 years old, who had been my classmate in school. They said he was a troublemaker who didn't submit to remolding. They had tied up my aunt so tightly that they'd broken her arms, because they said she had special kung fu skills that could break rope, and they'd broken my uncle Tu De's leg with a hoe. They would have been buried alive as well, but when asked if they admitted their crimes, they said they did, and when asked if they would behave, they said they would, so they were pulled out of the pit with ropes as a show of leniency.

At the time, I was too terrified to grieve. I ran home and told my youngest sister to tell my maternal uncle to come for us, because they were poor peasants. My uncle came over early the next morning, but he didn't dare enter our home and arranged to meet me in the tea grove out back. All my uncle could do was tell me to look after our home and be careful, and then nothing would happen to me. At that time I didn't know what had happened to my father, and only later learned that he had gotten word of what was happening and had run off during the night. I heard that after running away, my father was found by militia patrolling in Yao Mountain over by Hongtangying, and that they'd hacked him to death and left his body there in the wilderness. To this day I don't know exactly where he died.

The next day, the people who hadn't been killed the day before were captured again and killed, including my younger uncle and his wife and my elder uncle. Then they rounded up all of us class enemies and offspring, regardless of age or sex, tied us up, and locked us in the supply-and-marketing cooperative storehouse, dozens of us, old and young. . . . They finally decided to throw all of us into the pit. By then I was numb, feeling neither sadness nor fear; my mind was blank, and I just did whatever they told us to do. But fate was on our side, and as they dragged us out to be killed, a district cadre came along, and when he saw us he said, "Big tigers deserve to die for their crimes, but killing children is inconsistent with party policy." So for the time being they spared us 30-odd children and girls, while the older boys were still taken to the pit and killed like my mother. There were 20 to 30 people killed that way. Their bones and my mother's are still in that pit.

My parents and the males in my uncles' families all were killed. All that was left was my second uncle [Tu Hongsheng], who along with my cousin was spared because they'd gone to the city to get treatment for my uncle, and now they were working in Xinjiang. In 1982, my uncle was given a notice of rehabilitation and returned to Daoxian, but the production brigade still wanted to arrest him, so he ran back to Xinjiang and never returned.

After my parents were killed, the production brigade's Supreme People's Court of the Poor and Lower-Middle Peasants carried out a second "Land Reform" and confiscated my family's house, livestock, farming tools, food, and clothing. They left just one house for our families, and my cousins and I and my sisters lived there together. I was 17 years old at the time, and my sisters were 11, 8, and 4. We lived wretchedly, cold, hungry, and worse off than dogs or pigs. In September, the so-called judicial leaders, including public-security head Zhu Xianru, Li

Debing, and others, came and "arranged marriages" for us. I was to become the wife of a simpleton. I firmly refused, and as a result I was beaten on the spot and then denounced in large and small meetings and rallies, being paraded in the street and thoroughly humiliated until I was half dead. We couldn't even shed tears quietly at home, because there were always some ne'er-do-wells crowding around our doorway and teasing and insulting us. Several times I considered suicide, but when I looked at my little sisters, I knew I couldn't die. What would become of them? I later heard that in the county town there was an army called the 47th Army that could save us, and I thought that if we stayed at home, we would just starve to death, so it would be better to risk our lives trying to get to the county town for help.

One night, I took my three sisters and ran off in the direction of the county town. All my sisters were young, so we didn't get far before stopping to sleep under the eaves of a house along the way. When dawn broke, an old woman woke us up and said she was the mistress of the house. She asked where we were from and where we were going. Seeing that the old woman had a kindly face like my mother's, I tearfully told her of my family's tragic situation. The old woman said, "The 47th Army won't be able to help you. A lot of class enemies are already in the county town begging for food, and how can you manage there, a young girl looking after three children? I'll tell you where to go, and you can decide whether to go there." She told me about a young man in their village named He Weishun and suggested I marry him. She took me to He Weishun's home to meet him, and I saw that although the family was very poor and the elderly father was paralyzed in bed, He Weishun was a good man and not bad looking. If his circumstance had been better, he wouldn't have wanted to marry me, either. He Weishun, who is now my husband, agreed to raise my three sisters as well. I had no other options at the time, and for the sake of my young sisters and for my own stability, I agreed to marry him. My husband had been secretary of the Shuinan production brigade's Youth League branch, but because he married me, he was considered to have lost his class standpoint, and he was dismissed from his position.

In May 1968, I summoned up the nerve to visit my old home in Gongba with my husband. All that was left was four walls packed with pig manure. The head of our production team, Tang Huatong, had taken possession of our home, removed the partitions, and converted it into a pigsty.

PART FIVE

QINGXI DISTRICT'S
PAFD COMMANDER

15

High-Level Participation in Qingxi District

Qingxi District (Map 7) lies in Daoxian's eastern region, straddling the Xiaoshui and Lingshui (Ningyuan) Rivers. Here the famous Bajieda Mountains cross into Daoxian from Ningyuan and stretch southward, forming the eastern fringe of the Daozhou basin. The Xiaoshui River passes through the district's Dongmen, Qingxi, and Qingkou Communes to flow into Shuangpai County's Zijin (Purple) Mountain. The Lingshui River, originating in Ningyuan County's Jiuyi Mountain, pierces the Bajieda Mountains to enter Daoxian then follows the foothills of the Bajieda Mountains northward until it converges with two tributaries from Ningyuan and turns west to empty into the Xiaoshui (Shuangpai Reservoir) at Wujiatan. During the Cultural Revolution, this district was a major disaster area in terms of killings, with 617 fatalities (including 51 suicides)[1] and 24 households completely obliterated.

Understanding how the killings began and progressed in Qingxi District starts with the district's People's Armed Forces Department (PAFD) commander, Jiang Youyuan. Jiang was a straight-laced person with an explosive temper; unlike Zhong Changyou, a born political commissar, Jiang was born for battle. As the saying goes, there are no weak soldiers under a strong general; under Jiang Youyuan, the Qingxi People's Militia Self-Defense Corps made its presence felt wherever it went.

As a district PAFD leader, Jiang Youyuan was obliged to make frequent trips to Yingjiang, but he kept the district's leaders apprised of developments elsewhere in the county and closely monitored local operations, which he entrusted to district secretary Zuo Changyun and public-security deputy Nie Gaochun.

Qingkou Commune took the lead in the district's killings after commune PAFD commander Li Jingxue returned from accompanying Jiang Youyuan to the August 15 PAFD cadre meeting on August 15. At a "five chiefs" meeting back at the commune on August 17, Li exaggerated the "enemy situation" and instigated killings. After Jiang Youyun expressed his enthusiastic approval of the

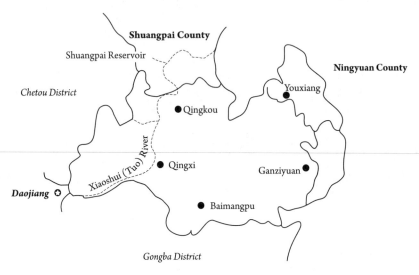

Map 7 Communes of Qingxi District

killings, Zuo Changyun telephoned the Qingxi, Qingkou, Ganziyuan, Youxiang, and Baimangpu Communes to transmit Commander Jiang's instructions to "do away with one or two troublemakers" and to notify the main leaders of each commune to attend a meeting for administrative cadres at the district headquarters on August 23.

Killing proceeded apace. Meanwhile, Jiang Youyuan acted with his usual speed and resolve to assemble the People's Militia that same day, and on the evening of August 23 he led the militia to Pingtang to block off the Lingdao Highway in preparation for an attack on the No. 2 High School. However, since the Gongba District militia didn't arrive in time, the attack on the Revolutionary Alliance headquarters was temporarily postponed. Qingxi District held its second killing-mobilization meeting that same day, and in short order a total of six people were killed in Qingkou and Baimangpu Communes. The other communes were somewhat slower to act but commenced their killings from August 25 onward.

The various levels of meetings and orchestration of killings in Qingxi District were virtually identical to the process in Qingtang and Gongba Districts. What made Qingxi distinctive was the active participation of Jiang Youyuan, the only district PAFD commander on the frontline of Daoxian's Cultural Revolution killings; all the others kept a discreet distance. Jiang Youyuan had his own take on this phenomenon: "I'm one of those ramrod-straight people. During the destructiveness of the Cultural Revolution, I was the tiger that didn't kill but looked the part. I wasn't like some people who hid themselves in the background concocting evil schemes and using me as their hatchet man."

So how was this hatchet man put to use?

After the attack on the No. 2 High School was postponed, District 1 PAFD commander Liu Houshan came to borrow guns from Jiang, because District 1 (Shangguan) had decided to hold a killing rally at Longjiangqiao on August 24 to execute a miscreant (six actually ended up being killed).[2] Fearing attempted sabotage by the Revolutionary Alliance, District 1 requested the support of the Qingxi militia.

Jiang Youyuan said, "It's no problem to send you men and guns, but we're short on bullets."

Liu Houshan said, "Leave the ammunition to me. Just make sure your troops turn up."

Jiang Youyuan was a dependable man, and whatever he promised he would do in spades. Early the next morning, he brought a dozen or so guns to Longjiangqiao, handed them over, and without even waiting for a thank you from Liu Houshan, he led his men back to the district militia headquarters at Baimadu.[3]

When the Qingxi militiamen set up their sentry points around three o'clock the next day, August 25, they looked across the river and saw Dongmen Commune's Gaoche brigade leading a group of class enemies to be drowned. Among the condemned was a class enemy offspring named Liang Xianyu, who suddenly jumped into the river and began swimming away. The Gaoche militiamen ran along the river hollering and chasing him. Watching from the other bank, the Qingxi militiamen joined in the chase. Militia platoon leader Li Xiancai raised his rifle, aimed it at the swimming "fugitive," and fired two shots, which missed their mark. An enraged Jiang Youyuan berated Li Xiancai: "You're going to pay for those two bullets you just wasted! And you claim to be a military veteran and a sharpshooter!" He went on and on until Li Xiancai blanched with shame.

I can't help but feel sorry for Liang Xianyu. He might have made a miraculous escape if he hadn't been unfortunate enough to encounter the Qingxi People's Militia Self-Defense Corps. During the Daoxian killings, most drownings were carried out by tying the victim's hands behind his back and then tying a large rock to him, or hanging a basket full of pebbles around his neck, and then throwing him into the river. Somehow Liang Xianyu had freed himself of this weight and had followed the current quite a distance downriver by the time the militiamen raised the alarm. When Li Xiancai fired his two errant shots, the cunning Liang Xianyu pretended to be hit and ducked under the water, emerging again a good 50 meters downstream.

Although still within shooting range of a rifle, Liang was far outside the range of a fowling piece, and with rifle bullets too precious to waste, the militiamen and cadres could only yell and chase after him along the river. After he'd swum for about a kilometer, an abandoned dam appeared before him, with two rows of fragmented wood posts protruding from the surface of the water. If Liang Xianyu could have beaten the militiamen to the dam, he might have survived. But a person can't swim as fast as someone can run, and the militiamen chasing along the riverbank arrived at the dam before Liang Xianyu.

When Liang Xianyu saw the militiamen blocking his way at the ruined dam, he began swimming toward the western side of the river, but militiamen were waiting there with fowling guns and sabers, and when he turned east he saw more of the same. By now the militiamen on the riverbanks were no longer worried, and they walked casually back and forth along the riverbank, watching their quarry's futile efforts. Exhausted and hopeless, Liang Xianyu let the current carry him to the base of the ruined dam and then struggled up the sloping embankment. A dozen fowling guns loaded with buckshot fired at once, and Liang Xianyu's body fell backward into the water, blood fanning out into the rushing current but soon swallowed up by the white spray.

On that same day, the Baimadu brigade decided to kill five miscreants (three class enemies and two poor peasants). Brigade CCP secretary Huang Mingyou (a delegate to the CCP's 10th Party Congress) sent public-security chief Zhu Rong'en to the Baimadu militia headquarters to request instructions from Jiang Youyuan. Jiang said, "If the masses say to kill them, then do it." Once granted permission, the Baimadu brigade arrested its targets that night; two had gotten wind of their intentions and fled, but the other three were captured and drowned on the 27th. In order to show his full support for the "revolutionary action of the poor and lower-middle peasants," Jiang Youyuan personally supervised the killings.

Later on August 27, Jiang Youyuan led more than 40 Qingxi militiamen to Youxiang Commune, and when cadres from the Youxiang brigade requested instructions, Jiang replied, "Go ahead and kill one or two black elements."

The next day, Jiang Youyuan presented a report at a meeting of production brigade cadres at Youxiang Commune. He first emphasized the "impurity" of the Revolutionary Alliance: "Of its nine leaders, seven have bad class backgrounds, and 70 percent of its armed personnel are black elements or their offspring. On August 8, they snatched the PAFD's guns for a counterrevolutionary coup d'état. If we let their scheme prevail, we poor and lower-middle peasants will suffer again under the revival of capitalism. They'll be just like the Kuomintang, coming down to steal our money and grain, killing our pigs, and committing various other evil acts." On the killing of class enemies, he said, "The killing of a few class enemies by poor peasants is a revolutionary act. When the Revolutionary Bandits object, it shows that they're breathing from the same nostrils as the class enemies. . . . Well-behaved black elements don't need to be killed, but it's all right to kill one or two troublemakers." He then told each production brigade to come up with a killing list.

This meeting was followed by a new upsurge in killings at Youxiang Commune, and the "killing sputnik" launched at the Yuejin (Great Leap) brigade was a direct result of this meeting.

The Great Leap brigade's killing sputnik

The Yuejin brigade recorded the largest number of killings of any brigade in Daoxian, largely due to the hands-on efforts of the brigade's CCP secretary, He Fangqian. Since the Yuejin brigade was a focal point of our reporting, we were able to gain an in-depth understanding of He Fanqian and the way he worked.

In Daoxian, there was no tradition of men helping their wives around the house, but He Fangqian was different; while CCP secretary of the Yuejin production brigade, he also managed things at home, which to him meant fetching the water, lighting the fire, and looking after the kids. Every woman in the village was green with envy, saying He's wife must have been outstandingly virtuous in her previous life to get such a good husband in this life.

The truth was that He Fangqian wanted to see things done right, even if it meant doing it himself. And as leader of a production brigade with such a revolutionary name, he felt all the more compelled to ensure that the brigade stood out.

After attending a meeting at Youxiang Commune on August 25, where public-security deputy Li Benyue reported on the "critical" class struggle situation, He Fangqian, deputy CCP secretary Zuo Longjiao, poor-peasant association (PPA) chairman He Juming, and other brigade cadres called a cadre meeting at the production brigade. Zuo Longjiao said, "Our production brigade has two scoundrels who are particularly unruly. One is the bad element Zuo Yongxiang, who's been attending clandestine meetings of class enemies, killing pigs, and drinking blood liquor.[4] The other is the landlord [offspring] Zuo Changyun,[5] who's preparing to assist a counterattack against the mainland by Chiang Kai-shek.[6] We need to impose dictatorship on these two and puncture the arrogant bluster of the black elements."

Zuo's words fired up the other cadres, who unanimously agreed to impose dictatorship, and when He Fangqiang telephoned the commune to report the brigade's decision, Li Benyue responded, "Excellent! The masses have been mobilized! Proceed with the killings."

The next morning (August 26), following a mass rally at the Youxiang High School, Zuo Yongxiang and Zuo Changyun were shot with fowling guns and dumped into the river, and 14 more black elements were locked up in the villages of Zhouzishang and Wulidong under the close watch of the militia.

That same morning, He Fangqian attended a cadre meeting during which district PAFD commander Jiang Youyuan delivered the "keynote speech," and Li Benyue said that given the serious situation of class struggle throughout the county, he was astonished to see Youxiang Commune so far behind, and his own Yuejin brigade behind the rest of the commune. He Fangqian was horrified. Although physically unprepossessing, he'd always held up his end of the work, and the criticism from the commune's leader made him break out in a cold sweat. As He Fangqian and the other brigade cadres walked home from the meeting, they reached an agreement to go all out to make up for lost time.

After dinner and a cursory washing, He Fangqian rushed off to another meeting. By the time He arrived, the grain-drying yard of the Wusheng production team was foggy with mosquito-repelling smoke and crowded with cadres, CCP, and Youth League members and activist poor and lower-middle peasants. He Fangqian hurried in to take his seat and instructed the militia guards to enhance their vigilance. Taking roll call, He Fangqian found that several people from distant Wulidong had yet to arrive, but when he saw their torchlights approaching, he relaxed enough to accept a proffered pipe.

Once everyone had arrived and the "Long live!" salute and Mao quotes were dealt with, He Fangqian reported, "I have good news for you all: at today's commune meeting, Director Li praised our brigade's elevated awareness and quick action. . . . Director Li said that by doing away with the arch-criminals Yongxiang and Changyun, we resolutely attacked the aggression of the class enemy. But we can't rest on our laurels. A lot of production brigades have surpassed us at this point, and we haven't taken any action since the 25th. Commander Li says that as an advanced brigade, we can't fall behind the others, and he wants us to decide what other troublemakers we can do away with."

After some discussion, it was agreed to kill all of the brigade's black elements, including the elderly and children. But when it came to drawing up a name list, a silence fell over the meeting; everyone bowed their heads, the scarlet embers glowing in their pipes like fireflies along a riverbank and imprinting the image of those honest and conflicted faces on the curtain of night. They all worked and lived together; of course there had been arguments and conflicts, but to kill off entire families for no reason was still a dreadful prospect. In this production brigade, most of the residents of Zhouzishang Village were surnamed He, while most in Wulidong were surnamed Zuo, and it had not escaped the attention of the Zuos that the previous killings had involved two with their surname. Was it really possible that all the bad eggs were Zuos and none were Hes?

When He Fangqian saw that no one was speaking up, he felt obliged to start things off by providing some names from his own production team. At that moment, all eyes were fastened on Wulidong, and a competition arose to see who could be most revolutionary. Finally all the black-element households were listed, totaling 61 people. When He Fangqian saw the name list, he became worried: "What are we going to do with so many people?"

It was finally decided that three pits near the Shitoushan Reservoir would suit the purpose, and that a judgment rally would be held there the next day. The roundup began at dawn the next morning, August 27, with the sounding of gongs at both villages.

Before moving forward, He Fangqian took the precaution of reporting to the commune's deputy CCP secretary, Bai Chengguang, who said, "This is a mass movement—of course you have to do whatever the poor and lower-middle peasants demand. But you should still request instructions from the two commanders [public security and PAFD] to see what they say."

He Fangqian quickly telephoned the commune, but PAFD commander He Wenzhi[7] was not there, and the person answering the phone was the commune's Cultural Revolution Committee (CRC) chairman, Zheng Laixi. After hearing of the brigade's plans, Zheng yelped, "Good job! That's a lot!" He Fangqian asked Zheng to also report the brigade's actions to public-security head Li Benyue as soon as possible.

By then, the brigade's black elements and offspring had been gathered up and bound. They included 10 class enemies and 51 offspring, 33 of whom were minors. At a little after nine o'clock in the morning, He Fangqian led the group escorting the 61.5 targets (one was a pregnant woman, and her fetus counted as half a person) in a grand procession to the Shitoushan Reservoir. When too elderly black elements slowed down the proceedings, CCP secretary He gave the militia permission to shoot them when they reached the Hejia River. This immediately sped up the procession as the terrified victims bolted toward their doom.

When the group reached the pits, the brigade's PPA chairman represented the peasant supreme court in handing down the death sentences, and the brigade accountant called each name in turn, after which the victims were pushed one by one into the pits. Burning rice straw was then tossed into the pits, and finally the victims were covered with dirt.

Counting the two killed on the 26th, the brigade killed a total of 63.5 people, half of the 128 people killed in Youxiang Commune during the killing wind. This campaign eliminated virtually all the "class enemies" in the Yuejin brigade; one class enemy managed to escape, and one young female landlord, who was in fact a poor peasant married to a landlord, was granted a way out through remarriage.

Looking at the fresh earth tamped down into the pits, the meticulous He Fangqian was still uneasy, and he and deputy CCP secretary Zuo Longjiao sat and smoked while they talked it over: was this thin layer of soil enough to cover so many people? What if someone wasn't dead and managed to dig his way out? They decided to take the extra precaution of posting militiamen to watch the pits overnight.

Campfire flames flickered, and the stars out in the wilderness were especially dazzling. Fish leaped playfully from the reservoir, their splashes startling the watchmen and making their hearts thunder. One militiaman with a middle-school education suddenly felt stirred to hum a song: "Raise your heads toward the Big Dipper, think of Mao Zedong, think of Mao Zedong. . . ."

Afterwards, He Fangqian bragged to everyone, "I killed until I was completely covered with blood!" This blood-soaked man was later promoted to commune CCP secretary.

Killings approved by the county organization department head

Another high-level leader involved in the killings in Qingxi District was Wang Ansheng, who at the time was director of the organization department of the county CCP committee. During the early stage of the Cultural Revolution, Wang came under attack for executing a "bourgeois reactionary line," and following the "January Tempest" of 1967, Wang was one of those hung out to dry as part of Daoxian's "erring ruling clique." Following the August 8 gun-snatching incident and the Red Alliance's withdrawal to Yingjiang, some leading cadres under the control (or "protection") of the Red Alliance were dispersed to various villages throughout the countryside. Wang Ansheng was one of those cadres, and he ended up at the Tuanjie brigade of Qingxi District's Qingkou Commune.

Wang Ansheng had been assigned to the Tuanjie brigade during the Socialist Education movement, so he and the local cadres and villagers were very familiar with each other. During an exceptional period such as the Cultural Revolution, finding this kind of port in the storm was immensely consoling, and while Wang arrived in Qingkou at a much lower status than on the previous occasion, the local cadres and villagers still regarded him as a paternalistic official in the most positive sense. A folk song popular during the Cultural Revolution went: "Molting, a phoenix is less than a chicken, but when its feathers grow back, a chicken is still a chicken and a phoenix is a phoenix!" To the villagers, Wang was just a phoenix temporarily without feathers.

When Wang Ansheng arrived at the Tuanjie brigade in mid-August 1967, he initially spent three days in the home of PPA chairman Jiang Xianfu and then shared a room with the deputy CCP secretary of Qingkou Commune, Zhou Shu, in the home of an elderly poor peasant named He Wenrao at Miaotou Village. At the time of Wang Ansheng's arrival, there had not yet been any killings in the Tuanjie brigade, but two rounds of killings occurred while Wang was staying in the home of He Wenrao.

Wang Ansheng and Zhou Shu were enjoying tea, cigarettes, and melon seeds at the home of Meihua Commune head He Changjin on August 23 when militia chief He Changkun and others hurried over and reported, "Director Wang, our production brigade wants to kill two miscreants today." In his usual fashion, Wang Ansheng nodded and smiled and said, "Great! That's great!" He Changjin invited He Changkun and the others to have a cup of tea first, but He Changkun waved him off, saying, "Next time!" Before the tea had time to cool, He Changkun and the others returned with a new report: "We've done away with the two bad guys." Wang Ansheng once again nodded and smiled and said, "Great! That's great!"

On September 4, Zhou Shu and Wang Ansheng presided over a meeting of CCP and Youth League members and cadres at the Tuanjie brigade, and Zhou led a recitation of quotes by Chairman Mao relating to struggle against the enemy. Militiaman and PPA chairman Jiang Xianfu was then asked to describe the experience of class struggle elsewhere, after which the attendees unanimously agreed that their brigade was too conservative and needed to catch up with the others. Some Youth League members in particular cried out for class enemies to be killed, and public-security head Zheng Sanxi and brigade leader Wei Zaihua expressed the view that all black elements should be killed. Wang Ansheng sat beside the door smiling and smoking, delighted to see the poor and lower-middle peasants so thoroughly galvanized. Nineteen people were killed the next day.

When Wang Ansheng encountered Zheng Sanxi on the way to Wangjiatan the next day, Zheng asked, "Director Wang, how do you feel we did?" Wang replied, "Your meeting was well run, and you did well! The problem is that if we don't kill them, they'll kill us."

After Wang Ansheng returned from Wangjiatan to his lodgings in Miaotou, his host, He Wenrao, asked, "Can we kill offspring?" He Wenrao asked this because some of the more softhearted poor peasants objected to offspring being killed the day before. Wang replied, "If it's not necessary to kill offspring, of course it's better not to. The problem is that this is a struggle between the two roads, and if we don't kill the enemy, they'll kill us."

A grassroots cadre from Qingkou Commune's Yishanping brigade (where seven were killed) also revealed that brigade CCP secretary Tang Fangming requested instructions from Wang Ansheng before killings had begun in the immediate vicinity, and Wang Ansheng replied, "Ha! Can't you see? If the masses demand killings, people should be killed. But you'll have to move fast; if you wait much longer it may not be possible." The next day, four people were killed.

This incident was uncovered during the "exposure study sessions" conducted by the 47th Army's 6950 Unit in 1968. Accused to his face, Wang Ansheng bowed his head and admitted his guilt, but when the Task Force investigated in 1984, Wang Ansheng denied everything. On instructions from the upper levels, the Task Force formed a "Special Investigation Group on the Comrade Wang Ansheng Problem" and carried out an in-depth and detailed investigation that confirmed some issues but left others unresolved due to the deaths of some of the persons involved.

It might appear that what I've recorded here breaches my basic principle of using only content corroborated by collateral evidence or the admission or confession of persons concerned. How can I include it when Wang Ansheng steadfastly refused to admit to it? However, I have in hand an informant's report from the 1968 "exposure study session," which in black and white records that Wang Ansheng and others admitted their guilt when confronted with the accusations. Can this be considered a confession by Wang? At the very least, it casts doubt on his subsequent retraction.

16

When the Pebble Rises
from the Water

Qingxi District's Baimangpu Commune was one of those that held its killing-mobilization meeting rather late, on August 25. In order to catch up with other localities, the commune that afternoon sent a group of cadres as "special emissaries" to each production brigade to oversee and push forward operations. Commune accountant Zuo Changqi was sent to the Zhushan brigade. Zuo Changqi was head of Baimangpu Commune's Red Alliance and was the commune's most enthusiastic student of Mao's works. It was said that he could recite from memory Mao's three pre-Liberation classics—"Serve the People," "In Memory of Norman Bethune," and "The Old Man and the Mountain," as well as 500 other Mao quotes. Upon arriving at Zhushan, Zuo Changqi immediately convened a meeting of brigade cadres and core militiamen to implement the spirit of the commune's three-level cadre meeting, but some cadres had reservations about killing people, and brigade Chinese Communist Party (CCP) secretary Bai Fuzhang noted that none of the brigade's black elements had aroused enough public indignation to warrant killing.

Zuo Changqi felt he needed to respect the views of the brigade's cadres, so he didn't impose his authority as "special emissary," but after returning to the commune, he discovered that he was the only emissary to have returned empty-handed, a severe loss of face. The next day, August 28, Zuo returned to the Zhushan brigade and sought to dilute the influence of opposition voices by calling an enlarged meeting that also included key production team cadres, core militiamen, poor-peasant association (PPA) members, and rebel faction leaders.

Appealing to the attendees' class consciousness, Zuo Changqi said, "Some comrades have been misled by the class enemies' semblance and don't recognize their counterrevolutionary nature. The Great Leader Chairman Mao teaches us that 'They haven't given up,' and if we allow them to successfully restore the old order, the first heads to roll will be ours."

As soon as he finished speaking, some people planted in the crowd began leading the others in chanting slogans: "Don't forget class suffering, remember blood vengeance!" "Sweep away all ox demons and snake spirits!" "Firmly suppress overthrow by class enemies!" At that point, cadres came forward to take a stand for killing, and those who had expressed reservations two days before were now among the most vehement supporters, afraid of committing a class standpoint error, which would put them at a great disadvantage.

Zuo Changqi left it to the brigade to decide whom to kill. It is said that he had a more realistic ideology and disagreed with killing as many people as possible; he particularly felt that killing suckling infants was excessive, and that CCP policy dividing lines had to be followed. As a result, the killing list ultimately included only two names: a man surnamed Bai and his wife (the parents of the protagonists of this story, Bai Yuanying and her three siblings).

Bai Yuanying's parents were harvesting rice in the field when several militiamen called them out, bound them, and took them away to be killed. The family's home was then ransacked, and all their farming implements, food, livestock, and other movable property were seized. The best rooms in the house were closed off, and Bai Yuanying and her siblings were forced to share the shabbiest room. At that time, Bai Yuanying was 17 years old (according to local custom, under which a girl's birth year was added to her age); her brother Bai Yuanzheng was 12, another brother, Bai Yuantan, was 8, and the younger sister was only 5. They couldn't waste time mourning but had to think of how to survive, starting with food. Bai Yuanying was an incredibly brave girl; where others would have stayed home trembling with fear, she went to the production team and requested an advance ration of unhusked rice, as was permitted in emergency situations. All she received was a harsh berating, however, and as she sat staring blankly at the family's cold stove, her brother Bai Yuanzheng quietly approached her and asked, "They won't kill us, will they?"

Perhaps it was these words that steeled Bai Yuanying's resolve: they had to flee rather than sit at home waiting to die. She washed up some sweet potatoes left behind by the looters, cooked them, and had her siblings eat their fill and then packed the remaining potatoes in a basket. Once night fell, she went out and quietly looked around, and seeing no sentries posted near their home, she hurried back, lit an oil lamp, and quickly packed a blanket, some clothes, an enamelware cup, and an aluminum bowl with the potatoes into a wicker basket. Finally, she dug out some money that her parents had concealed in a crack in the wall behind the stove and hid it inside her clothes. She told Bai Yuanzheng to carry their little brother, Bai Yuantan, and she placed their little sister in another wicker basket that she carried along with their belongings on a shoulder pole. Bai Yuanying and her siblings then slipped out the back door.

Between the village and the hills behind it lay a vegetable field where production team members raised their own vegetables, each household's plot marked off with waist-high stone walls. From there a path led to the main road outside the village, and Bai Yuanying decided this was their best route for escape. The four children crept along the low garden wall, winding their way out of the village and finally relaxing when they saw nothing stirring around them. When they passed the pond outside the village, Bai Yuanying picked up a pebble and tossed it into the water as a final farewell to this place that had brought them so much suffering, humiliation, and injustice; the saying in Daoxian is that a person won't return until a pebble rises from the water. Bai Yuanying and her siblings then quickly disappeared into the murky darkness of the night.

Bai Yuanying had no way of knowing that by the time they took flight, the 47th Army's 6950 Unit had arrived in Daoxian and had just held a telephone conference with all the communes, prohibiting further killing. The communes had notified their production brigades that no more indiscriminate killing was allowed and that detained black elements were to be released. On receiving these instructions, the brigade militias stood down; otherwise, Bai Yuanying and her siblings could not possibly have escaped—even if they'd managed to flee their brigade, they'd have been apprehended in some other locality.

Knowing none of this, the four siblings concentrated on getting as far from the village as quickly as they could.

As dawn began to break, they reached the home of an aunt, where they planned to seek refuge. The aunt was already up and performing various household tasks before going out to the fields. Upon seeing her nieces and nephews suddenly appear, she had an idea of what must have happened. "Where are your mama and papa?" she asked, and at that question, Bai Yuanying could no longer hold back her tears, and the other children began crying with her. Their aunt was alarmed: "Stop crying if you don't want to be killed!" Then she told them, "Go away now! I can't help you! You'll just kill us as well!" Bai Yuanying stared at her aunt with tear-filled eyes, hardly believing that this cold face belonged to the affable woman she'd always known.

Because the Zhushan brigade had started its killings relatively late, Bai Yuanying's parents had heard of killings in other brigades and prepared for the worst, telling Bai Yuanying that if anything happened to them, she should take the others to her aunt's home to hide for a while, because their aunt's family members were upper-middle peasants and less likely to be targeted. Now, after making their way there at such great risk, their aunt wouldn't even let them in the door. Deeply disheartened, Bai Yuanying said, "Aunty"—but her aunt said, "Don't call me aunty; I don't know you." There was nothing the children could do but turn and walk away.

After waiting for them to leave the village, the aunt crept out the back door of her house and caught up with them, giving them several cakes to eat and telling them to hurry home. But by then Bai Yuanying hated her aunt even more than the people who had killed her parents, and she refused the cakes without even looking at her. She was too young and too ignorant of life and of how terrible the world could be. All she knew was her aunt's rejection, never thinking of her quandary. Under the conditions at that time, even a poor or lower-middle peasant wouldn't have taken them in, much less an upper-middle peasant such as her aunt. Upper-middle peasants were regarded as fence sitters who could easily be pulled over to the side of the class enemy, and any false step would result in being treated as a class enemy. Their aunt had children of her own, and she, too, was afraid to die.

Ah, Bai Yuanying, you should have begged your aunt to have pity on you and help you or at least teach you how to survive! The older generation had experienced a great deal and had seen everything. Instead, Bai Yuanying took her siblings away and began a life of wandering and begging to survive.

Bai Yuanying is dead now, and her two brothers were too young at the time to remember clearly what their beggars' existence was like. What they remember most was that "Our sister had a bad temper and thin skin. She couldn't bear to beg, so she sent us two boys out to find food. Our little sister was too young to keep alive this way, so our elder sister had no choice but to give her away to someone else."

Begging was in any case not a long-term solution, especially for a girl Bai Yuanying's age. The killing wind was followed by an upsurge in marriages between impoverished old bachelors and the wives and daughters of victims, who often had no other way out. Someone noticed that Bai Yuanying was an attractive and decent girl and suggested arranging a match for her. Bai Yuanying probably knew this was her fate, and she said she'd be willing to marry as long as the man was from a lower social class and allowed her to bring her younger brothers with her. The first condition was easy enough, since men from higher social classes who had been spared death could hardly expect a wife as well. The second condition, however, narrowed her choices considerably. In my reporting I found that many young children from class enemy families were killed, in part to "destroy the roots and branches," but also because no one wanted surviving women to bring along extra mouths to feed in these hard times. Fortunately, Bai Yuanying was considered a desirable match in her own right, and since she wasn't particular, that gave her more room to maneuver. Eventually a 30-year-old poor peasant bachelor from Hongyan Commune's Shenxiantou brigade agreed to her terms, and Bai Yuanying and her brothers finally found a place to rest their heads.

Even so, the boys presented a problem. Bai Yuanying's husband had to be very poor to accept a beggar girl with two extra mouths to feed. Bai Yuanzheng and

Bai Yuantan were able to work but were still too young to support their own up-keep, and the production team refused to provide them with food rations. Poor to begin with, Bai Yuanying's husband now found his hardships compounded. He was used to eating sweet potatoes and congee all year, but now the congee was so thin that even a dog wouldn't lap it off the floor. His marriage wasn't look-ing like such a bargain anymore, and Bai Yuanying's husband began looking for ways to get rid of the two boys. Bai Yuanying already felt she'd married beneath her, and she would never have agreed to the marriage if not for her brothers. Husband and wife fought constantly, and the situation brought out the worst in Bai Yuanying's husband, who began to beat her.

When Bai Yuanzheng saw his sister being treated so badly, he told her, "You stay here. I'll take our brother and go out begging." But Bai Yuanying clutched the boys to her and wept: "I promised Father and Mother that I'd find a way to pre-serve the family line. . . . If it weren't for you, I'd have drowned myself long ago."

The days of fighting and crying continued, one after another, and after a year or so a new source of conflict arose: Bai Yuanying's womb remained empty. In the countryside, getting married wasn't like buying a painting to hang on the wall; it was for having children and another pair of working hands. Bai Yuanying satisfied neither requirement, and the brigade's busybodies buzzed around her like flies around a pile of manure, berating her as a jinx. Life was even harder for Bai Yuanying than for her brothers as she spent her days being chided and beaten.

Bai Yuanzheng and Bai Yuantan told me, "When our brother-in-law beat our sister, he wasn't beating his wife but rather a class enemy. One day, our sister somehow got him so angry that he hit her until she spit up blood and lay mo-tionless on the floor. The two of us ran out at that point, because if we'd stayed inside the house he'd have beaten her even worse. By the time we got back, our sister was dead. She couldn't take it anymore and hanged herself. She was too set on fighting her fate. She told us to hang on, but in the end she was the one who gave up."

With their sister dead, there was no way their brother-in-law would let the boys stay on. Bai Yuanzheng and Bai Yuantan took to the streets again and begged for a living. Now that they were experienced, they didn't find their situation so hopeless. As it happened, Daoxian was just launching its largest water management project, the Shangba Reservoir, which also involved constructing a simple highway from Qiaotou Market to the Shangba worksite along with dozens of big work sheds. Thousands of workers descended on the locality from surrounding districts and communes, along with engineers brought from outside; it was a grand spectacle. Because this was a priority project, apart from money and grain provided by the work teams the county was distributing cash and providing food subsidies, and begging was much easier here than in the villages. By the time the Bai brothers arrived at the worksite to beg, they'd gone a day and a night without eating and were half starved. A canteen cook, old and kindhearted, took pity on the beggar boys and scooped them two bowls of rice along with some vegetables. It was the most delicious and satisfying meal the boys had ever eaten. After all these years, they still don't understand what made this meal so wonderful and why it instantly spread warmth from their bellies to their limbs and refreshed their entire bodies so comfortingly. They told me, "We'd die for that feeling again."

The boys decided that the Shangba Reservoir was heaven on earth and that they'd stay there until they died. After eating their fill, the brothers immediately set about working for the cook. When the cook saw that the boys were clever, diligent, and compliant, he took a great liking to them, but he didn't have the authority to let them keep eating at the canteen, so he told the company commander of the situation. The commander looked askance at the scrawny boys and asked, "Can you carry a load?"

The boys immediately replied, "Yes, we can do it!"

The company commander gave Bai Yuanzheng a carrying pole and Bai Yuantan a hoe and took them to the worksite, and he saw that although small and thin, the boys were strong and energetic. Bai Yuanzheng could carry enough for half a laborer, and Bai Yuantan, while smaller, could handle odd jobs. The company commander said, "All right, you can stay, and we'll feed you, but you won't get work points." When the brothers heard that they'd be fed, they fell to their knees and kowtowed before the company commander. That's how the Bai brothers settled down at the worksite of the Shangba Reservoir. They continued to live and work there for many years.

When the Task Force began its aftermath work in Daoxian in 1984, the brothers heard the news and returned to the village they'd left 18 years before. Four of them had left the village, but only two returned. By then, Bai Yuanzheng was 30 years old and Bai Yuantan was 28. Their home and belongings were long gone, and they had nothing to their name. When the comrades in the Task Force learned of their situation, they were very sympathetic, and at their urging the Zhushan brigade provided the brothers with a responsibility field and a hillside where they could gather firewood. The Task Force also promptly provided the brothers with the various compensations they were entitled to and helped them settle in. The brothers shed tears of gratitude.

The brothers told us that their chief remaining wish was to move their sister's grave from Shenxiantou to the Bai ancestral plot. They couldn't allow her to remain alone outside. Bai Yuanzheng said, "Back then, our sister tossed a pebble into a pond and said she wouldn't return until it emerged from the water. Now that pond has gone dry and was turned into a field during the Learn from Dazhai campaign,[1] but our sister wasn't fated to come home."

PART SIX

XIANGLINPU DISTRICT'S MILITIA PUSH

17

The Shangdu Militia Headquarters

Situated in the southern portion of Daoxian, Xianglinpu District (Map 8) included Xianglinpu, Shenzhangtan, Xiajiang, Xinche, and Cenjiangdu Communes. The regional government office was in Xianglinpu Market, some 20 kilometers from the county seat, Daojiang. The south end of the district is fronted by the Tongshan, Heitou, Maor, and Ma'an Hills, while the Tuoshui River to its east and the Yongming River to its west join at Lianghekou to form a broad plain of fertile tea oil, rice paddy, and tobacco fields. The initiative of the district's deputy district head to establish a militia headquarters modeled on the Yingjiang Frontline Command Post led to Xianglinpu's recording the second-highest number of killings among all of Daoxian's districts.

After being notified of the Yingjiang Political and Legal Work Conference beginning on August 26, Xianglinpu District public-security deputy and district court cadre Jiang Guangde telephoned deputy district head Yuan Lifu, who had stayed behind to take care of business in Xianglinpu: "Quickly send all the commune public-security officers to Yingjiang for a meeting. It's urgent!" When Yuan Lifu asked Jiang Guangde about the conference, Jiang said, "We're going to discuss that [random killing] issue. From now on, if there are arch-criminals that the poor and lower-middle peasants insist on killing, they'll have to get permission first, and we have to adhere to the class line. It looks like they're about to put the brakes on things and it won't be so easy to take action in the future." After that, Jiang Guangde reported on the killings in other districts: more than 200 in Gongba, more than 100 in Yueyan and Simaqiao. He remarked, "The other districts have killed so many, but our district has fallen behind. . . . We need to catch up."

After the phone call, Yuan Lifu's brow furrowed with anxiety over Xianglipu falling behind the "advanced" districts. As the district's youngest leading cadre and an advisor to the district Red Alliance, Yuan Lifu had gone to the frontline command post of the Yingjiang Red Alliance in mid-August to observe the progress of the revolution, and soon after returning to the district, he'd arranged for the establishment of a district militia headquarters modeled on the Yingjiang

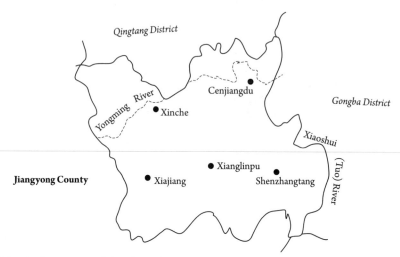

Map 8 Communes of Xianglinpu District

Frontline Command Post. Following the formal establishment of the militia
headquarters at Xianglinpu Commune's Shangdu production brigade on August
21, Yuan Lifu, Huang Shangsen, and other district leaders had on August 23
called a meeting of the district's cadres, Cultural Revolution Committee (CRC)
heads, and militia commanders to deploy manpower for the next stage of seize-
and-push work. A barricade set up that night at Xinche Market's pontoon bridge[1]
had nabbed three black-element offspring fleeing Shenzhangtang Commune,
and they were killed the next day, but in a very low-key manner that rankled
Yuan Lifu and other district leaders. The deputy commander of the Shangdu
militia headquarters, Huang Shangsen (who was also a member of the district
Chinese Communist Party [CCP] committee organization committee), had
the killings posted at Xianglinpu Market, creating a sensation that finally broke
through the stifling and muzzled atmosphere, and Yuan Lifu had called a mass
rally during which four scoundrels from the Shangdu production brigade were
killed, lending some dynamism and impetus to the district's operations.

Now, just as they were making headway, the brakes were being put on, and
Yuan Lifu couldn't bear to stand by and watch all his hard effort go down the
drain. Repeatedly analyzing and pondering the situation, Yuan concluded that
Jiang Guangde's telephone call was meant as a signal that if more people weren't
killed now, there would be little opportunity later. As one of Daoxian's up-and-
coming leaders, this dynamic young deputy district head felt compelled to show
what he was made of.

Huang Shangsen, who had been standing beside him during the phone call,
was alarmed by Yuan's serious expression and asked in a low voice, "District
Head Yuan, what did Director Jiang say just now?"

Perhaps it was at that instant that Yuan Lifu reached a decision. Tapping Huang Shangsen on the shoulder, he said, "Quickly contact headquarters and notify the administrative cadres and the militia cadres of platoon level and above that there will be an urgent meeting tonight at the rice-drying yard."

That night, two big gas lamps hissed at Shangdu Village's rice-drying yard. As people arrived for the meeting, Yuan Lifu called over Huang Shangsen, Xianglipu Commune Youth League secretary Li Shunyun, and other commune leaders for a preparatory meeting. He told them, "Comrade Guangde has told us to take measures to catch up. The suggestion from headquarters is to send militia to each commune and production brigade to supervise and push things forward. . . . What do you all think?"

Everyone agreed, and the men then returned to the drying yard and declared the meeting open. Yuan Lifu delivered the instructions: "Headquarters has decided that each production brigade should deploy two core militiamen for an assault action. . . . In the past, killing a scoundrel required writing up a lot of documentation and obtaining permission from the Supreme People's Court, but now the poor and lower-middle peasants are the Supreme People's Court and can authorize the death penalty. . . . But once the commune delegates return from Yingjiang, we'll have to obtain permission again, so we should grasp this opportunity for a thorough cleanup."

After the meeting, Yuan Lifu had Shangdu militia headquarters commander Yang Xiuzhi stay behind for a confidential briefing, and at an emergency rally of all the district's militia the next morning, Yang communicated the decision for core militiamen to coordinate the killing off of all deserving black elements in their production brigades. The meeting's presiding officer, Huang Shangsen, then warned them: "Take care to adhere to the class line and kill only black elements; no poor or lower-middle peasants can be killed, and there can be no indiscriminate killing."

Yuan Lifu delivered the concluding speech: "After you go back, the first thing you must do is seize revolution and push production for the 'double rush' planting and harvesting, and the second thing is to kill off the troublemaking black elements in your brigades. . . . The sooner the better; complete your missions within three days and then regroup in Shangdu for appraisal and commendation. We'll be here awaiting news of our comrades' victory." Yuan's speech was greeted with protracted applause.

After the meeting, a pig was butchered, and everyone dined together under a huge banner that the headquarters had quickly slapped together: "Enthusiastically sending our militia back to the frontline to carry out their glorious mission!"

Amid the deafening thunder of gongs, Yuan Lifu led the district and commune cadres in seeing off 126 militiamen (2 from each of the 63 production brigades) as they split off in all directions through the newly harvested fields. Standing with arms akimbo, Yuan Lifu buoyantly recited a famous line from one of Chairman Mao's poems: "The Golden Monkey wrathfully swung his massive cudgel / And the jade-like firmament was cleared of dust."[2]

After the shock brigade was sent back to the villages, Yuan Lifu made a special trip back to Yingjiang, where he reported to Red Alliance political commissar He Xia: "Class struggle in Xianglinpu is complex; people there have many overseas relations, and if we don't kill a batch, things will be difficult later on."

He Xia warned, "Killing has to be carried out discreetly. No matter who is killed, once the situation improves later on, someone may be called to account." Yuan didn't think there was any problem with killing a few black elements, and he found He Xia's skittishness a nuisance.

Three days later (August 30), 126 militiamen returned punctually to headquarters as ordered and reported the results of their mission: a total of 569 people killed in three days!

During those three days, Yuan Lifu and the other leaders at the Shangdu headquarters had maintained the pace of the catch-up effort. Yuan in particular took his work very seriously, and after the militia set out on August 27, he called over his most able lieutenant, Li Shunyun, and had him hurry off to Jiujiashan to report back to him on the killing (or, as he termed it, the suppression of black elements) so he would have a clear grasp on the situation on the frontline.

When Li Shunyun arrived at the Jiujiashan brigade, its cadres had already drawn up a preliminary killing list in accordance with instructions and were preparing to hold a mass rally. When they saw that the upper-level leadership had taken the trouble to send someone to direct operations, they immediately invited Li Shunyun to preside over the rally. Li demurred but agreed to give a speech in his capacity as emissary from headquarters, appealing for "the poor and lower-middle peasants to unite and impose the dictatorship of the proletariat over black elements." After the meeting, 16 black elements and offspring were escorted to the woodland alongside Wuzai Pond, where their "death sentences" were carried out.

His mission accomplished, Li Shuyun sped back to the Shangdu headquarters and reported to Yuan Lifu. Yuan said, "Well done! Well done! The poor and lower-middle peasants have truly been mobilized!"

The next morning (August 26), two cadres from Xianglinpu Commune's Zhufu brigade arrived at the Shangdu headquarters to clarify the policy on killing landlords and rich peasants, since there was some uneasiness within the brigade's CCP branch when they met to discuss their response. Deputy Commander Huang Shangsen replied, "The poor and lower-middle peasants are now the Supreme People's Court, and whatever they say goes. If you're afraid to carry out the killings, we'll send someone to help you out." Li Shunyun accompanied Zhang and He back to the Zhufu brigade and immediately convened a meeting of the brigade's cadres, followed by a mass rally during which the peasant supreme court pronounced death sentences on six black elements. Li Shunyun said, "You can't stop a dog from eating shit; if we don't kill them, they'll kill us." After the meeting, Li personally led the militia in escorting the six condemned people to a spot along the Yantiantang Highway, where they were shot with fowling guns and then were hacked with sabers and spears for good measure. Li and two militiamen then inspected the corpses, and on finding that one of the victims was still in a kneeling position, Li ran him through with a spear until he toppled over.

That night, Li Shunyun hurried back to Shangdu and reported to Yuan Lifu and another militia leader, Zhou Runzhen. Yuan and Zhou praised Li extravagantly and said, "Xiao Li, we have to trouble you with overseeing the killing of black elements in Dapan and Xiaopan tomorrow."

Early the next morning (August 28), Li Shunyun hurried to Dapan and Xiaopan. Since these villages were under the jurisdiction of Jianggong Commune, he had Jianggong Commune Youth League secretary Yang Shouyuan accompany him. At that time, the Xiaopan brigade had already locked up the 12 black elements and offspring they planned to kill, and as soon as Li and Yang arrived they organized a mass rally, during which Li Shunyun represented the district and commune leadership in calling for black elements to be resolutely suppressed. The 12 condemned people were then dispatched with fowling guns and sabers, and the meticulous Li Shunyun placed his finger under the nostrils of each victim to make sure they had truly expired.

Early in the morning on August 29, Yuan Lifu sent Li Shunyun on a new assignment: "Jiujiashan is a key area in your [Xianglinpu] commune; the class struggle there is very complicated. You're more familiar with the situation there, so I'm going to trouble you to run over today and get a grasp of the situation and come back with some numbers." After a quick breakfast, Li Shunyun rushed off to the Jiujiashan, where he helped the brigade's leaders finalize a killing list. A mass rally was then called to pronounce "death sentences" on 25 black elements, with Li Shunyun giving his usual speech. Each of the condemned was called by name and required to admit his or her guilt, and the few who protested their innocence were beaten until they complied. Li Shunyun personally led the brigade's militia in escorting the condemned to the execution ground, where they were killed with fowling guns and sabers. When two class enemy offspring continued to writhe on the ground, Li finished them off himself.

The Task Force designated Li Shunyun as someone acting under orders to organize the killings, which means that Yuan Lifu and other leaders took the brunt of the blame. Yuan was very unhappy about this: "That's too inconsistent with fact! When it came to killing people, he [Li Shunyun] was the most enthusiastic of anyone; how did he need my orders? And when did I direct him to kill anyone? All that I told him was to gather up figures and keep things in line. In fact, I repeatedly reminded him to be mindful of the party's policies and to draw a distinction between black elements and offspring, and not to kill indiscriminately."

The pressure to stay in the lead

Xianglinpu District racked up the second-largest number of killings of all of Daoxian's districts, with 916 killed (including 52 suicides), and 57 households obliterated.

The table below shows how the killings advanced in Xianglinpu District.

Date (1967)	Fatalities*	Event
August 24	8	District's Shangdu militia headquarters initiated killings. Xinche Commune held meeting to instigate killings.
August 25	24	Shenzhangtang and Cenjiangdu Communes held meetings to instigate killings.
August 26	105	
August 27	242	Shangdu militia headquarters sent militia to the villages to fuel the killings.
August 28	218	
August 29	109	Killing spree ended as the 47th Army's 6950 Unit entered Daoxian.
August 30	40	
August 31	55	
September 1	35	District held a meeting to transmit 47th Army's prohibition of killings.
September 2	13	
September 3	15	
September 4	2	
September 5	23	
September 6	4	
September 12	1	

* These figures were calculated at an early stage, and there is some discrepancy from the total of victims that was ultimately determined.

The above timetable shows that Xianglinpu was the last of all of Daoxian's districts to be struck by the killing wind, which started elsewhere on August 13 and reached its peak from August 21 to 25.

What led Xianglinpu District to bring up the rear? We asked several people in Daoxian for their views on this, and one heavyweight individual tied it to the need for a district-level cadre to be the frontman for the operations of the People's Armed Forces Department (PAFD):

> PAFD personnel originally had a relatively low status in their corresponding party committees, being at most members of the standing committees, so they invariably made certain party committee members the frontmen for everything they did. I'm not saying that party committee cadres held no responsibility for the killings, but the actual power lay in the hands of the PAFD. These people lacked local work experience and tended to be slapdash and excessively aggressive. . . .
>
> Xianglinpu District started its killings late because Chen Guobao [the Xianglinpu District PAFD commander] was an invalid recuperating at home, and the PAFD commander of Xiajiang Commune had temporarily stepped in for him. Obviously a PAFD militia commander was hardly in a position to orchestrate killings throughout the entire district—who would listen to him? This required someone to step forward at the district level. Ultimately Yuan Lifu came forward, but he was late in doing so. By the time the killings began in Xianglinpu, the killing wind had already spread throughout the county. By August 25, only 30-odd people had been killed in Xianglinpu, so after Jiang Guangde telephoned from Yingjiang on the 26th, Yuan Lifu had to "catch up" with a three-day killing spree that resulted in more than 500 deaths. In those three days, 60 percent of the district's victims died. You may not understand Yuan Lifu very well—on paper he looks like an out-and-out homicidal maniac, but in fact he was a very civilized and upright man. The same is true of Zheng Youzhi—the reports make him look like a cold-blooded killer, but he was actually very loyal and honest. When killing brings no risk of punishment and is considered a "revolutionary action," almost anyone can easily become a killer.

Although the killings started late in Xianglinpu District, the compulsion to make up for lost time resulted in round-the-clock killing campaigns in each commune, sending the death toll on an upward spiral.

18

Even Heaven Wept

Shenzhangtang Commune recorded the second-highest number of killings in Daoxian, but more significant, it launched the killings in Xianglinpu District. The posting of the commune's first killings on market day prepared the ground-work for Yuan Lifu's subsequent "catch-up killing spree."

The energetic participation of Shenzhangtang Commune's leaders in the kill-ings is highlighted in the accounts of some women who survived the killing wind. During the Cultural Revolution killings in Daoxian, male victims outnumbered females by a ratio of 3.5:1, but a case could be made that the harm suffered by women and girls was far greater. Survival is a human instinct, but it sometimes comes at great cost in terms of blood and tears, hardship, and degradation. Very few women stepped forward to demand justice on behalf of their relatives during the Task Force's investigations, and I can understand their heartbreaking silence. Many women from black-element households were forced to marry when their loved ones were killed—some even married the very men who had killed their husbands or parents. After 19 years, they'd raised families in their new house-holds and had made new lives for themselves, and their choice of silence was not so much for themselves as for their children. At the same time, I must express my profound respect for those women who stepped forward to speak on behalf of their unjustly killed loved ones. They chose to register their accusations for the sake of natural justice.

Zhu Guifang was 46 years old and living in Dongzishan, Dongmen Township, when I interviewed her in 1986. This is her recollection:

I was originally from Yapojing Village in the Dongfeng brigade of Shenzhangtang Commune and was married to Zhu Keneng, who at the time of the random killings was a doctor at the Xianglinpu public health clinic. Our brigade started killing people on August 26 [1967]. I'm not clear how the killing began, but it seemed very sudden—the word was given and then people were dragged out and killed. It was said that there were directives from above to once again kill landlords.

Because my husband came from a higher-class background, I was scared to death, but when I saw they weren't going after my family I began to relax a little. I thought that since my husband was a doctor in the district health clinic, he wouldn't come under the brigade's jurisdiction, so they wouldn't kill anyone in our household. What didn't occur to me was that because my husband worked outside and collected a salary, we had some extra income and perhaps lived better than others, and that drew envy. On August 28, the brigade held a meeting to discuss killing a second batch, and after CRC [Cultural Revolution Committee] chairman Ding Yunhua suggested killing my husband, party secretary Liu Jinchang sent militia commander Tang Mingsheng with some men to Xianglinpu to make the arrest. They arrested my husband at Xianglinpu clinic the next day and killed him on August 31.

I was too terrified to grieve, and I just sat at home trembling from head to foot. My two children, the youngest only three years old, understood enough not to cry or fuss; they just crept quietly to my side and pulled on my arms. Hugging them close, I found they were also trembling. How pitiful they were, at such a young age, to understand that disaster was looming!

Then I remembered that I still had more than 200 *kuai* in the cupboard, our life savings, which Zhu Keneng and I had hoped would tide us over in the future. When they'd killed class enemies a few days earlier, they'd ransacked their homes from top to bottom, so I took out the money and sewed it into my undergarments. Soon after that, Tang Mingsheng and the others came to my home and yelled, "Zhu Guifang, come out!" I thought they were going to kill me, and my head began buzzing and my legs turned to jelly. I thought it didn't matter so much if they killed me, but my children were so young, and who would take care of them? Then I heard Tang Mingsheng say, "Go to the clinic and bring back Zhu Keneng's belongings." When I realized they hadn't come to kill me, my heart dropped back from my throat and I hurried to accompany them to the Xianglinpu clinic. At the dormitory where my husband had been staying, I collected his luggage and bedding, his clothes, and his washbasin and thermos bottle, which they had me take to the brigade office to be confiscated as public property. They searched me and took the money I had hidden, and also took all our chickens, ducks, pigs, and grain. After ransacking my home, they forced me to produce my "hidden bankbooks." I swore to them: "We never deposited any money. If you don't believe me, go to the credit cooperative, and if they say we deposited any money, you can kill me." At that, they finally gave up.

After they left, I tidied things up a bit and then put the children to bed. At that time I suddenly felt a stabbing pain in my heart, and tears gushed from my eyes. I couldn't hold back, no matter how I tried, but I was afraid that my weeping would alarm the neighbors, so I bit down on my lips. All that day I had used all my effort to pacify them and preserve the lives of my family. Now I felt how unjustly we'd been treated. No one in our family had ever done anything wrong. Why should they kill my husband and ransack our home? I lit a lantern and looked at my two sleeping children, and I began to worry about how we would survive now that my husband had been killed and all of our money and belongings had been taken.

The next day, in the afternoon, Tang Mingsheng came back with several militiamen, and without saying a word, he dragged my two children away, and I realized they intended to obliterate my family root and branch. I held onto the three-year-old and begged them to spare one for me, but they tore the child from me and said, "Why spare one who could take revenge in the future?"

So they killed three out of the four of us in the space of two days. I was in utter despair, and no longer caring about anything, I screamed and wept until dark.

Finally, as darkness fell and I'd become hoarse with weeping and had no more tears left, I sat there in my empty house in a daze, feeling no hunger or thirst. That's when Tang Mingsheng came back. I thought he'd come to kill me, and I just sat there ignoring him, my eyes shut, thinking that if he was going to kill me, he should get it over with, and then our family could be reunited in the underworld and I wouldn't be left to suffer here alone. I never guessed that the bastard would drag me into the house and take off my clothes. I struggled to push away his hands, imploring him, "Brother Mingsheng, I beg you, don't do this. . . . Zhu Keneng has just died, I can't do this." That beast Tang Mingsheng held a knife to my throat and said, "You wife of a landlord, you should feel lucky I want you. Mind your manners or you'll end up like Zhu Keneng." Then he threw me on the bed and raped me.

After raping me, he looked at me lying on the bed weeping, and with a cheeky grin he said, "What do you have to cry about? I can give you a lot more satisfaction than Zhu Keneng! Be my mistress from now on, and I guarantee that no one will pick on you." He went on to say a lot of other smutty things that I can't bear to repeat.

That fellow was worse than a beast. After killing my husband and kids and taking possession of my body, he thought he could keep me under his control. Filled with hatred and fear, I decided I could no longer stay in Yapojing and that I had to find a way to escape.

While I was still working out a plan, on September 9 the brigade killed 16 more people, most of them the children of those killed in the first and second rounds. By that time, the upper level had already sent down a prohibition against further random killings, and the 47th Army had sent people to the village announcing that random killings were not allowed, but the brigade's accountant, Chen Youzhong, insisted: "We have to eliminate them root and branch. We don't have the manpower to defeat them, but if we kill them all now, we can rest assured that they won't avenge themselves on us later." At that time, it was just too easy to kill. It didn't take a brigade cadre—even a poor peasant could suggest killing someone, and if you had the wrong class background, you were as good as dead. After they killed you, your family couldn't say anything and had to behave themselves or they'd all be killed as well.

Yang Geng'e was 37 and a resident of Huangjiatian Village in Jiangyong County's Xianjie Township when I interviewed her in 1986. This is her story:

I was originally from Zhangjia Village in Daoxian's Shenzhangtang Commune, but my family is all gone now. My father, Yang Kaixi, was 41 when he died; my mother, Qiu Daixiu, was 38; my eldest brother, Yang Jingfang, was 21; my middle brother, Yang Faxin, was 12; and my youngest brother, Yang Zhengxin, was 9. They all died during Daoxian's killing wind, killed by a fellow villager named Jiang Dede. The most hateful of Jiang's accomplices was my sister-in-law, Zhu Jinjiao.

My brother Yang Jingfang married Zhu Jinjiao in 1965, and at first they got along well, but in the winter of the next year, Zhu Jinjiao began an illicit affair with Jiang Dede, and that caused conflict with my brother. At that time, our family had a high class ranking that caused us to be persecuted in the brigade. My dad was very decent, and my eldest brother was somewhat henpecked, so no one said anything. My mother couldn't hold it back, though, and she always made remarks about Zhu Jinjiao at home but didn't dare say anything outside. She never imagined that this would give Jiang Dede the idea of killing my brother and taking his wife.

In August 1967, the killing wind blew into our village. On August 25, Jiang Dede led a gang from the brigade in ransacking our house and taking our pigs, chickens, ducks, grain, and everything else of value. By then our brigade had begun killing people, but because my family was particularly well behaved, none of us had been killed. Then on

August 27, people came from the district to supervise operations and said we had to "catch up." Jiang Dede took this opportunity to drag out my mother, Qiu Daixiu, and my brother Yang Jingfang and have them killed. When my family saw this, we were horrified, but my father told us not to make a sound or let our faces reveal our feelings. He said, "They're dead and there's nothing we can do. The things that were taken don't matter, either—what matters is staying alive. Your brother is dead, and Zhu Jinjiao will marry Jiang sooner or later, so let her go."

We didn't dare even weep, much less say a word, as Zhu Jinjiao did what she pleased at home and flaunted her strength. Jiang Dede strutted in every evening and slept with Zhu Jinjiao in my brother's bed. We just pretended not to notice. But then one night, Zhu Jinjiao heard my middle brother cry out for our mother in his sleep. She told Jiang Dede, "When he's older, he'll take revenge. It's better to destroy them root and branch."

On August 30, Jiang Dede led a group of men who arrested my brothers Yang Faxin and Yang Zhengxin and killed them.

On September 3, Jiang Dede and Zhu Jinjiao had their wedding ceremony.

My father quickly sent me off to a relative's home to hide, and that saved my life. By then the upper levels had already sent down a directive forbidding random killings, but on that day, September 10, Jiang Dede used a hoe to beat my father Yang Kaixi to death. Everyone in my family was killed except me. Now he claims he was acting under orders, but I say he was killing people in order to take a man's wife, eliminate further trouble, and seize our goods! I insist that the government make Jiang Dede pay with his life. That's not too much to ask—his one life in return for five of ours.

At that, she broke down weeping.

The most important but also the hardest thing I did in Daoxian was interview survivors. Every interview was full of blood and tears. It was suffocating, like having the eyes of the victims drilling into the depths of one's soul. Although the pain belonged to others, its enormous weight and profound reality brought a sense of the common grief of mankind. We had an opportunity to interview a survivor whose husband was among the first batch killed in Xianglinpu Commune's Diaogaolou brigade.

Yan Shihai, a secondary-school librarian originally from Guang'an, Sichuan Province, was 54 when I interviewed her in 1986, but she looked much older, her hair gray and her spirit shattered. In a heavy Sichuan accent she said,

"Lao Yang has been dead all these years, but I still live that nightmare. I don't dare go out among crowds; the slightest movement sends my heart to my throat. I wake up terrified in the middle of the night and lie there weeping alone in my bed. Imagine what it was like, being locked in a cage and watching the people around you being taken out, one group at a time, to be slaughtered. The first group, then the second group—everyone killed. I was in the third group, and if they'd been quicker about it, my head would have rolled as well, and I'd be with Lao Yang. . . ." At this point she broke down and wept. We could only keep comforting her, hoping she could emerge from this shadow in the precious years remaining to her.

My husband's name was Yang Tianxun. He graduated from Chongqing's Central University[1] in the 1940s, but rather than engage in politics or follow the Kuomintang to Taiwan,[2] he returned to his native place, Daoxian, and served as head teacher in the county high school. Lao Yang was a versatile man and an excellent artist. In the early years of the Cultural Revolution, Chairman Mao's quotes and portrait were everywhere, and since Lao Yang was an artist, others asked him to produce a Mao portrait. At that time, Chairman Mao was called the Red Sun and was portrayed with light beaming from his head. Lao Yang did his best to reproduce these rays of light, but for some reason, some of the revolutionary masses didn't like the effect and said, "Those aren't rays of light, they're arrows; they're the poisoned arrows of the counterrevolutionaries aimed at our Great Leader Chairman Mao!" What a disaster! He was pulled out and struggled. With his political background, what could he say? Lao Yang gave a rational self-defense and raised plenty of comparable examples, so he was ultimately cleared of a "venomous attack"[3] but was labeled an "active counterrevolutionary," dismissed from his job, and sent back to his native village for labor reform. That was considered lenient. If he'd been convicted of a venomous attack, he would have been sentenced to at least 10 years of labor reform. The children and I were fortunate enough to be allowed to remain in town. Looking back now, he would have been better off imprisoned than being sent back to the countryside and killed.

Lao Yang's native place was Xianglinpu Commune's Datoushan production brigade. I'd been there before. It was an ancient town on a main thoroughfare from Hunan to Guangdong and Guangxi. I was very worried about Lao Yang being sent back to the village, because his health was not robust, and I didn't know how well he could bear up under labor reform. During the summer school break in 1967, I took the children to visit him, and he was overjoyed. After several months' absence, his gray hair, jutting cheekbones, sunken eyes, and straggly whiskers made him look at least 10 years older. He was still in good spirits, though, and said he needed to correct his thinking and remold himself, starting with labor. He told me he'd learned a lot about farming, and that we needn't worry, because he could look after himself. Even living alone, Lao Yang kept his home clean and tidy, especially his "loyalty altar," which in accordance with the county's requirements had a treasured image of Chairman Mao over a red paper cutout of the word *zhong*, for loyalty, and "Long live Chairman Mao!" and "Long live the Communist Party!" on either side. Under the *zhong* character, a small wooden shelf held four volumes of *Mao Zedong's Selected Works* and *Quotations of Chairman Mao* in a red plastic cover. Lao Yang had everything beautifully arranged, and this put me at ease. Since I wasn't from the countryside, I wasn't expected to work in the fields, and I planned to spend the summer break restoring his health.

I remember at noon on August 26, he came back from the fields after a "double rush" planting and harvesting, and after eating two big bowls of congee, he lay down for a quick nap. Just as he fell asleep, an urgent whistling sounded through the village. Coming from the county town, I was more up to date on current events, and I told him, "Lao Yang, I've heard there have been random killings in the villages; you have to be careful." Exhausted after his morning's labor, he lay on the bed and said languidly, "Don't be silly, I read the brigade's newspaper every day. The Cultural Revolution isn't targeting people like us. As long as we work hard and don't talk out of turn or do something foolish, nothing will happen." He'd barely finished saying this when militiamen armed with knives burst in our door and took him away. Our children and I were petrified, wondering what he could have done. The children began crying, but I urged them to be still. Before we could recover from our panic, another group burst in and wordlessly dragged us out as well.

I was taken to a primary school not far from Xianglinpu Commune, where I was held with Lao Yang and many others in a classroom used as a makeshift prison. It was hot and crowded, and the stench of sweat and urine was overwhelming. Many people had been grabbed right out of the fields and were still covered with mud. Around four o'clock in the afternoon, people outside carrying knives and guns began calling out names, while the rest of us were ordered to kneel with heads lowered in the classroom. The first person called out was my husband, and as soon as he walked out the door, militiamen grabbed him and bound him fast. It seems he felt compelled to say something, and the leader, a man surnamed Yang, raised a brick and slammed it into his head.

Lao Yang's skull was fractured, and he cried out in agony. That horrible sound still rings in my ears. I raised my head to look, but a man standing in the doorway with a knife yelled, "Head down!" Terrified, I lowered my head at once, and fearing I would cry out, I bit my lip until it bled.

Lao Yang was in the first batch to be killed. A dozen or so were pulled out, and seeing what had happened to Lao Yang, the others didn't dare utter a word but were dragged over to Niaozai Pond, not far from the school, and were hacked to death with sabers. Two days later, another 30-odd[4] people were called out and hacked to death beside the pond. All that remained were a few women who were to be killed in the third round.

I don't know how I passed those few days. After Lao Yang's death, I was so petrified that I couldn't shut my eyes, day or night, and any sound sent my heart to my throat. Desperately I told them that I was just Yang Tianxun's family member, that I was from the city and not from this county, and that I had a clean record and a good family background. I begged them to make their own inquires and free me. But who would listen? How I regretted ever coming to this nest of murderers! But what could I do now? Saying too much only increased their rage, so it was best to await death in silence.

When they killed the second batch, it was at noon under a blazing sun, but as they pulled those 30 people out, the sky suddenly darkened; thunder roared and rain came down in torrents for more than two hours. In the classroom, we women murmured to each other, "Listen, even heaven is weeping!"

I was never one to believe in fate, but from then on I became superstitious. I believed that fate decides life and death, honor, and riches, and that there was no escaping our fate.

The rain delayed burial of those 30-odd people, so the next day we women were ordered to go out and bury the corpses. I'd always been scared to look at the dead, but in order to save myself and my children, I immediately did what they told me. My God! My legs turned to jelly at the sight of that stack of corpses next to Niaozai Pond. I still remember clearly that the eyes of the dead were shut tight. It's said that when the innocent are killed, their eyes remain open in accusation, but I think that these people couldn't bear the sight of their own slaughter. The militiamen gave us wooden hooks and ordered us to drag the corpses into a pit next to the pond, and then we covered them with a thin layer of yellow soil.

There was a middle-aged woman among us whose husband had been killed in this group, and when she saw her husband's corpse, she fainted dead away. It's said that she subsequently went mad, constantly calling her husband's name.

Two more days passed, and just when the time came to kill the rest of us, Unit 6950 of the People's Liberation Army (PLA) arrived in the villages and stopped the killing. People in yellow uniforms drove away the people who were guarding us, and we were saved. In that week I aged 20 years, and by the time they released me I was unrecognizable. After my release I stopped menstruating, and although it eventually resumed after a great deal of time and medication, my general health was irretrievably broken.

From what we could determine, there was never any intention to kill Yuan Shihai and the other women; like the women in the above two narratives, they were to be distributed as the spoils of victory.

19

Two Classic Cases

Xianglinpu Commune's Diaogaolou brigade was distinguished by two particu-larly infamous cases that were eventually included on the Task Force's list of clas-sic cases. I remember the first time we went to do our reporting in Diaogaolou and asked a friend in the county seat how to get there; the first thing he said was "Oh, that's the brigade where a husband killed his wife."

This story circulated far and wide, and many people told it to me. This is how I recorded it at the time:

The Diaogaolou brigade had a young core militiaman, strong and manly, whose wife was the daughter of a landlord. She was pretty and virtuous and could sing and dance, and she had a middle-school education, which at that time qualified her as a midlevel intellectual in the Daoxian countryside. The two had been happily married for three years.

On August 26, 1967, the woman heard that people in her home village had been arrested and were being held in the brigade ancestral hall. In a panic she rushed to her native Jiujia brigade and ended up being arrested by the Jiujia militia. At that time her husband was passing by Jiujia in the line of duty, and someone rushed over and told him, "Your wife has been arrested by the Jiujia mi-litia. Go and save her!" Upon hearing this, the husband hurried over and found his wife bound hand and foot to a pillar in the ancestral hall. When she saw her husband, the wife believed he'd come to save her, but he ignored her imploring gaze and kept his distance. When the head of the Jiujia peasant supreme court asked him, "How should we handle this?," he replied, "She should be treated the same as those others [referring to the other black elements and offspring in the ancestral hall]. I'll leave it to you."

The woman was led off by the Jiujia militia and clubbed in the head but didn't die, and when she regained consciousness the next day, the Jiujia brigade cadres discussed the matter among themselves. They decided that since she had mar-ried a poor peasant, she should be considered part of a poor peasant family, and they sent her back to the Diaogaolou brigade. Since the Jiujia brigade had given her a way out, the Diaogaolou brigade should have been even more inclined to show her mercy, but against all expectation, her husband, the son of a poor peasant, showed the face of iron justice and refused to show any favoritism, insisting that she be killed. The woman knelt before her husband, begging him, "Look, I have your child inside me! If you don't believe me, feel my belly! It's moving! If you still don't believe me, I can go for an exam at the commune clinic. . . ."

The husband remained unmoved and with an expression of complete indifference said, "Then I'll do without the child." He personally tied his battered wife up like a rice dumpling and took her to the execution ground to be killed with the others. When it came time to kill his wife, the others just looked at him and didn't make a move. Seeing the hesitation of the others, he raised his carrying pole and brought it down twice on his wife's head. The others then took up their stones and fowling guns, and that's how this lovely young woman met her death at the hands of her own husband.

I originally regarded this case as one of putting duty above family, but when I made a subsequent visit to Daoxian for follow-up interviews, a friend gave me a petition written by the woman's family:

> My elder sister, Yang Jingui, married Neng Zi of Xianglinpu Commune's Diaogaolou Village in 1964. When she failed to produce a child after three years, Neng Zi blamed my sister, and when the killing wind began to blow in Daoxian in 1967, he had a discussion with his uncle about taking this opportunity to do away with my sister. They deceived her into leaving the village, and then his uncle shot her with a fowling gun. When my sister fell to the ground, Neng Zi stabbed her several times with a saber, and, thinking her dead, they went home. In the middle of the night, my sister regained consciousness and attempted to return to her home village, but she was discovered and sent back to Diaogaolou. The heartless Neng Zi used the excuse that my sister was a landlord whelp to kill her with a fowling gun.

After reading the petition, a multitude of feelings welled up in me. How superficial our reporting had been that first time! Of course, the cursory nature of the official investigations was also a factor. I remember one Task Force comrade saying, "Under normal circumstances, if there's no special evidence, we don't investigate the motives of the killers too much. If we did, there would be many more cases requiring the death penalty." Things we didn't pay much attention to back then ring like thunderclaps in my ears when I think back on them now.

My initial manuscript included the following exclamation: "This is simply inexplicable." It seems that apparently inexplicable matters often have less than cryptic reasons behind them.

The other "classic case" Xianglinpu District managed to claim credit for was the killing of six teachers from the Zhanjia Primary School in Cenjiangdu Commune.

Quite a number of Daoxian's primary- and secondary-school teachers were from landlord or rich peasant families, so it wasn't surprising that one county-level leader at that time summed up the situation of the local education community by saying, "Over the past 17 years [since the founding of the People's Republic of China in 1949], Daoxian's education community has been largely taken over by the bourgeois class. It's run by ox demons and snake spirits, and this phenomenon can absolutely not be allowed to continue." The Task Force's files reveal that during the 1957 Anti-Rightist campaign, 299 of the county's primary- and secondary-school teachers were designated Rightists and dismissed from the teaching ranks, while 201 "voluntarily" resigned and returned to their villages during the economic hardship from 1959 to 1966. During the Socialist Education movement and Cultural Revolution, 209 teachers were purged and dismissed. Likewise, teachers were particular targets of the killing wind, with 43 primary- and secondary-school teachers killed, including 34 who were still actively teaching.

The name Cenjiangdu refers to a major crossing on the lower reaches of the Yongming (Yanshui) River, as well as to a lovely village next to the crossing and the fertile stretch of land west of the Tuo River at the Yongming's lower reaches in Xianglinpu District. The crossing has a three-arched bridge about 100 meters long where the only national highway traversing Daoxian from north to south crosses the Yongming River on the way to Jiangyong and Jianghua Counties. Below the crossing, the confluence of the Yongming River with the Tuo creates a broad waterway containing 15 sandbars overgrown with old camphor trees, willows, and bamboo whose luxuriant foliage blocks the sun. Streamlets burbling among these groves create the unusual effect of land in the water and water on the land, and the azure water's rippling reflection of trees, clouds, and birds in the sky gives the scene a hallucinogenic quality. Local people call this place Lianghekou, the Mouth of Two Rivers, and it is renowned as the broadest and most beautiful stretch of Daozhou's river system. When reporting in Daoxian, we rowed here in a skiff, and as the boat glided into the dense green shade of the sandbars, I could hardly hold back my tears as my callused heart gradually softened and melted in a luxuriant distress. . . .

All the people involved in killing the teachers had left the area in the ensuing 19 years, so my reporting was limited to visiting the site and absorbing the atmosphere. Although mentally prepared, I still felt disappointed by the utter ordinariness of a school that had lost six teachers to the killing wind.

A comrade from the Daoxian Education Department explained that back in 1967, Daoxian's primary schools were divided into three types: the first type consisted of core primary schools, of which there were about five in the county. The second type comprised comprehensive junior-senior primary schools covering grades one through six, of which there was one for each commune. The third type included lower primary schools, of which there were more than 400 in the county; these covered only grades one through four, and the poorest of them had mixed classes in which one teacher taught several grade levels at once. Core primary schools typically included three years of middle-school classes, while lower primary schools were typically subordinate to the comprehensive junior-senior primary schools in their respective administrative divisions. The Zhanjia school was a comprehensive junior-senior primary school.

The deaths of the Zhanjia Primary School's teachers involved a wide range of individuals who shifted the blame onto each other, so it was difficult to determine who bore the main responsibility. The Task Force's repeated inquiries only compounded the complexity of the situation, so I will simply pull together the historical fragments to present a version as close as possible to the truth.

The first victim, Zhou Shenghong, came from a landlord family and was labeled a bourgeois intellectual at the outset of the Cultural Revolution. As an introvert, he took the usual public denunciation and beatings especially to heart. He might reasonably have felt flattered to be labeled a "bourgeois intellectual," given that he was merely a graduate of a teacher's college, but Daoxian had precious few college graduates at that time; county Chinese Communist Party (CCP) secretary Shi Xiuhua had only a middle-school education, and county head Huang Yida was only a high-school graduate. In any case, it wasn't the second term that mattered so much as the first; to be "bourgeois" rather than "proletarian" determined whether you were revolutionary or a target of revolution.

Zhou was the kind of fellow who in the best of times feared so much as a leaf falling on his head. This kind of sensitivity is fine when all is well, but once things go wrong it can be disastrous. In 1957, the county gathered all the primary- and secondary-school teachers together and asked them to submit their views to help the CCP rectify itself. Zhou could not be convinced to say anything more than that the Communist Party was great and socialism was good, which spared him having a Rightist cap slapped on his head during the subsequent political backlash against the CCP's critics. The tempest of the Cultural Revolution brought out the worst in him, however. On August 22, 1967, Zhou Shenghong somehow heard reports of killings, and it sent him into a panic. That afternoon he crept off to Cenjiangdu's Wantang Mountain with a rope, planning to hang himself. Reaching a ridge, he found a suitable tree, tied the rope to it, and placed a large, round rock beneath his feet. Just as he was about to kick it away, he was spotted by He Daixiu, a member of Cenjiangdu Commune's Shangqing production brigade, who was gathering mushrooms on the mountain. He Daixiu immediately shouted and ran over, and when he saw it was Teacher Zhou preparing to hang himself, he asked what could possibly drive him to take his own life. Weeping, Zhou Shenghong said, "Leave me alone and let me go in peace." He Daixiu said, "There's no way I'll let you die like this," and he began calling for help. Two militiamen patrolling the mountain at that time ran over, and when they heard what was going on, they urged Zhou not to be foolish. Finally the three men talked Zhou around, and the militiamen accompanied him back to the school.

After returning to his brigade, He Daixiu told brigade CCP secretary He Daiji what had happened. He Daiji leaped up and berated He Daixiu for his stupidity; the class enemy was attempting to commit suicide to escape punishment, but instead of sharpening their vigilance, He Daixiu and the militiamen had let him off.

Since Shangqing was close to Cenjiangdu and part of the same commune, He Daiji immediately ran to the Zhanjia Primary School and told principal He Juanshu about Zhou Shenghong's suicide attempt. He Juanshu was a stalwart communist with a high awareness of class struggle, and she took the matter very seriously: "Zhou Shenghong is a landlord. This is a major problem, and we have to put him under control right away. But our school doesn't have the authority. Could your brigade send people to take him to the commune headquarters?"

He Daiji said, "That's easy enough." He went straight back and sent public security chief He Guangzhong with several militiamen to the school to arrest Zhou Shenghong. He then telephoned the commune, where commune secretary Mo Rongxing instructed him to tie Zhou to the commune telephone pole. Since Zhou Shenghong was a member of Xianglinpu Commune's Shangdu brigade, Mo Rongxing then telephoned the Shangdu militia headquarters and told them to come posthaste to take Zhou away. Xianglinpu Commune security officer He Shiyuan arrived by bus with a militiaman, and they took Zhou back by the same route. When the bus dropped the group off at Xianglinpu, Zhou Shenghong refused to go any farther, kneeling on the ground and begging, "Please just get it over with quickly here!"

He Shiyuan said, "Teacher Zhou, don't be so paranoid. My superior didn't tell me to kill you, just to bring you back to Shangdu. Don't make things difficult for me." But Zhou Shenghong was unwilling to take another step, and He Shiyuan and the militiaman had to half-drag, half-hurl Zhou Shenghong back to Shangdu.

The next day, after permission was obtained from the Shangdu militia headquarters, He Shiyuan satisfied Zhou's request of the day before by executing him with a fowling gun along with three class enemy offspring who had fled from Shenzhangtang Commune's Songliu brigade.

The second Zhanjia Primary School teacher to be killed was Xu Zhishen, who was likewise a class enemy offspring, and whose killing was indirectly related to Zhou Shenghong's attempted suicide. Xu Zhishen and Zhou Shenghong were merely colleagues who had little contact with each other, and they had very different characters and were far apart in age. Even so, the close proximity of two people with problematic class backgrounds aroused unnecessary suspicion. Xu Zhishen was from the Shangqing production brigade, and since a member of the Shangqing brigade had discovered Zhou Shenghong attempting suicide, the brigade was subsequently notified when Zhou was killed. When the Shangqing brigade held a meeting on August 25 to discuss a list of people to killed, thoughts automatically turned to Xu Zhishen; since another brigade had killed this kind of bourgeois intellectual, why shouldn't they do likewise? Brigade CCP secretary He Daiji observed, "Principal He says Xu Zhishen is very reactionary. Such people shouldn't remain at the school to poison the minds of poor and lower-middle peasant children." On August 28, the Shangzing brigade went to the primary school, bound Xu Zhishen, and brought him back, and he was killed that same night.

The third teacher killed was He Rongzi, who came from Xianglinpu Commune's Langlong brigade. His demise came in a final round of killings resulting from Yuan Lifu's "big cleanup." The brigade had just killed a batch of nine class enemies the day before (August 26), and during discussions of the name list for the new round, Cultural Revolution Committee (CRC) chairman He Rongyue pointed out: "Chairman Mao has instructed us that taking control of a country requires both guns and pens, and retaining control also depends on both. Black elements also rely both on guns and pens to mount insurrections and restore the old order. We need to kill pen-wielding class enemies, because they're the most dangerous." On that basis, they included teacher He Rongzi among the 20 people on their killing list.

The next day, Youth League secretary He Yangzhu and four core militiamen went to Zhanjia Primary School to arrest He Rongzi. Clutching at a last thread of hope, He Rongzi said, "If you want to take me back, you have to get permission from the school's leadership." He Yangzhu went to see school principal He Juanshu, who said, "If the production brigade wants him arrested, take him away. We firmly support the revolutionary actions of the poor and lower-middle peasants." He Rongzi was killed with the 19 others the next day.

Killed along with He Rongzi was another teacher from the primary school, He Yan. A rich peasant who was also from the Langlong brigade, He Yan was terrified when he saw Zhou Shenghong and Xu Zhishen taken away and killed. Determined to avoid the treacherous He Juanshu, He Yan requested leave and returned to his production brigade, thinking he'd be safer there and knowing nothing about the plan to target pen wielders in a final batch of killings. He was doomed no matter what he did.[1]

The fifth teacher killed was Jiang Daiyi, who strictly speaking was a teacher at the Chibatang Lower Primary School, subordinate to the Zhanjia school. He was a member of Wanjiazhuang Commune's May 1st production brigade and a member of the landlord class. On August 29, Jiang Daiyi went to the Zhanjia Primary School to fetch his wages and grain rations, but Principal He Juanshu was not at the school, so Jiang went to the home of a cousin to borrow some rice and ask for news of his family back home. While he was there, his cousin's husband came in and told Jiang Daiyi to leave right away: "The principal of your school has put out the word that anyone who sees you has to tie you up and take you to the commune." Jiang Daiyi grabbed the rice and hurried back to Chibatang as fast as he could.

On the way, he encountered school principal He Juanshu, but she smiled at him as if nothing was amiss, and he wondered if the situation had been exaggerated. Jiang Daiyi asked He Juanshu to write him a certificate so he wouldn't have problems on the way home. He Juanshu replied, "Why do you want a certificate now? Go home first and we'll deal with it later."

After parting from Jiang Daiyi, He Juanshu hurried to the nearest production brigade and asked for two militiamen to detain Jiang Daiyi and take him to the commune. The militiamen caught up with Jiang at Guaiziling and escorted him straight to Cenjiangdu Commune, where commune secretary Mo Rongxing telephoned Wanjiazhuang Commune's May 1st production brigade and told them to come for Jiang Daiyi.

What I'm recounting here are the basic facts, without unconfirmed allegations of who did what or said what, but behind each victim are human forms, some distinct and others vague. For example, some reports link Jiang Daiyi's death to Huang Xisheng, the principal of Wangjiazhuang's Changxing Junior-Senior Primary School, who was behind the killing of another primary-school teacher in Wangjiazhuang's May 1st brigade, Liu Fucai.[2] In any case, the May 1st brigade took Mo Rongxing's telephone call very seriously and sent militiamen to bring Jiang Daiyi back.

On the way back to the brigade they reached Cenjiangdu's pontoon bridge at the Yongming River. The concrete highway bridge wasn't built until 1969, so the crossing consisted of the old pontoon bridge and a ferry large enough to carry one motor vehicle. At the other side of the pontoon bridge was a pavilion, and the militiamen decided to stop there to take a breather. The pavilion was in a state of disrepair, but its basic structure of stone pillars and green tiles was still intact, and its granite benches were cool and polished smooth by the rumps of numerous passersby. Travelers could refresh themselves with tea from two granite water vats filled by people hoping to accumulate merit through good works.

After sitting there for a short time, one of the militiamen cast his eyes up toward the roof of the pavilion and sighed with great emotion: "Daiyi, Daiyi, please don't blame us. We're under orders from our superiors, and if you want someone to blame, it's them. . . ."

Exchanging glances, the militiamen stood and led Jiang Daiyi to the hillside beside the pavilion. When they were halfway up the slope, a militiaman raised his blunderbuss and fired a single shot into the back of Jiang Daiyi's head. Each of the other militiamen then shot him in turn to put him out of his misery.

The last of the Zhanjia Primary School teachers to be killed was a man named Feng Yibo. I was never able to clarify the circumstances of Feng's death. He was a substitute teacher, and once classes were suspended for the Cultural Revolution, he was reportedly killed after returning to his production brigade in Lijiaping Commune. Since Lijiaping Commune was subsequently put under the jurisdiction of Shuangpai County, it's possible that the Task Force investigating events in that county has some record of the circumstances of his death.

The Banality of Evil

"The tough job is left to me"

We can better understand how the militia supervised and pushed forward the killings in the villages through the testimony of one of those responsible for the killings in Xianglinpu District. Given the opportunity to interview him, we found a small man of miserable aspect and in filthy clothing squinting at us timidly, his sickly face devoid of expression. I never would have dreamed this man capable of killing, and even less of wielding power over life and death; he came across more like a victim than a killer. His name was Zhou Guangyou, and at the time of the massacre he was the poor-peasant association (PPA) chairman of Cenjiangdu Commune's Chibatang production brigade.

The killings in the Chibatang brigade rated as only fair to middling in Xianglinpu District. The Task Force files recorded classic cases in other brigades with much-higher killing rates, but we were unable to visit some of these brigades, and in others, people claimed not to remember details or were unwilling to venture beyond generalities. It was only Zhou Guangyou who provided a vivid description of what happened in his brigade.

The Task Force's materials provide only a few simple sentences about what happened at Chibatang: "On August 28, 1967, Cenjiangdu Commune's Chibatang production brigade killed 13 people. The brigade's killing operation was influenced by the August 25 commune meeting (held by commune deputy secretary Mo Kunzhen) and was also related to the Shangdu militia headquarters. The major responsibility was held by the brigade's deputy secretary, Tang Shaoguang, militia head Tang Shaogong, and PPA chairman Zhou Guangyou, but Zhou Guangyou should bear the greatest responsibility. Recommendation: Zhou Guangyou should be expelled from the party; Tang Shaoguang and Tang Shaogong should be relieved of their positions." Without Zhou Guangyou's narrative, it would be impossible to know what rich material lay behind these bare facts.

At the time we interviewed Zhou Guangyou, he was recuperating at home after being gouged in the thigh by an ox. Limping and gritting his teeth with pain, he insisted on serving us tea and cigarettes. His expression was tense. After we repeatedly soothed him, he finally began to speak, albeit with lingering temerity, and once he began, he seemed compelled to continue:

> At that time, the situation was thoroughly chaotic; there was talk everywhere of killings, with multiple rumors reaching the village on any given day. Someone said that in one production team in Qingtang Commune, 20 class enemy households had risen up against the 10 poor-peasant households and wiped them out. Someone else said that many of the county's villages were killing class enemies, who in turn had fled to the No. 2 High School and snatched weapons in preparation for a bloodbath. The killing wind became increasingly intense. On August 26, our commune started killing people—there were killings in 13 of the 15 brigades, but not in ours. Every day there were rumblings about how many had been killed in such-and-such brigade, and why we hadn't made a move yet. At that time, everything was up to the poor and lower-middle peasants, and I was PPA chairman, so I called together several of our brigade's cadres and asked them: "There have been killings in other brigades, but we haven't taken action yet. What do you think we should do?" We were all unsure, and no one spoke up. Party secretary Zhou Yongbin noticed that not all party committee members were present, and he suggested that everyone gather at Tangjia Village that night to discuss the matter.
>
> That night at the meeting, I proposed a plan: "How about if we first round up the class enemies, and then we'll send someone to the commune to request instructions. If the higher-ups say we should kill them, we'll do it, but if they don't give the word, we'll let them go." Everyone thought that was a good idea.
>
> Early the next morning, party secretary Zhou went with Zhou Fating from the Zhou clan and Tang Shaogong from the Tang clan (one was brigade leader and the other the militia leader) to the commune to request instructions. Along the way, they ran into commune cadre Huang Renyi and asked him, "Comrade Huang, what are the commune's directives on killing people?" Huang Renyi said, "Outside they've been beating the war drums and you act like it's just chickens pecking at their food bowls! Don't waste time going to the commune—hurry back and start killing! The district has sent shock brigades down to the villages to supervise battle operations, and you're way behind!"
>
> At noon that day, I was taking my nap when Tang Shaogong rushed in and got me out of bed: "Guangyou, Guangyou! Someone's here from

the district militia headquarters berating us as cowards! What do you think we should do?" I said, "Since they've sent someone, all we can do is round people up." "Which ones?" "Just get started and we'll figure it out." As I got dressed, I told him to notify the poor and lower-middle peasants to come for a meeting, and I notified the militia to start rounding people up. Within two hours, the poor and lower middle peasants had gathered in the yard behind the Tangjia Village storehouse, and the militia had rounded up 12 class enemies and locked them in the storehouse. I saw that rich-peasant offspring Tang Shou'e was carrying a baby just two or three months old, and I told the militia to untie her.

After everyone had arrived, deputy party secretary Tang Shaoguang organized the key leaders to discuss who should be killed. He would name someone and then there would be discussion and a vote. The original idea was just to kill a few to satisfy the higher-ups, but the atmosphere suddenly became very intense. Our brigade included three villages divided among the Tang and Zhou clans, and members of one clan suggested killing someone from the other clan while protecting those from their own. It became a competition, and I could see that we'd need to kill either all or none of them, so we finally decided to kill all 12.

Next we held a rally to pronounce judgment. The militia leader whom headquarters had sent down to supervise operations was my cousin, and I invited him to speak. He'd spent the morning rushing down to our brigade, but we'd neglected to feed him and he was cranky with a bellyache, so he told me to speak instead. Obliged to mount the podium, I told everyone to raise their Little Red Books (you couldn't do anything back then without a Little Red Book) and read several quotes: "Whomever the enemy opposes, we must support. . . ." I don't remember the rest of it—I'm illiterate, but back then I'd memorized hundreds of quotes from that book. Then I said, "The main purpose of today's meeting is to kill landlords and rich peasants. If we don't, we'll lose out under the revival of capitalism. I suggest we agree to kill them!" I'm not much of a speaker, so I said just a few words, ended with "That's all!," and stood to the side.

After that, the death sentences were proclaimed. . . . After the meeting, I discussed with CRC [Cultural Revolution Committee] leader Tang Shaogong how we should carry out the killings. At first we considered doing it in the hills across the Cenjiang River, but this meant taking a busy road. If we killed them in the river, it would pollute the water. When the brigade upstream killed people and threw them in the river, the bodies floated downstream and blocked the dam over by us. It stank to high heaven, and we complained to that brigade. After talking it over, we decided to take them to the hills across from Zhoujia, and everyone else agreed. We decided that Tang Shaogong would arrange for a boat to cross the river, and I'd arrange for the militia to escort the class enemies, two for each so no one could escape.

The hill across from Zhoujia was an old graveyard overgrown with cogon grass. During the Learn from Dazhai campaign, some terraced fields had been cultivated, and some tea oil trees had been planted, but they were straggly and no taller than the cogon grass. After the boat crossed the river, we chose a grassy plain at the foot of the hill and had the class enemies kneel in a row. We had the 100-odd militiamen stand in five rows, with two facing each landlord and rich peasant. Those with fowling guns stood in the front three rows. Our brigade had feuded with other brigades in the past, so every household had a blunderbuss, and the militia later added some more. Those armed with spears and clubs stood in the back two rows, along with others who wanted to see the action. After we'd arranged everything, my brother Zhou Guangbao went weak and didn't want to take part in the attack, so I told him to stand to one side and give the orders. I was a core militiaman myself, so I stood in the front row with Tang Shaogong, my gun aimed at Zhou Yuliang.

Guangbao was about to call out the order when Tang Shou'e suddenly began to cry and begged, "Don't kill me, don't kill me! I have a three-month-old baby!" But by then, who dared listen to her?

"One, two, three, fire!" Guangbao shouted.

My hands were trembling, and it took a lot of strength to draw back the cock on the blunderbuss. After the first row finished shooting, they stood to the side and let the second row take over. After the second row fired, the third row came forward. Then the fourth and fifth rows went at them with their spears and clubs, and after that the people swarmed forward and stoned them. . . .

After I returned home, I felt as if I'd contracted malaria. I was weak from head to foot and so exhausted that I tumbled into bed, my heart pounding. It felt like being a bandit. After I'd lain down for a while, I heard someone shouting outside: some hadn't died and were standing up and untying each other's ropes. I got out of bed and ran outside and saw the brigade's leaders mobilizing militia to go finish them off. But no matter what they said, no one was willing to go, and when they told me to go, I said I was too sick. They had no choice but to cross the river themselves and deal with it. Public-security chief Tang Shaomu had spent some time in the Mao Zedong Thought Culture and Propaganda

Team and he was a great singer of mountain songs. He led the others while singing:

> Tell you to kill, you don't kill,
> Tell you to stab, you don't stab,
> The tough job is left to me. . . .

After crossing the river, they saw a man named Mao Tianguai hoeing weeds in the sweet-potato field. Party secretary Zhou Yongbin said to him, "Tianguai, over on the hill there are some class enemies that didn't get killed. If you take care of it for me, the brigade will pay you five *kuai*." At that time, five *kuai* bought a lot. Mao Tianguai was an old bachelor who'd fought in Korea. As a decommissioned soldier, he was brave as well as poor, and when he heard what Zhou Yongbin said, he wasted no words before picking up his hoe and setting off. When he reached the hill, he found that there were in fact some people who were still alive and groaning. He used his hoe to kill them all. He even took a couple of sweat rags off the corpses to take home. We have a saying here that the sweat rag of a dead man is a charm, and that keeping it with you will extend your life; the sweat rags of those who die violent deaths are the best. After Mao Tianguai finished, he came down the hill and crossed the river to the brigade office and filled out the form to get his five *kuai*. [That form became part of the Task Force's files in 1986.]

Now you're wondering about that little baby? No one dared to kill it, not even Mao Tianguai. It was just left there on the hill with no one taking care of it, and that night people heard it crying. . . .

Afterwards I left the village to work as a cook at the Dongsheng machine plant. When the Task Force began its investigation, I took the initiative to go to the factory party committee and confess. The factory party committee had someone take me back to the production brigade for a study class lasting more than 20 days. Because I'd been away, people in the brigade had pushed all the blame on me. That wasn't right—we had to seek truth from facts! I went to them, and in the presence of the Task Force, I clarified everything point by point, what I had done and what they had done, systematically and in full detail. There was no question of not admitting error—that was impossible. Saying you didn't remember was a lie—how could anyone forget what had happened? I remember everything clearly, times, places, witnesses— who can deny their wrongdoing? Afterwards, the comrades from the Task Force thanked me for helping them clarify how everything had come about in our production brigade.

A brigade secretary's story

The leading production brigades of Shenzhangtang Commune in terms of killing were the Qianjin brigade (39 dead, including 1 suicide), the Hongri (Songzhou) brigade (33 dead), and the Hongyan (also called Huluyan) brigade (30 dead, including 7 suicides). Among them, the Hongyan brigade stood out.

The Hongyan brigade, also known as Huluyan Village, lay nestled along a hill on the western bank of the Tuoshui River, where the Huluyan Crossing ferry traversed an ancient route to Jiangyong and Jianghua. The nearby hills, although rocky and barren, lent the village a picturesque charm.

On August 25, after brigade Chinese Communist Party (CCP) secretary Zhou Fu'ai and other leaders returned from the commune meeting at the Dongmin brigade, Zhou called a meeting of cadres and core militiamen to implement the spirit of the commune meeting. After the usual salute to Mao and the recital of relevant quotes from the Little Red Book, Zhou Fu'ai proceeded to the topic at hand: "In the previous phase, our brigade's seize-and-push operation was very successful, but other brigades started killing class enemies long ago and we still haven't taken action. The reason I've called you all together today is to discuss what we should do. Should we also kill a couple of our troublemakers?"

"Kill them! If we don't kill some troublemakers, our brigade's cadres can't claim any credit!"

"The higher-ups have given the word to kill, so we should do it!"

When Zhou Fu'ai saw the thinking was unanimous, he said, "Fine. So let's discuss which ones to kill."

When he said this, however, the meeting room fell silent. As in other brigades, once it became a matter of specific lives to take, the subject became much more difficult; the class enemies the brigade had left, while not absolute saints, hadn't done anything worthy of death. Confronted by this silence, Zhou Fu'ai said, "If none of you will make suggestions, I will: [Zhou] Fuwen and [Qiu] Shengfeng. Now let's discuss it."

After Zhou spoke, there was silence again. Even those who had previously been whispering to each other now sat ramrod straight. There was something odd about one of the two names Secretary Zhou had raised. Zhou Fuwen was understandable—as a rich-peasant offspring, he could be killed. But Qiu Shengfeng was a lower-middle peasant, and the crux of the matter was that his intimate relationship with Zhou Fu'ai's mother, Chen Mannü, was an open secret in the village. Zhou Fu'ai had been burning with anger over this for a long time, thinking it a blot on his reputation. Ordinarily, as the brigade's leader, he should have been able to do whatever he wanted with Qiu Shengfeng. But he was also a dutiful son who was somewhat fearful of his mother's wrath, and this made the situation particularly sticky. No one would miss Qiu Shengfeng, but no one wanted to get on the wrong side of the hot-tempered Chen Mannü.

When Zhou Fu'ai saw that no one was willing to speak up, he was furious, but he knew it was too late to take back what he'd said. Glaring at the crowd, he said, "Have you all gone mute? Or are you all unrevolutionary cowards?"

Even at that, no one spoke.

Pounding the table in fury, Zhou Fu'ai said, "No one can leave! Fuyu [Zhou Fuyu was the militia leader and a kinsman of Zhou Fu'ai], take some men and arrest Qiu Shengfeng and Zhou Fuwen. I can't believe revolution is really this difficult!"

Zhou Fuyu immediately led several of the attending core militiamen to apprehend Qiu Shengfeng and Zhou Fuwen, who were then dragged out to be executed in accordance with Zhou Fu'ai's orders. The meeting was then adjourned without anyone remembering to carry out the final shouting of slogans.

Early the next day (August 27), Zhou Fu'ai called another meeting to discuss the killing issue. Why had he woken up with an urge for more killing after purging his rankling hatred against those two? Several residents of Huluyan Village told us that after Qiu Shengfeng was killed, Chen Mannü wept all night and threatened to hang herself. Zhou Fu'ai repeatedly explained to his mother that it wasn't he who wanted Qiu killed, and he was only obeying instructions from above. But Chen Mannü wasn't buying it—the upper levels were calling for class enemies to be killed, so there had to be an ulterior motive to killing a lower-middle peasant such as Qiu when landlords and rich peasants weren't being killed. Her words made Zhou Fu'ai realize that letting off so many class enemies while rushing to kill Qiu Shengfeng would be very hard to explain to the upper levels. The more he thought about it, the more he realized that he had to quickly kill another batch—if the majority were class enemies, along with a few poor and lower-middle peasants who'd managed to change their class status, he would have no need to fear criticism from above.

That's why he woke up early and called a meeting of the brigade's cadres and militia. At the meeting, Zhou Fu'ai pulled out list of people to be killed, this time all bona fide black elements and their offspring. To his surprise, however, the others disagreed with his choices. Many objected to his actions the day before and accused him of selfish and unjust motives, high-handedness, and disregard for others. Cadres who had remained silent the day before now spoke out: "The higher-ups said we could kill one or two troublemakers, and we've done that. Anything more should wait for directives from above." The implication was that Secretary Zhou had acted without authorization. On hearing this, Zhou Fu'ai seethed internally but held it in; the others were speaking rationally and even-handedly, and it was hard to refute their insistence on upper-level directives. While inclined to wield his secretarial authority to force the issue, Zhou realized that he would have difficulty justifying repetition of his actions of the day before, however high his standing might be within the brigade. In any case, he had nothing to gain from killing these people, and it was enough that he'd made his views known. He responded, "Chairman Mao instructs us: the masses are the true heroes. If everyone feels there's no urgent need for killing, then we won't do it."

It appeared at this point that this second batch of victims would be spared. Nevertheless, at noon that day, two of the brigade's core militiamen who'd been deployed to the Shangdu militia headquarters hurried back to the brigade with directives from the district calling for "catch-up" operations: all class enemies should be killed within the next three days, or there would be no further opportunity to do so. For Zhou Fu'ai, the directive came just in time; the others had insisted on a directive from above, so what more could they say? Zhou Fu'ai immediately called another meeting that afternoon, and this time, cadres who continued to have reservations about the killings shrank like tortoises into their shells for fear of being labeled "Rightist deviationists." There was no further room for debate over the killings except on how they should be carried out.

Aware of appallingly drawn-out processes in other brigades, public-security head Qiu Shengyang recommended drowning as the simplest and least traumatic method, and everyone else endorsed this idea.

After assigning the manpower and deciding the rewards for those who carried out the killings, Zhou Fu'ai told the brigade accountant to lead the assembly in shouting slogans so this last order of business wouldn't be neglected again: "Long live the victory of the great proletarian revolution! Sweep away all ox demons and snake spirits! The revolution is not a dinner party or fancy needlework! . . ."

Everything had been carefully arranged and responsibilities assigned for each step, but one small problem remained: the rather long and drawn-out discussion resulted in word somehow leaking out, and by the time it came to arrest people, two class enemies had already "evaded punishment through suicide," and even one woman who was not on the list had panicked and hanged herself. The remaining nine were hogtied and taken to Huluyan Crossing, where Qiu Shengyang sentenced them to death in the name of the peasant supreme court. Several were paralyzed with fear and had to be dragged onto the ferry. Once the boat reached the middle of the Tuo River, the victims were tossed one by one into the water.

After that, on August 28, Shenzhangtang Commune coordinated with the Shangdu militia headquarters by again calling a cadre meeting to collect statistics on the killings and to supervise and encourage supplementary action.

After the meeting, the Huluyan brigade felt obliged to kill another batch, this time mainly black-element offspring, but Secretary Zhou felt it would be a waste to kill the young women, especially two who were especially attractive and hard-working. Zhou Fu'ai handed down a pronouncement: "The women of class enemies whose men have been suppressed can escape death if they're willing to marry poor or lower-middle peasants." The majority of cadres and villagers endorsed this decision, which reduced the number of deaths while also addressing the difficulties of some of the brigade's old bachelors. It was because of this local policy of Secretary Zhou that in the Huluyan brigade (and many others in Daoxian), many women from black-element households managed to survive. It could be considered a kind of dark virtue.

Nineteen years later, in 1986, while reporting in Huluyan Village, we heard the following story from villagers: During the random killings of 1967, Zhou Fu'ai and the other brigade leaders killed off the entire family of the landlord offspring Qiu Shengxiang except for Qiu's wife, Liu Guicui, who became the wife of Zhou's third elder brother, Zhou Fujin. Now that the Task Force was implementing the policy of compensating families for loss of life and providing them with housing subsidies and other funding, the compensation meant for Qiu Shengxiang's family was given to Zhou Fujin in the absence of other survivors. The villagers were indignant that this man who had taken part in killing Qiu and stealing his wife and assets should be the only one to enjoy the government subsidies.

On hearing this story, I felt like an overturned condiment bottle, many flavors mixing together. Perhaps I'd thought it through more than the villagers, or perhaps the villagers had also thought a lot about it but were unwilling to say what they felt. Although we were unlikely to be in complete agreement, it was certain that we all recognized this outcome as inevitable.

Whatever the Communist Party says

After repeated setbacks, we finally went through all the necessary procedures to interview Yuan Lifu and Zheng Youzhi[1] and found ourselves seated in the visitor's room of the Lingling Prefecture No. 3 Prison, staring out the window at the high walls topped with barbed wire. Our heads were packed with a muddle of data and heartbreaking stories, but we couldn't let this information give us any preconceived ideas about these men. If our reporting in Daoxian had taught us anything, it was that our imaginations were no match for the insane events of 19 years ago.

We first met Zheng Youzhi, whom we interviewed under the watchful gaze of a prison guard.

Zheng Youzhi was a big, imposing man with bright, piercing eyes and the lingering air of his former status as commander of the Frontline Command Post.

He was a coarse, uneducated, and inarticulate man, and what he said was largely consistent with what we'd read in the Task Force's files. I somehow felt he was basically honest, but without any basis for this belief beyond the intuition borne of my long experience as a journalist.

Zheng Youzhi had been sentenced to 10 years in prison.[2] The Task Force report on "Zheng Youzhi's incitement and tacit ordering of killings during the Cultural Revolution" quoted Zheng's remarks at various meetings, including one on August 31, after further killing had been prohibited. It also described a case on August 20 in which a postal and telecommunications officer had telephoned Zheng to ask how to deal with three fugitive black elements who had been captured. Zheng had the men brought to Yingjiang and then ordered militiamen to escort all three back to their home brigades: "These three wanted to blow up the postal and telecommunications office. Take them back and let the poor and lower-middle peasants decide what to do with them." All three were killed after being escorted home.

So what did Zheng Youzhi have to say about all this?

I enlisted in the army in 1950, returned to civilian life in 1958, and became a political instructor in the postal and telecommunications office. Originally the plan was to promote me to director of the office, but later, when the leaders saw that I was bold in my work, energetic, and hard-working, they sent me to Yueyan District, an air defense focal point, to serve as PAFD [People's Armed Forces Department] commander. In this district there was a place called Qianjiadong that was a focal zone for preventing air drops by enemy agents.... I was there for eight or nine years and racked up some accomplishments that drew commendations from the county, district, and province. In 1965 and 1967, I attended the Model Worker Conference for Learning and Applying the Works of Chairman Mao in the Hunan Provincial Military District and Guangzhou Military Region. On August 1, 1967, the county presented our district with a tractor as a reward for our work. I'm sure you've read my file, so you know I was never disciplined for anything. I always did whatever the party told me to. It's not that I never thought of myself, but I struggled against selfishness and revisionist thinking. Think about it: without the Communist Party and Chairman Mao, could a clod like me ever hope to become a cadre? Every day I was taught never to forget class struggle, and that class enemies were carrying out sabotage to stage an overthrow and restore the old order, that Chiang Kai-shek wanted to stage a counterattack against the mainland, so how could I ever lower my gun? On August 8, 1967, the county's minority faction raided the PAFD armory, and we heard that black elements were planning an overthrow to settle old scores [against the Red regime], and I automatically took the side of the Red Alliance. The county PAFD and old leaders also supported the Red Alliance. . . .

On August 16, while I was in Yingjiang, Zhou Renbiao came and said that our district had unearthed two counterrevolutionary organizations that had grown to more than a thousand members. Their plan was to "organize in August, rebel in September, and kill all the poor and lower-middle peasants and half of the middle peasants." When I heard this, I felt the situation was serious, and I went back and held a cadre meeting, where I transmitted this information. Later I heard it was false, but I didn't know that at the time and I never guessed that so many people would be killed. Really, I never imagined it at that time! In all fairness, I wasn't in favor of killing people. On August 19, district secretary Zeng Qingxuan telephoned me to report good news, saying Qingtang's Liaojia brigade had killed six black elements all at once. When I heard this I was shocked, and I said this kind of killing was wrong and I told him to quickly put an end to it. You can ask Zeng Qingxuan about this. The next day, Cui Baoshu, who was commander of the county militia at the time, came to Yingjiang, and I reported to him that our district had killed six people and asked what should be done about it. He said, "Right now the main issue isn't killings but weapons, and once that's resolved, everything else will be easier. Don't take any notice of what's happening in the villages for the time being." On the 21st, the military subdistrict's deputy commander Zhao and advisor Lu and the 47th Army's representative Liang came to Yingjiang, and I reported the killings to them. Deputy Commander Zhao asked how many people had been killed in the entire county. He Xia told him that around a hundred or so had been killed. Deputy Commander Zhao said, "Comrade Jiang Qing has said that this constitutes verbal attack and armed defense. In any case the killings have happened, and the problem now is how to safeguard the poor and lower-middle peasants."

You've asked if this is the truth. I've never been a person for careless talk; I tell it like it is, and I don't claim to have said something I didn't or deny saying something I did say. On the 23rd, He Xia and I once again discussed sending someone to ask Xiong Bing'en to personally call a meeting to stop the killings. On the 24th, He Xia told me that Xiong Bing'en said he couldn't do anything; the guns had been snatched, people had been killed, and he couldn't even guarantee his own safety, so how could he call a meeting? In fact, I didn't know how many people had actually been killed at that time. I noticed groups of Daojiang residents drawing water from the well of the Fanxianghao production brigade. I asked them why they'd come there to draw water, and they said the river was full of corpses and the water was undrinkable. That's when I realized how serious things were. Later we discussed holding a meeting to curb the killings, and originally we decided that district, commune, and Red Alliance leaders should report in on the 25th and then attend a three-day meeting starting on the 26th. Then He Xia and Huang Tao discussed it further and changed it into a meeting for political and legal cadres.

At the meeting on the 29th, someone asked how we should handle serious criminals whom the poor and lower-middle peasants insisted on killing. I telephoned militia political commissar Liu Shibin to request instructions, and Commissar Liu replied, "There's nothing I can do about it. . . ."

I didn't object to my sentence—even if they killed me I would have no objection. The consequences were just too serious! I tremble just thinking about it now. But the judgment says that I orchestrated the killings throughout the county, and I can't understand that. At the time, anything I said was just repeating what they said—not to mention that at the time, I requested instructions from this one and that one, and not a single person said the killings weren't allowed, and no one stepped forward to stop them. They all said we had to support the revolutionary actions of the poor and lower-middle peasants, and that one or two black elements could be killed. How could a district PAFD commander like me be responsible for such a major incident?

During the Cultural Revolution, I was beaten and locked up, and now they say I intentionally killed people and have to be imprisoned for it. . . . I feel I bear responsibility for the killings in Daoxian, but I absolutely don't bear the main responsibility.

Next came Yuan Lifu, sentenced to 13 years in prison.[3] In its report on "Yuan Lifu's organization and direction of killings during the Cultural Revolution," the Task Force described how Yuan "whipped up public opinion" and sent cadres from Xianglinpu District's Shangdu militia headquarters to push forward "catch-up" killings in the production brigades, resulting in 569 deaths in three days at the end of August. It might seem reasonable for Yuan Lifu to be remorseful and to have no complaints regarding his imprisonment for the killing of 569 people, but that was not the case.

Yuan presented a strong contrast to Zheng Youzhi, being a person of small stature with a glib tongue. His attitude seemed respectful and submissive, but everything he said contained hidden implications. After graduating from Hengyang Normal School in 1961, he underwent political training for an accelerated rise in the leadership ranks. By 1967, he was secretary and deputy head of Xianglinpu District. In 1984 he was transferred from his position as deputy secretary of the Daoxian commission for discipline inspection to become head of the Township Enterprises Bureau of Dong'an County. After being sent to prison, he joined the prison teaching team. What was it that turned this refined bookworm into a homicidal maniac? Here's his version:

> I was sentenced to imprisonment because of the killings in Daoxian in August 1967. My 13-year sentence was the highest for any state cadre; I can't understand it from the perspective of the party's line, policies, principles, and laws. We're a Marxist-Leninist party, and we're supposed to emphasize seeking truth from facts, respecting history, and respecting facts. The killing of black elements in Daoxian didn't come out of nowhere—meter-deep water doesn't freeze overnight. It arose out of many factors. No one person was capable of giving the word to start the killings; it had both contingency and inevitability. From 1957 onward, the party's line became increasingly Leftist, and the sense of class struggle in the countryside became increasingly strong, with the peasants feeling a steadily growing hatred for the class enemy; that was the ideological root. In 1962, Daoxian became deeply influenced by battle-readiness education. When Chiang Kai-shek started clamoring about a counterattack against the mainland, three meetings were held in Daoxian. Daoxian's party secretary at that time, Shi Xiuhua, told district and commune secretaries that at the first sign of trouble, all black elements should be killed off so that when Chiang Kai-shek invaded the mainland, he'd have no one to lead the way. There were also a lot of reactionary leaflets being dropped at that time. A great emphasis was placed on class education for the masses, and there was even a song that went, "Don't forget class suffering; remember deep-seated hatred." The masses deeply loathed class enemies.
>
> Then, at the outset of the Cultural Revolution, Daoxian descended into chaos. There was the gun-snatching incident on August 8, and all levels of the leadership as well as the public-security and judicial apparatus were paralyzed.
>
> The third reason was sabotage by a minority of class enemies—a counterrevolutionary organization here, a counterrevolutionary organization there, class enemy retaliation here, rumors and sabotage by class enemies there. Now you're saying these were all bogus cases, but at that time, who knew that? There were seven major cases in the county, with four resulting in arrests and killings.[4] Under the influence of an ideology in which it was better to be part of the Left than the Right

and the farther to the Left the better, we all believed that class enemies were genuinely plotting an overthrow. The whole county was in chaos, the masses were terrified, and from the time that the killings began until they ended, not a single leader stepped forward to say that killing people was wrong. They just said rebellion was justified and there was no crime in revolution; they just talked about trusting the masses and respecting the creative initiative of the masses. There's one more thing, which is that the 47th Army issued its "Cable on the Social Situation," but those below misconstrued it and just talked about the seriousness of class struggle and the poor and lower-middle peasants defending themselves, and that had a profound effect.

Speaking of myself, I was a very ordinary rural cadre. It was impossible for me to transcend my era, and it was inevitable that I would play a role in the killings. But the judgment departs too far from the truth and confounds right and wrong. Responsibility isn't clearly apportioned and has been misapplied. Jiang Guangde telephoned me and told me to catch up and act with urgency to even out the numbers, but he was sentenced to only five years. All I did was pass along his instructions in a meeting, but I was sentenced to 13 years. It's unreasonable to put the main blame on me. Jiang Guangde said he was reporting to me, but that is completely inconsistent with the facts. I was just a deputy district head and at that time a suspended leading cadre; how could I have that kind of authority? You say I gave some extra play to Jiang Guangde's words, and yes, perhaps I added the odd phrase, but under the circumstances at the time, I think you can understand that everyone in the country, from the highest to the lowest level, was exaggerating, so what difference would a few words make one way or the other? Besides, everyone in China was crazy at that time, so how could I be expected to be the only one keeping a cool head? The situation at that time was that when someone issued a directive, it would be carried out. At that time I even telephoned the county to request instructions, and they told me to stay out of it. Besides, I never said how to kill people or how many; instead, I declared that there were to be no random killings and that people would be held responsible. So I don't understand why I've been sentenced to prison now.

Yuan Lifu raised one important point: why did he, a deputy district head, have so much power, when in other districts the real power was held by seize-and-push groups with PAFD cadres at their core? The Task Force at one point assigned a group of people to carry out a special investigation on this very question, perhaps at Yuan's instigation. The conclusion the Task Force reached was this: after the 1967 "January power seizure," several leading comrades of the Xianglunpu district CCP committee and government came under heavy attack and were basically sidelined or "suspended," Yuan among them. But in March, the county's Red Warriors (forerunner of the Red Alliance) convinced two commune secretaries to join Yuan Lifu in establishing the Xianglinpu District headquarters of the Red Warriors, with Cenjiangdu Commune secretary Mo Rongxing as commander, Xinche Commune PAFD commander Fan Liangchun as political commissar, and Yuan Lifu as advisor. At that time, the district PAFD commander was at home recuperating from an illness, so Fan Liangchun took over his work. Two of the PAFD commanders of the district's other three communes joined the district Red Warrior headquarters, and the third was a recent transfer who was unfamiliar with the people and the place, so Xianglinpu District's CCP and government organs were all effectively controlled by the Red Warrior headquarters, of which Yuan Lifu was advisor. This is why Yuan Lifu wielded such great power in Xianglinpu.

After we interviewed Zheng and Yuan, we passed through that heavy metal gate and began walking down the bustling street. My heart was boiling with rage, especially from the horrible impression Yuan Lifu had left—all that talk about historical background and objective factors without considering personal or subjective causes, much less expressing any sense of conscience or regret. More than 500 people had died, and he still had the gall to complain about 13 years in prison! It was almost awe-inspiring.

I said to Zhang Minghong, "I don't believe Zheng Youzhi would have carried out a 'big cleanup' like that if he'd been in Yuan Lifu's place, do you?"

Zhang Minghong laughed and said, "Of course not! Someone like Zheng Youzhi kills without hesitation when his superior tells him to, and when his superior tells him to stop, he does so immediately. Yuan Lifu is different—he has to demonstrate his ability, go the extra mile, show some creativity."

"Everything that's wrong with China is because of people like him!" I fumed. "They read a few books, memorize a few quotes, and think the truth is in their hands and justice is in their breasts, and that they can provide guidance for the people. The fact is that he doesn't know shit and is totally superficial, but he's a self-taught master of officialese and ladder climbing. It's obvious he wanted to dye himself a red official's cap with human blood, but he can still go on about being treated unjustly. All this stuff about the enemy situation, major cases, and reactionary organizations—those guys concocted all of it out of thin air. New trends in class struggle, the vengeful hatred of the masses toward the class enemy; it was all stirred up by those kinds of people. For decades the cream of our national traditions and culture has been discarded like rubbish, while the dregs have taken on a new guise to confuse and poison the people's minds. When the dregs rose to the surface, farmers had nothing to eat and workers had nothing to wear, and yet they still wouldn't desist with their boasting and lies. . . ."

"Okay!" Zhang Minghong saw my indignation building and interrupted me: " 'Beware of heartbreak with grievance overfull.'[5] You're too excitable, and sooner or later it's going to bring trouble."

We never imagined how prophetic Minghong's remark would turn out to be.

PART SEVEN

DEADLY POLITICS

21

A Little Education Is a Dangerous Thing

The legend of Widow's Bridge

Why were all the roads so secluded, as if melting into those misty mountains and rivers? One village after another dotted the forks in the river like pieces of fruit. In search of Daoxian's killing fields, we took buses to places accessible by highway, and bicycles to those that were not, and where even bicycles couldn't go, we walked. Our backs streamed with sweat under the ferocious sun. It was the time of the double-rush planting and harvesting, and men and women crouching busily in the fields occasionally stood to stretch their backs and size us up, clearly unaccustomed to the sight of people who didn't grow our own food, and mystified as to what could bring us running around under the blazing sun instead of resting in the shade somewhere.

At Longjiangqiao, where a mass killing rally was held on August 24, we encountered a little girl, four or five years old, herding six or seven very dignified-looking examples of the Daozhou gray geese that are a major export product for Daoxian. Where people had been dispatched to the afterlife on a "homemade airplane" at Shangtangzui, we saw girls with colorful umbrellas and embroidered skirts herding cows through a grove of low masson pines. Continuing our way along the limpid Fushui River, we reached Guapoqiao, "Widow's Bridge," formerly an execution ground, where a group of laughing young peasant men and women crossed the river with shoulder poles laden with wet grain. It was almost impossible to visualize the horrors that had occurred among these blue rivulets, verdant mountains, and warm-hearted, simple, and honest peasants, and it seemed that everything we'd heard was just a legend written in ocher.

Widow's Bridge. We went there twice.

The first time, it was raining, and the Chinese Communist Party (CCP) secretary of the Dongsheng machine factory, Lao Liu, shielded us with an umbrella on the narrow path from the factory to Guapoqiao. We soon found ourselves on

261

the misty bank of the Li River, where the steady rain imparted a glossy azure tint to the mountains that jutted up on either side of the river. "It's as lovely as Guilin here," I felt compelled to exclaim.

"People always say that. This place used to be called 'Little Guilin.' We've lived here so long we don't even notice," said Secretary Liu with a smile.

Widow's Bridge was a five-arch stone bridge with tall trees shading each end. Legend had it that a wealthy widow from the nearby Tang clan had donated the funds for the bridge's construction in the Qing dynasty, after many people had drowned attempting to cross this stretch of the Fushui River.

Secretary Liu observed, "People were often killed at this bridge during the Cultural Revolution. At that time, our factory had just moved here, and our workers lived in the two villages nearby. They often stood here watching from a distance. We weren't clear what was going on, and didn't dare get too close or ask too many questions. People were escorted to the center of the bridge and made to kneel down, then all we could see was the flash of a saber. . . . The bodies were pushed off the bridge into the river. If someone didn't die and rose to the surface, militiamen posted at each end of the bridge would shoot them with fowling guns."

The documents we had in hand said that an administrator of the Daoxian Normal School was one of the people killed on this bridge. We went to the normal school and interviewed the old headmaster, comrade Yin Shao'e, who told us that the victim was He Pinzhi, the school's head teacher. This gray-haired intellectual held back tears as with evident distress he told us what happened:

> He was a fine comrade—enthusiastic, upright, long-suffering, helpful, able, responsible, and thoroughly devoted to the party's educational undertaking. Before Liberation, while still in secondary school, he had participated in the party's underground movement and had contributed significantly to the peaceful liberation of Daoxian. After Liberation, he started out as a district cadre and then worked in the county court. In the early 1950s, the party organization made use of his special abilities by transferring him to the Daoxian No. 2 High School as a language teacher. He never complained about being shifted from one job to another and always made the best of whatever work he was given.
>
> In 1958, the county established its normal school with me as headmaster and allowed me to choose my own staff. My first choice was He Pinzhi; he could be a bit stubborn, but he was always as good as his word. Constructing the school was onerous work, and he led students in digging the foundations, preparing the ground, and dredging sand until they were cross-eyed with exhaustion. Look there—he and the students hauled the wood used for that classroom building all the way

from Donggongyuan, 30 kilometers away. There isn't a brick, tile, blade of grass, or tree on this property that isn't stained with his sweat.

After the school was built, the party organization appointed him head teacher, and he was even more sincere and responsible in taking on education work. He was one of those people who would work without pausing to sleep or eat. He encouraged students to be worthy of their calling and said that teachers should always be the very best, not only in learning but also in character. He was very demanding of himself as well. At that time, our teachers could change the status of their family members from rural to nonrural (to live off state funds), but he transferred his quota to other teachers while not asking the party for anything for himself.

He was versatile and energetic, and he liked to spend his free time writing. It was his word mongering that became his downfall. In the latter half of 1958, he wrote a play called *The Red Flag Is Raised Ever Higher*, extolling the "Three Red Banners" of the Great Leap Forward and the People's Communes. From our current perspective, this play was deeply branded with the Leftism of that era, and we would regard some of it as exaggerated and fawning. After it was checked and approved by the county party committee's propaganda department, the school's teachers and students performed the play several times for the masses. But He came from a landlord background, and in those absurd times, someone criticized lines spoken by the play's villain as representing the reactionary thinking of teacher He Pingzhi. He was publicly denounced during the campaign against Rightist deviation in 1959, and again at the outset of the Cultural Revolution, when he was accused of being a "three-opposer" who "opposed the party, socialism, and Mao Zedong Thought." He Pingzhi was dismissed from his position and sent to the countryside for reform through labor.

Back in his home village, he obediently took part in agricultural production and regularly reported to the production brigade party branch on his ideological remolding. When the killings began, he continued to believe in the party's policies, and even as he was led to Widow's Bridge to be executed, he still didn't believe that indiscriminate killing was occurring. He repeatedly told his militia escorts, "I've been falsely accused. I love the party and Chairman Mao. Don't kill me—I'll go to Beijing and sort it all out with the party center." How would those militiamen pay any attention to him? They pushed him to his knees and hacked him to death with sabers. Before he could finish crying out, "Long live Chairman Mao!," his head was chopped off and tossed into the Fushui River. His 18-year-old son, He Shangming, was killed with him.

We asked, "Were his students among those who killed him?" We'd all been through the Cultural Revolution and knew it was common for students to beat and denounce their teachers. My own mother, a schoolteacher, had half her hair shaved off by her beloved students and was beaten so badly that she was bedridden for days.

Yin Shao'e gave a bitter laugh and said, "That's impossible to know, but back then, there was no longer any such thing as teachers and students."

A comrade in the Task Force confirmed that He Pinzhi had been held in very high regard by his students, to the point that even when he was labeled a "three-opposer," some students refused to distance themselves from him and shared his fate. This comrade told us of a county public-security cadre named Liu Liangyi who defended He Pingzhi at great personal risk during the 1959 campaign against Rightist deviation, and the two men were denounced together in July 1966. An official document described Liu as colluding with "the three-opposer element He Pinzhi, defending He, and regarding the party and the people with enmity." Liu Liangyi was finally rehabilitated 13 years later, and it isn't necessary to elaborate further on his attendant tribulations and castration of conscience. What mystified us was what kind of magic potion He Pinzhi could have used on Liu Liangyi to make him abandon all reason and refuse to strike his old teacher when he was down. Such people have become increasingly rare!

That night, back at the guest house, we read teacher He Pinzhi's play and the reports he'd written on his ideological remolding, as well as a poem he'd presented to a leader in the county government, all of which we found deeply depressing. How could anyone vilify, debase, and criticize himself to this extent? In He Pinzhi we saw the inherently tragic nature of Chinese intellectuals. Consciously and against his own convictions, he had sung the praises of policies such as the Great Leap Forward that had wreaked such devastation on the national economy (in his play *The Red Flag Is Raised Ever Higher*), and it was clear that he'd genuinely given his all to the CCP's undertakings. He never seemed to have reflected on the validity of the self-criticism and ideological remolding he'd undergone.

In particular, the poem that He Pingzhi offered to the county official brought us to the painful recognition of how profoundly this culture of sycophancy had embedded itself in the psyche of Chinese intellectuals. He not only extolled the Great Leader and the Great, Glorious, and Correct Party, but he seized on opportunities to fawn on his immediate superior, never dreaming that the promising young leader he'd so passionately eulogized would be the first person to label him a three-opposer.[1] His writings show clearly that long before he lost his life, He Pinzhi had already lost his independent character and capacity for independent thinking. His life was a tragedy all the more pungent for the depths of his sincerity. Over time, remolding and campaigning stripped China's intellectuals of their social authority, devastated their spirits and characters, and broke their spines."

China's literati have always aspired to self-improvement and to guiding their country toward peace and prosperity, but ultimately they've never been anything more than subjects, commoners, and slaves. Teacher He Pinzhi could be held up as a model for emulation or as a "class enemy" to be killed as a warning to others—it all depended on the needs of "revolution." He may have planned a hundred ways his life might end: martyring himself in the line of duty, dying for a just cause, giving his life for another, laying down his life for his country, dying at home at a ripe old age . . . but surely never the way he actually died. Others had taken He Pinzhi's road before; others are still taking it now and others will take it in the future. All we could think of was what lessons and reflections we intellectuals should draw from He Pinzhi's death.

A few days later, while reporting on another case, we came a second time to Widow's Bridge. This time it was a clear and sunny day, and the bridge was heavily trafficked by people on foot or on bicycles, as well as by lumbering cattle and a little yellow dog. Even under the brilliant sunlight, Widow's Bridge was shaded by the majestic canopy of a camphor tree, and the banisters of the bridge remained cool to the touch. The only trace of the killings was some faint knife marks on the granite rails. Rubbing the knife marks made everything around recede into a blur; this shouldn't have been a place where people died. I couldn't keep the tears from flowing down my face. I wasn't crying for He Pinzhi, but for myself.

As so-called intellectuals, we considered ourselves as having the capacity to think, reason, and analyze, but the moment a person's thinking comes under the control of any kind of power, a process of "dehumanization" occurs. This is true both of the killers and their victims. Indeed, rather than being dragged into the spiritual abattoir to undergo castration, it was more often that people struggled to be the first to squeeze into that slaughterhouse and then competed to see who could castrate themselves first and then as many others as possible. Vaclav Havel once said, "We are all—though naturally to differing extents—responsible for the operation of the totalitarian machinery. None of us is just its victim. We are all also its cocreators."[2]

For a long time, the social theories we believed in and energetically promoted provided a defense for atrocities, sustained the willpower of evildoers, and enabled them to whitewash their actions, ensuring that instead of being censured and reviled, they were extolled and their infamy was shrouded in a halo of righteousness, resulting in devastating calamity for millions of people (including ourselves). Ironically, we tumbled into the very ideological snares we fabricated for others. Long indifferent to the disasters suffered by others, especially other intellectuals, we sometimes even gloated at their misfortunes and saw them as opportunities for our own advancement. As each political movement purged one group of people, another group gained the wherewithal to sell their souls for their glorious ambitions. Contemplating our revolting performance is just too humiliating. A person might feel compelled to sell his soul for the sake of survival, but everyone should have a bottom line. Where was ours? Nurtured on the blood and sweat of the lower classes, we intellectuals repaid them with the creation of a totalitarian state in which the suffering of the lower classes outweighed our hardships a hundredfold; it was only that they lacked our gift for expressing it. China's intellectuals lack for nothing but independence of character and the spirit of free thought; this is our genetic flaw, and we will not be able to save ourselves or our country until we address it.

Widow's Bridge, oh Widow's Bridge, you're a testament to our dignity and shame!

Noticing my sudden loss of composure, the person accompanying us asked why I was crying. Wiping away my tears, I evaded the question by asking, "Among the people killed on this bridge, were any the descendants of that widow?"

Our companion thought this a very strange question to ask: "How would I know that? But the widow was so wealthy, it's likely that her descendants belonged to the upper social classes. If you really want to know, we can go to the village office and search the records."

"No, don't bother, I was just wondering."

Whether it was true or not, it might as well have been. Who knows but that the teacher He Pinzhi and his killers were both descendants of the same line, just as in Houtian Village, the native place of Zhou Dunyi.

If you loved the Communist Party, would the party kill you?

Similar to He Pinzhi's situation was that of a teacher at the Daoxian No. 2 High School, Li Jingxi. Born to a landlord family, Li was classified as an educator. He was 47 when he was killed on August 29, 1967.

After graduating in 1948 from Guangzhou's Sun Yat-sen University, Li Jingxi moved back to make an educational contribution to his native place, and by 1958 he had become the mathematics teacher for the graduating class at the No. 2 High School. He was always assessed as a model worker, active in every political movement, and was loved and respected by his students and trusted by parents.

During the 1965 Socialist Education movement, a decision was made behind closed doors to designate Li Jingxi as a "landlord who had slipped through the net." After the Cultural Revolution was launched in 1966, he was formally labeled a landlord element and sent back to his native village in the Tongxiwei brigade of Xianglinpu District's Xinche Commune for reform through labor.

I wondered how a man who had studied away from home since his youth and then worked as a teacher could be classified as a landlord. A Task Force comrade told us: "You can't use today's perspective on things that happened back then, or an urban perspective to view what happened in the countryside. There were actually plenty of reasons to label Li Jingxi as a landlord who had slipped through the net, and one or two was enough. You say Teacher Li never took part in exploitation, but let me ask you, where did the money come from to send him to school? Wasn't it the result of the exploitation his family engaged in? You can never really get to the bottom of these matters, but in any case, he's been rehabilitated now."

On September 27, 1966, Li Jingxi returned to the village he'd left years ago, wearing the cap of a landlord who'd slipped through the net, and with his mother, wife, and four young children in tow.

Tongxiwei is located on the border of Daoxian and Jiangyong Counties, sandwiched between the Dupangling and Tongshanling mountain ranges, where the Yongming (Yanshui) River enters Daoxian from its source in Liangsanjie, Jiangyong County. Before Liberation, this river was an important waterway between Daojiang Town and the county seat of Jiangyong (Yongming) County, carrying 4-ton wooden boats in the spring and summer, and 1- to 2-ton boats in the autumn and winter dry season. After Liberation, massive irrigation projects resulted in the construction of many overflow dams that made the river largely inaccessible to boat traffic but added to the beauty of the local scenery.

Villagers constructed the overflow dams where the riverbed was relatively even, building dikes of wood and stone around 2 meters high to raise the water level during the dry season, but allowing the water to flow over the dikes during the rainy season without causing flooding. In the gaps at either end of the overflow dams are placed archaic wooden waterwheels, typically 5 or 6 meters in diameter, which lift water into a trough that irrigates the fields beside the river. Historical material records the emergence of this automatic irrigation tool as early as the Southern Song period, about one thousand years ago, but the first time I saw one in real life was on the way to Tongxiwei, and my heart clenched in awe of the technical achievement it represented. The dry season had begun, and the waterwheels rotated at each end of the dam with a squeaking and clattering sound as they emptied meager bucketloads of water into the wooden troughs. No matter how slowly a waterwheel turned, it would never stop moving, and no matter how it groaned, it would never collapse.

This was the living environment that the teacher Li Jingxi returned to, a tremendous change from his previous existence. His family of seven was forced to live in a cattle shed measuring less than 20 square meters. The attic room where

Li's two daughters slept was stiflingly hot in the summer and bitter cold in the winter. Li's young son and mother slept in one corner of the downstairs, and Li, his wife, and second son slept in the opposite corner. (The eldest son, Li Dongde, had been sent down to Dapingpu Farm as an "educated youth.") The family took its meals at a small table in the middle of the room, and next to the entrance were two stoves, one for cooking rice and the other for cooking pig swill. Li had spent decades away from the farm, but he'd set his mind to thoroughly remolding himself and managed to bear up under the hard and exhausting work. Besides that, he had some former students who quietly looked out for him, along with some savings accumulated over the years and some relatives with good class backgrounds or serving as cadres, and all these things helped him get by about as well as any other local villager. The worst was when admonishment meetings were held for black elements, and he would have to bow his head or even kneel and admit his crimes, but after he got past the initial humiliation, it didn't bother him anymore.

By August 1967, after nearly a year in his home village, Li Jingxi was beginning to look just like any other wiry, 56-year-old peasant and had even come around to accepting the CCP's designation of him as a "landlord that slipped through the net." In the ideological report he submitted to the production brigade CCP branch, he wrote:

> Although before Liberation I was always studying elsewhere and never took part in my family's exploitative activities, from the time I was young, every mouthful of rice I ate and every penny I spent came from the exploitation of the blood and sweat of the poor and lower-middle peasants. . . . Let alone that before I went away to school, I helped keep accounts for my family's rent collection, which in fact was a thoroughly exploitative activity. In the past I didn't clearly recognize this and acknowledged only a disguised form of exploitation, but now I truly recognize that I am an utter parasite dependent on the blood and sweat of the poor and lower-middle peasants to support myself. Coming to this realization has undeniably been very painful for me, but if I am to thoroughly remold myself and make a fresh start in life, I must start with recognizing my reactionary nature first and foremost. I now truly realize this, and the organization's designation of me as a "landlord that slipped through the net" is both the inevitable result of my exploitative activities and the means by which the organization will ultimately educate and rescue me. . . . I am resolved, under the supervision, education, and assistance of the production brigade party branch and poor and lower-middle peasants, to thoroughly transform my worldview, completely reform myself, and struggle to become a new socialist person who lives off the labor of his own hands.

The village folk seemed to forget that Li had been handed over to them as a class enemy for penal labor under surveillance. Some even thought, "A high-quality, educated person such as Teacher Li will be taken back to the county seat sooner or later." So whenever the production team or individual villagers needed word-mongering skills, Li was the first person they went to.

Then the killing wind began blowing through Daoxian. On August 24, 1967, Xinche Commune's secretary, Zhang Guanghan, and People's Armed Forces Department (PAFD) commander, Jiang Liangchun, called a "five chiefs" meeting to incite and orchestrate killings. The Tongxiwei brigade's leaders returned to the brigade and immediately put all black elements under control, although they didn't kill anyone right away.

On August 26, commune CCP secretary Chen Pingri and commune secretary Zhang Guanghan arrived in Tongxiwei to "inspect operations," and Chen criticized the brigade for hanging back. Stung by the rebuke, the Tongxiwei brigade immediately decided to kill four "troublemakers." Li Jingxi was not among them, because his behavior had been exemplary; he smiled even when a three-year-old kid berated him, showing the progress he'd made in remolding himself.

After the first batch of four "class enemies" was killed, the Shangdu militia headquarters sent militiamen down to direct "military operations." The brigade held another meeting, during which Cultural Revolution Committee (CRC) chairman Li Xumei said, "The revolution hasn't been thorough enough! We killed only the fish swimming near the surface—we need to go after the ones hiding in the depths. Those are the most dangerous enemies." They therefore decided to kill another batch of 10 people, and one of them was the "landlord who slipped through the net," Li Jingxi.

When the name list was reported to the commune for approval, commune CCP secretary Chen Pingri said, "The poor and lower-middle peasants have discerning eyes and a demon-detecting mirror that exposes the true colors of the class enemy, no matter how well disguised or deeply hidden."

Li's son, Li Dongde, described his father's death to us:

In August 1967, the killing wind began blowing through Daoxian, starting over in Simaqiao. When it first started, no one was killed here in Xianglinpu, but the situation was fermenting. At this time, my uncle who lived over in Daokou Town was away from home peddling merchandise, and he sent someone with a verbal message to my father, telling him to meet him at Shangjiang Market [a town in Jiangyong County about 4 kilometers from Tongxiwei] because he had something important to tell him. Father was under a political cloud and it was difficult for him to request leave, so he asked my mother to go instead. My uncle told Mother: "Landlords are being killed all over Daoxian right now.

You have to devise a plan to escape as soon as possible." Mother rushed home and told this to Father. Father said, "How could that be? Don't listen to such lies. The party put the landlord label on us in order to compel us to reform our thinking and make a fresh start in life. They certainly won't resort to physical extermination. As long as we obey the party and remold ourselves, I'm sure this cap will be removed from us sooner or later."

My mother said, "This doesn't sound like a wild rumor to me. Since you've been labeled, you should think of a way to escape." My father said, "Where can I hide? What place isn't under the control of the Communist Party? And if I did run off, what about you and the children? The party's policy is that we don't choose our class background, but we can choose our path. Our generation has no hope, but the children can fight for a better future; at least I shouldn't have a further bad influence on their lives. I don't believe the party's policy will treat everyone the same; even if they're really killing landlords, I'm sure they'll kill only those who have really done something bad and not those who are honestly accepting remolding."

My mother usually accepted whatever my father said, but a woman's intuition is sometimes stronger than a man's, and she still felt uneasy.

My father said, "If a disaster is going to happen, we can't escape it, and if we can escape it, it's not a disaster. We have to be resigned to whatever comes. All we can do now is go out and work even harder and be even more careful in everything we say. We mustn't let anyone grab us by the pigtail."

My poor father never dreamed that the killing would be so indiscriminate. Just a few days later, on August 15 or 16, the production brigade called all the black elements in for a meeting, and as soon as Father arrived he was locked up with the others. During the day the militia escorted them to the fields to work, and at night they were locked up in the brigade's storehouse. My mother brought my father all his meals. A few days later, Father and the others were escorted to the river, where four class enemy offspring who had just turned 18 were pulled out and shot with a blunderbuss. Because a blunderbuss isn't a lethal weapon, rocks were taken from the river to crush their skulls. This time, Father and the others were only taken to observe and weren't killed.

By then, the killing wind was blowing even more ferociously, and people were saying that landlord families had to be destroyed root and branch. Two small children had just been killed in Xinche Commune's Bajia brigade, and this terrified us so much that none of us dared set foot outside our house.

On the evening of August 27, my father had been working in the fields for the double-rush planting and harvesting for two weeks without being allowed to take a bath. He was covered with dirt and sweat, his hair was matted, and he stank so much that the militiamen guarding him held their noses and stood far off. Father asked if he could go home and bathe, and the brigade agreed and sent a militiaman to escort him home. This militiaman was from a neighboring village and had studied at the No. 2 High School, and when classes had been suspended for the Cultural Revolution, Father had tutored him. He whispered to Father, "Teacher Li, you're in danger and I'm afraid they're going to kill you. Run off and I'll pretend I didn't see where you went." My father said, "I'm not going to run. I've done nothing wrong. I fervently love Chairman Mao, and I believe in the party's policies." In this way he missed the last opportunity to save his own life. It would have been better if he had run off; not only would he have lived, but the rest of us would also be better off now.

I asked Li Dongde, "Is it possible that your father feared that if he ran off, it would bring disaster on your mother and the rest of you?"

"Ai!" Li Dongde sighed. "That's what he was thinking. In fact, he should have just run. If they wanted to kill us, they would do it whether he ran off or not. But no one understood that at the time. Another reason was that Father was still harboring some hope. Brigade party secretary Li Chenglong's younger brother, Li Runlong, had graduated from the No. 2 High School in 1962, and he was very close to my father. He hadn't been a very good student, but Father had helped him so much that he ultimately passed the entrance exam to the Zhuzhou Metallurgical Institute, his gateway to success. Every year when he came home, he'd come to visit Father, and he was home on summer break just then. Father believed that at the key moment, the two brothers would speak up for him." Li Dongde went on:

After bathing, Father was escorted back to the storehouse. The next day, the higher authorities sent people down to direct operations, saying they needed to "stoke the fire." That night, the brigade called a meeting at the primary-school playground, and the Supreme People's Court of the Poor and Lower-Middle Peasants handed down a death sentence on my father and the others. They didn't kill them that day, but the next morning at nine or ten o'clock. When my Mother went to feed the pig as usual early that morning, she noticed it was gone. A well-intentioned neighbor told her, "They held a meeting last night and killed your pig to eat, and today they're going to kill your husband." Mother rushed over to the storehouse. Father's hands were bound tightly, and when he saw my mother, tears poured down his face. He said he'd been tied up all night, and this time he'd be killed for sure. Mother ran home and cooked four poached eggs, and she got out the woolen Mao jacket that Father wouldn't even wear when teaching. She wanted Father to eat the eggs so he wouldn't become a hungry ghost. Father said, "I can't eat them until you promise to remarry after I die and take the children away." Mother didn't cry; all she could think about was how to protect the rest of us— not to let anyone else be killed, or if the adults must be killed, how to protect the young, and if the boys couldn't be saved, to protect the girls. She said, "Please eat them. Who do you think will marry me? As long as I don't die, I'll take care of your mother for the rest of her life and raise the children till they're grown." At that, Father finally ate two eggs, but he couldn't eat the last two. Mother helped Father change into his good suit, and they didn't say anything more.

That day it rained hard, and the execution ground was across the river. The place was called Meihualuodi—"the place where the plum blossoms fall," and it was another half-hour walk after crossing the river. Even the executioners in their rush raincoats were soaked to the skin, not to mention the victims. While being led to the river to be killed, my father said to them, "I fervently love Chairman Mao and fervently love the party. I haven't done anything wrong." That irritated the killers, and one particularly low-class fellow, I think he was a poor-peasant association (PPA) leader, said to my father, "Go tell your jokes to the devil! If you loved the party and Chairman Mao, would the party kill you?" When my father heard this, he said, "Well then, get it over with. This rain makes things difficult for you as well." The executioners told my father to kneel down, but he said, "I've committed no crime, and I want to die standing." One of the militiamen said, "Don't talk nonsense! Who ever heard of someone being executed standing up!" He kicked my father to make him kneel. My father said, "I have a final request. Please make a clean job of it so I don't suffer." That request was granted. The executioner placed his fowling gun against my father's left temple and fired, and those on the scene said my father was dead by the time he hit the ground. The others were killed with fowling guns and sabers.

My mother was bold enough to ask several clan members to nail together a wooden box, and they collected my father's corpse. My father's skull was smashed to a pulp by the fowling gun, and his clothes had been stripped off, leaving him naked except for his underpants. Some of the dead were dumped in the Yongming River because their families didn't dare collect their bodies. Because of the overflow dams in the river, the bodies couldn't float away, and they bobbed on the surface of the water like fried crullers, giving off an unbearable stench. Some corpses pushed up onto the dam, and some became caught in the branches of the willow trees along the river, rotting into piles of white bones.

22

The Price of Truth

"That day, dozens of us were working in the sweet-potato fields at Shanmuling, about 2 kilometers from the production brigade." Zhou Fumei, from Xingqiao Township's Qiaotou Village,[1] was telling us about the killing of Zhou Wendong and his entire family:

> As we were about to finish for the day, our production team leader, Zhou XX, suddenly blew his whistle fiercely and shouted, "Come on, get to it!" Before I knew what was happening, a dozen male workers rushed over and grabbed Zhou Wendong and his wife, Chen Lian'e, who were still bent over their work, along with their son Zhou Hui, and pushed them to the ground and tied them up. I later learned that this had been discussed in advance, and that the family was to be killed because Zhou Wendong was a Rightist. Team leader Zhou then ordered, "Quickly push them into the cellar!" Realizing that disaster was at hand, Zhou Wendong knelt on the ground weeping and pleaded: "If you need to kill someone, just kill me. Don't kill my wife and son, they didn't do anything wrong. . . ." But what use was it? The others acted like madmen, grabbing all three of them and pushing them into an abandoned cellar. Someone brought out two bundles of rice straw that had been hidden among the pine trees, set the straw alight, and stuffed it into the cellar. We could hear heart-rending cries from inside as pine branches were piled at the mouth of the cellar to keep the smoke inside. It didn't take long for the cries to stop, and those three lives were ended. I couldn't bear to watch what was happening, and ran away. Before Liberation, I was a servant girl, and it was tough, but while class enemies could be harsh, they treated us well. People are always afraid of putting themselves in others' place. Zhou Wendong's family never had an easy day among us; how could they have done anything worthy of death?
>
> As the sun was about to set behind the mountains and it was time for us to go home, team leader Zhou recalled that Zhou Wendong still had

a son and a daughter at home, so he sent two men back to the village to bring the kids back to do away with them. The two who were sent back were normally very kind and honest men, but everyone changed back in those days. Zhou Wendong's eight-year-old daughter, Zhou Damei, was at home looking after her two-year-old brother, Zhou Xiaomei. When the two men arrived at their home, Zhou Xiaomei was asleep naked on a wooden bench in the main room of the house. Zhou Damei had just brought a bucket of water home, and when she saw the men she offered them a drink. The men said they weren't thirsty, and they lied to her: "Your mama wants you to take your brother to your grandma's house. They'll meet you on the way." Zhou Damei believed them and said, "My little brother is asleep. Let's leave him here and I'll go by myself." The men said, "It doesn't matter if he's sleeping, you can carry him." The little girl, suspecting nothing, lifted her brother onto her back and followed them. After they'd walked for a while, Zhou Damei realized they weren't heading for her grandmother's house, and seeing the thick smoke coming from Shanmuling, she became afraid and refused to go further. One of the men picked up Zhou Xiaomei, and the other dragged Zhou Damei, and they continued on to Shanmuling, where people were impatiently waiting. Everyone understood that with the parents dead, there would be no one to take care of the children. Team leader Zhou took Zhou Xiaomei and tossed him into the smoking cellar. Zhou Damei wailed in terror, but team leader Zhou paid her no mind and pushed her in as well. The fire was still burning, and the two kids roasted to death. Zhou Damei was a cute little girl with pigtails and a sweet smile who called everyone auntie and uncle. Only a black-hearted person could kill her! Who would think that such a nice family could come to such a bad end? It's a crying shame!

We have an old saying here: when someone dies, the rice steamer opens. That means when someone dies, the entire village goes to help and then eats all the dead person's rice. That night, the Zhous' home blazed with light as people from the production team slaughtered their chickens, ducks, a yellow dog, and a big, fat pig. Then there was the rice, the tea oil, the melon seeds and soybeans, the cotton and the farming implements, pots and pans, the floorboards of the house. . . . Whatever could be eaten was eaten on the spot, and what couldn't be eaten became the spoils of the victors, just like during Land Reform.

What kind of man was Zhou Wendong? From what I read in the "Rehabilitation Notice" that the Daoxian People's Government handed down regarding Zhou's family, Zhou was admitted to the 137 Army Military and Political Cadre School of the People's Liberation Army (PLA) in 1949, and after graduation he was retained to work in the army, later changing professions due to illness and returning to Daoxian as a teacher. After offering opinions during the Hundred Flowers movement in 1957, he was labeled a Rightist, dismissed from his job, and sent back to his home village to engage in agriculture. When the "Rehabilitation Notice" was issued, Zhou's family was paid 379 yuan as compensation for the property confiscated from them, as well as a home repair allowance of 300 yuan. Since the entire family had been killed, the funds were handed over to Zhou's younger brother. Team leader Zhou, who had directed the slaughter, was expelled from the Chinese Communist Party (CCP).

Our original intention was simply to present the record without further commentary and to let readers draw their own conclusions, feeling that anything we wrote would pale into insignificance before the blood-soaked facts. Even so, I feel compelled to add a few words about the price of truth.

There's a price to pay for speaking the truth in our country, and Zhou Wendong shows us just how high this price is. He first lost his future and his good life for trying to "help the party rectify itself," and to this price was added the lives of himself, his wife, and his children during the Cultural Revolution. I wonder how the poor peasants who killed Zhou and his family would have felt if they had known that one of the opinions Zhou had submitted to the CCP was that some rural cadres were trying to "secure their own advancement by falsely representing their achievements through exaggerated reports that increased the burden on the peasants." One cadre who had worked many years in Daoxian told us, "In Daoxian, if you did your work honestly and never made false claims, people would look down on you and think you had no real abilities, and you were less likely to be promoted or put in positions of importance." (This phenomenon was by no means limited to Daoxian.)

So what kind of people were promoted and put in positions of importance? Certainly not those with alternative views or who spoke the truth. What a pity!

It should be obvious that the courage and ability to put forward alternative viewpoints is the basic prerequisite of being a free person. A society that doesn't allow free persons to exist is a society of slaves, and a society of slaves is a savage, ignorant, brutal, and backward society, which in turn is a society without morality, mired in superstition and plagued with disaster.

The relevant data show us that in August 1957, in accordance with the CCP Central Committee's May 1 directive on its rectification campaign, Daoxian established a county CCP committee rectification leading small-group office, which initially carried out rectification campaigns in 43 work units and 31 CCP branches to mobilize the masses to assist the CCP in rectifying itself. The campaign then spread to the schools. In December, the CCP's internal rectification turned into an anti-Rightist struggle. Daoxian designated 293 people as

"Rightists," about a quarter of them cadres and most of the rest teachers, and many of these Rightists eventually became victims of Daoxian's killing wind. One Task Force leader told us with great sadness, "Reading through their dossiers breaks my heart. These were the best possible comrades. The views they raised were correct then and now and will be in the future as well."

After the Anti-Rightist campaign, Daoxian became one of the counties that advanced at double speed toward communism during the 1958 Great Leap Forward. From 1958 to 1960, Daoxian raised high the Three Red Banners (the General Line, the Great Leap Forward, and the People's Communes), and the Five Evil Winds of communism, exaggeration, coercive commandism, cadre privilege, and chaotic directives raged through the county and resulted in the Great Famine of 1959 to 1961, during which an estimated 10 percent of the local population died of unnatural causes. The Cultural Revolution reports of "counterrevolutionary organizations" being uncovered everywhere and other increasingly fantastical rumors were part of the same phenomenon of lies and exaggeration to win approval, and the results were similarly fatal.

For Chinese, lying is the inevitable result of a totalitarian society in which rulers preserve their power through violence and falsehood. "Bragging is not a crime." "Achievements are summarized, experience is unearthed." "You can't accomplish anything substantial without lies." These became the maxims of a generation of Chinese (including Daoxian residents). Many benefited from lies, and just as many suffered for the truth. The people of Daoxian summed it up most succinctly: "Telling the truth hurts only yourself, while lying hurts only others."

The destruction of two Rightist families

Tangjiashan Village in Qingxi District's Qingkou Township lies in close proximity to the Shuangpai Reservoir, and during the Cultural Revolution it fell under the jurisdiction of Chetou District's Meihua Commune. During the killing wind, the Tangjiashan production brigade killed 10 people (including one suicide), and the Rightist I want to talk about here was one of them. His name was Jiang Anmin, and three other members of his family were also killed, leaving only one survivor, his daughter, Jiang Lanju.

The reason for Jiang Anmin being labeled a Rightist was basically the same as for Tang Yu in Qingtang District's Jiujia Commune, whose story was related back in chapter 6; that is, he was a good talker, but what he said wasn't pleasing to the ear. Having little opportunity to express his views under normal circumstances, Jiang Anmin couldn't resist the opportunity in 1957 when he was invited to the county seat, provided with plenty to eat and drink, and asked to help the CCP with its rectification efforts. He differed from Tang Yu only in that after being labeled a Rightist and being dismissed and sent back to his home village, he basically tucked his tail between his legs and managed to stay out of trouble. Jiang Anmin came from a middle-peasant family, and although he'd been sent back to Tangjiashan as a Rightist, his fellow villagers didn't really understand what that was, so they initially didn't treat him like other black elements. Since he had some education and exposure to the outside world, other villagers often came to him for advice on all kinds of matters. As the saying goes, "It is easier to move mountains and rivers than to alter one's character"; over time, Jiang's tail became untucked, and forgetting his recent painful experience, he began offering opinions on things he felt were unfair in his production brigade and production team. This bred great resentment in brigade leader Jiang Lizhu, among others.

After Jiang Anmin was labeled a Rightist, his wife had divorced him. Back then, divorce was rare, but Jiang Anmin's ex-wife was apparently unwilling to spend the rest of her life sharing her husband's status as a "black element." The couple had a daughter, and Jiang Anmin's ex-wife would have had trouble remarrying if she brought the daughter with her, so she left the girl with him. This created difficulties when Jiang was sent back to his native village, so he handed his daughter over to the care of his elder sister while fulfilling his paternal responsibilities by covering her living expenses.

This daughter was Jiang Lanju, the only member of Jiang Anmin's family who survived. Jiang Anmin had chosen the girl's name in hopes that she would grow to be as elegant and refined as an orchid (*lan*), and as noble and unsullied as a chrysanthemum (*ju*).

Eventually Jiang Anmin remarried, and as two more children were born, he inevitably paid less attention to Jiang Lanju. Jiang Lanju grew up in her aunt's house, resembling the orchid and the chrysanthemum as her father had wished, but in her young heart, resentment grew against her father. She couldn't possibly understand his difficulties, nor could she forgive her father for abandoning her to her aunt rather than trying to forge a life with her. Whenever Jiang Anmin came with money and rice for his sister and tried to see his daughter, she would run away and hide. This was wounding to Jiang Anmin, but in those times of material shortage, people didn't have the time or energy to struggle over matters that didn't involve finding enough to eat.

The really hard times started for Jiang Anmin during the Socialist Education movement, which informed the poor and lower-middle peasants of Tangjiashan that "Rightists" were included among the black elements and were even worse than "counterrevolutionaries," opposing the CCP and socialism and wanting poor peasants to suffer another round of exploitation through the revival of capitalism. Jiang Anmin suddenly found himself in the front-row seat among the

Tangjiashan brigade's class enemies; no longer merely disadvantaged, Jiang was what his fellow peasant vividly described as "ground into the mire."

The killing wind began blowing in August 1967, and Meihua Commune started its killing-mobilization meetings on August 23.

On August 24, the commune's deputy CCP secretary, Wang Guoxiang, and commune head He Changjin made a special trip to Tangjiashan to see Zhou Yumei, vice chairman of the county women's federation, who had been seconded to Tangjiashan for work experience during the Socialist Education movement in 1965. After meeting with Wang Guoxiang and He Changjin, Zhou Yumei called a meeting of the brigade's cadres to discuss the killing issue, and brigade head Jiang Lizhu suggested that the first person to be killed should be the Rightist Jiang Anmin.

On the night of August 26, at the edge of the Shuangpai Reservoir, the Tangjiashan brigade used explosives provided by the commune to send Jiang Anmin and three others off on a "homemade airplane." Jiang Anming's wife and two sons were among five more people killed on August 31.

Jiang Lanju, then 16 years old, escaped her father's fate because she was in the care of her aunt. When she heard that her father had been killed, she broke out in sobs and heart-rending wails. Her aunt, in a panic, urged her to step crying or at least do it more quietly, but to no avail. Finally, Jiang Lanju's weeping gradually subsided, but some inner trauma caused her health to deteriorate after that, and she stopped menstruating. Later, hearing that this kind of illness would cure itself following marriage, Jiang Lanju's aunt hastily found a husband for her. After five years of marriage she was still childless, but eventually she recovered enough to give birth to four children, every one of them as sickly as a frost-blighted sprout.

The other Rightist family I'd like to mention is that of Wan Guangzhi in the Wanjia brigade of Qingxi District's Ganziyuan Commune. Someone observed that Wan Guangzhi's designation as a Rightist was thoroughly undeserved, because the Task Force found that his files contained not a single instance of "erroneous thought or action" that would qualify him as a Rightist. So how did this happen? The most reasonable explanation is that back then, when the county CCP committee handed down a quota of how many people should be labeled Rightists (as was done for each work unit throughout China), Wan Guangzhi's school didn't have enough proper Rightists to reach its quota and threw in his name to top up the number. As to why he was chosen rather than some other person, there may have been any number of reasons relating to family background, the impression he had made on his superiors, his everyday work performance, or even his relations with his colleagues.

One informed colleague said, "In any case, the man is dead, and a lot of times these situations can be summed up in two words: bad luck!"

Having been labeled a Rightist, this unlucky devil was dismissed from his job and returned with his wife and children to his native Wanjia Village. Since he'd been away teaching for so long, all he had left in that village was his landlord class designation. Quite apart from remolding his thinking and making a fresh start in life, the first problem he encountered was one of shelter. Fortunately a distant relative had a place to rent to him, resolving this most urgent issue, but housing remained a worry for the family from then on.

At that time, Wan Guangzhi and his wife, Li Meijiao, were still young and strong, and as long as they set their minds to remolding themselves, they could deal with the labor demands placed on them. By living frugally and gritting their teeth, they were able to get by. Besides that, they had three sons who would grow into able-bodied workers, and in the countryside, having adequate manpower always made things easier. Building their own home, however, was a different matter, requiring not only labor, but also wood, brick and tiles, a foundation, and hard cash. Back then, only a tiny minority of people in Daoxian, or anywhere in the Chinese countryside for that matter, had the means to build a new home; the vast majority of villagers lived in homes constructed before or shortly after Liberation. Mountain forests had been cleared during the Great Leap Forward to stoke backyard smelting furnaces, and during the communization movement, the construction of large-scale communal canteens and communal housing had resulted in the destruction of many homes, their crossbeams chopped into firewood. In short, wood had become a precious commodity. But the Wans had to build a house, not only for their own comfort but also to improve the marriage prospects of their sons. Wan Guangzhi summed up his resolve to be like "Iron Man" Wang Jinxi:[2] "I'll shed my skin if that's what it takes to build a house."

There's no need to go into what the family experienced during the Three Years of Hardship. Having survived that time, in 1962, Wan Guangzhi applied to the production brigade to lay a foundation for a house. From then on, after finishing work in the production team every evening, the Wan family could be seen at the site of their new home, making use of what little time was left before nightfall. Wan and his sons carried rocks from the mountain behind the village to lay the foundation, and in winter they would go to the hills to burn lime or saw wood planks. The family saved money for what they needed to buy by eating only congee in the morning and skipping the evening meal.

After many years of hard effort and self-deprivation, the Wan family had just about everything ready to build their house in 1967, and they planned to set to work once autumn arrived. Wan Guangzhi had long felt guilty about how his political fortunes affected his sons, and the prospect of providing them with a fine new home finally set his mind at rest. His wife and sons naturally shared his joy and looked forward to the fulfillment of their hopes.

In August 1967, the killing wind reached the Wanjia brigade, where the peasant supreme court sentenced Wan Guangzhi's entire family to death, along with the family of his cousin, Wan Guangli. In each family, the eldest son managed to escape. Wan Guangli's son, Wan Kaixian, fled deep into the mountains of Jiangxi's Yongxing County, where he earned a living making bricks and sawing wood. Wang Guangzhi's son, Wan Chaxin, ended up in a village of Hunan's Chaling County, also doing piecework.

It is said that Wan Guangzhi's second son, Wan Xiuxin, didn't die from the knife blows to his head and neck. That night, a breeze stirred him awake, and he climbed out from among the pile of corpses and crawled back to the village and into his home, climbed into the loft area, and hid among the construction materials that had been stored there for the new house. The next day, when members of the brigade arrived to confiscate the family's movable property, they discovered Wan Xiuxin on the brink of death among the wood planks, and thinking he was a ghost, they were scared half out of their wits. Finally they threw him out of the loft, and he died in the grain-drying yard. As he died, he kept saying the same word over and over: "My, my, my. . . ."

Death of a "little Peng Dehuai"

After the first Chinese edition of this book was published in Hong Kong, a number of additional cases reached my hands through various channels, many even more grisly and dramatic than those already included. However, I've maintained my ironclad rule that cases that can't be verified through original official (pre-1986) documents cannot be included, and even new cases verified through official documents have generally not been added to a book that is already too gory for many readers. This case is an exception, however: it has moved me and inspired my reflection more than any other.

The victim in this case was Liao Puzhan, a resident of the Nikouwan brigade of Lefutang Commune, at that time under the jurisdiction of Qiaotou District (but now under Shouyan District). Liao Puzhan was born to a rich peasant family in 1935 and received a year and a half of high-school education. He was 32 at the time of his death on August 21, 1967. The Nikouwan peasant supreme court sentenced him to death as a "reactionary rich peasant, Daoxian's biggest anti-CCP and antisocialist element, and a 'little Peng Dehuai.' "[3] Implicated and killed along with him were his father and elder brother.

How could a man who had been only 16 during the Land Reform movement, with no position or power—a semieducated, ordinary peasant—wear these three labels?

It all started with a letter that the 24-year-old Liao wrote to the CCP Central Committee Politburo on September 1, 1959. It has not been possible to ascertain what motivated him to write the letter, but in any case, he took the opportunity while at Shouyan Market to put it in the postbox.

Accompanying Liao's courteous letter to the Politburo members was a lengthy essay. It credited the CCP's focus on agricultural production with dramatically increased yields and bolstering the construction of socialism: "As a result, last year our country had bumper harvests both in industry and agriculture, this achievement of the party and the people marking a red-letter day in the annals of history." However, Liao noted, following the steel-forging campaign, agricultural production was faltering:

> The problem is that the people involved in production were returning from the factories and mines during the spring planting season and didn't have time to sow the seeds when they got home, much less to repair the slopes and ridges between fields. They just dropped the seeds into the unleveled fields. As a result, our crops here (in the county and prefecture) are somewhat worse than last year; according to current estimates, paddy yields average 180 kilos (per *mu*), a huge decrease from last year's 310 kilos. The main reason for the reduction in output is inadequate fertilizer and insect plagues. Originally the peasants here used the entire winter to mow grass for compost, to burn lime, and to put their fields in order in preparation for the next spring planting. In this way, when seeds were planted the next year, there were no weeds, the soil was loosened, and the crops could grow faster and more luxuriantly. In the past, in winter and spring alike, the caves[4] were full of wheat, barley, and compost, but with 90 percent of the workforce engaged in steel production and irrigation projects last year, the caves held just a few vessels of wheat and compost. . . . While our country urgently needs steel and coal, in order to better support our country's industrial construction, the countryside (with communes and counties as work units) needs to proceed in a way that takes account of the county's and commune's advantages (in terms of transportation and the production of ore sand). . . . Once we've gained a firm grasp of agricultural bumper harvests, satellites of steel production can also be launched.

Liao then turned to the "Eight-Point Charter for Agriculture," consisting of eight measures that Mao proposed in 1958 to increase agricultural output. He noted that in practice, the peasants suggested improvements on the points relating to "deep plowing" and "close planting."

The peasants observe that deep plowing has to be determined by the actual conditions of the soil, and that an inflexible standard of at least two-thirds of a meter is inappropriate. The peasants suggest that deep plowing is appropriate for good soil, but that poor soil requires shallow plowing, so that deep plowing is applied flexibly on the basis of the quality of the soil.

As for "close planting," following two years' experience, close planting . . . has several disadvantages: (1) it makes weeding more difficult, (2) it makes application of fertilizer more difficult, (3) it decreases the amount of sunlight that reaches the plants, leading to cooler water temperatures and more insects, (4) it is disadvantageous to pest control, (5) it increases manpower consumption (the original planting methods require only one unit of manpower per *mu*, but close planting requires five manpower units), (6) it uses more seeds (the original methods require 4 to 5 kilos per *mu*, while close planting requires 12.5 kilos), (7) it is not beneficial to the growth of the seedlings. . . . The peasants find that in promoting advanced techniques, the party and the government should consider practical conditions in the countryside, and not listen only to some professors of agriculture and other experts. . . . Requiring close planting exhausts peasants with work that can never be completed, while increased production has no scientific basis or effective outcome.

Turning to the communal kitchens, Liao noted that after large communal kitchens had proven unworkable, downsized versions were managing to meet local needs. However, he noted a lack of pork due to the practice of raising pigs communally:

When pigs were raised individually during the advanced agricultural cooperatives, after meeting the state's annual requisition quotas and sending more than 400 pigs to the state over and above the quota (and these pigs weighing 20 kilos more than the current ones), the cooperatives still slaughtered six pigs each month, and some meat even went unsold; now even if you have money, there's no pork to buy. . . . It turns out that the communist thinking of our country's peasants is not that advanced, and they're not responsible enough. The pig keepers don't pay attention to how well the pigs eat; they just dump fodder into the basins and leave it at that. If a pig dies, it's just taken to the communal kitchen to eat and is treated as a routine matter, without considering the relationship between loss and living standards. No thought, or not much, has been given to how to make the pigs eat more and grow faster.

It was different when pig rearing was dispersed among households (in the advanced cooperatives); if a pig wasn't eating, this was considered a grave misfortune to the household, and householders couldn't let it go.

As the saying goes, "Poor people rely on raising pigs." Although there are no poor people now, pigs have always been a major source of income for peasants and the state and are the most basic factor in improving the people's living standards. The party needs to think of a way to resolve this problem. The preliminary view of the peasants is to distribute the pigs for rearing by households, to distribute feed per pig, to establish a system of rewards and penalties, and to pay an appropriate remuneration. In this way, people will demonstrate more responsibility toward the pigs, the pigs will grow faster and better, and peasant incomes will increase.

Liao observed that peasants were also not being given their previous grain ration of 240 kilos per year, a problem compounded by the loss of small plots of land cultivated by individual households:

Piecemeal plots of land and small vegetable gardens around homes went fallow; the communes didn't manage these small plots (of 2 square meters or so), nor did individual households, fearing that the commune would just seize whatever was grown, so this was also a loss.

Liao went on to request a more appropriate balance of young village people recruited to work in factories:

Our country needs workers, but in order for the counties and communes to properly allocate assignments, each commune shouldn't lose too much or too little manpower. Regarding the establishment and expansion of local factories and industries, this should be decided in accordance with local conditions and advantageous conditions.

Massive irrigation projects also required more prudent planning:

During the great iron-smelting campaign last year, each locality also carried out irrigation projects such as irrigation canals and ditches, reservoirs, and dams, and this work was done splendidly, providing enormous and essential benefit to production. But the success or otherwise of such undertakings is the dividing line between happiness and disaster. On the basis of our country's current conditions, hydroelectric plants and large reservoirs cannot be built on each and every rivulet. Apart from the Yangtze, Yellow, Huai, Qiantang, Pear, and Xiangjiang Rivers, other rivers should not have such projects built for another one, two, or even four or five years. Every county was doing this kind of work last year, and some counties built five or six medium-sized reservoirs. Some reservoirs were built successfully and were a blessing to the people, reducing their hardship. But some reservoirs, due to a lack of long-term planning and examination, were swept away by river currents, and losses were immense. . . . In fact, building small reservoirs can solve the irrigation problem, but when the county made its plans, it wanted to construct communism and build large reservoirs, and the results were counterproductive. Therefore, going forward in irrigation construction, it would be best to first send a survey group and to approve and begin planning the project only after ascertaining that there will be no problems and that everything suits local conditions.

Finally, Liao drew attention to "a minority of lower-level cadres, who due to poor education have a less than thorough and comprehensive understanding of party policy": "Some have excessively Leftist or Rightist tendencies and engage in arrogant, ambitious, and impractical behavior. The party should transfer some cadres with poor educational and theoretical backgrounds to terms of study so they can better serve the people from now on." Liao also recommended that cadres be prohibited from reporting exaggerated crop yields. "Correcting this phenomenon will bring the people and cadres closer together."

Liao offered to provide further information and opinions if desired, and even to go to Beijing to report directly to the Politburo. He added, "If what I say is not beneficial to the development of agriculture and industry or to the party and the construction of socialism, please also send me a letter censuring and sternly criticizing me." By way of personal background, Liao wrote:

I'm 24 years old this year, and after beginning my schooling at the age of 8, I continued studying until high school, discontinuing my studies in the latter half of 1955 and returning home to engage in agricultural production (because both my grandfather and mother died within two months). I embarked on education work in 1956, and in 1957 I worked at the cadre school under the direct jurisdiction of this county while also in charge of the county Federation of Trade Unions library. At the end of the first lunar month in 1958, my application to return home to engage in production was approved. I have always worked hard in production and have gained a firm grasp of all farming techniques. Since I began taking part in production, I have never missed work except for seven days' sick leave; my work-point record contains not a single absence.

What pains me most is having said some things detrimental to the party and the people (saying that the literary value of *Journey to the West, The Dream of the Red Chamber, The Romance of the Tree Kingdoms, The Water Margin, Unofficial History of Confucian Scholars,* and *Romance of the West Chamber* is greater than that of all new books). I have clearly debriefed the government on everything I said, and I was sentenced to two years of production under surveillance (beginning on September 15, 1958). In the first lunar month of this year, I related this in a letter to the Central Committee Politburo and requested that my surveillance be rescinded. For some reason, the Politburo did not reply. Now in the course of my labor I have surmounted my Right-deviating conservative thinking and have further remolding my thinking, tempering myself into an ideologically resolute new person. . . . It is because I am loyal to the party and to the cause of socialist construction that I have reported the actual situation in the countryside to you, in hopes that you will know the true situation and formulate policies that will enrich and develop the countryside, make our country even stronger and the living standards of our people even more satisfying, further accelerate industrial and agricultural development, and further facilitate the cause of socialist construction.

Respectfully yours,

Wishing health and happiness to all of you in the Politburo!

Liao Puzhan, Nikouwan Village, Lefutang production brigade, Qiaotou Commune,[5] Daoxian, Hunan Province

From today's perspective, there is nothing problematic in the content of this letter, and indeed, it has much to recommend it. Official documents show that the actual situation in Daoxian was much worse than Liao's depiction. Although mass starvation had not yet occurred, many problems were already apparent. From his remote village, the young peasant Liao Puzhan could write only from his own experience, and fearing accusations of exaggeration, he minimized problems almost to the extent of untruth. In this way he earned his label of a "little Peng Dehuai," because like his namesake, he wished to speak the truth but didn't dare speak it fully.

Unfortunately, Liao's timing could hardly have been worse. The Eighth CCP Central Committee had just held its Eighth Plenum in Lushan in July–August

1959, and State Council Vice Premier and Defense Minister Peng Dehuai, whose personal observation of conditions in the countryside had led him to "plead on behalf of the people" for a rollback of China's disastrous Great Leap Forward economic policies, had been named ringleader of a "Peng, Huang, Zhang, and Zhou Anti-party Clique," which included Hunan provincial CCP secretary Zhou Xiaozhou. The influence of the purge spread throughout the country, and on September 21, 1959, just three weeks after Liao Puzhan wrote his letter, the Daoxian CCP committee held a meeting to implement the spirit of the Lushan Conference.

By then Liao's letter had been sent back down to county CCP secretary Shi Xiuhua, who ordered the secretariat to immediately print copies of it with his editorial comments. Shi accused Liao Puzhan of "persistently launched venomous attacks expressing his discontent with the socialist system" and said that Liao used "contemptible and shameless Rightist tricks of dual meaning, fabrication, rumors, and slander" to attack the CCP's policies on communal production and to attack the Great Leap Forward, while "promoting capitalist economics and individual economy, and dreaming of society's regression and the restoration of the evil capitalist system." Shi concluded:

> What difference is there between the rumormongering and attacks of this antisocialist element under surveillance and the anti-party program of the Right-opportunistic anti-party clique? It is very clear: whom does the anti-party program of the Right-opportunistic anti-party clique represent if not Liao Puzhan and his ilk? This letter from Liao Puzhan is nothing but a narrative of the anti-party, antisocialist words and actions of capitalists in the rural upper-class petty bourgeoisie, as well as of the landlords, rich peasants, counterrevolutionaries, bad elements, Rightists, and their proxies.
>
> Shi Xiuhua
>
> September 25, 1959

The Central Committee produced a Peng Dehuai, and Daoxian produced a Liao Puzhan. How perfectly these "Right opportunists" and "anti-party, antisocialist elements" inside and outside the CCP collaborated and echoed each other! Shi Xiuhua could only regret that this fellow Liao Puzhan had no official position or power and was just a country bumpkin; if he'd been a member of the county CCP committee or even just a CCP member, that would have been perfect!

The Daoxian CCP committee on September 29 embarked on an internal rectification to purge its "anti-party faction." On October 12, this became a struggle against "Rightist deviation" outside the CCP, during which 169 people were publicly denounced. Liu Puzhan was the lowest ranking among them (having no rank at all), but he was given the ultimate treatment of being named a "little Peng Dehuai." Among the 169 people who were denounced, 21 were designated "Right opportunists" and another 12 (including Liao Puzhan) as "anti-party, antisocialist elements."

After the ravages of the Great Famine, the Daoxian CCP committee in 1962 rehabilitated this group of people on a case-by-case basis, but seven were not rehabilitated, and one of them was Liao Puzhan.

When the Socialist Education movement was launched in 1965, the family background of the "anti-party, antisocialist element" Liao Puzhan was investigated, and he was determined to be a "rich peasant who slipped through the net," elevating his entire family to the level of class enemy. When the killing wind blew through Daoxian in 1967, there was no way Liao Puzhan and his family could emerge unscathed. The commune leaders said, "If we don't kill Liao Puzhan, there's no one else we can kill!"

After Liao Puzhan was killed, three of the village's bachelors vied to marry Liao's attractive young wife. Since none would back down, the production brigade decided they should cast lots for her. The wife's younger brother in Tangjia Commune's Bingtian production brigade heard about this, and he rushed to Nikouwan to take his sister home, only to be surrounded by local militiamen and narrowly escaping with his life. Fortunately, the wife's family was up to the challenge, and more than a dozen friends and relatives from Bingtian descended on Nikouwan before the shotgun wedding could take place, rescuing Liao's wife and their two children and bringing them safely home.

23

The Scapegoated Landlord Class

During our reporting in Daoxian in 1986, we took particular interest in the fortunes of the county's 290-odd "Rightists" as well as various other purged intellectuals, first of all because the situations of these people reflected the enormous tragedy of this era, and, second, because these people or their surviving family members provided us with large amounts of firsthand material. On the other hand, because of the limitations of our thinking at that time, we didn't engage at a deeper and more essential level with the taboo area of "class enemies" being "subjected to revolution," failing to recognize that this reflected an even-greater tragedy of the Chinese people. Although we later applied great effort to remedying this lapse, we were conscious of a lost opportunity, and I'm afraid that this is the greatest shortcoming of this book. I'd like to take the time for some reflections on the subject here.

Let me start by relating a story about one such class enemy. Lijiaping Commune (originally under the jurisdiction of Daoxian but now part of Shuangpai County) had an elderly landlord who was in his 60s at the time he was killed. Prior to Liberation he had served as head of the County Land Tax Bureau under the Kuomintang (KMT), and after Liberation he engaged in agricultural production. He survived the Land Reform movement and the Campaign to Suppress Counterrevolutionaries, either because he had expiated his crimes through meritorious service or because he served as a useful whipping boy for criticism and struggle; he was hauled out whenever there was a political campaign, and people referred to him as a "seasoned political survivor." But as the saying goes, "They'll get you sooner or later," and the peasant supreme court sentenced him to death during Daoxian's killing wind. The old landlord maintained his composure at the mass rally, unlike some black elements who were like scared chickens and even soiled themselves. When the chairman of the poor-peasant association (PPA), who was also chief judge of the peasant supreme court, asked him, "Do you admit your guilt?," he replied, "I have no idea what law I've broken."

"You're still dishonest! You said you wanted to 'kill all the party members, cadres, and poor and lower-middle peasants and half the middle peasants and just leave the landlords and rich peasants as the backbone.'"

"I don't recall saying any such thing."

"You're still dishonest! Tell us, have you ever thought such a thing?"

"Let me think if I've ever thought that."

"You're still dishonest!"

This was followed by a thunderous shouting of slogans.

"Tell us honestly, have you ever thought that?"

"I think I may have thought of killing party members and cadres, but I've never thought of killing poor and lower-middle peasants."

"You're still dishonest! You would kill party members and cadres but not us poor and lower-middle peasants?"

"You work the fields, and isn't it said that landlords rely on exploiting the poor and lower-middle peasants for their living? If I kill all of you, who can I exploit?"

"You, you're facing death and you still can't be honest!"

"It's because I'm facing death that I can be especially honest."

The old landlord's "arrogant bluster" infuriated his persecutors, and the indignant masses surged forward and tied him and the other black elements to wooden posts, after which Chinese Communist Party (CCP) and Youth League members and cadres stood in line with clubs and struck each of the condemned, one by one, while saying, "Will you be honest?" Before they'd completed a circuit, the heads of the old landlord and the others had been reduced to a bloody pulp.

During the Land Reform movement, there were reportedly also mass struggle sessions in which landlords were killed by people taking turns clubbing or stabbing them or throwing stones at them. At that time, the practice was mainly intended to dispel the misgivings of some individuals among the masses and to make them "undergo the baptism of class struggle"; if you were given a knife or a club, it was hard for you not to use it. But this time only those who were qualified could take part: people who were not CCP members, cadres, or activists were excluded. Notably, the participants displayed intense class hatred, as if their life depended on exterminating the old landlord. This raises an unavoidable question: what was the basis of this hatred?

While we were doing our reporting in Daoxian, whenever we encountered a killing involving a landlord or rich peasant, we nearly always asked: what misdeed had the victim committed before Liberation? The answer was almost always that there were no reports of any real misdeeds; they had mainly just collected rent, hired farmhands, and eaten the rice of exploitation. There was also this kind of answer: the person wasn't bad enough to be a landlord. The old landlord in the narrative above belonged to this category; he had committed no evil acts prior to Liberation and in fact had demonstrated a keen sense of justice and charity. A critical question then emerges: was that old landlord a representative figure of the landlord class, or an exception? Or to put the question more simply, what kind of people was the landlord class composed of? Where did their land and assets come from? What role did they play in China's villages before Liberation?

The textbook answer is that the landlord class was an exploiting class in feudal society. They profited from the toil of others and depended on renting out their land and exploiting the peasants to sustain their livelihood, and therefore represented the most reactionary and backward productive force. They had corrupt moral characters, sought profit in all things, and rampaged through the countryside, cheating men and tyrannizing women with their abundant capacity for evil. Their classic representatives were people such as Huang Shiren, Zhou Bapi, Nan Batian, and Liu Wencai.[1] In our youth, Minghong and I had read novels and watched movies featuring these infamous characters, and they truly instilled in us a teeth-gnashing hatred of the landlord class.

But with more social experience and as historical truth surfaced, and especially as we became increasingly immersed in reporting on the Cultural Revolution killings in Daoxian, we couldn't help but reexamine what we'd once regarded as "immutable precepts." That's not to say that the villainous landlords were fabricated out of thin air (although evidence indicates that facts were embellished and flaws were maximized to make them as hideous as possible), but they were a tiny minority. In Daoxian, at least, we found not a single such example.

The landlord class consisted of Chinese peasants whose land and assets exceeded a certain limit, and it would be more accurate to call them a gentry class. There were bad people among them, but the vast majority were decent and law-abiding. Their land and assets generally came from three sources: (1) family property handed down through the generations, (2) money made while serving as an official or doing business elsewhere, which was used to establish themselves upon their return to the village, or (3) prospering through hard work, usually due to a talent for management or a certain craft or skill. China's small-scale farming economy had a 2,000-year history, during which agriculture was always emphasized over commerce, and the thinking of people in that era was very different from now. The well-to-do laid particular emphasis on working and studying and handing property down from one generation to the next. A poor person who managed to accumulate any amount of money immediately used it to buy land. Land was not movable and could not be stolen, and its value increased over time; it could be left to one's sons and grandsons so one's family never had to go without. This was the way of the world, not only in China, and in the transactions and ownership transfers of such land and assets, deeds were signed and taxes were paid, and the competent government departments issued land warrants, demonstrating that such dealings were generally recognized and accepted at that time.

Naturally there were also people who prospered through immoral means such as dominating the market or practicing usury, but Confucianism was the mainstream ideology of that era; anyone whose path to riches involved dishonest practices would be condemned by public opinion and shunned. At the same time, most people believed in some sort of deity and in karma, putting an emphasis on the accumulation of merit by good deeds and believing that heaven would punish unconscionable acts. Society was for the most part stable and harmonious; rich and poor relied on each other and didn't engage in the kind of "fight to the death" class struggle we know today. On the contrary, while wealth could be inherited, it also migrated, as reflected in the old saying, "Wealth lasts no more than three generations."

The fact is that the so-called landlord class was actually the middle class in the small-scale farming economy.

The value system back then focused on the words "scholar, farmer, worker, merchant." The highest ranking was accorded to scholars. The well-to-do, specifically landlords and rich peasants in the villages, invariably did everything in their power to send their children to school, thereby raising the landlord class to the most educated grouping in the countryside. Economic advantage and educational advantage thus combined to make the landlord class the mainstream in society at that time and, in particular, made it the core power in rural society.

When we were reporting on the Cultural Revolution killings in Daoxian, we learned in passing that many of the class enemies who were killed, or members of their family, had been prominent local leaders before Liberation. They contributed to the support of widows, orphans, and the disabled; helped establish schools; provided disaster relief; built bridges and mended roads; financed irrigation projects; mediated in disputes; and sponsored cultural activities (dragon dances, lantern displays, temple fairs, opera performances). In short. they played a leading role in their villages' public welfare and charitable enterprises, enthusiastically initiating and supporting such projects with their own funds and personal effort. At that time, government organs were very weak, especially at or below the county level, and there was no concept of "social relief" or any local economic capacity to speak of. The management of local affairs in the countryside therefore fell to rural gentry of noble character and high prestige. Generally speaking, the landlord class managed rural society through clan law, village laws, and folk law, with Confucian teachings as its guiding ideology. Mencius said, "Property ownership brings a steady heart"; that's why the landlord (or rural gentry) class took up the social responsibility that was missing from government and performed a stabilizing role in society.

In short, the rise of the landlord class was the result of a balancing out of the long-term collision of many kinds of social forces in the small-farm economy society. Social practice in the 20th century proves that the method of tumultuous attacks on "local tyrants" (killing landlords) and distribution of land did not achieve the desired objective of social justice but instead concealed the ill effects of even-greater social injustice.

What we observed while reporting in Daoxian was that when the massacre occurred in 1967, black-element families were already generally living below the poverty line, and the poor and lower-middle peasants who served as their assassins didn't live much better. All of them toiled year in and year out for 20 to 30 cents a day or even less, subsisting on watery congee, sweet potatoes, and pickled vegetables, their coarse homespun clothes raising boils on their skin. The mass of poor and lower-middle peasants had nominally become the masters, but their actual living conditions had not improved substantially, nor was there any substance behind their title of masters of society. The enhancement of their political status was manifested only through the consignment of black elements and their offspring to the 18th Circle of Hell; while a level higher than such people, poor peasants were still an underclass. The only hope of improvement in their living situation derived from the limited opportunity of joining the CCP and becoming an official or cadre released from production work, and even some of these people lived very poorly.

While in Daoxian, we focused on the Cultural Revolution killings, but since the vast majority of victims were landlords or rich peasants and their offspring, we inevitably heard scattered reports about the situation during the Land Reform movement. These reports indicated that the movement had been carried out on a grand scale in Daoxian, with horrific violence involving the use of fists, feet, shoes, and clubs to inflict massive physical trauma on landlord elements. Some especially headstrong landlords were beaten to death on the spot. The slogan raised at the time was "Smoke billowing from every home, every village seeing red"—that is, every village had to kill at least one class enemy.

Legal stipulations required killings to be authorized at the district level. Taking Daoxian as an example, the total population of the county at the time of the Land Reform movement was around 350,000 distributed among nine districts, with some 40,000 people in each district. Power over the life and death of those 40,000 people lay in the hands of district CCP secretaries and district heads, all young men in their 20s, who drew up killing lists solely on the basis of the reports submitted by each township. If it was someone such as Xianzijiao District's Wang Xianzhi making the decision, fewer would be killed, but if it was someone such as Xianglinpu District's Yuan Lifu, the killing could go on indefinitely. Killing landlords involved practically no standard of guilt or innocence, only of necessity. Some villages who lacked individuals qualifying as landlords promoted rich peasants to landlord status, and if even rich peasants couldn't be found, some unlucky upper-middle peasant would have his status raised. The main thing was to ensure that "every village saw red."

There are no detailed reports on how many landlords and reactionary rich peasants were killed in Daoxian during the Land Reform movement, but the population data for Daoxian from 1949 onward kept by the county's Family Planning Commission show that from 1949 to the present there were three periods in which the population experienced negative growth. One of those periods was 1952, when Land Reform took place, the second period was from 1961 to 1962 (during the three-year "natural disaster"), and the third was during the massacre in 1967. Simple calculations employing statistical principles produce the result that around 2,500 people died of unnatural causes in Daoxian in 1952. Official reports state that more than 800 were killed at that time in campaigns to rid the county of bandits, local despots, and counterrevolutionaries. That reduces the number attributable to Land Reform to 1,700. Comparing this with the official policy requiring "every village to see red," Daoxian had more than 1,400 natural villages at that time, so averaging 1,400 and 1,700 produces an estimate of around 1,550 landlords who were killed.

When people told us stories from the Land Reform era while we were in Daoxian, we sensed a common origin with the Cultural Revolution killings. Some grassroots cadres even referred to the killing wind as a "second Land Reform." Of course, there were many ways in which the first Land Reform movement differed from the second, which can be specifically summed up in six aspects: (1) the first instance was governed by a Land Reform Law, (2) killing people required compiling dossiers and obtaining permission from the district level, (3) at that time there were in fact attempts by KMT remnants to subvert the regime, (4) there were policy limits on whom to attack, whom to isolate, and whom to bring into the fold, (5) women and children were basically not to be killed, and (6) most people were executed by shooting, and while people were also stabbed, clubbed, or stoned to death, this was not common.

I am not a theoretician, and my scholarship and the materials I have in hand are not adequate to carry out an evaluation of the Land Reform movement of the 1950s. No major historical incident can be explained by the aspirations and the words and actions of those who participated in it, nor can an appropriate conclusion be reached by observing it from close proximity. It is necessary to observe such an incident from a historical height and distance that allows for a broader perspective in order to define its actual historical function and significance. Major events are affected by the choices people make on the road to survival as well as national development trends. Taking a historical and nationwide perspective, we can see that people who influenced China's historical process from the mid-1800s to the mid-1900s, such as Kang Youwei, Liang Qichao, Tan

Sitong, Cai E, Cai Yuanpei, Hu Shi, Lu Xun, and figures both from the KMT and CCP, such as Sun Yat-sen, Huang Xing, Chiang Kai-shek, Chen Duxiu, Mao Zedong, and Deng Xiaoping, all were born to the landed gentry (landlord) class. What does this phenomenon show us? Without going into an in-depth exploration that would easily give rise to controversy, I suggest that at the very least, acceptance of the advanced culture of the West and inheritance of the best of Chinese culture gave the landed gentry (landlord class) a unique advantage.

Scholars have written theses showing that small-scale farm economy and the Arcadian rural society of the Qing dynasty's Mid-Qianlong period began developing a process in which "the rural gentry became tyrants and the peasantry became thugs." This process continued right up into the Land Reform movement of the 1950s, during which the rural gentry or landlord class was eliminated and the rural leadership class deteriorated and was declared obsolete. On the other hand, the land system of China's rural society, which hadn't changed in a thousand years, also accumulated very serious social contradictions that seriously obstructed the development of productive force and the pace of society's advancement toward modernization. In a sense, this land system was headed for collapse, which makes the Land Reform movement that swept through China's countryside in the early 1950s easier to explain. And there is no denying that its initiators and participants were striving for social justice and resolution of the problems of increasing class disparity and underdeveloped productive force.

It must be said that at that time, this movement was heartily embraced by the vast majority of China's people, as well as the vast majority of intellectuals in what could be considered an overwhelming national consensus. If there was any difference of opinion, it was over the form that Land Reform should take. Even the opposing CCP and KMT were not essentially antagonistic on the general principle; it was only that the communists wanted reform imposed by force, while the nationalists sought a peaceful land reform of "land to the tiller." After losing the war and retreating to Taiwan, the KMT engaged in what was called a "land to the tiller" reform movement in Taiwan, using the land reform that General Douglas MacArthur imposed on Japan as a blueprint. Although it took the form of a "buyout," it was still essentially "forcible expropriation and redistribution."

The Land Reform movement carried out in mainland China from 1950 to 1953 adopted the violent and tumultuous method, and the notion of peaceful redistribution of land came under heavy political attack. Evidence indicates that the majority of those who led the assault in Land Reform were designated as poor peasants and farm laborers but were in fact rural *lumpenproletariat*. Already marginalized due to a variety of personal failings (theft, gambling, vagrancy, idleness, gluttony, etc.), these people grasped the historic opportunity of the Land Reform movement to display their "revolutionary character" and "fighting spirit" with matchless intensity. These resentful "taproots of Land Reform" joined the CCP and became officials during and after the campaign, and many became leading grassroots cadres holding positions such as CCP secretary, CCP committee member, chairman, or township or village head. Most were semi-literate at best, lacked a sense of public welfare, and were unrestrained by moral standards. Personal experience had convinced them of one thing: tagging along with the CCP would allow them to do whatever they wanted. In their unques-tioning obedience to those above, predatory attitude toward those below, cliqu-ishness, braggadocio, short-sightedness in production goals, and instinctive talent for political campaigns, they consciously or unconsciously carried their *lumpenproletariat* ethos into the political and productive life of China's villages. Of course there were also good cadres, but they were woefully outnumbered and repeatedly purged and enfeebled in subsequent political campaigns. Actual practice has repeatedly made clear that those who are adept at destroying an old world are never good at building a new one.

I've read the Land Reform Law and some theoretical essays from the Land Reform period, and in practical terms, the law's content is reasonable. Violent land reform did in fact achieve its objectives of shattering the old production relations, eliminating economic inequality, and "giving land to the tiller," and it won the support of the majority of China's people at the time. However, it also destroyed the productive force in the countryside and obliterated the traditional moral concepts of the Chinese people (which was arguably also one of its objec-tives). What it brought about was a rural society in which everyone was equally poor rather than one in which everyone enjoyed equal prosperity or in which a minority who prospered could improve the fortunes of the rest. Experience has shown that countries or regions that impose the rule of common poverty can rely only on violence, lies, and terror to maintain social order. Theories that divide people into classes, manufacture class struggle, encourage violent revolu-tion, and call for the elimination of one group of people by another group have inflicted greater calamity on the Chinese people than all previous disasters of history combined.

In a sense, property is like freedom: it is a genuine power, and the pursuit of wealth is a common human desire and a motivating force for productivity. Taking a step back, even if there were injustices attached to private ownership, given that this system existed under feudalism for 2,000 years, the possessors of land (the landlord class) should not be made to bear responsibility for his-tory, and even less should they be condemned to death for it. Statistical data indicate that China currently has more than 10 million people whose assets are valued at more than one million yuan, composing 0.8 percent of the population. If official policies were to change and these people were labeled as regenerated bourgeoisie, and a decree were issued that they should be subjected to public criticism, struggle, and reform and that their assets should be redistributed to poor working people whose incomes are less than 1,000 yuan per month, would that be reasonable? Would it be supported by the majority of China's people? The answer is obvious.

While reporting in Daoxian, I half-jokingly asked some people whether "peaceful land reform" might have been possible. Liu Daixiu, the PPA chairman who will reappear later in this book as leading the killing of 13 members of "master petitioner" Li Niande's family, hardly gave me a chance to draw a breath before saying, "How is it that you educated people just keep getting dumber? Would you agree to give me your stuff if you weren't dead?"

Perhaps there's a simple truth in what Liu Daixiu said, but my point is that Liu Daixiu, a taproot of the Land Reform movement, had seen his family enter its fifth generation as poor peasants when I interviewed him in 1986. In standing up and being liberated, they'd made revolution and killed people, but where was the prosperity they'd been promised? Where was the power of masters and the social justice they'd been promised? And yes, where was the land that was to be apportioned to them? Liu Daixiu gained nothing and perhaps lost even more.

PART EIGHT

THE KILLERS

24

Beyond the Pale

The Task Force handled 401 cases that occurred during Daoxian's killing wind, and every one of them could be described as "utterly inhumane and heinous." Compared with fictional villainous landlords such as Huang Shiren, Zhou Bapi, Nan Batian, and Liu Wencai, these real-life cases outstrip the human imagination. In the previous sections of this book, I've examined these cases from the perspective of the victims. In the next few chapters I want to focus on the killers and what motivated them. While some were genuine criminals, the majority were law-abiding tillers of the soil. The following questions should be answered: what would lead them to display such savage brutality, and what did the ancient Chinese race lose in this mass frenzy?

This chapter deals with particularly bestial behavior. Much as I'd prefer to avoid the spectacle of gore, violence, wretchedness, ignorance, and ugliness, this is an organic aspect of the Daoxian massacre that cannot be ignored and, indeed, should be a starting point for soul-searching by all Chinese.

The "big rice pot"

The *Xinhua Dictionary* defines the term "big rice pot" as a meal shared by many. It can be considered a specifically Chinese term originating in the 1958 Great Leap Forward, when cooking pots were confiscated and smashed for the great backyard iron- and steel-forging campaign, and everyone ate from the "big rice pots" of communal kitchens in the People's Communes. The story that follows shows how this term became endowed with new meaning in Daoxian in 1967.

The story takes place in the Tianguangdong brigade of Xianglinpu District's Xiajiang Commune. This locality has a deeply mysterious flavor. A little more than a kilometer northeast of Tianguangdong Village is a place called Guizailing— Demon Whelp Ridge—covered with a dense deciduous forest. In the middle of this forest is a clearing full of human-shaped rocks ranging in height from 10 centimeters to 1 meter, with their forms diverse and lifelike, some scattered on the ground and others half-buried. Local people say the stone carvings are the remains of a ghost army that turned to stone at daybreak after their wizard commander was defeated in a battle with an immortal being. A provincial archaeological team eventually determined that the site was a sacrificial altar dating back more than 2,000 years to the Warring States period. Visiting this secluded and umbral spot with its petrified denizens sent a chill down my spine.

The victim in my story is Li Jincui, the daughter of a poor peasant family from the Zhujiawan brigade in Jiangyong County, just across the border, who married a man in the Tianguangdong brigade, Chen Gaoxiao, in October 1966. The Chen family was of a higher social class, and the lovely Li Jincui must have had better options than a class enemy, but the matchmaker made a strong case, saying that Chen Gaoxiao's father, although a Kuomintang (KMT) party secretary before Liberation, had ensured the People's Liberation Army (PLA) a warm reception in Daoxian[1] and therefore was not considered a black element. Added to that, Chen Gaoxiao was a handsome, good-natured, and hard-working man, so ultimately Li Jincui agreed to the marriage. They turned out to be a loving and well-matched pair, and some envious types cursed the landlord whelp for his good fortune.

On August 26, while Chen Gaoxiao was cleaning up for dinner after work, a brigade militiaman named Chen Gaoyou, whose nickname was Qinggou, or "Black Dog," came calling for him. Li Jincui felt instinctively uneasy and asked, "What do you want him for, Gaoyou?"

Chen Gaoyou replied, "Don't worry, it's nothing bad—I'm on such good terms with Gaoxiu, you can't think I would hurt him!"

Chen Gaoxiao got dressed and hurried off with Chen Gaoyou to the brigade office. As soon as he entered the door, militiamen tied him hand and foot. The chairman of the brigade's poor-peasant association (PPA), Chen Dengyi, whose nickname was Potato Head, walked up to Chen Gaoxiao without a word and stabbed him in the leg with a spear, after which seven or eight others lunged forward and beat Chen Gaoxiao to death as if he were a wild animal. Chen Dengyi cut off the heads of Chen Gaoxiao and two other class enemies who had already undergone similar treatment and stuck them on poles for public display to demonstrate the brigade's revolutionary resolve.

Upon hearing the news, Li Jincui fainted dead away in terror. Only 21 years old and four months pregnant, she had suddenly become a widow. First thing the next morning, she packed up her belongings and the household's chickens and ducks and fled to her home village. But her family was unable to protect her. The Tianguangdong brigade's militia commander, Yi Zhengxi, sent militiamen to Zhujiawan to deliver a "general order" demanding that "the landlord woman Li Jincui be escorted back to the brigade within 12 hours, failing which revolutionary action will be taken." The people of Tianguangdong were tough and known for their ferocious fighting, so the Zhujiawan brigade felt compelled to ignore the entreaties of Li Jincui's family and sent her back to Tianguangdong late that night.

Why did the Tianguangdong brigade insist on bringing this woman back? In Chen Gaoyou's words, "My friends, all landlord women in the Zhujiawan and Daoshuidong area have been made 'big rice pots' shared by the poor and lower-middle peasants, so why shouldn't we do the same?"

Chen Dengyi put it even more explicitly: "If we can kill, why shouldn't we screw?"

By then, Tianguangdong had assembled a militia under military-style management, and all core militiamen lived and ate together in the primary school. A temporary pigsty in the small exercise yard held the pigs, chickens, and ducks of the dead. That afternoon, the militiamen killed another pig and brought out a bottle of rice wine as 30-odd men gathered to feast and drink.

One particularly ugly and disreputable fellow in his 40s named Chen Xiwei winked and said, "After a meal like this, we'll have plenty of energy to share the big rice pot." Everyone laughed.

By the time they'd sated themselves, it was midnight, and with their energy fully recharged, they dragged Li Jincui from the school's main hall, where she was being held. Prior to Liberation, this structure was where the villagers would come together to worship their ancestors and celebrate the Qingming Festival. After Liberation, it became the place where villagers held meetings, and then a primary school. With classes suspended, the school served as the brigade militia headquarters.

A militiaman named Chen Gaohe suggested, "Let's take her to the dry gulley next to the village." Another worried, "You can muzzle a pig but not a woman. We can't do this." Chen Gaohe untied the sweat rag around his waist and said, "I'll muzzle her with this." A third militiaman suggested, "It would be better to take her to the little thatched cottage outside the village."

By then, Li Jincui had collapsed on the floor, trembling with fear.

Chen Xiwei said, "It's so late already, let's save trouble and just do it here."

So the men dragged Li Jincui below a stage that had been erected in the school. Chen Xiwei brought a barn lantern and shined it in Li Jincui's face as she was surrounded by 30-odd leering men armed with sabers and fowling guns. Chen Xiwei tore open Li Jincui's clothes as the men started arguing over who would get her first. When Li Jincui resisted, Chen Xiwei held his saber against her neck: "Move again and I'll slaughter you."

Li Jincui pleaded with the men to go easy on her since she was pregnant, but Black Dog sneered, "Who cares if we crush some landlord whelp!"

One by one, the men took their turns with her, and by the time the 12th man had "shared the big rice pot" and crawled off her motionless body, a rooster was heralding the dawn. In any case, the 12th rapist was suspected to have leprosy, so the rest passed up their opportunity. As the sun rose, the men dragged the battered and half-dead Li Jincui to the home of an old bachelor named Chen Gaoyue and coerced her into marrying him. "She's worth 10 doses of leprosy," Chen Xiwei assured him. Chen Gaoyue ravaged Li Jincui that same night.[2]

After recovering her wits, Li Jincui took the first opportunity to flee again to her home village and salvage what was left of her life. She had already miscarried her unborn child.

So who were these beasts who raped Li Jincui? At first glance they all bore the label of poor and lower-middle peasants with "strong roots and red shoots." A closer look shows what kind of men they really were:

The instigator, Chen Gaoyou (Black Dog), was a gambler. Chen Dengyi, known as Potato Head, the main killer, was originally the brigade's PPA chairman but had been dismissed for corruption.

Chen Xiwei was a man of multiple vices who had served eight months in prison for corruption, rape, and hounding someone to death while serving as the brigade's deputy Chinese Communist Party (CCP) secretary, and more recently he had been disciplined for corruption and in "assembling a crowd for gambling." During the Cultural Revolution, he became a head of the brigade's rebel faction (Red Alliance) and colluded in the killing of 16 people.

Chen Gaohe perpetrated a revenge killing against a man surnamed Guo during the Cultural Revolution. Another of the rapists, only 15 or 16 at the time, was the son of a loafer known as Demon Pig, while yet another was a gambling addict who once poisoned his production team's fishpond. Another, known as Hound Dog, was an inveterate thief who had stolen and slaughtered his work team's plow ox. The others consisted of gamblers and idlers, and Chen Gaohui, the alleged leper, had raped other women as well.

In the Task Force's files we read that a member of the organization committee of Xiajiang Commune's CCP committee, Zhu Fenxiang, personally went to Tianguangdong on August 25, 1967, to instigate and orchestrate the killings. During the killing wind, the Tianguangdong brigade killed 22 people (including five suicides). The main people responsible included deputy CCP secretary Chen Denglu and militia deputy commander Chen Gaoxin, who led the killing of 16 people and committed multiple rapes. One report alleged that brigade schoolteacher He Jianhua committed suicide after being gang-raped by Chen Gaoxin and others.

During the Daoxian massacre, it was common for the men in black-element families to be killed and the women to be raped. However, while there were explicit provisions for the Task Force to investigate cases of rape, these cases were typically not pursued unless they involved murder as well. Many rape victims subsequently remarried and had children and didn't want to resurrect these old matters, and some had submitted to their abuse to preserve their lives, making subsequent pursuit of their cases far from clear-cut. If leniency was extended even in cases of killing, what was the point of investigating rapes? It made more sense just to let everyone off. Women such as Li Jincui who were given the "big rice pot" treatment and managed to survive could consider themselves lucky—many women treated with similar brutality ended up dead.

One such case is that of Chen Guozhen, 19, born to a landlord family in the Bailutang brigade of Xianglinpu District's Cenjiangdu Commune. Chen Guozhen was to be married in a few months, after the autumn harvest. In accordance with local custom, she had visited her fiancé's family accompanied by her mother, and her fiancé had also come to her home to present the bride price. An auspicious day on the lunar calendar had been chosen, and the nuptials awaited only the passing of the busy late rice harvest period. Her fiancé's family circumstances weren't the best, but all that mattered to Chen Guozhen was that her fiancé was a poor peasant; she'd already suffered enough from being born to a landlord family. Her marriage would make her part of a poor-peasant household, and her children would be poor peasants who could walk with their heads held high all their lives. Thinking of this made Chen Guozhen anxious for the arrival of her wedding day.

Chen Guozhen's parents were also happy to have their worries ended by their daughter marrying into a good family. Their main task now was to live frugally enough to provide her with a dowry that would ensure her a warm reception in her husband's family. Focused on their modest goals, they knew nothing of what was going on in Beijing, Changsha, or even elsewhere in Daoxian, nor did they dare take an interest.

Fate played a cruel trick on them, however. If one is to believe that people get their just deserts, this family must have committed some great evil in a previous life to deserve such terrible retribution. But since ancient times it has all too often been the case that "a righteous man perishes in his righteousness, and a wicked man prolongs his life in his evildoing."

On August 25, 1967, the deputy CCP secretary and organization committee member of Cenjiangdu Commune, Liu Qifu, went to the Bailutang brigade with commune secretary Mo Rongxing and called a meeting to transmit the upper-level directive to kill more class enemies. Several class enemies and offspring were then dragged out and killed, Chen Guozhen's parents among them. Core militiamen Zhang Enzhong and Zhang Xianhua then arrested and raped Chen Guozhen. Chen Guozhen reportedly implored the men, "I beg of you, don't do this! I'm about to be married!" Zhang Enzhong and Zhang Xianhua said, "You think you can still get married, landlord woman? Your man doesn't want you anymore!" They then proceeded to assault her continually over the next two days and nights.

By then, Yuan Lifu had sent down militiamen for the three-day "catch-up" killing spree, and Chen Guozhen was included in the new batch of victims on August 28. Zheng Enzhong and Zhang Xianhua had promised to spare Chen Guozhen's life while raping her, and as she was led to the execution ground, she kept asking, "Where's Brother Enzhong? He said I wouldn't be killed."

A head of the brigade's peasant supreme court said, "No one can save you! Don't think you can use your feminine wiles to sabotage the ranks of us poor and lower-middle peasants."

Word went around that Chen Guozhen was a seductress and fox spirit, and when it came time to kill her, many core militiamen who normally displayed great revolutionary resolve shrank back. One militiaman struck at her with his spear with his eyes shut but barely penetrated her skin. Enraged by the sub-standard performance of his men, militia deputy commander Zhang Qisheng roared out, "Step aside and watch me!" He tore off Chen Guozhen's trousers and thrust the spear deep into her vagina.

Chen Guozhen's case was not unique in Daoxian at that time. For instance, in the Wujiashan production brigade of Shangguan District's Dongmen Commune, a woman named Huang Langen was gang-raped by four militiamen and then speared through her vagina. Her three-year-old son was then grabbed by the legs and hurled to his death.

In another case on August 25, 1967, a cadre in the Daoxian public-security apparatus waylaid a young woman from a landlord family in Wutian Commune, dragged her to a tea hill, and raped her. He then stuffed a detonator cap into her vagina and ignited it. Because the detonator cap had only limited explosive power, the woman didn't die immediately but lay there writhing in agony until she bled to death. The cadre later spread the rumor, "That woman had a mini radio transmitter in her snatch, and it exploded inside her." Because too much time has passed and "evidence" is insufficient, it has been impossible to ascertain the specific culprit, but the report bringing the case to light clearly stated the location and the persons involved, and a genuine investigation could have clarified everything.

I have other similar cases in hand:

In the Qianjin brigade of Simaqiao District's Yangjia Commune, landlord offspring and sent-down cadre Peng Tao was killed along with four family members, leaving behind two daughters, 18-year-old Peng Wumei and her 13-year-old sister. The plan was to marry Peng Wumei off to one of the brigade's poor peasant bachelors. The chairman of the brigade's Cultural Revolution committee, Peng Jiaming, and his cousin, Peng Jiazhi, both wanted Peng Wumei, so they gang-raped her and then covered up their actions by killing both sisters. With the whole family destroyed, there was no one left to seek redress for them.

In the Second Shuguang brigade of Shouyan District's Niulukou Commune, Cultural Revolution committee chairman Jiang Shibao and others killed the husband of landlord offspring Li Xinrong and then dragged Li to a tea hill, where they gang-raped her and killed her with a saber.

In the No. 2 production team of the Junmin brigade of Qingxi District's Youxiang Commune, the entire seven-member family of landlord element Chen Shutang was exterminated. Chen, his wife, and their three sons, aged 11 to 16, were initially killed, leaving Chen's two daughters, 19 and 3 years old. A few days later, brigade CCP secretary Xiang Zhiqing told the production team's cadres, "If you don't take action against Chen Shutang's daughters, you'll take the blame if problems arise in the future." The two girls were then killed, reportedly after the elder was gang-raped.

All these women and girls suffered just as much as Chen Guozhen and the others, even if the manner of killing was less horrific. Even worse than their tragic and humiliating ends was the prolonged physical and mental devastation that came before.

Having reached this point, I can't go on. How pitiful it is to be a Chinese woman, and how lamentable to be a Chinese man! None of us emerged from a crack in a stone; we all passed through our mothers' birth canals, so why should there be such deep-rooted hatred toward a woman's reproductive organs? This destruction of a woman's reproductive organs through rape and murder was not unique to Daoxian; it occurred all over the country. Surely it is not only the Chinese race that commits such atrocities? Just thinking about it makes me shudder. On further thought, I find that three factors give rise to this phenomenon: one is a worship of violence at all levels of society; the second is the sexual constraint and repression imposed on the lower classes over the long term, giving rise to a distorted sexual psychology among the entire citizenry; the third is the cultural bias against women. Our traditional culture has always regarded women as property, and when this kind of property is not one's own, the first impulse is to hate and destroy it in accordance with the logic that if I can't have it, then neither can anyone else. I've mentioned that the ratio of men to women killed in the Daoxian massacre was nearly four to one and that a major factor was the need of many poor and lower-middle peasant bachelors for a wife. Even more essentially, these women were the spoils of "revolutionary victory," and the first consideration was distribution. Killing became a consideration for those presenting less value or convenience, or those who refused. Once a decision was made to kill a woman, the first thing to be destroyed was the part of her body considered most valuable.

Yet, why is it that before these women were killed, no one stepped forward and asked: why must they be treated this way? This is the even-greater tragedy of our people.

Between humans and beasts

In just a week, 19-year-old Tang Shuilan was to become a mother. Like all first-time mothers, she was both elated and nervous, carefully feeling for the movement of the child in her womb and guessing whether it would be a boy or a girl. She hoped for a boy; if her husband's family felt she'd brought them some benefit, her life would be that much easier. . . . Everything was ready for the baby's arrival—a cradle, diapers, tiny clothes—and her parents had sent over a chicken and eggs.

If Tang Shuilan's baby had been born just a few days earlier, it might have been able to root itself in this world and push out a shoot of life. But just at this time, in the latter half of August, the killing wind began blowing through their production brigade, and Tang Shuilan, born into a higher social class, could not escape her fate. The peasant supreme court of Xingqiao Commune's Xiaoliu brigade, where she was born and raised, issued a "general order" for Tang Shuilan to be brought back to her village to be "tried." The peasant supreme court of her husband's brigade had militiaman Zhang Tiansha escort her back to Xialiu Village to undergo trial with the rest of her family, and the Xialiu brigade sent a militiaman to receive her.

The late summer sun blazed overhead, soaking everyone in perspiration. Heavily pregnant, Tang Shuilan could only walk slowly in spite of the militiamen's urging. When they reached a tea hill, the sun was already sinking in the west. The militiamen were impatient and said to each other, "At this rate, how long will it take us to get there?" Since they were just bringing her back to be killed, it made sense to save trouble and just do away with her. At that time, Zhang Tiansha was just over 20, strong and stubborn as a bull. He pulled out a razor-sharp steel wire that he always carried with him, and ripped it through Tang Shuilan's sweating midriff from back toward front.

Tang Shuilan may never have expected to be killed, since through marriage she was no longer part of a landlord family. Now she screamed and turned horrified eyes on her assailant, but Zhang Tiansha just tore off her trousers and sawed his steel wire across her belly until the flesh opened and the baby slid out in a flow of blood. Tang Shuilan instinctively reached out to clutch the baby to her as they tumbled together into a pool of blood.

After returning to the brigade, Zhang Tiansha went around bragging! "Fuck her mother! When I tore off Tang Shuilan's pants, the baby was moving, so I cut her twice and the baby slid right out, still alive! Hah hah!"

The cave lay amid a stretch of rocks and weeds, deep and slanted and very wide, and an underground river ran through it. Local people said that during the War of Resistance, people hid here when the "Jap Devils" invaded Daoxian. But the cave's real claim to fame arrived on August 26, 1967, when it became a natural execution ground into which groups of people were kicked into a ready-made grave. After one group was killed that morning, another was led there in the afternoon, including a woman in her 60s named Tang Changfeng. Four militiamen armed with sabers and fowling pieces escorted the old woman, bound hand and foot, to the mouth of the cave.

A widow for decades, Tang Changfeng had managed against all odds to raise three sons, who in turn had raised two boys and two girls. By now she should have been allowed to enjoy a happy old age, but that afternoon, Tang's three sons and four grandchildren were all "sentenced to death" along with her; not a single one was spared. Two of her daughters-in-law were being spared, apparently to allow them to "change classes" through remarriage. Tang Changfeng knew she was on her way to the netherworld, but she went calmly. With her sons and grandchildren dead, what point was there for her to keep on living? Once she was dead, the family would be reunited in the underworld. She had been a secret Buddhist for many years and accepted her fate.

So it was that she approached this natural grave without weeping or wailing, but when she was nearly there, something unexpected happened. Perhaps because of brambles along the road, her trousers tore and slipped down her legs, leaving her half-naked. I should explain that women's trousers in Daoxian (and the rest of China) were not the snug type common today but were made of coarse, homespun cloth with large waistbands that were rolled under and then held in place with a belt. Tang Changfeng instinctively cried out and bent while clenching her legs, but her pants continued to slide down, and with her hands bound, she had no way to hold them up. All she could do was plead with the young men escorting her, "Please untie me so I can pull up my pants."

The militiamen just laughed and said, "What do you care? You'll be dead soon anyway. Just keep going!"

All that day, even upon hearing of the deaths of her sons and grandchildren, Tang Changfeng hadn't shed a tear as she accepted her fate. But now she wept as she knelt down and pleaded, "I'm old enough to be your mother. I've never done anything indecent in all my life. Don't send me to my ancestors half-naked!"

A militiaman said, "That will make your ancestors even happier to see you!," and the rest joined in raucous laughter. "Revolution isn't a dinner party! Who cares if you're half-naked!" The young men pulled her up, scolding and laughing as they dragged her to the cave and sent her hurtling trouserless to the end of her life.

His name was He Hengchang, and before his arrest he lived in Lefutang Township's Shiqiaotou Village. We interviewed him in prison. Largely illiterate, he was gluttonous and lazy, his hands and feet unwashed, and he was regarded with contempt by those around him. His brigade didn't even think enough of him to assign him a part in the killing wind, but no one could hold him back. Everyone had to be allowed to be revolutionary, after all, and He Hengchang's issues were too trifling to deprive him of an opportunity to express his revolutionary character.

We asked He Hengchang, "What were you thinking when you volunteered to kill people?"

He replied, "I wasn't thinking anything. It was just an impulse; when I saw others killing people, I wanted to do it, too." He added that there were rewards for killing, and poor as he was, how could he pass up this opportunity?

The peasant supreme court of his production brigade sentenced 21 black elements and offspring to death. When discussion turned to who would carry out the executions, He Hengchang jumped up and volunteered. When it came to actually escorting the "criminals" to the hills and carrying out the death sentences, some of the executioners couldn't go through with it, but He Hengchang stepped forward, beat his breast, and said, "Just watch me!" He grabbed a saber from a militiaman's hand, swung it through the air, and in the blink of an eye hacked seven people to death. When he reached the eighth, his blade was too dull, and cursing that it was like using a hoe, he brought it down on his victim's skull, spraying blood and brain matter all around. When the killing was finished, he imitated the executioner in traditional operas, raising his bloodied saber in both hands and running around in a circle for all around to see. By then the other 12 "criminals" had also been dispatched by the militia. He tried sticking one of the heads on his saber and marching around with it, but the head kept dropping off, so he grabbed it by the hair and lifted it up as the others cheered.

Feeling a need to keep going, He Hengchang suddenly remembered that one of the dead had children. He suggested to the CCP branch secretary, "Tang XX still has three brats at home; let's get rid of them, too." Without waiting for permission, He Hengchang raced back to the village, burst into Tan's home, and thrust his saber through the body of seven-year-old Tang Caixia and then the girl's younger brother. He was about to do the same with the last of the children when their grandmother, tottering on bound feet, rushed forward and clutched the child to her. He Hengchang gave the old woman a fierce push and then dashed the child's head against the floor, covering his legs with blood and brains as the old woman wailed.

That day, He Hengchang earned 55 yuan for killing these people, more than the dividend he'd been paid at the end of the previous year.

When the case was investigated, He Hengchang was sentenced to three years in prison. According to the unwritten rules in Daoxian, three lives cost a CCP membership, and those who killed only two or three people were usually not brought to justice. Where victims were more numerous, the killer had to have acted on his own initiative rather than under orders, and then the sentence was typically half a year for each life. He Hengchang was not a CCP member and had killed 11 people, so a three-year prison sentence could be considered letting him off lightly. Even so, He Hengchang was dissatisfied, saying, "I wasn't the one who decided to kill those people, and if I hadn't killed them, someone else would have, so why am I the one who was punished instead of the ones who made the decisions?"

Fengmu'ao Village in Simaqiao District's Dapingling Commune had a class enemy offspring named He Yongyi, an obedient and intelligent boy who was only 14 at the time of his death. After his parents were sentenced to death by the brigade's peasant supreme court, the brigade sent a militiaman to tie up He Yongyi and do away with him as well.

As he was being tied up, He Yongyi tried to save his life by telling the militiaman, "There's money in our chest at home. If I lead you to it and give all the money to you, will you let me live?" The militiaman promised not to kill He Yongyi, and upon reaching the boy's home, he forced open the chest and took all the money inside. He Yongyi said, "Brother, now the money is all yours, please let me go." The militiaman said, "I won't kill you. I'll just take you to Hongmen'ao Cave with the others and then let you go." Innocent He Yongyi believed the militiaman and obediently accompanied him to the cave.

When they reached Hongmen'ao Cave, the militiaman's expression suddenly changed, and he pushed the boy down onto a heap of corpses. He Yongyi tried to climb out, but the cave walls were too steep and tall, and after climbing part of the way he just slid back down. Pointing a bleeding finger at the militiaman, he shouted, "You took my family's money, so why are you still killing me?"

The militiaman lied, "What money did you give me? Your family doesn't have a pot to piss in!"

He Yongyi cursed the militiaman as a swindler and an animal, and when the leaders of the brigade's peasant supreme court saw the landlord whelp in such a frenzy, they set a pine branch on fire and threw it in. Even that didn't kill He Yongyi, who after coughing for a while began cursing the militiaman again: "Fuck your mother! I'll come back and haunt you!"

The militiaman and the others standing nearby mixed rice straw with insecticide, set it alight, and threw it into the cave, and immediately toxic smoke filled the cave. After the smoke dispersed, they found that He Yongyi was still alive and moaning. Shocked, a brigade cadre berated the militiaman, saying, "You obviously did something immoral. Hand over the money! Taking private possession of movable property is against the law!"

They then tied dynamite to a stone, pushed it into the cave, and detonated it. A great explosion followed, after which there was silence at last.

The Xiushuidong brigade of Xianglinpu District's Xinche Commune had a young man from an upper-middle peasant family named Chen Zutian who normally wouldn't have been a target of the killing wind, but he'd had a falling out with the brigade's Cultural Revolution Committee (CRC) chairman, Chen Zude, who carried a grudge. When it came time to kill class enemies, Chen Zude represented the brigade's peasant supreme court in ordering Chen Zutian rounded up with the others, demanding that he confess to joining a "counterrevolutionary organization." When Chen Zude denied the allegation, he was brutally tortured until he confessed. Chen Zude said, "Since he's confessed, there's nothing more to say. Take him out and kill him."

By then, however, the 47th Army's 6950 Unit had already entered Daoxian to halt the killings, and the commune had handed down a directive prohibiting further "random killing." Someone said, "Wouldn't it be better to send him to the commune and let them handle it?"

Chen Zude said, "If we send him to the commune, they'll just send him back and tell us to handle it. His family was already lucky enough not to be designated landlords during the Land Reform movement. We're not letting him off so easy this time. I'll take responsibility if any problem arises."

He then took Chen Zutian to the tung oil ground outside the village to carry out the "execution."

Seeing that things were not going well for him, Chen Zutian knelt down at Chen Zude's feet and begged, "Brother Zude, whatever I did to offend you in the past, please tell me and I'll promise to make amends."

Chen Zude said, "It's too late!" And without letting Chen Zutian say anything more, he shot him with his fowling gun.

Because fowling guns had limited killing power, Chen Zutian rolled on the ground in his death throes and cried, "Chen Zude, you're avenging a personal grudge in the name of public interest. You'll meet a bad end. After I die, I'll come back for you. . . ."

When Chen Zude heard this, he took up his saber and cut off Chen Zutian's hands, while improvising a poem:

> Others stretch out and die,
> But you gave me the evil eye.
> Sending you handless to the King of Hell,
> I, Zude, will treat you well.

After killing Chen Zutian, Chen Zude went home but couldn't sleep, feeling he hadn't covered all the bases. He had no need to fear Zutian, who could come back only as a handless ghost, but his elderly father and older brother might try to take revenge. The more he thought about it, the more convinced he was that they would have to be done away with.

Early the next morning, Chen Zude took a group of men to arrest Chen Zutian's father and elder brother. Guessing Zude's intentions, the brother had run off, so only the father was apprehended. When Chen Zude and the others took Chen Zutian's father to the tung oil ground, the old man tearfully begged, "Chen Zude, please aim well so I don't suffer."

Moved by the old man's plea, Chen Zude loaded pellets for killing wild boar into his blunderbuss and pointed it at the back of the old man's head. The gun blasted, and Chen Zutian's father was dead when he hit the ground.

Brainwashed

The Communist Party secretary who killed
a poor-peasant association chairman

The Chinese Communist Party (CCP) secretary of Xianglinpu Commune's Diaogaolou brigade, He Daiyu, became famous during Daoxian's killings and even in the Task Force investigations, not because his brigade had an especially high fatality rate (only 16 were killed), but because he killed the brigade's poor-peasant association (PPA) chairman. Quite a few poor and lower-middle peasants were killed during the killing wind, but only one PPA chairman, and for that reason this case was numbered among the notable cases of the Daoxian Cultural Revolution killings.

He Daiyu had served as CCP secretary of Diaogaolou Village since the Land Reform movement, but with little to show for it. His occasional overindulgences of his sexual and physical appetites were considered long-time vices handed down to him from the multiple evils of the Old Society, and on the critical questions of political performance, obedience to the CCP, and reliable class standpoint, Secretary He couldn't be faulted. When the village engaged in the Socialist Education movement in 1964, the only person who raised any criticism about Secretary He was a poor peasant named He Daijing, who exposed He Daiyu's failings,[1] cuffed him in the head, and killed one of his pigs as restitution. The CCP secretary was broken-hearted: criticism by upper-level leaders was to help and educate him, but he had helped He Daijing in the past, and now his kindness was being repaid with a box in the ears and the loss of a pig.

When the killing wind blew in, CCP secretary He summed up his years of experience by saying, "It's not enough to do away with black elements; we also have to do away with rascals who disobey the party so that Chairman Mao's radiance can shine on our Diaogaolou brigade!" He Daiyu wasn't an educated man, but he'd studied Chairman Mao's works and understood that wars were fought one battle at a time. When he called a meeting of the brigade CCP branch to discuss killing black elements, he particularly arranged for his hated enemy He Daijing to take a frontline role in the extermination. When He Daijing demurred, He Daiyu accused him of an unreliable class standpoint and of collaborating with black elements and declared that if he didn't correct his attitude, "revolutionary discipline" would be applied. He also sat down with He Daijing to study Chairman Mao's highest directive: "Should local tyrants, evil gentry, despots, and counterrevolutionaries who have committed heinous crimes be put to death? Yes! Some democratic personages say it's wrong to execute them, but we say it's fine. . . ."[2]

The CCP secretary's ideological work was effective, and the old peasant radiated revolutionary fervor as he awed the brigade by hefting his gleaming saber and killing people inside and outside the village. When most of the black elements were exterminated and the upper levels ordered an end to the random killings, He Daiyu immediately called in militia commander He Zhenshu and Cultural Revolution Committee (CRC) chairman He Daixin for an inner-circle meeting on how to resolve the problem of He Daijing's toxicity. The three unanimously agreed that the Diaogaolou brigade would have no peace unless He Daijing was eliminated. Worried that He Daijing would put up a fight, they decided to lure him to the brigade office with an offer of peanuts and melon seeds, at which time he could be put under arrest.

He Daijing suspected nothing and appeared bright and early at the brigade office with a bamboo basket to collect his peanuts and melon seeds, only to have his arms and legs shattered by wooden poles wielded by He Daiyu and the others. The brigade leaders then convened a mass rally and declared that He Daijing had committed multiple murders, not even sparing small children. The masses boiled with righteous indignation and called for his death. CCP secretary He had He Daijing's broken legs tied to a bull, after which he was dragged like a plow over a kilometer of rocky hills, the skin on his back disintegrating into a red pulp. Finally a dozen militiamen shot He Daijing with fowling guns. That was really excessive.

He Daiyu was subsequently expelled from the CCP, and during the Task Force's investigation of the killings at the Diaogaolou, He Daiyu described how the brigade had arranged killings at the instigation of the Shangdu militia command post. Regarding the killing of He Daijing, He Daiyu is recorded as saying:

> I actually was responsible for killing Daijing, but I don't agree that it was a revenge killing. I've received so many years of education from the party, my consciousness couldn't be low enough for me to kill someone on a grudge in the name of public interest. It was He Zhenshu who first suggested killing Daijing, and I agreed because he was playing a destructive role in the brigade, and the masses were infuriated with him. I'm not defending myself. The leaders taught me to be honest and

faithful to the organization—I say it as I see it. I will accept whatever punishment the organization sees fit to give me.

Duty before family

After hearing of the incident that follows, I became lost in thought about the mystery of human nature. People like to say that greed and fear are the two flaws most difficult to surmount, but they are hardly our only weaknesses. In this case, a female member of the militia put duty above family and stabbed her adoptive mother with her own hand.

She was in the prime of life then, and a core member of her brigade militia. Fate had deprived her of both parents at an early age but had provided her with a good-hearted aunt to raise her. The aunt was married to the girl's paternal uncle, and while the family belonged to the landlord class, her circumstances were far from comfortable, especially after her husband died of edema during the famine in 1961. Daoxian maintained a traditional emphasis on education, and any family that could make ends meet would find a way to send its children to school. Coming from a higher social class, the aunt saw no sense in educating her children, but her niece was classified as a poor peasant, so she scrimped and saved to send her to school. The girl flourished, able to recite large swaths of Chairman Mao's works and quotations and to understand the major principles of class struggle. If not for the Cultural Revolution, she might have gained admittance to a university, no small accomplishment for a village girl.

One day, the girl made a painful and terrible discovery: her apparently kind-hearted aunt was actually an unpardonably vicious landlord woman! This girl, a bona fide poor peasant, had been reared at the teat of a wolf! This became a source of great anxiety to her.

When the brigade held its meeting to draw up its killing list, someone said of the aunt, "That woman is good-hearted and helped us raise a poor peasant girl, so let's not kill her."

But when it came time to act, the girl tied up her aunt with her own hands. Watching from a distance, the brigade militia commander called out, "You've made a mistake—didn't we say we wouldn't kill your aunt?"

The girl replied, "This is no mistake! She's not my aunt but a class enemy! Social class takes precedence over blood. The farmer who pitied the poisonous snake was bitten and died." She pushed her aunt in among those who were to be killed, and they were escorted to the edge of a pit.

Still nursing a faint hope, the aunt turned and looked at her stern-faced, saber-holding niece and asked with tears gleaming in her eyes, "My dear, where did I fail you in all these years? I just want to hear you tell the truth."

The girl glared at her aunt and barked, "Who cares about failing or not failing? Today I'm a revolutionary!" She brought down her saber, and the aunt's head dropped to the ground like a melon. After killing her aunt, the girl took part in subsequent killings and was personally responsible for six deaths.

Eventually the girl paid a price for her "revolutionary action." In those days, Daoxian girls married young, usually between the ages of 18 and 20, and this girl, 18 years old in 1967, was already engaged. Prior to Liberation, here, as elsewhere in China, marriages were arranged by parents and matchmakers, and while love matches were encouraged after Liberation, the traditional arrangements continued in disguised form in the countryside. They involved a lengthy process of escorted meetings and visits, mutual approval by the couple and their families, and then the delivery of a series of monetary and material gifts from the groom's family, which would not be returned if the groom backed out. In this case, the girl had reached the stage of formal betrothal, which meant the groom's family had already spent quite a lot of money, but the groom's parents decided to withdraw from the match. They worried that if a conflict should arise between the couple, the girl might get "revolutionary" in the middle of the night and that would be a disaster!

Once this happened, there wasn't a young man anywhere around who would marry this young woman, and she reached her 30s as an old maid. She finally married a primary-school teacher in another county who was in his late 30s but still unmarried because of an undesirable family background. The villagers pitied her and kept her history as a killer a close secret, and her husband knew nothing about it; if he'd known that the woman sleeping next to him had stabbed seven people to death, he probably couldn't have slept a wink. I've also declined to reveal her name out of pity for her and her husband. She was not the first person to have done such a thing, nor the last. Since ancient times, China has had people who put duty before family, and many young people from illustrious households threw themselves into revolution and cut all ties with their wealthy families. It was not unheard of for such young people to prove how thoroughly they'd been revolutionized by escorting their own parents to the execution ground. That's why we shouldn't cast too much blame on this country girl, who is as pitiful as she is disgusting.

Reportedly, when the Task Force comrades called her in and asked why she'd insisted on killing her aunt, she couldn't give a clear answer, but just kept saying, "I was insane, completely insane!"

The Iron Maiden of Daoxian

A story circulated in Xianglinpu District of the leader of an "iron maiden shock brigade" who killed 18 people.

The iron maiden shock brigade was a product of the 1963 "Learn from Dazhai in Agriculture" campaign, which was carried out at the same time as campaigns to "Learn from Daqing in Industry" and for the whole country to "Learn from the People's Liberation Army." The Dazhai production brigade in Shanxi's Xiyang County had an iron maiden shock brigade led by the celebrated Guo Fenglian, who led heroic rescue efforts during a flood. The leader of Daoxian's iron maiden shock brigade (whom I'll refer to now as the Iron Maiden) didn't achieve the same level of fame as Guo Fenglian, but her name was still known throughout Xianglinpu District.

The Iron Maiden was as tall and husky as a man. Young scamps in her village referred to her behind her back as Prize Sow or Door Plank, but none dared say it to her face, because she was amazingly strong and would undoubtedly teach them a painful lesson.

The first time the Iron Maiden rose to fame was when production teams began assigning work points on the basis of evaluation of labor in 1964. At that time, her production team called a meeting to assign a work point base for each person. Men typically received ten points, and women eight points or less. The Iron Maiden received eight points, the highest level for women, but she disputed it on the spot: "Why do you men get ten points and I get only eight? What can you do that I can't do?" The production team didn't know how to respond. Everyone knew she worked as well as or better than any man; she didn't seem to know the meaning of the word "slacking," harvesting half a *mu* of rice without stopping for a breath, and being able to work at the limekilns two days and nights without sleeping and with more energy than male workers. The production team was in a predicament; it was traditional for men to earn more work points than women, and if they gave in to her, what could they say to other women?

At that point, a robust young man said, "Let's see who's the real man here. Empty talk is useless; let's see actual results."

"Fine," said the Iron Maiden, "You choose the work, and if I can't beat you, I'll cook three of my fingertips for you to eat!" That made it official.

The next day, the production team leader and several cadres called her and the young man over, and pointing to a pile of ox dung, they said, "Get a move on—carry it over to that field." The two set to work without another word. After working all morning, neither conceded defeat.

The young man said, "There's no skill involved in this. Let's compete on plowing in the afternoon." That afternoon, each of them chose an ox and they worked until night fell and their water buffalo were foaming at the mouth with exhaustion, but still they were evenly matched.

The Iron Maiden spoke up: "Light the lanterns and let's keep going."

The young man said, "Forget it, I'm done! I'm not afraid you can outwork me, but I don't have your layer of fat to keep me going."

That should have made her 10 work points a foregone conclusion, but when another meeting was held, a new problem emerged: other women were also demanding to compete with men for work points. The matter was debated all the way to the commune level, and the commune leaders said equal work points for equal work was Chairman Mao's policy. As a result, not only did the Iron Maiden receive 10 work points, but the base work points for all other women were raised by half a point. All the women were grateful to the Iron Maiden for sticking to her guns. Later, when the production brigade decided to Learn from Dazhai by establishing an iron maiden shock brigade, the Iron Maiden inevitably became the leader.

In 1965, the Xiyuan Reservoir[3] began leaking because it hadn't been properly stripped when it was built. The iron maiden shock brigade was sent to the work-site to help out with emergency repairs. Around a thousand people were living at the worksite, and there was a bustling competition to see who could get the most work done. The young women in the iron maiden shock brigade challenged the young men to a "socialist work competition." At that time, the worksite issued an extra ration of rice to workers who carried two shoulder poles. The Iron Maiden told headquarters she wanted to be paid this way, and she took up two shoulder poles and walked as if on wings, breaking several poles from the weight of her loads and creating a new record for the worksite. She became an instant heroine cited as an example throughout the commune and the district.

The Iron Maiden's parents were middle peasants, so when the killings began, she didn't qualify for a prominent role. Nevertheless, the commune had established her as a model, and she was also the leader of the core militia, so when the production brigade held a meeting to discuss killing people, she had to be notified as well. At the meeting, the brigade leader said, "Chairman Mao has taught us that 'The times are different; men and women are equal, and female comrades can do whatever male comrades can do.' Our brigade's iron maiden shock brigade is a Red Flag for our commune, and today we'll hand this mission over to them!"

As soon as he finished speaking, the Iron Maiden stood up and said, "I pledge to complete this mission."

But when it came to the actual killing, the other members of the iron maiden brigade shrank back, and the Iron Maiden had no choice but to deal with it herself. The condemned class enemies were tied and lined up at the execution ground, and after the brigade's PPA chairman pronounced the death sentences in the name of the peasant supreme court, the Iron Maiden stepped forward. She had worked hard all her life and knew the importance of a sharp knife and good aim in cutting firewood, so she had honed her machete to razor sharpness. People might wonder how she could be so professional and calm when she had never killed before, but perhaps it was because she had cut so much wood, and this was much the same process only with different and indeed softer material. Gripping her machete in both hands, she walked to the victim at the end of the line and told the militia escorts to step aside. Then she raised her gleaming machete and brought it down with a forceful swing. There was a snapping sound, a head hit the ground, and the body crumpled spurting blood, but none of it splashing on the Iron Maiden. A clean job indeed! Within a short time, a dozen heads had found new homes. At that point, however, a problem arose: the blade was losing its edge with each cut, requiring more strength for each blow; this increased tension, which in turn made each execution proceed less smoothly.

If the Iron Maiden had been more experienced, she might have anticipated this problem and brought an extra knife. Refusing to be put off, she just exerted the superhuman strength she was known for. When she came to the 16th victim, the machete became jammed in the bone, and the Iron Maiden braced her foot on the back of the "class enemy" as she dislodged the blade with a forceful pull. Blood sprayed out and drenched her from head to toe. The last two class enemies had long fallen paralyzed to the ground, so she grabbed them by the hair and chopped at their necks like firewood. After she had killed all 18, the machete slid from her hand and she slumped to the ground. By then she was so covered with blood that even her eyes and nose were indistinguishable from the rest of her face. Several cadres ran over and carried her to one side.

Eventually the Iron Maiden's boyfriend was promoted in the army, and after they married, the Iron Maiden left Daoxian for Guangxi as an army wife. When the Task Force began its work, it called her back from Guangxi to attend the exposure study sessions. When asked what motivated her to kill, the Iron Maiden replied, "I felt it was like any other work in the production team—if I did it, I had to do it well."

PART NINE

THE OUTLIERS

26

The Anomalous Xianzijiao District

While reporting in Daoxian, we took particular notice of production brigades where there were no killings and the districts and communes where killings were fewest, hoping to find something in common between them. One reason was to satisfy our reporting assignment, which included finding some bright spots rather than painting the events in Daoxian as uniformly bleak, but the other was to meet our own psychological needs. During our reporting in Daoxian, all the props of our mental world were in ruins, toppled and crumbled as if from a psychic version of the Tangshan earthquake. The result was an utter despair in the way we regarded others, ourselves, and even humanity in general—or at least the Chinese portion of it. Many were the nights when I would awake from a fantastical dream that I could not recall, but which left me with a lingering sense of disaster and dripping with a clammy sweat. We needed something positive to preserve us from utter collapse.

One production brigade had missed out on the killings simply because it was too remote. Located deep in the mountains, the Lucaoping brigade didn't receive notices of meetings or send anyone to attend them, and didn't receive any killing orders. This reason for the lack of deaths we referred to as the "Lucaoping phenomenon." But what about other districts, communes, and brigades where there had been few or no killings? It was with this question in mind that we went to Xianzijiao District (Map 9).

Xianzijiao District is situated at the foot of the Dupangling Hills in western Daoxian, and its district government lies 32 kilometers from the county seat in Daojiang. Marking the highest point in the Daozhou basin, the district's southwestern corner hosts Jiucailing, the second-highest peak in Hunan Province. Zijin Mountain lies on the north end of the district, and at the demarcation line between the two great mountain systems is Daoxian's most strategically located and inaccessible mountain pass, Yong'anguan, on the border with Guangxi.

Xianzijiao, which means "immortal's footprint," gained its name through a beautiful legend. According to tradition, when the legendary monarch Shundi journeyed to the south, he lost a shoe at Caoxieling (literally, Straw Sandal Ridge)

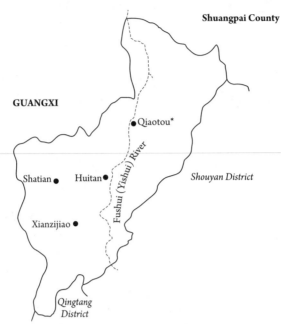

* At the time of the massacre, Qiaotou was part of Qiaotou District.

Map 9 Communes of Xianzijiao District

and changed into a new pair of straw sandals after arriving here, leaving behind a huge imprint. Shundi's two concubines came south searching for their husband, and upon discovering his footprint they blessed the surrounding land with abundant harvests and a flourishing population. The locality's scarlet azaleas are hailed in a Mao cult anthem that was playing over our transistor radio just as the rioting blooms of the "land where the Red Sun rose" appeared before our eyes.

Xianzijiao District had not only the fewest killings, but also eight production brigades with no killings at all. A total of 152 people were killed in the district (including 32 suicides). It should be noted that most of the deaths occurred in Qiaotou Commune, which at that time was actually part of Qiaotou District. That exclusion makes the number of killings carried out under the direct administration of Xianzijiao District truly minuscule, and Xianzijiao was the only district where no households were obliterated. Even so, the mortality rate of 0.36 percent, if applied to China's total population at that time of 700 million, would have meant at least 2.5 million deaths. Of course, there's no comparison with Gongba District, where the proportion of killings, if applied to the entire country, would have resulted in 35 million deaths!

Xianzijiao lagged in numbers but not in timing, and it was one of the first districts to experience killings. The first victim, a black element named Hu Xiang in Xianzijiao Commune's Qijiawan brigade,[1] was killed on August 21,

1967. Since the killing wind had just begun blowing at that time, the brigade's Chinese Communist Party (CCP) secretary was rather uneasy and requested instructions three times from district secretary Hu Guangxue, who according to the Task Force investigation was one of the main people responsible for the killings in this district. Hu Guangxue's first reply was, "You decide for yourselves." His second reply was, "I told you that you have to decide this for yourself. Now everything is up to the poor and lower-middle peasants." His third reply was "If you've decided you want to kill someone, put a file together and call a meeting to announce it." He also loaned the handgun of district People's Armed Forces Department (PAFD) commander Wang Xianzhi to the Qijiawan brigade to carry out the execution.

A typical pattern in Daoxian's Cultural Revolution killings was for the grassroots unit (typically the production brigade) to compile a file and then petition the next higher level (typically the commune) for permission before carrying out the killing, or for the grassroots unit to kill someone and then write up a report to submit to the higher level. The latter method was especially common in districts and communes with fewer killings and seems to be the reason that killings were fewer in these localities. Few of these files were preserved, but the report relating to black element Qi Zhengma, related to Hu Xiang's case, miraculously fell into our hands. The report stated that Qi Zhengma, 55 years old, came from a poor-peasant background but had served as a "puppet" official before Liberation and, following Liberation, had been sentenced to five years of reform through labor for counterrevolutionary crimes. The report stated that Qi's behavior didn't improve following his release, and that he spread rumors of an impending attack by Chiang Kai-shek, occupied collective land, engaged in highway robbery, and took to the hills as a bandit. Most recently, he was accused of colluding with Hu Xiang in a plot to kill poor and lower-middle peasants, and he was apprehended while returning from Guangxi on August 24. "After being brought back, he still refused to honestly confess the facts or acknowledge his errors, pretending that his foot ached and gripping a walking stick. While passing by the stone bridge at the school, he hit out at the masses with his cane and then jumped onto the bridge and ran off. Through the efforts of our militia, he was apprehended once again, but he still refused to make an honest confession. In order to defend social order and safeguard the construction of socialism, and under the pressing demands of the poor and lower-middle peasants, he was sentenced to death, and the sentence has been carried out."

According to a villager in Qijiawan, Qi Zhengma was actually beaten to death. After he was captured in Guangxi and brought back, the brigade carried out a "rigorous interrogation" on Qi, during which his leg was broken. "Fortunately he kept his lips tight and didn't make careless accusations against others, otherwise even more people would have shared his fate."

The killings in the Qijiawan brigade opened the floodgates in Xianzijiao District, but how did the situation actually develop?

On August 24, 1967, the head of the district's seize-and-push group, public-security deputy Jiang Zhengtian, "paged through all the books by Marx, Lenin, and Chairman Mao and could find nothing that allowed for indiscriminate killing." He knocked on the door of Wang Xianzhi, the district PAFD commander and also a leader of the seize-and-push group, and declared his stand: "Let the others kill first, and we'll just watch for the time being."

It is undoubtedly because of these men that Xianzijiao District was alone in Daoxian in not holding a district-level killing-mobilization meeting. When the district called a meeting to discuss the issue of killing on August 25, the stand taken by Jiang and Wang prevented a consensus being reached. After the meeting, district secretary Hu Guangxue telephoned Red Alliance heads Tang Mingzhi, Liu Changlin, and others to report on the meeting, saying, "They said they wouldn't kill anyone." As long as the core authorities wouldn't budge, those below them didn't dare make a move.

Later, the Yingjiang Frontline Command Post telephoned the district twice to push for killings, but its orders weren't passed on for implementation at the lower levels. Jiang Zhengtian's "Right-deviating thinking" enraged Zheng Youzhi and the others: "That bastard is just three inches away from being a class enemy!" In order to save him and straighten him out, Zheng Youzhi requested instructions from the upper level and then had Jiang Zhengtian surrender his gun.

Regrettably, we didn't get an opportunity to directly interview Jiang Zhengtian or Wang Xianzhi. They didn't want to be interviewed because they felt they'd done nothing but follow their conscience, and all they wanted now was to live in peace.

Comrade Zhou Renzhe, who was CCP secretary of Xianzijiao Commune at that time, did accept our interview. This is what he said:

> The killings in our district [District 5] occurred mainly under the influence of the killings in neighboring districts and communes. Of course there were a few district and commune cadres who bear responsibility, but the majority objected to this kind of indiscriminate killing. In the latter half of August, our commune's Xiashitang, Qijiawan, Laofudi, and other production brigades began to experience killings of black elements. When I learned of this, I immediately discussed the matter with commune PAFD commander Zhou Guizhang, and we held six meetings for cadres of production team leader and above to halt the killings. When the 47th Army's notice [prohibiting random killing] was handed down, our commune's cadres went to each production brigade to disseminate and implement the order. By the time the killing wind arrived

here, all kinds of people were being killed. At that time, I went down to the Laofudi brigade and overheard rumors that the brigade's poor-peasant association and rebel faction were planning to do away with someone at midnight that night.

Back then, very few people in the village owned watches. A little after eleven o'clock that night, a rebel faction leader telephoned the commune's postal and telecommunications office to ask what time it was. The duty officer asked, "Why are you asking the time this late at night?" That man laughed and said, "We're killing a big pig at midnight." The duty officer picked up on his meaning and told me. Although I didn't know whom they intended to kill, I quickly called in PAFD commander Zhou Guizhang and public-security deputy Zheng Qibing,[2] and we groped our way along 4 kilometers of mountain paths to reach the Laofudi brigade before midnight. When we got there, we learned that the target was Mu Daoyi, a former brigade leader who had stepped down during the Four Cleans campaign. We promptly prevented the killing and placed Mu Daoyi under the commune's protection, and we didn't let him go home until the killing wind died down five days later.

During the Daoxian massacre, the fewest fatalities occurred at Xianzijiao District's Huitan Commune, where only 17 people were killed. We went to Huitan Commune hoping to learn that people there had resisted the killing wind. Our hopes were dashed, however, when we learned the simple reason for the small number of deaths: Huitan Commune had not held a killing-mobilization meeting. The same district's Shatian Commune, which was in a more remote location deep in the highland forests, had a relatively high number of killings because it had held a killing-mobilization meeting.

We hurried off to Shatian Commune to see why holding a killing-mobilization meeting had made a difference there.

On August 21, 1967, Shatian Commune public-security duty officer Jiang Rigang and others held a "seize-and-push" meeting for commune and production brigade cadres, during which they talked up the "current situation of class struggle" and the "enemy situation" and focused on the issue of killings. Jiang Rigang said, "The trees can't keep the wind from blowing; comrades, don't kid yourself that it's possible to keep black elements from careless talk and actions! Locking up, struggling, and killing all are appropriate—use these tactics against any who deserve them." After this meeting, the commune killed 26 people. At the time, commune cadres Fu Guan'ai and Wang Xufu objected to killing people in this way. Calling them turncoats, Jiang Rigang ordered the militia to string them up for seven hours. The next day he called a special meeting to "educate them" and compelled the two men to "hang their heads and confess their guilt."

Fortunately, Fu and Wang were "born Red"; without their "revolutionary roots" they might have lost their lives.

After Jiang Rigang returned from the Political and Legal Work Conference at Yingjiang on August 29, he held another cadre meeting, during which he said, "Now that I've come back I want to catch some big fish; I'm not interested in minnows." He added, "Make it quick; you won't have another opportunity as good as this." After the meeting, some production brigades hurriedly killed another batch, and some brigades that hadn't killed anyone did so this time.

Shatian Commune's Xiaowei brigade decided to deal with a well-behaved rich-peasant offspring named He Hancun by just making him pay some protection money. It couldn't be put in such blunt terms, however, so production team cadres said to He Hancun, "You belong to the class that could be killed or not killed, but we want to save you, so think about what you should do."

During the Land Reform movement, some class enemies had escaped death by handing over their movable assets and land deeds, so He Hancun hurried home and took out all the money he had, 90 yuan, and handed it over to the production team. But this paltry amount only infuriated the cadres, who told him, "If you genuinely intend to turn over a new leaf, you have to strip off your trousers and lop off your tail!"[3] Upon hearing this, He Hancun ran home and collected his pig, two quilts, 10 kilos of oil, nine chickens, four sheets, eight garments, his washbasin stand and silver ornaments, and everything else in his house and handed them over as communal property. This saved his life, but He Hancun's wife was so traumatized by the incident that she died soon afterwards. He Hancun quickly married off his 16-year-old daughter for fear that he might still end up being killed.

When the Task Force eventually arrived in the village, He Hancun was the first person to come forward, and he remembered every item on this old account. When it was alleged that he had offered up all his belongings on his own initiative and against the wishes of the production team, he broke down in tears and said he'd been forced to hand over money to save his life. The production team cadres were infuriated: if they'd known he'd be this way, they would never have spared him!

Qiaotou Commune's mass-killing rally

When we started out our reporting in Xianzijiao District, we were initially confused by the fact that among the district's four communes (Xianzijiao, Shatian, Huitan, and Qiaotou), Qiaotou Commune not only had the most killings but exceeded the killings of all the other three put together. Qiaotou also started killing earlier, did it with greater fanfare, and held a mass-killing rally like

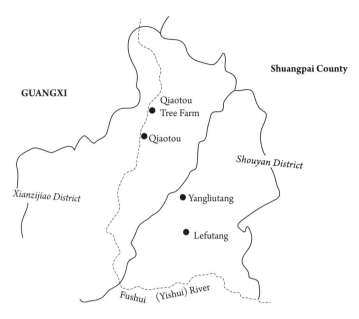

Map 10 Communes of the former Qiaotou District

Shangguan Commune. This all made sense after a Task Force comrade explained that Qiaotou Commune was actually part of Qiaotou District (Map 10) at that time. Qiaotou District (District 4) not only held killing-mobilization meetings, but each of its communes also held meetings to incite and plan killings. The Task Force comrade went on to observe:

> District PAFD commander Liao Mingzhong[4] was one of the main people orchestrating the killings in Qiaotou District, and he person- ally authorized the killing of two poor peasants. District public-security deputy Huang Laishun was even worse—he not only orchestrated kill- ings throughout the district, he also personally authorized the killing of 12 people. The mass-killing rally at Qiaotou Commune was planned by Huang Laishun and Qiaotou Commune public-security deputy Yang Xunqing, who was the main person orchestrating the killings there.

The Task Force comrade told us that initially there were only scattered killings in Qiaotou Commune, but after Huang Laishun returned from a meeting in Yingjiang on August 21, he called in Yang Xunqing to discuss the local situa- tion, and the two decided to mobilize the masses to hold a mass struggle rally at Qiaotou Market on August 23, where a "troublemaking class enemy offspring" named He Guangxian was condemned to death before a packed crowd. In his speech at the rally, Yang Xunqing said, "We need to take note of retaliatory attacks and reactionary organizations in other brigades. After the meeting, every brigade needs to start taking action and get rid of everyone like this!" (pointing to He Guangxian). After He Guangxian was taken out and shot, district and commune cadres went to each production brigade to oversee and push forward killings, which spread to Lefutang and Yangliutang Communes as well.

The Task Force comrade told us a story about Yang Xunqing going to the Dajiangzhou brigade to supervise killings after the mass rally. Although it involved the deaths of only two people, it shook our souls a hundred times more intensely than the rally that prompted it.

When Yang Xunqing went to the Dajiangzhou brigade on August 24,[5] he was furious to learn that the August 23 mass rally had had little effect on the brigade's "sluggish and ideologically conservative" leading cadres. Yang immediately called a meeting of the brigade's cadres and core militiamen, after which they killed two people.

What kind of people did they kill? A 75-year-old woman named Qin Xiurong and a 5-year-old boy named He Guoxin.

Why give an old woman and a little boy priority over the many other black elements and offspring? It turns out that someone claimed that during the Land Reform movement, the landlord element Qin Xirong had failed to hand over a large quantity of silver dollars, and that she also had money deposited in an account. Qin Xiurong's husband had served as an official elsewhere, and the family was educated, so they must have money; an elderly former hired hand for the family said that in the old days, even the hired hands had eaten well. The brigade's cadres recalled that Qin's younger son, a teacher in another county, had cut off all relations with her, and if things weren't played right, once the old lady turned up her toes, those silver dollars might be left to Chiang Kai-shek to use for his attack on the mainland. The brigade therefore decided to go after the old woman and her grandson.

Sadly, old Madam Qin put an end to their fevered imaginings: her family had handed over all their silver dollars during the Land Reform movement, and the old woman and boy scarcely managed to scrape enough together to put food on the table, much less put anything aside in a bank account.

Yang Xunqing decided that if the old lady was so bull-headed, he'd have to threaten the boy: if he didn't hand over the silver dollars, he'd be tied up and executed! As Yang said this, he pulled his gun out of his holster and aimed it at the little boy, saying, "bang!"

The 5-year-old He Guoxin was so alarmed that he ran wailing to his grandmother: "Granny! Give them your silver dollars so they won't kill us!"

Qin Xiurong was stiff as a statue; there was something almost offensive about her impassivity. It's often said that people grow more afraid of death as they age, but this old woman was staring at her coffin without so much as a tear. It's well enough to seek your own death, but how could she bear to have her little grandson die with her?

When his grandmother didn't respond, He Guoxin turned to the heavily armed men and said, "Uncles, don't kill me! I'll be a good boy, I'll work for you! I'll tend your cattle. . . ."

He grabbed one of the men around the leg, but the man kicked him off. He knelt before another, but that one turned his back. One man, wanting to give the boy a chance, said, "Go tell your grandma to give us the silver dollars and bank book, and I promise we won't kill you."

He Guoxin ran back and grabbed his grandmother's leg and wept and pleaded himself hoarse: "Grandma, Grandma! Please give them the silver dollars! I'm afraid to die! I want to live. . . ."

Reaching out her withered hand, Qin Xiurong patted the boy on the head and said, "My dear boy, don't think there's much to be gained in living. After I'm gone, who will take care of you? When the nest is crushed, can the eggs remain unbroken? It's better for you to go with Granny. We'll keep each other company."

And so they were buried alive together.

The last victim

While reading through the Task Force's files before coming to Xianzijiao, we had learned that the last victim of Daoxian's killing wind was He Yuxiang, a middle peasant from Qiaotou Commune's Shangba brigade, but there were no details in the files regarding why or how he was killed. We wanted to find out more about this case, which would allow us to put a period at the end of our reporting on the Daoxian killings.

When I asked the Task Force comrade about this case, he smiled and said, "I knew you'd ask about it. He Yuxiang's death was the 'parting shot'; after he was killed, the killing wind stopped blowing, and no one else was killed. In fact, this was a classic case of killing someone for his property and wife. He Yuxiang was killed on October 17 [1967]. By then, the killings had ended in Daoxian. The 47th Army's 6950 Unit had entered Daoxian on August 29, and by the latter half of September there were hardly any more killings. The two main culprits behind He Yuxiang's killing were brigade head Yi Changjin and militia commander Tang Guiting. Tang Guiting had served in the Kuomintang army and was a man of many vices. He and He Yuxiang had become enemies over some petty matter, and Tang decided to take advantage of the random killings to wreak his revenge. As it happened, brigade leader Yi Changjin had his eye on He's home, so the two of them used their authority to concoct a false accusation that He Yuxiang had joined a reactionary organization called the China Freedom Party, and they killed him with a blunderbuss at the pavilion at Ma'anqiao. After killing He Yuxiang, Yi Changjin not only took possession of his house but also raped his wife. . . . Prior to this, Yi and Tang had been involved in a number of killings in the brigade, and Tang had taken part in the gang rape of a 15-year-old girl."

We proposed going to Shangba Village to interview the people involved, but the Task Force discouraged us, saying Yi and Tang had already been brought to justice, and Shangba Village was remote and hard to reach. He offered to provide a car to take us there the next day, but Zhang Minghong and I wanted to fit the trip in that day. When the Task Force comrade saw we were determined, he managed to borrow two bicycles and said we could make it to the village in two hours, but since he'd been able to borrow only two bicycles, he'd be unable to accompany us. In fact, that was just what we wanted—most of our interviews had been carried out in the company of Task Force comrades, and while this greatly facilitated our access, it also limited our freedom and imposed enormous limitations. Now we felt like baby birds spreading their wings and attempting to fly.

As it turned out, the gravel road and undulating mountain paths soon exhausted even seasoned cyclists such as us, and it took three hours of alternately walking and riding before we finally reached Shangba Village. There we learned that the village's CCP secretary was away on business, and without this connection, no one else was prepared to help us. As in so many other places, the families of victims were suspicious and avoided us, while the grassroots cadres claimed not to recall the killings, and people who'd been involved either defended their actions in every way possible or flatly refused to see us. When all was said and done, the people who most clearly understood what had happened were the Task Force comrades. It had taken a long and circuitous route for us to finally arrive at this conclusion.

By then night was falling, and as we faced the uninviting prospect of the long ride back, Minghong suggested, "The Qiaotou tree farm is nearby. Let's go there and see if we can find another way."

Zhang Hongming's local connections proved invaluable. When the leader of the Qiaotou tree farm saw the local radio station's chief reporter standing before him, he welcomed us effusively, killing a chicken and preparing a feast for us. We were in fact ravenous and didn't waste time on empty ceremony before digging in. I've always been partial to big hunks of chicken and pork, but the liquor went straight to my head, although the others didn't seem affected. By the time we finished dinner, the moon had reached the meridian and the tree farm officials urged us to stay the night. We insisted on returning to the district, however, so they arranged for a jeep to take us back to Xianzijiao Town.

The swaying of the jeep on the meandering mountain roads soon lulled me toward slumber, but, bloated and achy, I forced myself to stay awake. Suddenly the jeep stopped for a wild hare caught in its beaming headlights. The others jumped out to kill it while I stepped out to relieve myself, moving toward a pitch-black shadow along the side of the road. Suddenly a hand grabbed me from behind and I heard Zhang Minghong's voice say, "Xiao Tan, what are you doing?"

"It's nothing, I just need to pee." I tried to pull away, but he gripped me even harder and hauled me back into the jeep before I could finish my business. I had no idea what happened after that.

I woke up in the hostel at Xianzijiao at noon the next day, and Zhang Minghong walked into my room laughing: "Come on, let's shake hands again. Last night you rubbed the nose of the King of Hell and almost forced us to hold a funeral for you today." Seeing my mystified expression, he told me that when he'd grabbed me, I was at the edge of a cliff. "You're a lucky fellow. The driver from the tree farm said that precipice was about 40 meters deep—if you'd fallen, you'd have been a dead man."

After all this, we gave up on our idea of returning to Shangba Village and instead hurried back to the county seat. We were thinking we still had plenty of time and opportunity, but subsequent events proved that some things missed the first time are gone forever.

27

The Zhenggangtou Phenomenon

This book won't be complete without a description of the situation in production brigades where no one was killed. I originally planned to focus on this while writing about Xianzijiao District, but ended up writing about the killings there instead. In Daoxian, murder cases were plentiful while instances of no killings or outright resistance to them were few and far between, and we devoted a great deal of effort and energy to this aspect, with minuscule returns. Still, what we learned is an essential addition to the record.

(1) The Chinese Communist Party (CCP) secretary of Shouyan District's Niulukou Commune, Tang Renhan, had been sidelined as soon as the Cultural Revolution began, but he was still called in for commune cadre meetings. At one such meeting, he heard the commune People's Armed Forces Department (PAFD) commander suggest, "Other places have already taken action, so we should discuss whether we want to get rid of a couple [black elements]." Tang immediately rose to his feet and declared his stand: "What Commander Liu said just now is wrong and has to be ignored." Because of his relentless opposition, the commune's other cadres were ashamed to raise the matter again, so no killings were arranged on this occasion. Among that commune's 23 production brigades, the cadres of two brigades held the same views as Tang Renhan, and as a result, no one was killed in those two brigades.

(2) Qin Tingliang, dismissed as head of the Daoxian Agricultural Bureau for being a "capitalist roader," had been "sent down" to Jiujia Commune's Jianshe brigade to oversee the rush planting and harvesting. When the killings began, the other 15 cadres who had been sent down with him all fled, and he was left on his own to continue his ideological remolding. The brigade CCP secretary and militia commander had already called two meetings to discuss killing people and had drawn up a name list, planning to take action the next day. When Qin Tingliang learned of this, he risked accusations of "taking the side of the class enemies" and went to

talk with those two grassroots cadres: "Killing has never been allowed. Since ancient times, killing has brought the death penalty, and wounding has brought imprisonment. Chairman Mao has taught us that people are not like chives to be cut down as we please. Sooner or later, people will be called to account for what's happening now. If someone's calling for killings, tell them do it themselves. We absolutely cannot get involved in this nonsense!" The CCP secretary and militia commander saw the reason in Qin's words and changed their minds, releasing those who had been detained. As a result, no one was killed in that production brigade.

(3) In Youxiang Commune, cadres of the Huangjin brigade returned from a commune meeting on August 28 and called a meeting during which it was decided that 26 people should be killed. Throughout the discussion, the brigade's CCP secretary, Jiang Renjun, sat to one side smoking and said nothing. When the poor-peasant association (PPA) chairman solicited Jiang Renjun's opinion as a representative of the CCP leadership, Jiang said, "If you insist on killing people, I can disregard it, but that's the most I'll do. If you want me to give the word to kill people, I absolutely refuse." Seeing Jiang Renjun's attitude, several others from the brigade's CCP committee came forward and said that if Secretary Jiang didn't support the idea, it should be dropped. Jiang Renjun said, "In that case, this meeting is adjourned." As a result, the killings never took place. Even so, word got out, and among the 26 people on the death list, 3 were so terrified that they killed themselves, while several of the bolder ones fled.

On August 31, the commune's public-security deputy telephoned the brigade and told militia commander Chen Yuxian that one of the brigade's fugitive class enemy offspring, Deng Jiansheng, had been captured, and that the brigade should send someone to fetch him. By then, the upper levels had handed down the directive prohibiting further killings, so Chen Yuxian and brigade public-security head Deng Jiangqing were sent to the commune to bring Deng Jiansheng back. While they were there, the commune's public-security deputy, Li Benyue, asked them, "What's going on with the lack of activity in your brigade?"

Deng Jiangqin said, "It's mainly because Jian Renjun is so conservative. He's the party secretary, and if he won't give the word, there's nothing we can do."

Li Benyue said, "He can represent only his own views. Party leaders still have to listen to the views of the masses. In my opinion, a person like Deng Jiansheng can be killed."

Encouraged by Li, and convinced that they'd be unable to kill Deng Jiansheng once they returned to the brigade, Chen Yuxian and Deng Jiangqing killed him on the way back.

(4) In Yingjiang Commune, where the Red Alliance Frontline Command Post was located, there was a village called Zhenggangtou, which at that time was called the Heping (Peace) production brigade. The brigade had nine class enemy households as well as more than 20 offspring and other "elements," yet not a single person was killed during the Cultural Revolution, allowing the brigade to live up to its name. Why was this?

We interviewed the elderly Jiang Liangzhong, who was the brigade's CCP secretary during the Cultural Revolution. When we arrived in Zhenggangtou, he was busy building a new house, but when he heard that "leading comrades from the provincial capital" (at the time we were being described as provincial cadres) had come to talk to him about the Cultural Revolution killings, he dropped everything he was doing and came to receive us. He was the classic image of an old Daoxian peasant—of modest stature and noticeably stooped, his feet bare. He was obviously a person accustomed to manual labor, although his experience as a cadre had also left its mark. He wasn't terribly expressive and simply gave us a bland smile by way of greeting.

We expressed amazement that he'd been able to hold back the killing wind during that dark and oppressive time. He replied, "That was quite a wind! As soon as the leaders called for killings, those below went about it energetically and wantonly. The 'Five Evil Winds' had blown up just that way, and look how many starved to death! After I came back from the meeting at Yingjiang, they asked me, what should our brigade do? The way I saw it, even killing a pig required a permission slip, so how could it be so easy to kill a person? Even during Land Reform killing hadn't been that easy—the Land Reform Law had to be followed, and the higher authorities issued written directives. Ever since ancient time, killing people required official authorization as well as supervision of the execution and specifying exactly which law had been broken, so how could we be so unruly? The ones stirring up the killing were pushing for promotion, but I didn't want promotion, so I just hung back. Since the higher authorities were paralyzed, we just joined them in their paralysis. Poor-peasant representative Jiang Zhongshang supported my views. He told me, 'If the other brigades want to kill people, let them; we're not activists, so we won't kill.'

"Later, the killing wind became increasingly fierce, and other brigades were killing more and more people. Some people in our brigade couldn't sit still any longer, and they tied up landlord Jiang Fubao and his son and called a cadre meeting at the grain-drying yard to force me to take a stand. Jiang Fubao and his son figured they were dead men and had changed into their best clothes to meet their fates. I don't know what class enemies were like in other brigades, but hadn't everyone here seen with their own eyes how Jiang and his son had behaved? Apart from Jiang Fubao having benefited from exploitation before Liberation, he'd never done anything bad, and now we were supposed to go through Land Reform all over again? I refused to take a stand. They began to press me on it, and I said it was getting chilly and I needed to put on some more clothes, and I ran home and hid. When they couldn't find me, they didn't dare make the decision themselves, and after discussing the matter for a while they finally let Jiang and his son go."

With sincere admiration, we said, "Secretary Jiang, you are a man of elevated awareness and high standard."

Jiang Liangzhong shook his head like a rattle. "You say I had elevated awareness and a high standard, but deputy county head Pan, who is now chairman of the county People's Congress, came here and gave me a hiding, saying I was a cowardly devil and unrevolutionary."

We were stunned. We could believe that deputy county head Pan might feel that way, but for him to act so brazenly was surprising. After a brief pause, all we could say was, "History will judge."[1]

In the context of the Cultural Revolution, I refer to the situation here as the Zhenggongtou phenomenon. As with the Lucaoping phenomenon, it tells us as much as those brigades that racked up the most killings, only from a different perspective. In our investigation of brigades with few or no killings, we discovered a universal phenomenon, which was that they almost without exception met the following five conditions: (1) the brigade's grassroots CCP organization was rather lax, (2) the brigade was relatively behind other brigades in all its operations, (3) the brigade's geographical location was relatively distant from the administrative hub, (4) the brigade didn't have commune cadres sent down to direct operations, and (5) the brigade's leading cadres had a rough time of it in the years that followed; for example, Jiang Renjun was dismissed from his post as brigade CCP secretary. Discovering or rather recognizing this last point dealt a heavy blow to us; I felt physically and mentally sapped as if by a serious illness.

I swear that our original intention was to write a report that would find something positive to praise in this dark time. Unfortunately, that proved impossible.

28

The Miracle of Life

In our reporting, we sometimes came across individual stories so astonishing that they took on the quality of myth. As we near the end of the narrative of the killing wind, I would like to present two such stories. This is the first.

Her name was Zhou Qun. In 1986 she was 51 years old, a teacher at Daoxian's Gongba Central Primary School, and a member of the county political consultative conference. Tall and thin, she retained traces of youthful charm on her wan face. Only large and deep-set eyes like iced-over lakes suggested the profound grief behind them. When she spoke, her voice was somewhat hoarse, and even her weeping was voiceless. I wept three times while carrying out my reporting in Daoxian, and one of those times was when Zhou Qun told her story. How much strength must heaven have bestowed upon this woman for her to survive? This was truly the miracle of life.

With repressed grief she said, "I never imagined they would kill people. Never in a million years. . . ."

I came from a poor peasant family, so by rights I shouldn't have had any problems during the Cultural Revolution. But my father had been a traffic police section chief in Nanjing under the Kuomintang, so I was labeled a counter-revolutionary offspring. After I graduated from normal school, I was assigned to teach at the Hongtangying Primary School in Daoxian's mountain region, and I married another teacher named Jiang Hanzhen. Hanzhen had been transferred to civilian work from the military because he came from a bad class background. Soon after the Cultural Revolution began, Daoxian launched a cleansing of the class ranks, and the two of us were dismissed from our teaching positions and sent back to Hanzhen's native village in Simaqiao District, the Tuditang production team of Dapingling [Hengling] Commune's Xiaoluwo brigade.

The Tuditang production team was in a remote mountain area, and when the killing began outside, we knew nothing about it.

On the evening of August 26, 1967, I'd already gone to bed with our three children when I heard an urgent pounding on our door. I quickly pulled on some clothes, but before I could open the door, brigade Chinese Communist Party

(CCP) secretary Tang Xinghao and the militia commander kicked it open. "Get up! You have to attend a meeting." I had a sense of foreboding but never thought they'd actually kill people. I got dressed while telling my eldest son, Linhai, who was weeping with fear, "Look after your brother and sister here. I'll be back soon."

They tied me up and dragged me to the threshing yard next to the brigade's storehouse. By then, dozens of militia carrying sabers, fowling guns, and torches had gathered around the threshing yard, encircling the village's class enemies and offspring, 14 people in all. My husband was among them; he'd been captured the night before. He saw me and struggled to come over to where I was, but poor-peasant association chairman Zhang Guangsong shouted, "Jiang Hanzhen isn't behaving! Tie him up with iron wire!" They brought out iron wire and bound him with it, the wire digging into his flesh, and Hanzhen cried out in pain. Under the light of the torches, I saw his forehead covered with sweat, and it was like a knife stabbing my heart. Zhang Guangsong shouted, "Let's go! Off to the district!" I still thought they were actually taking us to the district, and Hanzhen and I, having some education and analytical ability, thought they'd at most put us into a concentration camp. We'd just have to do our best to look after our kids. Our generation was finished, but if our children obeyed the party, they should still have a future.

We were getting ready to leave when Tang Xinghao said, "Slow down, Jiang Hanzhen has three kids at home. Send someone to get them." When I heard this, an explosion went off in my head. There were no children among those who were tied up; why did they have to bring our children along? Heartless Tang Xinghao, what did we ever do to deserve this from you? When we first came back to the village, Hanzhen had seen that Tang's family was having financial difficulties and loaned him 100 yuan without being asked. Back then, 100 *kuai* was an impressive sum.

Tang Xinghao led a group of men to our home and coaxed or dragged our three children to the threshing yard. The children were sobbing with terror, but they stopped when they saw me. My children's names were all taken from my favorite novel, *Tracks in the Snowy Forest*.[1] Our eight-year-old son was named Linhai, our six-year-old daughter was named Xueyuan, and our four-year-old son was named Linsong. I decided it was better for them to be taken to the district with us, rather than being left at home alone and worrying.

We set off, escorted by the militia. It was a difficult road, and the night was dark, and only the two militiamen at the front were holding flashlights. We couldn't see a thing and could only follow the people in front of us. Because my hands were bound, my daughter, Xueyuan, had to hang on to my shirt, and Linhai staggered along behind us with Linsong on his back. I can't imagine where he got the strength, such a small boy carrying another and still able to keep up. As we walked, the children started crying again, and my ropes were so tight that my hands went numb. I was greatly distressed and sweat poured down my face, but I did my best to act like everything was fine and coaxed the children, "Don't cry, just stay with Mama and we'll be there soon."

I don't know how we managed on that hard road. My head turned to wood, and all I knew was to keep on walking. When we'd gone a kilometer or so, the militia stopped for a while. I later learned they were discussing where to take us. Soon after that, we set off again.

When we reached Fengmu Mountain, they ordered us to stop, and then Tang Xinghao jumped up on a rock and announced, "I now represent the Supreme People's Court of the Poor and Lower-Middle Peasants in sentencing you to death!" We were paralyzed. At that moment, the moon came out, deathly pale. The militiamen surrounded us and pointed their fowling guns and spears at us. That was when I finally realized they were going to kill us. My heart sank. Killing us didn't matter so much, but who would take of our three children when we were gone?

They'd decided to push us into a limestone cave. These were very common in our area, and so deep that you couldn't see to the bottom of them. Tang Xinghao called out names, and as each name was called, the militiamen would lead that person to the cave and push him or her in. The third to be called was my husband, and two militiamen grabbed my husband like a chicken and dragged him toward the cave. The children cried out, "Papa! Papa!" and ran after him, but the militiamen pushed them fiercely away. Hanzhen was already as numb as a block of wood and didn't react in any way. I was afraid the children would be killed, so I quickly called them back to me, thinking only of saving them.

The fourth to be called was a prominent doctor of traditional medicine named Jiang Wenfan, 60 years old. He was from a landlord family, but he was famous for his treatment of illnesses. Facing his death calmly, he asked a militiaman for a drink of water. The militiaman said, "You're about to die and you want a drink of water?" He said, "It's not too much to ask, is it? In the old days, they would give a man three warm buns before they beheaded him. . . ." Before he could finish speaking, one of the militiamen, a gluttonous and lazy old bachelor, struck him down with an iron club and then dragged him to the cave and threw him in.

I was the eighth one called, and when the militia commander came to get me, the three kids began pitifully crying, "Mama! Mama!" Seeing their distress, I steeled myself and told them, "Be good now and stay here and wait. Mama will be back in a little while and take you to Grandma's house." The children weren't fooled and cried even harder. I was still harboring the illusion that they would kill only the adults and not the children. Worried that if I didn't cooperate, the children might also be killed, I went submissively. I felt a coolness wafting from the mouth of the cave, which was so dark that I couldn't see a thing.

"Kneel down!" someone ordered. Two people pushed me until my legs buckled and I knelt. I heard air move behind my head, and something hard struck me from behind. I felt the world spinning around me and knew nothing more. . . .

I don't know how long it was before I woke up in terrible pain. There was a groan, and I heard someone beside me call, "Mama," and I thought I'd woken up in hell. The person calling me was my daughter, Xueyuan. My three children and another four-year-old girl had also been thrown into the cave, but with so many bodies piled up there, we'd been cushioned by corpses and hadn't died. I later heard from someone at the scene that when they pushed the children in, it was absolutely heart-rending. After Xueyuan saw her elder brother pushed in, she grabbed someone near her and wouldn't let go, crying, "Uncle, uncle! Don't throw me in! I'm afraid!" After that man pushed her away, she crawled to another and hugged him, crying, "Uncle, don't throw me in, please! I'll be good!" But finally she was thrown into the cave.

When I heard her call me, my head cleared and I quickly called out, "Xueyuan! Xueyuan, come untie Mama!" The cave was pitch dark and we couldn't see a thing. Xueyuan groped her way over to me and was able to untie me. By then, a member of my husband's family, Jiang Hanyuan, had also regained consciousness, and he said, "Sister-in-law, come help me!" My wrists were broken from being bound, so I used my teeth to loosen his ropes. After untying him, I told him to crawl out and find some way to save us. Jiang Hanyuan was a nimble teenager, and through a tremendous effort he managed to climb out of the cave. I breathed a sigh of relief, believing there was hope we could be saved. As it turned out, however, he encountered a search party and had to go into hiding instead of rescuing us.

We couldn't tell if it was night or day, but I guess it was the second day that people started throwing rocks into the cave. The cave had many layers, and we'd fallen onto the upper layer, which is why Jiang Hanyuan had been able to climb out. But the rocks that were thrown in destabilized that layer, and it collapsed, sending us down to the second layer. There I found Hanzhen and our two sons, all still alive. Our family was reunited. That layer of the cave was full of corpses—apart from the people from our brigade, quite a few from the Fengmushan brigade had been pushed in several days earlier. The cave was dark and cold, and my family sat and slept on corpses. I can't imagine hell being worse than this! With my injured hands, I couldn't undo the wire around Hanzhen's wrists, and that's what killed him in the end.

I don't know how much time passed before the children began crying for water. I told the children, "Just sleep; sleep and you'll feel better." The two older ones understood and lay down beside me. I held the youngest, Linsong, close to me, but he kept crying, "Mama, Mama! I'm thirsty! I'm hungry!" His cries tore at my heart.

Sometimes drops of water oozed out of the cave walls and dripped down on our faces. The children jumped up and cried, "Mama, there's water!" They opened their mouths and stuck out their tongues, but after waiting a long time with no water dripping, they became tired and closed their mouths in disappointment.

Linsong cried nonstop for water, and there was nothing I could do but urinate into my hands and give it to him. He drank it thirstily. By then, my husband had become deranged. He stood unevenly on the corpses and paced back and forth, saying, "I'll water the sorghum." At one point he stepped on our youngest, who began crying. I said, "Hanzhen, what are you doing?" He said, "If I don't grow the sorghum, the kids will have nothing to eat and the poor things will starve! Look, you see? The sorghum is growing. . . . Now we're all set!" I said, "Hanzhen, come to your senses! There's no sorghum here, we're in a pit!" When he heard this, he fell silent and dropped to the ground, and he didn't get up again.

I don't know how many days passed, but the children gradually grew silent, and it was only when cold water dripped down and startled them that I knew they weren't dead. Linhai lay down next to me and said haltingly, "Mama, why am I not dead? I wish I were dead!" What mother can hear an eight-year-old child say this and not be heartbroken? All I could do was comfort him by saying, "Go to sleep, son, go to sleep." I stroked the faces my children, reduced to skin and bones. I wished I could tear my heart from my body to feed them. But all I could do was silently watch as they died one by one at my side. And yet I didn't die. Why not? Why not? What was God sparing me for?

Linhai went first and then Linsong. I laid their bodies together so they could accompany each other to the netherworld. Xueyuan was on the verge of death. I clutched her to me and sat next to Linhai and Linsong. By then I was calm. My children had been released and could suffer no more, and we had managed to die together, which made us more fortunate than many others.

On August 30 (I was later told), there was a rainstorm. Inside the cave, I heard water running down and quickly placed Xueyuan to one side, groping blindly around the cave until I felt a puddle. I carefully drank a couple of mouthfuls and then filled my mouth with water to give to Xueyuan. At first she was able to swallow, but then all she did was choke; it was too late. Just then, I heard someone moaning off to the side, and found that it was Hanzhen. He was still alive! Perhaps he was still clinging to me and the children and was unwilling to leave without us. I quickly gave him some water. There wasn't enough in the puddle to scoop up, so I took off some of my clothing and soaked it in the water and wrung it into his mouth. His throat moved a few times, but then he couldn't swallow any more, and his head tilted to the side and he died. This time he was really dead; I felt under his nose, and there was no more breath.

Now there was only me left out of our family of five. Over the last few days, I hadn't been able to think about what had happened, preoccupied with looking after the children. Before the children died, I'd still wanted to live, but now, looking at the bodies of my family around me, I felt it was meaningless to go on living alone. What's strange is that I didn't cry or feel any pain or fear. My head was very clear, and I just sat there calmly waiting to die. I didn't think any more about my husband or my children, but rather about the past, back when I was still a girl in my parents' home, and when I was in college. . . .

Then I suddenly discovered that someone else was still alive in a branch cave in the level above me. Her name was Jiang Fugui, and she was a rich-peasant offspring, 17 or 18 years old. For some reason, the women endured longer than the men. I had been so busy looking after my children that I hadn't noticed her. She seemed to be deranged, because she kept calling out, "Mama! Quickly light the lamp! I'm thirsty!" I called to her, "There's no use shouting, we're in a cave. It rained just now—see if there are any water puddles near you." She kept crying out for a while and then I heard nothing more. I called to her several times, but when she didn't answer, I stopped. In any case, we were going to die sooner or later.

When I felt I was near the end, I suddenly heard someone call my name at the mouth of the cave. At first I thought I was dreaming, but when I listened carefully, I recognized the voices of my former student, Lü Biaofeng, and a clansman of my husband's, Jiang Hanyang. Apparently someone had heard me talking to Jiang Fugui and realized that people were still alive in the cave. Jiang Hanyang called down, "Sister-in-law, it's me, Hanyang! We've come to rescue you. No one's allowed to kill people anymore." They tied four lengths of rope together and dropped it down, but by then I had given up on life. My entire family was dead in this cave, so what point was there in coming out? They stayed by the cave all morning persuading me, and they even lowered a bamboo tube full of water for me to drink. Then my former student, Lü Biaofeng, said, "Teacher Zhou, Teacher Zhou! You can't die in there for no reason. This is an enormous crime, and the government has to pass judgment." I decided he was right; I had to go on living. I agreed to let them lift me out, but the cave was too dark, and I couldn't see the rope. Finally they found a water pot and placed some rocks in it, and when they lowered the rope they rattled it. I followed the sound to the rope and wound it around my waist. Pulling with all their strength, they managed to lift me out of the cave. When I saw daylight, I fainted under the dazzling brightness. By then I'd been in the cave for seven days and seven nights. God kept me here so I could tell the world about this horrific tragedy.

After Lü Biaofeng and Jiang Hanyang saved me, they were afraid that moving me might kill me, so they laid me down in a shady spot near the cave and hurried off for a doctor. They also cooked some congee and fed it to me a spoonful at a time. I later learned that they went on working all night to save Jiang Fugui, but the girl was so out of her senses that she couldn't grab the rope, and they were unable to get her out.

As day broke and Lü Biaofeng and Jiang Hanyang and others were discussing how to save Jiang Fugui, our brigade's poor-peasant association chairman, Zhang Guangsong, heard what was going on and rushed over with his fowling gun. He scolded the villagers, saying, "Who told you to pull her out?" and he pointed his gun at me. The villagers who had rescued me were from the Fengmu brigade, and they snatched the gun from Zhang Guangson, saying, "If you want to lord it over people, go back to your own brigade!" When Zhang Guangsong ran back for reinforcements, the villagers scattered, and one of them, Zhang Hanfan, carried me to nearby Lutang Village and hid me in a gulley.

Zhang Guangsong telephoned the commune and requested armed militiamen to fetch me from the Fengmu brigade. Everyone in the village said they didn't know where I was, but the militia looked everywhere and finally found me.[2] They tried to force the people who'd rescued me to throw me into the cave again, but the masses objected, saying, "The order has already come down prohibiting any more killing." At that point, an old poor peasant known as "the Mute" came forward and said, "You can see the shape she's in—if you don't kill her she'll die anyway, so why waste the energy? Let's just lock her up for now, and then we won't have to worry if one of the higher-ups asks about her." That made sense, so they had someone carry me back to Tuditang Village, and I was locked up in the production team's storehouse with Jiang Hanfan and Jiang Hanyuan.

I was extremely frail by then, covered with wounds and lice. Those two young men washed my hair and cleaned the blood from my body. Some former students secretly brought me a change of clothes. We were locked up there for two days. On the third day, Hanyuan was released because he had an elder brother working elsewhere as a regiment-level cadre. That left just me and Hanfan in the storehouse, and this seemed worrying. I asked Hanfan, "Why did they release Hanyuan but not you and me? There's something wrong. I have a feeling we're not going to get away." Hanfan was also anxious, and he asked me what we should do. I said, "Run away as fast as you can. You might still have a chance. Don't sit here waiting to die." Hanfan said, "Then let's go together. I'll carry you on my back." But I was afraid of dragging him down with me once again, so I said, "How can I escape in this condition? You're still young and have a long life ahead of you. After you escape, they'll see what bad shape I'm in and maybe they won't kill me." That night, Jiang Hanfan broke the bars on the storehouse window and escaped. The next day, when Tang Xinghao came to the storehouse with others to get us, they found that Jiang Hanfan was gone. Tang Xinghao said the lucky devil had gotten off easily and declared, "Zhou Qun is a landlord's wife, and anyone who gives her food from now on is a counterrevolutionary and will end up just like her!"

From then on, none of my friends or relatives dared to come see me openly. Some kind people sent their children to drop sweet potatoes through the window, or they wrapped rice balls in pumpkin leaves and slipped them through the cracks in the door at night. In that way, sometimes famished and sometimes fed, I stayed alive for half a month. During this time, Tang Xinghao came twice to see me, sneering, "Zhou Qun, you're quite something to still be alive!" I don't know why he hated me so much.

The day of the Mid-Autumn Moon Festival arrived, and the moon was shining its brightest. I looked at the moon through the storehouse window and thought of other families celebrating while everyone in my family was dead, and I felt so sad. My physical injuries had me hovering at the brink of death, and I didn't have the courage to go on living. I straightened my hair with my fingers and then sat down, ripped up my quilt, and braided the pieces into a rope to hang myself, all the while crying, "Oh God, why are you so unjust?"

My actions were noticed by the mother-in-law of the production team's accountant, Jiang Yuanluan. She was from Simaqiao Market and was spending the Mid-Autumn Festival with her daughter's family. When she heard about me, she wondered how a woman could spend seven days and nights in a cave without dying, so she came to see me. While standing outside the window of the storehouse, she saw me braiding the rope and said, "I thought you must be an old lady, but I see you're just a young woman. You're young enough to have another family; don't end things this way! I'll talk to my son-in-law, and tomorrow we'll think of a way to rescue you."

Hearing what the old woman said revived my despairing heart. I still don't know why I wanted to keep living, when death would have ended all my suffering, trouble, and fear.

The next day, Jiang Yuanluan heeded his mother-in-law and took advantage of market day at Simaqiao to send word to my family. My family members were all genuine poor peasants, and my friends and relatives had influence. My younger brother went to the commune, and after repeated negotiations they were finally able to bring me home. After returning to my home village, my body began to break down. There's a saying that if you're not going to die, you need to shed your skin, and I actually shed a layer of skin off my entire body. My younger brother went deeply into debt to get me cured; he even sold off his clothing and quilts.

Now I've remarried and I have a child. After rehabilitation I was allowed to teach again. I've been named a "model teacher" three times now, I've attended a county conference for advanced worker representatives, and last year I was elected to the county political consultative conference. . . . My view of the Daoxian killings is that although we don't need to demand a life for a life, those who took the lead must be dealt with severely; otherwise, someday they might kill again.

Brigade CCP secretary Tang Xinghao was expelled from the party in 1985. After initially refusing to acknowledge owing Jiang Hanzhen 100 yuan, under questioning by the Task Force he finally had someone repay the money to Zhou Qun.

The Story of an Execution
Ground Survivor

If Zhou Qun is the most miraculous female survivor of Daoxian's killing wind, Xiao Weiren must be counted among the most miraculous male survivors, having managing to escape from the execution ground.

The first time I saw Xiao Weiren was at Simaqiao Market, which I happened to be visiting on market day. As I roamed through the bustling market to gain a sense of what county market days were like, I noticed a dignified man of around 50 with bushy eyebrows and large eyes, wearing a white shirt and black trousers and a rather formal-looking narrow-brimmed straw hat of a type seldom seen on local villagers. Wondering if he was a vendor from outside the county, I surreptitiously kept an eye on him, but he quickly noticed that someone was watching him, and turned to me with a smile that made my heart tremble—it was the same expression I'd seen on the faces of prisoners I'd interviewed in Changsha Prison. Who was this man? I went up to him and said, "You don't look like a local man."

"Actually, I'm from here, but I've just come back recently," he replied with a typical Daoxian accent.

"So you've been working elsewhere for a long time?"

"No, not working, hard labor. Do you often come to this market?"

I told him, "I'm a journalist and I've come down to report on the Task Force's work."

His eyes glowed and he said, "I'm a survivor. Can I tell you about some problems?"

"Of course! But you have to know that we don't have the authority to resolve any issues."

Assuring me he understood, he led me to a home near the market, presumably belonging to a friend or relative, and fetched two stools for us to sit on as he told his story.

The problems Xiao Weiren brought up were these: compensation for confiscated property, and punishing those responsible for the killings. These same problems were raised by all the survivors I'd been in touch with, but Xiao Weiren was an educated man, so he made his points differently: "The government is compensating us for homes

*that were torn down, belongings that were taken, and people who were killed. I feel
it shouldn't be the government but rather the killers paying the compensation. They
shouldn't have to pay for more than what they originally took, but they shouldn't
enjoy any economic benefit from killing people or taking their wives. Killers needn't
pay with their lives or even go to prison, but they should admit their wrongdoing and
make a formal public apology. Otherwise, how can we distinguish right from wrong
and bring order out of chaos? It shouldn't be like now, where they flaunt their power
in our faces and warn us not to talk or act irresponsibly. When did we ever do that?"*

What follows is Xiao Weiren's narrative of how he escaped from death.

I'm a native of Hanhetian Village in Yangjia Township of Simaqiao District,
born in 1932 to a rich peasant family. After graduating from Lingling Junior
Normal School in the 1950s, I was assigned to teach physical education at the
Jinshi'an Primary School in our commune [Yangjia]. After the "years of hardship" ended in 1962, I was sent back to my village; the actual reason was that
I was purged from the teaching ranks because my family's class status was too
high. At the time I didn't worry too much about being sent down; I had a big
appetite and taught physical education, so my teacher's food ration of 13.5 kilos
of rice really wasn't enough, and I'd wanted to go back to the village but hadn't
dared request it. They wanted me to write an application volunteering to be sent
down to the countryside, and I did. My thinking was that I was physically fit and
strong, and I also had some bone-setting skills handed down in the family, so I'd
be better off there than as a primary-school teacher.

After returning to the production team, I lived well enough. My wife was a capable woman, and quite a few people came to me for bone setting, which brought in
a little extra money. Generations of my family had practiced martial arts; my father
was quite a famous local kung fu master, and I'd started learning kung fu as a boy.
Anyone who practices martial arts knows bone setting, because they're bound to
be injured, and if they can't heal their injuries, how can they continue to fight? Our
family was known far and wide for a secret bone-setting formula handed down
through the generations. Eventually when the tail of capitalism was lopped off,[1]
I wasn't allowed to take money for bone setting, but people would bring me things
such as chickens, ducks, pork, or oil. This gave us a better life than many others.

The Cultural Revolution killings began very suddenly. I don't know about
anyone else, but I never saw it coming; otherwise, I wouldn't have sat at home
waiting to die. I remember that day clearly. It was the 14th day of the seventh
lunar month in 1967, just after the Festival of Hungry Ghosts, and the moon
was bright. I'd come home from work and had just finished dinner when militiamen from the production brigade came and notified me to attend a meeting at
the brigade headquarters. When I reached the headquarters, only the brigade's
public-security chief, Xiao Xinjue, was there with a team of militiamen—Xiao

Xinjue was also a leader of the rebel faction [Red Alliance]. As soon as I stepped inside, Xiao Xinjue shouted, "Tie him up!" The militiamen grabbed some rope and tied me very tightly, and I yelled in pain while asking, "What's the matter? What is this?" Xiao Xinjue said, "What is this? Kneel down and confess all the crimes you've committed!" What else can a person do in this situation? I knelt down and said, "I haven't broken any laws. If you've seen me doing anything wrong, please tell me."

This made him lose his temper completely. He stood up and grabbed a piece of firewood—a chunk of pine almost a meter long with sharp edges, weighing 2 kilos or more. "You dishonest son of a bitch! You dare ask me what laws you've broken!" He swung that hunk of firewood at me, and as I instinctively turned, the firewood struck me square on the left side of my forehead. I heard the impact and saw stars, then fainted dead away. Xiao Xinjue and the others splashed water in my face, and I felt like my head was about to explode. Blood plastered my hair and half my face. Xiao Xinjue told me again to confess my crimes, and I bent my head, afraid that if I said the wrong thing, I'd be hit again. Xiao Xinjue sneered, "You capitalist roader persisting in your reactionary standpoint, death is too good for you!" To be honest, at that point it still hadn't occurred to me that they might kill me. I just wanted to get through it with as little suffering as possible.

Around midnight, they took me and some others, all class enemy offspring, to the reservoir at the base of Luojia Mountain. I later learned there were several abandoned pits there, and they intended to throw us in. When we got there, the militiaman escorting me ordered me to kneel down, and at that moment, my brain swelled and my heart leapt to my throat. Seeing a saber gleaming in his hand, I stammered, "Are—are you going to kill us?" Then I heard my cousin Xiao Weiyi, who had also been led there, shout out, "They're going to kill us! Run for it!" I saw someone throw off his ropes and run toward the field. There was a steep ridge next to me, and I jumped down with the intention of running as well. Seeing me take off, the militiaman swung his saber at me. I ducked my head while twisting at the waist, and the knife missed my head but struck me in the back. I later realized that this stroke of the knife saved my life, because while injuring me, it also sliced through the ropes around my arms. I scrambled up and ran for the hills.

Several militiamen chased after me. I was still bound, so I couldn't run fast, and they soon caught up with me and stabbed me in the right foot. This gave me a burst of energy, and I fought my way out of my ropes. Less panic-stricken now, I saw the Luojiashan Reservoir ahead and ran toward it. I was a good swimmer, so my plan was to jump into the reservoir, where they wouldn't be able catch me. I was wearing canvas army shoes, and one fell off as I ran. When I stopped to pick it up, the militiamen caught up with me. I pulled myself together and grabbed a rock off the ground, telling them, "Don't come any closer. We don't have any grievance among us in the past life or now, so don't force me to fight you to the death." They knew I was skilled in martial arts, so they just stood there shouting as I ran up the hill. When I reached the reservoir, I stripped off my clothes and shoes and jumped into the water, swimming across the reservoir to the mountain on the other side.

I got away, but my cousin Xiao Weiyi didn't. He shouldn't have run into the field. The uneven ground slowed him down, and he hadn't been able to loosen his ropes, so the killers caught up with him and hacked him to death there in the field.

Our village was near the border with Ningyuan County, and on the other side of the reservoir was Jiuyi Mountain. When I reached the Ningyuan border, I was soaking wet, wearing only a pair of shorts and an undershirt, and wounded. Fortunately the cut on my back wasn't deep, but the injury to my head was serious and ached in the mountain wind. My head swimming, I wondered if I'd grabbed my life back from the gate of hell only to die in the mountains. Then I recalled an old man, nicknamed Old Fang, who lived in the mountains there in Suoyichong. He was from a poor peasant family, and I had once saved the life of his young son. I could think of nothing else to do but ask him for help.

I had no ties of kinship or friendship with Old Fang and hadn't even known him until a few years earlier, when his son had gone up the mountain to collect medicinal herbs and had fallen off a cliff and been badly injured. Local medics couldn't heal the boy and told them to hurry to the county. Old Fang had no money, so he brought his son to me. The boy looked like he might not make it, and I was afraid to take him, but Old Fang pleaded with me and said he would blame fate and not me if the boy died. Hearing him say that and pitying him, and seeing that the boy was young and healthy, I brought him inside. After a month of treatment, the boy was able to walk again. Seeing how poor his family was, I considered it a charity case and didn't ask for payment. Old Fang told his son to regard me as his godfather, but I said that was inappropriate, given that I wasn't much older than the boy, but Old Fang said that someday he'd repay my act of mercy. After they went home, the boy continued to come to my home for herbal medicine for half a year, and he always brought me local products from the mountains. I never took any payment from them, and in that way we became like family.

I hurried to Suoyichong and found Old Fang's home, knocked at the door, and went in. My appearance shocked him. He joked, "Aiya! Doctor Xiao, whose woman did you grab to get beat up like that?" I told him about my situation, and because there had not yet been any killings in Ningyuan, Old Fang simply couldn't believe it. He just kept saying, "Don't joke around with me!" He called for his wife to boil some water, and they washed my wounds and gave me a clean change of clothes.

First thing the next morning, Old Fang said he'd go down to the village to see what was going on there. I was still trying to figure out why they wanted to kill me, and I didn't know what had happened to my wife and three children, so I hoped he could find out.

Grinning, I asked him, "Weren't you afraid Old Fang would go fetch the militia to arrest you?"

He replied, "I wasn't afraid, and even if I was, it would be no use. I was in fate's hands. I didn't think Old Fang was that kind of person, and if he brought the militia back, then it was my fate to die. At that time, leaving Old Fang's home would have meant death to me. I didn't think any more about it, but I put my life in Old Fang's hands." He then continued:

Around mid-afternoon, Old Fang returned, shaking his head. "I never guessed they'd really be killing people. When I arrived in your village, they said a big-time criminal got away last night, and they'd sent people out to catch you. They also said you had kung fu skills that could cut through rope, and the militia would kill you where they caught you. When I heard this, I didn't dare go see your wife for fear of being found out." When I heard this, I was so anxious that I wept, and I said to Old Fang, "I never did anything wrong or broke any law." Old Fang said, "I know that. You can't go back to Hanhetian. Just stay here with us and let your wounds heal. You saved my kid's life, and now I'll repay you by saving yours." When I heard him say this, I kowtowed at his feet.

I stayed in Suoyichong for five or six days, and as my wounds began to heal, it occurred to me that I couldn't stay much longer. By then killings had begun in Ningyuan as well, and the reports were horrifying. Old Fang said nothing, but I could see he was really worried. Old Fang told me he had friends who were stonemasons and were preparing to go to Guangxi to earn extra money. He asked if I'd be willing to go with them, in which case I could learn a new profession and also find safety. He said I could tell them I was his relative. I immediately agreed to go but said I first wanted to go home late at night to look in on my family. He scolded me: "Are you looking to be killed? A husband and wife are like birds in the forest—when disaster strikes, the best thing is to scatter. If you don't go back, they'll get along fine, but if you go back and something goes wrong, you'll not only lose your own life but bring disaster on them as well." Anyone could understand his reasoning, of course, and I reluctantly abandoned my idea of returning home.

Old Fang was truly a good man, and I'll never be able to repay his kindness. He insisted on accompanying me down the mountain, and that's how I went with a group of Ningyuan stonemasons to Guangxi's Fuchuan County. We did our stonework in a place called Xianglujiao. Stonemasonry was hard work, but easy in its own way. It required a certain amount of skill, but mostly it required hard labor. In Fuchuan I mostly worked on irrigation ditches and stone bridges. I learned fast and did my job well.

Many people from the Yao minority lived in Fuchuan, and Xianglujiao was a Yao stockaded village. A villager surnamed Pan had six daughters and no sons. The daughters were all fine girls who had been married off except for the youngest, who was scarred from a childhood case of smallpox. In the village they called her Pan Mamei, or Pockmarked Girl. I'd been working in Xianglujiao for a long time when one day a matchmaker approached me and asked if I had a family back home. Thinking of my home back in Daoxian that I'd never be able to return to, I said my family was poor so I'd never been able to marry. The matchmaker asked if I was willing to marry Pan Mamei. As a roving craftsman, I longed to settle down. I knew Pan Mamei, and while disfigured, she was a good person, young and capable, and 10 years younger than I. Added to that, she came from a poor peasant family, and I'd suffered all my life from my high class status. If I married into the Pan family, I would become a poor peasant, and no one would bother me anymore. So I agreed to marry Pan Mamei, but I told them honestly that I was from the rich-peasant class. My father-in-law felt that was unimportant as long as I was a good man. So we went to their commune and carried out the formalities for me to marry Pan Mamei.

I thought I'd be able to spend the rest of my life peacefully in Xianglujiao, but fate was toying with me. Right after the Spring Festival in 1970, there was a major purge in the villages as Fuchuan County sent down cadres for the "One Strike and Three Antis" campaign.[2] They found out that I was a fugitive black element and arrested me and sent me back to Daoxian. Somehow, even after marrying into a poor peasant family, I'd been elevated from an offspring to a full-fledged element.

After I was sent back to Daoxian, the production brigade sent militiamen to fetch me. Taking a ferry on the way back to the brigade, one of them said, "There's no use taking this fellow back—he'll just cause problems for the production team. Let's drown him here." I was bound, and I thought I'd die for sure this time, but the ferry captain said, "You can't do that. Indiscriminate killing is prohibited now. There will be consequences." The militiamen decided it wasn't worth the risk, so they took me back to the brigade.

After I returned to the brigade, things got tough for me. Before they'd treated me as a black-element offspring, but now I was a full black element. They subjected me to public denunciations and ordered me to reform myself through labor. My first wife had long ago married our brigade PPA [poor-peasant association] chairman, Li Sineng, and had taken our children and belongings with her. I didn't have so much as a roof tile to shelter me or an inch of ground to stand on. This isn't figurative, but my actual situation at the time. The production team gave me a place to live that was little more than a cattle pen. I worked like a beast of burden and ate like a pig or a dog. My former wife turned away if she saw me at a distance, and my children cut off all relations with me. Sometimes I'd see them from afar and just want to die. I wondered what the point was of living, and to what end I'd escaped from the execution ground. I felt it would have been better if they'd chopped me up and thrown me in the pit.

Fortunately, just at that time my wife, Pan Mamei, came to Daoxian looking for me, very pregnant. At first my brigade wouldn't accept her, but she had a certificate from her commune and was a poor peasant, so finally they accepted her. That wife of mine! Without her, I wouldn't be alive today. After I was sent back to Daoxian, my father-in-law advised her to forget me and find someone else. But she was unwilling and had a falling-out with her family, and she came looking for me. Being a bachelor is hell, and having a woman in your home changes everything. I was still a strong worker and not afraid of hardship, and Mamei was used to making do. After that we had a daughter, and we gradually turned our home into something acceptable. There's no need to go into the rest; under the circumstances back then, you bent yourself to fit under the eaves.

In September 1971, our district built the Yongquan Dam at Fushitang in order to improve irrigation in Yangjia Township, and I was part of the crew our production team sent to work on it. Since I had stonemasonry skills, I was assigned to build the Yongquan Canal. At that time, a major event occurred in the upper level of government, which you must know about—Lin Biao's attempt to betray our country and go over to the enemy. At first we didn't know anything about it, but news finally reached our village at the end of the year. We black elements weren't informed, but we knew something major had happened. The situation was extremely tense, even more than during the 1967 killings. Every time something happened at the upper level of government, the village would have to engage in class struggle, and we'd be in trouble again. I was educated and experienced, so I understood this. At that time, rumors circulated at the worksite and in the village that black elements would be killed again. In Simaqiao Commune's Mawan brigade, a class enemy offspring who had fled the "killing wind" returned to his production team in 1971, and the brigade's militia commander had beaten him to death with a hoe. When I heard of this, I couldn't sleep all night. At that time, my wife came to the worksite looking for me and said people in the village were saying I'd be killed, and that this time I wouldn't get away. She said the brigade had sent someone to the county to buy iron wire so I couldn't break through it with my kung fu skills.

I can state here that this information was not entirely accurate. There were people in the brigade calling for Xiao Weiren to be killed, but it wasn't the brigade leadership's idea, and the iron wire was being bought for production purposes.

As the saying goes, when you've been bitten by a snake, you're scared of even a rope. I felt I couldn't sit there waiting for death and should run off immediately. I told my wife what I thought, and her response was simple: if I was going to run off, we'd go as a family. I told her to take our child back to Fuchuan but she refused, saying that if we were to die, we'd die together. I knew that if she went back to Fuchuan she'd become part of someone else's family, and we'd never see each other again, and I couldn't bear that. So we agreed to flee together. In any case, she was a poor peasant, and if the worst happened, she was unlikely to be killed.

I devised a careful plan for escape, telling my wife to return to the brigade and quietly carry out the necessary preparations without attracting attention. Then I requested leave from the worksite, saying I had to go back to collect my grain ration. I had arranged to meet my wife outside the village. We owned nothing of value, so all we needed was two bags and some extra clothes, and we took our child and ran off. Afraid of being followed, we detoured around Yejipu and set off from Jianghua. Since Mamei was from the Yao minority, and Jianghua was a Yao area, that seemed a good place to start. From there we went to Guangxi, stopping off in Liuzhou, where we made a living by cutting hay for horse feed and gathering scrap. Later we went to Yuezhou (Yueyang), where we cut reeds for a living and pulled handcarts, all heavy labor. We just needed to earn enough to support our family.

In 1984, we heard that rehabilitation was being carried out in Daoxian, so I brought my family back. Now there's been some redress, but a lot of things are still not right. . . . In short, those people at the higher levels are still treating me differently. For example, reporting our situation to a prefectural leader, I've repeatedly told him of the attempt to kill me and the snatching of my first wife, but he just gets impatient and says, "Fine, you say they tried to kill you and someone took your wife. Do you want me to tell Li Sineng to give your wife back to you?"

What are we supposed to say to people like that?

PART TEN

THE CRACKDOWN

30

The 6950 Unit Arrives in Daoxian

As the killing wind made its way through Daoxian in gradually increasing waves, it soon crossed the county's borders, sparking killings in surrounding counties and cities and threatening the entire province and even other parts of the country. People were killed not only throughout Lingling Prefecture, but also in the neighboring Guangxi and Guangdong Provinces.

On August 25, Unit 6950 of the 47th Army of the Chinese People's Liberation Army (PLA), stationed in the Mailing region on the border of Hunan and Guangxi, received an urgent cable from the 47th Army headquarters in Huangtuling, just outside the provincial capital, Changsha, requesting confirmation of reports of indiscriminate killing in Daoxian.

The 6950 Unit was an artillery unit, smaller than a regiment, with only 10 companies of troops. The unit was stationed at Mailing because there had been several instances of Taiwan's Kuomintang (KMT) government dropping reactionary leaflets in that region, and the Central Military Commission stationed the unit there for "anti-airborne defense." In accordance with Chairman Mao's highest directive to "be prepared against war and natural disasters," the unit had reclaimed thousands of *mu* of undeveloped land to grow peanuts in this hilly and sparsely inhabited region. A large sign posted at the entrance to the unit's encampment proclaimed: "Carrying out air defense as well as production." Because there had not yet been any sign of the KMT airdropping enemy agents, the unit's chief task at this time was growing peanuts, and the troops hadn't the slightest idea what was going on locally.

On August 26, the unit received an urgent follow-up cable: "According to reports, indiscriminate killing is in fact occurring in Daoxian. It is hoped that your unit will rapidly investigate and halt this phenomenon."

After receiving this cable, the unit's leaders immediately called a Chinese Communist Party (CCP) committee meeting to discuss the matter, and given the urgency and uncertainty of the situation, they decided to send deputy chief of staff Liu Zhaofeng with three political and ideological cadres to investigate the situation and then formulate an action plan.

Early the next day, Liu and the others sped off in a dark-green Army jeep. Arriving in Daoxian less than three hours later, Liu and the others proceeded straight to the county People's Armed Forces Department (PAFD) headquarters. The PAFD leaders vaguely confirmed that killings had occurred in the villages, but they provided no details regarding the reasons, how many had been killed, or whether the killings were still ongoing.

After leaving the militia headquarters, the four soldiers set out to make further inquiries. They found the streets all but deserted, with little to see apart from gaudy posters and banners proclaiming the life-and-death class struggle between the Red Alliance and Revolutionary Alliance. Two posters juxtaposed on a bulletin board gave a sense of the explosive atmosphere pervading the county. One was a Revolutionary Alliance poster, which accused the Red Alliance of "openly misappropriating Chairman Mao's lofty prestige, forging CCP Central Committee documents, and using various meetings to deceive the masses . . . manufacturing a white terror in the villages that is killing people like flies!" The Red Alliance poster, on the other hand, asserted that "the Revolutionary Alliance has relied on the guns it unlawfully snatched from the county PAFD as reactionary capital and has run rampant, committing all kinds of outrages, and in Daojiang Town it has engaged in widespread beating, smashing, looting, grabbing, and killing, suppressing our Red rebel faction and the poor and lower-middle peasants generally and creating a white terror throughout the county."

Daojiang was shrouded in an atmosphere of terror, and every door was barred. With great difficulty, the four soldiers managed to persuade one resident to talk to them, and they learned that the killings had begun long ago and had reached bloodbath proportions, with deaths numbering in the thousands, that the killings were continuing, and that floating corpses filled the Xiaoshui River like crullers in a vat of oil. . . .

The four soldiers hurried to the riverside, and, climbing onto the steel cable bridge behind the No. 2 High School, they immediately saw corpses drifting with the current. Liu Zhaofeng raised his wrist and began timing the flow of corpses, calculating an average of two per minute over the space of half an hour. Liu adduced that at this rate there would be 120 corpses per hour or 2,880 per day, which meant the local person they'd talked to hadn't been exaggerating in the slightest.

Just as they were about to leave, a group of people who looked like peasants ran over to them sobbing. Most of these ragged, unkempt people were black-element offspring who had escaped from Daoxian's villages and were packed into the bus stop shack across from the No. 2 High School, or they were hiding in the upper floor of a hostel next to the county guest house. One had escaped after being shot with a blunderbuss. They'd rushed over after hearing that the

PLA was sending people to inquire into the Daoxian killings, and the first thing they said was, "PLA comrades, we beg you to arrest us and lock us up in prison!"

Liu Zhaofeng told them to stop the wild talk and to slow down and tell him what they wanted to say. One young man, who looked well educated, said, "Under the direction of the party's capitalist roader faction in power, Daoxian's villages have engaged in a catastrophic massacre. They're ostensibly killing black elements, but in fact they don't draw any distinctions and are indiscriminately killing black-element offspring and people whose views diverge from theirs. They haven't even spared suckling infants, and entire families have been slaughtered. . . . We're the ones who have managed to escape. Although we have bad family backgrounds, we're willing to obey Chairman Mao and follow the party, to reform our thinking and make a fresh start in life. We beg you, PLA comrades, give us a way out. . . ."

The others chimed in, "We're willing to go to prison, we're willing to reform. . . ."

After listening to the tearful pleas of the black-element offspring, the four soldiers felt their hearts sink like lead. They sensed that these people were telling the truth, but the CCP's fundamental line required dealing with all matters according to the guiding principle of class struggle. This meant they had to be wary of anything said by these people and must carry out further inquiries through all available channels.

One after another, upstanding people in Daoxian told the soldiers stories of appalling violence and bloodshed. The Revolutionary Alliance also seized the opportunity to send over reports and evidence they'd collected on the incitement and implementation of killings in the villages by the "Red Fogies." What they saw and heard gave the four soldiers a profound sense of the seriousness and urgency of the problem. That night, in the county labor union office where they were staying, the four men stayed up almost the entire night writing up their report.

Taking into consideration the killing activities and the partisan fighting between the Red and the Revolutionary Alliances, the next morning Liu Zhaofeng and the others went to see the heads of both factions and called an "urgent countywide telephone conference." Deputy chief of staff Liu Zhaofeng represented the 6950 Unit in emphasizing over the telephone, "Anyone who engages in arbitrary killing without authorization from the political and legal departments is in breach of the law. This must stop immediately!" However, his words met with resistance from some people in the Red Alliance.

That afternoon, the four soldiers wired the results of their inquiries to the Mailing regimental headquarters and requested that the regiment send people to Daoxian to end the killings—the sooner the better! When the regimental leader received the urgent telegram from Liu Zhaofeng and the others, he immediately reported it to army headquarters and also called a meeting of the regiment's CCP committee to discuss an action plan.

The inquiries undertaken by Liu Zhaofeng and the others gave the 6950 Unit's leaders an understanding of the scale and seriousness of Daoxian's killing wind. However, the troops were right in the middle of harvesting several thousand *mu* of peanuts, and under the extreme material shortages of that time, they couldn't abandon this task. In order to ensure due attention both to the peanuts and the killings, the regimental leaders arrived at a plan: two battalions would remain in Mailing harvesting the peanuts, and one battalion would be sent to Daoxian to halt the killings. This plan was approved by army headquarters, which also ordered them to take over the county PAFD's role in local "Support-the-Left" work. After receiving these orders, the regiment selected two companies from the first battalion and several dozen of the stronger political and ideological cadres from the second and third battalions to strengthen the leadership, and ordered them on an urgent mission to Daoxian to stop the killings.

Early in the morning of August 29, the first group of 6950 Unit officers and men boarded trucks bound north for Daoxian. The trip from Mailing was about 100 kilometers—not an excessive distance, but the roads were poor, and the soldiers were bumped and tossed around for more than three hours before reaching their destination. When the trucks stopped at Xiaojiangkou on the outskirts of the county seat, the officers and men climbed out and slapped the dust from their clothes, lined up in proper military columns, and marched into town behind the red flag.

One resident described the scene this way: "When the PLA entered the city, it was around ten o'clock in the morning. Upon hearing the news, everyone was overjoyed and ran about spreading the word, spontaneously pouring into the streets to welcome the troops. Someone said, 'The 47th Army has arrived in Daoxian, the 21 black categories can stop worrying!' In fact, even those of us who weren't in the black categories could stop worrying. If the killing had continued, heaven only knew how far it would have gone! When I heard the news and reached the street, both sides were packed with people, some so agitated that they broke down into tears. Because we hadn't heard the news in advance, no preparations had been made. There were no banners or posters for flags, and no one knew what slogans to shout, so all people could do on seeing the PLA arrive was clap their hands—clap with all their might."

Yet, once the 6950 Unit arrived in Daoxian, the first problem they had to address was a major battle between the Red and the Revolutionary Alliances on August 30.

According to what the Task Force was able to ascertain, it appears that the Red Alliance provoked this battle. Destroying the "fortified village" of the No. 2 High School where the Revolutionary Alliance was headquartered had been the guiding principle set when the Red Alliance Frontline Command Post was established, and the Red Alliance had carried out a great deal of preparation to this end. Of course, the Revolutionary Alliance had also been busy reorganizing their leadership ranks and had been promoting those with experience as demobilized servicemen and core militiamen to the frontline leadership, while also organizing an "armed working detachment" (modeled on the anti-Japanese guerrillas of an earlier time) made up largely of former soldiers and militiamen. It was under these conditions that Revolutionary Alliance leader Liu Xiangxi was elected the person with overall responsibility for the alliance, yet at that time, no one imagined that his rise to prominence would spell such disaster for the Red Alliance. Both sides had mounted intense publicity in preparation for the battle that was sure to happen sooner or later. The arrival of the 6950 Unit triggered the battle on August 30. After the Red Alliance, which enjoyed a decisive advantage in terms of armed force, heard that the 6950 Unit would be taking over the county PAFD's "Support-the-Left" operations, it decided to take the No. 2 High School in one fell swoop and make the Red takeover of the entire county a fait accompli that would force the 6950 Unit to take its side.

Perhaps because their defeat in this battle constituted such a major loss of face, few well-informed people on the Red Alliance side were willing to talk to us about it, and we were obliged to rely on the Revolutionary Alliance as the main source for this brief synopsis of the battle. Li Chenggou, commander of the Revolutionary Alliance's "verbal attack and armed defense" headquarters, provided us with the following account:

> Two days before the battle, on the evening of August 28, we received word that the Red Alliance was holding more than 200 innocent people in several residential areas . . . and was preparing to kill them. They included members of the county people's political consultative conference who are now prominent people in Daoxian. . . . Liu Xiangxi ordered me to send people to order their release, and told me that the Red Alliance wanted to provoke a large-scale battle, so he wanted me to send a military scouting party to reinforce defense work in Daojiang Town. So I told Xiong XX to take a group to the Temple of the Town God, and the people held there were rescued on the spot. We never guessed that one of the minor ringleaders of the Red Alliance, militia commander Nie Guangbao, would secretly arrest nine of them first thing the next morning, kill them next to the southern gate of Daojiang Town, and dump their bodies into the Xiaoshui River.[1] The families of the victims included four underage children. Nie Guangbao and the others pushed them into a big vat and put a huge rock on top of it,

intending to suffocate them to death. Some good people rescued the children, but by then, one child had already died.

That night [the 29th], our scouting party clashed with an advance force that the Red Alliance had sent to Daojiang. Many of our men were wounded and ten were captured, and only two made it back to the No. 2 High School. By then we had gotten word that the Red Alliance was planning a bloodbath at the school, and was coming with thousands of ropes to bind us up. Some of the Revolutionary Alliance leaders panicked and asked Liu Xiangxi what we should do. These leaders were all teachers who were very able with pen and paper but terrified of dealing with this kind of situation. Liu Xiangxi told them not to panic but to prepare for battle. I remember Liu Xiangxi said at the time that retreat would be a dead end road, and the only hope of survival lay in fighting our way out.

Early in the morning on August 30, The Red Alliance fired three cannon shots at the No. 2 High School from the direction of the porcelain factory. The first shot hit the canteen, another landed on the sports field and the third landed on the riverbank behind the school. None caused any casualties.[2] The militia that the Red Alliance had assembled at Yingjiang and elsewhere then advanced on the county town with three point companies made up of demobilized servicemen, including some who had fired real guns and ammunition against the Yanks on the Korean War frontlines. These fighters were armed with light and heavy machine guns and rifles and pulled a heavy-duty cart loaded with explosives and crates of hand grenades. Inside the No. 2 High School, the Revolutionary Alliance had fewer than 300 people and a little more than 100 guns, putting them at an absolute disadvantage. Red Alliance head Zhang Mingchi telephoned Liu Xiangxi and gave the Revolutionary Alliance the ultimatum of laying down their weapons and surrendering in return for guarantees of their personal safety. Liu Xiangxi responded, "Excellent! The guns are all polished up and waiting for you."

Just then, the 6950 Unit's deputy chief of staff, Liu Zhaofeng, arrived at the school with several cadres, and raising his Little Red Book, he called out, "Don't shoot! Don't shoot!" Liu Xiangxi issued an order for Liu Zhaofeng and the others to be allowed in, and once inside, Liu advised the Revolutionary Alliance to put down their weapons and allow the PLA to take over defense of the No. 2 High School. Liu Xiangxi agreed to do so if the Red Alliance withdrew to Yingjiang, so Liu Zhaofeng went out to negotiate with the Red Alliance.

While Liu Zhaofeng was out working on the Red Alliance, the sound of intensive gunfire erupted like firecrackers being set off. While Liu Zhaofeng and his men were advising both sides to lay down their weapons and stop their fighting, the leaders of both sides were saying one thing while doing something completely different. The Red Alliance's three point companies had already stealthily approached the No. 2 High School and were awaiting the order to start their general offensive. Unbeknownst to them, however, the Revolutionary Alliance's fighters were not all holed up inside the school; an intrepid detachment led by Li Chenggou had been sent out with the Revolutionary Alliance's best weapons, including two machine guns and seven or eight semi-automatic rifles and plenty of ammunition, and navigating up the city's network of waterways in a matt-covered houseboat, they had crept up behind the Red Alliance's point companies, cutting off the advance force from the large detachment of troops at its rear.

Li Chenggou recalls, "Liu Xiangxi told us to quietly climb to the upper floor of the Postal and Telecommunications office building and set up our machine guns, allow the Red Alliance advance force to enter first and then block their retreat and annihilate them. He said that occupying this command point would bring us halfway to victory. He told us to ignore the Red Alliance's main detachment and to concentrate our firepower on the advance force and knock them out, and then we would win. When I reached the top of the Postal and Telecommunications building, I saw that the advance force was just where we could box them into Lijia Lane, and that one cartridge clip of bullets could kill a lot of men. Keeping in mind that they were our class brothers, I told the other men not to shoot to kill, but to fire into the air. As soon as we started firing, the trapped point companies were thrown into complete confusion, and the main detachment in the rear threw down their spears, sabers, and blunderbusses and turned tail and ran. Some were in such a hurry that their shoes fell off . . ."

After about an hour of intense fighting, the 6950 Unit imposed a ceasefire and called for negotiations. The Revolutionary Alliance suffered ten casualties, including three fatalities, while the Red Alliance had two fatalities among a large number of casualties that including county PAFD section chief Yu Hexiang with an abdominal wound. More than 300 others were taken prisoner. The Revolutionary Alliance's "(Draft) Summary of Events of the Proletarian Great Cultural Revolution in Daoxian," published on November 11, 1967, records: "At 9:15, we were compelled to strike back in self-defense and captured 660 Red Alliance personnel, releasing 360 on the spot and taking the rest back to the No. 2 High School as prisoners to undergo education. Within four days these were all released. In this battle we seized two light machine guns and more than 80 other guns of various types, a cartload of explosives, daggers (striking knives), and a cartload of other materials." The Red Alliance claimed this was exaggerated.

A political instructor with the 6950 Unit, Guo Xuegao, died in the line of duty after being struck in the chest by a stray bullet while attempting to halt the fighting. At noon that day, the Red Alliance called together more than 400 people for a memorial ceremony mourning the dead on their side as martyrs. In a speech at the ceremony, Qingtang District PAFD commander Zheng Youzhi said, "If the black elements dare stage an overthrow, we'll destroy them root and branch! Let's see them try!" Then He Xia gave a speech in which he paraphrased Mao: "Daoxian belongs to the people of Daoxian, not to the reactionary faction;[3] the people of Daoxian will assuredly achieve the final victory." Fearing that the Revolutionary Alliance would follow up their victory with hot pursuit, the Red Alliance Frontline Command Post then hastily withdrew from Yingjiang to Qingtang.

The entry of the 6950 Unit marked what the Task Force regarded as stage 4 of Daoxian's killing wind, following the first three stages marked by the August 8 gun-snatching incident, the August 21 Yingjiang reporting meeting, and the August 26 Yingjian Political and Legal Work Conference. One of the top cadres in Daoxian at that time summarized this historical interlude thus:

> After the 6950 Unit entered Daoxian, they didn't betray expectations but immediately issued an order and posted the prohibition against killing issued by the provincial revolutionary committee preparatory group and the 47th Army in all the towns and villages. They also mobilized the broadcast apparatus in a grand propaganda campaign. At the same time, they arranged for the two factional mass organizations to sit down face to face for consultation and negotiation and to take a clear stand against violence and killing, and they sent troops deep into the towns and villages, where the killing was worst, for a face-to-face effort that resulted in the situation rapidly stabilizing. Although the occasional unlawful element still went against the wind and committed offenses, the overall situation throughout the county was quickly stabilized and the "killing wind" gradually subsided. After that they helped the masses resume production and resolve factional violence. They set about establishing a new revolutionary regime—the county revolutionary committee—so the leadership ranks that had been paralyzed for years could gradually recover and resume exercising their functions and powers. Step by step, the situation took a turn for the better. This was the historic achievement of the 6950 Unit, and it was a blessing to the people of Daoxian.

The hard task of halting the killing

Once the 6950 Unit reached Daoxian, it immediately put its hand to three matters: the first was to end the fighting between the Red and the Revolutionary Alliances, the second was to halt the killings in the countryside, and the third was to investigate the truth behind the indiscriminate killing.

After the CCP Central Committee handed down its "September 5 Order," the 6950 Unit called a meeting during which the unit's comrades repeatedly stated, "Both the Red Alliance and the Revolutionary Alliance are mass organizations. The two factions should be united."

After the meeting, the unit issued a notice for a telephone conference and sent propaganda trucks with propaganda teams to "publicize the party's policies and strictly prohibit killing." At the same time, a military patrol party patrolled the streets of Daojiang to restore stability and peace of mind among the residents.

The two sides had become irreconcilable, however. In plain language, the Red Alliance regarded the Revolutionary Alliance as the "chief representative of black elements, ox demons, and snake spirits," and the Revolutionary Alliance designated the Red Alliance as the ringleaders of "counterrevolutionary butchers and oppressors of the revolutionary people," and neither could be happy until the other was utterly destroyed. On top of that, the killings had become as uncontrollable as a prairie blaze, and stamping out the flames was no easy matter.

By this time (the first half of September), the 6950 Unit's second and third battalions left behind in Mailing had harvested their peanuts and compressed them into nearly 150,000 kilos of peanut oil, which had been delivered to the Guangzhou Military Region. Just as they finished this task, they received orders from headquarters to set off for Daoxian and its adjoining counties to stop the killing wind.

Because this was still a particularly chaotic stage of the Cultural Revolution, in order to prevent mishaps the regimental headquarters ordered the troops to bury all excess guns and ammunition underground and also to hide the cannons, and to leave a small number of soldiers behind to protect these arms while the others accompanied the regimental headquarters to Daoxian. Four 122-millimeter howitzers, which due to their size could not easily be concealed, were brought along to Daoxian. With the regimental headquarters stationed there, Daojiang became the hub for dispatching personnel throughout the county and to nearby counties and towns where killings were occurring.

Given the chaotic situation, the major interference caused by factional fighting, and rumors that one organization or another was preparing to snatch the PLA's weapons, the regimental leaders came up with a master stroke: they ordered the troops to haul the four howitzers to a barren hill at Xiaojiangkou on the southern end of Daojiang and then invited the revolutionary masses of the entire county to observe the PLA testing the howitzers. On the morning of the test firing, people crowded the hillside at Xiaojiangkou as flames issued from the howitzers, followed by a roaring sound and thick smoke billowing up from the barren southern face of Zijin Mountain at Daguping. Each howitzer fired two shots, raising eight columns of smoke. The observers cheered, and those familiar with the topography guessed the range of the howitzers at about 10 kilometers. A rumor quickly circulated in Daojiang Town: "Whichever faction starts fighting again, the PLA will use its cannons to bombard their headquarters."

On September 9, the 6950 Unit called an urgent meeting in the assembly hall of the county CCP committee office. The theme of the meeting was resolutely ending armed struggle; preventing indiscriminate arrest and killing; executing the Central Committee's September 5 "Order Prohibiting the Snatching of People's Liberation Army Weapons, Equipment, and Other Military Supplies"; and joining forces to maintain social order in Daoxian. Attending the meeting were Revolutionary Alliance representatives Liu Xiangxi, Pan Xingjiang, Zhou Donglin, Lu Chengchu, and Song Zhouneng and Red Alliance representatives Zheng Youzhi, Zhong Changyou, He Xia, Liao Mingzhong, and Liu Houshan, with Liu Zhaofeng, deputy chief of staff of the 6950 Unit, presiding.

They first studied the Central Committee's "September 5th Order," after which Liu Zhaofeng read out a written statement of agreement discussed in advance with the Revolutionary Alliance. It contained seven clauses:

(1) Both sides would work together to immediately end indiscriminate killing in the villages; killers would be investigated and punished.

(2) The people's militias were to be disbanded, and the militiamen were to return to their communes and production brigades to seize revolution and push production. All weapons were to be handed over to the commune PAFDs within seven days and would be locked away for safekeeping under the supervision of representatives of the 6950 Unit. Further manufacture of lethal weapons would be severely punished.

(3) All checkpoints were to be dismantled, and unimpeded transportation by land and water was to be maintained.

(4) All of the Revolutionary Alliance's guns and ammunition were to be locked up in the No. 2 High School under the supervision of PLA representatives, and no one could break the seal without an order from the 6950 Unit's senior officers.

(5) Transportation, post, telecommunications, and electrical generation were to be promptly restored.

(6) The two sides would work together to allow official organs to resume normal operations, to allow shops to resume business, and to allow students to return to their schools to make revolution.

(7) The routine operations of speaking out, airing views, and creating big-character posters should carry on, and further effort should be made to expose and criticize capitalist roaders and bring the "Proletarian Great Cultural Revolution" to completion.

After Liu Zhaofeng read out these seven items, the Red Alliance representatives objected, stating that handing over the militia's weapons to the commune and under the supervision of the troops without making the Revolutionary Alliance hand over theirs was in defiance of the "September 5th Order," and that Red Alliance personnel in the villages would not feel safe returning to the county seat. Liu Zhaofeng said he would add an eighth item guaranteeing the personal safety of Red Alliance personnel returning to Daojiang from the countryside.

After the eighth point was added, the leaders of both sides signed what came to be known as the "September 9th Agreement."

The 6950 Unit then carried out a parade in the streets with representatives of the Red and the Revolutionary Alliances to celebrate the signing, and the four-vehicle convoy wound through the streets and was applauded by the masses all the way. When they stopped to rest at noon, the county PAFD's political commissar, Liu Shibin, went to see the Red Alliance representatives at the county CCP committee office and criticized Zheng Youzhi, saying, "The Revolutionary Alliance's representatives all were from the masses, but four of our five representatives were PAFD commanders. Wasn't this really a negotiation between the PAFD and the Revolutionary Alliance? What do you want Liu Zhaofeng and the others to think of us?"

After the September 9th Agreement was signed, the people's militia formed by the Red Alliance was declared disbanded, and the district and commune PAFD commanders and 500-odd core militiamen assembled in Shouyan all returned to their districts, communes, production brigades, and production teams.

The killings in the villages were rapidly declining, but the killing wind hadn't completely died out, and in a few places, such as Xianglinpu District, killings actually escalated as people "seized a last opportunity to kill another batch."

The head of the 6950 Unit's regimental headquarters organization section, Wu Ronghua (now political commissar of a military-run farm in Shaanxi), recalled:

> After we arrived in Daoxian, we quickly formed several Mao Zedong Thought propaganda teams and worked nonstop to publicize the party's policies and national laws and decrees and to end the indiscriminate killing. We faced enormous resistance, especially in the countryside, where we regularly encountered all kinds of people carrying sabers, spears, blunderbusses, and other weapons who surrounded, threatened, and jeered at us. They cursed us as "Liu Shaoqi's army" and as "working for the black elements," and they threatened to "fight us to the bitter end." Once when we were carrying out propaganda in Gongba, we were besieged for more than four hours. On another occasion near the county forestry bureau, our propaganda team was carrying out

propaganda to the masses when we saw a group of people carrying blunderbusses and broadswords with two bound middle-aged men, and when we went over and stopped them, we were subjected to attacks and invective. After we repeatedly disseminated Mao Zedong Thought and did our utmost to obstruct them, they were finally compelled to release the two men.

Deputy battalion commander Liu Fu'an (now retired from the Fujian provincial grain apparatus) recalled:

One afternoon, we received word from the ground that people were going to be killed in Qingtang District. Political commissar Sun Runqing sent me with comrades from the second company to rush over to prevent it. By the time we arrived it was already nightfall, and the people had been killed, the corpses placed alongside a well. Several people holding melon knives and blunderbusses blocked our way, but after our repeated propaganda work, they finally let us enter the village. Without having eaten dinner and with no place to stay, we went to a small shop, but the man there quickly packed away all his edible items and wouldn't sell any to us. We took out money and asked why he wouldn't let us buy anything. He said, "It's not that I don't want to, but I don't dare. The brigade said that anyone who gives you anything will have their home ransacked and lose their head." In spite of that, we worked against all odds and rescued many victims from under the knife and prevented repeated killing campaigns. . . .

Deputy chief of staff Liu Zhaofeng (now a cadre at a military academy in Beijing) recalled:

The work was extremely difficult back then; the situation was very complicated, and killings took place every day. There was a man surnamed He whose father had been a puppet village chief, and at that time he was hiding in the county town. His production brigade sent three people to Daojiang to apprehend him, and when he screamed for help, someone ran over and reported it to us. I led several soldiers to run over and stop them, and I asked the three why they wanted to kill him. They said he was a counterrevolutionary. I asked what proof they had. They hemmed and hawed and couldn't come up with anything. After going on for a while they said his father had been a puppet village chief, and he himself had been a slacker and then had gone off to become a vagrant. I threatened them by saying, "If I think you're counterrevolutionaries, can I kill you?" The three of them were so scared that they knelt on the ground weeping and said, "We're not counterrevolutionaries, we're poor and lower-middle peasants; we have elderly parents at home, and if you kill us, who will support them?" I said, "Do you think you're the only ones with elderly parents? The truth is that the way you're killing people is intolerable and it's a serious criminal act." They said, "It's not our fault, the brigade sent us." I said, "The brigade is also at fault for sending you." At that time, however, we didn't have the authority to punish people, so we could only educate and release them.

During our reporting, we heard many stories of the 6950 Unit preventing killings, but it was all hearsay and in principle we couldn't include them. We did gain access to one relatively firsthand account in the form of a mimeographed report, yellowed with age, written on October 17, 1967, by a female educated youth sent down to Shouyan District's Datanghu Farm. The account describes the horrific beatings inflicted on the writer and several other educated youth on September 9:

> After they'd beaten us for a while, they took us to Shouyan's Huangtuling Hill. The murderers used a fowling gun to shoot Zeng Botao and then they stabbed him with a saber, and blood spurted all over. That nice young man who had answered Chairman Mao's call to go up to the mountains and down to the countryside fell into a pool of blood and died tragically under the executioner's knife. Next the executioners killed Yi Xucheng with a fowling gun. In the face of these atrocities, we could only wait to die. At this moment the executioners used even more ruthless fascist methods, telling one of the educated youth, Zhou Jiran, to kill the other educated youths with his own hand. The murderers threatened him, saying, "If you don't kill them, we'll kill you!" How could he bear to kill his own brothers and sisters! Fortunately, just at that moment, someone came to the killing ground and called the executioners to the commune for an urgent meeting; the people's army had heard the news and rushed over, and they had issued an order prohibiting random killing. We were freed from the grasp of the King of Hell and escaped death by sheer good luck. . . .

Figure 1 shows that after the 6950 Unit arrived in Daoxian on August 29, the killings immediately went into sharp decline and gradually stopped. In a sense, the arrival of the 6950 Unit in Daoxian was the main event that ended the Daoxian massacre.

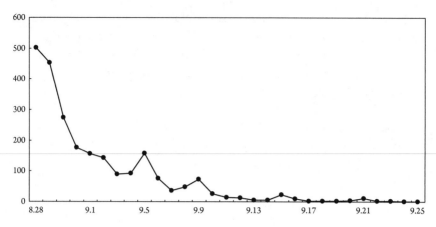

Figure 1 Number of killings in Daoxian from August 28 to September 25, 1967

Even so, there are those who criticize the 6950 Unit for not doing enough to stop the killings in Daoxian and the surrounding areas. Especially after being besieged and jeered when they went to the countryside to dissuade people from killing, they didn't dare keep going there, and there were more measures they could have taken but didn't. I discussed this point with cadres from the 6950 Unit. They said they were appalled at the inhuman slaughter occurring before their very eyes, but "class struggle and violent revolution" was the CCP's fundamental line, and they simply didn't know how to deal with "poor and lower-middle peasants killing class enemies."

A local cadre who paid a heavy price for opposing the killings told us:

> Why was it that before the 47th Army arrived, Daoxian's killing wind grew in intensity, but after they came it quickly subsided? Could it be that everyone in the 47th Army had superhuman powers while we county cadres were completely useless? Is it possible that before the army arrived, the masses had such a weak grasp of law and discipline, and that it rapidly strengthened after the army arrived, or that before the army arrived, everyone's thinking had been confused by the Gang of Four, but it was all straightened out after the army arrived? Is it possible that before the army arrived, the public-security and judicial organs were paralyzed, but they revived as soon as the army appeared, or that before the army arrived, class struggle was severe, but after the army arrived all was stability and unity? In fact, the reason was very simple: the source of the Daoxian killings was not from below, but from above. As soon as the 47th Army arrived, that bunch in the county, districts, and communes became afraid and withdrew their hands, and once they withdrew their hands the killing wind naturally subsided.

While biased, these words provide much food for thought. I have in hand two urgent telegrams dated September 15 and September 22 that the 47th Army and the Hunan Provincial Revolutionary Committee Preparatory Group sent to the Central Military Commission and Central Cultural Revolution Small Group, which describe the 6950 Unit's efforts in Daoxian but acknowledge that "attempts to halt the random killing phenomenon have fallen short." The September 22 telegram states "On the basis of the above circumstances, we are taking further measures to halt the killings."

On September 27, 1967, the PLA's 47th Army and the Hunan Provincial Revolutionary Committee Preparatory Group issued a joint urgent notice regarding the Daoxian killings:

> . . . Recently, some parts of Daoxian, Jianghua, Jiangyong, Ningyuan, Lanshan, Lingling, and other counties have experienced ongoing counterrevolutionary incidents of continuous killings and sabotage of communications and transportation. In order to . . . ensure the people's safety . . . in light of the aforementioned incidents, the following notice is issued:
>
> (1) It is necessary to resolutely execute the CCP Central Committee and State Council's "Certain Stipulations regarding Strengthening Public-Security Work in the Proletarian Great Cultural Revolution" [dated January 13, 1967] . . . and resolutely prevent the occurrence of killings or sabotage of communication and transportation.
>
> (2) The so-called Supreme People's Courts of the Poor and Lower-Middle Peasants . . . are illegal and must be resolutely banned. The minority of ringleaders and chief instigators of the killings must be investigated with severity and dealt with in accordance with law.
>
> (3) All weapons in the hands of conservative organizations must be promptly and immediately recalled and turned over to the troops of the local People's Liberation Army 47th Army. . . . Following confiscation of the weapons in the hands of conservative organizations, take control of the weapons of the revolutionary rebel organizations and have them placed under seal.
>
> (4) All the masses and cadres who have been compelled to leave their work units should be guaranteed that upon returning to their units they will take part in struggle-criticism-transformation, and under no pretext may they be subjected to attack from all sides, violent struggle, or death. Checkpoints set up on thoroughfares must be immediately dismantled, and roadblocks and searches are strictly prohibited so as to ensure the safety of travelers and unimpeded post, telecommunications, and transportation.

The day that the notice was issued, every county in southern Hunan reprinted and posted it. The 6950 Unit's Mao Zedong Thought propaganda teams set off for Daoxian and surrounding counties and went into the districts, communes, and even production brigades to notify people of the content of the notice and stop further killing.

On the sunny morning of September 25, a roaring sound filled the sky as a Soviet-made aircraft flying in a northeasterly direction pierced a bank of clouds and suddenly reduced altitude as it circled over Daoxian. Wondering if an enemy aircraft was preparing to land, peasants working in the fields laid aside their tools and raised their faces to squint with wary and apprehensive eyes at the aircraft gleaming in the sunlight. The red star and numeral on the fuselage clearly identified it as a Chinese aircraft, but why had it come here, and why was it flying so low? Suddenly the tail of the aircraft expelled something white that slowly drifted through the air like snowflakes.

"Airplane, airplane!" a group of children shouted joyfully as they chased after the plane with their hands outstretching to capture the fluttering leaflets.

After obtaining approval from the Central Military Commission and Central Cultural Revolution Small Group, the Hunan Provincial Revolutionary Committee Preparatory Group and 47th Army Support-the-Left troops, in co-operation with the 6950 Unit, had dispatched the aircraft to distribute leaflets prohibiting further killings: "Those who kill will be punished under national law." The aircraft dropped another batch of leaflets the next day.

Tens of thousands of leaflets blanketed Daoxian and the towns, villages, and fields of peripheral counties. Some hit the ground still tied in bundles. There were so many leaflets that people didn't even bother to pick them up. Many were rolled into the crude, trumpet-shaped cigarettes the peasants liked to smoke. Not a single one can be found now; the Daoxian People's Government at one point offered a reward of 5,000 yuan (equivalent to 10 months' wages for a college graduate) to anyone who could hand over a leaflet, but without result.

After the October 1 National Day celebration, the "revolutionary rebel faction" organizations of Daoxian and 10 surrounding counties and towns formed a "Southern Hunan Petition Delegation to Changsha" to deliver a report on the killings to the Hunan Provincial Revolutionary Committee Preparatory Group.[4] On October 8, 47th Army commander Li Yuan and other top leaders of the provincial preparatory group received the members of the petition delegation and issued an important directive:

> The killing incident in the southern Hunan region was extremely serious and was instigated by black elements and a smattering of capitalist roaders within the party . . . who used the pretext of killing black elements to sabotage the dictatorship of the proletariat and the Proletarian Great

Cultural Revolution. Although specific circumstances differed in each county, the general nature was identical: it was a reactionary incident.

Upon gaining an understanding of the Daoxian killings, the provincial preparatory group and 47th Army . . . held more than a dozen meetings, sent several cables, made many telephone calls, and dropped leaflets from airplanes, yet the killings continue. We are aware of the circumstance you have reported to us; troops stationed in Daoxian, Jiangyong, Lingling, and Dong'an have reported very much the same thing. In the previous stage, we followed Premier Zhou [Enlai]'s directive to resolve it from the inside outward, first concentrating our strength to resolve the problem in Changsha, Xiangtan, Liuyang, and such places. As a result, fewer troops were sent to Lingling Prefecture, and manpower was inadequate.

On the basis of the current circumstances, the provincial preparatory committee and 47th Army took resolute measures to end the killings. . . . Dictatorial measures must absolutely be taken against the party capitalist roaders and evil ringleaders and black elements who instigated the killings, and, following authorization, several have been arrested and dealt with according to law. When you go back, you must assist the troops in carrying out their work, but be careful not to engage in revenge massacres. Toward the hoodwinked poor and lower-middle peasants, chiefly disseminate Mao Zedong Thought and clearly explain policies, patiently carry out political and ideological work, and teach them to genuinely follow Chairman Mao's revolutionary line. Another measure is to bring in the leaders of all district militias for centralized study sessions. Since the party's Central Committee has stated its position on the Hunan issue, some have transformed their thinking, but others have not been completely transformed, and for this reason it is necessary to organize effective study sessions for them.

With the signing of the order on October 9, 1967, the shocking Cultural Revolution massacre in Daoxian and surrounding counties completely subsided. The verdict was by no means cut and dried, however, and as the Cultural Revolution progressed, the official version of this incident remained in flux.

In October, Daoxian became tranquil. Because of the protective screen formed by the mountains on all sides, autumn comes late to Daoxian, and the green of summer hadn't yet retreated before the multicolored splendor of autumn. Even so, the breeze had become gentler and the waters calmer, and it seemed that the killing was over. Then suddenly, on October 17, there was the sound of gunfire in Qiaotou Commune's Shangba production brigade as militia commander Tang Guiting used a fowling gun to kill middle peasant He Yuxiang at the Ma'anqiao pavilion. As if at heaven's will, first blood was drawn "below the dam" (Xiaba) and last blood was drawn "above the dam" (Shangba): after the smoke cleared on this stretch of flatland at the Hunan-Guangxi border, the giant hand of history finally placed a blood-colored full stop at the end of this Cultural Revolution atrocity.

31

No Regrets

An interview with Revolutionary Alliance leader Liu Xiangxi

After the Gang of Four was crushed, family members of victims of the Daoxian massacre made thousands of trips to Changsha and Beijing to petition the authorities for redress; tens of thousands of written complaints flooded prefectural, provincial, and central government offices. All these complaints identified county Chinese Communist Party (CCP) secretary Xiong Bing'en as the orchestrator of the massacre and "chief justice" of the peasant supreme court and demanded that he be brought to justice. These denunciations likewise implicated the head of the county CCP committee organization department, Wang Ansheng, the deputy head of Xianglinpu District, Yuan Lifu, the commander of the District 6 People's Armed Forces Department (PAFD), Zheng Youzhi, and Red Alliance heads Zhang Mingchi and He Xia, among others.

The Task Force took these petitions and written complaints very seriously and established special investigation teams to ascertain the facts behind them. However, no strong evidence was ever found that Xiong Bing'en had directly ordered killings.

Deng Youzhi, who was CCP secretary of Lingling Prefecture at the time, personally sought out Huang Yida, who during the Cultural Revolution was Xiong Bing'en's opponent as county deputy CCP secretary and county head, and asked him, "Comrade Huang Yida, you have a better understanding of the Cultural Revolution killings in Daoxian, so I want you to tell me honestly, did Xiong Bing'en direct any killings?"

Huang Yida replied, "I worked with Xiong Bing'en for many years, and he was always a highly circumspect person, never saying or doing anything out of line. He committed serious errors during the Cultural Revolution killings; as the county's main leader, he didn't stop the killings and even supported them, but there's no evidence that he ever planned or directed any killings. At that time, he was mainly in charge of production, and the actual power was not in his hands."

The question then arises how the Daoxian massacre could have proceeded with such coordination and speed without some kind of centralized planning and arrangement.

At considerable risk, we managed through an intermediary to interview the commander in chief of the Revolutionary Alliance and ringleader of the armed violence in Daoxian, the former chairman of the county grain bureau labor union, Liu Xiangxi. I already knew that Liu had spent a total of seven years in prison during the Cultural Revolution and had nearly been handed a death sentence, and that he subsequently served a long term of penal labor under surveillance. We were afraid he'd be jittery and unwilling to talk, but on meeting him all our apprehensions were shattered. This was no timid and overcautious man, but rather someone who had long ago set aside any considerations of life and death.

Liu was a wiry man of modest height, and what left the deepest impression on me were his eyes, which gleamed with an enigmatic and somewhat ghastly smile, and the long, deep creases alongside his mouth. Unlike the connotation of the Western term "laugh lines," the classic Chinese *Guide to Physiognomy* refers to these creases as "winged snakes" and says that if they "enter the mouth," the bearer will "starve to death in an alien land." Liu's "winged snakes" curved dangerously close to the corners of his mouth but then extended downward. One look at him suggested that this was a very intelligent, capable, obstinate, and conceited man. I had to remind myself to maintain my objectivity and not let him lead me by the nose.

Liu Xiangxi was a native of Daoxian, born in 1931 to a poor peasant family and receiving a primary-school education. He joined the volunteer army in 1951 to fight in the Korean War, and he joined the Chinese Communist Party in 1953. He graduated from the People's Liberation Army (PLA) General Staff Headquarters Xuanhua Institute of Communications in 1957, and most of his army postings were in the communications field. Following a back injury during training, he transferred to civilian work in February 1966 and returned to Daoxian, and the Cultural Revolution began soon after that. Perhaps his years in prison had frozen his speech and thinking in the patterns of the early Cultural Revolution. He referred to himself as a soldier of the Maoist revolutionary rebel faction, to his opposition, the Red Alliance, as the "counter-revolutionary killing faction," and to Xiong Bing'en as "Daoxian's biggest capitalist roader."

Liu was housed in the grain bureau's residential quarters, the shabbiness of which evidenced the poverty of its occupant. What stood out were the many scrolls that hung in the living room, all poems of Liu's own composition and in his own calligraphy. Following his release from prison, Liu had begun practicing calligraphy as a means, he said, of improving his character and healing his wounds. He had suffered enormous physical injury in prison, nearly losing the use of both arms. He seemed to emulate the calligraphic style of Yan Zhenqing, and although of a clearly amateur standard, his writing was bold and firm. One scroll in particular caught my attention:

Qilü:[1] **The Cultural Revolution Catastrophe**
White Terror August 13
Saving people and city;
The school guarded with hardship,
Gelian[2] skill repelled slayers.

Bullets rained August 30,
Honglian[3] bloodbath in Daozhao;
Valiant resistance one hour,
Three rebel corps captured.

Riot on Sept 23,
Rushing the school to snatch guns,
Against the Sept 5 Order;
Ruthless in evil designs!

These three stanzas of doggerel depict three major battles between the Red and the Revolutionary Alliances that resulted in Liu Xiangxi being designated a "beating, smashing, and looting element." These dramatic battles are not the focus of this book, however, so I will not go into the details here.

Our main objective in interviewing Liu Xiangxi was to listen to him, or more precisely, to hear about the Daoxian massacre from the perspective of the Red Alliance's opponents, the Revolutionary Alliance.

It appeared that Liu Xiangxi approached the interview with the greatest possible wariness. This was understandable for someone who'd learned of the treachery of human beings through hard experience.

Our interview or, strictly speaking, our conversation revolved cautiously around his experiences during the Cultural Revolution, but shrewd as he was, he couldn't help but know what we really wanted, and for all the lack of trust between us, I believe that what we wanted was what he was most willing to provide. When we raised the topic of the killings, Liu Xiangxi gave a sardonic laugh and said, "You came to the right person. I'm a 'living fossil' of the Daoxian massacre, and I can give you whatever you need."

He let us read an "exposure report" he'd written on the Cultural Revolution killings in Daoxian, and while he wouldn't let us take it with us, he did let us take notes. The petition ended with this impressive statement: "If a single word I've written is false, may I be beheaded in the public square." We read this report very carefully and conscientiously, and apart from the different perspective, the basic facts it presented differed little from the Task Force's investigation files.

Liu Xiangxi told us that when a revolutionary committee was established in Daoxian in early 1968, with the political commissar of the 6950 Unit as chairman and county CCP secretary Huang Yida as first vice chairman, Liu Xiangxi was appointed to the Revolutionary Committee's standing committee in charge of finance and trade. In March 1968, the 6950 Unit and the county Revolutionary Committee held an "exposure study session" attended by more than 250 people, including work unit leaders, representatives of both alliances, and people implicated in the killings:

> This study session lasted 21 days and carried out in-depth and detailed exposure and confrontation regarding the massacre. We sent people into each district and commune and carried out a very thorough and solid investigation. We wrote up an investigative report and a register of individuals, all supported by ironclad evidence. I remember that we printed off dozens of copies of this report and sent it to the prefecture, the province, and the party center. The original draft was preserved in Zhang Fushan's hands; he was also a Revolutionary Alliance leader, a native of the Northeast who has since returned there. The development of the Great Cultural Revolution in Daoxian was excellent then, and the inside story of the massacre was crystal clear. At the time, I went to see Secretary Huang Yida and suggested that he quickly put the material in order and report it to the Provincial Revolutionary Committee, and then kill a few of the arch-criminals and imprison another batch. But Huang Yida was too softhearted, saying such things as "There's no rush, let's leave it for handling at a later stage of the campaign," and "The material is here, it's not going to fly away." The result was that those fellows were spared and allowed to carry out a counterrevolutionary restoration of the old order. . . .

At that time, Lin Biao's anti-party clique wanted to make Hunan the strategic base of their counterrevolutionary coup d'état. The Hunan provincial military district's political commissar, Bo Zhanya, was one of Lin Biao's "black operatives," and in order to securely control Hunan as a strategic base, they pushed the 47th Army out of Hunan. In September 1968, the 6950 Unit that was supporting the Left in Daoxian suddenly withdrew secretly overnight, without giving us any kind of notice. Once the 6950 Unit left, the PAFD began to throw its weight around again. The world turned upside down in an instant, and the homicidal maniacs in the Red Alliance took control again. Those fellows feared and hated us, and they came up with a plan to fabricate accusations and arrest me, Secretary Huang Yida, and the other Revolutionary Alliance leaders and send us to prison, where we were bound, beaten, and tortured. Zhang Fushan was also imprisoned, and no one knows what happened to the report and register of implicated individuals following his arrest.

Because I had opposed their arbitrary killings, exposed their true counterrevolutionary colors, and resolutely fought them, they considered me a thorn in their side and would have liked to see me dead. They arrested and imprisoned me twice for a total of four years. They were calling for the death penalty for me, but I hear they repeatedly submitted reports to the upper level and couldn't get authorization. I, Liu Xiangxi, was loyal to the party and Chairman Mao; I was upright, open, and aboveboard, and it was no easy matter to frame me for some fabricated crime. By the time I got out of prison, both my arms were almost completely disabled, and I healed myself by constantly massaging my hands and practicing calligraphy every day. They wanted me to die, but I insisted on living; every day I live is another day to fight them. I don't believe there's no justice in this world. The overlord of this gang of crazed killers, Lin Biao, once said, "Sooner or later, people always get what they deserve, for good or for ill." I believe that, too, and one day, they'll receive retribution, just as their overlord did.

We asked, "From what you know, who orchestrated the Daoxian massacre at the county level?"

He answered decisively, "Xiong Bing'en!"

"Is there evidence?"

"Of course there's evidence. First of all, his August 5 speech and August 11 telephone conference directive were general mobilization orders for the Daoxian killings."

"But in his speech, he didn't explicitly order anyone killed, did he?" I countered.

"You're a reporter. How can you not understand how things work in China? When does any leader make his directives that explicit? They always depend on those below understanding and acting accordingly. Isn't it always the case that when a leader says something, each level downward ups the stakes?"

"Back then, it wasn't only him saying this kind of thing. Secretary Shi Xiuhua, who had been unseated at that time, said 'Chiang Kai-shek wants to launch a counterattack on the mainland, and we have to kill people so he won't have anyone leading the way for him.'"

"Then you have to distinguish the time, place, and target: when Xiong Bing'en said what to whom, and what district PAFD commanders and public-security cadres were doing."

"All right then, please go on to the second point of evidence."

"The second is that his wife, He De'e, was 'honorary chief justice' of the 'Supreme People's Court of the Poor and Lower-Middle Peasants' in Dongmen Commune's Fengjia production brigade, and she was very active in the killings."

"Can what his wife did be attributed to him?"

"Why not? If he hadn't advocated killing people, why would his wife be so involved? This is just like corruption and bribe taking—you send your wife in your place. You think I don't understand Xiong Bing'en's schemes?"

"And the third piece of evidence?"

"The third is the most important: during the killings, his secretary, Wang Enchang,[4] telephoned the lower levels many times to get progress reports on the killings and to supervise and push forward the killings."

"But Wang Enchang won't agree with what you said. That was the time of the double-rush planting and harvesting, and Xiong Bing'en was in charge of production. If his secretary telephoned each district and commune to check on how production was progressing, and in passing expressed interest in the killings, that can't be equated with supervising and pushing forward the killings, can it?"

Liu Xiangxi looked rather anxious: "Why can't you understand even that much? Sometimes all that's needed is one mispronounced word and the meaning changes completely. Those people were his people, and of course they'll protect him. Xiong Bing'en was a county head, and when the head of a county supports killings, that's the same as directing them!"

"You can say that, but there's still a need for evidence. Besides which, this all happened nearly 20 years ago, and a clear and thorough investigation is easier said than done."

"Easier said than done? Give me a chance to investigate, and within a month I guarantee that I'd get to the bottom of it. No one who engineered the killings would get off. They'd all end up confessing to me."

I looked at Liu Xiangxi and laughed: "No wonder they wanted to sentence you to death!"

Liu Xiangxi said, "I don't blame them for wanting me dead. If I were in power, I'd sentence them to death. I'm not as softhearted as Huang Yida. 'An eye for an eye and a tooth for a tooth.' I would take out each article of law and party discipline and act accordingly and without apology. I long ago prepared myself to fight them to the bitter end to protect Chairman

Mao's revolutionary line. After Chairman Mao passed away in 1976, they imprisoned me for another three years, and on the day they released me after I was exonerated, I rushed over to the county party committee and grabbed that old counterrevolutionary Yang XX, the head of the county special-investigation group, wanting to throw him into the Nanmen River and turn him into turtle food."

As we prepared to leave, Liu Xiangxi suddenly said, "Let me give you another clue: you should go and interview He Xia. That fellow is a reactionary scholar and theoretician, and he has evidence."

"How do you know?"

"Last time [1985] when they held the study sessions at the XX guest house, three leaders from the Task Force, Director Liao, Headmaster Guo, and Secretary Chen, went to get him to confess. He was very arrogant and said he had original records, but he wouldn't hand them over until they arrested him. Now they don't dare arrest him, because they're afraid of what he has. You can go ask him for it."

"If he wasn't willing to hand it over to the Task Force, why would he give it to us?"

Liu Xiangxi smiled and said, "That's not my problem."

The things that Liu Xiangxi said were also in the Task Force's files, but it wasn't enough to designate Xiong Bing'en as the main orchestrator of the Daoxian killings. There was plenty of evidence that Xiong supported the killings, but very little suggesting that he directly ordered them. In our heart of hearts, we secretly hoped that Xiong was the main leader of the Cultural Revolution killings in Daoxian. That would make the matter so simple: the ringleader identified and all the cause and effect wrapped up neatly for presenting the public with a clear and complete answer. Of course, Xiong Bing'en had already been transferred away from Daoxian to serve as assistant director of Lingling Prefecture. We hoped to interview him and hear his side, but he refused. I guess he thought we wanted to interview him as the main behind-the-scenes instigator of the killings, but if so, he was wrong; we didn't bring preconceived assumptions to interviews with anyone, whether members of the Task Force, the family members of victims, or even those involved in the killings. We felt only that if he were willing to talk, it would be more profound and essential than what anyone else could say.

An interview with Red Alliance leader He Xia

The first time we came to Daoxian to carry out our reporting, our plan included interviewing He Xia and other Red Alliance leaders, but because interviewing them presented even-greater difficulties than interviewing Revolutionary Alliance head Liu Xiangxi, they were left for last. When problems arose that resulted in our reporting being suspended midway, our interviews with He Xia and others also went by the wayside. The opportunity to meet He Xia finally came 20 years after my first reporting trip to Daoxian, and 40 years after the killings. By then, He Xia was an old man of 76, and I myself was becoming rather long in the tooth.

He Xia was passing his twilight years in leisurely comfort and indifference to fame. Since retiring as a department head, the orbit of his daily life was simple: after rising in the morning, he would go to the market to buy vegetables and then to Zhou Dunyi Square to exercise, after which he would read the newspaper and watch television to keep up on national current events. Apart from this, his main interest and favorite topic of conversation was maintaining his health. He never talked about what had happened during the Cultural Revolution, and even when asked by leaders of the prefectural and county CCP committees, he always politely declined comment.

During my fourth visit to Daoxian at the end of 2007, I finally made contact with He Xia through the help of a friend who was close to him. However, he would not accept an interview or provide information: this was only a "conversation on topics of mutual interest, as between friends." I felt this suggestion was a good one, because by then interviewing He Xia was no longer so important, and meeting him was merely the fulfillment of a long-cherished wish. I only wanted to hear his observations and thoughts about the social changes over the past 40 years, and whether his views regarding the killings had changed. The Revolutionary Alliance had referred to him as a "hack," a "theoretician," a "reactionary scholar," and a "dog-headed advisor," presumably an indication of his outstanding qualities. I didn't know what considerations had led He Xia to agree to see me, but my wish to see him was as simple as that.

My friend took me to He Xia's home. It was a small, two-story house, spacious and immaculately clean, located along the Lianxi River. He Xia himself lived on the second floor above a little computer school. He came downstairs, opened the heavy security grate, and very graciously invited me to his parlor upstairs.

A diminutive old man less than 1.6 meters tall, he had a kindly and gentle appearance. His eyes, although somewhat clouded, retained the self-confidence of a former department head, and one caught glimpses of the intelligent and capable official he'd once been. He spoke at a moderate pace and in an orderly and logical fashion. His recollection of the Cultural Revolution killings was amazingly clear: names, dates, and places were all accurate.

We sat down as guest and host, exchanged conventional greetings, and eventually parted as friends. Because we both were mentally prepared, I didn't ask what I shouldn't ask, and he didn't talk about what he shouldn't talk about, so the atmosphere was one of mutual understanding.

He Xia first spoke of the killings as he saw them, and although from a different perspective, the basic contours of the process he described differed little from what I knew. Without waiting for me to ask, he took the initiative in talking about his own role during the killings:

> I know there have been a lot of rumors about me, and many petitions by survivors have lumped me together with Zheng Youzhi and Yuan Lifu as a ringleader of the "killing wind." I can responsibly state that I never at any time or any place ordered any killings; rather, on many occasions I gave speeches calling for adherence to the party's policy boundaries that prohibited indiscriminate killing. I also saved people on four occasions: the first time, on the morning of August 28, a cadre from the Yingjiang seed multiplication farm, Wang Shoubo, told me the farm wanted to kill Zeng Mengyun and Zhou Dejun and had already bound them and taken them out. I told Zheng Youzhi to hurry and save them. Zheng Youzhi told Zhang Mingchi, "You're tall and a fast runner, so go with Liao Mingzhong to save them." Zhang Mingzhi yelled as he ran, "Stop the execution! Death sentence suspended for three days!" By the time he got there, Zeng Mengyun had already been blown up with dynamite, but Zhou Dejun was saved. When the three days were up, the poor and lower-middle peasants of the seed multiplication farm went to Zhang Mingchi demanding that he hand Zhou over. Zhang telephoned Zheng Youzhi for instructions. Zheng said, "If they really insist, hand him over but tell them to save on bullets." As a result, Zhou Dejun was ultimately executed.
>
> The second time, on the morning of August 30, it was Wang Shoubo who told me again that the farm wanted to kill its director, Long Yunfu. Having learned a lesson from attempting to save Zhou Dejun, I found a way to have Long Yunfu handed over to me, and his life was saved.
>
> The third time, on the evening of August 29, core members of the Daojiang Town militia had prepared dynamite and rope for an attack on two men in Chengguan Street. When I learned of this, I told them firmly that I wouldn't allow any killing in Daojiang Town, and that anyone killing under any circumstances would be called to account. This not only saved the two men—more important, it prevented Daojiang residents from killing anyone. Once the taboo against killing was broken, who knew how many people would have met with disaster.
>
> The fourth time, on the morning of September 9, Revolutionary Alliance "Rulers of Destiny"[5] commanders Xu Jiayu, Zhou Jiaming, and

another educated youth sent down to Dapingpu Farm were seized by Dapingpu functionaries in the county seat, and after being beaten they were taken back to the farm and locked up in cages in the cotton press machine room, with the intention of killing them. When I heard of the matter, I immediately went to the farm's director, Zhou Yuan'en, and worked on him, saying that they were sent-down educated youth who absolutely could not be killed and must be released right away and given money for treatment of their injuries. After thinking it over for a while, Zhou said they could be released but they wouldn't be given money for medical treatment. I quickly found the farm's driver and asked him to take the three educated youth back to Daojiang overnight, and I took 30 yuan out of my private funds to pay for their medical treatment.

You may not know this, but all the leaders and comrades know that I, He Xia, have always been a moderate in everything I've ever done over the decades. After the Task Force began its work in 1984, it opened a file on me, and the party organization came to talk to me. At the time I took the stand that if they identified any instance in which I directed killings in any place, they should execute me. They carried out repeated investigations, and when they finally reached a formal conclusion, the prefectural party committee sent the county party committee's deputy secretary, comrade Hu Canzheng, to carry out the final interview with me. Secretary Hu said, "Old He, they originally treated you as a focal case, but after repeated inquiries they ascertained that you weren't involved in the killings and even found ways to save people. When so many other county leaders got carried away, only you were a solid moderate."

I wasn't a hothead like Zhang Mingchi and Zheng Youzhi. I've never done anything against party policy. On the night of the battle on August 13, Zhang Mingchi and Zheng Youzhi rounded up more than a thousand militiamen and piled explosives around the enclosing walls of the No. 2 High School, planning to blow it up. I was in a panic thinking how many would be killed—only a few among them were really bad, and all of them were class brothers. I kept trying to dissuade them, but they wouldn't listen, so I ran to the PAFD headquarters and asked them to come forward and put a stop to it. This averted a disaster—you can ask around and confirm this.

At this point I interjected, "Since that's the case, why was everyone pointing the finger at you?" He Xia continued:

That was because of rumors. For example, it's always said that I was political commissar for the Red Alliance—even official documents state this. But in fact, I was never the Red Alliance's political commissar. During the Cultural Revolution, I was just an ordinary cadre in the county party committee's rural work department. When the Cultural Revolution started, I was still in the countryside carrying out "socialist education," and by the time I returned to the county seat, the Cultural Revolution was going full blast. At the direction of the county party committee, I joined the rebel corps of the "Red Warriors," and I served as political commissar for the Fifth Unit of that rebel corps. That's the only capacity in which I served as a political commissar in the Red Alliance. After the Red Alliance headquarters withdrew to Yingjiang and established its frontline command post there, they gave me the official title of deputy political commissar, but the actual people in charge were Zheng Youzhi and Zhong Changyou. My assignment was to take charge of the everyday needs of the Red Alliance masses. When the PAFD's political commissar Liu and Commander Cui arrived in Yingjiang, people always went to them and not to me, and we were never let in on what was said behind closed doors.

The reason I became so well known in Daoxian was because after the January power seizure, the operations of the county party committee organs were suspended for a time. At that time, the Lingling military subdistrict and county PAFD were in charge of Support-the-Left work, and in mid-February, the Lingling military subdistrict's deputy commander Kuang assumed command in Daoxian, establishing two groups: a "seize revolution and push production headquarters" and a "Cultural Revolution office."

The seize-and-push headquarters was under the command of county PAFD political commissar Liu Jinbin, and Xiong Bing'en and another county deputy party secretary, Yu Shan, served as deputy commanders. The Cultural Revolution office, due to a failure to reach consensus among various conflicting parties, wasn't formally established until April 20. County PAFD commander Cui Baoshu was director, and I was first deputy director, with a Revolutionary Alliance member named Zhou Donglin serving as second deputy director. Originally both sides had agreed on this, but the Revolutionary Alliance went back on its word, and as soon as the office was established, the streets were plastered with posters calling for me to be unseated, saying I was Shi Xiuhua's proxy and Daoxian's biggest royalist. They also organized people to attack the Cultural Revolution office and smashed up its sign. Less than a week after it was established, the Cultural Revolution office was forced to disband, so I served as first deputy director for less than a week. After the Cultural Revolution office was disbanded, Cui Baoshu called a meeting of the leaders of all of Daojiang's Red Alliance organizations and said that the Cultural Revolution office couldn't be established, and the Red Alliance hadn't set up a headquarters, so from now on comrade He Xia would be convener of the Red Alliance, and that the PAFD's views would be communicated through comrade He Xia. In that way I was transformed into a Red Alliance leader without portfolio, and that's how the county came to know that there was a person named He Xia.

"From what I understand, the main leaders of the Red Alliance Frontline Command Post in Yingjiang all were PAFD commanders of various districts," I said. "What was their relationship with the Red Alliance?"

"They could be considered members of the Red Alliance. They joined the Red Alliance collectively under orders from the county PAFD headquarters. . . . After they joined the Red Alliance, they naturally took over its leadership. After the Frontline Command Post was established in Yingjiang, it replaced the Red Alliance headquarters."

"I see. Director He, as someone who experienced the Cultural Revolution in Daoxian, in your view, what was the main reason the killing wind emerged there?"

"There are six main reasons, and I discussed all of them with the Task Force as well as with the leaders of the prefectural and county party committees. The first was the Revolutionary Alliance's gun-snatching incident on August 8, which sent shock waves through the whole county." He Xia sounded as if he'd spent a lot of time thinking about this question.

"Gun-snatching incidents were widespread throughout China during the Cultural Revolution," I interjected. "Why didn't massacres result from gun snatchings in other counties?"

"Don't be in such a hurry, and listen to what I have to say! After the August 8 gun snatching, the PAFD gave off the wrong signal. At that time, the county PAFD headquarters designated the August 8 gun snatching as a counterrevolutionary coup d'état by the class enemy and an attempted takeover by black elements. The poor and lower-middle peasants became very anxious, truly believing that black elements were planning an overthrow. After hearing this news on August 9, I immediately ran to the county PAFD headquarters to learn more. I saw Commander Cui Baoshu in his room, and he was very upset, actually crying, and he told me a lot of things, the gist of which was that this gun-snatching incident was class enemies organizing and planning a counterrevolutionary coup d'état, and he wanted us to organize the poor and lower-middle peasants and revolutionary masses to defend the Red regime. While we were talking, people arrived from the Revolutionary Alliance. Many of the guns they'd taken didn't have firing pins, so they'd run back to the PAFD to get them.

Commander Cui lowered the mosquito net and had me hide in his bed while he went to deal with them. At that time, everything was very simple and crude, and the PAFD office was right outside Commander Cui Baoshu's bedroom, a very large room furnished with many tables where everyone was squeezed together working. I hid in the bed and listened to them negotiate outside. I stayed there until the Revolutionary Alliance people left."

"Did they give the firing pins to the Revolutionary Alliance?" I asked, already knowing the answer.

"Yes. The Revolutionary Alliance people took them from the ceiling of the PAFD headquarters."

"How did they know the firing pins were stored in the ceiling?"

"There must have been a traitor in the PAFD."

The second reason He Xia gave was the 47th Army's "Cable on the Social Situation" being misconstrued to encourage further killing of "troublemakers." The third was the "tense situation of class struggle" in Daoxian and the discovery of counterrevolutionary organizations and KMT [Kuomintang] agents operating in the county.

"But I hear all these were bogus cases," I pointed out.

"Bogus? They may have been exaggerated, but it's not possible that they all were bogus! I personally saw some of those reactionary leaflets defaming Chairman Mao and the Communist Party, and the language was truly venomous. Some of them are still on file at the Public Security Bureau."

"All right. And the fourth reason?"

"The fourth reason was the influence of Left-deviating thinking. Class struggle had long been a guiding principle under the interference and sabotage of Lin Biao and the Gang of Four, and it had become absolute. The truth taken a step further becomes error. The fifth reason was that the public-security, procuratorial, and judicial organs were in ruins, and the legal system had been severely compromised. The sixth reason was that rumors were circulating everywhere that the class enemies had organized 'black killing squads' and were planning an uprising, that they wanted to kill the poor and lower-middle peasants and Communist Party members. Some cadres and masses didn't make inquiries in accordance with party policy but instead took extreme measures that resulted in the killing getting out of control."

After hearing He Xia list out the six reasons, I couldn't help laughing inwardly. How ludicrously naive I'd been to hope for even the slightest expression of regret! It was too difficult to change a person's thinking. Likewise, a nation's advancement requires the untiring effort of generations of people over a very long time frame. Many matters simply cannot be turned around by those who were involved. Repentance, like democracy and science, requires genuine study and effort on the part of the Chinese people as a whole.

I decided to put my question in more-concrete terms: "Director He, what responsibility do you feel Xiong Bing'en should bear for the killing wind in Daoxian? He's dead now, so this isn't a matter of calling him to account but rather of rethinking the question." This is what I'd wanted to ask him 20 years earlier.

"He doesn't bear a great deal of responsibility, in my opinion. If he's to be blamed for anything, it's for his ambiguous attitude."

"When the leader of a county takes an ambiguous attitude toward what's going on in his jurisdiction, shouldn't he bear responsibility for what happens as a result?"

"From our present perspective, what you say is absolutely correct. But the Cultural Revolution created a special situation. Comrade journalist, you experienced the Cultural Revolution, so you should know what I mean."

"Can we say that Xiong Bing'en sympathized with and supported the killings?"

After being immersed in thought for a long time, He Xia said, "You could say that. In the situation of that time, a person's attitude was determined by the position he was in. Xiong Bing'en wasn't the only one in the county party leadership who maintained that attitude at that time; you could say the vast majority held basically the same views. The 'killing wind' had its fortuitous and inevitable aspects. This can be seen from the way that it drew in so many party members and cadres, and from the way that once the killings began in Daoxian, they spread to surrounding counties and towns. Surely it can't be said that someone in the prefectural party committee gave the order? This is a historical tragedy and the inevitable result of expanding the scope of class struggle. It couldn't be bent by human will; no one person could give the word to start the killings, and no one could end them just by saying so."

I asked, "So who do you think bears the greatest responsibility?"

I expected him to say Zheng Youzhi, and didn't expect his swift and straightforward reply: "the PAFD headquarters."

"What makes you say that?"

"Comrade journalist, I can see you're very well informed about the killing wind. Tell me, which district or commune had killings that weren't carried out through the PAFD? At that time, they were the ones who had the say in Daoxian. As for people such as us, whether we wanted people killed or didn't want people killed, what could we actually do about it?"

At this point I suddenly recalled the clue that Liu Xiangxi had given me years earlier, so I tossed out my last question: "I hear you still have some original records of meetings that were held back then."

He Xia was immediately put on guard: "Comrade journalist, didn't we agree not to talk about this kind of thing?"

I knew that I was in the wrong, and fearing that I would cause problems for my go-between, I quickly smiled and changed the subject. We talked about some irrelevant matters, and sensing there was nothing left to be said, I stood and took my leave.

Leaving He Xia's home, I strolled to Zhou Dunyi Square, a new landmark construction in Daoxian, situated on the west bank of the Xiaoshui River and with a concrete bridge leading to Xizhou Park in the middle of the river. The square was immense and paved with granite, and a granite statue of Zhou Dunyi towered more than 20 meters high in the middle of the square. This was Daoxian's busiest spot, filled with elderly people early in the morning, swarming with people going about their daily business during the daylight hours, and at night becoming a sea of gleaming neon, music, and dancing. Daojiang is rather strange that way—a small county town that no one talks about much, so tranquil and carefree, can give such a sense of radiating vitality. Leaning on a carved stone railing, I looked down at the Xiaoshui River flowing peacefully below my feet. Ever since knowing its story, I never came to Daoxian without walking along this river and sitting and gazing at it as if visiting an old friend, but a visit that produced agitated feelings, like weeping without tears. The river was always calm, rippling, and silent, but at night, when people were at home resting, if you came quietly up alongside it, you could hear its labored panting.

I suddenly recalled something that happened in 1988. That year, a publishing house in Beijing expressed strong interest in this historical record and wanted to publish it but needed to confirm the veracity of its contents, so the publisher sent two editors, Yue Jianyi and Huang Xiaozhong, to accompany me to Daoxian. Arriving at noon, we stopped at a small restaurant at the end of town. This little restaurant specialized in wild game, and coming from Beijing, Xiao Yue and Xiao Huang had little opportunity to eat such food, so we ordered platters of pheasant, bamboo rat, catfish, smoked pork, and wild mushrooms, as well as a flask of warm rice wine, taking our time to enjoy the feast. Pointing to the plate of fish, Xiao Yue jokingly asked me, "Did this fish ever eat human flesh?" I said, "If it had, it would have become immortal by now." We ate and drank and joked together, but Xiao Yue and Xiao Huang kept glancing sideways at the people who hustled along the road. I knew they were thinking the same thing I had thought when I first came to Daoxian, trying to see how people here were different from those anywhere else.

Across the road was a supply-and-marketing cooperative, where a peasant in his 50s was carrying a load of bamboo products to sell. After the peasant was paid for his wares, he took his money to the cooperative's sales counter, where he bought a bowl of liquor and a packet of crispy snacks and sat on the steps of the cooperative to enjoy them while basking in the sun. It was winter, but the temperature wasn't very cold, in the mid-40s, and the peasant was wearing unlined trousers and an unbuttoned old quilted jacket, squinting in the sunlight as he snacked. Once the liquor put him in a good mood, he began crooning to himself.

Xiao Huang asked me, "Do you think that old guy knows about the killings?"

Looking at the peasant, I said, "On the basis of his age, I'd say he not only knows about them but personally experienced them."

"Do you think he's related to a victim, or that he was one of the killers?"

"That's hard to say. But seeing him so happy and pleased with himself, I'd say he's unlikely to be a surviving family member."

"Can I go ask him?"

"Of course!"

Carrying his bowl of wine, Xiao Huang crossed the road and struck up a conversation with the old peasant. Suddenly he stood up, walked to in the middle of the road, and cried up toward heaven, "The wretched ignorance!"

We were more than a little startled.

When Xiao Huang came back, I asked him what had happened. He said, "I asked him if he knew what happened during the Cultural Revolution. He said he knew. I asked if anyone had been killed in his village, and he said yes. I asked who had been killed. He said it was class enemies and bad guys. I asked how they were killed and he said they were dragged out and stabbed. I asked if it was right to kill them and he said yes. . . ."

Now, pulling my gaze back from the Xiaoshui River, I turned toward the square and watched people walking back and forth, and the thought suddenly occurred to me: if I went up to someone right now and asked them about the Daoxian killings, how would they respond? I knew this was a taboo topic in Daoxian, but I couldn't restrain the impulse to do it just as Xiao Huang had done years ago.

I purposely selected a fairly young man wearing fashionable glasses, and intercepting him I asked, "Excuse me, but during the Cultural Revolution, there were mass killings here, and I was wondering if you knew about it."

He looked at me and said, "I know about it. Everyone in Daoxian knows about it."

"Are you clear about how the killings happened?"

"Not too clear. I wasn't born when it happened."

"Do you think that during that particular historical period, it was reasonable to kill people this way?"

"It wasn't reasonable. It's never reasonable to kill people." He looked at me and asked, "What is it you want? Why are you asking these questions?"

I said, "I came here on a trip, and when I heard about this matter I was curious."

He said, "It happened decades ago. It's hard to be clear about what happened at that time, and people don't like to talk about it now. It's a disgrace to us here in Daoxian."

The young man's words made me somewhat heavy-hearted. Since my reporting in 1986, I had come to Daoxian three more times, and it seemed different each time. This county town was changing too much too quickly, and so were its people. If this young man were transplanted to a big city such as Changsha or Beijing or even a coastal city such as Shanghai or Shenzhen, he wouldn't stand out in a crowd. Still, a thought lingered in my mind and was hard to dispel: if one day some senior official called for the killing of China's newly regenerated bourgeoisie, would people respond to the call with another bloodbath?

Anything that could occur on such a grand scale could not possibly die out so easily.

It takes personal awakening and historical enlightenment to allow a nation to leave behind its wicked propensities and tragic disposition. This can't be avoided, nor is there a shortcut.

After my reporting trip to Daoxian in 1986, I didn't write poetry for a very long time, but after interviewing He Xia, I wrote this poem at Zhou Dunyi Square:

> The branch bears less fruit
> But it's sweeter,
> My mind bears more fruit
> But more bitter,
> Love's wasteland has no seasons,
> Harvest songs are always sung
> Toward the horizon
> I have the patience to wait,
> To wait
> For when the ancient lotus blooms.

32

The Petitioners

Although the killings ended, a new saga began for survivors who were determined to obtain justice for their murdered family members. Among them was a woman whose family was among the last victims of the killing wind at Dapingpu Farm, and whose fate intersected with that of a young boy orphaned in the killings in Futian Commune's Dongyang production brigade.

The killings at Daoxian's Dapingpu Farm started with a poster of a Mao quote. While the killing wind was blowing throughout Daoxian's countryside in late August 1967, no one had been killed here yet, because "educated youth" who had been "sent down to the countryside" were under a separate administrative jurisdiction. Even so, a former "educated youth" who had been sent down to Dapingpu at the time told us, "The killings in the communes around us stirred up calls at our farm to kill people. Without a concrete directive, no one made a move right away, but we were like a pile of kindling waiting for someone to strike a match."

That match was finally struck after the Red Alliance's defeat in the armed confrontation on August 30. After the Red Alliance lost its turf in Yingjiang, Zheng Youzhi and the other leaders led the militia's withdrawal to Qingtang, but, still feeling vulnerable, Zheng Youzhi called a meeting of district People's Armed Forces Department (PAFD) commanders at Dapingpu Farm and decided to establish a militia contingent at the No. 3 High School in Shouyan, from which they could stage attacks but also retreat to Guangxi's Guanyang County. After the meeting, Zheng Youzhi sought out the director of the Dapingpu Farm to gain an understanding of local battle-readiness, and found it sorely lacking. Zheng warned, "If you don't kill a few troublemakers, you're going to have big problems later." After discussion, they decided to puncture the arrogance of the class enemy by "suppressing" a counterrevolutionary named Xie Zhishang, who had once been a medical officer in the Kuomintang Army (although subsequently serving in the Korean War as a People's Liberation Army [PLA] medical officer), and a counterrevolutionary offspring named Yu Zhen'e.

That very day, one of the revolutionary masses had discovered a Mao quote poster in the latrine, and the entire farm exploded in outrage; this action constituted at least two major crimes: the crime of "current counterrevolution" and the crime of "venomously attacking the Great Leader," either of which could draw a death sentence. The farm's Red Alliance immediately organized a search for the culprit, and suspicion ultimately fell on Xie Zhishang's 11-year-old son. The inference was that Xie had instructed his son to throw the poster into the toilet as a means of venting his deep-seated hatred toward Chairman Mao. In accordance with this logic, Xie Zhishang, his wife, and their son and second daughter all were taken into custody. The eldest daughter, Xie Shuxiang, who had been crippled by polio as a child, was spared, since she had already married by then and lived in Daojiang, and the two younger daughters, aged 16 and 13, were "treated with leniency." The condemned family members were taken to the hillside behind the farm and blown to smithereens with dynamite, along with a young doctor, Yu Zhen'e, who apart from his problematic family background was allegedly a member of the Revolutionary Alliance.

Xie Zhishang's surviving eldest daughter, Xie Shuxiang, was mentioned many times in the course of our interviews and was referred to as Big Sister Xie. This frail and crippled woman, repeatedly battered by fate, spent years petitioning government departments in Yongzhou, Changsha, and Beijing demanding justice for her parents, sister, and brother. She was like a little drop of water constantly dripping from an eaves onto a solid rock foundation, sustained by the conviction that there must be some kind of justice in this world. Her husband, a simple and kindly ceramics factory worker, didn't completely understand his wife's actions, but he silently gave her his full support even as her ceaseless petitioning drove the family ever further into penury. In order to bring in more money, Big Sister Xie operated a book rental stall next to the long-distance bus station across from the No. 2 High School. This stall became a meeting place for family members of victims who came to the county seat on business or to petition. Naturally it also attracted the close surveillance of the Daoxian public-security bureau and letters-and-visits office.

At her book rental stall, Big Sister Xie became acquainted with a street kid who foraged around the bus station. This was Liang Yueming from Futian Commune's Dongyang brigade, whom I mentioned in chapter 10 in connection with the killing of his father, mother, and aunt, when as a toddler he was left to the care of his 46-year-old grandmother. His grandmother remarried a worker at the Daojiang Shipping Company surnamed Jiang, and Liang took his step-grandfather's surname. Jiang Yueming, as he was now known, grew up in Daojiang bereft of the love and discipline of his parents, an "artful dodger" who eventually gained a criminal record as a thief. Mencius believed that people are born good, while Xunzi believed they are born evil, but neither of these absolutist philosophies can fully explain the complexity of life. Although people have the power to choose the road they take, fate also plays a role.

Big Sister Xie was very sympathetic toward Jiang Yueming and treated him like her own son. While not insensible to the boy's vices, she was firmly convinced that he would go straight. Jiang Yueming once told someone, "No one in this world has been as good to me as Big Sister Xie," and I'm sure this was true.

In March 1985, more than 80 family members of victims of the Daoxian massacre secretly planned to travel together to Beijing to petition the authorities, setting Shuinan Village as their gathering place. But the Daoxian Public Security Bureau (PSB) got wind of their plans and staged a roundup the day before, with a dozen leading members, including Big Sister Xie, arrested and prosecuted. Big Sister Xie was sentenced to two years of reeducation through labor but was released after eight months. Following her release, she heard that Jiang Yueming had been the PSB's "earphone," but she adamantly refused to believe it.

Of all the surviving family members in Daoxian, Big Sister Xie and Jiang Yueming were the people I most hoped to interview, but because of the trouble they'd been in, I didn't dare approach them. When I visited Daoxian a third time in 2006, I learned that Big Sister Xie had become ill and died. Meanwhile, Jiang Yueming had managed to turn his life around, owning a small business and driving a Chery sedan.

Master petitioner Li Niande

While I never got to meet Big Sister Xie, I eventually established contact with an even more notoriously intractable petitioning family member who led others on petitioning drives. Reading through his file, I learned that he had petitioned Deng Xiaoping regarding 76 major cases from the killing wind, that he had posted an antithetical couplet on the injustices of the era at the entrance of the State Council's Office of Letters and Visits, and that he had waylaid the limousine of the provincial Chinese Communist Party (CCP) secretary, Mao Zhiyong, at the entrance to the Hunan provincial CCP committee's office building in order to make his complaint. . . . In sum, he was not considered a law-abiding citizen.

I'd wanted to interview Li Niande right from the outset, but well-meaning people warned me off. A leading comrade from the Task Force who had provided enormous support to our reporting opposed the suggestion outright: "This man is very cunning and knows how to use policy loopholes to go around petitioning. It's taken an enormous effort to get him settled down, and if you interview him now, he could get the wrong idea and trigger another mass petitioning incident."

In any case, we had the investigation file on the killing of Li Niande's 13 family members, so a face-to-face interview wasn't essential. But as it turned out, I encountered Li Niande by chance at the home of a friend during my third visit to Daoxian in 2006. By then Li had a family and had become a lawyer, and he cut an imposing figure with gray hair that he didn't bother to dye. "My hair went completely gray 20 years ago," he told me. It turned out that for all his petitioning, Li knew no more about the specifics of his family members' deaths than I did as an outsider. This was not unusual, however; very few of the survivors we interviewed were able to describe the circumstances of their family members' deaths.

Li Niande fled Daoxian right at the outset of the killings, when he was 21 years old. While in Daojiang on business in August 1967, Li had learned from an old classmate that black elements were starting to be killed in the villages, and he relayed the news to his parents after returning home. Killings had started in Shouyan and their own Yangjia Commune at the time, but the news hadn't spread, and Li's parents were skeptical. As one of the commune's less well-behaved black-element offspring, however, Li was nervous and proposed going into hiding for a while, and his parents finally agreed that it made sense. Early the next morning, Li Niande left Jinshi'an Village with 40 yuan his parents had given him.

Li Niande made his way to Jiangyong County's Taochuan Township, which had a dozen brick-and-tile factories requiring large quantities of firewood. Collecting firewood from the hillsides was hard work, and most who did it were people from poor areas who were trying to make some extra money. Young and strong, Li Niande built himself a thatch shack and supported himself by collecting firewood for the kilns.

About 10 days after Li Niande left, the killings began in his brigade. On August 22, 1967, at the height of the "double rush" planting and harvesting, Li Niande's father, Li Guangwei, as well as his two uncles and a cousin, were executed along with three other men. A week later, on August 29, the brigade began "eliminating roots and branches" by killing nine more members of Li Niande's extended family, including his mother, Wang Manzhen. This was the very day that the PLA 47th Army's 6950 Unit entered Daoxian and held its telephone conference ordering a halt to the killings, but by the time the order reached the Jinshi'an brigade, the death sentences had been pronounced. "Tell the commune that we've already killed them," said the brigade's poor-peasant association (PPA) chairman, Liu Daixiu, and he ordered the militiamen to take the condemned out and kill them quickly, saying, "If we're blamed, I'll take responsibility."

After the killings, the Jinshi'an brigade established a movable-property disposal group headed by accountant He Xiuwen, and they ransacked all the belongings of the murdered families. That night, the brigade's leaders held a feast in the brigade hall to celebrate their victory.

A total of 19 people died in the Jinshi'an brigade during the killing wind, including two who committed suicide. Among the 17 people who were murdered, 13 were members of Li Niande's family, including all of the family's men except for Li himself. Li's remaining family consisted of his two sisters and a female cousin. For Li Niande, the only remaining male descendant, real suffering had just begun.

A mansion and a family's fate

What kind of family could bring on this kind of annihilation? A famous architect once said, "A building is a piece of history." We can observe the rise and fall of the Li family through its mansion in Jinshi'an Village.

Li Mansion was built by Li Niande's grandfather, a doctor of traditional Chinese medicine, who, while the richest man in Jinshi'an, ranked much lower in Yangjia Township and lower yet in Simaqiao District, not even making the grade for Daoxian as a whole. Dr. Li built the house around 1941 with a bereavement pension awarded to his third son, who had laid down his life resisting the Japanese invasion at Lugou Bridge on July 7, 1937. It was the largest residence in all of Jinshi'an Village at the time, standing out like a Daozhou gray goose in a flock of ducks. By the time I visited in 2006, however, it was woefully shabby and dwarfed by several new concrete and red-brick villas that had been built around it. Now it housed only pigs and cattle and a single human occupant, the former brigade PPA chairman, Liu Daixiu. Some said Li Mansion was a haunted house and that anyone who lived there was jinxed. Liu Daixiu was not afraid, however. He said, "Screw that! I've been through enough that the worst that can happen to me now is death, and that would be almost a relief."

Calling it a haunted house was reasonable enough, given that most of the people who lived there came to a bad end. Reportedly, when Dr. Li built the house, he had a geomancer come to check out the *feng shui*, so it's hard to know the exact source of the family's woes. During Land Reform in 1951, most of Li Mansion was divided up among several of the village's poor peasant families, leaving just some side rooms for the Li family. Li Niande's grandmother was beaten to death during a denunciation rally, and his second uncle was killed along with an aunt.

Doctor Li, an old man by then, was spared because of his medical skills, and when the Lijia Commune Health Clinic was established, Dr. Li was employed there along with his son Li Guangwai (Li Niande's father), who served as his apprentice. However, the family still wore the landlord label, so even working in the health clinic they were considered to be serving penal labor under surveillance and had to keep their heads down and their tails between their legs.

When the Great Famine struck Daoxian in 1960, Dr. Li drowned himself in the Gongba River after being humiliated while trying to buy some meat.

Somehow the rest of the Li family made it through the famine, but during the Socialist Education movement in 1964, Li Guangwei and his wife were purged from the health clinic and sent back to their village, where they once more took up residence in the side rooms of Li Mansion.

In spite of their grim circumstances, the Li family seemed to have an innate ability to take root even in the rockiest soil and lived nearly as well as anyone else—right until the family was largely wiped out during the killing wind of August 1967.

The poor peasant families who were allotted portions of Li Mansion during Land Reform enjoyed no better fates. It goes without saying that some died of starvation during the Great Famine, but even in ordinary times they were scarcely better off than Li Niande's family. Former PPA chairman Liu Daixiu was eventually sentenced to 10 years in prison on February 3, 1986, for killing nine members of Li Niande's family. Liu's crime was exacerbated by the fact that he'd carried out the killings after being explicitly directed not to, and Li Niande had ensured that Liu Daixiu wouldn't fall through the cracks, filing complaints at the highest possible level so that even the leader sent by the Central Committee to inspect the Task Force's operations had asked after the matter. Liu Daixiu had to be sentenced, and his sentence could not be too light.

I can say with confidence that Liu Daixiu truly bore enormous culpability, but there were many people like him in Daoxian, and few served any prison time, while Liu was handed the heaviest prison sentence of all of them. No wonder Liu Daixiu hated Li Niande so much and stamped his feet and beat his breast while saying, "It's too bad we didn't kill all of them. Then the government wouldn't have to pay compensation to anyone, and I wouldn't have gone to prison." He accepted his sentence calmly, however: "I'm not as bad as some who were involved in all kinds of dirty dealings for personal gain. I killed people to defend Chairman Mao and the Red regime, and to be imprisoned for that is an honor."

In 1994, after growing vegetables in a Hengyang Prison for eight years, Liu Daixiu was released early for good behavior, but he was expelled from the CCP and barred from any further role in village affairs. From then on, Liu Daixiu lost his erect bearing and resonant voice. His wife left him for another man, and his sons became estranged from him. The poverty that had plagued the family for three generations extended through another two. Liu Daixiu was left to pass a hard and lonely existence in Li Mansion. The Lijia Township government established an old folk's home for unsupported elderly people, but since Liu Daixiu had two sons, he didn't qualify for aid. Fortunately, Liu was used to hardship and was still fit and able, so he didn't let his problems get to him, but his hatred of Li Niande only grew. He said, "I'm in no hurry. Let him enjoy himself now. Next time the higher-ups call for killing, the first one I kill will be him!"

Rise of a master petitioner

The place where Li Niande settled in Yaochuan, Jiangyong County, was called Liushigong, and as it happened, another person from Yangjia Commune was also working there and reported him to the commune. The brigade sent men to apprehend Li Niande and bring him back, but the head of the Liushigong brigade brick kiln refused to hand Li over. Although Jiangyong County had also been influenced by Daoxian and was also killing black elements, the situation was less serious, and in remote areas such as Yaochuan, almost no one was being killed.

Li Niande was hard-working, honest, and nimble, and the brick kiln head thought well of him, so he told Li Niande that someone had come for him and also that his family had been killed. Li Niande was shocked and terrified, but he didn't know where to go, so he decided to stay and work until it came time to pay his wages. He remained on the alert, however, and when people came again from the Jinshi'an brigade, he managed to escape into the Dupangling Hills and travel by bus to Guilin. In Guilin he took a train to Beijing.

Li Niande had an uncle, Li Guanglun, who had been a low-level cadre in the Beijing Railway Department but was now relegated to cleaning toilets at Yongdingmen Station, near Beijing's Temple of Heaven. Li Guanglun was shocked when his nephew burst into his home, and gaped in horror when Li Niande told him what had happened back at home. The uncle and nephew decided that what was going on in Daoxian couldn't possibly be in accordance with CCP policies, so Li Niande wrote out a formal complaint and took it to the Central Cultural Revolution Small Group reception office to report the problem. When the PLA comrade at the reception office saw this landlord whelp who'd dared to file a complaint against the poor and lower-middle peasants, he flushed with anger and roared, "Get the hell out of here!" When Li Niande didn't move fast enough, the man kicked him out the door.

Li Niande managed to make his way back to his uncle's home, and when Li Guanglun heard what had happened, he bowed his head and said nothing. From then on, the two of them had a tacit understanding never to mention what had happened in Daoxian.

After several days, Li Niande saw that he couldn't stay with his uncle much longer, and when he proposed leaving, his uncle silently bought him a ticket for Lengshuitan. The household registration system made it impossible to do anything without a certificate issued by his local CCP organization. However vast the world might be, Li Niande could only go home to Daoxian.

By the time Li Niande circled back to Daoxian, the killing wind had subsided, but Li still didn't dare return to Jinshi'an. Recalling an uncle at the Yueyan Tree

Farm with whom the family had lost contact, Li sought him out. The uncle knew about the killings, so he was very sympathetic to his nephew and helped him find temporary work planting pines on the hills. Li Niande had finally found a place to settle down.

In October of his second year at the tree farm (1968), Li Niande had reason to go to Daojiang, and while there he ran into Old He, whom he knew from working on the Jinshi'an road repair team. Old He was a "historical counterrevolutionary," so Li Niande immediately clasped his hand and asked about his family's circumstances. Old He told him that his two sisters were still alive, and he invited him to a small restaurant for a bowl of noodles. While the noodles were cooking, Old He said he had to go out for a minute and Li Niande said he'd wait for him. But the next person who came through the door was an inspector with the county public-security bureau. After confirming Li Niande's identity, the inspector pulled a rope from behind his back and said, "You're under arrest."

Li Niande was taken to the PSB's temporary custody center and placed in a cell designed for 4 people but now holding at least 20. There was only about a foot of space for each person, and the most recent arrival had to sleep next to the waste bucket in the corner. Fortunately, Li Niande was willing to sleep anywhere. Meals consisted of 280 grams of rice each day, but inmates confined to the cells had to give up 30 grams of their ration to those who worked outside.

After a few days in these conditions, the military policeman in charge of the custody center called Li Niande to his office and asked, "What crime did you commit?"

Li Niande said, "I don't know." He explained how he had come to be arrested, but before he could finish, the supervisor said, "All right, that's enough. Tomorrow you'll start carrying water."

Few places in Daoxian had running water at that time, and all the water used at the custody center had to be carried from the Xiaoshui River. Li Niande considered this a stroke of luck: not only would he get a double portion of rice, but he'd be able to enjoy the comforts of the outdoors instead of spending all day and night in the stench of the cell.

After Li had spent a month fetching water for the custody center, the supervisor called him into his office and said, "You can go home."

Li Niande said, "I don't want to go home. I like it here, and if I go back I might be killed."

The supervisor said, "This isn't a hotel where you can stay as long as you want. If you're unwilling to go home, I'll have to take you to the detention center."

That's how Li Niande came to spend 17 months in prison. He was offered release on two occasions but refused to leave, having come to find life in the detention center much more congenial than outside. Here all he needed to do was bow and scrape to a few guards, while he could be as arrogant as he liked to others, and by the end he was even allowed to serve as team leader.

One day in March 1970, the new county PAFD commander and county CCP secretary, Chen Fengguo, came to inspect the detention center, and he mobilized Li Niande to return to his production team. Li Niande raised three demands: (1) not to be killed, (2) to be given a grain ration, and (3) not to be publicly denounced.

Chen Fengguo laughed and said, "I can guarantee you all three. But you have to promise to work hard in production and reform your thinking and not go running off."

Chen Fengguo was as good as his word and immediately assigned two militiamen to escort Li Niande back to Simaqiao, where in accordance with Secretary Chen's instructions, district government secretary Yan wrote a letter of introduction for Li Niande to take back to Jinshi'an.

I'll summarize Li Niande's return to Jinshi'an Village with a passage from one of Li's own petitions: "They said I 'attacked the newborn Red regime' and 'opposed the proletarian headquarters.' I was beaten four times until I spit up blood, my left arm was broken, and my skull was fractured. I was diagnosed with post-traumatic brain injury, and I'm now disabled."

In April 1974, when the production brigade planned another public denunciation, Li Niande fled once again, making a living through manual labor and as an "illegal medical practitioner."

In 1979, the CCP held the Third Plenum of its Eleventh Central Committee, and order was brought out of chaos throughout China. Li Niande took a train to Beijing and began his long and arduous career as a petitioner in hopes of gaining justice for his dead family members. He became the most famous petitioner in Daoxian.

In winter 1981, as Beijing lay covered in snow, the vagrant Li Niande, suffering from hunger and exposure, posted an antithetical couplet on the door of the State Council's Letters and Visits Office:

> Another year sighing in regret, hair gray and still a bachelor, with no shelter in the dead of winter, alas!
> Sleeping in the streets half my life, only my shadow for company as I petition, with no department accepting my complaint, alack!

The couplet remained on the door of the Letters and Visits Office for four days.

In early 1982, Li Niande was taken into custody and repatriated to Daoxian. Near Gongba Bridge he ran into Teacher Xu, a Rightist he'd met in the detention center in 1968. The two men were ecstatic to find each other alive. In particular, Teacher Xu had already been near 50 while in prison, and his constitution was weak, making it hard for him to adjust to the prison rules, so he'd been constantly punished with kneeling and being beaten more than anyone else, his four limbs numb and nearly paralyzed. The prison provided no medical treatment, but Li Niande had pitied him and used his knowledge of traditional Chinese medicine, massaging him every day. Discussing their experience since prison made both men break down weeping. Teacher Xu had been slightly more fortunate in having his Rightist cap removed during the rehabilitation campaign and receiving his teacher's salary again. The two sat alongside the road and talked for more than two hours, and during this conversation, Li Niande became aware of two problems: first, Daoxian's killing wind was not a batch of scattered killings but a complete historical incident, and if the problem of the killing wind wasn't resolved, no individual cases of justice could be resolved. Likewise in the case of "Rightists," the entire issue had to be addressed; otherwise, those whose Rightist caps were removed were still "rehabilitated Rightists." Second, if the Communist Party continued to regard class struggle as its guiding principle, it would be impossible to resolve the issue of the killing wind. If the Communist Party was to truly focus on building the economy, the issue of the killing wind must be resolved.

After returning home, the minimally educated peasant Li Niande took up his pen, and by the light of an oil lamp he wrote a letter to the vice chairman of the CCP Central Committee, Deng Xiaoping, asking the Central Committee to investigate the Daoxian massacre and prosecute its perpetrators in accordance with law. Li listed dozens of cases. That same year, hundreds of family members of victims went in a group to Beijing to "cry out their grievance and file their complaints."

The petitions were the "straw that broke the camel's back" as pressure mounted to investigate the killing wind. In March 1968, the 47th Army's 6950 Unit and the Daoxian Revolutionary Committee had conducted its "exposure and study session," but the investigation work came to a premature end, and most of those involved came under attack in varying degrees. In 1974, the Daoxian county CCP committee had carried out a token handling of a small number of criminal cases, but the killings were still largely defined as revolutionary actions that followed the correct general orientation. Then, in winter 1978, Lingling prefectural CCP secretary Deng Youzhi led a small task force deep into Daoxian to carry out investigations and submitted an investigation report to the provincial CCP committee. This was followed by visits to Hunan by two native sons, CCP general secretary Hu Yaobang and Chief Justice Jiang Hua. In 1982, the petitions Li Niande and others wrote were included in the agenda of the Chinese People's Political Consultative Conference. The Task Force to Deal with the Aftermath of the Cultural Revolution Killings was formed two years later.

33

Change of Plans

As our reporting progressed, we experienced an encounter with petitioners such as Li Niande that impressed on us the risk we were taking and indirectly precipitated the end of our reporting. The world is like that—things go so smoothly at first that you become complacent and expect it to continue right through to the end, but in fact it's just a snare and a delusion.

When we had been reporting for three weeks or so, we came back to our guest house after interviews in a village and had barely had time to catch our breaths in our room when we heard someone knock. When we opened the door, a dozen or so people surged in—men and women, old and young, filling our small room to bursting. At first we couldn't figure out who these people were and nervously asked, "Who are you looking for?"

One of the men[1] replied, "We're family members of victims of the killing wind and we want to report to the leaders." The others then pulled out their own petitions and chorused, "Please, leaders, resolve these for us!"

Zhang Minghong and I asked them to sit down on the bed and tell us everything slowly, but when they saw there wasn't enough room, they insisted on standing: "Leaders, you should sit. We're used to standing."

I was at a loss over what to do. On the one hand, interviewing the family members of victims had been one of our greatest desires all along, but we'd never gained access to them, so wasn't this a heaven-sent opportunity to have so many seek us out? To interview them here and now and listen to what they'd experienced during the massacre, to see through their eyes what things were like at the time, would be so meaningful! On the other hand, interviewing them under these circumstances might result in our reporting being forcibly halted, and even in our losing everything we'd done up to now. We had no chance to consider the options or confer with each other, however.

I explained to them, "You're mistaken. We're not leaders, just ordinary reporters. We have no power to intervene in the Task Force's cases, or any power to resolve them."

To our amazement, one family member said, "Please don't be so modest! We heard early on that you're a senior official from the province. They say that Liu Shaoqi's son sent you."

I couldn't help but recall an incident several days earlier, while we were in Simaqiao, and a village cadre had challenged me to my face: "Are you really reporters for the Communist Party? Who cares if a few black elements got killed? They got killed during Land Reform and no one said anything about it. The killing was a little more chaotic this time, but the government has already paid compensation and rehabilitated them, so what more do they have to say about it? Why do you feel you have to speak up for class enemies?"

I'd never spoken a word on behalf of landlords and rich peasants but had merely asked this cadre what kind of people had been killed, who proposed killing them, how they were killed, and what crimes they'd been accused of, and the cadre had drawn his own conclusions. The truth was that I'd begun reconsidering the entire Land Reform movement by then, seeing it as part of the theoretical foundation of Daoxian's killing wind, but the very thought made me feel seditious and terrified. I took care in my interviews to purge my questions of emotional bias, and I took the same precaution even in discussions with Zhang Minghong. Although the family member's comment had come out of the blue, it made me extremely uneasy. Perhaps it was only wishful thinking that made them imagine that we were officials going around incognito, but it was also possible that a hidden implication lay behind what they said.

I braced myself and told them, "Don't listen to other people's nonsense. We're just ordinary journalists." I showed them my work ID and said, "We really have no authority to deal with your problems. Whatever injustices you wish to report, or whatever demands you have, you should talk to the comrades on the Task Force. They're the people the party and the government have sent to resolve this issue."

I'd barely finished when all the family members began speaking at once: "We went to see them a long time ago, but it's no use." One young woman clutching an infant said tearfully, "After I exposed several men who attacked me, their wives came barging into my home cursing me as a vixen who'd seduced their men, and they tried to beat me. The men who killed my parents and brothers and raped me haven't been punished in any way."

My heart pounded like a drum as I struggled to respond. Luckily at that moment, Zhang Minghong addressed the people in the local dialect: "We're deeply sympathetic to what you've all gone through, but you've really come to the wrong place. Our assignment in coming to Daoxian is to report on the launch of rural cultural activities. We're not authorized to inquire into the Task Force's work. You might as well ask for help from some random person you encounter on the street—we're of no use to you. I myself work in Lingling—if I could really help in any way, wouldn't I have done so already?"

The family members said nothing, but disappointment showed on their faces. One of the men who seemed to have seen something of the world said grudgingly, "So you're reporters?"

"We're reporters."

"Then can I ask you comrade reporters to pass my petition on to the provincial authorities?"

I didn't have the courage to refuse his request, so I said, "That much I can do." The other family members also thrust their petitions at us, after which we saw them to the door. Zhang Minghong and I then sat down and stared at each other without speaking for a very long time.

Zhang Minghong suddenly asked, "Leader Tan, what do you think happened just now?"

I said, "It's because during our reporting you once said I was a leader sent down from the province."

"Aiyoh! Don't blame me for this! I said you were a leader, but you acted more leaderly than a real leader!"

"Don't joke about it," I said. "I'm really worried and I don't know where our reporting went wrong. It's very detrimental to have this kind of rumor going around!"

Zhang Minghong looked at me with a forced smile and said, "Tan, my friend, you don't have to pretend with me. I noticed long ago that you have a rebellious streak, and it's probably obvious to others as well. Who can believe that you've come here to write an article about bringing order out of chaos? You're just an atom bomb waiting to explode against the party and socialism. You think the comrades on the Task Force are a bunch of idiots and can't see it? Have you ever thought about why some people have just handed us photocopies of confidential documents, not even following the most basic party protocol? They object to the killing incident and to the Task Force's work and hope to get the truth out through you and raise the concern of society at large. But . . . I'm going to be frank with you, my views of the Daoxian killings weren't entirely the same as yours at the outset. . . . For me, this reporting has been like going through the Tangshan earthquake. It's changed my views of everything. Our party has been using these kinds of people for so many years to do this kind of thing! If reform doesn't come, we're finished!"

At first I was shocked by Minghong's words, but then my respect for him grew. He'd been engaged in the rough and tumble for years and was much more mature, so I sought his advice: "What do you think we should do next?"

"We need to speed things up and finish our reporting as soon as possible. If you spend too long on a dark road, you're going to run into a ghost."

"What about the petitions from the family members?"

"Keep them as reporting material."

"But we promised to submit them."

"Xiao Tan, you know what I like about you? You're smart but still so innocent. If you have to submit them, go ahead, but wait until we finish our reporting. It'll just make you feel better without serving any real purpose. Those petitions have been submitted at least a hundred times, if not a thousand, to the province and even to the central government, and what good has it done? Xiao Tan, let me remind you that the Public Security Bureau has informants among those family members."

"How do you know?"

"How could I not know? Only people like you who spend their lives in an ivory tower don't know such things." Seeing the shocked expression on my face, Zhang Minghong added, "Okay, try to stop gaping like that, will you? My point is we have to be very careful in our contact with them. It's a good thing you handled things well today, or we'd be in real trouble. Okay, it's getting late. Let's clean up and go to bed, and we'll continue our reporting tomorrow."

After Zhang Minghong went to bed, I followed my usual practice of putting my daily reporting material into some kind of order. There were too many petitions for me to read through them all in detail, but I found the one from the young woman carrying the baby. The petition stated her name as Jiang Luanrong, originally from the No. 7 production team of the Xinyouzha brigade of Gongba Commune. She was only 17 years old when the brigade's peasant supreme court sentenced her parents and younger brothers to death. That same night, two men broke into their home and raped Jiang, sparing her 12-year-old sister only because the girl was so stunted that she appeared much younger. The men then took everything of value in the house. It wasn't until 1987 that one of the rapists was finally arrested and punished.

I met Jiang Luanrong once more when I went to Daoxin again in 2006 to interview the "master petitioner" Li Niande. When Li Niande took me to her home and pointed out a plump, meek-looking old woman with short hair, I simply couldn't connect her with the delicate, pretty young woman in my memory, but she remembered me immediately: "Comrade journalist! You bought me a bowl of noodles. Do you remember?" In fact, I'd nearly forgotten.

Jiang Luanrong was still living in poverty, but she seemed to have accepted whatever life gave her. She said, "Let's not talk about the past. I have children and grandchildren, and bringing up these matters is an embarrassment to them. I really don't want to talk about it anymore."

I sighed to myself. What that senior Daoxian cadre had said was true: all things fade with time—suffering, hatred, shame, and grief, even memory. I casually shifted the topic of conversation to her current existence, and while life was still very hard for her, it was better than before. All her children were working in Guangdong Province, leaving her alone to tend a "responsibility field." Money was tight, but she had enough to eat, and she believed that as long as she worked hard, things would gradually improve.

When I rose to take my leave she suddenly said, "Comrade journalist, don't keep on with this. You'll only hurt yourself and your kids. Leave the past alone. It's enough if they never kill anyone again."

At first I couldn't think of what to say to this simple and honest village woman, but finally I smiled and said, "Aunty Jiang, I think they're the ones who are afraid of being killed now."

I could tell from the expression on her face that she hadn't understood me, and I didn't want her to.

A drinking mishap

After the encounter with the petitioners in our room, we were extremely nervous and sped up the pace of our interviews: first, because we were afraid that hitches would arise from further delay; second, because I'd already spent far more time reporting in Daoxian than originally planned; and third, because the more reporting we did, the more we felt there were even more places we needed to go to. Fortunately, several days passed with nothing unusual happening, and we allowed ourselves to gradually relax.

One day we went to a particular district to carry out reporting, and the district's youthful deputy head received us. He had recently returned from studying at the Chinese Communist Party (CCP) school and had been put in charge of dealing with the aftermath of the killing wind in his district. He was very forthright and enthusiastic, and at lunchtime he insisted on us eating with him. "I'm not inviting you to a big feast, just ordinary peasant fare that will give you a feel for what life is like here." We felt compelled to accept.

He took us to a peasant home at the edge of the town, where a middle-aged woman hurried out with tea and a bowl of red melon seeds. The deputy district head conversed with her in the local dialect, after which the woman grabbed a net and headed off. Sensing this was being turned into some kind of occasion, I quickly objected: "Please don't go to any trouble."

The deputy district head insisted, "It's no trouble. There's a pond right out back where she can net a nice fresh fish, and there's pork hanging in the kitchen. Things are different in the countryside now—people have food readily available."

In two hours the village woman presented us with a bountiful meal that included the famous Shangguan chives, meatballs mixed with special local chili peppers, and chicken fried in tea oil. A small iron wok, heated red hot on a clay charcoal stove, contained a bubbling mixture of mountain mushrooms, cured meat, and fried bean curd, accompanied by two big plates of leaves wrapped around sweet-potato flour and fresh fish cut in pieces. The fragrance of the food filled the air and had our fingers twitching for our chopsticks. In spite of what the deputy village head had said, I knew this was a lavish meal at a time when basic living needs were still not being met in the countryside.

The deputy district head went into the house and brought out a bottle of the local rice wine, which went in sweet and mild with a delicate aftertaste but had a real kick to it. Zhang Minghong immediately said, "I can't drink liquor. I didn't even drink when I accompanied Secretary Youzhi last time."

With Zhang Minghong using prefectural CCP secretary Deng Youzhi as a shield, the deputy district head conceded, "Very well, Station Head Zhang, I'll just share a drink with journalist Tan." Back then I was still young, enjoyed my food and liquor, and considered myself to have a decent drinking capacity, so I was up to the challenge.

The deputy district head filled three bowls with rice wine, then lifted his own in a toast: "I welcome the two of you to our district to direct operations!"

"Take it easy!" I reached out and stopped him. "We're not here to direct operations, we're just here to learn."

"Sure, sure, then I welcome you here to direct learning." He guzzled down his wine and turned his bowl toward us to show it was empty.

I lifted my wine bowl and said, "We thank you, deputy district head, for your great support for our work," and then I also emptied my bowl. Minghong took a swallow out of politeness.

The deputy district head's heartiness was contagious, and he and I accompanied our eating of fish and pork with bowl after bowl of wine. Zhang Minghong wasn't a big drinker, but he sipped at his bowl to keep us company, and the atmosphere was very congenial.

Wine is this way: when you first start drinking, you pace yourself and say what the other person likes to hear and are very clear about what you shouldn't say. Once you get warm all over and start feeling buoyant, you still know better, but your mouth starts spouting all sorts of nonsense. Minghong and I had decided not to talk about the aftermath efforts so as to avoid trouble, but after a while the subject came up, and I asked, "Deputy district head, do you have some good examples of work being done to help heal psychological wounds in your district?"

Why did I ask this? Reflecting on the matter afterwards, I believe it was for two reasons: one was that we needed content of that sort for our reporting assignment, and we hadn't found any examples yet. The other was that the dinner had made me favorably disposed toward the deputy district head, and I wanted to find some examples here that would allow me to put in a good word for him. He immediately replied, "We have lots of examples—they're every-where. We've been very determined in our aftermath work and we've put a lot of effort into solving problems for the families of victims. First of all, on the political front we've issued each with rehabilitation notices. We've provided subsidies to help them with their living difficulties; we've provided funding to support widows, orphans, and the handicapped; and we've helped the homeless build new homes.

"For those who left for other places, we've used various methods to invite them back. Those who've returned have been treated like everyone else, without discrimination, and we've allocated personal garden plots, responsibility fields, and hillsides to them and have helped them develop their production and establish a stable living. When a small number have made unreasonable demands, we've patiently carried out ideological work and have helped them understand that the blame belongs to Lin Biao and the Gang of Four. The vast majority of surviving family members have expressed satisfaction with our work and are deeply grateful to the party and the government. They've expressed understanding toward the comrades who committed the earlier errors, and the two sides have broken down barriers and reconciled their contradictions, and an excellent situation has emerged for carrying out the Four Modernizations in stability and unity. For example, we have two brothers in a production brigade here whose parents and elder sister were killed. They were very young at the time, and they went off wandering outside the district. This time we brought them back and provided them with a responsibility field and a hillside for gathering firewood, and we helped them build a new home. These brothers were so moved with gratitude that they wept. After they received their aide payments, they used the money to hold a dinner, inviting the people who had killed their parents."

"Why invite them to dinner?" I found this incomprehensible.

"The two sides talked the matter over face to face and expressed mutual understanding and their wish to let bygones be bygones."

I was no longer in full control of my tongue, and the deputy district head's word seemed to ignite the wine in my stomach. I said sardonically, "This is called wound healing? It sounds like they were afraid of being killed a second time!"

The deputy district head cried out, "Ai ai, journalist Tam, did you really just say that?"

I admit I was the one who became offensive first: "What else should I say? Here in Daoxian you have a saying that killing a father brings vengeance for three generations. If I killed your parents, would you invite me to dinner?"

The deputy district head said sternly, "We're a Marxist-Leninist political party. We have to view problems from a historical and dialectical perspective. During the Cultural Revolution killing wind, those who were killed were victims, but the killers were also victims. The vast majority of those who killed did it out of public-spiritedness and ardent love for the party."

"If killing people was as reasonable as you suggest, why the rehabilitation and why deal with the aftermath?"

"Journalist Tan, I would like you to note that I never said the killing was reasonable! I only said there were two sides to the killings. Whatever you may say, this matter was essentially poor and lower-middle peasants rising up to kill landlords and rich peasants. Those who killed committed very serious errors, even serious crimes, but at the same time, they were demonstrating their love for the party and Chairman Mao and the spirit of poor and lower-middle peasants as masters of their own affairs."

I began tittering. "Don't say anything more about the poor and lower-middle peasants as masters of their own affairs! That's not some kind of certificate of merit or medal of honor you can hang on your wall or pin to your jacket. It has to have real meaning. Does poor peasants being masters of their affairs refer to the way they spend all year with their faces toward the ground and their backs toward the sky, struggling to earn 10 cents a day? Does it mean that when you public servants arrive on their doorsteps, they have the honor of bringing out their beds, wives, and daughters for your use? Does it mean that when you cadres point east and they face west, it demonstrates 'the serious problem of educating the peasants'?[2] When exactly did the poor peasants act as masters of their affairs during the Cultural Revolution killings? Which incident wasn't instigated by the district cadres?" I went on and on with more such belligerent comments.

The deputy district head had also had more than enough to drink, and he said sternly, "Journalist Tan, what do you mean by those comments? Why did most party members and cadres become involved in what happened back then? Were they all evil? Were they all murderers? The point is that back then, obeying the party meant killing people, and those who didn't kill were disobeying the party!"

When those words came out, we stared at each other, dumbstruck. Perhaps we both sensed that the conversation had gone too far.

Zhang Minghong spoke from off to the side: "Xiao Tan, Xiao Tan, you're drunk and talking nonsense."

I muttered, "It takes more than this to get me drunk," and raised my bowl for more.

Zhang Minghong snatched the bowl from my hands and said, "You've overestimated your capacity and you don't have the sense to take good advice." To the deputy district head he said, "I'm really sorry. Journalist Tan is drunk. I'm going to take him back."

The deputy district head was himself so drunk that he could hardly stand, and he just said, "Sure, fine, go ahead. I won't see you out."

Such a wonderful dinner had ended so badly. Our afternoon reporting trip was out of the question, and we headed back to Daojiang instead.

As soon as we got into the car, Zhang Minghong sighed, "What a mess!"

Knowing I hadn't a leg to stand on, I said, "Why didn't you stop me?"

Zhang Minghong said, "Why didn't I stop you? I was kicking you like mad under the table, but you just ignored me and got even more full of yourself."

"I just couldn't stand that look on his face."

"Do you think you looked any better? If you hadn't had your journalist's mantle draped over you, he would have had you arrested. Do you know that?"

The aftereffects of the wine began to hit me, my legs turning rubbery and my head spinning as if I were floating in air. "I don't believe it! He wouldn't dare. . . . Aiyah, I feel like I'm going to pass out."

Zhang Minghong said, "I just wish you'd have passed out sooner!"

We made our way back to the guest house with considerable difficulty, and I collapsed on my bed and slept like a dead pig. By the time I finally woke after nine o'clock the next morning, it was too late for breakfast, but Zhang Minghong had risen early and brought some food back for me. Feeling chastened, I said to Zhang Minghong as I ate, "I'm sorry. I screwed up again."

Zhang Minghong said, "We won't even talk about screwing things up. The main thing is that you've shown your true colors. A philosopher once said that in discussing any controversial topic, it's essential to cast off your personal emotions, including hatred, sympathy, anger, and pity. You have too much sympathy for the victims' family members."

"No, no, Lao Zhang, I'm not as superficial as you imagine. Of course I sympathize with the family members, but I also sympathize with the people who were used to kill people, and I even sympathize with the deputy district head. . . ."

"Fine, whatever, don't try to make yourself look like a hero. The person you pity most is yourself."

"You're right. I do pity myself."

As I said this, there was a knock at the door, and a female room attendant said, "Room 205, comrade Tan, you have a long-distance call."

Back then, guest houses didn't have telephones in the individual rooms. Surprised, I immediately hurried to the reception desk to take the call. It was a leader from my work unit saying that something had come up and I had to end my reporting immediately and return to Changsha.

When I got back to the room, Zhang Minghong saw the grave expression on my face and asked, "What's wrong?"

"My work unit telephoned. I have to go back right away."

Zhang Minghong sighed. "The Communist Party is usually so inefficient, but I guess it depends on the circumstances! What are you going to do?"

"I can try to ignore it for a while and do what I can first."

Zhang Minghong said, "All right, so we won't go to XX District" (where the deputy district head was posted). "We'll go someplace else instead."

As we were preparing to go out, there was another knock, and when we opened the door, we saw two middle-aged men, one stocky and the other wiry.

Startled, Zhang Minghong said, "What brings you two gentlemen here?"

The stocky man said, "We've committed the error of bureaucratism. Station Head Zhang and journalist Tan have been in the county seat all this time, and we haven't come to see you until now. That's very wrong of us." He laughed as he spoke.

Zhang Minghong said, "You officials have so many important affairs to attend do, we didn't dare impose on you."

"Station Head Zhang, don't stand on ceremony. No matter how busy we are, we can't slight our VIP visitors."

"How can our paltry business compare with the heavy responsibility you bear for the well-being and happiness of so many people!"

"Station Head Zhang, you're talking nonsense. We're incapable of the work you do; otherwise, we'd love to change places and give you a taste of our difficulties!"

Hearing this dialogue, I got an idea of who these two visitors were, and as I secretly blamed myself for bringing this trouble on us, Zhang Minghong turned to me and said, "Journalist Tan, this is Secretary Zhou of the county party committee" (indicating the stocky man), "and this gentleman is County Head Li" (indicating the thin man).

I quickly went over and shook their hands. "Very pleased to meet you."

After we all sat down and exchanged conventional greetings, Secretary Zhou asked us, and me in particular, our impressions of Daoxian, whether we'd been able to get used to conditions here, whether the guest house was treating us right, whether we had any requests. . . . They didn't bring up our reporting, and this made me nervous, because in my heart I knew that this studious avoidance indicated how serious the matter was.

At this point, a man walked in and said softly to Secretary Zhou and County Head Li, "Everything's ready. When should we start?"

Startled, I wondered if they were taking "organizational measures" against us, but then Secretary Zhou glanced at his watch and said, "How about this: we haven't arranged any kind of reception since you arrived, so we're going to make up for it. County Head Li and I have a meeting in the afternoon, so we'll start the banquet a little early."

So they were just inviting us to lunch. I breathed a sigh of relief, even though I knew we weren't going to enjoy this meal.

We went to the guest house's top-VIP dining room to find a lavish banquet of all the best food Daoxian had to offer. Zhang Minghong clicked his tongue and said, "Aiyahyah, you're treating us like the prefectural secretary!"

We sat down according to our status as hosts and guests, just six of us for such a feast: apart from Secretary Zhou, County Head Li, Zhang Minghong, and myself, there were two comrades from the county CCP committee propaganda department. One of those comrades said, "Secretary Zhou, County Head Li, you asked for two bottles of good liquor. The best the guest house has is Huiyanfeng" (a hard liquor produced in Hengyang).

Zhang Minghong said, "Secretary Zhou, I don't drink."

I quickly chimed in, "I can't drink, either. I had too much yesterday and I still have a headache."

Secretary Zhou said, "Friends can't get together without drinking! We won't push you to drink too much, only as much as you want, all right?"

"If you insist."

Secretary Zhou raised his glass and said, "I raise this first toast on behalf of the county party committee and county government welcoming the two of you to our county to guide our work." He then downed the glass in one swallow.

By then I'd learned my lesson, and I just dipped my tongue in the liquor without actually drinking it, but Zhang Minghong downed his in one gulp and showed his empty glass: "After drinking this glass, I'd like to start out by reporting to the county party committee and the county government on this stage of our work."

Secretary Zhou said, "Station Head Zhang, don't use the word 'report.' Today we're not sharing this meal as station head and secretary but as friends. Anything we say here will be like words on a chalkboard that can be wiped away. Today we're just having a friendly chat as we eat, all right?"

"That's fine."

"Come on, dig in!"

I slowly ate and drank while reminding myself to mind my manners and also thinking of what to say when Secretary Zhou brought up yesterday's incident. But Secretary Zhou just said with a confidential tone, "Li and I want to tell you something that's on our minds. We want to heartily welcome the two of you coming here to report on the Cultural Revolution killings. It's hardly surprising that you should care about this matter—everyone cares about it. But this matter is too involved and complicated, and it's been extremely hard to handle. Station Head Zhang, you know that my predecessor demanded to be transferred when he heard that this aftermath work was going to be carried out. He just didn't want to deal with it, so I got stuck with it! We're all educated men, and hearing what happened here must appall you. It's more fascist than the fascists! Before you arrived, some political and legal cadres from the central government and the province organized an inspection team that went to the districts to hear reports, and everyone was outraged and said this had be dealt with severely.

"But when they reached the county and had to deal with the specifics, what standard could they apply? If you sentenced someone to death for killing ten people, what about someone who killed nine? Was it right to kill another one or two thousand people because four or five thousand had already been killed? When Khrushchev spoke of the Soviet Union's purge of counterrevolutionaries, he said, 'We forgive them not because they are innocent, but because they are too many.' There were 10,000 to 20,000 people involved in the killing wind, and careful analysis shows that most of them were essentially decent people. If you met some of the killers, your heart would ache for them. For example, the county party committee was preparing to promote a comrade who was excellent in terms of personal character, abilities, revolutionary experience, and public reputation, but back when he was very young, he became embroiled in the killings, so we couldn't make use of him. It's a real pity.

"They finally decided that the principle for the aftermath work had to stress 'the big picture, not the details, magnanimity rather than severity, and fewer rather than more.' The objective of this work isn't to punish people, but to bring order out of chaos and correct the messed-up thinking that Lin Biao and the Gang of Four created, educate the cadres and masses to accept this serious historical lesson, enhance the concept of rule of law, and consolidate and develop the excellent situation of stability and unity to ensure that reform and openness can proceed smoothly. It's like a doctor carrying out an operation, not to kill someone but to save his life. The majority of family members of victims have shown good sense. They understand what we're doing, and they're deeply grateful to the party and the government for rehabilitating them and helping them resolve their difficulties. I sympathize with their misfortune from the bottom of my heart. I know very well that the subsidy the state is providing for them is paltry, but the government's finances are strained at the moment, and we can't provide them with more. All we can do is help create the conditions for them to rebuild their homes and reconstruct their lives through their own efforts. A minority have made demands that I would not call unreasonable, but which we simply can't meet. So what should we do? We can resolve problems only within the scope that policy allows, however much we may wish to do more. Not to mention that if we do more for those who make trouble and less for those who don't, the county will be in an uproar.

"History has to record this matter. We can't pretend to be the famous Judge Bao, but at least we're not some kind of clowns. We've strictly complied with the directives of the party center and the provincial and prefectural party committees. We thoroughly welcome you coming to Daoxian to report on the aftermath work here, but we ask only that you safeguard our hard-won stability and unity. If any trouble arises, the two of you can just run off, but we'll be left behind to deal with it!"

Zhang Minghong quickly interjected, "Secretary Zhou, we can't just run off. Where would we go? My wife and kids and parents are in Lingling. We came to Doaxian to provide appropriate publicity to the impressive accomplishments and valuable experience of the aftermath work, which has been so highly praised by the Central Committee and the provincial party committee."

"We're extremely grateful and appreciate your kindness. Reaching the current stage has really not been easy. You can't imagine the resistance we faced when the aftermath work first began two years ago. The origin and development of the killings were still unclear, and the thinking of the masses was very confused. Some even said that the Task Force had been sent by the Kuomintang. When the Task Force comrades went to speak with one grassroots cadre, he ran out and ate pesticide and killed himself, and his family claimed we'd persecuted him to death. The Task Force comrades have had to withstand enormous pressure to carry out a large amount of hard and painstaking work, but just between us, writing about it won't do anyone any good. The best way is to let the matter slowly fade with time and to allow future generations work out who was right and who was wrong. Lao Zhang, I've always been a bookish person myself, but since taking this yoke on my shoulders, I've come to understand that there are many things we can't explain in our lifetimes."

Zhang Minghong and I quickly joined in, "That's very profound."

"Don't try to feed my vanity. I don't claim to be profound, but I speak from the bottom of my heart." Turning to County Head Li, Secretary Zhou said, "County Head Li, I have an idea, and see what you think of it. It's hard work for Station Head Zhang and journalist Tan to come here to do their reporting and support our work. Although we're short on motor vehicles, we should provide them with a car, and the propaganda department should also find a couple of people to help them out. What do you think?"

County Head Li said, "That's a great idea."

Zhang Minghong said, "Secretary Zhou, that's much too much trouble."

Secretary Zhou said, "It's no trouble at all. This is what the party should do. Here, let's drink another toast."

After dinner, Secretary Zhou and County Head Li took their leave to attend their afternoon meeting. After we saw them out, I asked Zhang Minghong, "What should we do?"

Zhang Minghong said, "As the saying goes, running off is the best of all plans. Let's make a sweep of the other counties before word gets out, and after we've collected all our material we can decide."

I said, "All right, I'll call the county party committee's propaganda department and tell them our work units have called us back and we have to leave right away."

We checked out of our room, bought two tickets to Jianghua at the long-distance bus station, and left Daoxian.

34

Killings in the Counties and Cities Surrounding Daoxian

The Daoxian killings detonated a "spiritual atomic bomb" (in Cultural Revolution terminology) that sent out shock waves in every direction. Most heavily influenced were the counties and cities in Daoxian's immediate vicinity. Our cursory sweep through these localities lacked detail, depth, and completeness but was enough to illustrate the problem.

Ningyuan County

Ningyuan County is located northeast of Daoxian. The first killings in that county occurred in the Xiao'oujia brigade of Meigang Commune, which was separated from the Zhengjia brigade of Daoxian's Yangjia Commune by a single mountain. After the Zhengjia brigade began killing people, some black elements or offspring, fearing that they would be killed, took refuge on the Ningyuan side of the mountain. Some members of the Xiao'oujia brigade who were collecting firewood on the mountain discovered traces of their encampment and reported the matter to the brigade's Chinese Communist Party (CCP) branch. A rumor soon spread throughout the commune of a "black killing squad from Daoxian" holding a meeting in Ningyuan to prepare for a massacre of CCP members, cadres, and poor peasants. The return of a local craftsman and two strangers for the Festival of Hungry Ghosts sparked a panic, and four men were killed on August 18. That is how the killing wind spread from Daoxian to Ningyuan County.

From then on, killings multiplied throughout the county, using methods as cruel and gruesome as those in Daoxian. In Xiaomutang Commune's Xiaomutang brigade, all 68 of the brigade's class enemies and offspring were buried alive, making the brigade Lingling Prefecture's top killer and outranking Daoxian's Yuejin brigade by five deaths.

This county held another record for exterminating the largest number of members of one family. In the Lüjia brigade of Qingshuiqiao Commune, the ten-member family of Lü Chenggao was killed, exceeding the killing of the nine-member family of Tang Congjiao in the Hongxing brigade of Daoxian's Ganziyuan Commune.

The special characteristic of killings in this county was that entire families were killed without distinguishing by sex or age. There was a popular saying in Ningyuan County at that time: pumpkins have to be gutted, even to the smallest seed.

A total of 1,092 people were killed (including suicides) in Ningyuan County from August 18 to October 25, 1967 (when killings throughout the prefecture stopped), putting the county in second place in Lingling Prefecture.

The Jianghua Yao Minority Autonomous County

Jianghua County is located south of Daoxian. When four members of landlord offspring Yang Jieqiao's family were killed in Hongtangying Commune in the latter half of August 1967, Yang managed to escape and sought refuge with relatives in the Miaoziyuan brigade of Jianghua County's Xiangjiang Commune. Hongtangying Commune repeatedly sent people to fetch Yang back. The Miaoziyuan brigade cadres held a meeting to discuss the matter, and they felt that if Daoxian could kill troublemaking black elements, so could they. On August 29, a rich-peasant offspring with problematic romantic proclivities was taken into the hills and thrown into a cave. This launched a wave of killings that spread rapidly throughout the county.

In Beijiang Commune's Beijiang brigade, nearly all the brigade's class enemies and others with historical problems were killed. At Dashiqiao Commune, some class enemies seen conversing along a roadside were accused of holding a secret meeting (in fact, they were taking a cigarette break while working on road repairs). After they'd been strung up and beaten for three days and nights, one of them fabricated a story about joining the "Anti-Communist Salvation Army" and named another 131 "members," 14 of whom were eventually killed.

Jianghua County started its killings relatively late, after the 47th Army's 6950 Unit arrived in Daoxian, and continued well into autumn. Although the death toll didn't match Daoxian's, the deeper causation was very similar, with the seize-and-push leading group that held actual governing power in Jianghua County and the main leaders of the county People's Armed Forces Department (PAFD) tacitly supported the killings.

A total of 898 people were killed (including suicides) in Jianghua County between August 29 and October 25, 1967.

Jiangyong County

Like Jianghua, Jiangyong County is south of Daoxian, separated from it by the Tongshan mountain range.

The killings began in Jiangyong County on August 17. The first victim, a sent-down educated youth in Taochuan Commune's Shiyan brigade, was killed that morning, and that evening, the Yuejin brigade of the Tongshanling Farm shot two old "landlords" and two "landlord whelps" and hanged a young woman who had lost her class status by marrying a landlord. Hundreds of the farm's workers and nearly a hundred educated youth were notified to appear at the grain-drying yard to observe the executions and "undergo the baptism of class struggle."

The killings reached a climax under the instigation of the CCP secretary of Jiepai Commune, Yang Xiuyu. Yang was from Daoxian's Xianglinpu District, and while visiting relatives he was inspired and encouraged by the sight of bodies floating in the rivers and hanging from trees. After returning to his commune, he called a "five chiefs" meeting on August 25 and told leaders of the commune's brigades all about what he'd seen in Daoxian. Within three days, 126 people were killed throughout the commune.

After that, the public-security deputy at Yunshan Commune, Zhang Wende, orchestrated the execution of three black elements in the name of the commune's peasant supreme court on market day, with at least a thousand people watching, and drafted a "killing report" that he ordered distributed throughout Jiangyong County and the Longhu Pass on the border with Guangxi. The report caused an uproar throughout the county.

A total of 325 people were killed in Jiangyong County (including suicides).

Shuangpai County

Shuangpai County, separated from northern Daoxian by Zijin Mountain, wasn't established until the 1970s. During the killing wind, this area consisted of the Xiaoshui Forestry Management Bureau as well as Daoxian's Lijiaping Commune and the Shuangfeng brigade of Chetou Commune. During the Cultural Revolution, the killing wind was mainly concentrated in Lijiaping and Jiangcun Communes. The killings in the Xiaoshui Forestry Management Bureau began on August 23 in the Hexianguan brigade (village), which had been brought under the jurisdiction of Yongzhou City. The killings there followed the pattern in Daoxian.

Part of our reporting task was to particularly focus on communes (farms or forests) or brigades where no one was killed, both in Daoxian and in other counties. In Shuangpai County we came across a particularly noteworthy example, the Yangmingshan Tree Farm. This was a densely wooded mountain with complex social relations and a considerable population outflow, and the Xiaoshui Forestry Management Bureau had focused its most effective class struggle efforts there. During the Cultural Revolution, the tree farm was engaged in intense partisan struggle, seizing and publicly criticizing the largest number of people, but not a single person was killed. The reasons were similar to those in Daoxian's Xianzijiao District: the tree farm's PAFD commander, CCP committee secretary, and deputy CCP secretary all shared the view that others might kill as they liked, but without an explicit directive from the upper level, they would not take action.

A total of 345 people were killed in Shuangpai County (including 48 suicides). The killings were notable for being scattered, piecemeal, and brutal.

Xintian County

Xintian County was one of Lingling Prefecture's smaller counties, with a population of just over 200,000.

The county was notable for the mass rally that launched its killings, which started relatively late, on September 8, but in a spectacular fashion. All of the county's 21 communes killed people in the 40 days from September 8 to October 18. Among them, 18 communes (including Chengguan Town) orchestrated 19 mass killing rallies led by commune CCP secretaries, commune heads, and PAFD commanders. A total of 786 people were killed in the county (including 180 driven to suicide), composing 0.35 percent of the county's total population.

Xintian differed from Daoxian in that its killings began in its county seat, Chengguan Town, where the county's rebel faction staged a mass rally on September 8 and executed five class enemies. After the mass rally, the leader of a mass organization under the "Alliance Headquarters" drafted an "Urgent Proposal" that was distributed throughout the county, encouraging the spread of killings in every village.

As in Daoxian, Xintian's county PAFD headquarters, which held the actual governing power during the killings, passed along the first part of 47th Army's "Cable on the Social Situation" concerning the "aggressive activity" of Daoxian's black elements and the "spontaneous" action of the county's poor and lower-middle peasants, but not the second part prohibiting indiscriminate killing and requiring that offspring be handled differently from black elements. Within the next four days, 15 of the county's communes killed a total of 129 people. A second wave of slaughter involving 230 deaths followed a meeting during which the county PAFD transmitted the latter portion of the 47th Army's cable but still didn't call for measures to halt the killings. County PAFD commander Jia Chun finally called an emergency telephone conference during which he emphasized that the killings had to stop, and that anyone involved in further killings would bear the consequences. After that, the killing subsided.

Lengshuitan City and Yongzhou City (Lingling County)

During the Cultural Revolution, these two cities had not yet been established and were under the direct jurisdiction of Lingling County.

Apart from coming under the influence of Daoxian's killing wind, the killings in Lengshuitan were set off by a criminal case on August 12. A private dispute resulted in a landlord offspring killing a production team head in Haopiqiao Commune. After militia apprehended and killed the perpetrator, the commune convened a mass rally to commemorate the victim, condemn the heinous crimes of the black elements, and call for puncturing the arrogant bluster of the class enemy. After the memorial ceremony, every brigade began killing black elements.

The killings in Yongzhou started in Fujiaqiao in the latter half of August. After the Yongxingqiao brigade of Fujiaqiao District's Fujiaqiao Commune killed three black elements under the influence of Daoxian's killing wind, the district PAFD commander called a cadre meeting to discuss how to prevent further random killings. However, the meeting devolved into a discussion of class struggle and the enemy situation, with agitated cadres beating their breasts, stamping their feet, and weeping. During a break in the meeting, some cadres pooled their funds to buy liquor, and when a class enemy offspring working at the supply-and-marketing cooperative refused to lend them bowls to drink with, the cadres dragged him to the river, hurled him over the bridge, and drowned him.

This incident was like a spark dropping into a pile of kindling. "Fuck his mother! A landlord whelp dared to bully us!" The commune and brigade cadres attending the meeting were outraged and rushed back to their communes and brigades. A total of 158 people were killed in three days, composing more than half of all the killings that occurred in the city during that period.

Lanshan County

Lanshan County was the last in Lingling Prefecture to begin killing people. The killings there began on September 10 and resulted in 145 deaths. The special feature of killings in this county was the high awareness of class struggle among grassroots cadres, and the spontaneous tracking down of counterrevolutionary organizations at the production brigade level. Subsequent investigations established that all these cases were bogus.

The classic killing in this county occurred in the Qingshui brigade, where the peasant supreme court had the village simpleton carry out the executions. As in Daoxian, executioners received a "commission" in the form of cash or millet, and after the simpleton killed 19 people, he went to the brigade cadres to collect his grain. The brigade accountant said, "Nineteen is too hard to calculate. Kill another so we have a round number." The simpleton then ran back and randomly killed a child from a landlord family to bring his total to 20.

Qiyang County

Qiyang County, under the jurisdiction of Hengyang Prefecture, is famous as the place of origin of Hunan's Qi Opera. During the Cultural Revolution killings, the county's Zhoutang Commune, which adjoined Lingling County, used the method of trussing up, hanging, and beating to force confessions regarding a so-called black killing squad. A member of the commune's organization committee, Li Xinming, and others enhanced their results by organizing a witch hunt that soon identified more than 600 members of this bogus killing squad. Other communes responded enthusiastically in kind, with the county's 33 communes killing a total of 218 people and torturing more than 1,000, some of whom were rendered permanently incapacitated.

Dong'an County

Dong'an County, known throughout China as the home of martial arts, is located relatively far from Daoxian, along the Hunan-Guangxi Railway, and the county killed only 11 people during the 1967 killing wind. Instead, the county's most serious killings took place eight months later, during the campaign to Rectify the Class Ranks.

PART ELEVEN

THE END OF
THE KILLING WIND

35

Huang Yida and the Fall of the Red Alliance

Midnight run to the provincial capital

The reader may remember that back in chapter 4 I mentioned a particular individual and promised to devote a chapter to him later in the book. I believe that without this man, many more than 4,500 people would have lost their lives in Daoxian's killing wind, and that the killings would have spread far beyond the surrounding 10 counties and cities.

Let's return to Daoxian's No. 2 High School at time that the killing wind began on August 13, 1967, where we will resume our story of a "capitalist roader" locked up inside the school, county head and deputy county Chinese Communist Party (CCP) secretary Huang Yida. Huang had come under attack by the revolutionary masses at the outset of the movement for executing "Liu Shaoqi's bourgeois reactionary line,"[1] and after the "January power seizure" he had been apprehended by the Revolutionary Alliance and confined in the No. 2 High School for struggle and criticism. Initially Huang was subjected to daily public denunciation rallies, but as the movement progressed and attention shifted to the conflict between the Revolutionary and the Red Alliances, he was left to reforming his thinking through the study of Central Committee documents, the editorials of the CCP's official publications, and the works of Mao Zedong, Karl Marx, and Vladimir Lenin.

While Huang Yida was studying the works of Mao on the morning of August 13, 1967, a Red Guard strode into his room and told him the "Red Fogies" were planning a bloodbath at the No. 2 High School that day: "If you do or say anything rash, you'll bear the consequences."

After the Red Guard left, Huang Yida wondered what he should do. Although sidelined, he was still county head, and he didn't feel he could just stand by and watch. Aware of the numerical superiority of the Red Alliance, and unfamiliar with the martial skills of Revolutionary Alliance commander in chief Liu

Xiangxi, Huang was sure that the Red Alliance would force its way into the No. 2 High School, giving rise to countless fatalities.

A little after ten o'clock, whistles sounded throughout the No. 2 High School, and armed men scrambled everywhere. Seeing an old schoolmate surnamed Jiang pass by his window, Huang Yida asked what was going on, and Jiang replied, "The Red Alliance is holding a meeting and will soon attack the school. We have to defend ourselves."

Huang Yida said, "Please tell comrade Liu Xiangxi that no matter what happens, he shouldn't fight! Tell him I want to give him some suggestions face to face."

After Jiang left, a Revolutionary Alliance leader surnamed Zhu arrived and said, "Comrade Liu Xiangxi is very busy at the moment. Tell me what you have to say."

Huang Yida urged him to send someone to report the situation to the county People's Armed Forces Department (PAFD) headquarters: "They're the only ones who can speak with authority right now."

Zhu agreed this was a good idea and said he'd send two men over with a letter right away. But around noon, Huang heard the sound of gunfire outside and sensed that the situation had become grave. He sat motionless in his room, deciding to let fate direct him.

A little after one o'clock, Liu Xiangxi came to his room with several others and said, "Comrade Yida, Jiang gave me your message. The Red Alliance has sent troops to attack us today and apprehended two female comrades at the Chengguan grain depot. We didn't open fire to defend ourselves until the situation became untenable."

Just then, Jiang came in and said, "Two people just got killed. Militia from the nearby towns and villages are amassing toward the county seat. Things are going to get really bad by nightfall!"

Huang Yida said anxiously to Liu Xiangxi, "Commander Liu, now that the situation is so serious, why not report it to the PAFD headquarters and ask them to resolve the matter?"

Liu Xiangxi said, "I sent two people to the PAFD headquarters, but they just ignored them."

Putting on his county head demeanor, Huang said "The Central Committee just issued its 'July 13 Notice' explicitly stipulating that the peasants aren't allowed to enter the cities and engage in violence. Why isn't the PAFD headquarters implementing it? Let me go to the PAFD headquarters to personally speak with Commander Cui and political commissar Liu and ask them to immediately send men to deal with this."

Liu Xiangxi eagerly accepted Huang's offer, and around four o'clock that afternoon, Huang Yida arrived at the county PAFD headquarters, where he told a functionary, "I've just come from the No. 2 High School. It appears that armed fighting has resulted in two deaths there already, and we hear a large number of villagers are arriving tonight to place the school under siege. I'm afraid even worse fighting will break out, and I'd like to report this personally to Commander Cui and political commissar Liu."

After disappearing inside for a moment, the functionary emerged and he said, "Commander Cui is indisposed and all the other leaders are out on business. Tell me what you want to say, and I'll pass it on to him."

Huang Yida could only relay his suggestions, which were to broadcast the content of the "July 13 Notice" to prevent the peasants from entering the city, and to have PAFD leaders come to the No. 2 High School and arrange talks between the leaders of the two factions to curb the violence.

After the functionary promised to pass on his message, Huang Yida rushed to his home near the PAFD headquarters to see his wife, Sun Meijiao. Huang Yida and his wife had been apart since the "January power seizure," and they had a great deal to tell each other, but it wasn't safe to talk at home, so they arranged to meet at the citrus grove near the east gate. Huang had just reached a stone gate less than 300 meters from the PAFD headquarters when he heard his wife call from behind him, "Huang Yida, run! They're coming for you!"

Huang Yida turned and saw the functionary from the PAFD headquarters and seven or eight cadres and staff from county CCP committee organs chasing him with clubs and fire tongs and yelling, "Catch Huang Yida! Beat him to death!"

Huang Yida took off running as fast as he could with the others close on his tail. Risking a 1.5-meter leap from the city wall, he dashed off to the Dongyang brigade's Liangtian Village, where he took refuge in the home of an acquaintance surnamed Jiang.

Huang hardly slept a wink, and after spending all night thinking, he had Jiang send word to the No. 2 High School the next morning, expressing his wish to return. It was a hard decision for Huang to make; although he'd reached the conclusion that the Revolutionary Alliance's actions were more compatible with Chairman Mao's revolutionary line, most of his dealings over the years had been with people in the Red Alliance, and he felt a kinship with them. But it had also become clear that the Red Alliance wanted him dead; even Cui Baoshu and Liu Shibin, who had always bowed and scraped to him, had sent people out to kill him. He had been driven to join the "outlaws."

After receiving Huang Yida's message, Liu Xiangxi quickly sent one of his most capable subordinates, the commander of the "verbal attack and armed defense" command post, Li Chenggou, with a dozen armed men to escort Huang Yida and villager Jiang to the No. 2 High School.

That day (August 14), the Revolutionary Alliance received intelligence that core militiamen from every district and commune were amassing under the Red

Alliance's direction at the Yingjiang Commune seed multiplication farm on the outskirts of Daojiang, and that they were preparing an all-out siege to capture the No. 2 High School. After conferring with county CCP committee propaganda department head Jiang Quanyi, who was staying at the No. 2 High School, Huang Yida went to see Liu Xiangxi. Huang felt that with the county PAFD supporting the Red Alliance, the only way to resolve the situation in Daoxian was for him and Jiang to go to the provincial capital to report to the provincial CCP committee leaders and ask them to step in. Huang Yida had two strong connections in the provincial capital: Hua Guofeng, at that time vice chairman of the provincial revolutionary committee preparatory group, had been assigned to Chetou Commune for work experience while Huang Yida was county head. Another preparatory group vice chairman, Zhang Bosen, had been Huang Yida's leading cadre when Huang served as a bank president in Hengyang, and they'd been in close contact up until the Cultural Revolution.

Liu Xiangxi accepted their suggestion even more readily than they'd hoped, and he said, "That's an excellent idea, and I'll send a representative along with you. But we're completely surrounded now, and the villages are blockaded with sentry posts, so you have to consider how dangerous this will be—the Red Alliance has already issued an order for comrade Huang Yida to be killed on the spot."

Huang Yida said, "This situation has passed the point of considering individual safety."

Liu Xiangxi said, "I'm grateful to you both and will arrange for you to be escorted out of Daojiang Town, but once you leave the city, there's nothing I can do. When you reach the provincial capital, please tell the provincial revolutionary committee preparatory group and the 47th Army that we're a revolutionary mass organization defending the safety of the people's lives and property, and we're not engaged in beating, smashing, or looting or staging an overthrow. Please report the facts to the upper-level leaders—tens of thousands of lives are at stake!"

The men then discussed the specific route Huang and Jiang should take, and a rudimentary outline for their report.

Liu Xiangxi wanted to accompany them to Changsha himself, but Huang Yida said, "You can't go. With things so tense at home, you need to stay here to manage operations." It was finally decided to send another Revolutionary Alliance leader, a teacher at the No. 2 High School, Huang Chengli.

At that point, the Revolutionary Alliance still objected to Huang Yida; he was particularly resented by some alliance members who had earlier been attacked as "little Deng Tuos,"[2] "Rightists," or "political pickpockets" in the campaigns Huang led. Some suspected that Huang Yida's trip to Changsha might be another capitalist-roader intrigue, or that he was using it as a pretext to escape

the struggle and criticism of the revolutionary masses. Outnumbered and surrounded by the Red Alliance, however, the Revolutionary Alliance was in an
extremely weak position and was in urgent need of outside help, especially from
the provincial revolutionary committee preparatory group. Huang Yida was
the only top county-level leader taking the side of the Revolutionary Alliance,
so even if they regarded him as a "capitalist roader," they could only hope that
he'd genuinely returned to "Chairman Mao's revolutionary line" and support his
suggestion.

At 10:45 on the night of August 15, under cover of darkness, Li Chenggou
led an armed escort that took Huang Yida, Jiang Quanyi, and Huang Chengli
out of Daojiang Town over the cable bridge behind the No. 2 High School. Upon
reaching Shangguan, Li Chenggou shook their hands and said, "I can take you
only this far. Take extra care on the road ahead."

According to the intelligence the Revolutionary Alliance had received, checkpoints had been set up on all the roads out of Daoxian, and only the road through
Xiaojia to Shuishi in Ningyuan County was still passable. As it happened, Jiang
Quanyi was a native of Xiaojia and familiar with this road. In spite of the summer heat, the three were dressed in blue uniforms to avoid detection. The night
was dark and moonless, and since they didn't dare use flashlights or take the
main road, they had to grope their way across mountains and fields; if not for
Jiang Quanyi having grown up in these parts, they would soon have become
hopelessly lost. They reached Shuishi before dawn, their legs torn by thistles and
streaming with blood. Even at that, they were not yet out of danger, because
Ningyuan County's Red Alliance had close ties with its Daoxian counterpart.
Deciding it would be safer to keep walking and catch a bus in Lanshan County
instead, they set off in that direction after putting their clothes in order and grabbing a bite to eat. After walking a day and a night and crossing more than 50
kilometers of mountain paths, they finally reached the county seat, Lanshan, at
noon the next day and were able to breathe easy.

That same day (August 16), they arrived in Chenzhou, where they raced
to the train station and squeezed onto a train bound for Changsha. There was
nothing to eat or drink on the train, and no sign of an attendant, and even
the toilets were packed with people. People sat below seats, on luggage, and
on the floor, and some even climbed on top of the train carriage. All around
them was fighting and the sound of gunfire, and the train lurched forward at
a snail's pace; if there was fighting ahead, the train stopped until the fighting
ended, while the passengers fainted and wailed in distress in the oppressive
August heat. The train proceeded in this halting fashion the entire 200 kilometers from Chenzhou to Changsha, chugging along for nearly two full days
until it reached Yijiawan on the afternoon of August 18. There, within sight of
Changsha, the train stopped.

This time the train seemed rooted in place, and when evening arrived with no further movement, Huang Yida ran forward to get some news. What he learned was that the provincial Workers Alliance and Xiang River Storm were engaged in an armed battle with the Xiangtan Revolutionary Rebel Alliance, and both sides had mobilized tens of thousands of people, bringing the railways and highways to a standstill. No one knew when traffic would begin moving again. Huang Yida and the others were out of their minds with anxiety, but all they could do was climb off the train to stretch their legs and lie down to rest on some discarded posters beside the tracks. In the darkness they heard the sound of constant artillery fire, and tracer bullets lit the sky with their long tails of light like a meteor shower, ripping the night air with their piercing whistle. Huang Yida wondered how many were dying in such a large-scale battle, which made even the conflict in Daoxian fade in comparison. And then, the battle suddenly stopped.[3] When dawn broke, the train blew its whistle and set off on its way.

On the afternoon of August 19, Huang Yida and his companions arrived in Changsha.

Hua Guofeng's directive

Upon arriving in Changsha, Huang Yida and his companions rushed off to report to the leaders of the provincial revolutionary committee preparatory group and the commander of the 47th Army.[4] By then violence had reached fever pitch in Changsha. While battling the College Command Post faction, the Worker Alliance faction had parted ways with Xiang River Storm, and an even more intense conflict had developed on the groups' shared battlefront. The normally bustling May 1st Avenue was deserted apart from roadblocks and sandbags piled into fortifications, while heavily armed fighters roared through the streets in vehicles, firing their guns into the air and making the populace tremble with fear. The leaders of the revolutionary committee preparatory group and the 47th Army were frantically busy from morning till night. As vice chairman of the preparatory group, Hua Guofeng spent every day shuttling back and forth for negotiations with the heads of the two mass organizations, his meals consisting of crackers and a canteen of water he carried in a yellow satchel wherever he went. Zhang Bosen was in a similar situation, and it was exceedingly difficult to arrange to see either of them.

On the evening of August 24, 1967, Huang Yida telephoned the Revolutionary Alliance headquarters to learn about the latest situation in Daoxian, and Deputy Commander Pan Xingjiang told him, "People are already being killed in the villages! Some places have even established 'supreme people's courts of the poor and lower-middle peasants' and have arrested and brutally killed people without authorization from higher-level organs! According to incomplete figures, more than a thousand people have been killed throughout the county, and corpses are floating down the Xiaoshui River. . . . The situation is still developing and expanding. . . ."

Horrified at the news, Huang Yida rushed to the preparatory group office with Jiang Quanyi and Huang Chengli to report the critical situation, and then went to the home of preparatory group member Liang Chunyang (a former secretary of the Provincial Planning Commission, whom Huang knew very well) and reported the situation to him as well. Deeply shocked, Liang Chunyang quickly telephoned Zhang Bosen and Hua Guofeng,[5] who agreed to meet Huang Yida and the others at the preparatory group's office the next morning.

Huang and the others arrived at the preparatory group's office at eight o'clock the next morning (August 25), but as soon as they entered, Liang Chunyang said, "It appears that what you reported last night may not be quite accurate. After you left, I had our office telephone the Daoxian PAFD, and PAFD commander Li Yonghua said, 'Nothing of the kind has happened. In the mountain areas of Simaqiao District near the Ningyuan border, some black elements who were planning an insurrection fled into the hills, and militiamen surrounded them and shot some of them with fowling guns and then threw their bodies into the river.' So it's unnecessary to look any further into this matter, and comrades Guofeng and Bosen have gone out on other business."

There was nothing Huang Yida and the others could say, since they knew nothing about the random killing of black elements in the countryside.

That night, livid with rage, Huang Yida telephoned Daoxian again and demanded to know why Pan Xingjiang had given him a bogus report. Pan immediately cried out, "Heavens! How can Daoxian's situation be the way Commander Li says it is! Wholesale massacres are being carried out in all of the county's villages, and according to multiple sources, at least 2,500 people have been killed. This morning, we stood for a short time on the cable bridge behind the No. 2 High School and saw 17 corpses float by in 20 minutes. The killing is spreading, and in some places it's become factional. The Xiaoshui River reeks of death and no one can drink the water any more. People are lined up day and night at the Anjia Well next to the PAFD headquarters to draw drinking water. How can the PAFD headquarters claim to know nothing about what's going on under their very noses? It's obvious they're intentionally ignoring it."

After hanging up, Huang Yida discussed the matter with Jiang Quanyi and Huang Chengli. By then, some people from Daoxian had made their way to the provincial capital, and some had put up big-character posters proclaiming a "bloodbath in Daoxian." The three men agreed that there could be no further delay and that they were in a race against time to save lives. They went again that night to Liang Chunyang's home, and the next morning, with Liang's assistance, they were able to meet with Zhang Bosen in the preparatory group auditorium, where they reported on the killings in Daoxian and exposed the lies of PAFD commander Li Yonghua and the others.

At that time, Zhang Bosen was busy presiding over a meeting, but he squeezed in some time to hear a report from Huang Yida and the others next to the rostrum. Huang told him, "We've come here at great risk to our lives to request that the provincial leaders and the 47th Army Support-the-Left Unit take action as quickly as possible to halt the killings. We've done everything we can to fulfill our responsibility, and if the provincial government doesn't take decisive action, the consequences will be too dreadful to contemplate."

When Zhang Bosen asked what measures Huang recommended to end the killings, Huang had an answer ready: "The first step is to revoke the county PAFD's Support-the-Left leadership authority and send in PLA [People's Liberation Army] troops to support the Left in Daoxian. Second, Chairman Mao personally issued the June 6th General Order (forbidding random killings) and the Central Committee's July 13th Notice (forbidding organized groups of peasants from entering the city to fight), but the PAFD hasn't disseminated or executed them, and most of Daoxian's cadres and poor and lower-middle peasants have been completely hoodwinked. The province should dispatch aircraft to disseminate the June 6th General Order and July 13th Notice so the masses will come into direct contact with the Central Committee document and Chairman Mao's directive.

"Third, it's essential to immediately take down all checkpoints and declare that all 'supreme people's courts of the poor and lower-middle peasants' are unlawful and banned, and to issue a general order to end the killing. The death toll needs to be calculated by class ranking and factually reported to the provincial revolutionary committee preparatory group and the 47th Army's Support-the-Left Unit. Any killings from now on should be harshly punished.

"Fourth, the Lingling Military Subdistrict and the Daoxian PAFD should recall all arms in the hands of conservative organizations, withdraw the PAFD militia surrounding the county seat, and prohibit peasants from entering the city to fight. Disagreements between the two opposing mass organizations can be resolved through consultation and negotiation under Chairman Mao's revolutionary line."

Zhang Bosen commended the suggestions and said he'd discuss them with Hua Guofeng and Li Yuan, commander of the 47th Army and chairman of the provincial revolutionary committee preparatory group, and that they'd notify the Lingling Military Subdistrict to move in and end the killings. Meanwhile, Zhang told the men to draft two cables on behalf of the preparatory group and the 47th Army describing the situation in Daoxian and their proposals for ending the conflict. One cable would be sent to the Central Cultural Revolution Small Group and the other to the Lingling Military Subdistrict and Daoxian PAFD. "Once you've drafted the cables, get them to me, the sooner the better. I'll get back to you as soon as I've discussed your suggestions with comrades Li Yuan and Guofeng."

After returning to their hostel, Huang Yida and the others discussed and drafted the content of the cables. The cable to the Central Cultural Revolution Small Group reported the killings in Daoxian and stated that the provincial revolutionary committee preparatory committee had charged the Lingling Military subregion and the Daoxian PAFD with immediately halting the killings. The cable to the military subregion and PAFD then laid out the specific measures Huang Yida had recommended to end the killings.

The draft cables were delivered to the provincial preparatory group office to be passed along to Zhang Bosen and Hua Guofeng.

At noon the next day (August 27, 1967), Huang Yida and the others were told to come to the preparatory group's office at two o'clock that afternoon to meet with comrade Hua Guofeng. The three men arrived promptly, and after hearing their report, Hua Guofeng said, "Your report and suggestions are excellent. Comrade Li Yuan intended to come, but he's busy writing a report, so he's entrusted me with representing the provincial revolutionary committee preparatory group in voicing some preliminary views."

After some preliminary remarks assuring Huang and the others that the CCP Central Committee and Chairman Mao attached great importance to the problems in Hunan, and that the two roads were clearly delineated and the problem was easy to resolve, Hua Guofeng issued a five-point directive.[6]

(1) The Central Committee had approved the suggestion to send aircraft to Daoxian to disseminate the Central Committee's June 6th General Order and July 13th Notice in the near future.

(2) The provincial preparatory group and the 47th Army would send the drafted cable to the lower levels ordering them to end the killing, but punishment of the killers would have to be resolved at a later time.

(3) The Central Military Commission had approved a transfer of troops to carry out Support-the-Left work. But Huang and the others were expected to make a greater effort to win over cadres in the county PAFD. "Once you've effectively dealt with the county PAFD, it will be easier to win over and unify the district and commune PAFD cadres."

(4) Likewise, more ideological work should be carried out on the Red Alliance organizations rather than suppressing them. "In particular, the two of you [referring to Huang Yida and Jiang Quanyi] must work harder on the leading cadres following your return, and get them to switch sides."

(5) After the situation improved, a revolutionary committee preparatory group was to be established to address the lack of a leadership core. "Two matters require attention in the future: The first is the need to focus on internal unity, and the second is the need to assist the hoodwinked masses. The peasants have suffered great harm through fighting and random killings, and we need to organize a transport of material goods to help restore productivity. The three of you can first return to Lingling and see Comrade Guo Zhi'an, who will help you resolve the problems in Daoxian as soon as possible."

The September 23 Tragedy

Two days later, the finalized texts of the cables to the Central Cultural Revolution Small Group and the Lingling Military Subdistrict and Daoxian PAFD were approved and signed by Hua Guofeng and Li Yuan. Once they were sent out, Huang Yida and the others were finally able to prepare for their return.

They left Changsha early in the morning on August 29 and arrived in Ningyuan on September 1, preparing to take the long way back to Daoxian from there. When their return was prevented by massacres and roadblocks, they decided to go back to Changsha and focus on reporting on the massacres. During their second stay in Changsha, Huang and the others submitted reports to Liang Chunyang, Hua Guofeng, and Zhang Bosen, as well as preparatory group members Tan Wenbang (also political commissar of the provincial military commission), Ye Weidong (also head of Xiang River Storm), Li Zhenjun (also political commissar of the 47th Army), and others.

While reporting to Liang Chunyang, Huang Yida made a point of asking about the August 8 gun-snatching incident, which still troubled him: "Chairman Liang, was the rebel faction following the spirit of the higher levels by seizing the PAFD's weapons?"

Liang Chunyang replied, "The party center called a meeting of military region commanders, and Premier Zhou [Enlai] said this was a lesson to us to take note of which side people were on. If they're on the side of Chairman Mao, weapons can be handed over to the rebel factions." He also said, "The provincial military region also called a meeting of subregion commanders. . . . As a result, three situations have emerged in our province: one is that guns were handed over to the rebel faction, the second is that the situation became worse when weapons were handed over to the conservative faction, and the third is that once both sides were armed, they fight." Huang quickly put this in writing and sent it to Daoxian.

After the CCP Central Committee issued its September 5th Order, the Revolutionary Alliance telephoned Changsha to consult Huang Yida and the others: "The 6950 Unit wants us to hand over our guns. What should we do?"

Huang consulted Xiang River Storm leader Ye Weidong along with Zhang Bosen at the provincial preparatory group office, and both advised against the rebel faction turning over their weapons unless the conservative faction did as well. Huang passed on the gist of Ye's and Zhang's comments in a telephone call to Pan Xingjiang and the others at the Revolutionary Alliance and came up with an idea: "In order to take the political initiative, we can make a show of handing over some of our malfunctioning guns to the 6950 Unit." He added, "Under the current conditions, it would be suicidal for the Revolutionary Alliance to hand over its guns. On the basis of the experience of the rebel faction in the provincial capital, we can organize some Mao Zedong Thought propaganda teams to go down and liberate the territory occupied by the Red Alliance district by district."

Huang and the others stayed on in Changsha for a few more days, mainly to pay their respects to some old leaders, observe the situation of the Cultural Revolution there, and learn from the experience of the proletarian rebel faction in the provincial capital. Around September 13, the three of them left Changsha and embarked on their return journey to Daoxian. Upon arriving in Lingling, Huang and the others followed Hua Guofeng's instructions by meeting with Guo Zhi'an to discuss measures to solve Daoxian's material supply problems, after which they prepared to hurry back to Daoxian. Guo Zhi'an told Huang Yida that Daoxian's villages hadn't yet dismantled their blockades and checkpoints and were still sealed up tight. The mountain pass at Shuangpai was basically impenetrable, and all the land routes were perilous. For that reason they decided to return to Daoxian by water.

This water route had once been Daoxian's main connection with the outside world, but since the construction of the Ling-Dao Highway, road traffic had gradually increased while water traffic decreased. The water route followed the Xiaoshui River through Zijin Mountain, then passed through Shuangpai to Pingzhou in Lingling and then into the Xiang River. By this time, the killing wind had caused a shutdown of Daoxian's ferry services, so Huang Yida and the others traveled by road to Jiangcun and arranged for a small boat to take them upstream to Daoxian.

Daoxian's killing wind had begun to subside at that point, but the Xiaoshui River still reeked of death, and there were piles of corpses where the river forked and bent. The floodwaters had begun to recede, and the roots of willows and other trees along the banks had emerged from the water like boney fingers, creating the horrifying image of a hand reaching into the muddy banks in its death throes while another hand clutched the swollen corpses to the land where they'd been born and bred. As the dinghy labored its way upstream, Huang Yida sat at the prow, wondering how this kind of killing could have happened. Suddenly two corpses with bellies swelled to the size of barrels floated by, and the men on the boat began sobbing in unison, but the boat's captain nonchalantly used his punt pole to jab at the bellies of the corpses and force them below the water. With a popping sound, the bellies burst open, and a pasty film trailed after the punt pole and adhered to the boat's prow. At that moment, one of the men cried out in fear as another corpse jammed against the stern of the boat. The boat captain turned and extended his punt pole again and lightly pushed the corpse away. Huang Yida felt his heart thundering in his breast and choked back vomit as the Xiaoshui flowed by, dimly mirroring the green mountains on its banks in water that rippled like fish scales in the cool autumn wind.

The day Huang Yida returned to Daoxian was the day of the shocking "September 23 Tragedy."[7]

A man who experienced the Cultural Revolution in Daoxian said, "The Cultural Revolution here in Daoxian was like a pancake, flipped from one side to the other and then back again." (In fact, that was the case throughout the country.) "During the first stage, the Revolutionary Alliance took the heat, but now the 6950 Unit took over the Support-the-Left work and explicitly expressed its support for the Revolutionary Alliance, so it was the Red Alliance's turn to feel the heat."

In a show of force, the Red Alliance leaders called a "seize-and-push mass effort pledge rally" on September 23 at the Dongfeng Cinema (formerly the county labor union assembly hall), which was filled to the rafters. County deputy CCP secretary Huang Shiyou gave a speech assuring the 1,200 attendees of the county leaders' support for the Red Alliance, followed by a grand parade through the streets.

Cadres from the county CCP committee and county people's committee marched at the front of the parade shouting inoffensive slogans authorized by the Support-the-Left troops, but then someone began yelling, "Down with the Revolutionary Alliance bandits!" and "Down with the Royalist faction!,"[8] and the entire contingent joined in. As the demonstration passed the entrance to the No. 2 High School, the slogan-shouting became thunderous. The demonstration then proceeded to the county Goods and Materials Office (where the 6950 Unit was stationed at the time), after which Red Alliance heads Zhang Mingchi, Liu Changlin, and others led the contingent back along the same route and past the No. 2 High School again. Infuriated beyond endurance, 20-odd Revolutionary Alliance members burst out of the No. 2 High School and grabbed county CCP committee deputy secretary Ouyang Yingxiong and county CCP committee united front department head Li Mingde from the procession and pulled them into the school. Chaos broke out as the Red Alliance masses burst into the school grounds to grab their people back. More than 300 people flooded the school's sports ground as the situation spun out of control. Some Red Alliance heads took the opportunity to urge the masses to rush into classrooms where guns were being stored and "seize back some guns."

They underestimated Liu Xiangxi's vigilance, however; the Revolutionary Alliance had turned over and sealed up only a token number of their weapons, while retaining a considerable number. As the Red Alliance poured into the school, the Revolutionary Alliance's security force under the direction of Deputy Commander Zhang Fushan opened fire. Twelve people were killed on the spot, and dozens more were wounded. Two 6950 Unit military representatives stationed at the school also suffered serious injuries. The incident sent shock waves throughout the county.

At the time that the September 23 Tragedy occurred, Huang Yida was having a drink at the home of a teacher from the No. 2 High School. When he heard the sound of machine gun fire from the direction of the sports field, he ran out to learn what had happened, and upon being told of the incident he became deeply distressed.

That evening, he visited Ouyang Yingxiong and Li Mingde at the No. 2 High School, and since they'd normally gotten along well, Huang Yida made a special effort to work on them, passing on the directive from Hua Guofeng and the other leaders of the provincial preparatory group and describing what he'd seen and heard at the provincial capital and advising them to switch sides.

The September 23 Tragedy threw the entire county into chaos, but it didn't lead to further killing. The chronology of the Daoxian killings shows there was not a single death in the days immediately afterwards, and the killing wind continued to subside.

At this time, the standpoint of the Hunan provincial preparatory group and the 47th Army became increasingly clear-cut, and the Red Alliance began to disband. Especially after the preparatory group and the 47th Army issued their joint notice on September 27[9] and aircraft dropped leaflets throughout the county, the Red Alliance collapsed.

One old Daoxian cadre (not Huang Yida) said, "After the killing wind subsided, the executioners, especially those behind the massacre, were like dogs who had lost their master. They became panic-stricken, and some absconded to their home villages and the homes of friends and relatives, while others kept silent and laid low, no one having any idea where they'd gone. Just a few people continued to put up a stubborn resistance; for example, the PAFD commander of District 6, Zheng Youzhi, who took men and guns to Dapingpu Farm. But overall, the chaotic situation in the county calmed down and steadily improved."

From the end of October to early November, the 6950 Unit stationed in Daoxian issued notices calling on all work unit leaders and cadres to return to their units as soon as possible to seize revolution and push production. Some leaders and cadres of county CCP committee organs began returning to the county seat and gathered in the county CCP committee guest house on Douzi Street for a period of collective study during which everyone could express their thoughts and feelings regarding recent events and undergo ideological transformation. The great majority were "educated and rescued."

While the situation was still in flux, some surviving Revolutionary Alliance members and family members of victims believed that the ringleaders of the massacre had returned, and they burst into the guest house and beat and denounced some of the leaders and cadres. When the 6950 Unit troops learned of this, they quickly dispatched cadres and soldiers to safeguard the guest house, and the situation didn't deteriorate further. Even so, some county CCP committee leaders and cadres were badly beaten. For example, county deputy CCP secretary Yu Shan was blinded in one eye after being bound, blindfolded, and whipped with a leather thong. Likewise, the head of the county CCP committee's organization department, Wang Ansheng, was dragged onto a basketball court in the depth of winter, stripped down to his shorts, blindfolded, and made to kneel in the snow while he was punched and kicked until his assailants tired and went home to warm themselves. Wang Ansheng lay in the snow, afraid to move for a very long time before finally crawling home.

The exposure study sessions

In December 1967, the 47th Army's Support-the-Left force and the Hunan Provincial Revolutionary Committee Preparatory Leading Small Group held Hunan's first Mao Zedong Thought Study Group, the main task of which was to select leading cadres for Hunan's county and municipal revolutionary committees. Huang Yida represented Daoxian at this session of the study group, which was to last for two months.

One evening about 10 days into the study session, Hua Guofeng called Huang Yida to the provincial garrison headquarters and told him, "Daoxian doesn't have any leading cadres qualified to handle Support-the-Left operations. I'd like you to go back and take charge of the first stage in coordination with the army."

Huang said, "I'm grateful for the provincial leadership's trust in me, but I feel there are many problems I'm powerless to resolve, and I'm not capable of meeting the provincial leadership's demands." When pressed on the matter, Huang pointed to the need to restore the county's leadership core and recommended the establishment of a revolutionary committee to gradually train up a new group of cadres. The second issue was to provide for the material needs of surviving victims of the massacre and for some 20,000 people who had fled the county. Finally, there was the matter of satisfying calls for punishment of the instigators and perpetrators of the killings. "My view is that those who killed black elements should be let off for the time being and dealt with later. We first need to go after those who killed out of revenge or to snatch women or property, and those who instigated killings or who directed them behind the scenes, and punish them according to law, showing no mercy to the most heinous offenders."

Hua Guofeng said, "You can move faster on establishing organs of power. There's no need for preparatory groups or such things—just set up a revolutionary committee and shorten the process. Regarding how to handle the killings, after you've established the revolutionary committee, clarify the situation and work out the various categories so you can get an idea of the scope of handling it through legal processes. Write a report with recommendations and send it up, but for the time being don't deal with anyone except those who continue to harm the people or particularly heinous offenders who are preparing to flee. The rest can be handled in a uniform fashion once a policy has been formulated. As for bringing back family members who have fled and making proper arrangements for them, this is a very important practical issue. I think that no matter what, you must first get them to come back and not allow them to continue roaming around the country. For current hardships, you'll need to take relief funds back with you. How much do you think you'll need?"

Huang Yida said boldly, "Let's start with 400,000." (That was a considerable sum at the time.)

Hua Guofeng made no objection and told his secretary to write a memo to the provincial Department of Civil Affairs approving the sum.

Huang Yida returned to Daoxian on January 6, 1968. Apart from assigning staff to handle relief requests and settlement arrangements for the families of victims, Huang focused on establishing leadership groups in each district and commune to take charge of production and operational matters in the countryside, and on lifting the lid off the massacre.

The 6950 Unit focused most of its energies on quickly establishing Daoxian's revolutionary committee on March 1, 1968. Huang Yida was appointed vice chairman, while 6950 Unit political commissar Sun Runqing served as the committee's chairman. The revolutionary committee's power structure remained military in nature, and the heads of each organ under the revolutionary committee were comrades from the 6950 Unit, with deputy heads drawn from the community through direct appointment by the military.

Soon after the revolutionary committee was established, Huang Yida and two leaders of the 6950 Unit convened "exposure study sessions" at the county grain depot (the county CCP school in Dongmen) for all work unit leaders, representatives of the two mass organization factions, and more than 250 people involved in the killings. The study session consisted of establishing fact and talking reason and didn't involve beating, struggle, or extorting confessions through torture. People who had engaged in serious errors that involved killing others were given an equal opportunity to defend themselves and expose the errors of others. At the same time, each district and commune established a special investigation team to investigate and verify issues brought to light during the exposure study sessions.

News of the exposure study sessions spread rapidly, and an increasing number of people began attending. Some used their personal experience to expose and accuse others, while others hurried to the county seat from remote regions to make tearful denunciations. The study sessions continued for 21 days at various levels and, combined with investigation and verification work, resulted in a series of reports submitted to the prefectural and provincial revolutionary committees, which established that some 6,000 people had been killed. The classic cases I've highlighted in this book came to light during these study sessions.

Not long after the sessions began, an eye-catching piece of doggerel appeared on the wall between the county PAFD headquarters and the county CCP committee offices:

> Little cockerel, don't strut too much,
> Your crowing days are done;
> The left hand grabs you to cut off your head,
> The right hand grabs you for the fattening cage.

The people running the study sessions were shocked. Refusing to be intimidated, Huang Yida went to the leaders of the 6950 Unit's Support-the-Left group and said, "So many people died in the massacre, and the methods were so brutal, it defied every human and divine law. If we don't thoroughly expose it and deal with it, it will bring our party into disrepute and plague future generations. We have to continue these sessions until the truth becomes clear." The leaders of the 6950 Unit were in full agreement.

Liu Xiangxi's responsibilities in the county CCP committee standing committee covered finance and trade, and at first he had little interest in the study sessions, especially since he felt slighted at only being appointed to the revolutionary committee's standing committee. Now, reading the doggerel painted on the wall, he was so angry that he reverted to form, telling Huang Yida, "Secretary Yida, what are we waiting for? Submit the reports quickly, and then let's kill some of those fellows, while arresting some and removing others."

Huang Yida said, "At this point we're still investigating the problem and raising awareness. Dealing with those responsible will have to wait for later."

Liu Xiangxi said, "Secretary Yida, you're too softhearted."

Huang Yida said, "Comrade Xiangxi, I'm not softhearted. Chairman Mao instructs us to be extra careful in dealing with people; a human head isn't like a leek that can grow back again after it's cut off. Comrade Guofeng has also directed us to leave the handling of those responsible for a later stage when the provincial leadership comes out with a unified policy. Don't worry. We have this material and ironclad evidence, and there's no way they'll escape."

Why was Huang Yida so reluctant to follow through? I asked him this at one point. He muttered ruefully, "I just didn't want to take things too far. . . ."

I posed the same question to an old Daoxian cadre who knew Huang Yida very well. He said, "I've thought about this question for a long time. In the final analysis, I think it boils down to six reasons: one was that Huang had the material in hand and ironclad evidence, and he could take it out at any time. He never guessed that the upper-level leaders might not understand the truth as clearly as we did. The second reason was that there were still false rumors misrepresenting the killings as an overreaction by the poor and lower-middle peasants to a genuine threat by class enemies. The third was that people were killed under the banner of defending the Red regime. The fourth was our failure to recognize the nature and ruthless repetitiveness of line struggle within the party, and our belief that the larger picture was settled. The fifth was underestimating the social influence of the killers. The sixth was that Huang Yida had been too heavily influenced by the teachings of Confucius and Mencius. In a word, he was too naive and too shallow in his understanding of Chinese society and politics."

36

Reversals

One day in September 1968, the 6950 Unit stationed in Daoxian withdrew overnight without giving even cursory notice to the other members of the revolutionary committee that it had formed. Many explanations circulated in Daoxian regarding the reasons for the unit's withdrawal, but none was authoritative. One thing for certain was that the withdrawal was related to line struggle at the upper levels, which took precedence over all else.

Upon arriving at work the next morning, Huang Yida was dumbstruck to find the office empty, and an ominous feeling overcame him. He quickly conferred with other members of the revolutionary committee, who agreed that even without the 47th Army, they must hold the fort and continue with the tasks the 6950 Unit had left unfinished, especially reviving production. The peasants didn't have the benefit of the iron rice bowls that cadres and masses enjoyed in the cities; if they didn't bring in the harvest, they'd have nothing to eat.

At that time, the original leaders of the Daoxian People's Armed Forces Department (PAFD) had been replaced with a new batch of leaders. People noticed that the original leaders hadn't been dismissed for their errors but had been transferred or even promoted. The reorganized Daoxian PAFD took over the 6950 Unit's leadership of the Support-the-Left work, and the cadres and PAFD officers who had supported the Red Alliance were once again wielding authority over Daoxian's Chinese Communist Party (CCP), political, military, and financial affairs. The pancake had flipped once again, and the Revolutionary Alliance was once more taking the heat, with a considerable number of its members coming under investigation. Huang Yida nevertheless remained vice chairman of the county revolutionary committee.

At that time, Liang Chunyang ran into trouble back in the provincial capital, Changsha, under allegations of "bombarding the three reds"[1] with the intention of "destroying our Great Wall"[2] along with another provincial CCP committee leader named Shang Chunren. Big-character posters proclaiming "Down with Huang Yida!" appeared in Daojiang Town, claiming that Huang was the "black hand" of the "Liang-Shang clique" that extended into Daoxian and that he had begun colluding with "Liang-Shang" on "shady dealings" while in the provincial capital. The posters also accused Huang of being "the main behind-the-scenes backer of Daoxian's class enemies" and "a loyal offspring of black elements."

While pressured by the ominous implications of these big-character posters, Huang maintained his composure, confident that he'd committed no major errors and had always complied with CCP principles and Chairman Mao's revolutionary line.

A few days after the posters appeared, PAFD deputy commander Liu Rong and deputy political commissar Fan Shulin came calling at Huang's home. Military men like to get straight to the point, and after the conventional exchange of greetings, they said, "Recently we held a study session for district and commune PAFD commanders to arrange tasks for the coming period. Morale was high, but everyone felt under great psychological pressure because various parties have been alleging they were involved in the killings. We've looked into the issue, and it was nothing to do with them. We're hoping you'll come forward and exonerate them so they can cast off this burden and carry on with confidence."

Huang Yida said, "How can I say that when the recent exposure sessions revealed that certain PAFD commanders were directly involved in the Daoxian killings? My saying otherwise won't make it true."

At noon the next day, the county's revolutionary committee chairman and PAFD political commissar, Liu Kuan, came to see Huang and said, "Yesterday comrades Liu and Fan came to talk with you and asked you to say some words at the study session for district and commune PAFD commanders, but I hear you're unwilling. I suggest that it would be good for you to go. First, it would take a load off their minds so they can carry on with confidence, and second, it would improve relations and facilitate future work, which would be good for everyone. You'll be depending on these people for operations in the countryside. You bear the main responsibility for operations in Daoxian from now on. The PAFD's participation in Support-the-Left work is only temporary, and you'll be handling it over the long term."

Huang Yida stood firm, however: "Commissar Liu, even in the short time that the exposure study sessions have been held, countless facts have shown that the killings were in fact related to some of these men, and that some will eventually become targets of investigation. I'd be lying if I went to the meeting and said they had nothing to do with it, and I couldn't say it in good conscience." When he saw that he was getting nowhere, Commissar Liu left in a huff.

Huang Yida's attitude caused deep resentment within the county PAFD and among some cadres in the county CCP committee and government, who didn't see any problem with killing a few black elements and felt that Huang was an upstart hatching some nefarious plot against them. They recalled errors Huang had committed during the Great Leap Forward that resulted in even more deaths through starvation—and most of those victims had been poor and lower-middle peasants, but now the CCP had put Huang in charge in spite of that. Huang was obsessing over the deaths of a few black elements because he'd been born to a well-off middle peasant family and was really just a rich peasant who'd slipped through the net. That made this conflict a life-and-death class struggle, and Huang wasn't the only one who could wield his pen to report on others.

In short order, a report on "Huang Yida's Anti-party, Anti-socialist Errors" was compiled in the name of the Daoxian Revolutionary Committee and Support-the-Left Leadership Office and submitted to the Lingling prefectural and Hunan provincial revolutionary committees.

This report summarized Huang Yida's four great "errors": (1) concealing his class status and social relations, (2) reversing the verdict on cadres unseated during the Socialist Education movement and villainous Kuomintang remnants, (3) false and exaggerated reports resulting in starvation, and (4) stirring up controversy and sowing division within the revolutionary committee and turning the spearhead of struggle against the "three Reds."

Any one of those four accusations was a major issue at that time, and it looked like these people had a tactical advantage over Huang Yida's cohort: Huang Yida knew what to do, but he was too softhearted, while Liu Xiangxi was ruthless enough, but a poor strategist.

Huang was particularly vulnerable to the third allegation relating to starvation during the Great Leap Famine in the late 1950s and early 1960s. To date there are still no official figures on how many people died of unnatural causes during the Great Famine, but all the authoritative estimates put the death toll in the tens of millions. Hunan Province didn't suffer the greatest number of fatalities, but Daoxian was one of Hunan's hardest-hit areas, and Lingling Prefecture was near the top of the list. During our reporting, we obtained official data stating that in Daoxian alone, more than 34,000 people died of unnatural causes, and informed sources said the actual number was much greater. It took nine years for the population to regain its 1959 level.

In winter 1961, the Hunan provincial CCP committee sent a rectification work team to survey the consequences of famine in each county, and Huang Yida admitted to having underreported Daoxian's deaths under orders from county CCP secretary Shi Xiuhua. In his "Preliminary Self-Criticism and Admission of Error," dated December 3, 1967, Huang wrote, "I duped the party and the people, and this is extremely despicable and shameful. We committed monstrous crimes against more than 40,000 people who died in our county and truly deserve ten thousand deaths."

"Did you bear any responsibility for these deaths?" I asked him during our interview. I'd read in some related files that Huang Yida had committed serious errors during the famine. In particular, he'd been complicit in a bogus report of a paddy field producing 55,000 kilos per *mu*, as well as sweet-potato yields of 100,000 kilos per *mu*, which led to higher requisition orders from the state and left less food for the farmers. He also led 7,000 villagers in a steel-forging campaign, which like most at that time produced nothing but worthless scrap iron while diverting manpower and resources from agricultural production. Many cadres had committed similar errors at that time, and Huang Yida had been no exception.

"I bear the main responsibility," Huang admitted frankly.

"How about Xiong Bing'en? Was he more responsible, or you?"

"I was. He was a rather overcautious person."

"How about Shi Xiuhua?"

"His responsibility was greater. I was his right-hand man. I'm not trying to make him bear all the blame, but he was the top man and bore overall responsibility. Comrade Xiuhua was very high-handed; everything had to be done according to his orders, and anyone who disobeyed would be punished. Besides that, Comrade Xiuhua had promoted me to important positions, and I was grateful to him and followed his directions in all matters, and of course I came up with quite a few bad ideas of my own so he would think well of me." He added, "In spite of my selfish motivations, in my heart of hearts I genuinely believed in the superiority of the socialist system and that collective economy could liberate productive force and create a man-made miracle."

Many years later, Huang Yida retired from his position as chairman of the standing committee of the Xintian County People's Congress and returned to Daoxian to spend his twilight years. Whenever it rained or the seasons changed, his old injuries from being bound and beaten during the Cultural Revolution flared up with a piercing ache, and lying sleepless at night, he recalled the day he visited his home village in Xianglinpu during the famine and found wayside pavilions full of people who had starved to death sitting on the stone benches, and the production brigade's ancestral hall piled high with unburied corpses. He told me, "I deserved to be sent before the firing squad twice over for the crimes I committed against the people of Daoxian and the disaster I brought down on them. The party has forgiven me and the people have forgiven me, and I'm grateful."[3] Shi Xiuhua, however, was unrepentant to the end.

Those memories of starvation and hardship were still fresh on October 12, 1968, when banners went up in the streets of Daojiang: "The upper levels have authorized the dismissal of Huang Yida as member and vice chairman of the revolutionary committee and from its standing committee!"

The banner created a sensation throughout Daoxian—the Revolutionary Alliance was doomed.

What followed was a series of criticism rallies, which eventually spread to every district and commune. The main slogan of the day was, "We will eliminate the poison wherever Huang Yida spread it."

Huang Yida recalled, "Those criticism rallies were worse than the ones against the capitalist roaders. You would be taken up and hog-tied and then beaten and kicked until you were half dead."

Liu Xiangxi was treated just as badly as Huang Yida. The first time they met on the stage of a criticism rally, Liu Xiangxi said to him, "Your softheartedness will kill us!" Huang Yida said nothing but only bowed his head.

On November 14 the weather was turning cold, and Huang Yida had put on a quilted jacket and had just finished his breakfast when several people arrived and took him to the sports field behind the No. 1 High School. The county revolutionary committee was holding a mass rally for all the county's cadres, workers, and residents to announce the decision of the county's public-security, procuratorial, and judicial military control group to formally detain Huang Yida and the others. The rally was carried out with great ceremony and under the tightest security, with armed militiamen posted everywhere. After Huang Yida's name was read off, militiamen tied his arms behind his back, pressed his head down, and pushed him onto the stage. Then amid the thunderous shouting of slogans, Huang was hog-tied and taken to the detention center.

The detention center of the Daoxian public-security bureau was in the county government compound. Back when Huang Yida had been county head, he'd heard the cries of detention center inmates from his office, but he'd never gone there. The detention center's leaders had repeatedly invited him to inspect their work, but he'd always politely declined, reluctant to set foot in that inauspicious place. Now as Huang was brought in, the old warden, Ou Chunlin, untied him and said, "Huang Yida, this is good. I invited you here several times to make an inspection but you always said you were busy, and now you finally have time to sit here all day. If you'd known you'd be staying here, maybe you'd have allocated more funding to enlarge the cells. Now that you're here, read the prison rules carefully and be sure not to break them."

Huang Yida had expected this to be only a brief detention, and the old warden's words came as a shock. He realized how complicated and serious the situation had become.

Arrested and sent to detention along with Huang Yida were county CCP secretary Shi Xiuhua (for the crime of being an incorrigible capitalist roader and degenerate), public-security bureau chief Song Changxin, chief procurator Yan Weisheng, deputy county head Liu Bao'an, and others (mainly for choosing the wrong side). Liu Xiangxi was also brought in, as anyone would have expected, but surprisingly Zheng Youzhi was also detained, along with He Xia.

In prison

Huang Yida heard the heavy metal prison door slam shut behind him, and raising his head, he saw pasted to the wall a paper with the "prison regulation system" printed on it: "Frankness will be treated with lenience and resistance with severity, so make a truthful debriefing of your problems; no whispering in each other's ears or shouting and creating a disturbance; no matches or hard objects inside the jail cells, and no smoking or drinking; submit to the control of the guards in all things; report everything to the guards," and so on.

At this moment, Huang Yida's new life began.

No one had told him why he was here, but it was written clearly in the prison rules: he'd been brought in to "make a truthful debriefing of his problems."

This outmoded detention center had 12 cells of around 10 square meters each that were originally designed to hold 14 prisoners but now held around 30. Each prison cell had only one barred ventilation window in the outer wall 3 meters off the ground, which was so small that even with the bars removed, it would be difficult for a person to crawl through it. The concrete floor was damp, especially in late spring, when the walls dripped with moisture. Anyone staying in the detention center for a year or more suffered from arthritis.

Among the inmates was the former head of the county broadcast station, Tang Houwen. During the Great Famine in autumn 1959, Tang had risked his life to report on the "excellent situation" at Shouyan Commune's Xialongdong production brigade, where Huang Yida was stationed, and had been shocked by what he'd seen. He recorded a poem in his notebook: " . . . China's excellent situation is desolate and bleak; there's little smoke in village chimneys and the landscape weeps. Corpses young and old lie scattered, food for beasts." This poem was discovered during the 1964 Socialist Education movement, and in 1966, Tang Houwen was labeled a "little Deng Tuo" and repeatedly subjected to public criticism, after which he was sent to the detention center as a major political criminal. Now, after less than a year in detention, he was crippled by arthritis so painful that his groans kept his cellmates up at night. The first time he saw Tang Houwen, Huang Yida felt as if he'd been punched in the face. He'd never guessed that 16 months in prison could reduce a person to such a state, and even less that after personally sending this man to jail, he would join him there. Even stranger was that all he could remember was that Tang was Daoxian's biggest "little Deng Tuo," while he hadn't the slightest recollection of what "anti-party, anti-socialist crimes" Tang had been accused of.[4]

The prisoners slept on wooden planks, with a large chamber pot in the innermost corner of the cell. Prisoners were allowed out for just five minutes every day, during which they focused all their energy on breathing fresh air and using the outdoor toilets. Tardiness in returning to the cell was punished with kneeling on the ground outside for one or two hours, no matter how broiling or frigid the weather.

Because the air inside the cells was so foul and the sanitary conditions were so poor, there were always several prisoners suffering from diarrhea, and the smell in such confines can only be imagined. During the first few days, the stench made Huang Yida so nauseated that his head spun and he couldn't eat, and he just stared at the other prisoners wolfing down their food.

The 30-odd prisoners in Huang Yida's cell included people involved in "factional struggle," clan heads and grassroots cadres involved in clan feuds, and various petty criminals and the occasional fugitive murderer. Hunger was a constant torment, with the small allotment of rice, turnips, and cabbage having a portion deducted as an extra ration for prisoners engaged in outside labor. Each cell was given one bucket of water per day, enough for a small cupful for each person, resulting in intolerable thirst during the hot summer months. Prisoners were allowed to bathe at most once a month, so part of their daily allotment of water was used for superficial washing. Most hoped to be sent to a labor reform farm, where a harsher sentence would be offset by more food and exercise.

Liu Xiangxi suffered even more than Huang Yida. The moment he landed behind bars, Liu resolved to die: "I can't think that I'll get out alive, because if I do, I'll lock all those killers up!" This attitude inevitably brought him under greater attack.

Eventually "master petitioner" Li Niande was sent to this same detention center but was held in the labor cell for prisoners accused of lesser crimes. As related earlier, Li Niande adapted much better to prison life than Huang Yida or Liu Xiangxi. Conditions were more relaxed in the labor cell, and he was out in the sunlight every day and given more to eat, but even when he wasn't assigned work, Li Niande managed very well. He was young and strong, capable, clever, and tough. If there had already been a system of trustees or cell bosses back then, he might well have become one.

Among the 30 people in Li Niande's cell were two key people implicated in the killings: the Red Alliance's deputy political commissar, He Xia, and Revolutionary Alliance commander Zhang Fushan.

He Xia's crime was being a "ringleader of the massacre" and an "alien-class element" (a counterfeit poor peasant, capitalist, and traitor to China). The label of "alien-class element" was hardest to bear for someone who had always considered himself to have "red roots and shoots," an unshakable class standpoint, and the highest consciousness of class struggle. He Xia was like someone punished by castration; although the physical hardship was not severe, his spiritual suffering was worse than death. But even in his jail cell, He Xia resolutely maintained a clear distinction between himself and the others, and in accordance with the strict standards of a Communist Party member, he took the initiative to monitor the activities of the "class enemies" around him. Li Niande recalled, "That man loved ratting on others."[5]

Zhang Fushan was accused of being the "evil head of a reactionary organization; a beating, smashing, and looting element; and commander in chief of the tragic September 23 shooting." Upon entering prison, he suffered extreme anxiety over his future, and his health gradually deteriorated. Li Niande looked on him with pity and used the advantages of his own physical strength to help Zhang whenever he could, and gradually the two became friends. The night before Li Niande was to be released from jail, Zhang Fushan crept over and whispered to him, "Xiao Li, I need you to do something for me. I have some material regarding the killings that I left with my wife. This is very important evidence. I can't take care of it myself, and it's not safe to leave it with my wife. After you get out, go to the salt company and find my wife. . . . Tell her I sent you. You have to put the file in a safe place—sooner or later it'll be useful."

After his release, Li Niande kept his word and fetched the file from Zhang's wife. It was material collected during the "exposure study sessions." As soon as he saw it, Li Niande knew that his friend had entrusted him with his life, and he immediately found a safe place to hide it. Later, because of his transient existence, he changed the hiding place 10 times before finally taking the file out in 1982. The petition Li wrote to Deng Xiaoping was based on this material.

Regarding Huang Yida's life in prison, I'd like to quote from something Huang Yida himself wrote:

My detention and investigation were all the more devastating because the jail was run by the [county] PAFD, and they considered me an absolutely irreconcilable enemy. They believed that their killing of black elements was a revolutionary act, and that as a Communist Party member and county head of Daoxian who had run off to the provincial capital and reported on them to the 47th Army and provincial revolutionary committee preparatory group leaders, I had spoken up for the black elements and acted as the main backstage supporter of the "ox demons and snake spirits," and that made me an "alien-class element." Accordingly, they requested that Liu Xianxi and I be sentenced to death, and had already obtained permission from the Lingling prefectural Support-the-Left leading small group (i.e., the Lingling military subregion) and had sent their request under seal to the Hunan provincial revolutionary committee; because I was a cadre under provincial management, the prefecture wasn't authorized to execute me. Comrade Hua Guofeng reportedly heard of this matter and said, "I know this man. When the killings arose in Daoxian, he came to Changsha to see me, and he made a great effort to solve the serious problems in Daoxian. If there's a problem, have him make a self-criticism. . . ." The provincial government's refusal to authorize the death sentence pulled me back from the brink.

But if someone like me, who held the evidence of their murders and was preparing to call them to account for their crimes, wasn't disposed of, wouldn't that bring them endless trouble? How could they let me off so easily? They therefore adopted the even-crueler method of locking me up for life.

Huang Yida was cut off from all contact with the outside world, and unlike other prisoners, his family was forbidden to bring him food. His wife and children also suffered hardship due to the loss of most of his income. Huang and Liu Xiangxi were tortured daily. Huang lost his appetite and ability to sleep, and the trauma to his blood vessels and ribs devastated his formerly hale physique to the point where he could no longer use his left hand and began to suffer from heart disease and other ailments. In spring 1969, Huang Yida and Liu Xianxi were taken to the auditorium of the Daoxian No. 1 High School for a "seize-and-push rally" for village militia leaders, where Huang expected to be permanently disabled or even killed.

> At eight o'clock that morning, we were taken to the rally and led onto the stage amidst a burst of yelling. . . . I was surrounded by a dozen or so people pushing my head and pulling my hair, kicking me in my vital parts and tearing off my clothes. . . . While they were beating me, I no longer felt any pain and only sensed things going black and a great wave of sound rolling back and forth over me. I seemed to be aware of only one thing: I'm still alive, I'm still alive. . . . At that point someone below the stage stood up and shouted, "You can't do this! What crime did Huang Yida commit? It would be better for you to take him out and execute him!" People on the stage shouted, "Down with the pro-Huang faction! Protecting Huang is a crime worthy of 10,000 deaths!" But people below the stage shouted, "Fight with words, not violence!" The people in charge of the rally, seeing things devolve into chaos, went to the microphone and shouted, "That's enough! Don't do anything unless directed!" But everything was in chaos now, and the masses were protesting the nonsensical policies. The public denunciation rally couldn't continue, so they declared it adjourned and took Liu Xiangxi and me back to the detention center.

Huang Yida's wife, seeing him led bloodied from the rally, ran to the county PAFD headquarters and demanded to see the newly appointed political commissar and revolutionary committee chairman, Chen Fengguo. "What crime has Huang Yida committed?" she demanded. "Does he deserve a death sentence? If so, it should be carried out through a court judgment. How can you just persecute someone until he's half dead?"

Claiming to know nothing about the rally, Chen said he'd look into it, and Huang Yida and Liu Xianxi weren't taken to criticism rallies for a long time after that. Nevertheless, Huang spent 40 hellish months in prison, and throughout that time no one questioned him or brought him before the court or carried out even the most basic legal procedures. Finally, after the "Lin Biao Anti-party Clique" fell from power, Huang Yida was released from prison on April 1, 1972, and placed under house arrest at the Dongwei coal mine, more than 30 kilometers from the county seat:

> By then, Wang Ansheng had become vice chairman of the county revolutionary committee and head of the military control group. He personally ordered that I be sent into the mine to dig for coal. When the head of the mine saw that my health was so fragile, he went to the county seat to see militia commissar and county revolutionary committee chairman Chen Fengguo and said, "On the basis of Huang Yida's current physical condition, I absolutely cannot allow him into the mine or there's sure to be an accident."[6] Commissar Chen replied, "Then arrange for work that he can handle. Don't force him to go to the mine if he can't do it." After this they had me tend the pigs and raise vegetables.
>
> After I'd spent a year under house arrest at the Dongwei coal mine, full exposure of the crimes of the Lin Biao Anti-party Clique resulted in many issues being gradually clarified. I was declared a free man and allowed to rejoin my family.

In May 1981, the Daoxian CCP committee's Commission for Discipline Inspection carried out a review of Huang Yida's case, and with the authorization of the Lingling prefectural CCP committee and Hunan provincial CCP committee, the commission overturned the false allegations, rehabilitated Huang Yida, and restored his good name.

Heaven's unfathomable will

After public-security chief Song Changxin was ferreted out and sent to jail along with Huang Yida and the others, the public-security bureau was reorganized, and a new director, Wu Guiwen, was moved up from the ranks. Likewise, the education department promoted a young cadre named Zhong Changbin to strengthen its leadership. Zhong Changbin and Wu Guiwen had worked together in Shangguan District, Wu as district head and Zhong as CCP secretary, and they had always gotten along well. After being transferred to the county seat, being in unfamiliar surroundings and temporarily separated from their families, the two of them regularly met up in the public-security bureau office after work to drink and chat. On one such evening, Zhong Changbin noticed a large stack of files piled up along the office wall, and out of curiosity he picked one up to have a look. He was shocked by what he read, and asked Wu what all this was. Wu said, "These are documents the 6950 Unit left behind. They're useless."

Zhong Changbin said, "Oh, I don't think you can call them useless. Sooner or later someone's going to look into this matter, and in your position you're sure to be blamed."

The two of them found a filing cabinet, an old wooden type with two doors, and stuffed the files inside. Then they found several bed boards and nailed them over the cabinet doors, which they sealed with a paper strip for good measure. On the strip they wrote "Save permanently" and then took the precaution of stamping it with the public-security bureau's seal.

The years passed in a series of political ups and downs, and the incident gradually faded from memory.

In 1982, Deng Xiaoping's reform and opening policy called for the cadre ranks to become "younger and more intellectual, professional and revolutionary." Zhong Changbin happened to fit all four criteria. When the Daoxian CCP committee and county government were reorganized, Zhong underwent vetting by the prefectural CCP organs and county CCP committee, with the intention of appointing him county deputy CCP secretary and secretary of the commission for discipline inspection. But on the very day that his superiors came to discuss this appointment with Zhong, someone reported to the county CCP committee that Zhong Changbin's family (still living in the village) had cut down 23 of the production team's trees to build their house. Although a thorough investigation vindicated Zhong and his family, the case scuppered Zhong's promotion to deputy CCP secretary.

This was a hard blow to Zhong Changbin, and he felt depressed and discouraged for a very long time. Just then, Daoxian established its task force to deal with the aftermath of the Cultural Revolution massacre, and after lengthy consideration the county CCP committee leaders decided Zhong Changbin was the best choice to lead this work. The first time they approached Zhong, he refused, and he refused the second time as well. The third time they approached him, the county CCP committee leaders said, "This is revolutionary work and the county has already made its decision. It's inappropriate for you to refuse a third request." At that, Zhong Changbin finally relented.

Upon taking on this task, Zhong Changbin felt dejected and at a loss; such a large county with a population of more than 400,000, and an incident that had occurred 16 years before under very different circumstances—how could he even begin to deal with it? Then Zhong remembered the filing cabinet. But that had been so long ago—did it even still exist? He rushed over to the county public-security bureau and saw the filing cabinet right where he and Wu Guiwen had left it, nailed shut and with the writing on the seal paper still faintly legible. He opened it up, and apart from being yellowed with age, the documents inside were completely intact. No one had disturbed them in all those 16 years.

Zhong Changbin bowed his head into his hands: "This was heaven's will. . . ."

AFTERWORD: LIVING FOR TRUTH

1

The first draft of this historical record was completed in November 1986. The second draft was completed in 1989. I shelved the second draft for a long time, partly due to the social environment at that time, but even more because of my own need for soul-searching. But I never stopped thinking about the Daoxian massacre, and I continued my inquiries because it had become part of my life and even part of me. With the help, support, and concern of many friends, I finally finished adding and verifying the material that allowed me to complete the third draft in August 2007, just before the 40th anniversary of the Daoxian massacre.

After the Chinese edition of *The Killing Wind* was published in Hong Kong and was allowed to circulate online in mainland China, I made a special trip to Daoxian to gauge the book's reception there. I was gratified to learn that among survivors of the massacre who were still alive and well, the majority opinion was that the book was fair and objective. Inevitably there were other views as well, but these were generally differences of opinion rather than fact. Synthesizing the views of various parties, I took the opportunity to produce this revised and expanded edition to bolster, correct, or clarify content that others disputed, and to restore some passages that had been edited out. Various parties antagonistic to each other are in basic agreement that *The Killing Wind* provides an authentic depiction of the massacre in its outline and through its individual vignettes.

Several scholars and readers coincidentally raised the same two questions with me:

(1) What happened to those chiefly responsible for the Daoxian massacre, and why does the book avoid this issue?
(2) What's the story behind the sudden withdrawal of the 47th Army's 6950 Unit that was sent to Daoxian to halt the killing?

I'll start with the first question.

It's not that I avoided this subject, but rather that at the outset I wasn't sufficiently aware of its significance, and I missed the best opportunity to cover it in the course of my reporting. Fortunately I was eventually able to make some follow-up inquiries.

After the Cultural Revolution massacre in Daoxian and the 10 counties and cities around it, there were two rounds of dealing with the people responsible for the killings. The first round occurred from 1968 to 1974; the second, during the aftermath work from June 1984 to December 1986.

As mentioned before, apart from collective killings of black elements and their offspring, the Daoxian massacre included a substantial number of "purely" criminal homicides. From 1968 to 1974, while the Cultural Revolution was still in progress, the Daoxian Chinese Communist Party (CCP) committee and revolutionary committee tried 12 people who had aroused particularly intense public reactions, and against whom there was irrefutable evidence of rape and murder or of revenge killings against poor and lower-middle peasants or revolutionary cadres. These people were sentenced to prison terms of 5 to 15 years or more. Even so, the official assessment at the time was that the revolutionary general orientation of poor and lower-middle peasants killing black elements in order to defend themselves and the Red regime "had always been correct," even if it resulted in the deaths of a few innocents, so apart from those 12 people, others who had been detained and investigated for such crimes were rehabilitated. Individuals who had taken a leading role in organizing, planning, and directing the killings were largely untouched. In all of Lingling Prefecture, 77 people were tried and imprisoned (including the 12 from Daoxian), and 13 were sentenced to death.

After the Task Force began its formal inquiries in June 1984, it was able to gain a sense of the origin and development of the killings. The investigation concluded that 9,093 people had been killed in Lingling Prefecture, including 4,519 in Daoxian, that not one of the 9,000-plus victims had engaged in any kind of counterrevolutionary speech or actions, and that the dozens of "counterrevolutionary organizations" supposedly unearthed at that time (including seven in Daoxian) all were fictitious. A total of 15,050 people in the prefecture were found to have direct involvement in the killings (through organizing and planning, supervising, and encouraging, or actual killing), including 7,281 in Daoxian.

Handling such a large number of perpetrators was a very thorny problem; failing to deal with them would be irresponsible to society and history, but dealing with them too harshly would plant the seeds of instability. In accordance with directives from the CCP Central Committee and Hunan provincial CCP committee, the Lingling prefectural CCP committee proposed a guiding principle of "the big picture rather than the details, magnanimity rather than severity, and fewer rather than more."

Emulating reparation work carried out in Guangxi, the Task Force recommended criminal charges and CCP discipline against those responsible for major killing incidents. Apart from the groups dealt with in the first round, these included three kinds of people: the main planners of killings at the commune level and above, under circumstances that were especially horrific and had particularly serious consequences; those who enthusiastically volunteered to kill people under circumstances that were especially horrific and had particularly serious consequences; and those who continued to kill people after the upper levels had explicitly forbidden further killing.

Daoxian announced the arrest of 9 people on May 26, 1985, and another 21 were arrested on October 4. Following vehement demands by the family members of victims, another 12 were subsequently arrested, for a total of 42. Among them, 24 had been state cadres prior to their arrest. Among the 23 arrested for planning killings at the commune level and above, 11 were accused of revenge killings against poor peasants or revolutionary cadres; 3, of raping their victims before killing them; 1, of enthusiastically volunteering to kill people; another, of continuing to kill following the official prohibition; and 3, of acting under orders to organize killings under especially horrific circumstances and with particularly serious consequences.

A total of 124 people were arrested in Lingling Prefecture, which combined with the 77 convicted during the first round made a grand total of 201.

The Lingling prefectural CCP committee produced sentencing guidelines that required the rate of criminal prosecution to be kept under 2 percent and for the majority of those convicted to be handed prison terms of 10 years or less. These guidelines quickly encountered a major technical problem, however: China's Criminal Law, no matter how leniently applied, required prison sentences of 10 years or more for all these crimes.

On December 26, 1985, the Lingling prefectural CCP committee sent several of its most senior judicial officials to the provincial capital to report to the Hunan Province Politics and Law Committee, which held a special meeting to discuss the matter. The Politics and Law Committee agreed in principle with the prefectural CCP committee's guidelines and called for the application of Article 59 of the Criminal Law (1979 edition), which gave the courts leeway to pass sentences below the statutory limit if circumstances warranted, thereby making the guidelines legally tenable. Hunan's leaders then issued a major directive: "On the question of sentencing, consider the policy implications and extensive scope of this matter and unite everyone's understanding."

After the technical problems were resolved, the Daoxian People's Court in late 1985 and early 1986 tried Jiang Wenjing, Yuan Lifu, Zheng Youzhi, and 39 others accused of major responsibility for the killings. One was sentenced to life in prison; seven, to prison terms of eleven to fifteen years; fifteen, to prison terms of eight to ten years; twelve, to prison terms of four to seven years; and two, to prison terms of three years. Among the 24 former state cadres, the most harshly sentenced was Yuan Lifu, at 13 years, followed by Zheng Youzhi, sentenced to 10 years, and then Jiang Wenjing, Zhou Renbiao, and others, sentenced to 8 years. Huang Shangrong, Jiang Guangde, Zeng Qingsong, and Zheng Jitian were among those sentenced to five years. The lightest sentence of three years went to He Tian. Added to the 12 people sentenced during the first round, 54 people were convicted and sentenced, just 0.74 percent of the total number of people responsible for the killings. Among the 42 prosecuted in the second round, not one protested his innocence or appealed his conviction or sentence.

Another 948 people were disciplined by the CCP or government, composing 13 percent of those held responsible for the killings. Among them, 631 were CCP members, 449 of whom were expelled from the CCP and 181 of whom were forbidden to register as members during CCP rectification, while one other was stripped of probationary CCP status. Among 402 local administrative cadres (i.e., "cadres released from production") who were directly implicated in the killings, 209, or just over half, were disciplined; 108 were expelled from the CCP, 2 were forbidden to register, and 1 was stripped of probationary status, while 98 were dismissed from their official positions, demoted, or handed demerits. Among the 114 who committed serious errors during the killings and subsequently joined the CCP, 96 were expelled, 10 were forbidden to register, and 1 lost probationary status.

The popular saying in Daoxian that "three lives cost party membership" was no exaggeration.

As some of those imprisoned for the massacre began to be released in 1989, someone pointed out that arrangement had to be made for them, or they might become a source of future instability. Following a request for instructions form the Lingling prefectural CCP committee, the Hunan provincial CCP committee's organization department on December 20, 1989, issued its Document No. 55, stating, "Taking into consideration that these people committed their crimes under the special historical conditions of the Cultural Revolution, it is appropriate to follow the principle of strict handling on the political side while providing them with a way out in respect of livelihood, and following completion of their sentences, they should be settled appropriately."

Following the release of this document, state cadres and workers punished for the Cultural Revolution killings were typically released before completion of their sentences on a variety of pretexts, with people such as Zheng Youzhi serving only three years and Yuan Lifu serving only five years. Initially provided with temporary work, they eventually resumed their official positions as a matter of course. A small number met premature deaths. He Tian died of cancer soon after his release. Zeng Qingsong died after falling off a scaffold while building a new house. The unluckiest of them was Zheng Youzhi; badly beaten in prison during the Cultural Revolution, he was imprisoned again by the Task Force, at which point his wife divorced him. Following his release, his health went from bad to worse and he died within a few years, his body rotting for three days before it was discovered. Apart from these few, however, the majority of those convicted of the killings ultimately retired with honor. From what I've heard, the situation in the other 10 counties and cities was much the same.

Now for the second question: why did the 47th Army's 6950 Unit withdraw from Daoxian overnight in September 1968? This remains a mystery to the present day.

I took a strong interest in this matter all along, but given the Chinese People's Liberation Army's revered status as the cornerstone of the dictatorship of the proletariat, the chances of a direct interview were close to nil, and I could only prod the topic through indirect methods. The first time I did my reporting in Daoxian, informed sources gave me three explanations: (1) the Task Force said it was simply a routine transfer to relieve the garrison, (2) the Red Alliance said it was because the unit committed the error of "supporting a faction instead of supporting the Left," and (3) the Revolutionary Alliance said the unit was pushed out by Bu Zhanya (at that time political commissar of the Hunan Provincial Military Region), described as a backstage manipulator planted in Hunan by the Lin Biao Counterrevolutionary Clique. No one produced evidence to support any of these theories.

A book called *Record of the 47th Army's Three Supports and Two Militarizations in Hunan*, published as a pamphlet for internal circulation, is effectively an official history of the 47th Army's Support-the-Left work in Hunan.[1] The author, Li Zhenxiang, was head of the 47th Army propaganda department and a Support-the-Left cadre, and the consultant, Li Yuan, was head of the Hunan Provincial Revolutionary Committee Preparatory Group, chairman of the Revolutionary Committee, and commander of the 47th Army. The book includes a section relating the official version of the Daoxian Cultural Revolution massacres, which departs little from the facts but connects some incidents with no actual causality between them, and uses the exquisite succinctness and ambiguous but logical construction of the Chinese language to create a misreading of the incident as largely the result of factional struggle and intensified class struggle.

Although *Record of the 47th Army's Three Supports and Two Militarizations in Hunan* provides no account of the 6950 Unit's withdrawal from Daoxian, the book does provide one additional piece of information, which is that after the Hunan Provincial Revolutionary Committee was formally established in April

1968, it made the military districts and subdistricts responsible for "Support-the-Left" work in all 15 prefectures and cities under the direct jurisdiction of the province, with the exception of the cities of Zhuzhou, Xiangtan, and Hengyang. It would be natural under those conditions for the 6950 Unit to be ordered out of Daoxian and for the reorganized county People's Armed Forces Defense Department (PAFD) to take over the county's Support-the-Left work.

Even so, why did the unit leave in such a hurry and without prior notice to other leading members of the county revolutionary committee that it had single-handedly organized? There should have been at least a routine hand-over process.

Through personal connections, I made a special effort to consult several former 47th Army Support-the-Left cadres who had worked in the provincial revolutionary committee and remained in Hunan. Most pleaded ignorance or hazy memories, but one old comrade's recollections shed some real light. During the Cultural Revolution, Zhong Zhenhua had accompanied 47th Army commander Li Yuan to Daoxian as his confidential staff officer, so he had an in-depth understanding of the situation. He read the earlier edition of my book from start to finish and wrote many comments in the margins. This is what he told me:

> When I heard about the situation in Daoxian at the time, I was deeply shocked, but the Cultural Revolution was full of violence and there were many major incidents. In comparison, the Daoxian killings didn't seem all that extraordinary, but they came to be regarded with increasing importance later [after the Cultural Revolution]. At the time, it was felt that this was just a small and localized countercurrent to the Cultural Revolution, and that once troops were sent there, the situation would be quickly resolved.
>
> After taking up Support-the-Left work, the 6950 Unit was supporting the Revolutionary Alliance—on this point we requested instructions from the 47th Army's senior officers and the provincial leadership. At that time, the opinions of the provincial military district differed from those of the 47th Army command, so the Lingling Military Subdistrict (and Daoxian PAFD), being under the jurisdiction of the provincial military district, was naturally in conflict with the 6950 Unit. The crux of the disagreement was the composition of the county revolutionary committee, and the 6950 Unit and Lingling Military Subdistrict became deadlocked over the issue. Some members of the county revolutionary committee were in fact problematic; the county PAFD reported issues relating to them to the provincial military district, and many were at a particular disadvantage since the province had

just ferreted out the "Liang-Shang Counterrevolutionary Clique. The senior 47th Army officers and the provincial leaders ultimately decided to put the Lingling Military Subdistrict in charge of the Support-the-Left work, which meant that the 6950 Unit had to be transferred out.

Why leave in such a hurry, without giving notice? It's because time was too tight and the situation was too complicated. The evacuation order came very suddenly—Comrade Li Yuan personally telephoned and ordered the troops to report to army headquarters [in Changsha] within three days, saying the provincial military district would take over Support-the-Left duties. That was a very tight deadline at a time when transportation was so inconvenient, and there was no time to waste. In any case, the local troops taking over the Support-the-Left work had different views from ours, and we had no way of knowing what they would do, so what was the point of giving notice?

When asked if the 6950 Unit's Support-the-Left work had been criticized or if the unit could be said to have been "pushed out," Mr. Zhong said very decisively, "No. At that time, the armed forces placed the greatest emphasis on unity and mutual assistance and on not undercutting each other. The focus wasn't on the Daoxian killings but on restoring revolutionary order. Chairman Mao said there could be no more chaos. The [47th] Army leaders and provincial leaders were focusing on the game plan for the entire province."

Mr. Zhong provides us with the key to a historical puzzle that is ripe for future inquiry.

2

While reporting in Xianzijiao District, we read a poem in the notebook of one of the Task Force comrades.

Qilü on the Task Force's Work
Based on the Chairman's "Long March"[2]
The Task Force fears no hardship,
Lab'ring without food or sleep.
Endless stacks of lawless death,
Human heads roll like clay orbs,
The Xiaoshui full of corpses,
Chilling hearts even today.
The Third Plenum guides the course,
Order brought out of chaos.

I copied down this poem, not because it is particularly well written or profound, but because it revealed a particular attitude and emotional inclination and reflected the difficulties the Task Force faced. Was it merely by chance that such a poem appeared in the notebook of a Task Force official in Xianzijiao District, where the killings were fewest and the issue was uncovered with relative thoroughness? We found that the knowledge and attitude of individual investigators determined the scope and depth of what they uncovered. In some localities, members of the Task Force socialized with people responsible for the killings, sometimes even staying in their homes, and in these localities little was uncovered; indeed, some cases became even more unclear the more they were investigated.

The Daoxian CCP committee's summary report on dealing with the aftermath of the unlawful Cultural Revolution killings states: "Through this work, we accomplished three things: the first was to ascertain the origin and development of the killings, the second was to make appropriate arrangements for the family members of victims, and the third was to properly deal with the crimes and errors of those responsible. Through this work, we established the facts, drew important historical lessons, and enhanced the sense of law and discipline. The vast majority of the surviving family members are satisfied, and the vast majority of those responsible have admitted their guilt and error." I feel this summary lacks basis in fact. What we saw while reporting in Daoxian was that the origin and development of the killings were basically ascertained, but important historical lessons were not truly drawn. The majority of surviving family members felt frustrated in their efforts for justice. Most of those responsible for the killings refused to admit error, much less guilt. It grieves me to write this, and I feel it is letting down the comrades in the Task Force, especially those who gave us so much support in our reporting; I know they will be deeply disappointed and consider me ungrateful.

We know very well that the Task Force's work was enormously difficult, and without their effort, Daoxian's Cultural Revolution killings may well have disappeared into the fog of history.

One of the leading comrades of the Task Force told us: "The Cultural Revolution killings that occurred in Daoxian and surrounding counties left enormous scars— quite apart from the dead, the survivors were also profoundly damaged. Especially since 1982, because of the new situation and new problems accompanying the implementation of the production responsibility system in the countryside, some of the ways for collectively supporting and looking after surviving family members have disappeared. According to preliminary figures, more than 40,000 family members of victims in this region are in dire financial straits. Some are homeless and sleep with cattle or pigs or in public toilets or under the eaves of other people's homes or under trees. They rummage through garbage piles or beg for food, and some even resort to robbery. When we first arrived in Daoxian, we saw beggars everywhere in Daojiang Town. It was impossible to sit down in a restaurant and enjoy a peaceful meal. The minute you raised your rice bowl, you would be surrounded by ragged and famished-looking beggars staring at the bowl of rice in your hands. You could only set your bowl down and leave. Then the beggars would swarm over it, and the bowl would be licked clean."

There was still a big market for the notion that killing black elements had been justified, that it was meritorious, and that it aided the preservation of the Red regime. As soon as the Task Force arrived at the scene, its members were surrounded by a chorus of opposition. Some said, "It was just a few black elements killed more than 10 years ago, why are you stirring up trouble?" Some said, "There's so much work to be done, but you come here for this bullshit!" Some said, "Chairman Mao is dead and now the landlord restitution corps has come!" Some said, "Why are you speaking up for the class enemies?" Some went about day and night crying at the top of their voice, "Chairman Mao! Chairman Mao! Come back and save us!" Some even took poison or hanged themselves in protest, while others fled, fearing they'd be called to account. One commune secretary put it most concretely: "If you'd come here to help us manage our crops or deal with family planning, we'd have feasted you with chickens and ducks. But no one's going to support you on this."

When the Task Force came to talk to one man who helped orchestrate the killings, he said, "I killed on order from above. I was acting under orders." His wife, standing next to him, broke in: "It was you higher-ups who gave the word to carry out the killings, so what the hell are you investigating? If the higher-ups told us to kill you Task Force members right now, I'd do it!"

At the same time, conflict was intensifying between those responsible for the killings and surviving family members.

The Lingling prefectural CCP committee and various county CCP committees held a special meeting to discuss the situation and proposed a series of measures for the task forces in each county to carry out. The Daoxian Task Force went down to the grassroots and held symposiums and study sessions refuting the Cultural Revolution and impressing on the cadres and masses that the killings had resulted from the ultra-Leftist thinking of the Lin Biao-Jiang Qing Counterrevolutionary Cliques, the serious breakdown of the legal system, and paralysis in CCP and government organs, and that the aftermath had to be handled on the basis of the specific historical conditions and in accordance with specific policies. No one was allowed to take things into his own hands or raise additional demands.

The Task Force members ran themselves ragged and talked themselves hoarse as they carried out what would now be called "truth and reconciliation" efforts, while also resolving the livelihood issue of survivors of the massacre. The Task Force provided new homes to 40,000 survivors, and 401 investigation groups carried out focused investigations.

Given this prodigious effort, it may seem presumptuous for me to question the outcome of the Task Force's work. Yet, dear friends in the Task Force, what choice do I have? How much say did you have in what you did? How much of it transcended or even acknowledged the limitations of that era? In facing the darkest chapter in our nation's history, it is only through "the longing for love, the search for knowledge, and unbearable pity for the suffering of mankind"[3] that we can save ourselves. We have no choice but to bravely and loudly state the truth about this incident.

3

There is so much more to write, and that I would like to write, but completing this historical record requires the effort of all Chinese society and its people. The only purpose I can serve is as a camera and recorder.

Chinese history, especially modern history, is full of erasures and falsification and portions inked out or obscured by mold. Discussion, reflection, or even recollection of appalling incidents of violence has repeatedly been made taboo, while the vacuum is filled with monstrous lies and the brainwashing of one generation after another. Each of these junctures has sealed the tragic fate of China's people. Once a group or even a generation of the duped and misled regains consciousness through personal experience, the creators of lies can easily find a new group of victims and of the credulous in the next generation. Truth is a tonic for the conscience of a nation. There is nothing more toxic to a society than the lies imposed by those above on those below.

We must treat all bogus truths, bogus history, bogus incidents, and bogus models as we treat fake merchandise and tainted food, relegating them to the rubbish heap of history. Only then will our people truly have hope.

This is living for truth.

We need to reflect on the Cultural Revolution massacre in Daoxian for the sake of the survivors, for posterity, and for the future of our people. New problems and conflicts will continue to arise, and although we can't foresee what methods will solve these problems and conflicts, we should know which methods must never be used.

In a sense, the Daoxian massacre can become a precious national legacy, depending on how we deal with it. Societies that refuse to acknowledge and reflect on history have no way to establish a stable value system and sense of ethics and therefore have difficulty producing a sense of security and belonging.

The best test of a nation's strength comes through confronting the darkest chapters of its history.

With the onset of the 21st century, the grand spectacle of the mass movements of the 1960s and 1970s is mentioned less and less, and scenes from the Cultural Revolution that appear on television or in the movies are so superficial and stereotyped as to become a running joke. There's nothing even remotely funny about an episode involving so many human lives and so much blood. The Cultural Revolution provided a 10-year performance space for China's politics, economy, culture, and even national character; all the absurdity and evil of China's past and present finds its fountainhead and footnote here. Yet, distracted by the lures of progress and prosperity, we've missed a prime opportunity for a radical overhaul of Chinese culture and a rejuvenation of our people's spiritual health as we've emerged black and blue from physical and mental trauma only to swarm onto the next train to our desires, final destination unknown, trampling all remaining morality, justice, conscience, and shame into oblivion.

Who was actually the chief instigator, and what was the real reason for this barbarous slaughter? The victims have the right to demand that the truth be brought to light; otherwise, how can we be sure that another such horrific incident won't occur? Most of those responsible for the killings had no personal grievances against their victims. Who sparked the fire of hatred in their hearts? Who opened the door to their animal passions? Who gave them guns and knives and entrusted them with the power over life and death? A family member of a Daoxian victim put it well: "They were pathetic. They were slaves with only one pair of trousers controlling slaves like us who had no trousers at all." The reason all this happened was the slave mentality that had become entrenched among the Chinese people, which grew from the soil of the autocratic system, planted there by autocrats for their use.

How long must we wait for the day when it will be possible to fairly and objectively bring the actual perpetrators of the Daoxian massacre to the court of history, giving justice to the victims and comfort to their families, as well as a clear explanation for future generations?

The Chinese national spirit is often described as one of pressing resolutely forward under the greatest difficulties. But this spirit requires "iron-shouldered torchbearers of justice," intellectuals with a profound and critical mentality, not theorists for hire. The British philosopher Bertrand Russell once said, "Men fear thought as they fear nothing else on earth—more than ruin, more even than death. Thought is subversive and revolutionary, destructive and terrible; thought is merciless to privilege, established institutions, and comfortable habits; thought is anarchic and lawless, indifferent to authority, careless of the well-tried wisdom of the ages. Thought looks into the pit of hell and is not afraid. . . . Thought is great and swift and free, the light of the world, and the chief glory of man."[4] In a sense, the history of humanity is the history of human thought. Without thought, we would still be eating raw meat and clawing our way up the evolutionary ladder through natural selection. A nation that holds that "the more intellectual a person is, the more reactionary" is doomed for self-destruction, while an emphasis on cultivating educated people to become mere parrots and yes-men results in a castration of the soul.

I've left these words so that posterity will not be duped by history, because there's nothing in the world more duplicitous and mercurial than the human condition.

4

The Buddha said: Lay down your butcher's knife and become a buddha.

Appendix I

BASIC STATISTICS ON THE VICTIMS OF THE DAOXIAN CULTURAL REVOLUTION KILLINGS

(For the county's 36 villages and towns)

District Name (Number)		Meihua (2)	Xianzijiao (5)	Qingtang (6)	Xianglinpu (7)	Simaqiao (8)	Qingxi (9)	Gongba (10)	Shouyan (11)	Daojiang Town	County jurisdiction	Total
Scope	No. of communes/towns	3	4	5	5	4	6	4	4	1	12	36
	Production brigades	32	43	56	63	54	59	72	72	5	24	468
	Production teams	90	99	163	250	153	217	336	250	8	24	1590
	Households	135	134	269	543	270	358	643	396	17	63	2828
Sex	Male	138	143	288	725	400	446	897	443	23	64	3567
	Female	19	9	64	191	133	171	299	92	4	10	992
	Total	157	152	352	916	533	617	1196	535	27	74	4559
Class	Black element	86	71	202	346	213	239	531	281	13	12	1994
	Black element offspring	49	49	107	520	287	304	575	201	12	49	2153
	Poor or lower-middle peasant	22	28	40	31	32	70	75	46		6	350
	Other		4	3	19	1	4	15	7	2	7	62
Political affiliation	Communist Party member		1	2	2		1	2	1			9
	Communist Youth League member	2			5	2	3	2			3	18

Occupation	State cadre	2	2	2	5	1	1	4	3		9	29
	Teacher	8	8	10	25	11	21	29	6		7	125
	Medical worker	1	2	2	2	3	3	2			8	23
	Worker	1	1	1	5	6		5			19	37
	Villager	145	140	337	879	518	586	1156	526	27	31	4345
Killing method	Shooting	53	103	189	495	86	74	145	241	4	38	1428
	Stabbing	40	4	46	152	126	93	442	155			1058
	Drowning	17	47	88	1	180	90	13		16	1	453
	Explosion	21	17	28	14	21	7				10	118
	Pushed from a height			9	38	19	137					203
	Burial alive	3	1	3	128	108	130	6			5	384
	Beating	1	12	8	88	22	18	68	15		2	234
	Strangulation			1	4	1	57	4		1		68
	Burning	3	5		23	59	37					127
	Suicide	19	32	37	52	52	51	121	97	6	18	485
Households eradicated		5	7	57	55	24	46	12			1	207
Forced to flee		58	26	23	106	56	71	102	133	12	1	588

Note: In 1967, the population of Meihua District was around 29,000, so the number of deaths composed 0.54 percent of the total population. Lijiaping Commune was part of Meihua District at that time but was put under the jurisdiction of Shuangpai County after the Cultural Revolution, and the fatalities in that commune were also transferred to Shuangpai County for statistical purposes. For missing Districts 1, 3, and 4, see the explanation in chapter 6.

Appendix II

OFFICIAL CULPABILITY IN DAOXIAN'S KILLING WIND

I have in my possession a report submitted to the Lingling prefectural Chinese Communist Party (CCP) committee by the Task Force, which I at one point excised from the book on the advice of some comrades. There were a number of reasons for this, including requirements relating to publication, the need to protect people who had provided information, and the wish to preserve stability and unity, but the fundamental reason was that it was too shocking and subversive. In the course of the current revision, I decided to restore it for the sake of posterity.

Before quoting this report, I took the precaution of giving it to Liu Xianxi, who paid a heavy price for his participation in the 1968 "exposure study sessions" on the Daoxian killings. After reading this report, Liu said, "The actual situation was much more serious than this. The lid was never truly lifted off the Daoxian killings. In particular, this report doesn't touch on the PAFD [People's Armed Forces Department] cadres involved, and without bringing them into it, it's impossible to uncover the truth of the Daoxian killings. During the 1968 'exposure study sessions,' He Xia, Zhang Mingchi, and others wrote confessions that pinpointed several PAFD commanders and a small number of county party committee leaders. In particular, [county PAFD political commissar] Liu Shibin circulated reports on the enemy situation at every meeting and incited killings. [County PAFD commander] Cui Baoshu deceived his superiors and pressured his subordinates, lying about the situation and hiding the truth of the killings from the 47th Army and the provincial Cultural Revolution Committee. There was also a deputy political commissar, Qiu Qinglong, who was very substandard and sloppy, and he spoke a lot of nonsense. PAFD military affairs section head Zhou XX and logistics section head Liu XX, who assumed command of the Red Alliance's Yingjiang headquarters, were very problematic. . . . These people all bear an inescapable responsibility for the Daoxian massacre. None of them is named in this report, and that is manifestly unfair to those who are named. The reason these people weren't investigated and punished was because they were in military uniform. I've never been able to understand why people who committed errors while wearing a blue Mao suit could be pursued, but not those wearing yellow military uniforms."

Following are excerpts from the Task Force report:

Some Circumstances Relating to Cadres Implicated in the "Killing Wind"

There are many people implicated in the "killing wind"; state cadres alone number 215 (the actual number is in fact much greater). Among the 150 people who have been investigated, 95 are cadres of the level of commune deputy director or above, including 25 reporting directly to the prefectural level or above.

Cadres had three main types of involvement in the killing wind:

First, they incited and orchestrated the killings, personally proposed names, and authorized and mobilized killings. These people included 188 state cadres, of whom 78 were at the level of commune deputy director or above (including 10 reporting directly to the prefectural level or above). The most problematic of these include:

[Thirteen cadres are listed, with details of their participation as narrated in this book.]

Second, they took arbitrary stands sympathizing with and supporting the killings. Preliminary information indicates that such people included 27 state cadres, 20 of whom are currently cadres of commune vice director or above (and 11 reporting directly to the prefectural level or above), in particular the following:

[Six cadres are listed, with details of their participation.]

Third, preliminary information indicates 25 cases of killings for the purpose of personal revenge or to obtain the assets or wives of others.

According to preliminary information, 90 cadres at the level of commune deputy director or above are implicated in the "killing wind," including:

(1) Five who killed with their own hands;
(2) Twenty-nine who authorized killings or specified persons to be killed;
(3) Eight who participated in discussions about killings;
(4) Fifteen who mobilized killings;
(5) Eight who supervised or urged killings;
(6) Twenty-five who took a stand in support of killings.

Role Position	Killed	Authorized	Suggested names	Participated	Orchestrated	Supervised and urged	Supported	Revenge killing	Total
Commissioner							1		1
Provincial/prefectural department director							4		4
County CCP secretary/deputy secretary		1					1		2
County director/deputy director		1							1
County bureaucracy	2		1		1		1		5
County department director	1		1						2
County department deputy director		1		1			3		5
District CCP secretary/deputy secretary		2	1		1		2		6
District director					2		2		4
District deputy director	2		1	2			1		6
Section chief	1	10	2	2	3	3	2	1	24

(continued)

Role Position	Killed	Authorized	Suggested names	Participated	Orchestrated	Supervised and urged	Supported	Revenge killing	Total
Commune CCP secretary/deputy secretary	1	1	3	2	2	3			12
Commune director/deputy director	2	6	2		2		2		14
District CCP committee member		5	2	1	1	2	1		12
Ordinary cadre	6	10	5	13	11	5	2		52
Unknown	3	19	5	10	15	7	5	1	65
Total	16	58	23	31	38	20	27	2	215

	Formerly reporting to the prefecture or above	*Currently reporting to the prefecture or above*
Killed	1	3
Authorized killings	4	4
Proposed names	1	3
Sympathized with or supported	7	11
Participated or arranged		1
Total	13	25

Name list:

Sympathized with or supported killings: Xiong Bing'en, Yu Shan, Wang Ansheng, He Rongyu, Li Mingde, Zhu Guangrong, Xiao Fuzhi, Zhang Renda

Authorized killings: Li Laiwen, Zheng Jitian, Yang Junxian

Proposed victims: Wu Ronggao

Killed: Ou Caiqing

NOTES

Foreword: Blood Awakening

1. Zhu Houze (1931–2010), appointed propaganda head in 1985 under Hu Yaobang, was widely respected for his fresh approach during a time of unprecedented openness in China, and for introducing a "three broadenings" policy of "generosity, tolerance, and lenience." He was deposed along with Hu in 1987.
2. "*Quanli shichang jingji zhidu*" is a term Yang uses to refer to an economic system in which political power is the key market factor (as opposed to a plutonomy, in which the economy is controlled merely by the richest regardless of their political power).

Introduction

1. The article, titled "A True Record of the Massacre in Dao County, Hunan Province, in Late Summer and Early Autumn 1967," which was published under the byline Zhang Cheng in Hong Kong's *Open Magazine* in 2001, was written jointly by myself and Zhang Minghong.

Chapter 1

1. Black elements included landlords, rich peasants, counterrevolutionaries, and bad elements. Landlords and rich peasants were classified by the possession of property; counterrevolutionaries could be categorized on the basis of activities prior to Liberation, such as service to the Kuomintang regime, or current resistance to the CCP or to socialism by word or deed. "Bad element" was an all-inclusive term applied to thieves, swindlers, murders, arsonists, hooligans, and others causing serious violations of public order.
2. Translator's Note (TN): The Socialist Education movement, which some scholars regard as a dress rehearsal for the Cultural Revolution, was launched by Mao in 1963 to remove "reactionary" elements from the bureaucracy. Its goal was to "cleanse" politics, economy, organization, and ideology, as a result of which it was also referred to as the Four Cleanups campaign. The campaign, which lasted until the Cultural Revolution began in 1966, required intellectuals to go to the countryside to be reeducated by peasants.
3. This is the first of many appearances that Chen Zhixi will make in this book in connection with the killings in Daoxian. I will provide more-thorough background on him later in the book.
4. There are many versions of these 21 categories, but generally speaking, they consisted of landlords, rich peasants, counterrevolutionaries, bad elements, Rightists, capitalists, and spies; people who had served in the police, military police, or Youth Corps or as military officers or functionaries under the "puppet" Kuomintang regime; and moneylenders, concubines, peddlers, prostitutes, sorcerers, monks, Daoist priests, nuns, and vagrants.

5. TN: The official name for the Great Famine that occurred during the Great Leap Forward, killing an estimated 36 million people.

Chapter 2

1. Translator's Note (TN): The "smashing of the four olds" was a campaign that began in mid-August 1966, aimed at destroying "old customs, old culture, old habits, and old ideas."
2. The Task Force later verified that Xianglinpu, Qingtang, and Shangguan Districts all posted notices of their killings.
3. TN: The Celestial Maiden is a Buddhist deity bringing blessings, depicted in a famous Peking Opera of the same name.
4. TN: In October 1933, Mao wrote "How to Differentiate the Classes in the Rural Areas" to clarify the classification of individuals and households during Land Reform. Mao delineated the rural classes as landlord, rich peasant, middle peasant, poor peasant, and hired laborer on the basis of possession of land and other assets. This classification, further refined with breakdowns into upper-middle and lower-middle peasant, formed the basis for the treatment of individuals and families (through inherited status) through the decades that followed.
5. TN: For an account of the notorious Guangxi killings, which included instances of cannibalism, see Zheng Yi, *Scarlet Memorial: Tales of Cannibalism in Modern China*, edited and translated by T. P. Sym (Boulder, CO: Westview, 1996).
6. TN: Zhou Enlai first called for the modernization of agriculture, industry, national defense, and science and technology at the 4th National People's Congress in 1963. The "Four Modernizations" were officially launched by Deng Xiaoping in 1978, marking the beginning of the reform era.
7. TN: The Third Plenum, held December 18–22, 1978, marked the launch of "reform and opening" under Deng Xiaoping and put an emphasis on economic development under the "Four Modernizations" and "seeking truth from facts," while initiating a repudiation of the Cultural Revolution (which was finally publicly negated in 1981, five years before Tan Hecheng was assigned to report on the Daoxian killings) and ending the Maoist personality cult. The catastrophic Tangshan earthquake occurred in 1976, the same year as the deaths of Premier Zhou Enlai and Chairman Mao Zedong. An accurate death toll has never been reported, but estimates range from around 250,000 to 700,000.
8. TN: President Liu Shaoqi advocated this approach in his speech opening the CCP Central Committee's Lushan Conference on July 16, 1959, which was marked by enormous conflict over the drawbacks and accomplishments of the Great Leap Forward. Liu reversed the order of discussing problems and accomplishments out of fear of offending Mao—a fact that contributes to the irony of this quote.
9. Wen Yu, *China's "Leftist" Disaster* (Beijing: Chaohua chubanshe, 1993).

Chapter 3

1. Xiong Bing'en was county CCP secretary, but at this time, the top CCP official at the county level was the party first secretary, Shi Xiuhua, making the CCP secretary the equivalent of a deputy CCP secretary. When the appellation of party first secretary was abolished during the middle period of the Cultural Revolution, many subsequent county CCP committee documents referred to Shi Xiuhua as CCP secretary and Xiong Bing'en as deputy CCP secretary. For the sake of consistency in this book, Xiong will be referred to by the formal title he held at the time, which was CCP secretary.
2. Translator's Note (TN): Nan Batian was the name of a villainous local despot in the 1960 film *The Red Detachment of Women*.
3. While I was reporting in Daoxian, one of those responsible for the killings told me, "The incident shouldn't be referred to as one of killing people, but of killing black elements." I asked, "Aren't black elements people?" "Of course they're people." "So what's the difference between killing people and killing black elements?" "Now it looks like there's no difference, but at that time the difference was enormous."

4. TN: The "three types of people" who after the Cultural Revolution were investigated for ties with the Gang of Four included "rebels who succeeded by following the Lin Biao and Jiang Qing counterrevolutionary groups, people with strong factionalist tendencies, and people who took part in beating, smashing, and looting."

Chapter 4

1. In Toad Grotto, in the hills about 3 kilometers from Shouyan Town, an archaeologist in December 1993 discovered the remains of rice grains planted by human beings more than 12,000 years earlier, as well as a large number of earthenware pottery sherds dating back at least 14,000 years.
2. The words and actions of individuals in this narrative were recorded from the oral accounts of persons involved in the incidents, or are drawn from the files of the Task Force, and they have been corroborated through collateral evidence. This applies throughout the book.
3. When I wrote the first draft of this book around 1987, it was very hard to get a copy of the Bible in mainland China. Someone managed to skirt official restrictions by publishing a volume called *Bible Stories*, based on the Bible. When I read this passage in this book, it moved me so much that I recorded it in my notebook, and its inclusion here struck me as appropriate.
4. It is said that Zheng Shengyao slept outside Secretary Zheng Fengjiao's doorway because the latter had raped his wife. Zheng Shengyao managed to run off to the Xiangyuan tin mine, but he was arrested on August 30 and brought back to Yangjia Commune, where commune cadres beat him to death and then placed a massive stone on his body to signify that he would never rise again.
5. Translator's Note (TN): For a breakdown of the killing methods, see Appendix I.
6. Referring to the order issued on September 5, 1967, by the CCP Central Committee, State Council, Central Military Commission, and Central Cultural Revolution Small Group, which prohibited further killings. This order will be described in detail later in this book.
7. Zheng Yuanzan served under the KMT regime as Daoxian's county head in 1948, and as Ningyuan's county head in 1949. He organized his uprising in Ningyuan on March 29, 1950, and eventually died in Taiwan.
8. The files of the Task Force contain the following text: "Zheng Guozhi, male, born 1945, landlord class, main problems: (1) in order to save his own family, he personally killed one landlord element, (2) he concocted facts and compiled false information on several victims in order to exonerate people who directed killings behind the scenes, or who were themselves killers."
9. TN: When the Great Famine exposed the disastrous consequences of the commune system, some localities began assigning households responsibility for cultivating certain plots of land and allowed them to retain crops in excess of the state quota. These fields came to be known as "responsibility fields." Mao ordered that the practice be terminated by spring 1964, and it was not officially reinstated until 1978, but in the meantime, many localities continued to implement the responsibility field system in some form. See Yang Jisheng, *Tombstone: The Great Chinese Famine 1958–1962*, edited and translated by Stacy Mosher and Guo Jian (New York: Farrar, Straus and Giroux, 2012), pp. 315–19.

Chapter 5

1. For a breakdown of the killing methods, see Appendix I. These statistics are somewhat overstated because they include Lefutang Commune and Yangliutang Commune, which at the time of the massacre were part of Qiaotou District, but which by the time of the Task Force investigation had become part of Shouyan District due to an adjustment of district boundaries in 1984.
2. "Five chiefs" (or "four chiefs") meetings typically related either to class struggle and killings or planting and harvesting. In the context of this book, I will be referring only to the former type.
3. The top three were Youxiang Commune's Yuejin production brigade, Qiaotou Commune's Shengli production brigade, and Gongba Commune's Yanhetang production brigade. Coming in fourth was Lefutang Commune's Longcun production brigade, with 51 killings.

4. According to statistics from the People's Republic of China Agricultural Ministry's People's Commune Management Bureau, the average per capita annual income in China's rural areas in 1967 was less than 70 yuan, among which some 200 million peasants had an average annual income of under 50 yuan, and 120 million earned only 10 cents per day. There were also a considerable number of peasants who labored all year without having any monetary payment distributed to them, and who were actually indebted to their production teams. In Daoxian, official data indicate that the average rural per capita income in 1967 was 64 yuan, with most work teams paying their laborers about 40 cents per day, and a small number paying less than 10 cents. Generally speaking, Daoxian was above average in terms of rural incomes nationwide.

5. Translator's Note (TN): Throughout this book, the term "class enemy" will be employed in place of the more cumbersome designation of "landlord / rich peasant."

6. TN: Xiong is employing the same language Mao Zedong applied to Chiang Kai-shek after the War of Resistance against Japan.

7. TN: The actual Chinese term used here is *tuochan ganbu*, or "cadre released from production." It applied to cadres who were relieved of physical labor to handle administrative duties. We use the translation "administrative cadre" throughout the book for the sake of brevity and clarity.

8. A primary document regarding Deng Jiayu's criminal acts states that Deng referred to himself as director of the "Commune Supreme People's Court of the Poor and Lower-Middle Peasants," and that apart from directing or authorizing the killing of 23 people, he personally tied up 10 victims.

Chapter 6

1. Readers will notice that there is no District 3 in the above list. Before the Cultural Revolution, Daoxian had a District 3, Jiangcun District, which included Jiangcun, Shangwujiang, Tangdi, and Linjia Communes. On March 25, 1965, the Hunan provincial CCP committee issued a document that made Jiangcun District part of Shuangpai County. Notably, the largest number of killings in Shuangpai County occurred at Jiangcun Commune, which was formerly part of Daoxian.

2. Evidence indicates that county deputy CCP secretary Yu Shan also took part in this killing mobilization meeting and praised it as having been "run well, promptly, and with initiative."

3. Translator's Note (TN): Referring to Lin Biao, whom Mao had designated his successor until Lin was killed in an airplane crash while attempting to flee China on September 13, 1971.

4. Daoxian includes some well-populated natural villages (those that existed spontaneously rather than being created for administrative purposes) with long histories, and the largest of these is Dacun, with more than 1,000 households totaling 4,000 people (during the Cultural Revolution, the county seat, Daojiang, had only a little more than 4,000 people). Because Dacun had too many people for a production brigade, it was divided up into two administrative villages known as Dayicun and Da'ercun (literally, First and Second Da Village). During the Cultural Revolution killings, Dacun acted in strict accordance with the spirit of the upper-level directive stating that "one or two troublemaking bad elements could be killed," and only two people were killed, one in Dayicun and another in Da'ercun.

5. Someone testified that the Yingjiang Red Alliance headquarters also had a "Supreme People's Court of the Poor and Lower-Middle Peasants" with formal trials and a sign, which the Revolutionary Alliance was said to have confiscated and displayed at the entrance to the No. 2 High School. However, the Task Force's files made reference only to the peasant court at Ganziyuan, so the sign displayed at the No. 2 High School might have been the Ganziyuan sign.

6. *Authentic Record of the People's Republic of China* (Jilin People's Publishing) states that from October 2 to 4, 1967, some localities in the Guangxi Zhuang Autonomous Region had "supreme people's courts of the poor and lower-middle peasants" that randomly seized black elements and their offspring. On December 24, with the authorization of the CCP Central Committee, the Guangxi Revolutionary Committee Preparatory Committee and Military Subregion jointly declared the peasant supreme courts illegal and ordered them disbanded. TN: The notorious cases of Cultural Revolution killings and cannibalistic practices in Guangxi are described in Zheng Yi's *Scarlet Memorial: Tales of Cannibalism in Modern China*, translated by T. P. Sym (Boulder, CO: Westview, 1996) began in July 1968.

7. The Task Force identified one local supervising cadre (Ou Caiqing, former director of the CCP committee office of the Lengshuitan Paper Mill), one politics and law cadre (Zhou Renbiao), and one commune CCP secretary (Deng Yaochun, former deputy CCP secretary of Simaqiao District's Yangjia Commune) who personally took part in the killings.

Chapter 7

1. This banner was eventually seized by the Revolutionary Alliance and displayed at the entrance of Daoxian's No. 2 High School along with a plaque for the "Supreme People's Court of the Poor and Lower-Middle Peasants."
2. Jiang Weizhu, born in 1948 to a landlord family in Qingtang Commune's Jiangjia production brigade, was imprisoned in 1967 in connection with the New People's Party case, ultimately saving her from being killed in the massacre. Rehabilitated after the Cultural Revolution, she became a teacher.
3. Translator's Note: The political jargon "unify" (*tuanjie*) meant to win someone over so he or she could be included in the revolutionary ranks.
4. Zheng Youzhi specially arranged for logistics department head Zheng Mingchi to purchase several copies of the *Investigative Report on the Hunan Peasant Movement* to distribute to the conference attendees.
5. Referring to the Central Cultural Revolution Small Group's official reply to the 47th Army's "Social Situation Cable" forwarded by the Lingling Military Subdistrict.
6. Starting in February 1967, a meningitis outbreak in Daoxian's villages affected 1,730 people in a year's time, killing 212.
7. This includes Lijiaping Commune, which was still under Daoxian's Chetou District at that time, although it fell under the jurisdiction of Shuangpai County by the time of the Task Force investigation.

Chapter 8

1. Chetou District was renamed Meihua to commemorate the female revolutionary He Baozhen (1902–1934), the first wife of former president Liu Shaoqi and a native of Daoxian's Meihua Township. She joined the CCP in March 1923 and married Liu Shaoqi that same year. After being arrested by the Nationalist authorities in 1933, she was executed in 1934 at the age of 32. When Liu Shaoqi was labeled the CCP's "biggest capitalist roader of the faction in power," He Baozhen lost the respect of her home village, but when Liu Shaoqi was posthumously rehabilitated in 1978, He Baozhen likewise regained her good name.
2. He Wencheng earned less than 30 fen per day, so 180 yuan was the equivalent of two years' pay.
3. Translator's Note: Lijiaping Commune's killings aren't included in the total for Chetou/Meihua District, because the commune was under the jurisdiction of Shuangpai County by the time of the Task Force's investigation.
4. During the Cultural Revolution, the Zhangwufang production brigade was under Chetou District's Meihua Commune, but when the administrative areas were restructured in 1984, it was made part of Qingxi District's Qingkou Township. The Zhangwufang production brigade killed 33 people during the Cultural Revolution.
5. At that time, commune members were highly restricted in their movements, and leaving the village to work required permission from one's production team and production brigade as well as a certificate. Income from a sideline occupation had to be handed over to the production team according to a quota and was converted into work points, which were then distributed at the end of the year.
6. The Task Force files reveal that the production brigade's deputy head, He Kaixian, was also implicated in the revenge killings of He Dingxin and his son because during the Socialist Education movement, He Dingxin had followed his work team's directive to publicly criticize He Kaixian. During this "random killing," when the brigade discussed the name list of people to be killed, the majority were against killing He Dingxin, but He Kaixian insisted, and militia head He Ziliang supported him.

7. Hua Guofeng (1921–2008) was first secretary of the Hunan provincial CCP committee during the Cultural Revolution. He was appointed premier of the State Council in 1976 and became China's supreme leader in October following Mao's death. Because he adhered to "whatever Mao directed or ordered" and committed "ultra-Leftist line errors" by maintaining conservative policies and rejecting reform, he was removed from his position as state council premier in September 1980, and as chairman of the CCP Central Committee and Central Military Commission that December.

Chapter 9

1. Two were provided by the Dongjin brigade, and one each by the Dongfang and Dongfeng brigades, but none were provided by the Dongyuan brigade, where cadres were unable to reach a consensus.
2. According to what the Task Force was able to ascertain, brigade CCP secretary Jiang Shiming had additional motivation for killing He Shanliang, who had criticized him during the Socialist Education movement.
3. Translator's Note: To make the text less confusing for a non-Chinese readership, the translators have removed many names of minor figures, but we wish to state here that Tan did include the names of the perpetrators, with a few stated exceptions.
4. On August 8, 1966, the 11th plenum of the Eighth Central Committee passed the "Stipulations regarding the Proletarian Great Cultural Revolution," which defined and elaborated on the nature, aims, targets, and methods of struggle and policies pertaining to the Cultural Revolution. It was divided into 16 clauses and therefore came to be known as the "Sixteen Articles."

Chapter 10

1. He Shaoji was from a prominent family of officials and scholar farmers. His father, He Linghan, served as a top-ranking official in the court of the Qing emperor Jiaqing. He Shaoji himself was a successful candidate in the highest imperial examination in the Daoguang era, and he served as a minor official in other parts of the country. He's three younger brothers, Shaoye, Shaoqi, and Shaojing, were all master calligraphers in the Qing dynasty, resulting in the appellation of the "four outstanding He brothers." He's grandson, He Weipu, was a nationally famous artist during the Republican era.
2. From what the Task Force was able to ascertain, during the Cultural Revolution killings, Guo Chengshi repeatedly raped women and served as an executioner. Among the 14 people killed in his brigade, seven died by Guo Chengshi's hand.
3. During our reporting in Wanjiazhuang, an informed source told us that Liu Fucai had a dubious relationship with CCP secretary Jiang Fangru's wife, and since Jiang wasn't able to satisfy his wife, he was forced to tolerate it. When the killing wind blew up in 1967, Jiang Fangru took this opportunity to have Liu killed.
4. Translator's Note: The "Five Winds" referred to "unhealthy tendencies" of "communist wind," "exaggeration wind," "coercive commandism wind," "cadre privilege wind," and the "chaotic directives wind," relating to production that arose during the commune movement in 1958 and contributed directly to the Great Famine.
5. The Task Force investigated the rape and killing of Liang Xianlian, but due to lack of evidence they were unable to ascertain the facts or reach a conclusion. What I have recorded here is drawn from the original complaint. As a matter of principle, this book recounts only what the Task Force was able to verify, but because the story of what happened to Liang Xianlian was circulated so widely in Daoxian, I decided to make an exception and include it here.

Chapter 11

1. See Appendix I for a breakdown of killing methods. In the course of repeated statistics gathering, inaccuracies crept in. The figures here are from the final written record, but the totals don't add up neatly.
2. Subsequent investigation determined that this allegation was false.

3. Zhou Renjie's story was told to me by a surviving family member after my book was published in Hong Kong. This family member, who was still badly shaken by the events of that time, also told me stories of many other victims, but I didn't add them to the revised version of the book, in accordance with my principle of including only those stories backed up by official documentation. I made an exception for Zhou Renjie's story, because there are very few accounts relating to suicide cases.

4. Some have challenged the details I provide in these narratives: "You write in such detail; did you see it yourself?" On this I am willing to make the following declaration: first of all, before black elements were killed, all of them had persons assigned to keep watch over them—"Their every word and action was under close surveillance by revolutionaries." Second, these details were told to me by villagers when I did my reporting in 1986, and they all gave the same version of events. Third, historical records need to place an emphasis on detail in order to portray as much as possible the real feelings of those times. The truth is that I haven't reproduced villagers' descriptions of the killings verbatim, because it would be too overwhelmingly horrific for readers.

Chapter 12

1. Translator's Note (TN): This is a different person from the Qingxi District PAFD commander of the same name.

2. After Yang Meiji ran off, he was killed in Simaqiao's Henglinggaoqiao Village while the local militia was searching the hills. It remains a mystery how he learned he was on the killing list. Yang's son, Yang Yanggu, was subsequently also sentenced to death by the brigade's peasant supreme court.

3. The information concerning Gongba Commune is drawn from the Task Force's files.

4. TN: Aesop's fable: One winter a farmer found a snake stiff and frozen with cold. Pitying the creature, he picked it up and tucked it into his shirt. Revived by the warmth and resuming its natural instincts, the snake bit its benefactor. With his dying breath, the farmer lamented, "I am rightly served for pitying a scoundrel." Moral: the greatest kindness will not bind the ungrateful.

5. The Task Force's files reveal that Tian Zibi was killed at the instigation of two "revolutionary teachers" and the principal of the school where he taught.

Chapter 13

1. Translator's Note (TN): Mao in late 1956 initiated a campaign to "let a hundred flowers bloom and a hundred schools of thought contend" to encourage people to speak out about how the CCP should improve its operations. Once too many criticisms were raised, however, the movement turned into an Anti-Rightist campaign in July 1957, resulting in the persecution of hundreds of thousands of those who had spoken out.

2. TN: The "Communist Wind," "Exaggeration Wind," "Coercive Commandism Wind," "Cadre Privilege Wind," and "Chaotic Directives Wind" that arose and then were combated during the Great Leap Forward.

3. TN: This encounter is mentioned by Xu Zhensi in his narrative below.

4. TN: This encounter with Zhu Xianhou and several companions (not actual brothers) is also referred to in Zhu Xianhou's narrative below.

5. TN: See the narrative by Xu Zhenzhong above.

6. TN: Lei Feng was a PLA soldier who after his death in 1962 was promoted as a model of selfless and modest devotion and became the subject of a nationwide propaganda campaign to "learn from comrade Lei Feng."

7. The Task Force's investigation confirmed that Jiang Rutian took part in the killing of 19 people during the Cultural Revolution massacre.

8. TN: See Xu Zhenzhong's narrative above.

Chapter 15

1. Translator's Note (TN): See Appendix I for the breakdown of killing methods.

2. See chapter 9.
3. Baimadu is one of Daoxian's eight main markets and is where the Qingxi District government has its offices. The marketplace was relocated to a hill 200 meters back when the original location was flooded with the construction of the Shuangpai Reservoir in 1961.
4. TN: Liquor into which blood has been dripped, which is shared among a group to signify an oath of loyalty.
5. TN: Not to be confused with the district secretary, whose name has the same pinyin spelling.
6. The Task Force's investigations determined that all these accusations were unfounded.
7. The Task Force's files reveal that Youxiang Commune PAFD commander He Wenzhi was one of the main people responsible for organizing, planning, and carrying out killings at the commune.

Chapter 16

1. Translator's Note: In 1963, Mao arranged a campaign to encourage all of China's peasants to follow the example of self-sacrifice and political awareness set by farmers in Dazhai, Shanxi Province. The campaign was reinforced in the later stage of the Cultural Revolution.

Chapter 17

1. The Xinche pontoon bridge, 100 meters long and composed of 23 conjoined boats, spans the Yanshui (Yongming River) between Xinche Market and Bajia Village in Daoxian's southwest region. The Zhu clan of Bajia Village contributed the funds to construct the bridge in 1795.
2. Translator's Note: Mao Zedong, "Inscription on a Picture Taken by Comrade Li Chin" (November 17, 1961), in Mao Zedong, *Poems* (Utrecht, The Netherlands: Open Source Socialist Publishing, 2008).

Chapter 18

1. Translator's Note: This university was an important Kuomintang training ground before the Cultural Revolution.
2. One of Yang Tianxun's brothers, Yang Tianbao, was a high-ranking officer in the Nationalist Army. He went to Taiwan in 1949 and reportedly served as a deputy commander of the Quemoy (Jinmen) defense force. When mainland China bombarded Quemoy in 1958, the local county government sent Yang Tianxun to the Xiamen frontline to try to convince his brother to change sides.
3. A "venomous attack against the Great Leader Chairman Mao and the Glorious, Great and Correct Chinese Communist Party" was the greatest crime that could be committed during the Cultural Revolution.
4. The number killed was actually 25.

Chapter 19

1. According to the Task Force's files, Xianglinpu Commune's Langlong brigade killed two other schoolteachers who were still in service: the principal of Shenzhangtang Junior-Senior Primary School, and a locally funded schoolteacher in the brigade.
2. See chapter 10.

Chapter 20

1. Translator's Note (TN): Although involved with Qingtang rather than Xianglinpu District, Zheng Youzhi is included in this chapter because he was interviewed at the same time as Yuan Lifu.
2. The Task Force file on Zheng Youzhi describes him thus: "Zheng Youzhi, male, 50 years old [in 1985], Han, CCP member, upper-primary-school education. Enlisted in the Army in 1950,

transferred to civilian work in 1955, served as commander of Daoxian's Qingtang District PAFD from 1962 to 1968. During the Cultural Revolution he was commander of the Daoxian Red Alliance Frontline Command Post and is now an ordinary cadre in the Daoxian sugar refinery."

3. The Task Force file described Yuan Lifu thus: "Yuan Lifu, male, 45 years old [in 1985], university education, CCP member, native of Daoxian, currently a cadre in the Dong'an County township enterprise bureau. During the Cultural Revolution, he was deputy district head and secretary of Xianglinpu District, and leader of the district militia headquarters in Shangdu."

4. All of them unjustified.

5. TN: Mao Zedong, "Reply to Mr. Liu Yazi," 1949.

Chapter 21

1. The name of this leader was Huang Yida, whose story I'll tell at the end of this book.

2. Translator's Note: Vaclav Havel, "New Year's Address to the Nation," January 1, 1990 [http://old.hrad.cz/president/Havel/speeches/1990/0101_uk.html].

Chapter 22

1. Daoxian has two places called Qiaotou ("bridge head"); one is Qiaotou Market in Qiaotou Township, and the other is Qiaotou Village in Gongba District's Xingqiao Township.

2. Translator's Note (TN): Wang Jinxi gained his nickname for his heroic exploits laboring in the punishing environment of Liaoning's Daqing oil field in the early 1960s.

3. TN: Defense Minister Peng Dehuai (1898–1974) was purged and replaced by Lin Biao after criticizing Mao's disastrous Great Leap Forward during the Lushan Conference in July 1959. Held under house arrest until vindicated by an official investigation and the obvious failures of the Great Leap, Peng was once again assigned work in September 1965, only to become one of the first public figures attacked when the Cultural Revolution was launched in 1966. Accused of being a "great warlord, ambitionist, and conspirator" who had "infiltrated the party and the Arm," Peng spent the rest of his life in prison, dying after a protracted illness.

4. In Daoxian, land basins surrounded by hills were referred to as "caves."

5. Twelve People's Communes were initially established in Daoxian under the communization movement, but after Liao wrote this letter, in May 1961, these communes (with the exception of Daojiang People's Commune) were subdivided into 40 communes. Qiaotou Commune became Qiaotou District, and the Lefutang production brigade became Lefutang Commune.

Chapter 23

1. Translator's Note: Huang Shiren was the despotic landlord character in the Chinese opera, film, and later ballet *The White Haired Girl*. Zhou Bapi ("Zhou the skin-peeler) was a semi-fictionalized landlord who reputedly stirred up the roosters to wake up his laborers earlier. Nan Batian is the evil landlord in the revolutionary film and ballet *The Red Detachment of Women*. Liu Wencai (1887–1949) was the brother of a warlord, reputed to cheat peasants in their leases to ensure they remained permanently in debt.

Chapter 24

1. Daoxian was peacefully liberated on November 15, 1949, and some officials of the KMT county party committee and county government rendered meritorious service in the liberation.

2. I have another similar case in hand, which occurred in the Shijia brigade of Xianglinpu District's Xianglinpu Commune. Yang Xiyou and Yang Xilian, among others, carried out a revenge killing

on landlord offspring Yang Juejin and his four minor children, then gang-raped his wife, Yang Damei (age 25), and forced her to marry a 60-year-old poor peasant named Yang Xixuan.

Chapter 25

1. According to the Task Force's files, He Daijing criticized He Daiyu only because the Socialist Education movement work team put him up to it.
2. Translator's Note: This quotes Mao's speech at the Second Plenum of the Eighth Central Committee on November 15, 1956.
3. The Xiyuan Reservoir is located in Xiaojia Township in eastern Daoxian. Construction began in October 1958 and was completed in February 1959. As soon as water was stored in it, the dam began leaking and required emergency repairs every year. Early in the morning on June 20, 1968, the reservoir burst and inundated four communes downstream, destroying 5,420 *mu* of paddy fields and 309 homes. The reservoir was rebuilt later that year, with work completed at the end of 1970.

Chapter 26

1. Early on in the Cultural Revolution, during the campaign to "smash the four olds" in August 1966, Xianzijiao Commune was renamed Hongyan Commune, and the Qijiawan production brigade was renamed Qixing. However, the original geographical names were subsequently restored, so they will be used here.
2. According to the Task Force's files, Zhou Guizhang and Zheng Qibing, as well as the commune's deputy CCP secretary Wu Yaozhi and others, all were implicated in the killings at Xianzijiao Commune, either by inciting, directing, or authorizing the killings. For example, when production brigades requested instructions from Zheng Qibing, he said, "It doesn't matter if you kill a few troublemakers."
3. Translator's Note: Referring to the slogan "lopping off the tail of capitalism."
4. This is the same Liao Mingzhong who was deputy commander of the Red Alliance Frontline Command Post in Yingjiang.
5. During the Cultural Revolution killings, 16 people were killed in the Dajiangzhou brigade.

Chapter 27

1. The person referred to here is Pan Xingyue, who was vice chairman of Daoxian's county revolutionary committee during the Cultural Revolution and later became county deputy head. Like the vast majority of the county leadership, Pan explicitly supported the killings, although his overall performance during the Cultural Revolution was relatively moderate. During the subsequent investigations of the killings, the only county-level leaders called to account were people such as Xiong Bing'en and Wang Ansheng—and only because of the persistence of their opponents in the Revolutionary Alliance.

Chapter 28

1. Translator's Note: A very popular novel by Qu Bo, published in 1957 and made into a movie in 1960. The novel related the thrilling tale of soldiers sent into the mountains to search for bandits and brigands.
2. Inquiries subsequently found that the militia grabbed Zhang Hanfan and forced him at gunpoint to say where he'd hidden Zhou Qun.

Chapter 29

1. Translator's Note: That is, when peasants were no longer allowed to earn income from private enterprise. This prohibition came into effect in the late 1950s.

2. A campaign to attack counterrevolutionaries and oppose corruption, extravagance, and waste, carried out from 1968 to 1970.

Chapter 30

1. According to the Task Force's files, most of those killed were former KMT military personnel who had taken part in the peaceful liberation of Daoxian in 1949. The question that needs to be answered is who exposed the histories of these people and ordered them targeted.
2. The Revolutionary Alliance believed they were under mortar attack by the Revolutionary Alliance, but in fact the Red Alliance was firing homemade cannonballs that Zheng Youzhi and others had manufactured at Dapingpu Farm and delivered to Daojiang on the afternoon of August 29. Zheng ordered the cannons to fire at the No. 2 High School at midnight, but since lack of accuracy diminished their lethal power, the barrage was discontinued.
3. Translator's Note: The original quote by Mao is "China belongs not to the reactionaries but to the Chinese people" ("The Foolish Old Man Who Removed the Mountains," June 11, 1945, in *The Selected Works of Mao Zedong*).
4. The Hunan Provincial Revolutionary Committee Preparatory Group was established on August 19, 1967, after a delegation from Hunan was received in Beijing by Premier Zhou Enlai. Under the authorization of the CCP Central Committee, the members of this group were:

> Chairman Li Yuan (commander of the 47th Army); Vice Chairman Hua Guofeng (Hunan provincial CCP secretary); Zhang Bosen (alternate Hunan provincial CCP secretary and provincial vice governor); members Liang Chunyang (vice chairman of the provincial economic commission), Jia Yong (deputy commissioner of the provincial water and electricity department), Zheng Bo (deputy commander of the 47th Army), Liu Shunwen (director of the PLA political cadre school), Tan Wenbang (political commissar of the Hunan provincial military district), Lin Guoxing (deputy political commissar of the Hunan provincial military district), Hu Yong and Tang Zhongfu (leaders of the Changsha Workers' Alliance), Ye Weidong (leader of Xiang River Storm), Zhu Shunxiang (leader of the University and College Revolutionary Rebel Headquarters), Zhang Chubian (leader of "Changsha Workers"), and Xie Ruobing (leader of "Jinggang Mountain"). On September 5, 1967, the provincial preparatory group issued its Proclamation No. 1, which "invested all of Hunan's party, government, financial, and cultural authority in the Hunan Provincial Revolutionary Committee Preparatory Group."

Chapter 31

1. It appears that Liu Xiangxi lacked the most basic understanding of China's classical poetry. Claiming that this doggerel follows the strict prosodic rules of *qilü* heptasyllabic verse reflects his rudimentary education.
2. Translator's Note (TN): Abbreviated pinyin for the Revolutionary Alliance.
3. TN: Abbreviated pinyin for the Red Alliance.
4. Wang Enchang was also the secretary in charge of the county CCP committee's rural work committee.
5. TN: "Rulers of Destiny" comes from a phrase in a poem by Mao titled "Changsha—in the Rhyme Pattern of Qingyuanchun" ("Who rules over man's destiny in this boundless land?")

Chapter 33

1. I later learned that this was Yang Qingxiong from Gongba Commune's Guangjialing brigade, whose story was related in chapter 12.
2. Translator's Note: A quote by Mao referring to the difficulty of turning the peasantry into a proletariat with advanced consciousness.

Chapter 35

1. When the CCP Central Committee launched the Cultural Revolution with its "May 16 Notice," some people in Daoxian's county CCP committee treated it like a more advanced stage of the Socialist Education (Four Cleans) movement, continuing with the traditional campaign methods of dispatching work teams to schools and major cultural work units to mobilize the masses, develop class struggle, etc., which Mao Zedong subsequently referred to as Liu Shaoqi's "bourgeois reactionary line." Huang Yida was targeted for his involvement in such activities as an official who supervised cultural and educational frontline work and as a leader of the Socialist Education movement at the county and prefectural level.
2. Translator's Note (TN): Deng Tuo, Beijing's municipal secretary in charge of culture and education, became caught up in the controversy over the historical play *Hai Rui Dismissed from Office*, which sparked the Cultural Revolution, and he was driven to suicide in 1966.
3. This was the August 18 Battle of Yijiawan, famous in the history of the Cultural Revolution in Hunan.
4. They presented two reports, one on the state of the struggle between the two roads in Daoxian's Cultural Revolution, and the second on the Daoxian PAFD's support of the conservative faction and suppression of the rebel faction. Huang Yida wrote the first report; Huang Chengli, the second one.
5. From 1958 to 1966, Zhang Bosen served as alternate secretary of the Hunan provincial CCP committee, and vice governor of Hunan Province. In 1967 he became vice chairman of the Hunan Provincial Revolutionary Committee Preparatory Group, and in 1968 he became vice chairman of the Hunan Provincial Revolutionary Committee. In March 1984, he was expelled from the CCP and was dismissed from all positions inside and outside the CCP due to errors he committed during the Cultural Revolution.
6. Subsequent inquiries established that Liang Chunyang gave a similar five-point directive. The directive was probably decided by the main leaders of the provincial revolutionary committee preparatory group after a special meeting and discussion.
7. Members of the Revolutionary Alliance such as Liu Xiangxi referred to the "September 23 Tragedy" as the "Battle of September 23," while the Red Alliance said it wasn't a battle but a massacre. In my humble opinion, referring to it as the "September 23 Tragedy" is more appropriate.
8. TN: The Chinese term for "Royalist" sounds the same as the term "protect Huang [Yida]."
9. For the content of the notice, see chapter 30.

Chapter 36

1. Translator's Note (TN): "Bombarding the three reds" consisted of "opposing the Great Leader Chairman Mao and the proletarian headquarters under his command, opposing Chairman Mao's revolutionary line, and opposing the Great Proletarian Cultural Revolution personally launched by Chairman Mao."
2. TN: The "Great Wall" was typically a reference to the People's Liberation Army.
3. Huang Yida spoke this sentence the first time I interviewed him, focusing at that time on the killings. I wasn't aware of the full implications until he later told me the rest.
4. In his "Self-Criticism and Admission of Guilt" (December 3, 1967), Huang Yida reported that during the Socialist Education movement in July 1966, the prefectural leader of the movement ordered him to come up with a list of the county's "little Deng Tuos": "In the phase of arresting 'little Deng Tuos' alone, 73 people from county organs and secondary schools were struggled, and after large and small rallies, 29 were labeled anti-party anti-socialist elements, while another 24 were not labeled and 20 were helped."
5. It is an irrefutable fact that the relevant authorities arranged for He Xia and others to secretly monitor other inmates. Someone told me that he felt a compulsion to strangle He Xia.
6. The Dongwei coal mine was relatively backward and accessed by a wooden ladder dozens of meters long. Even the strongest laborer, not to mention someone in Huang Yida's condition, could easily fall to his death while lugging a sack of coal. Such accidents had already occurred at the mine.

Afterword: Living for Truth

1. Li Zhenxiang (Li Yuan, consultant), *Record of the 47th Army's Three Supports and Two Militarizations in Hunan*, April 2004, Hunan publication permit No. 2004-021. The title refers to supporting the Left, the workers, and the peasants, and providing military control and training. The section on the Daoxian massacre is in chapter 2, section 5.
2. Translator's Note (TN): The Chinese poem matches the seven-syllable cadence and some of the words in Mao Zedong's poem "The Long March."
3. TN: Bertrand Russell, "Prologue," in *Autobiography* (London: George Allen & Unwin, 1951).
4. TN: Bertrand Russell, *Why Men Fight: A Method of Abolishing the International Duel* (New York: Century, 1917), p. 179.

INDEX

Page numbers in italics refer to tables or figures; emboldened page ranges refer to chapters.